*Don't read
Ch. 2, 4, +8*

CONCEPTIONS OF SOCIAL LIFE

A Text-Reader for Social Psychology

William A. Gamson
Andre Modigliani
University of Michigan

University Press
of America™

University Press of America, Inc.™

P.O. Box 19101, Washington, D.C. 20036

All rights reserved

Printed in the United States of America

ISBN: 0-8191-0854-5
Library of Congress Number: 79-89925

To Our Kids:
Julie and Leah,
Josh and Jenny

Printed in the United States of America

Published originally by Little, Brown and Company in 1974.

PREFACE
THE PROMISE OF A
SOCIAL PSYCHOLOGY COURSE

Students beginning a social psychology course have lived intimately with the subject matter they are about to study. They may, as a consequence, take too much of it for granted, but they also come with ample curiosity. Unfortunately, this curiosity is easier to stimulate than to satisfy.

Many students are eager to find in social psychology a body of knowledge about various aspects of social life, from the pleasantly social to the grimly political—a knowledge that explains how babies become people, how people affect and influence each other, and how they transact their business in groups or organizations. By body of knowledge, they mean a set of generally accepted and interrelated principles—supported by careful research—about the phenomena which the field purports to deal with. Some, of course, are skeptical from the outset and suspect that the alleged body of knowledge in social psychology will be heavily inflated with hot air—but then others are quite trusting and not skeptical enough.

We believe that a course which attempts to satisfy these expectations by undertaking to transmit a well-organized collection of facts is doomed to confirm the skeptics and disillusion all but the hardiest of believers. The body of knowledge in social psychology contains few widely accepted answers and those that exist often seem narrow, specific, factual, non-cumulative, and of intramural concern. And our own excitement about the field is not usually at its peak as we study some narrow hypothesis just confirmed by a new piece of research. We find our excitement at another level, in discovering a fresh, new way of looking at some common phenomenon. Social psychology at its best offers us a vision, a window on social life that suddenly makes perceptible things which were always there but had escaped our notice. Our ideas about what is relevant to understanding a given phenomenon are sharply juggled. "Yes, I see," we say, "I hadn't looked at it that way before," and we then see other, related things that were previously invisible to us.

This is the promise, we think, that a social psychology course should offer students in place of the body of knowledge they are expecting to find: not facts or laws about social life, but new ways of looking at their experiences and social encounters. We should offer not answers but conceptual frameworks—ways of thinking about a phenomenon, strategies of answering questions about it, and examples of research that illustrate and exemplify underlying perspectives.

If there were a single overarching viewpoint in social psychology, the distinction we are making between presenting a body of knowledge and conceptual frameworks would not be useful. Such an overarching viewpoint would contain a commonly agreed upon way of looking at social phenomena—of asking questions about it—and would identify the examples of existing research that have successfully attacked some of these questions. If this were the state of social psychology, then the task of an introductory social psychology course and text would be to present students with the dominant framework in as interesting and provocative a manner as possible.

No such single framework exists in social psychology. How then should one present the field to introductory students? One approach is to forego broad conceptual frameworks, relying instead on isolated clusters of hypotheses by presenting a collection of the best known, most widely accepted, "classic" research studies in the field. Many collections of readings of such studies are available for the instructor who adopts this approach.

The advantages of such a tack are clear. It allows the instructor to go "where the action is"—to present his version of the best available empirical work in the hopes of communicating not only interesting hypotheses and concrete findings, but also a feeling for the research process itself. We have often used this approach ourselves. But what is the students' experience of the field in such a course? We have found that it comes to them as a series of discrete pieces written by a parade of researchers who appear to be addressing overly narrow issues in discordant fashion. Even the set of studies within a single content area—for example, social influence—may focus on topics as diverse as "conformity in social judgment" and "the effects of forced-compliance," and will invariably address different issues using different concepts drawn from a variety of theoretical traditions. There will be little or no interdependence among the studies within a content area, let alone across them. The proof of this is that the order in which one takes up a series of classic studies is typically arbitrary and can be readily changed without affecting comprehension.

It is difficult to see what lasting value a student can derive from such a course. Many studies assume prior knowledge of a conceptual tradition. Their importance is invisible to the student who does not really understand why the questions addressed are significant ones. And if he begins to sense the conceptual framework underlying study A, there is no guarantee at all that study B, reflecting a different approach, will also make sense. We believe that such an approach leaves a student with answers to questions he has not learned to ask, and that answers without questions are quickly forgotten.

As an alternative, one may choose some single conceptual framework from among the available ones and present the field in terms of it. There are, after all, some broad analytic perspectives that span many content areas: social learning/exchange is one, cognitive and interpersonal consistency another, symbolic interaction a third. This approach has some advantages over the series of isolated studies. Some research, at least, will make good sense within the chosen framework and the student will receive a glimpse of the forest as he looks at certain trees. But it is our premise that no overarching framework exists that can do justice to the field. To adopt one is either to ignore much exciting work or to force it into an artificial framework. For example, to present Goffman's subtle analyses of the social construction of interpersonal reality in a behaviorist framework is nearly as grotesque as to translate the bold simplicity of Homans' or Adams' exchange framework into the delicate complexities of a symbolic meaning, "definition of the situation" framework. But worse, the student is encouraged to think he has explored the forest when in fact he has only glimpsed it from a special angle. He has not been allowed to see what many other social psychologists—using different angles of vision and a different lens—have been able to see. If there is no shared vision, it fosters an illusion to pretend one exists.

APPROACH OF THIS BOOK

How then do we propose to fulfill the promise we see possible in a social psychology course? First, we start with a set of interesting and fundamental questions about social life—questions whose challenge for us is as genuine as we hope it will be for new students of the field.

Our book is not about social psychology but about the things that social psychologists try to understand. Social psychologists tread this turf, but they have company from clinical psychologists, sociologists, anthropologists, political scientists, novelists, and anyone else whose life experiences have led him to think seriously about such phenomena—with or without conventional credentials. Our starting point is a set of questions—and we take the answers where we find them, without concern for the labels their authors may wear.

Perhaps answers is a misleading term to describe what we have collected here. Take a question such as, "Why do people rebel?" We present some divergent perspectives on this issue, each of which tells us something quite different about the elements of the puzzle. Each points to certain key elements, tells what is important about them, suggests critical matters that require study, and points to the sort of research that can best accomplish this. Thomas Kuhn's term "paradigms" comes closest to describing what we have attempted to bring together here.

In his provocative analysis of the history of science, Kuhn (1962)* argues that at the core of those major breakthroughs that he calls scientific revolutions is the overthrow of an existing paradigm by some newer one. Paradigms are implicit ways of viewing the subject matter of a field. They are organizing vehicles, vantage points, overarching frameworks that give meaning to the subject matter. For Kuhn, it is a sign of scientific immaturity when there exists a babble of competing paradigms in a field. In the more mature sciences, such as physics or astronomy, a single paradigm is ordinarily dominant in an area—one that permeates the pages of every textbook and that supports the taken for granted assumptions underlying each piece of research. At the same time, it is precisely this accepted view that is subject to overthrow during extraordinary times of scientific revolution.

---

* Complete reference for each acknowledgement falls at the end of the section or reading in which it appears.

For better or worse, by Kuhn's standards at least, social psychology is an immature science. As we have noted repeatedly, there are as yet no universally shared visions of the phenomena we study. Instead, a plurality of visions co-exist—not exactly in harmony, but not in antagonistic confrontation either. It is not that proponents of different paradigms have great sympathy for one another; it is rather that debating across paradigms is a very slippery business precisely because there is insufficient common ground on which to mount telling arguments. Cross-paradigm debates sometimes resemble dialogues of the deaf.

At any rate, faced with a field that does not yet have shared paradigms, we propose to make a virtue of necessity by making competing paradigms the keystone in the teaching of social psychology. Our experience as teachers (and as students) has been that students get more involved in the subject matter, and are more likely to master it in a creative manner, when the material through which it is presented contains a certain amount of tension—a degree of controversy and incongruity that the students must resolve for themselves, either on their own or through class discussion.

This book tries to create that tension by offering a series of visions on different aspects of social life that are both compelling in their own right and competitive with each other. Each paradigm represents a new gestalt—a reorganization of the separate elements into a whole with a different meaning. They compete with each other not in the sense of being contradictory—although they sometimes are—but in the sense of being incapable of merging. A paradigm shift is a shift in consciousness. One can move back and forth between the different ways of viewing a phenomenon but these views cannot be used simultaneously, at least not without considerable strain.

Each chapter of the book deals with a different phenomenon of interest to social psychologists. First, we try to make the question we are attempting to understand concrete and vivid; usually we employ a vignette for this purpose. The trick is to illustrate the phenomenon without assuming one of the competing paradigms in the process. Fortunately, our descriptions can be guided by a knowledge of what each competing perspective considers important. We can thus include elements central for each of the views, even though any particular element may be wholly irrelevant to some.

Having highlighted the phenomenon of a chapter, we then present three or four paradigms as radically different from one another as possible. At the same time that we search for contrast, we try to make each as persuasive and plausible as we can. Any given perspective is likely to seem natural to some student but, if we are successful, he will find another that seems equally natural and that entices him to look at the same thing in a new and different way. The "natural way", then, can no longer be taken for granted in an unexamined fashion.

A believer in a paradigm is likely to be its most persuasive advocate. Although we present each paradigm in our own words trying to make its unstated assumptions explicit, we have included in each chapter a set of readings as well. Each reading is chosen to illustrate and represent one of the paradigms discussed in the text but the manner in which a given one does so differs. In some cases, the reading is a direct and explicit statement and defense of the paradigm. In others, it is a piece of research premised on the paradigm—one that exemplifies it in use without necessarily stating it directly. In still other cases, it is a theoretical explanation in which the paradigm is used implicitly, perhaps not even recognized by the author who is using it.

The book addresses itself to twelve questions and includes three or four perspectives on each, for a grand total of some three or four dozen paradigms. Needless to say, the paradigms presented in one chapter are not necessarily in conflict with those included in another. To the contrary, certain paradigms have greater span than others and are thus able to deal with more of the phenomena treated in this book. But even when the same basic paradigm re-surfaces in another chapter, it reappears in a different form, especially molded to fit the subject matter of that section. Thus, it is not always easy to spot the family resemblances, nor have we been deliberate in planting them. Whenever possible and useful we have sought to point out connections between the paradigms covered in different sections of the book, but we are certain that some have eluded our grasp. Had we been able to get a handle on all these connections, we would surely have organized our book around them. At one time, we contemplated doing this. But we became persuaded that the task of linking up all the related ways of viewing all the different phenomena covered amounted to nothing less than a theoretical integration of the entire field of social psychology. In the face of such a task, our valor, such as it was, quickly gave way to discretion.

This brings us to a final matter. *Within* each chapter we have made a special effort to show how the several paradigms presented there relate to one another by mapping their basic assumptions on certain important dimensions of contrast. How well we have succeeded in this remains to be seen, but our intent was to sharpen both the contrasts and overlaps, thus helping to maintain a proper degree of tension. We see no virtue in ambiguity produced by lack of clarity. But we feel that the residual uncertainty about the most fruitful way of looking at a given phenomenon is a healthy one whose resolution is better left to the student and instructor. The integration of the different paradigms in a section we must leave to the future of the field. We have not always succeeded in finding paradigms that fundamentally conflict, but, where we have, we feel rather certain that no eclectic integration of the viewpoints is possible without doing serious violence to at least one of them. The integration, if it comes, must be precisely in the form of a new paradigm that somehow reorganizes the combinations of elements spotted by each perspective, thereby making them compatible. If we cannot yet glimpse the shape of such a future resolution, we can at least take heart in the faith that it will come as surely as it came to the more mature sciences—there are scores of cases in which unrelated as well as incompatible facts were dramatically drawn together by new breakthroughs in perspective. Perhaps the day of a single dominant paradigm in social psychology is not so very far off.

The intent of this book, then, is to preserve some of the advantages of a classic studies approach to the field while controlling the oft associated confusion and intellectual chaos. The readings in each chapter do permit some of our most astute thinkers and researchers to present their thought and work in their own words, within their own framework. At the same time, the introductory section to each chapter seeks to place each of these disparate formulations into broader perspective to create a meaningful forum in which they can be discussed simultaneously.

The book is intended for an introductory or middle level course taught in part through class discussion. It covers most of the traditional topics of a social psychology course, although some areas of work appear with unaccustomed bedfellows. Hopefully, the user will emerge with a deeper understanding of the subject matter we study and, where this cannot be, at least with a greater ability to formulate good, answerable questions about it. If he ends up with no neat package containing the field as a whole, he is, after all, no different from those of us spending our lives working in it.

REFERENCE

Kuhn, Thomas S. *The Structure of Scientific Revolutions.* Chicago: University of Chicago Press, 1962.

CONTENTS

PART
ONE
SOCIALIZATION

CHAPTER ONE
WHAT IS THE NATURE OF MAN?

THE ISSUE OF HUMAN NATURE

Before we move too hastily to examine how man acts, we should consider what man is. What basic needs and capacities must be understood before we can begin to make sense of how people operate in a social environment? The answers offered by social psychologists are typically implicit. Few of us are bold enough to walk in such a brier, preferring clearings where the footing is more comfortable. Nonetheless, we all make assumptions about the underlying issues and carry with us some operating images of man.

It is misleading to ask which of these competing images is more or less true. The question, rather, is which is more or less useful and for what purposes. Some images of man seem particularly helpful in highlighting an issue that is left obscure by others; these others, in turn, have their own uses. Indeed, some seem to us to have little use at all, but still they will have their defenders and we prefer to let the reader make the judgment. We are content with presenting the different images and drawing attention to the underlying issues that each must confront.

THE MAJOR VIEWS

Man, the Animal

"An ape's an ape, a varlet's a varlet,
Though they be clad in silk or scarlet."

In *The Naked Ape*, Desmond Morris takes pains to remind us that, though we may fly to the moon, we are still very much a primate:

There are one hundred and ninety-three living species of monkeys and apes. One hundred and ninety-two of them are covered with hair. The exception is a naked ape self-named *Homo sapiens*. This unusual and highly successful species spends a great deal of time examining his higher motives and an equal amount of time studiously ignoring his fundamental ones. He is proud that he has the biggest brain of all the primates, but attempts to conceal the fact that he also has the biggest penis, preferring to accord this honour falsely to the mighty gorilla (1967, p.9).

It is not a lesson that most social psychologists are wont to take to heart. Typically, they are more impressed by the fact that man can uniquely speak with symbols and can regard his own person as an object than by the equally undeniable fact that "even a space ape must urinate" (Morris, 1967, p.23).

By itself, the fact that we have biological needs can be accepted and ignored. It is only when such needs are seen as central influences on our social life that they can be said to be part of an image of man. This is exactly the place Freud gives them in *Civilization and Its Discontents.** We live with ever present, powerful, instinctive biological drives—especially sexual and aggressive ones. "The passions of instinct are stronger than reasoned interests," Freud argues. "Culture has to call up every possible reinforcement in order to erect barriers against the aggressive instincts of men."

It is true that we are able to contain and divert such drives but only with difficulty and never completely in this view. At every opportunity, such drives slip through our defenses and color our activities in countless forms. If our social institutions fail to allow for their partial expression and successful sublimation, the basic strains will prove overwhelming and social life will be crippled. Schemes for social organization that fail to recognize this intractable fact of human nature are, in Freud's view, founded psychologically on an untenable illusion.

This view imparts a fundamental pessimism to Freud's writing. Most of us would like to think that we can transcend such a biological inheritance and Freud's emphasis on instincts has proved one of the least palatable parts of his thinking to most contemporary social psychologists. But the line between pessimism and realism is frequently invisible and the unpleasantness of an image is no test of its value in helping us to understand man's social life.

Man, the Profit-seeker

If Freud holds a disturbing mirror up to us, this next image of man is hardly more exalted. Blau states its central assumption: "Human beings tend to be governed in their associations with one another by the desire to obtain social rewards of various sorts, and the resulting exchanges of benefits shape the structure of social relations" (1964, p.18). "The theory itself," writes Kenneth Boulding (1962, p.454) in a review of Homans' *Social Behavior: Its Elementary Forms,** "is a mixture of the economist's theory of exchange with the psychologist's theory of learning by rewards and punishments. Economic man is crossed with the psychological pigeon to produce what the unkind might call the Economic Pigeon theory of human interaction."

---

* A segment is included in the readings for this chapter.

Homans is unperturbed by the squelch that his view of man as a seeker of rewards and minimizer of costs is nothing more than common sense. "Modern social science has been so sensitive to the charge that its findings are old or obvious, ... that it has ended by painting a picture of man that men cannot recognize. ... I am not out to destroy common sense but to make explicit and general the wisdom it embodies."

There is nothing basically wrong with economic man in Homans' view except that his goals are too narrowly construed. "The trouble with him," Homans points out, "was not that he was economic, that he used his resources to some advantage, but that he was antisocial and materialistic, interested only in money and material goods and ready to sacrifice even his old mother to get them." The rehabilitated man of social psychological exchange theory can have any goals including altruistic ones. But given that he has picked up some goals along the way, he will engage in those social relationships that help him to get what he wants in an economical way.

Because the image of man here is so close to common sense, the following reminder is especially in order: One shouldn't judge a paradigm knowing only its assumptions about the nature of man. We will encounter "exchange theory" again in attempting to answer many other questions in this book. It can be and has been used to uncover many non-obvious implications. Blau (1964), especially, has used it to understand the development of quite complex social processes. If the underlying assumptions are simple, then it is all the more to its credit if subtle insights can come from such humble origins.

Man, the Symbol Interpreter

It is easiest to convey this paradigm by discussing an episode from the television program, Candid Camera. It took place at a hamburger stand in which an impressive piece of machinery had been installed on the lunch counter for the occasion. The apparatus had a number of blinking lights and a large red light at the top under which a sign was appended. The sign bore the legend "Eating Recorder" and carried instructions asking the diner to stop eating when the red light was on and to resume eating again when the light went off.

Several patrons were shown confronting the machine. The ones selected by Candid Camera were frequently caught with mouth open and cheeseburgers suspended in midair. When this occurred, they waited patiently until the light went off before taking a bite, only to be caught again with a mouthful that they obediently refrained from swallowing while the light remained on. One man put his food down on his plate when the light was on and picked it up to transport it to his mouth each time the light went off. However, the light always went on again just before he could get a bite and the sandwich remained inviolate during the sequence shown. None of the victims showed much visible irritation during the sequence, but they frequently looked around to see if others were noting their actions. Some made remarks or asked questions of the counter-man (a Candid Camera stooge), but everyone around the victim conspired to maintain the impression that nothing untoward was occurring.

We asked a number of students in an introductory social psychology class to interpret this episode. Many of their explanations ran something like the following. The red light is a conditioned stimulus and the response has been acquired quite naturally in American society. A red light means stop. Failure to make this response has been negatively reinforced by traffic tickets or other unpleasant consequences in the past. The students saw the response as involving no conscious thought and tended to be rather contemptuous of the foolish passivity of the responders.

There is an alternative interpretation of this episode rooted in a social psychological tradition that emphasizes the interpretation of meanings as man's most central and distinctive characteristic. The seminal figure in this tradition is George Herbert Mead and, because of its strong emphasis on the exchange of symbols which have shared meanings, it bears the label "symbolic interaction." The selection by Blumer outlines the central ideas and premises.

To see it in operation, take the lunch counter example. The logical starting point from this perspective is to assume that people need to make sense of their environment. Then, one can ask what set of shared meanings a person at the counter might find to make this situation comprehensible. It is as if we ask ourselves, how would I have interpreted this situation if I were there in his or her place? If we saw such a complicated apparatus, we would recognize that someone had gone to a good deal of trouble and expense to install it. Normally, people don't go to such trouble unless it is important to some goal they wish to pursue. While we don't always know the exact purpose of someone else's behavior, such knowledge is unnecessary as long as there is no reason to doubt that the goal is a legitimate one. Just because one doesn't know the precise reasons for the machine does not imply that there *are* no good reasons for its existence.

Of course, we might be puzzled and seek further information from the people around us. We might ask the counter man what the machine is for if the delays become annoying. Or, we may decide not to cooperate if we become suspicious of the purpose or if cooperation becomes too onerous. In this particular instance, of course, the purpose of the machine *was* harrassment and a good faith interpretation was mistaken. But, cooperation makes a great deal of sense given the interpretation that a normal person would make. He puts himself in the position of the person who installed the machine, attributes intentions to this person's actions and evaluates these intentions in terms of the norms of a larger community in which both parties share membership. Man is not a passive responder to stimuli in this view but is always interpreting and rendering them meaningful.

Man, the Noble

Finally, we reach that point in the hall of mirrors in which man looks pretty. Things have been looking up, it is true, from the image of the animal with his barely concealed lust. But the bargain hunter calculating advantages was not much prettier. The interpreter made a respectable appearance but was perhaps a bit more rational and cool than we'd like to see ourselves—not very intense, loving, and creative, for example.

Well, we have some friends among the humanistic psychologists who see us basically as a pretty attractive lot. Of course, our behavior is another thing entirely and they would not deny the greed and viciousness that we constantly exhibit. The issue is the source of such behavior and they are kind enough to see it as a distortion rather than a revelation of our true nature.

What is this true nature? As Maslow puts it in his selection, "creativeness, spontaneity, selfhood, authenticity, caring for others, being able to love, yearning for truth are embryonic potentialities belonging to [man's] species-membership just as much as are his arms and legs and brain and eyes."

But these potentialities are frequently not realized. Despite the fact that they are biologically based and instinctoid, they are, unfortunately, easily overcome, suppressed or repressed. We are left with instinct-remnants which must be carefully nurtured if man is to realize his intrinsic potential. Social institutions can encourage the growth and development of this potential but frequently they inhibit or suppress growth and self-actualization.

CONTRASTING THE VIEWS OF HUMAN NATURE

These images of man can be contrasted by examining their treatment of four issues:

1. How important are biological needs?
2. How much tension is there between man's intractable nature and society's intractable demands?
3. How much is man a passive responder rather than an active chooser?
4. How unique is man compared to other animals? How similar or different are the principles that shape human nature compared to those that shape the nature of other animals?

Importance of Biological Needs

For Freud, such needs are clearly central, but for the rest they are attenuated or ignored. Rose, for example, in presenting the symbolic interactionist perspective, claims that it does not exclude biological influences but concedes that it "does not incorporate them into [its] theory" (1962, p.14). If the utilitarian creatures of Homans' paradigm have a body, it is not of much interest although, presumably, it leads to some of the goals they seek in social exchange. They seek pleasure, to be sure, but it is not satisfying basic biological drives that provides the animus for their activity.

Maslow's position is somewhat more complicated. Man's core nature is indeed biological and inherited, but the need for self-actualization is a great deal weaker and more easily diverted than are sexual and aggressive drives for Freud. When instincts become instinct-remnants, the biological theme is muted and Maslow's human doesn't look very much like a naked ape.

Tension between Man's Nature and Society's Demands

How malleable is the material that society molds? How stubborn or intractable? Are we plastic, easily shaped and altered to meet the needs of different social institutions? Or are we marble with a hidden form that the skillful sculptor gradually reveals (or the clumsy one destroys by forcing an inappropriate form)? How much harmony is there between our basic needs and the demands of organized social life?

The sociologist's answer to this question tends to emphasize much less tension than the psychologist's. "For most of us," Berger writes, "the yoke of society seems easy to bear. Why? ... Because most of the time we ourselves desire just that which society expects of us. We *want* to obey the rules. We *want* the parts that society has assigned to us . . . . Society not only determines what we do but also what we are" (1965, p.93).

The symbolic interactionists, for example, see no tension at all. If man has a dominant tendency in his nature it is to become a social creature. Our humanity emerges as we take our place in a meaningful set of social relationships and learn the meanings and values by which we interact with others. The dichotomy between individuals and society is a false one. A person becomes most fully himself by making society part of him, by bringing it inside his head.

Nor is there any more tension for a social exchange theorist such as Homans. We seek rewards and other people are the primary source of these rewards. Our pleasures are more social than biological. Reward seeking creates no inevitable tension. In fact, many other individuals have complementary needs and this makes social life possible.

Neither of these perspectives assumes, of course, that all social life will be harmonious. Tensions arise because of imperfect social forms that are ultimately remedial, or they reflect the fact that nature has endowed us unequally with socially valued characteristics. But they are not inevitable tensions, produced by an intractable nature, that cannot be subdued by some social institution.

Wrong (1961) has taken sociologists to task for this view which he characterizes as "The Oversocialized Conception of Man." He turns the usual sociological argument on its head. Typically, sociologists argue that man feels strain when he violates the expectations of others. He, thus, finds it more psychologically comfortable to meet the expectations of those around him—it brings him social support, acceptance, meaningful relations with others. But Wrong argues that, "the person who conforms may be even more 'bothered,' that is, subject to guilt and neurosis." He may experience more discomfort from suppressing his natural inclinations than from violating some norms that he is uneasy and ambivalent about.

Wrong reminds sociologists of the Freudian image of man. For Freud, the tension between man's nature and society's demands is always there. The tensions of social life are not aberrations and, at some level, are irreducible. Some social institutions may make them worse, but the quest to remove them entirely is a chimera.

For Maslow, some of the tension is there, but the battle is an uneven one. Society has all the big guns; man's nature is easily bullied or seduced into inauthentic paths. Still, when institutions distort man's nature in such a manner, they will produce pathologies in individuals and society will ultimately pay the price in social strains. Only when we develop a set of true, growth-encouraging institutions will the tension subside and man realize his potential.

Passive Responder versus Active Chooser

Are we the passive resultant of the many forces that play upon us? Or, is it more useful to think of man as the chooser and initiator, the goal seeker who modifies the physical and social environment or compromises with it, if need be, as he pursues his various ends? There is a red herring here which it is best to get beyond rapidly. The issue is not whether man is free or his behavior is determined. All explanations assume that his behavior is determined; this is the nature of explanation. But some include in their explanation the notion of choice, volition, or will. These volitional explanations are, in an important sense, determined; the goals or end states that man seeks are givens. They may come from his inner nature or be learned from the culture, but he does not choose them.

Real differences remain on how much emphasis should be given to the conscious seeking of some end, whether it is an emotional state of being or some material reward. In some views, man emerges as a basically passive responder to forces he does not fully comprehend. In Freud, for example, there is an important dynamic between biological drives and the demands of civilization, but man is essentially at the mercy of both—and suffers from their inevitable contradiction. He may work the problems out— for example, by sublimating biological drives in a manner that begets social rewards— but he is hardly a master of his fate. He may walk the tight rope between the pleasure and reality principles with varying degrees of skill, but the path is still straight and narrow.

Man, the chooser, comes back in for Homans. He is a seeker of rewards and an avoider of punishments and he soon learns that most of the significant rewards and punishments in his life are mediated by other people. He gradually learns which strategies will bring him what he wants, subject, of course, to all the errors of judgment to which fallible human beings are prone. But choice is at the center as he weighs costs and gains, avoids situations where the cost-benefit ratio looks poor, and takes a flyer now and then on an unknown situation that promises a pot of gold.

The symbolic interactionist position on this issue appears at first to place man in a fairly passive role. He is engaged in a process of attributing meanings to the world but he is born into a world of established meanings and learns these as he interacts with others. However, Blumer emphasizes an additional element that gives a much more active role to the interpreter. He is not a passive product of either his psychological make-up or his positions in the social world—for example, his social class, religion, ethnic group, and the like. Although his interpretation of the world ultimately grows out of social interaction, it is not received directly and unproblematically but is treated by the individual. He does not mechanically apply the social meanings that he has learned from others, but intervenes in a highly active way. Blumer describes the process: *

> The actor indicates to himself the things toward which he is acting; he has to point out to himself the things that have meaning. The making of such indications is an internalized social process in that the actor is interacting with himself.... The actor selects, checks, suspends, regroups, and transforms the meanings in the light of the situation in which he is placed and the direction of his action. Accordingly, interpretation should not be regarded as a mere automatic application of established meanings but as a formative process in which meanings are used and revised as instruments for the guidance and formation of action.

---

* From the Blumer segment included in the readings for this chapter.

It is this process of interacting with oneself that makes the image of man in this paradigm an active one.

Maslow and the humanistic psychologists also employ an active view of man. The organizing dynamic is self-actualization, an active, striving tendency aimed at realizing our potential. When institutions fail to foster human growth and development, we struggle with the constraints and seek a more suitable growth environment.

Similarity of Man to Other Animals

Man necessarily shares with other animals many characteristics—most notably biological ones—that stem from a common evolution. The issue here is whether these common characteristics are central to human nature or whether, instead, man must be understood in terms of capacities or traits that are unique to the human species. Are the principles, processes, and abilities that shape human social behavior essentially similar to those that shape the behavior of other animals, or are they of a qualitatively different sort?

The view of man as symbol-interpreter is clearest in stressing capabilities not shared with "lower" animals. Only humans have the mental capacity to interpret abstract symbols, an ability demonstrated by that uniquely human form of communication, language. The utterances that make up human speech are abstract compared, say, to the growl of a dog or the slap of a beaver's tail. The sound denoting a particular object is not only arbitrary (in the sense that the object could be renamed by common agreement), but it can be used with a conscious intent to communicate. Beavers, in contrast, are incapable of changing their natural danger-signal and it is not clear that they enact it with the intent of communicating danger. They would issue the same sign in the absence of other beavers who could interpret it. But a person who talked aloud when alone would be considered a bit odd to say the least. In the symbolic interaction view, it is precisely this unique ability to make abstract interpretations that is the essence of the human species. When a person enters a social situation, he does not respond directly to that situation but to a complex interpretation of it.

The view of man as profit-seeker, in contrast, puts the smallest emphasis on uniquely human capacities. The central principle—that a person will seek out and repeat rewarded behaviors while avoiding punished behaviors—is one that applies to all animals. To be sure, people may strive for certain uniquely human rewards and are capable of far more sophisticated calculations and planning; but, ultimately, a human travelling the social path in search of profit in the world and trying to avoid adversity is no different from a rat travelling a maze, seeking the shortest path to food while avoiding a painful shock.

On the surface, it might seem obvious that the view of man as animal would emphasize continuities across species, but for Freud, at least, the picture is complex. Clearly biological factors—especially sexual and aggressive instincts—are emphasized, but he also recognizes man's unique capacity to moderate these drives, to repress and rechannel them in accord with the dictates of civilized social life. Biological needs cannot be completely suppressed. They must find some outlet, but they need not be expressed in the same direct and straightforward fashion as is the case for other animals. Especially in his later work, Freud gave considerable attention to special human capabilities that permit man to deflect and defend against his animal side as well as to incorporate the moral dictates of his society. We shall encounter some of this work in Chapter Three where we take up Freud's views on moral socialization. For the moment, it is sufficient to note that Freud takes an intermediate position on man's similarity to other animals—yes, man has a definite animal side, but, no, his social behavior cannot be understood without central attention to uniquely human psychological characteristics.

Chart 1 Underlying Issues on What is the Nature of Man

Questions	Man, the Animal (*e.g.,* Freud)	Man, the Profit-seeker (*e.g.,* Homans)	Man, the Symbol Interpreter (*e.g.,* Blumer)	Man, the Noble (*e.g.,* Maslow)
How important are biological needs?	Very important, central to man's nature	Exist but not fundamental to man's nature	Exist but not fundamental to man's nature	Exist and are important but are easily overcome, suppressed, or repressed.
How much tension is there between man's intractable nature and society's intractable demands?	Plenty and inevitably	None worth emphasizing	None worth emphasizing	Frequently some but not inevitably; depends on how well society adapts to man's basic needs
How much is man a passive responder rather than an active chooser?	Primarily a responder	An active chooser seeking a goal or end state	An active interpreter engaged in self dialogue	An active chooser seeking a goal or end state
Is man similar to other animals?	Yes and No: Similar biological needs but unique capacity to modify and control them.	Yes: Shares tendency to seek rewards and avoid punishments.	No: Unique capacity to use and interpret abstract symbols	Mainly No: Other animals may self-actualize but man has some unique potentials.

Finally, the view of man as self-actualizing seems to stress the uniqueness of the human species but the issue is not clear-cut. Maslow puts a somewhat paradoxical emphasis on inborn "instinctoid" tendencies. If these tendencies come to us by way of evolution, then perhaps we share them with other animals. On the other hand, perhaps each species has unique potentialities of its own; the characteristics emphasized by Maslow may be of this sort. A glance at his list, which includes "creativeness, spontaneity, selfhood, caring for others, being able to love, yearning for truth," suggests a set of traits at least some of which seem uniquely human. But the central theme in Maslow's argument is self-actualization—a drive to develop to their fullest whatever natural tendencies we possess. Such a drive is probably common to all animals. Anyone who has watched young animals at play has seen them exercising their repetoire of not yet mastered abilities, apparently for the sheer fun of it. The tendency to utilize and develop those potentials of which we are capable is not unique to the human species although there may be some specific potentials that are.

These are the central issues we see running through these contrasting images of man. They are summarized in Chart 1.

REFERENCES

Berger, Peter L. *An Invitation to Sociology*. Garden City, New York: Doubleday & Company, Inc., 1963.

Blau, Peter M. *Exchange and Power in Social Life*. New York: John Wiley & Sons, Inc., 1964.

Boulding, Kenneth E. "Review of George C. Homans, *Social Behavior: Its Elementary Forms*," *American Journal of Sociology*, 67 (January, 1962), pp. 454-461.

Morris, Desmond. *The Naked Ape*. New York: McGraw-Hill, 1967.

Mead, George Herbert. *Mind, Self, and Society*. Chicago: University of Chicago Press, 1934.

Rose, Arnold M. "A Systematic Summary of Symbolic Interaction Theory," in Arnold M. Rose (Ed.), *Human Behavior and Social Processes*, Boston: Houghton Mifflin Co., 1962.

Wrong, Dennis H. "The Oversocialized Conception of Man in Modern Sociology," *American Sociological Review*, 26 (1961), pp. 183-193.

THE NATURAL TENDENCY
TO AGGRESSION

SIGMUND FREUD

The existence of this inclination to aggression, which we can detect in ourselves and justly assume to be present in others, is the factor which disturbs our relations with our neighbour and which forces civilization into such a high expenditure [of energy] in consequence of this primary mutual hostility of human beings, civilized society is perpetually threatened with disintegration. The interest of work in common would not hold it together; instinctual passions are stronger than reasonable interests. Civilization has to use its utmost efforts in order to set limits to man's aggressive instincts and to hold the manifestations of them in check by psychical reaction-formations. Hence, therefore, the use of methods intended to incite people into identifications and aim-inhibited relationships of love, hence the restriction upon sexual life, and hence too the ideal's commandment to love one's neighbour as oneself—a commandment which is really justified by the fact that nothing else runs so strongly counter to the original nature of man. In spite of every effort, these endeavours of civilization have not so far achieved very much. It hopes to prevent the crudest excesses of brutal violence by itself assuming the right to use violence against criminals, but the law is not able to lay hold of the more cautious and refined manifestations of human aggressiveness. The time comes when each one of us has to give up as illusions the expectations which, in his youth, he pinned upon his fellowmen, and when he may learn how much difficulty and pain has been added to his life by their ill-will. At the same time, it would be unfair to reproach civilization with trying to eliminate strife and competition from human activity. These things are undoubtedly indispensable. But opposition is not necessarily enmity; it is merely misused and made an *occasion* for enmity.

The communists believe that they have found the path to deliverance from our evils. According to them, man is wholly good and is well-disposed to his neighbour; but the institution of private property has corrupted his nature. The ownership of private wealth gives the individual power, and with it the temptation to ill-treat his neighbour; while the man who is excluded from possession is bound to rebel in hostility against his oppressor. If private property were abolished, all wealth held in common,

Reprinted from *Civilization and Its Discontents* by Sigmund Freud (Volume XXI of *The Standard Edition of the Complete Psychological Works of Sigmund Freud*). Translated from the German and edited by James Strachey. Copyright © 1961 by James Strachey. By permission of W.W. Norton & Company, Inc., Sigmund Freud Copyrights Ltd., The Institute of Psycho-Analysis, and The Hogarth Press Ltd.

and everyone allowed to share in the enjoyment of it, ill-will and hostility would disappear among men. Since everyone's needs would be satisfied, no one would have any reason to regard another as his enemy; all would willingly undertake the work that was necessary. I have no concern with any economic criticisms of the communist system; I cannot enquire into whether the abolition of private property is expedient or advantageous.* But I am able to recognize that the psychological premises on which the system is based are an untenable illusion. In abolishing private property we deprive the human love of aggression of one of its instruments, certainly a strong one, though certainly not the strongest; but we have in no way altered the differences in power and influence which are misused by aggressiveness, nor have we altered anything in its nature. Aggressiveness was not created by property. It reigned almost without limit in primitive times, when property was still very scanty, and it already shows itself in the nursery almost before property has given up its primal, anal form; it forms the basis of every relation of affection and love among people (with the single exception, perhaps, of the mother's relation to her male child). If we do away with personal rights over material wealth, there still remains prerogative in the field of sexual relationships, which is bound to become the source of the strongest dislike and the most violent hostility among men who in other respects are on the equal footing. If we were to remove this factor, too, by allowing complete freedom of sexual life and thus abolishing the family, the germ-cell of civilization, we cannot, it is true, easily foresee what new paths the development of civilization could take; but one thing we can expect, and that is that this indestructible feature of human nature will follow it there.

It is clearly not easy for men to give up the satisfaction of this inclination to aggression. They do not feel comfortable without it. The advantage which a comparatively small cultural group offers of allowing this instinct an outlet in the form of hostility against intruders is not to be despised. It is always possible to bind together a considerable number of people in love, so long as there are other people left over to receive the manifestations of their aggressiveness. I once discussed the phenomenon that it is precisely communities with adjoining territories, and related to each other in other ways as well, who are engaged in constant feuds and in ridiculing each other—like the Spaniards and Portuguese, for instance, the North

---

* Anyone who has tasted the miseries of poverty in his own youth and has experienced the indifference and arrogance of the well-to-do, should be safe from the suspicion of having no understanding or good will towards endeavours to fight against the inequality of wealth among men and all that it leads to. To be sure, if an attempt is made to base this fight upon an abstract demand, in the name of justice, for equality for all men, there is a very obvious objection to be made—that nature, by endowing individuals with extremely unequal physical attributes and mental capacities, has introduced injustices against which there is no remedy.

Germans and South Germans, the English and Scotch, and so on. I gave this phenomenon the name of 'the narcissism of minor differences', a name which does not do much to explain it. We can now see that it is a convenient and relatively harmless satisfaction of the inclination to aggression, by means of which cohesion between the members of the community is made easier. In this respect the Jewish people, scattered everywhere, have rendered most useful services to the civilizations of the countries that have been their hosts; but unfortunately all the massacres of the Jews in the Middle Ages did not suffice to make that period more peaceful and secure for their Christian fellows. When once the Apostle Paul had posited universal love between men as the foundation of his Christian community, extreme intolerance on the part of Christendom towards those who remained outside it became the inevitable consequence. To the Romans, who had not founded their communal life as a State upon love, religious intolerance was something foreign, although with them religion was a concern of the State and the State was permeated by religion. Neither was it an unaccountable chance that the dream of a Germanic world-dominion called for antisemitism as its complement; and it is intelligible that the attempt to establish a new, communist civilization in Russia should find its psychological support in the persecution of the bourgeois. One only wonders, with concern what the Soviets will do after they have wiped out their bourgeois.

If civilization imposes such great sacrifices not only on man's sexuality but on his aggressivity, we can understand better why it is hard for him to be happy in that civilization. In fact, primitive man was better off in knowing no restrictions of instinct. To counterbalance this, his prospects of enjoying this happiness for any length of time were very slender. Civilized man has exchanged a portion of his possibilities of happiness for a portion of security. We must not forget, however, that in the primal family only the head of it enjoyed this instinctual freedom; the rest lived in slavish suppression. In that primal period of civilization, the contrast between a minority who enjoyed the advantages of civilization and a majority who were robbed of those advantages was, therefore, carried to extremes. As regards the primitive peoples who exist today, careful researches have shown that their instinctual life is by no means to be envied for its freedom. It is subject to restrictions of a different kind but perhaps of greater severity than those attaching to modern civilized man.

When we justly find fault with the present state of our civilization for so inadequately fulfilling our demands for a plan of life that shall make us happy, and for allowing the existence of so much suffering which could probably be avoided—when, with unsparing criticism, we try to uncover the roots of its imperfection, we are undoubtedly exercising a proper right and are not showing ourselves enemies of civilization. We may expect gradually to carry through such alterations in our civilization as will better satisfy our needs and will escape our criticisms. But perhaps we may also familiarize ourselves with the idea that there are difficulties attaching to the nature of civilization which will not yield to any attempt at reform.

SOCIAL BEHAVIOR
AND PROFITABLE EXCHANGE

GEORGE C. HOMANS

Both behavioral psychology and elementary economics envisage human behavior as a function of its pay-off: in amount and kind it depends on the amount and kind of reward and punishment it fetches. When what it fetches is the behavior, similarly determined, of another man, the behavior becomes social. Thus the set of general propositions I shall use in this book envisages social behavior as an exchange of activity, tangible or intangible, and more or less rewarding or costly, between at least two persons. . . .

My set of general propositions gets no high marks for originality. In its vulgar form it must be the oldest of all theories of social behavior, and it is one we still use every day when we say, "I found so-and-so rewarding," or "I got a great deal out of him," or even "Talking to him took a great deal out of me." Men have always explained their behavior by pointing to what it gets them and what it costs them. That mine is an explanation of the same sort I claim as one of its positive advantages. Modern social science has been so sensitive to the charge that its findings are old or obvious, so ready to go out of its way to show how common-sense explanations are wrong, that it has ended by painting a picture of man that men cannot recognize. Thus of all our many "approaches" to social behavior, the one that sees it as an economy is the most neglected, though it is the one we use every moment of our lives—except when we write sociology. But even then, in our unguarded moments, sociologists find words like *reward* and *cost* slipping into what we say. Human nature will break in upon our most elaborate theories, but we seldom let it have its way with us and follow up systematically what these words imply. If you will read any writing in sociology, you will find all sorts of theories and explanations, besides the one the sociologist says he is using, slipping in surreptitiously to plaster up cracks in the argument and dropping out again as soon as the need for them has passed. The economic explanation seems so far to have been kept under the table for use in this way. I intend to bring it out into the open.

From *Social Behavior: Its Elementary Forms* by George C. Homans, © 1961, by Harcourt Brace Jovanovich, Inc., and reprinted with their permission.

I am not out to destroy common sense but to make explicit and general the wisdom it embodies . . .

Let not a reader reject our argument out of hand because he does not care for its horrid profit-seeking implications. Let him ask himself instead whether he and mankind have ever been able to advance any explanation why men change or fail to change their behavior other than that, in their circumstances, they would be better off doing something else, or that they are doing well enough already. On reflection he will find that neither he nor mankind has ever been able to offer another—the thing is a truism. It may ease his conscience to remember that if hedonists believe men take profits only in materialistic values, we are not hedonists here. So long as men's values are altruistic, they can take a profit in altruism too. Some of the greatest profiteers we know are altruists.

We have also tried to show how, given the special conditions of exchange that economics chooses to confine itself to, our propositions and corollaries are wholly compatible with those of elementary economics. Indeed we are out to rehabilitate the "economic man." The trouble with him was not that he was economic, that he used his resources to some advantage, but that he was antisocial and materialistic, interested only in money and material goods and ready to sacrifice even his old mother to get them. What was wrong with him were his values: he was only allowed a limited range of values; but the new economic man is not so limited. He may have any values whatever, from altruism to hedonism, but so long as he does not utterly squander his resources in achieving these values, his behavior is still economic. Indeed if he has learned to find reward in *not* husbanding his resources, if he values *not* taking any thought for the morrow, and acts accordingly, his behavior is still economic. In fact, the new economic man is plain man.

Some readers may feel that in making men profit-seekers we have made them more or less "rational" than they really are. If "rational" behavior means conscious rather than unconscious behavior, the question of rationality is irrelevant for us. In the fields of endeavor we shall be interested in, conscious and unconscious behavior come out at the same place. Person can offer Other more lavish praise in return for more valuable help, his behavior can be utterly economic, without his being any more conscious of what he is doing than the pigeon is.

But two other and somewhat more interesting meanings have been given to rationality. The first is this: behavior is irrational if an outside observer thinks that its reward is not good for a man in the long run. A man is irrational if he likes what he ought not to like. In this sense, a man who takes some drugs, including tobacco, is behaving irrationally. So is a masochist, a man who finds punishment rewarding, though the criterion of "goodness" or "health" is not as clear. But since for the purposes of this book we take a man's values as simply given, we care not here—though we surely do care elsewhere—if they be rational. What we are interested in is what he does with them once he has somehow picked them up. Suppose a man is a masochist—is it still true that if he has taken a lot of punishment lately, he will find further punishment less valuable? Will the first kick in the teeth give him more kick than the last? Although we have not experimented, we have no doubt it will.

The second meaning of rationality is a little different. Whatever a person's values may be, his behavior is irrational if it is not so calculated as to get him the largest supply of these values in the long run. Here the emphasis is not on the kind of value being pursued—it may be capital gains or eternal salvation—but on the way it is being pursued: the emphasis is on calculation and the long run—the longer the better. An irrational man is either unwilling to forgo some immediate reward in order to invest in some greater future, or unwilling to acquire the knowledge and make the calculations that would show him how to reach that future. A large part of many sciences, from divinity to the Theory of Games, is devoted to providing him with this knowledge and enabling him to make the calculations. The Theory of Games should, for instance, make him better able to choose a strategy among alternative courses of action, when the risks and returns of each are matters of probability, not certainty.

Even without the benefit of a science, there are of course people whose elementary social behavior is rational in this sense. The social climber is an example. Using his implicit knowledge of the propositions we try to make explicit here, and prepared to accept—this is his characteristic heroism—certain immediate costs in self-respect, he may well wind up in a far higher social position than he would have attained without his calculations and his peculiar asceticism. A developing science of elementary social behavior should enable a social climber who will study it to reach the top more surely—so long as it does not also help other people to see through his schemes. Indeed it should help anybody who has some long-term social goal in mind, selfish or unselfish. But let the reader be warned: though he himself may draw conclusions from this book that will enable him to act more rationally, we shall not draw them for him. This is not a book on applied sociology.

Although calculation for the long run plays its part in human affairs, we make no allowance for it in our propositions, which are to this extent incomplete. We do not rule it out; neither do we rule it in. Our first justification is that we shall not often need it to explain the research results considered in this book. And our second lies in plain sight: calculation for the long run is the exception and not the rule. The Theory of Games is good advice for human behavior but a poor description of it.

But we have a still better reason for our lack of concern with rationality. All the good advice, from ethics to economics, that wise men give their fellows is meant to change behavior and not to explain it; but our business is with explanation. The advice tries to answer the question: Given that you value the attainment of certain ends, how could you have acted so as to attain them more effectively? But what men or pigeons could have done is what they did do, and much social science has gone to show some of the surprising reasons why they cannot do in fact what some wiseacre says they could. This does not mean that all the advice goes for nothing. So far as men will take it, so far as they will learn from it, it may change the way they behave the next time. But behavior observed is behavior past, and for the purposes of explaining how men have indeed behaved, it is seldom enough to ask whether or not they were rational. The relevant question is what determined their behavior—though of course the advice they have listened to may be among the determinants.

The people who will appear in this book are, if you like, no less rational than pigeons. If it be rational of pigeons to learn and take the shortest of two paths to a reward, so it is of our men. They choose among a few alternatives immediately open to them; they choose with little regard for the really long-term results of their choice, which sometimes surprise them. But the short-term results they do know, and they know them less as matters of probability than of certainty. If Person will only praise Other enough, he is pretty sure of getting help: the question is not whether he can get the result but whether he finds it worth the price. Within these limits, our men do not choose foolishly—that is, at random— but only in the way our propositions say they do. All we impute to them in the way of rationality is that they know enough to come in out of the rain unless they enjoy getting wet. To be sure, such rationality as we have now left them may not amount to much, for rational behavior in the present sense is only behavior that is determined.

Let us make sure we are not snobs about the common pigeon or the common man. When the future is uncertain and science weak, the pursuit of immediate reward is by no means irrational even by the austere standards of the Theory of Games. "A bird in the hand is worth two in the bush" is by no means always an unintelligent policy. And so far as the pursuit of rationality entails study, forethought, and calculation, and such things hurt, as they often do, the pursuit of rationality is itself irrational unless their costs are reckoned in the balance. The costs of rationality may make rationality irrational.

THE NATURE OF
SYMBOLIC INTERACTIONISM

HERBERT BLUMER

Symbolic interactionism rests in the last analysis on three simple premises. The first premise is that human beings act toward things on the basis of the meanings that the things have for them. Such things include everything that the human being may note in his world—physical objects, such as trees or chairs; other human beings, such as a mother or a store clerk; categories of human beings, such as friends or enemies; institutions, as a school or a government; guiding ideals, such as individual independence or honesty; activities of others, such as their commands or requests; and such situations as an individual encounters in his daily life. The second premise is that the meaning of such things is derived from, or arises out of, the social interaction that one has with one's fellows. The third premise is that these meanings are handled in, and modified through, an interpretative process used by the person in dealing with the things he encounters. I wish to discuss briefly each of these three fundamental premises.

It would seem that few scholars would see anything wrong with the first premise—that human beings act toward things on the basis of the meanings which these things have for them. Yet, oddly enough, this simple view is ignored or played down in practically all of the thought and work in contemporary social science and psychological science. Meaning is either taken for granted and thus pushed aside as unimportant or it is regarded as a mere neutral link between the factors responsible for human behavior and this behavior as the product of such factors. We can see this clearly in the predominant posture of psychological and social science today. Common to both of these fields is the tendency to treat human behavior as the product of various factors that play upon human beings; concern is with the behavior and with the factors regarded as producing them. Thus, psychologists turn to such factors as stimuli, attitudes, conscious or unconscious motives, various kinds of psychological inputs, perception and cognition, and various features of personal organization to account for given forms or instances of human conduct. In a similar fashion sociologists rely on such factors as social position, status demands, social roles, cultural prescriptions, norms and values, social pressures, and group affiliation to provide such explanations. In both such typical psychological and sociological explanations the meanings of things for the human beings who are acting are either bypassed or swallowed up in the factors used to account for their

From Herbert Blumer, *Symbolic Interactionism: Perspective and Method,* © 1969.
Reprinted by permission of Prentice-Hall, Inc., Englewood Cliffs, New Jersey.

behavior. If one declares that the given kinds of behavior are the result of the particular factors regarded as producing them, there is no need to concern oneself with the meaning of the things toward which human beings act; one merely identifies the initiating factors and the resulting behavior. Or one may, if pressed, seek to accommodate the element of meaning by lodging it in the initiating factors or by regarding it as a neutral link intervening between the initiating factors and the behavior they are alleged to produce. In the first of these latter cases the meaning disappears by being merged into the initiating or causative factors; in the second case meaning becomes a mere transmission link that can be ignored in favor of the initiating factors.

The position of symbolic interactionism, in contrast, is that the meanings that things have for human beings are central in their own right. To ignore the meaning of the things toward which people act is seen as falsifying the behavior under study. To bypass the meaning in favor of factors alleged to produce the behavior is seen as a grievous neglect of the role of meaning in the formation of behavior.

The simple premise that human beings act toward things on the basis of the meaning of such things is much too simple in itself to differentiate symbolic interactionism—there are several other approaches that share this premise. A major line of difference between them and symbolic interactionism is set by the second premise, which refers to the source of meaning. There are two well-known traditional ways of accounting for the origin of meaning. One of them is to regard meaning as being intrinsic to the thing that has it, as being a natural part of the objective makeup of the thing. Thus, a chair is clearly a chair in itself, a cow a cow, a cloud a cloud, a rebellion a rebellion, and so forth. Being inherent in the thing that has it, meaning needs merely to be disengaged by observing the objective thing that has the meaning. The meaning emanates, so to speak from the thing and as such there is no process involved in its formation; all that is necessary is to recognize the meaning that is there in the thing. It should be immediately apparent that this view reflects the traditional position of "realism" in philosophy—a position that is widely held and deeply entrenched in the social and psychological sciences. The other major traditional view regards "meaning" as a psychical accretion brought to the thing by the person for whom the thing has meaning. This psychical accretion is treated as being an expression of constituent elements of the person's psyche, mind, or psychological organization. The constituent elements are such things as sensations, feelings, ideas, memories, motives, and attitudes. The meaning of a thing is but the expression of the given psychological elements that are brought into play in connection with the perception of the thing; thus one seeks to explain the meaning of a thing by isolating the particular psychological elements that produce the meaning. One sees this in the somewhat ancient and classical psychological practice of analyzing the meaning of an object by identifying the sensations that enter into perception of that object; or in the contemporary practice of tracing the meaning of a thing, such as let us say prostitution, to the attitude of the person who views it. This lodging of the meaning of things in psychological elements limits the processes of the formation of meaning to whatever processes are involved in arousing and bringing together the given psychological elements that produce the meaning. Such processes are psychological in nature, and include perception, cognition, repression, transfer of feelings, and association of ideas.

Symbolic interactionism views meaning as having a different source than those held by the two dominant views just considered. It does not regard meaning as emanating from the intrinsic makeup of the thing that has meaning, nor does it see meaning as arising through a coalescence of psychological elements in the person. Instead, it sees meaning as arising in the process of interaction between people. The meaning of a thing for a person grows out of the ways in which other persons act toward the person with regard to the thing. Their actions operate to define the thing for the person. Thus, symbolic interactionism sees meanings as social products, as creations that are formed in and through the defining activities of people as they interact. This point of view gives symbolic interactionism a very distinctive position, with profound implications that will be discussed later.

The third premise mentioned above further differentiates symbolic interactionism. While the meaning of things is formed in the context of social interaction and is derived by the person from that interaction, it is a mistake to think that the use of meaning by a person is but an application of the meaning so derived. This mistake seriously mars the work of many scholars who otherwise follow the symbolic interactionist approach. They fail to see that the use of meanings by a person in his action involves an interpretative process. In this respect they are similar to the adherents of the two dominant views spoken of above—to those who lodge meaning in the objective makeup of the thing that has it and those who regard it as an expression of psychological elements. All three are alike in viewing the use of meaning by the human being in his action as being no more than an arousing and application of already established meanings. As such, all three fail to see that the use of meanings by the actor occurs through a *process of interpretation*. This process has two distinct steps. First, the actor indicates to himself the things toward which he is acting; he has to point out to himself the things that have meaning. The making of such indications is an internalized social process in that the actor is interacting with himself. This interaction with himself is something other than an interplay of psychological elements; it is an instance of the person engaging in a process of communication with himself. Second, by virtue of this process of communicating with himself, interpretation becomes a matter of handling meanings. The actor selects, checks, suspends, regroups, and transforms the meanings in the light of the situation in which he is placed and the direction of his action. Accordingly, interpretation should not be regarded as a mere automatic application of established meanings but as a formative process in which meanings are used and revised as instruments for the guidance and formation of action. It is necessary to see that meanings play their part in action through a process of self-interaction.

It is not my purpose to discuss at this point the merits of the three views that lodge meaning respectively in the thing, in the psyche, and in social action, nor to elaborate on the contention that meanings are handled flexibly by the actor in the course of forming his action. Instead, I wish merely to note that by being based on these three premises, symbolic interaction is necessarily led to develop an analytical scheme of human society and human conduct that is quite distinctive. It is this scheme that I now propose to outline.

Symbolic interactionism is grounded on a number of basic ideas, or "root images," as I prefer to call them. These root images refer to and depict the nature of the following matters: human groups or societies, social interaction, objects, the human being as an actor, human action, and the interconnection of the lines of action. Taken together, these root images represent the way in which symbolic interactionism views human society and conduct. They constitute the framework of study and analysis. Let me describe briefly each of these root images.

Nature of Human Society or Human Group Life.

Human groups are seen as consisting of human beings who are engaging in action. The action consists of the multitudinous activities that the individuals perform in their life as they encounter one another and as they deal with the succession of situations confronting them. The individuals may act singly, they may act collectively, and they may act on behalf of, or as representatives of, some organization or group of others. The activities belong to the acting individuals and are carried on by them always with regard to the situations in which they have to act. The import of this simple and essentially redundant characterization is that fundamentally human groups or society *exists in action* and must be seen in terms of action. This picture of human society as action must be the starting point (and the point of return) for any scheme that purports to treat and analyze human society empirically. Conceptual schemes that depict society in some other fashion can only be derivations from the complex of ongoing activity that constitutes group life. This is true of the two dominant conceptions of society in contemporary sociology—that of culture and that of social structure. Culture as a conception, whether defined as custom, tradition, norm, value, rules, or such like, is clearly derived from what people do. Similarly, social structure in any of its aspects, as represented by such terms as social position, status, role, authority, and prestige, refers to relationships derived from how people act toward each other. The life of any human society consists necessarily of an ongoing process of fitting together the activities of its members. It is this complex of ongoing activity that establishes and portrays structure or organization. A cardinal principle of symbolic interactionism is that any empirically oriented scheme of human society, however derived, must respect the fact that in the first and last instances human society consists of people engaging in action. To be empirically valid the scheme must be consistent with the nature of the social action of human beings.

Nature of Social Interaction.

Group life necessarily presupposes interaction between the group members; or, put otherwise, a society consists of individuals interacting with one another. The activities of the members occur predominantly in response to one another or in relation to one another. Even though this is recognized almost universally in definitions of human society, social interaction is usually taken for granted and treated as having little, if any, significance in its own right. This is evident in typical sociological and psychological schemes—they treat social interaction as merely a medium through which the determinants of behavior pass to produce the behavior. Thus, the typical sociological scheme ascribes behavior to such factors as status position, cultural prescriptions, norms, values, sanctions, role demands, and social system requirements; explanation in terms of such factors suffices without paying attention to the social interaction that their play necessarily presupposes. Similarly, in the typical psychological scheme such factors as motives, attitudes, hidden complexes, elements of psychological organization, and psychological processes are used to account for behavior without any need of considering social interaction. One jumps from such causative factors to the behavior they are supposed to produce. Social interaction becomes a mere forum through which sociological or psychological determinants move to bring about given forms of human behavior. I may add that this ignoring of social interaction is not corrected by speaking of an interaction of societal elements (as when a sociologist speaks of an interaction of social roles or an interaction between the components of a social system) or an interaction of psychological elements (as when a psychologist speaks of an interaction between the attitudes held by different people). Social interaction is an interaction between actors and not between factors imputed to them.

Symbolic interactionism does not merely give a ceremonious nod to social interaction. It recognizes social interaction to be of vital importance in its own right. This importance lies in the fact that social interaction is a process that *forms* human conduct instead of being merely a means or a setting for the expression or release of human conduct. Put simply, human beings in interacting with one another have to take account of what each other is doing or is about to do; they are forced to direct their own conduct or handle their situations in terms of what they take into account. Thus, the activities of others enter as positive factors in the formation of their own conduct; in the face of the actions of others one may abandon an intention or purpose, revise it, check or suspend it, intensify it, or replace it. The actions of others enter to set what one plans to do, may oppose or prevent such plans, may require a revision of such plans, and may demand a very different set of such plans. One has to *fit* one's own line of activity in some manner to the actions of others. The actions of others have to be taken into account and cannot be regarded as merely an arena for the expression of what one is disposed to do or sets out to do.

We are indebted to George Herbert Mead (1934) for the most penetrating analysis of social interaction—an analysis that squares with the realistic account just given. Mead identifies two forms or levels of social interaction in human society. He refers to them respectively as "the conversation of gestures" and "the use of significant symbols"; I shall term them respectively "non-symbolic interaction" and "symbolic interaction." Non-symbolic interaction takes place when one responds directly to the action of another without interpreting that action; symbolic interaction involves interpretation of the action. Non-symbolic interaction is most readily apparent in reflex responses, as in the case of a boxer who automatically raises his arm to parry a blow. However, if the boxer were reflectively to identify the forthcoming blow from his opponent as a feint designed to trap him, he would be engaging in symbolic interaction. In this case, he would endeavor to ascertain the meaning of the blow—that is, what the blow signifies as to his opponent's plan. In their association human beings engage plentifully in non-symbolic interaction as they respond immediately and unreflectively to each other's bodily movements, expressions, and tones of voice, but their characteristic mode of interaction is on the symbolic level, as they seek to understand the meaning of each other's action.

Mead's analysis of symbolic interaction is highly important. He sees it as a presentation of gestures and a response to the meaning of those gestures. A gesture is any part or aspect of an ongoing action that signifies the larger act of which it is a part—for example, the shaking of a fist as an indication of a possible attack, or the declaration of war by a nation as an indication of a posture and line of action of that nation. Such things as requests, orders, commands, cues, and declarations are gestures that convey to the person who recognizes them an idea of the intention and plan of forthcoming action of the individual who presents them. The person who responds organizes his response on the basis of what the gestures mean to him; the person who presents the gestures advances them as indications or signs of what he is planning to do as well as of what he wants the respondent to do or understand. Thus, the gesture has meaning for both the person who makes it and for the person to whom it is directed. When the gesture has the same meaning for both, the two parties understand each other. From this brief account it can be seen that the meaning of the gesture flows out along three lines (Mead's triadic nature of meaning): It signifies what the person to whom it is directed is to do; it signifies what the person who is making the gesture plans to do; and it signifies the joint action that is to arise by the articulation of the acts of both. Thus, for illustration, a robber's command to his victim to put up his hands is (a) an indication of what the victim is to do; (b) an indication of what the robber plans to do, that is, relieve the victim of his money; and (c) an indication of the joint act being formed, in this case a holdup. If there is confusion or misunderstanding along any one of these three lines of meaning, communication is ineffective, interaction is impeded, and the formation of joint action is blocked.

One additional feature should be added to round out Mead's analysis of symbolic interaction, namely, that the parties to such interaction must necessarily take each other's roles. To indicate to another what he is to do, one has to make the indication from the standpoint of that other; to order the victim to put up his hands the robber has to see this response in terms of the victim making it. Correspondingly, the victim has to see the command from the standpoint of the robber who gives the command; he has to grasp the intention and forthcoming action of the robber. Such mutual role-taking is the *sine qua non* of communication and effective symbolic interaction.

The central place and importance of symbolic interaction in human group life and conduct should be apparent. A human society or group consists of people in association. Such association exists necessarily in the form of people acting toward one another and thus engaging in social interaction. Such interaction in human society is characteristically and predominantly on the symbolic level; as individuals acting individually, collectively, or as agents of some organization encounter one another they are necessarily required to take account of the actions of one another as they form their own action. They do this by a dual process of indicating to others how to act and of interpreting the indications made by others. Human group life is a vast process of such defining to others what to do and of interpreting their definitions; through this process people come to fit their activities to one another and to form their own individual conduct. Both such joint activity and individual conduct are formed *in* and *through* this ongoing process; they are not mere expressions or products of what people bring to their interaction or of conditions that are antecedent to their interaction. The failure to accommodate to this vital point constitutes the fundamental deficiency of schemes that seek to account for human society in terms of social organization or psychological factors, or of any combination of the two. By virtue of symbolic interaction, human group life is necessarily a formative process and not a mere arena for the expression of pre-existing factors.

Nature of Objects

The position of symbolic interactionism is that the "worlds" that exist for human beings and for their groups are composed of "objects" and that these objects are the product of symbolic interaction. An object is anything that can be indicated, anything that is pointed to or referred to—a cloud, a book, a legislature, a banker, a religious doctrine, a ghost, and so forth. For purposes of convenience one can classify objects in three categories: (a) physical objects, such as chairs, trees, or bicycles; (b) social objects, such as students, priests, a president, a mother, or a friend; and (c) abstract objects, such as moral principles, philosophical doctrines, or ideas such as justice, exploitation, or compassion. I repeat that an object is anything that can be indicated or referred to. The nature of an object— of any and every object—consists of the meaning that it has for the person for whom it is an object. This meaning sets the way in which he sees the object, the way in which he is prepared to act toward it, and the way in which he is ready to talk about it. An object may have a different meaning for different individuals: a tree will be a different object to a botanist, a lumberman, a poet, and a home gardener; the President of the United States can be a very different object to a devoted member of his political party than to a member of the opposition; the members of an ethnic group may be seen as a different kind of object by members of other groups. The meaning of objects for a person arises fundamentally out of the way they are defined to him by others with whom he interacts. Thus, we come to learn through the indications of others that a chair is a chair, that doctors are a certain kind of professional, that the United States Constitution is a given kind of legal document, and so forth. Out of a process of mutual indications common objects emerge—objects that have the same meaning for a given set of people and are seen in the same manner by them.

Several noteworthy consequences follow from the foregoing discussion of objects. First, it gives us a different picture of the environment or milieu of human beings. From their standpoint the environment consists *only* of the objects that the given human beings recognize and know. The nature of this environment is set by the meaning that the objects composing it have for those human beings. Individuals, also groups, occupying or living in the same spatial location may have, accordingly, very different environments; as we say, people may be living side by side yet be living in different worlds. Indeed, the term "world" is more suitable than the word "environment" to designate the setting, the surroundings, and the texture of things that confront them. It is the world of their objects with which people have to deal and toward which they develop their actions. It follows that in order to understand the action of people it is necessary to identify their world of objects—an important point that will be elaborated later.

Second, objects (in the sense of their meaning) must be seen as social creations—as being formed in and arising out of the process of definition and interpretation as this process takes place in the interaction of people. The meaning of anything and everything has to be formed, learned, and transmitted through a process of indication—a process that is necessarily a social process. Human group life on the level of symbolic interaction is a vast process in which people are forming, sustaining, and transforming the objects of their world as they come to give meaning to objects. Objects have no fixed status except as their meaning is sustained through indications and definitions that people make of the objects. Nothing is more apparent than that objects in all categories can undergo change in their meaning. A star in the sky is a very different object to a modern astrophysicist than it was to a sheepherder of biblical times; marriage was a different object to later Romans than to earlier Romans; the president of a nation who fails to act successfully through critical times may become a very different object to the citizens of his land. In short, from the standpoint of symbolic interactionism human group life is a process in which objects are being created, affirmed, transformed, and cast aside. The life and action of people necessarily change in line with the changes taking place in their world of objects.

The Human Being as an Acting Organism.

Symbolic interactionism recognizes that human beings must have a makeup that fits the nature of social interaction. The human being is seen as an organism that not only responds to others on the non-symbolic level but as one that makes indications to others and interprets their indications. He can do this, as Mead has shown so emphatically, only by virtue of possessing a "self." Nothing esoteric is meant by this expression. It means merely that a human being can be an object of his own action. Thus, he can recognize himself, for instance, as being a man young in age, a student, in debt, trying to become a doctor, coming from an undistinguished family and so forth. In all such instances he is an object to himself; and he acts toward himself and guides himself in his actions toward others on the basis of the kind of object he is to himself. This notion of oneself as an object fits into the earlier discussion of objects. Like other objects, the self-object emerges from the process of social interaction in which other people are defining a person to himself. Mead has traced the way in which this occurs in his discussion of role-taking. He points out that in order to become an object to himself a person has to see himself from the outside. One can do this only be placing himself in the position of others and viewing himself or acting toward himself from that position. The roles the person takes range from that of discrete individuals (the "play stage"), through that of discrete organized groups (the "game stage") to that of the abstract community (the "generalized other"). In taking such roles the person is in a position to address or approach himself—as in the case of a young girl who in "playing mother" talks to herself as her mother would do, or in the case of a young priest who sees himself through the eyes of the priesthood. We form our objects of ourselves through such a process of role-taking. It follows that we see ourselves through the way in which others see or define us—or, more precisely, we see ourselves by taking one of the three types of roles of others that have been mentioned. That one forms an object of himself through the ways in which others define one to himself is recognized fairly well in the literature today, so despite its great significance I shall not comment on it further.

There is an even more important matter that stems from the fact that the human being has a self, namely that this enables him to interact with himself. This interaction is not in the form of interaction between two or more parts of a psychological system, as between needs, or between emotions, or between ideas, or between the id and the ego in the Freudian scheme. Instead, the interaction is social—a form of communication, with the person addressing himself as a person and responding thereto. We can clearly recognize such interaction in ourselves as each of us notes that he is angry with himself, or that he has to spur himself on in his tasks, or that he reminds himself to do this or that, or that he is talking to himself in working out some plan of action. As such instances suggest, self-interaction exists fundamentally as a process of making indications to oneself. This process is in play continuously during one's waking life, as one notes and considers one or another matter, or observes this or that happening. Indeed, for the human being to be conscious or aware of anything is equivalent to his indicating the thing to himself—he is identifying it as a given kind of object and considering its relevance or importance to his line of action. One's waking life consists of a series of such indications that the person is making to himself, indications that he uses to direct his action.

We have, then, a picture of the human being as an organism that interacts with itself through a social process of making indications to itself. This is a radically different view of the human being from that which dominates contemporary social and psychological science. The dominant prevailing view sees the human being as a complex organism whose behavior is a response to factors playing on the organization of the organism. Schools of thought in the social and psychological sciences differ enormously in which of such factors they regard as significant, as is shown in such a diverse array as stimuli, organic drives, need-dispositions, conscious motives, unconscious motives, emotions, attitudes, ideas, cultural prescriptions, norms, values, status demands, social roles, reference group affiliations, and institutional pressures. Schools of thought differ also in how they view the organization of the human being, whether as a kind of biological organization, a kind of psychological organization, or a kind of imported societal organization incorporated from the social structure of one's group. Nevertheless, these schools of thought are alike in seeing the human being as a responding organism, with its behavior being a product of the factors playing on its organization or an expression of the interplay of parts of its organization. Under this widely shared view the human being is "social" only in the sense of either being a member of social species, or of responding to others (social stimuli), or of having incorporated within it the organization of his group.

The view of the human being held in symbolic interactionism is fundamentally different. The human being is seen as "social" in a much more profound sense—in the sense of an organism that engages in social interaction with itself by making indications to itself and responding to such indications. By virtue of engaging in self-interaction the human being stands in a markedly different relation to his environment than is presupposed by the widespread conventional view described above. Instead of being merely an organism that responds to the play of factors on or through it, the human being is seen as an organism that has to deal with what it notes. It meets what it so notes by engaging in a process of self-indication in which it makes an object of what it notes, gives it a meaning, and uses the meaning as the basis for directing its action. Its behavior with regard to what it notes is not a response called forth by the presentation of what it notes but instead is an action that arises out of the interpretation make through the process of self-indication. In this sense, the human being who is engaging in self-interaction is not a mere responding organism but an acting organism—an organism that has to mold a line of action on the basis of what it takes into account instead of merely releasing a response to the play of some factor on its organization.

Nature of Human Action.

The capacity of the human being to make indications to himself gives a distinctive character to human action. It means that the human individual confronts a world that he must interpret in order to act instead of an environment to which he responds because of his organization. He has to cope with the situations in which he is called on to act, ascertaining the meaning of the actions of others and mapping out his own line of action in the light of such interpretation. He has to construct and guide his action instead of merely releasing it in response to factors playing on him or operating through him. He may do a miserable job in constructing his action, but he has to construct it.

This view of the human being directing his action by making indications to himself stands sharply in contrast to the view of human action that dominates current psychological and social science. This dominant view, as already implied, ascribes human action to an initiating factor or a combination of such factors. Action is traced back to such matters as motives, attitudes, need-dispositions, unconscious complexes, stimuli configurations, status demands, role requirements, and situational demands. To link the action to one or more of such initiating agents is regarded as fulfilling the scientific task. Yet, such an approach ignores and makes no place for the process of self-interaction through which the individual handles his world and constructs his action. The door is closed to the vital process of interpretation in which the individual notes and assesses what is presented to him and through which he maps out lines of overt behavior prior to their execution.

Fundamentally, action on the part of a human being consists of taking account of various things that he notes and forging a line of conduct on the basis of how he interprets them. The things taken into account cover such matters as his wishes and wants, his objectives, the available means for their achievement, the actions and anticipated actions of others, his image of himself, and the likely result of a given line of action. His conduct is formed and guided through such a process of indication and interpretation. In this process, given lines of action may be started or stopped, they may be abandoned or postponed, they may be confined to mere planning or to an inner life of reverie, or if initiated, they may be transformed. My purpose is not to analyze this process but to call attention to its presence and operation in the formation of human action. We must recognize that the activity of human beings consists of meeting a flow of situations in which they have to act and that their action is built on the basis of what they note, how they assess and interpret what they note, and what kind of projected lines of action they map out. This process is not caught by ascribing action to some kind of factor (for example, motives, need-dispositions, role requirements, social expectations, or social rules) that is thought to initiate the action and propel it to its conclusion; such a factor, or some expression of it, is a matter the human actor takes into account in mapping his line of action. The initiating factor does not embrace or explain how it and other matters are taken into account in the situation that calls for action. One has to get inside of the defining process of the actor in order to understand his action.

This view of human action applies equally well to joint or collective action in which numbers of individuals are implicated. Joint or collective action constitutes the domain of sociological concern, as exemplified in the behavior of groups, institutions, organizations, and social classes. Such instances of societal behavior, whatever they may be, consist of individuals fitting their lines of action to one another. It is both proper and possible to view and study such behavior in its joint or collective character instead of in its individual components. Such joint behavior does not lose its character of being constructed through an interpretative process in meeting the situations in which the collectivity is called on to act. Whether the collectivity be an army engaged in a campaign, a corporation seeking to expand its operations, or a nation trying to correct an unfavorable balance of trade, it needs to construct its action through an interpretation of what is happening in its area of operation. The interpretative process takes place by participants making indications to one another, not merely each to himself. Joint or collective action is an outcome of such a process of interpretative interaction.

REFERENCE

Mead, George Herbert. *Mind, Self, and Society*. Chicago: University of Chicago Press, 1934.

BEING AND
SELF-ACTUALIZATION

ABRAHAM MASLOW

Man demonstrates *in his own nature* a pressure toward fuller and fuller Being, more and more perfect actualization of his humanness in exactly the same naturalistic, scientific sense that an acorn may be said to be "pressing toward" being an oak tree, or that a tiger can be observed to "push toward" being tigerish, or a horse toward being equine. Man is ultimately *not* molded or shaped into humanness, or taught to be human. The role of the environment is ultimately to permit him or help him to actualize *his own* potentialities, not *its* potentialities. The environment does not give him potentialities and capacities; he *has* them in inchoate or embryonic form, just exactly as he has embryonic arms and legs. And creativeness, spontaneity, selfhood, authenticity, caring for others, being able to love, yearning for truth are embryonic potentialities belonging to his species-membership just as much as are his arms and legs and brain and eyes.

This is not in contradiction to the data already amassed which show clearly that living in a family and in a culture are absolutely necessary to *actualize* these psychological potentials that define humanness. Let us avoid this confusion. A teacher or a culture doesn't create a human being. It doesn't implant within him the ability to love, or to be curious, or to philosophize, or to symbolize, or to be creative. Rather it permits, or fosters, or encourages or helps what exists in embryo to become real and actual. The same mother or the same culture, treating a kitten or a puppy in exactly the same way, cannot make it into a human being. The culture is sun and food and water: it is not the seed.

"Instinct" Theory

The group of thinkers who have been working with self-actualization, with self, with authentic humanness, etc., have pretty firmly established their case that man has a tendency to realize himself. By implication he is exhorted to be true to his own nature, to trust himself, to be authentic, spontaneous, honestly expressive, to look for the sources of his action in his own deep inner nature.

But, of course, this is an ideal counsel. They do not sufficiently warn that most adults don't know *how* to be authentic and that, if they "express"

From *Toward a Psychology of Being* by Abraham H. Maslow. © 1968 by Litton Educational Publishing, Inc. Reprinted by permission of Van Nostrand Reinhold Company.

themselves, they may bring catastrophe not only upon themselves but upon others as well. What answer must be given to the rapist or the sadist who asks "Why should I too not trust and express myself?"

These thinkers as a group have been remiss in several respects. They have *implied* without making explicit that if you can behave authentically, you *will* behave well, that if you emit action from within, it will be good and right behavior. What is very clearly implied is that this inner core, this real self, is good, trustworthy, ethical. This is an affirmation that is clearly separable from the affirmation that man actualizes himself, and needs to be separately proven (as I think it will be). Furthermore, these writers have as a group very definitely ducked the crucial statement about this inner core, i.e., that it *must* in some degree be inherited or else everything else they say is so much hash.

In other words, we must grapple with "instinct" theory or, as I prefer to call it, basic need theory, that is to say, with the study of the original, intrinsic, in part heredity-determined needs, urges, wishes and, I may say, values of mankind. We can't play both the biology game and the sociology game simultaneously. We can't affirm *both* that culture does everything and anything, and that man has an inherent nature. The one is incompatible with the other.

And of all the problems in this area of instinct, the one of which we know least and should know most is that of aggression, hostility, hatred, and destructiveness. The Freudians claim this to be instinctive; most other dynamic psychologists claim it to be not directly instinctive, but rather an ever-present reaction to frustration of instinctoid or basic needs. The truth is that we don't really know. Clinical experience hasn't settled the problem because equally good clinicians come to these divergent conclusions. What we need is hard, firm research. . . .

Some Propositions about the Nature of Man

1. We have, each one of us, an essential inner nature which is instinctoid, intrinsic, given, "natural," i.e., with an appreciable hereditary determinant, and which tends strongly to persist. . . .

I include in this essential inner nature instinctoid basic needs, capacities, talents, anatomical equipment, physiological or temperamental balances, prenatal and natal injuries, and traumata to the neonate. This inner core shows itself as natural inclinations, propensities or inner bent. . . .

2. These are potentialities, not final actualizations. Therefore they have a life history and must be seen developmentally. They are actualized, shaped or stifled mostly (but not altogether) by extra-psychic determinants

(culture, family, environment, learning, etc.). Very early in life these goalless urges and tendencies become attached to objects ("sentiments") by canalization but also by arbitrarily learned associations.

3. This inner core, even though it is biologically based and "instinctoid," is weak in certain senses rather than strong. It is easily overcome, suppressed or repressed. It may even be killed off permanently. Humans no longer have instincts in the animal sense, powerful, unmistakable inner voices which tell them unequivocally what to do, when, where, how and with whom. All that we have left are instinct-remnants. And furthermore, these are weak, subtle and delicate, very easily drowned out by learning, by cultural expectations, by fear, by disapproval, etc. They are *hard* to know, rather than easy. Authentic selfhood can be defined in part as being able to hear these impulse-voices within oneself, i.e., to know what one really wants or doesn't want, what one is fit for and what one is *not* fit for, etc. It appears that there are wide individual differences in the strength of these impulse-voices. . . .

4. Even though "weak," this inner nature rarely disappears or dies, in the usual person, in the U.S. (such disappearance or dying is possible early in the life history, however). It persists underground, unconsciously, even though denied and repressed. Like the voice of the intellect (which is part of it), it speaks softly but it *will* be heard, even if in a distorted form. That is, it has a dynamic force of its own, pressing always for open, uninhibited expression. Effort must be used in its suppression or repression from which fatigue can result. This force is one main aspect of the "will to health," the urge to grow, the pressure to self-actualization, the quest for one's identity. It is this that makes psychotherapy, education and self-improvement possible in principle. . . .

5. If this essential core (inner nature) of the person is frustrated, denied or suppressed, sickness results, sometimes in obvious forms, sometimes in subtle and devious forms, sometimes immediately, sometimes later. . . .

6. Self-actualization does not mean a transcendence of all human problems. Conflict, anxiety, frustration, sadness, hurt, and guilt can all be found in healthy human beings. In general, the movement, with increasing maturity, is from neurotic pseudo-problems to the real, unavoidable, existential problems, inherent in the nature of man (even at his best) living in a particular kind of world. Even though he is not neurotic he may be troubled by real, desirable and necessary guilt rather than neurotic guilt (which isn't desirable or necessary), by an intrinsic conscience (rather than the Freudian superego). Even though he has transcended the problems of Becoming, there remain the problems of Being. To be untroubled when one *should* be troubled can be a sign of sickness. Sometimes, smug people have to be scared *"into* their wits." . . .

7. From this point of view, a society or a culture can be either growth-fostering or growth-inhibiting. The sources of growth and of humanness are essentially within the human person and are not created or invented by society, which can only help or hinder the development of humanness, just as a gardener can help or hinder the growth of a rosebush, but cannot determine that it shall be an oak tree. This is true even though we know that a culture is a *sine qua non* for the actualization of humanness itself, e.g., language, abstract thought, ability to love; but these exist as potentialities in human germ plasm prior to culture.

This makes theoretically possible a comparative sociology, transcending and including cultural relativity. The "better" culture gratifies all basic human needs and permits self-actualization. The "poorer" cultures do not. The same is true for education. To the extent that it fosters growth toward self-actualization, it is "good" education.

As soon as we speak of "good" or "bad" cultures, and take them as means rather than as ends, the concept of "adjustment" comes into question. We must ask, "What kind of culture or subculture is the 'well adjusted' person well adjusted *to*?" Adjustment is, very definitely, *not* necessarily synonymous with psychological health.

CHAPTER
TWO

HOW DO PEOPLE
PERCEIVE AND ORGANIZE THEIR
SOCIAL ENVIRONMENT?

THE ISSUE OF SOCIAL PERCEPTION

Four-year-old Jimmy Smith sits before the television watching the flickering screen with open-mouthed intentness. A man picks up a ball and tosses it directly into the camera. Jimmy blinks but does not flinch. The scene changes. A cartoon figure of a cow dominates the screen urging Jimmy to have a glass of delicious, cold milk. He glances briefly toward the kitchen and returns his gaze to the television.

From upstairs he hears his mother's voice: "Jimmy, turn off the TV and come pick up your room. It's almost time for dinner."

He hesitates momentarily, then turns to the stuffed bear sitting in the chair beside him: "Teddy, I have to pick up my room. Can you wait here for me all alone?"

He watches the bear briefly and then walks slowly to the foot of the stairs. "Mommy," he calls, raising his voice above the television, "Teddy wants me to stay with him and I don't want to leave him alone, so I can't pick up my room now."

His mother's reply is firm: "James, please stop talking nonsense. Teddy is very nice but he's just a stuffed animal. Now you pick up your room like a good boy."

Jimmy returns to the television and turns it off. "Oh, O.K." he says sulkily and saunters into his room. He begins picking toys off the floor and placing them on shelves, paying little attention to what he is placing where, so that the disarray on the shelves gradually grows. A marble rolls back off the shelf and falls on the floor. He picks it up and replaces it more firmly. Again it rolls off.

"Mommy!" he shouts angrily, "The marble doesn't want to stay on the shelf."

"Well, put it someplace else," she says.

"I think it wants to stay on the floor—Mommy, where should the red truck go?"

"Put it in the toy chest."

"What about this other car?" He picks up a turquoise-colored racing car.

"Which one?"

"This one. It's blue—no green—no, I don't know."

"Well, just put it in the toy chest, too."

The mother comes downstairs and enters his room. "Jimmy, these shelves are a mess," she exclaims, "try to put your things away more neatly."

"I can't," he whines, "why don't you do it mommy, you're better."

"I'm busy, Jimmy, I have to vacuum the floor now."

"But you can do both, Mommy. It's easy for you to do it."

He watches carefully as his mother wheels in the vacuum cleaner and flicks on the switch. The machine comes alive filling the room with its loud whining sound. As it begins to glide across the floor, Jimmy edges away into a corner and watches uneasily. His mother notices and turns off the machine.

"What's the matter," she asks.

"Mommy," he whines, "I don't like the vacoming cleaner."

"Why, it helps me a lot. See how it sucks up all the dirt off the floor?"

"Yes, but it might suck me up too, Mommy."

"No, it won't. It can't pick up a big boy like you. It only picks up tiny things."

"But what about my toys?"

"It can't pick them up either. Now you get back to work and let me finish up."

Somewhat reassured, Jimmy turns his attention to the nearest shelf and his mother once again starts the vacuum cleaner.

Jimmy is wrestling with the complex task of learning to perceive and organize his social environment. The fact that he sometimes makes mistakes, that he does not always interpret and react in a manner that accords with our conception of reality, should not obscure the more important fact that Jimmy is already able to carry on this tremendously complex task reasonably successfully. If we were to place ourselves in Jimmy's room and attempt to experience his world completely passively—as a mere input of sense perceptions—we would experience little more than a booming, buzzing confusion: lights, colors, sounds, smells, movements, and feelings. This is the world of the new-born: nothing has meaning, nothing is related, nothing is any more real or relevant than anything else. Clearly, Jimmy is well beyond this point. His world is, by and large, orderly and meaningful. He can screen out irrelevant inputs, anticipate upcoming events, and act on his environment in such a way as to produce intended and predictable outcomes. With time, his ability to carry out these tasks and more will continue to improve.

But how has Jimmy acquired these skills? Just what has he learned? What factors or principles underlie the process by which a child (or adult) comes to perceive and organize his social environment? The readings in this section deal broadly with these questions. Specifically, we shall examine four somewhat different frameworks that have been used in studying how people code their world. In part, each framework represents an emphasis on somewhat different aspects of the problem, but in part each also represents a different way of approaching or construing the entire process.

THE MAJOR VIEWS

Social Realism

The central premise of this first perspective is that *reality, or the world as we know it, is essentially a product of social consensus.* One of the earliest coherent exponents of this perspective was a philosopher/social psychologist named George Herbert Mead. He founded a school of social psychology known as symbolic interaction whose adherents today take this central premise very seriously. We had occasion to encounter the symbolic interactionists in the preceding section dealing with the nature of man. Here, the social realist perspective is represented by Tomatsu Shibutani.

What would a social realist be most likely to note in the vignette about Jimmy? Probably he would be most intrigued by the manner in which Jimmy is learning to distinguish among various levels of reality. It is clear from Jimmy's behavior that he distinguishes between the reality of events on television and the reality of events around his house. The latter are part of reality par excellence—he cannot and does not ignore the wishes of his mother in the same way that he can and does ignore the wishes of the cartoon cow. As yet, however, he has not quite learned that the wishes of his teddy bear are imaginary and will not be treated by others as being on a par with the reality of everyday life.

A social realist would, of course, be quick to point out that this is purely a matter of social convention. To Jimmy, his teddy bear is a very important companion—a sort of ritual object or fetish with which he sleeps every night—whose wishes seem quite real. It is not difficult to find cultures in which the wishes of such ritual objects, *e.g.,* gods, statues, relics, are considered part of the paramount reality of everyday life to be indulged as faithfully as those of any authority. It just happens that American culture does not treat teddy bears in this fashion—at best they are considered very important toys, somehow related to a child's sense of security. The child's need for such toys, or related objects like security blankets, is treated as real, and parents may go to some length to assure that such objects are brought along on trips. At the same time, these objects are not considered to have any needs of their own. It is not surprising, then, that Jimmy has not yet fully understood the rather subtle distinctions that apply to his teddy bear.

In similar fashion, he may as yet have difficulty in distinguishing between his night dreams and the reality of everyday life. Both seem very real to him. Both seem to involve very definite interactions with significant persons in his life. He is as frightened by a nightmare as by any unpleasant experience in his waking life. Again, it is not difficult to find cultures that treat dreams as real in the sense that they must be heeded and understood as faithfully as any important everyday event. But again, it just happens that American culture treats dreams as imaginary and classifies them together with the wishes of teddy bears and cartoon cows.

Before Jimmy can be said to be fully capable of perceiving and organizing his social environment, he must learn a myriad of such social conventions that distinguish between real and unreal events and objects. Nor is the learning of these conventions a trivial matter. However arbitrary they may seem in cross-cultural perspective, if Jimmy by a certain age fails to adhere to them, he will in all probability be considered mentally ill and will be forced to undergo appropriate treatment. Most people simply do not consider it healthy for a grown man to introduce the wishes of his teddy bear in ordinary, polite conversation.

For the social realist, then, one important aspect of learning to code the world properly is that of learning to identify the level of reality to which various objects and events belong. And this is only a particularly interesting part of a larger whole. More generally, the social realist is interested in the process by which events and objects in the environment come to have meaning for the individual. Realness is but one important aspect of meaning and the speciality of social realists is their belief that this, as well as all other aspects of meaning, is very largely a matter of social convention. The meaning of any object–the way it is to be perceived, used, treated, and reacted to–is *not seen as an intrinsic property of the object but rather as something imposed upon it by social convention.* A chair and a coat may have certain intrinsic properties of weight and mass, but the fact that one is sat upon in certain ways while the other is worn to keep warm on certain occasions is a matter of convention, and for an ordinary person it is the latter features that are important.

In effect, the social realist sees the individual as inhabiting a world of events and objects which, though they may have certain basic physical properties, are fundamentally social in nature. Herbert Blumer (1969, p.11), whom we encountered earlier as presenting the symbolic interactionist view of man, puts it this way:

> . . the 'worlds' that exist for human beings and for their groups are composed of 'objects' and these objects are the products of symbolic interaction . . . . The nature of an object–of any and every object–consists of the meaning it has for the person for whom it is an object. This meaning sets the way in which he sees the object, the way in which he is prepared to act toward it, and the way in which he is ready to talk about it. . . . The meaning of objects for a person arises fundamentally out of the way they are defined to him by others with whom he interacts.

Peter Berger and Thomas Luckman (1967, pp. 21-22), taking a more phenomenological tack, put it this way,

> . . . the reality of everyday life appears already objectified, that is, constituted by an order of objects that have been designated *as* objects before my appearance on the scene. The language of everyday life continuously provides me with necessary objectifications and posits the order within which these make sense and within which everyday life has meaning to me. I live in a place that is geographically designated; I employ tools from can openers to sports cars, which are designated in the technical vocabulary of my society. . . .In this manner, language marks the co-ordinates of my life in society and fills that life with meaningful objects.

The analytic framework used by social realists points not only to the ultimate arbitrariness of any culture's system for coding the world, but also to the extreme malleability of our sense impressions. Things are real not because they really impinge on our senses, but because we collectively agree to define them as real. Perhaps a "rose by any other name would smell as sweet," but if a rose were called a stinkweed, at the very least, its sweetness might be experienced as a bit cloying. Scotch and beer are considered fine beverages in our society, but still it takes considerable time to acquire a "taste" for them. Tomatoes were once considered poisonous, and there is every reason to believe that a person forced to eat them then would have become violently ill.

In short, the social realists put us on our guard against the over-simple assumption that our way of perceiving and organizing the environment is somehow in accord with some natural, objective reality. It is in accord only with our social reality. It permits us to navigate smoothly in an environment populated by others who share that coding system with us. For example, Berger and Luckman (1967) discuss two different cultural frameworks for viewing mental illness: the psychiatric framework used in America and the voodoo framework used in parts of Haiti. They note that, as theoretical frameworks, one or both of these may prove to be empirically inadequate; that is, important predictions that each makes within its conception of reality may prove false. But they also note that, as interpretive frameworks used to diagnose mental illness within a specific cultural setting, each has an important claim to validity in that each can make some sense of *its* clients' symptoms. Indeed, a psychiatrist who planned to practice among rural Haitians would probably do well to learn the voodoo framework for the simple reason that his clients live in a voodoo culture and, hence, would be more likely to act as if they were "possessed" than to act as if they were "neurotic."

Apart from noting and comparing the different conceptions of reality that arise in different cultures, the social realists have another and much more difficult task. This is the task of determining how and why these different conceptions evolve and hang together. Why do rural Haitians believe in possession while middle class New Yorkers believe in neurosis? What other parts of their respective schemes for coding the world are consistent with these views? In short, what determines the meanings that different cultures will attach to objects and events?

Linguistic Relativism

We turn now to a second perspective that offers a partial answer to the social realists' question of how and why different cultures evolve different conceptions of reality. The central premise of linguistic relativity is that *our conception of reality is shaped by the particular language system that we happen to use.* This position is associated with the psycho-linguist Benjamin Lee Whorf, and an excerpt from this man's seminal book, *Language, Thought and Reality,* is included in the readings for this chapter.

What would a linguistic relativist be likely to notice in the story of Jimmy? Obviously, he would be most intrigued by the manner in which Jimmy's native language shapes the way he deals with the world. It is apparent, for example, that Jimmy's conception of how to put his room in order is shaped by his mother's favorite phrase for this, *i.e.,* "pick up." Indeed, Jimmy concentrated primarily on picking objects up off the floor while putting his shelves into disarray. Had his mother regularly used different words such as "clean up" or "straighten up," his behavior might have differed accordingly. Other languages may have radically different words for referring to the process of putting something in order, and their concept of this process can be expected to vary accordingly. Whorf gives an example of how the English phrase "cleaning (a gun) with a ramrod" is expressed in Pawnee as "making a dry space in the interior of a round hole by motion of a tool." Thus, it is more a process of drying something off than of cleaning it.

A linguistic relativist might also note with some interest Jimmy's difficulty in finding a word to express the color of the turquoise racing car. Although turquoise is a place on the light spectrum like any other, the English word for this color is used infrequently—much less frequently than blue or green or red or orange. As a consequence, we can expect that Jimmy will have more difficulty in remembering the color of the racer than, say, the color of the red truck. If we presented him with an array of colors and asked him to select the one closest to his racer, we would probably find that he erred in the direction of blue or green, nearby colors that have clear linguistic labels in English. It is not that Jimmy cannot see the subtle differences between blue and turquoise and green and turquoise. It is that, in trying to recall the color of his racer, he is likely to assimilate it to those nearby categories that his language happens to use for carving up the color spectrum. Systematic cross-culture studies by Brown and Lennenberg (1965) have in fact shown that people are much better able to remember and match colors for which they have linguistic labels. Thus, in a sense, we see the colors in our world in terms of our readily available linguistic categories.

The framework of the linguistic relativists is not *so* different from that of the social realists. Both believe that the events and objects that populate our world have much less intrinsic or objective meaning than we ordinarily assume. Both also believe that these events and objects take on meaning through social processes. The specialty of linguistic relativists is that they see language systems as paramount factors in shaping our conceptions of the world. As Whorf puts it " ... the background linguistic system (in other words, the grammar) of each language is not merely a reproducing instrument for voicing ideas but rather is itself the shaper of ideas, the program and guide for the individual's mental activity, for his analysis of impressions, for his synthesis of his mental stock in trade."

A social realist might not really disagree with this view, although he might argue that language is not so much a cause as merely another manifestation of certain underlying social conventions. In other words, he would argue that language does not really produce the meaning system we use for coding the world, it merely reflects it. While there is a difference here, it is probably sufficiently subtle that we shall never be able to prove one over the other. Who can say whether we and the Pawnee have different concepts of cleaning a gun because we use different linguistic expressions, or whether, instead, we use different linguistic expressions because we have different concepts of such operations? Language and meaning are learned together and the only thing we can say for certain is that different linguistic systems are associated with different conceptions of the world. We can speculate that, historically, concepts probably came first, but at the same time it is highly likely that each succeeding generation learns these concepts in and through their language system.

For present purposes, let us assume that this is correct and let us examine some of the basic ways in which linguistic relativists see language affecting our coding of the environment.

1.   Capturability. The language categories (the particular words available to us) affect our ability to code, capture, express, or remember events. We have already discussed this feature with respect to colors. As another example, Whorf notes that Eskimo has a great many different words that correspond to our one word snow. These words express what, to us, are fairly subtle differences in types of snow. Hence, if one had to obtain information on skiing conditions in a certain area from a non-skier, one would probably be much better off asking an Eskimo than an American. The Eskimo would

be able to remember and express the quality of the snow in a much finer-grained way. An American would probably not even notice its quality.

2.   Relatedness. Linguistic systems affect the perceived similarity or relatedness of particular objects and events. For example, English divides up the world into objects (denoted by nouns) and actions or states of being (denoted by verbs). For us, all things referred to by nouns have a certain concrete quality in common, and all things referred to by verbs have a certain active quality in common. But the Hopi divide up the world differently. They use verbs to refer to certain entities of short duration that we refer to with nouns. For them, flames, lightning and fists are denoted by verbs and, hence, are evidently more active and less concrete than they are for us. As another example, the Hopi have a single word to refer to all flying things (including airplanes) except birds. For us, an airplane is a type of machine that planes through the air. To the Hopi, it is probably seen as having something more in common with insects, butterflies, and bats. In general, one can say that the range of entities denoted by a single word in a particular language become linked together by a common concept. Thus, our cognition of the world is carved up into relatively arbitrary sets that correspond to our language.

3.   Abstraction. Linguistic systems affect the way we conceive of, or formulate, certain abstract concepts such as time, causality, and existence. We noted earlier how the English phrase "pick up" led Jimmy to conceive of the process of putting his room into order as a matter of getting objects off the floor. In a similar fashion, language can affect our concept of time. In English, we denote future events by using a future tense in our verbs. But the Hopi have no tenses. To them, future events are different from past and present ones primarily in that they are less valid, less certain to occur— they are only expected. Thus, the Hopi use the same tense to refer to past and present events, and an "expected tense" to refer to future events. Evidently, then, they do not conceive of time as a dimension that runs from past to future. For them, past and present are more closely related, and are contrasted with the future on a dimension of probability that is not even particularly salient to us. In discussing the Hopi concept of time Whorf goes on to show how its use would necessitate reformulating other scientific concepts, such as velocity and acceleration, both of which depend on our own special view of time.

As another example, consider again the fact that English, like other European languages, divides up the world into objects (nouns) and actions (verbs). This means that, for us, the world is a place in which certain objects act upon certain other objects. Clearly, such a conception is very conducive to thinking in terms of causal relations. Perhaps this is why science has flourished so well in the Western World, and why we still measure our progress in terms of our ability to predict and control the environment. Some languages do not make the above distinction. For example, Nootka, a language of Vancouver Island, denotes *all* entities by verb-like terms: a house "houses," a flame "flames," and a table "tables." It is clear, at the very least, that such a language will lead to a formulation of causality that is different from our own.

As a final example, consider Descartes' famous proof of his own existence: "Cogito ergo sum." Translated into English this becomes, "I think. Therefore I am." In this form, it is rather easy to see the validity of Bertrand Russell's criticism of the proof: Descartes assumes his premise in the first word—he postulates the "I" whose existence he is attempting to prove. However in the Latin version, where the pronoun is incorporated in the verb ending, it is much harder to see the fallacy. Thus, again, we see how language can blur distinctions and influence our abstract logic.*

Perhaps, then, linguistic relativists have contributed a partial solution to the issue left unresolved by social realists: why do different cultures adopt different conventions for assigning meanings to objects and events? Perhaps language systems, by grouping and construing entities in different ways and by being subject to their own laws of evolution, are a major force in shaping meaning systems rather than being merely a reflection of them. At any rate, the major thrust of the work undertaken by linguistic relativists has been to suggest a distinct correlation between a people's linguistic system and their cognitive map of the world.

Semantic Mapping

The third perspective to be reviewed here takes quite seriously the notion that a person's conception of the world can be viewed as a cognitive map. Indeed, the basic premise of semantic mappers is that *meanings can be plotted and compared in a topographical field known as "semantic space."* The early work in this area was done by a psychologist named Charles Osgood and one of his papers is included in the readings for this chapter.

A semantic mapper would be most interested in that portion of the story about Jimmy that deals with the vacuum cleaner. Here we see Jimmy attempting to arrive at a proper understanding of this superficially frightening machine. A theorist of the semantic mapping school would view this process by analogy to map-making. What is being mapped in this case is the concept "vacuum cleaner," and where it is being mapped is in an abstract space of meanings known as "semantic space." In effect, Jimmy is re-locating the concept of vacuum cleaner into a more appropriate place in semantic space.

Before one can usefully speak of mapping concepts into "meaning space," it is necessary to know the co-ordinates or dimensions of such a space. Researchers of the semantic mapping school have spent a great deal of time and effort on this issue. If we look carefully at Jimmy's reactions in the story, we can discern two of the basic dimensions uncovered by these researchers. It is apparent that Jimmy initially sees the vacuum cleaner as bad (he doesn't like it) and as extremely potent (it may suck him up). Thus, good-bad and potent-impotent can be seen as two dimensions of meaning that serve to locate the concept for Jimmy and that summarize his responses to it. It is also apparent that Jimmy's mother is attempting to alter his coding on these two dimensions by pointing out that the machine is really good (it helps her) and relatively weak (it cannot even suck up his toys).

One can imagine a master map for Jimmy that would contain his concept of vacuum cleaner as well as many other salient entities in his environment: Mother

---

* It should be noted that some do not agree with Russell's critique. They argue that Descartes meant simply that, although one can doubt the existence of everything, one cannot doubt that *something* is doing that doubting. Hence, that something must exist—call it "I."

teddy bear, television, marble, etc. If we could get Jimmy to describe these objects using a set of carefully chosen adjectives, we could then plot them accurately and be in a position to say which concepts have similar meanings to him and on what dimensions. For example, we might expect both Mother and teddy bear to be much higher on the goodness dimension than vacuum cleaner; and Mother to be very high on the potency dimension followed by vacuum cleaner and then teddy bear. (The adjective scales that semantic mappers actually use to collect their data are called semantic differentials. Each scale consists of a pair of polar-opposite adjectives connected by a line, for example:

Hot  Cold

A subject is asked to mark that point on the line which best describes the entity he is rating.)

Unlike the two schools described earlier, semantic mappers are not particularly concerned with the origins of meaning. They do not much care *why* Jimmy conceives of Mother and vacuum cleaner the way he does, but only with *how* he conceives of them. Their central focus is on the measurement of meaning. Indeed, *The Measurement of Meaning* is the title of the original book written by Charles Osgood and his co-workers (1957) describing their initial work on semantic space. The major contribution of this book was their discovery that there are three basic dimensions, or co-ordinates, of semantic space: Evaluation (good-bad), Potency (strong-weak) and Activity (active-passive). They found that a remarkable amount of the meaning inherent in almost any concept could be captured by these three dimensions, and they developed methods for accurately plotting any concept in terms of them. Moreover, as Osgood discusses in the paper included here, later research revealed that these three dimensions hold up across different cultures using different languages. In other words, the dimensionality of semantic space is not a consequence of some special feature of English language or culture; it is the same everywhere. This does not mean that translation equivalents from two languages will necessarily occupy the same position in semantic space. The Hopi may perceive airplanes as less good, more potent, and more active than we do, but nonetheless both our conceptions can be captured by the same basic dimensions.

Although semantic mappers are not directly concerned with origin of meanings, the measurement techniques they have developed can contribute to the exploration of this and related problems. No matter what one may wish to learn about meaning, it is always useful to have accurate assessment devices. To be able, for example, to measure and compare with precision the American and Haitian conceptions of mental illness is an important step in understanding the possible source of these conceptions. Thus, semantic mapping provides a way of delineating a culture's conception of the world and, thus, of relating it to other factors of interest such as their linguistic system. It makes it possible to test whether (and to what extent) the Hopi convention of denoting both airplanes and insects by the same word leads them to perceive the two as more similar than, say, Americans perceive them.

Beyond contributing certain measurement techniques, the work of semantic mappers points to some fundamental features in our mode of coding the world. The apparent universality of the three dimensions of meaning suggests that they must represent basic information needed by human beings to cope with their environment. Evidently, our reactions to objects are very much affected by whether we perceive them as good or bad, potent or impotent, active or passive. Indeed, each of these dimensions does contain a great deal of useful information: good objects can be safely approached, potent ones can be a major source of help or danger, and active ones have an inherent behavioral tendency that must be taken into account. Since this type of information is so useful, we can expect it to be transmitted to an offspring quite early, and to remain of basic importance in shaping our later coding of the environment.

Attribution Theory

The final perspective to be considered here is concerned less with how people perceive the environment and more with how they organize it. In particular, it is concerned with how people explain events by identifying causal agencies. The term attribution refers to the attribution of causality. The basic premise of this school is that *such processes are subject to systematic psychological biases.* In a paper included here, Edward Jones and Richard Nisbett illustrate this school as they explore some striking differences in the causal inferences typically made about an actor's behavior by the actor himself and by a neutral observer.

In examining the story of Jimmy, an attribution theorist would be most intrigued by Jimmy's efforts to make sense of sequential events in his environment. It is apparent that Jimmy sees many such events as linked together by cause-effect relationships. For example, he understands that the marble rolled off the shelf because 'it wanted to.' Eventually, he will put aside such animistic attributions and learn that the proper causal agent in this case is gravity. Yet, despite such errors, it is clear that Jimmy is learning about causality. His world is filled with more or less powerful causal agents. Even the vacuum cleaner threatens to suck him up, and he probably believes that there is almost nothing his Mother cannot do if only she sets her mind to it—surely she can help him pick up his room and do her own work as well. He experiences his own causal power as limited—many of his intentions are thwarted by a resistant environment and by more powerful adults. Gradually, his sense of agency will grow and he will learn the proper conventions for attributing causality but, as Jones and Nisbett show in their paper, he may never entirely outgrow the belief that his own behavior is more constrained by the environment than is that of others.

Attribution theorists, then, are concerned with a very special type of meaning—with the meaning we give to sequences of events by identifying causal agents. Among the first to study this process systematically was a psychologist named Fritz Heider. Heider (1944) approached the problem from a perspective he termed "naive psychology" because he was interested not in the correct way to infer causality but in the way naive observers did so. His enduring contribution was to show that everyday causal inferences are governed not so much by a logic of objective correctness as by a psycho-logic of simplicity, wholeness, and salience. Heider began by noting that virtually any moving perceptual field is organized in terms of phenomenal units—that is, into units consisting of causal origins and their effects. He then went on to show how the perception of phenomenal units could be analyzed using principles of Gestalt Psychology—principles that make for elegant, parsimonious, or practical perception. For example, even Jimmy's incorrect attribution of intentionality to the marble can be seen as a parsimonious way of understanding a complex event. The marble, after all, is doing the moving and, as Heider noted, active entities are likely candidates for causal origins; because they are so salient, they tend to dominate our perceptual field. If an active entity is also animate, *e.g.*, a person, then it is especially likely to be seen as an origin because animate entities are assumed to have intentionality or will. One consequence of these tendencies is that an observer surveying a scene which includes an acting person will tend to overestimate the causal role of the person while underestimating the role of inanimate objects. Thus, if we observe a person who trips and falls on the sidewalk, we tend to attribute this to his clumsiness whereas the victim is more likely to attribute it to an unexpected protrusion in the sidewalk.

Another Gestalt principle that Heider utilized is the Law of Assimilation and Contrast: the tendency to perceive entities in a perceptual field as either maximally similar or maximally different. For example, in surveying a woodland scene, we tend to assimilate parts that are obviously related, such as the parts of a tree, and to contrast these with other parts of the scene, such as the sky or a stream. Phenomenal units are governed by the same principle. If we see a vicious person engaging in hostile acts, we can easily form a unit and attribute the act to his vicious disposition. But if we observe a kind person engaging in hostile acts, we get a contrast effect and are unable to form a person-act unit. Instead we must search for another form of organization, perhaps grouping his act with certain frustrating factors in the environment.

Heider's seminal article on attribution theory was published in 1944, but despite the provocative nature of many of his ideas, little further work was done in this area for the better part of 25 years. The resurgence of interest that came in the late 60's was due in large measure to two stimulating papers—one by Edward Jones and Keith Davis (1965) entitled "From Acts to Dispositions," and another by Harold H. Kelley (1967) entitled "Attribution Theory in Social Psychology." In sharp contrast to Heider, Kelley began his analysis with a careful examination of the information and rules of inference needed to make correct causal inferences. Once having established the nature of these rules, he was in a position to study systematically how and why naive observers deviate from them.

It is easiest to follow Kelley's analytic framework in the context of a concrete example. Suppose we learn that Frank Smith, a college sophomore, has just failed his mid-term exam in chemistry. To what shall we attribute this event: to Frank's own ineptness, to the notorious sophomore slump, or to the objective difficulty of the mid-term exam? Of course, Kelley would say that to make a correct causal inference we need much more information. In particular, we would need to know how the event "performance on the exam" would be altered by substituting other students for Frank Smith, other points in his college career for sophomore year, and other types of exams for chemistry mid-term. If we could systematically vary these three dimensions (persons, time/modality, and objects) we would be in a position to arrive at valid conclusions.* For example, if we found that only Frank Smith failed the chemistry mid-term,

---

* When these three dimensions are used simultaneously to work out an attribution problem, they can be seen as defining a three-dimensional analytic space. Because Kelley's original paper contained pictures of this space resembling a cube, it has come to be called "Kelley's cube."

that he failed it three years running, and that he failed many other exams as well, we would be in a strong position to make an attribution to Frank's ineptness. On the other hand, if we found that almost everyone failed the chemistry mid-term, that Frank failed it three years running, and that he never failed any other exams, we would be on solid ground in attributing his problems to the objective difficulty of the chemistry mid-term. Of course, we are not ordinarily in a position to generate all the data required to make absolutely correct causal inferences though we might have certain equivalents of it. For example, to know that Frank Smith is none too bright is equivalent to knowing that he regularly fails other exams, and to know that chemistry midterms are generally quite difficult is equivalent to knowing that many students regularly fail them. But neither of these pieces of information is by itself a sufficient data pattern for solving our original problem. Lacking sufficient data we are forced to make an educated guess. And, indeed, we do so continually—we are forever making causal inferences on the basis of partial information.

Are the errors we make as a result of these educated guesses, random in nature, or are they subject to systematic biases? From Heider to Kelley and beyond, attribution theorists have been prone to point to many systematic biases although, particularly in Kelley's work, these biases are not necessarily seen as irrational—often they represent reasonable inferences given the data at hand. Among the less rational biases are: (1) a persons bias, *i.e.*, a tendency to attribute events to persons rather than to their inanimate environment, (2) a self-enhancing bias, *i.e.*, a tendency to attribute our successes to our own efforts and our failures to a resistant environment, (3) an ego-centric bias, *i.e.*, a tendency to treat our own judgments as accurate and to discount the possibility that they might be colored by personal quirks. As an example of the last case, if we enjoy a movie we are likely to conclude that the movie is good and not that we are particularly easy to please. These and other biases combine to produce one of the most intriguing phenomena in attribution theory: the tendency for observers and actors to make different causal inferences—the former giving more weight to person-factors and the latter more weight to environmental factors. This is the issue explored by Jones and Nisbett in their paper reprinted in this chapter.

In sum, attribution theorists are concerned with the ways in which we organize our environment through cause-effect relations. While they see this ability as developing with age and as being partly a matter of learning, they also believe that our causal attributions are less a matter of social convention and more a matter of individual psychology. Thus, they typically analyze the problem in terms of principles of Gestalt Psychology, or perceptual defenses, or information-processing biases. It may yet turn out that our patterns of attributing causality are more culture-bound than we think, but for the present, attribution theorists are betting they are based to an important degree on certain universal psychological principles.

CONTRASTING THE VIEWS OF SOCIAL PERCEPTION

These ways of looking at how people perceive and organize the environment can be compared by examining how they address themselves to five questions:

1. What is the raw material of perception? What are the primary entities whose nature is being studied?

2. What is the core puzzle that researchers must solve? What aspect of the raw material presents the central problem?

3. What is the locus of the answer to this puzzle? Where should we look to discover the principles that govern the solution to the problem?

4. Are the governing principles likely to be primarily social or primarily psychological in origin?

5. What research questions does each paradigm suggest?

Meaning versus Inference

The world presents us with varying raw stimuli that we must take sense of in some manner. As a starting point, each paradigm must identify some class of these primary entities with which it will deal. Social realism, linguistic relativism, and semantic mapping all focus on the meaning of objects and events. They share the view that meaning is neither inherent in the entity being perceived, nor built into the perceptual apparatus of the organism. Meaning is, therefore, a problem to all of them, though the aspect singled out for special attention differs.

Attribution theory has a slightly different focus. Here the primary entities are sequences of events—event A followed by event B. Starting from such pairs or larger groupings, their focus is on the inferences we make about their inter-relatedness—on meaning only in the sense of deduction.

Origin or Organization

What is the primary puzzle to be resolved about this raw material? For social realism and linguistic relativism, it is the origins of meaning. Since meaning cannot be deduced either from the entity or from its perceiver, it must come from somewhere else. The major problem then is to explain why objects and events have the meaning they do for observers, and why the same objects and events may have different meanings in different cultures.

Semantic mapping parts company here. The issue for this view is not so much the origin of meaning as the codification and organization of it. Obviously, meanings have an origin, but this is not taken as especially problematic. The major question is whether these meanings can be decomposed into a few basic elements, or factors, that can then be used to define the coordinates of a map of meanings, and thus can be used to measure the distance between two entities in meaning.

Attribution theory is also concerned with an organization of meaning. It takes the how and why of causal inference as its puzzle. In observing chains of events, we must continually make complex judgments about their causal relatedness. The central question is what organizing principles underlie our adaptive, but imperfect, ability to make such judgments.

The Locus of Solutions

Having identified a puzzle, each paradigm then suggests where we must look to solve it. For social realism, we must understand the principles that govern the making of social consensus or conventions. Reality is what we agree to regard as real. Witches are as real as mountains if the consensus about their existence is equally unchallenged. The apparent presence of mountains could be re-interpreted as illusory just as easily as we can deny that the sun moves across the sky even though we see it with our own eyes. What we must understand, then, is why certain things are accorded the status of reality while others are denied it—and how such conventions are established and changed.

For linguistic relativism, it is our language that determines the manner in which we give meaning to events. Every linguistic system is an implicit way of coding and organizing the world and we are all captives of such a system. In a sense, we perceive only what we can say; and what we can say is a product of constraints built into our language. To understand social perception, we must understand these constraints.

For semantic mapping, we can understand meaning if we can discover and use the coordinates of the space of meanings, thereby creating a universal map on which any concept from any culture can be measured and located. By thus lifting to an empirical level any debate about the meaning of this or that entity, one can systematically study the manner in which people perceive and organize the world.

For attribution theorists, the basic organizing principles are those psychological processes by which we make causal inferences. Lacking sufficient data (and probably the capacity to handle it were it available) we are constantly forced to rely on a variety of heuristic devices—some biased, some unbiased, some partially learned, and some entirely wired into us. The key to understanding how we organize our experience, then, is through understanding these devices—these psychological processes, by which we attribute causal meaning to sequences of events.

Social versus Psychological

Is the process of organizing and coding the world primarily social—something which must be understood in terms of social interactions, institutions, and values? Or is it a more psychological and, by implication, universal process which must be understood in terms of the internal functioning of the human mind?

Social realism, of course, makes the social process paramount. Learning what is real is simply a process of learning what other people think is real. Those who resist these social definitions in major ways are considered insane and are put in institutions until they acknowledge the conventional view of what is real. What is considered conventional varies from society to society but the process is the same.

Linguistic relativism is equally social since the language system has a reality of its own outside of the psychological processes of the individual. Since linguistic systems vary, we should expect to find that views of reality differ in societies having fundamentally different linguistic systems.

Semantic mapping emphasizes a much more psychological process. It hypothesizes that individuals use common dimensions in mapping objects, regardless of their culture and language. Where they place any given object on the map will vary, of

Chart 2 Underlying Issues on How People Perceive and Organize the Social Environment

Questions	Social Realism, *e.g.*, Shibutani	Linguistic Relativism, *e.g.*, Whorf	Semantic Mapping, *e.g.*, Osgood	Attribution Theory, *e.g.*, Jones and Nisbett
What is the raw material under study?	Meanings of objects and events	Meanings of objects and events	Meanings of objects and events	Inferences about sequences of events
What aspect of this raw material is treated as problematic?	The origin of meaning	The origin of meaning	The organization and structure of meanings	The organization of causal inferences
What is the locus of the answers?	Principles of social consensus (convention)	Principles of linguistic systems	The basic dimensions of meaning, *i.e.*, the coordinates of semantic space	Principles of causal attribution
Are the principles primarily social or psychological in origin?	Almost entirely social	Almost entirely social	Basic dimensions of semantic space are psychological, but location of concepts in this space is social	Primarily psychological
What is a typical research question?	How is homosexuality perceived and treated in this society; how and why is this different from other societies?	Do languages containing masculine and feminine articles lead its users to perceive and treat objects in accordance with their denoted sex?	How do Blacks and Whites differ in their conception of ghetto riots?	What sorts of attribution biases are present in paranoid disturbances?

course. Fire and water, for example, may have very different locations in different cultures. But, it is argued, the dimensions of evaluation, potency, and activity are the basis for mapping in each case—the semantic space is constant and apparently part of the nature of man's cognitive processes.

Finally, attribution theory also emphasizes psychological processes. The process which makes the actor's attribution systematically different from the observer's attribution is rooted in the psychology of the individual. Presumably it will be independent of the social conventions and linguistic systems that surround the actor and observer.

Typical Research Questions

Each paradigm points to different issues and Chart 2 illustrates typical research questions that might be investigated by a social psychologist operating within the particular paradigm. However, it is also true that they can provide a different perspective on the same problem and can, therefore, be considered contrasting views of the same fundamental phenomena.

Consider, for example, the research question listed under social realism—the perception of homosexuality. Social realists might concentrate on specifying the social conventions that govern the perception and treatment of homosexuals in different societies, showing how these relate to institutions or cultural values. Linguistic relativists might emphasize the linguistic categories and their implications. For example, if male homosexuals are called by words connoting woman-like, this may imply a different way of acting toward them than would the use of terms connoting criminality or sickness.

Semantic mappers would attempt to locate conceptions of homosexuality in semantic space. They might find that its position on, say, the evaluative and potency dimension tells us a great deal about how homosexuals will be dealt with in different societies. Finally, attribution theorists might concentrate on studying the inferences that are made about the causes of homosexual behavior and find, for example, that it is more tolerated when seen to stem from environmental factors and more persecuted when seen to stem from purely personal factors. In any event, it is clear that each paradigm can contribute a special vantage point.

These then are the central issues we see running through the contrasting views of perceiving and organizing the social environment. They are summarized in Chart 2.

REFERENCES

Berger, Peter and Luckman, Thomas. *The Social Construction of Reality*. Garden City, New York: Doubleday & Company, Inc., Anchor Books, 1967.

Blumer, Herbert. *Symbolic Interactionism: Perspective and Method.* Englewood Cliffs, New Jersey: Prentice-Hall, Inc., 1969.

Brown, Roger and Lennenberg, Eric. "Studies in Linguistic Relativity," in E. Maccoby, T. Newcomb and E. Hartley, (Eds.) *Readings in Social Psychology*, Third Edition, New York: Holt, Rinehart and Winston, Inc., 1958.

Heider, Fritz. "Social Perception and Phenomenal Causality," *Psychological Review*, **51** (1944), pp. 358-374.

Jones, Edward E. and Davis, Keith E. "From Acts to Dispositions: The Attribution Process in Person Perception," in L. Berkowitz (Ed.) *Advances in Experimental Social Psychology*, 2, New York: Academic Press, 1965.

Kelley, Harold H. "Attribution Theory in Social Psychology," *Nebraska Symposium on Motivation*, **14** (1967), pp. 192-241.

Osgood, Charles E., Suci, G.J. and Tannenbaum, P.H. *The Measurement of Meaning.* Urbana: University of Illinois Press, 1957.

MEANING AND THE
ORGANIZATION OF EXPERIENCE

TOMATSU SHIBUTANI

The effective environment in which men live and act is made up of all kinds of meanings—meanings of physical objects, of people, of colors, of emotional reactions, of images, of various types of activity. Since meanings are generally believed to depend upon the characteristics of the objects themselves, those who have somewhat different backgrounds of experience often get into arguments over what things "really" are. A rancher whose holdings are so extensive that he must rely upon horses to do his work views these animals quite differently from a city dweller who rarely sees a horse except in motion pictures. Some people use books primarily for decorative purposes, and others use them only as paperweights; such persons are frequently condemned by those who actually read books as not appreciating their "real" significance. It is often assumed that such variations in "interpretation" arise from differences in the capacity of people to appreciate the inherent properties of objects.

Meanings, however, can be identified more fruitfully from a behavioristic standpoint—in terms of what people *do* with objects. This is particularly noticeable in the early definitions of children, who refer to a table as an object "to put something on," a chair as something to "sit on," or an automobile as something "to ride." This suggests not only that we initially learn meanings through action but also that *meanings are primarily a property of behavior and only secondarily a property of objects.* Seen in this light it is not strange that the same object can mean different things to different people. One need only note the differences in the meaning of the identical dog to its owner, to the operator of a pet shop, to an employee of the city pound, and to the postman to get some appreciation of the extent to which the meaning of an object with identical attributes can vary. A cross has a very special meaning for Christians; but there are many parts of the world in which it would be meaningless, for there are no organized ways of acting towards it. The significance of any object arises, then, from the manner in which it is used. Charles Pierce (1923) once declared that there was no distinction of meaning so fine as to consist of anything more than a possible difference in practice. The physical properties of objects are important only in that they place limitations upon what men can do with them. . . .

The Social Validation of Meanings

Meanings, once they have been formed, tend to be self-sustaining. Even though new events are continually taking place, each man is able to conceive of his world as being reasonably stable. Although nothing ever happens twice in the same manner, men are able to ignore differences in particulars, to classify objects and events into categories, and to characterize each class in terms of given attributes. They are prepared to act in understood ways, and their environment remains meaningful as long as everything happens in accordance with their expectations. The relative stability of the orientation of men toward their world is assured by the very character of human perception.

Men attempt to cope with their environment through perception. Although it is generally assumed that what is experienced is a mirror-like reflection of what is "out there" in reality, all perception is selective. Perception is also *cumulative* and *constructive.* It is not so much a reaction to stimuli but a serial process in which men note and respond to cues to which they are already sensitized, form hypotheses about the characteristics of the object with which they are confronted, and then confirm these expectations by making further observations.

In general, then, men do not react passively to what happens; they approach their environment through a succession of hypotheses. These expectations, which are derived from the meanings of various objects, are indications of the kinds of experiences one would have if his assumptions about this aspect of the world are correct. When dealing with a familiar object each person has a working conception of its attributes, and the various stimuli are selected and organized into cues which serve as the basis for inference. For a man who is going for a walk toward evening, a hazy blue in the sky is not simply a color but a cue indicative of how much time he has left to return without difficulties. A hungry man does not react to a mere mass of soft fibres but sees food which can bring him pleasure as he devours it. What men are inclined to see in any situation depends upon what they anticipate, and what they anticipate depends upon the meanings with which they have entered the situation.

Once such hypotheses have been projected, men become acutely sensitized to those cues which will enable them to test their expectations. The perceptual field is organized to maximize the possibilities of noting cues that are relevant to the hypotheses and to minimize reacting to cues that are not. Thus, perceiving is never just receiving; there is always discrimination and selection. A person walking alone at night by a graveyard or through a dark alley is especially alert to sounds indicative of the presence of an assassin. It is taken for granted that assault and robbery could occur under such circumstances, and the possibility that such a criminal may be lurking in wait is a hypothesis that is seriously entertained. All this suggests that the manner in which anyone perceives his environment depends upon the meanings that various objects have for him as well as upon what he is doing.

Since meanings are products of past experience, people from different cultural backgrounds should perceive identical situations in somewhat different ways. Those with different meanings will project different hypotheses; hence, they will be responsive to different cues and construct different perceptual objects. This was demonstrated by Bagby (1957) in an ingenious experiment comparing Mexican and American subjects. He set up ten pairs of slides to be viewed through a stereoscope. On one side he mounted a picture of an object that would be familiar to most Mexicans— such as a bullfighter , a dark haired girl, and a peon—and on the other side a similar picture of an object with which most Americans would be acquainted—such as a baseball player, a blonde girl, and a farmer. The corresponding photographs resembled one another in form, contour of the major mass, texture, and the distribution of light and shadows. In some cases the subjects saw a mixture of the two pictures, and in other cases they saw the two superimposed; and there were even instances in which they saw only the picture that was culturally strange. In the vast majority of cases, however, the Americans saw only what was already familiar to them, and the Mexicans likewise saw only the scenes placed in their own culture. This study thus supports the contention that the selection and interpretation of cues depend upon one's expectations, which in turn are learned while participating in an organized society.

Further evidence of the extent to which perception depends upon meanings, especially upon values, is provided by an experiment by Bruner and Goodman (1947). A group of children from prosperous families and another group drawn from the slums were asked to indicate the size of various coins. All children overestimated size, but the amount of overestimation increased regularly with the monetary value of the coins and not with their actual size. Thus, a dime is smaller than a penny but is worth more, and the deviation between actual and judged size for the dime was greater than that for the penny. Furthermore, it was found that the poor children, who are presumably much more preoccupied with money, overestimated the size of coins considerably more than the rich ones. In addition, the exaggerated appraisal became relatively greater as the value of the coins increased. Several attempts have been made to repeat this study, sometimes with refinements in technique, and the findings have not always been consistent. In no case, however, have the data supported the view that perception is a direct response to stimulation. . . .

While we are able to characterize those we know personally in terms of their distinctive traits, most of our contacts, especially in urban communities, are with strangers. Strangers are usually perceived as instances of some category. Human beings may be classified in many ways, but the most commonly used categories are the various stereotypes found in all communities. A *stereotype* is a popular concept, designating a rough grouping of people in terms of some easily noted mark, supported by widespread beliefs concerning their attributes. Such abstractions are formed by combining the accentuated forms of conduct on the part of some of `the people so classified. People in ethnic minorities are often approached as if they were all alike. Negroes are often characterized as lazy, ignorant, unreliable, having a good sense of rhythm, prone to fight with razors, and having strong preferences for chicken and watermelon. Jews are frequently regarded as crafty, aggressive, and constantly preoccupied with money. Other common stereotypes include the woman driver, who can be counted on to do the wrong thing, and the spinster, with her sublimated interest in sex, predilection for cats, and vulnerability to attentive males. . . . Such categories are perpetuated in spite of the numerous inaccuracies because some of the features in terms of which they are lumped together are sometimes acknowledged by the people themselves. Those who are stereotyped often consist of people who identify themselves as being of a kind. Even when such beliefs are completely unjustified, they may serve as the basis for invidious distinctions, for they provide definite hypotheses with which to approach people about whom nothing else is known.

The category into which a person is placed is a matter of considerable importance, for the motives that can be plausibly imputed to him depend upon it. If those in a given category are assumed to have certain characteristics, they are expected to act in a particular way, and others become sensitized to cues indicative of such conduct. If a person is labelled as a "good" woman, it is assumed that she has no sex interests outside of marriage; if she should make gestures which appear to have erotic overtones, they are dismissed as irrelevant. In contrast, a woman who is reputed to be "bad" may have difficulty in persuading others that she is not making seductive overtures. Studies of political campaigns by Berelson *et al.* (1954) show that partisans tend to perceive the stand taken by candidates of their own party as being like their own, whether in fact this is the case or not. Similarly, the position of the opponent is seen as unfavorable. Therefore, once a speaker is classified as representing the opposition party, nothing that he says seems to matter. If there are no particular items to which objections can be made, his sincerity is questioned. When listening to speakers of one's own party, however, only the best motives are imputed. Thus, the kind of hypotheses that can be projected to people depends upon the manner in which they are classified and the evaluation placed upon the category. Much of the tension characterizing modern society becomes more understandable once we get an appreciation of some of the weird assumptions with which people approach one another.

If men perceive familiar objects of all kinds by projecting expectations and then becoming sensitized to cues relevant to them, the question arises as to whether their respective worlds are not entirely in the imagination. After all, each man does construct his working conception of his surroundings, even creating fictional meanings having no counterpart in reality. They can never be directly aware of the real world as such, only of the nervous impulses emanating from their organs of sensitivity. How, then, can the correspondence between what is perceived and what is "out there" be explained? To the extent that the hypotheses constitute the basis for behavior, most of them must be reasonably accurate if they are to remain effective foundations for adjustment. This suggests that all hypotheses are subject to repeated confirmation of some kind.

The most common form of confirmation is reality testing. Meanings constitute generalized relationships between a living organism and an object. Because an object is assumed to have certain properties it is approached with fixed expectations, and the relationship can be sustained only as long as these expectations are fulfilled. Men would not continue to regard a tiger as a dangerous object if each tiger they met smiled and licked their hands, nor would they regard a speeding automobile as something to be avoided if the vehicles splintered upon coming into contact with human bodies. . . .

Confirmation may also arise from consensus. Whenever one is uncertain about what he has perceived, he turns to others to see whether they have had the same experience. How is one to be certain that he is not dreaming? How does one differentiate between hallucination and reality? It is largely through a comparison of experiences with others. If others agree that something has happened, however unexpected it may have been, one has greater confidence in his own sensations. Furthermore, confirmation comes not only from such explicit communications but also from the observation of deeds. When confronted by a horrifying scene a person also notes the shock on the faces of others around him, and if for any reason they do not appear as upset as he feels they should be, he re-examines the situation. When one overhears an uncouth remark but sees that no one else appears to be offended, he concludes that he did not hear correctly. Thus, people do not always "trust their eyes and ears"; they need direct and indirect assurances from other people in whom they have confidence. Even when one feels positive about his own experience, if all others insist that he is mistaken, he may begin to raise questions about his sanity. In the last analysis, then, consensus may prove to be the crucial criterion of reliability. In our highly technical society there are many scientific hypotheses which laymen cannot test for themselves. Often they are inconsistent with popularly accepted beliefs, and yet the scientific account of the world is often accepted as true. . . .

Meanings are constantly reaffirmed in action. Since most deeds are performed by men in their capacity as participants in some kind of collective enterprise, virtually all meanings are subject to some measure of social control. Most meanings are social in that what any man is likely to do with reference to a given object is largely circumscribed by group norms concerning its appropriate use. Especially in the evaluation of objects there are accepted criteria for ascertaining what is wise or unwise, economical or extravagant, effective or futile. On the basis of such understandings certain modes of conduct are adjudged silly, dangerous, or sensible. Meanings are patterns of potential activity, and the responses that might be elicited in various situations are limited by social considerations. . . .

In the case of meanings that enjoy a high degree of consensus the anticipated reactions of other people are a part of the expectations with which one approaches the object. A person anticipates tacit approval when conforming to customary usage, praise if he acts correctly even at considerable sacrifice, and condemnation or some other kind of negative sanction when he does not act properly. Such expectations are a part of his orientation toward the object. As an illustration let us take the case of a man suffering from a severe cold who discovers just as his nose begins to run that he has misplaced his handkerchief. If an American flag hanging nearby were the only piece of cloth available, it is very unlikely that he would use it, even though its physical properties might be admirably suited for such a purpose. Indeed, it probably would not even occur to him that the flag might be suitable for blowing his nose, and even if it did, he would reject the possibility at once. He can easily anticipate the shock and dismay, if not the outrage, of others were they to observe him committing such a sacrilege. Thus, the American flag has a conventional meaning as a symbol, and this special meaning precludes many acts which are physically possible. Most of the hypotheses through which familiar objects are perceived include such reactions on the part of others. Many of the things that men do are social, then, not only in that they constitute responses to other people but also in that *the anticipated responses of other people are incorporated into the actual organization of conduct.*

These observations suggest that *man's conception of reality is largely a social process.* This is not to imply that there is no real world "out there" but that what men know about it is a product of group participation. Men approach their world through expectations learned as participants in organized groups, hypotheses which may even be reaffirmed without reality testing. Thus, man's conception of his environment is something that is constructed. Each person learns to participate in this world by having his behavioral tendencies corrected and by having the appropriate acts appreciated, until finally he learns to behave as others expect him to behave. Although categories are revised or replaced from time to time and inaccurate beliefs are successfully corrected, at any given time most meanings are essentially what people in a given universe of discourse agree that they are. What people generally call "reality" is a working orientation over which there is a high degree of consensus.

The Symbolic Organization of Experience

Behavior consists of adjustments to changing life conditions, but the environment to which men adjust is essentially a substitute environment. Men do not live in the world of immediate sensory impressions, for their effective environment has spatial and temporal extension. What a man does depends upon his definition of the situation. Much that is actually present is ignored; one simply does not notice many features of the world around him. Definitions also include much that is not physically present. A man who has just missed a bus need not run after it. He is reasonably certain that another will come along in time even though he cannot see it. In making decisions he may worry about the probable reactions of his mother, who has been dead for several years. One talks meaningfully about foreign countries he has never visited, and he bases many decisions upon considerations of which one knows only indirectly through reading. Furthermore, men avoid doing all sorts of things in anticipation of future consequences, events that have not yet occurred. Thus, the world in which men live and act includes the present, past, and future; it includes the remembered and the expected, the potential as well as the actual. The definition of the situation is a reconstruction from sensory experiences; it arises from selecting what is pertinent and bringing to bear upon it memories of other events thought to be relevant. . . .

Sensory data are organized into conceptions not only of things and their qualities but also of the order of things in spatial coexistence and of the order of things in time. Men do not walk through walls, and one can see more accurately in bright light than in the dark. There are assumptions about appropriate sequences. If a spectator at a baseball game were to see a ball flying toward center field before the bat is swung, he would be quite upset. A perspective, then, consists of premises concerning what is plausible and what is possible. What is called "knowledge" is not simply a collection of things with which we are familiar; it is an orientation toward a real or imaginary order of the possible—a scheme of space and time, of relations between objects, an order governed by rules. It is on the basis of this order and within its rules that men act. Without it life would be chaotic; even doubts and questions are possible only within an unquestioned frame of reference. As Riezler (1951) puts it, one's perspective is an outline scheme, which, running ahead of experience, defines and guides it. By assuming such regularity, even when they know that events are not absolutely predictable, men are able to pursue their interests with reasonable assurance that the world of tomorrow will be much the same as it is today.

The construction of perspectives is greatly facilitated by the capacity of men to use symbols, especially linguistic symbols. The world is presented in sensory experience as a kaleidoscopic flux of impressions, which are organized in terms of the categories that each person learns in his group. Nothing ever happens twice in exactly the same manner; yet men are able to adjust to each occurrence with some assurance that things will happen much as they had in the past. Because men can break up their experiences, classify them into units, and use words to refer to these segments, it becomes possible to give organization to the inchoate sequences of sensation. By abstracting out of historical reality they can hold a segment of the totality constant, relive it in memory, and compare it with similar occurrences in the past. Most experiences are thus classified.

Human life takes on some of its distinctive characteristics because men have the ability to use symbols to refer to meanings. But what is a *symbol?* Roughly speaking, a symbol is anything that stands for something else. A flag is a symbol for a nation. The piece of colored cloth often evokes patriotic sentiments and plays an important part in the mobilization of millions of men for war. Seeing someone treat the flag with disrespect can arouse the most violent emotional reactions, for men often regard the piece of cloth as if it were the nation with which they identify themselves. Hence, the discourtesy is experienced as a personal insult. In our society a kiss is widely accepted as a symbol of affection; therefore, the willingness of a girl to kiss on a first date is taken as an indication of her desire to continue the association. Most important are the linguistic symbols, the combinations of articulated sounds as well as written marks which are used to represent almost all meanings. A symbol, then, is any object, mode of conduct, or word toward which men act as if it were something else. Whatever the symbol stands for constitutes its meaning.

Although there are some exceptions, in most cases the connection between a symbol and the meaning it represents is arbitrary; the meanings designated are generally a matter of convention. Therefore, the meaning of a symbol cannot be derived from an examination of the symbol itself. There is nothing intrinsic in a piece of colored cloth that would necessitate or even suggest its standing for a nation, and to a person unfamiliar with the practice even the most exhaustive study of the cloth would not lead to its meaning. A wink may be an indication of knowing something that others do not know or in some contexts may be an invitation to seduction, but there is nothing in the shutting of the eyelids which points to either meaning. . . . Nowhere is this principle better illustrated than in linguistic symbols. The various sound combinations that make up our words are of themselves of little significance, but within each universe of discourse there are a number of common understandings as to what is represented by each word.

The actual significance of a symbol, then, is out of all proportion to the apparent triviality of meaning suggested by its intrinsic properties, for men perceive symbols and then act toward the meanings they represent. Soldiers risk their lives on battlefields to save a flag from falling into the hands of the enemy; the cloth in itself is of little value, but what it stands for is of great importance. Similarly, the sounds used in human speech are commonplace; almost anyone can articulate most of them with relative ease. Under some circumstances, however, these symbols can move men to engage in holy wars, to undertake dangerous pilgrimages, to participate in brutal lynchings, or to lay down their lives in the heroic defense of a hopeless cause. In such behavior there is an imputation of significance which goes far beyond what is inherent in the symbol itself.

The capacity to form abstractions and to refer to them by symbols frees human beings from the dictates of their immediate environment. Only infants, other animals, and some psychotic patients are confined to the world of the "here and now." Others are not directly dependent upon their sensory experiences, for they live in a substitute world. . . .

One cannot understand what is happening around him unless he can categorize his experiences and place them within a larger frame of reference. Without appropriate symbols this is extremely difficult, and adjustment takes on a hit or miss character. The uneducated often cannot comprehend many things that educated people find quite simple, and scientists can understand many things that puzzle even well read laymen. Doctors can diagnose disorders that their patients cannot recognize even when they themselves are suffering from the symptoms; most patients do not have the vocabulary to sensitize them to the various transformations in body conditions. Effective action rests upon clear understanding, and the clarity of one's conception of his world rests upon the adequacy of his stock of symbols. Much depends, then, upon the adequacy of the symbols available in a group for delineating significant categories of experience.

Role-taking and self-control, which make coordinated action possible, are greatly facilitated by the fact than men live in a common symbolic environment. Such shared perspectives constitute the culture of each group. Since the norms that make up these perspectives constitute the premises of action, it is not surprising that men who share a common culture are characterized by common modes of action. All cultures are products of communication. Perspectives are organized in terms of symbols, and those who can communicate with these symbols come to share one another's views. Hence, they form a common outlook which serves as the basis for concerted action.

Summary and Conclusion

The Greek philosopher Protagoras is said to have proclaimed that man is the measure of all things, and this observation seems to be borne out by current research. The effective environment in which men live may be viewed as consisting of meanings, ordered ways of acting which have evolved through past experience and are constantly reaffirmed in new experience. Although we ordinarily think of meanings as the property of the various objects with which we come into contact, they are actually characteristic ways of approaching various aspects of the environment. The meaning of anything is an organized orientation that can be identified as a configuration of behavioral tendencies, all predicated upon the assumption that the object has certain characteristics. Thus, familiar objects are perceived in terms of expectations, and each person's conception of these objects is reinforced as these hypotheses are confirmed. What is significant about human beings is that both the expectations and the confirmations usually include the reactions of other people.

Human beings actually live simultaneously in two environments—the natural environment, which consists of all the things that are actually present, and a symbolic environment. Viruses are a part of the natural environment of all men, and they affect life processes whether their victims know about them or not. But viruses are not a part of the symbolic environment of many peoples; and when one of their number dies, his demise is explained in other terms—the anger of evil spirits, the violation of some taboo, or weakness of the blood. The symbolic environment is not a mere reproduction of the external world; by virtue of their capacity for using symbols men are able to reconstruct their surroundings. Fleeting sensations that blend almost imperceptibly into one another are categorized and labelled so that they can be recalled for comparison. Even though nothing ever happens twice in exactly the same manner, each man is able to form an orderly outlook, and those who utilize the same symbols are able to develop a common orientation. Since they approach their respective worlds with similar expectations, they can understand and reinforce one another. Men live, then, in a substitute environment, one that is largely a product of communication.

Although social psychologists generally write from the standpoint of a disinterested observer, as if they were among the proverbial men from Mars, they cannot, of course, escape the fact that they are human beings living in an organized society. The concepts used, to the extent that they differ from the general vocabulary, refer to special distinctions not ordinarily made in daily discourse. Each theoretical scheme, then, is a symbolic environment, a special way of looking at human contact which, it is hoped, will prove more effective than the common sense view. There would be no point in studying social psychology unless its mastery made possible the comprehension of many phenomena which otherwise would remain strange.

REFERENCES

Bagby, James W. "A Cross-Cultural Study of Perceptual Predominance in Binocular Rivalry," *Journal of Abnormal and Social Psychology,* **54** (1957), pp. 331-334.

Berelson, Bernard, Lazarsfeld, Paul and McPhee, William N. *Voting: A Study of Opinion Formation in a Presidential Campaign.* Chicago: University of Chicago Press, 1954.

Bruner, Jerome S. and Goodman, Cecile C. "Value and Need as Organizing Factors in Perception," *Journal of Abnormal and Social Psychology,* **42** (1947), pp. 33-44.

Peirce, Charles S. *Chance, Love, and Logic.* Morris R. Cohen (Ed.) New York: Harcourt, Brace & Company, 1923.

Riezler, Kurt. *Man: Mutable and Immutable.* Chicago: Henry Regnery Company, 1951.

Stratton, George M. "Some Preliminary Experiments on Vision without Inversion of the Retinal Image," *Psychological Review,* **3** (1896), pp. 611-617.

LANGUAGE, THOUGHT, AND REALITY

BENJAMIN LEE WHORF

Every normal person in the world, past infancy in years, can and does talk. By virtue of that fact, every person—civilized or uncivilized—carries through life certain naive but deeply rooted ideas about talking and its relation to thinking. Because of their firm connection with speech habits that have become unconscious and automatic, these notions tend to be rather intolerant of opposition. They are by no means entirely personal and haphazard; their basis is definitely systematic, so that we are justified in calling them a system of natural logic—a term that seems to me preferable to the term common sense, often used for the same thing.

According to natural logic, the fact that every person has talked fluently since infancy makes every man his own authority on the process by which he formulates and communicates. He has merely to consult a common substratum of logic or reason which he and everyone else are supposed to possess. Natural logic says that talking is merely an incidental process concerned strictly with communication, not with formulation of ideas. Talking, or the use of language, is supposed only to "express" what is essentially already formulated nonlinguistically. Formulation is an independent process, called thought or thinking, and is supposed to be largely indifferent to the nature of particular languages. Languages have grammars, which are assumed to be merely norms of conventional and social correctness, but the use of language is supposed to be guided not so much by them as by correct, rational, or intelligent thinking.

Thought, in this view, does not depend on grammar but on laws of logic or reason which are supposed to be the same for all observers of the universe—to represent a rationale in the universe that can be "found" independently by all intelligent observers, whether they speak Chinese or Choctaw. In our own culture, the formulations of mathematics and of formal logic have acquired the reputation of dealing with this order of things: i.e., with the realm and laws of pure thought. Natural logic holds that different languages are essentially parallel methods for expressing this one-and-the-same rationale of thought and, hence, differ really in but minor ways which may seem important only because they are seen at close range. It holds that mathematics, symbolic logic, philosophy, and so on are systems contrasted with language which deal directly with this realm of thought, not that they are themselves specialized extensions of language. . . .

From *Language, Thought, and Reality: Selected Writings of Benjamin Lee Whorf,* edited by John B. Carroll. (Cambridge M.I.T.Press, 1956), pp. 207-219. Reprinted by permission.

Natural logic contains two fallacies: First, it does not see that the phenomena of a language are to its own speakers largely of a background character and so are outside the critical consciousness and control of the speaker who is expounding natural logic. Hence, when anyone, as a natural logician, is talking about reason, logic, and the laws of correct thinking, he is apt to be simply marching in step with purely grammatical facts that have somewhat of a background character in his own language or family of languages but are by no means universal in all languages and in no sense a common substratum of reason. Second, natural logic confuses agreement about subject matter, attained through use of language, with knowledge of the linguistic process by which agreement is attained: i.e., with the province of the despised (and to its notion superfluous) grammarian. Two fluent speakers, of English let us say, quickly reach a point of assent about the subject matter of their speech; they agree about what their language refers to. One of them, A, can give directions that will be carried out by the other, B, to A's complete satisfaction. Because they thus understand each other so perfectly, A and B, as natural logicians, suppose they must of course know how it is all done. They think, e.g., that it is simply a matter of choosing words to express thoughts. If you ask A to explain how he got B's agreement so readily, he will simply repeat to you, with more or less elaboration or abbreviation, what he said to B. He has no notion of the process involved. The amazingly complex system of linguistic patterns and classifications, which A and B must have in common before they can adjust to each other at all, is all background to A and B.

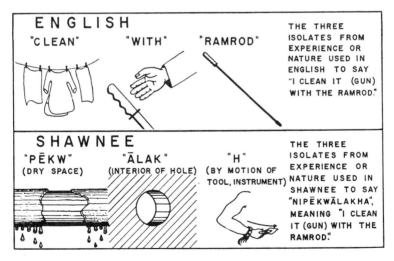

Figure 1 Languages dissect nature differently. The different isolates of meaning (thoughts) used by English and Shawnee in reporting the same experience, that of cleaning a gun by running the ramrod through it. The pronouns 'I' and 'it' are not shown by symbols, as they have the same meaning in each language. In Shawnee ni- equals 'I'; -a equals 'it.'

These background phenomena are the province of the grammarian—
or of the linguist, to give him his more modern name as a scientist. The
word linguist in common, and especially newspaper, parlance means something entirely different, namely, a person who can quickly attain agreement about subject matter with different people speaking a number of
different languages. Such a person is better termed a polyglot or a multilingual. Scientific linguists have long understood that ability to speak a language fluently does not necessarily confer a linguistic knowledge of it: i.e.,
understanding of its background phenomena and its systematic processes
and structure, any more than ability to play a good game of billiards
confers or requires any knowledge of the laws of mechanics that operate
upon the billiard table.

Figure 2 Languages classify items of experience differently. The class corresponding
to one word and one thought in language A may be regarded by language B as two
or more classes corresponding to two or more words and thoughts.

The situation here is not unlike that in any other field of science. All
real scientists have their eyes primarily on background phenomena that
cut very little ice, as such, in our daily lives; and yet their studies have a
way of bringing out a close relation between these unsuspected realms of
fact and such decidedly foreground activities as transporting goods, preparing food, treating the sick, or growing potatoes, which in time may become very much modified, simply because of pure scientific investigation
in no way concerned with these brute matters themselves. Linguistics

presents a quite similar case; the background phenomena with which it deals are involved in all our foreground activities of talking and of reaching agreement, in all reasoning and arguing of cases, in all law, arbitration, conciliation, contracts, treaties, public opinion, weighing of scientific theories, formulation of scientific results. Whenever agreement or assent is arrived at in human affairs, and whether or not mathematics or other specialized symbolisms are made part of the procedure, *this agreement is reached by linguistic processes, or else it is not reached.*

As we have seen, an overt knowledge of the linguistic processes by which agreement is attained is not necessary to reaching some sort of agreement, but it is certainly no bar thereto; the more complicated and difficult the matter, the more such knowledge is a distinct aid, till the point may be reached—I suspect the modern world has about arrived at it—when the knowledge becomes not only an aid but a necessity. The situation may be likened to that of navigation. Every boat that sails is in the lap of planetary forces; yet a boy can pilot his small craft around a harbor without benefit of geography, astronomy, mathematics, or international politics. To the captain of an ocean liner, however, some knowledge of all these subjects is essential.

When linguists became able to examine critically and scientifically a large number of languages of widely different patterns, their base of reference was expanded; they experienced an interruption of phenomena hitherto held universal, and a whole new order of significances came into their ken. It was found that the background linguistic system (in other words, the grammar) of each language is not merely a reproducing instrument for voicing ideas but rather is itself the shaper of ideas, the program and guide for the individual's mental activity, for his analysis of impressions, for his synthesis of his mental stock in trade. Formulation of ideas is not an independent process, strictly rational in the old sense, but is part of a particular grammar, and differs, from slightly to greatly, between different grammars. We dissect nature along lines laid down by our native languages. The categories and types that we isolate from the world of phenomena we do not find there because they stare every observer in the face; on the contrary, the world is presented in a kaleidoscopic flux of impressions which has to be organized by our minds—and this means largely by the linguistic systems in our minds. We cut nature up, organize it into concepts, and ascribe significances as we do, largely because we are parties to an agreement to organize it in this way—an agreement that holds throughout our speech community and is codified in the patterns of our language. The agreement is, of course, an implicit and unstated one, *but its terms are absolutely obligatory;* we cannot talk at all except by subscribing to the organization and classification of data which the agreement decrees.

This fact is very significant for modern science, for it means that no individual is free to describe nature with absolute impartiality but is constrained to certain modes of interpretation even while he thinks himself most free. The person most nearly free in such respects would be a linguist familiar with very many widely different linguistic systems. As yet no linguist is in any such position. We are thus introduced to a new principle of relativity, which holds that all observers are not led by the same physical evidence to the same picture of the universe, unless their linguistic backgrounds are similar, or can in some way be calibrated.

OBJECTIVE FIELD	SPEAKER (SENDER)	HEARER (RECEIVER)	HANDLING OF TOPIC, RUNNING OF THIRD PERSON
SITUATION I a.			ENGLISH... "HE IS RUNNING" HOPI... "WARI" (RUNNING. STATEMENT OF FACT)
SITUATION I b. OBJECTIVE FIELD BLANK DEVOID OF RUNNING			ENGLISH... "HE RAN" HOPI... "WARI" (RUNNING, STATEMENT OF FACT)
SITUATION 2			ENGLISH... "HE IS RUNNING" HOPI... "WARI" (RUNNING, STATEMENT OF FACT)
SITUATION 3 OBJECTIVE FIELD BLANK			ENGLISH... "HE RAN" HOPI... "ERA WARI" (RUNNING. STATEMENT OF FACT FROM MEMORY)
SITUATION 4 OBJECTIVE FIELD BLANK			ENGLISH... "HE WILL RUN" HOPI... "WARIKNI" (RUNNING, STATEMENT OF EXPECTATION)
SITUATION 5 OBJECTIVE FIELD BLANK			ENGLISH... "HE RUNS" (E.G. ON THE TRACK TEAM) HOPI... "WARIKNGWE" (RUNNING. STATEMENT OF LAW)

Figure 3 Contrast between a "temporal" language (English) and a "timeless" language (Hopi). What are to English differences of time are to Hopi differences in the kind of validity.

This rather startling conclusion is not so apparent if we compare only our modern European languages, with perhaps Latin and Greek thrown in for good measure. Among these tongues there is a unanimity of major pattern which at first seems to bear out natural logic. But this unanimity exists only because these tongues are all Indo-European dialects cut to the same basic plan, being historically transmitted from what was long ago one speech community; because the modern dialects have long shared in building up a common culture; and because much of this culture, on the more intellectual side, is derived from the linguistic backgrounds of Latin and Greek. Thus this group of languages satisfies the special case of the clause beginning "unless" in the statement of the linguistic relativity principle at the end of the preceding paragraph. From this condition follows the unanimity of description of the world in the community of modern scientists. But it must be emphasized that "all modern Indo-European-speaking observers" is not the same thing as "all observers." That modern Chinese or Turkish scientists describe the world in the same terms as Western scientists means, of course, only that they have taken over bodily the entire Western system of rationalizations, not that they have corroborated that system from their native posts of observation.

When Semitic, Chinese, Tibetan, or African languages are contrasted with our own, the divergence in analysis of the world becomes more apparent; and, when we bring in the native languages of the Americas, where speech communities for many millenniums have gone their ways independently of each other and of the Old World, the fact that languages dissect nature in many different ways becomes patent. The relativity of all conceptual systems, ours included, and their dependence upon language stand revealed. That American Indians speaking only their native tongues are never called upon to act as scientific observers is in no wise to the point. To exclude the evidence which their languages offer as to what the human mind can do is like expecting botanists to study nothing but food plants and hothouse roses and then tell us what the plant world is like!

Let us consider a few examples. In English we divide most of our words into two classes, which have different grammatical and logical properties. Class 1 we call nouns, e.g., 'house, man'; class 2, verbs, e.g., 'hit, run.' Many words of one class can act secondarily as of the other class, e.g., 'a hit, a run,' or 'to man (the boat),' but, on the primary level, the division between the classes is absolute. Our language thus gives us a bipolar division of nature. But nature herself is not thus polarized. If it be said that 'strike, turn, run,' are verbs because they denote temporary or short-lasting events, i.e., actions, why then is 'fist' a noun? It also is a temporary event. Why are 'lightning, spark, wave, eddy, pulsation, flame, storm, phase, cycle, spasm, noise, emotion' nouns? They are temporary events. If 'man' and 'house' are nouns because they are long-lasting and stable events, i.e., things, what then are keep, adhere, extend, project, continue, persist, grow, dwell,' and so on doing among the verbs? If it be objected that 'possess, adhere' are verbs because they are stable relationships rather than stable percepts, why then should 'equilibrium, pressure, current, peace, group, nation, society, tribe, sister,' or any kinship term be among the nouns? It will be found that an "event" to us means "what our language classes as a verb" or something analogized therefrom. And it will be found that it is not possible to define 'event, thing, object, relationship,' and so on, from nature, but that to define them always involves a circuitous return to the grammatical categories of the definer's language.

In the Hopi language, 'lightning, wave, flame, meteor, puff of smoke, pulsation' are verbs—events of necessarily brief duration cannot be anything but verbs. 'Cloud' and 'storm' are at about the lower limit of duration for nouns. Hopi, you see, actually has a classification of events (or linguistic isolates) by duration type, something strange to our modes of thought. On the other hand, in Nootka, a language of Vancouver Island, all words seem to us to be verbs, but really there are no classes 1 and 2; we have, as it were, a monistic view of nature that gives us only one class of word for all kinds of events. 'A house occurs' or 'it houses' is the way of saying 'house,' exactly like 'a flame occurs' or 'it burns.' These terms seem to us like verbs because they are inflected for durational and temporal nuances, so that the suffixes of the word for house event make it mean long-lasting house, temporary house, future house, house that used to be, what started out to be a house, and so on.

Hopi has one noun that covers every thing or being that flies, with the exception of birds, which class is denoted by another noun. The former noun may be said to denote the class (*FC-B*)—flying class minus bird. The Hopi actually call insect, airplane, and aviator all by the same word, and feel no difficulty about it. The situation, of course, decides any possible confusion among very disparate members of a broad linguistic class, such as this class (*FC-B*). This class seems to us too large and inclusive, but so would our class 'snow' to an Eskimo. We have the same word for falling snow, snow on the ground, snow packed hard like ice, slushy snow, wind-driven flying snow—whatever the situation may be. To an Eskimo, this all-inclusive word would be almost unthinkable; he would say that falling snow, slushy snow, and so on, are sensuously and operationally different, different things to contend with; he uses different words for them and for other kinds of snow. The Aztecs go even farther than we in the opposite direction, with 'cold,' 'ice,' and 'snow' all represented by the same basic word with different terminations: 'ice' is the noun form; 'cold,' the adjectival form; and for 'snow,' "ice mist."

What surprises most is to find that various grand generalizations of the Western world, such as time, velocity, and matter, are not essential to the construction of a consistent picture of the universe. The psychic experiences that we class under these headings are, of course, not destroyed; rather, categories derived from other kinds of experiences take over the rulership of the cosmology and seem to function just as well. Hopi may be called a timeless language. It recognizes psychological time, which is much like Bergson's "duration," but this "time" is quite unlike the mathematical time, *T*, used by our physicists. Among the peculiar properties of Hopi time are that it varies with each observer, does not permit of simultaneity, and has zero dimensions; i.e., it cannot be given a number greater than one. The Hopi do not say, "I stayed five days," but "I left on the fifth day." A word referring to this kind of time, like the word day, can have no plural. The puzzle picture (Fig. 3, page 66) will give mental exercise to anyone who would like to figure out how the Hopi verb gets along without tenses. Actually, the only practical use of our tenses, in one-verb sentences, is to distinguish among five typical situations, which are symbolized in the picture. The timeless Hopi verb does not distinguish between the present, past, and future of the event itself but must always indicate what type of validity the *speaker* intends the statement to have: (a) report of an event (situations 1, 2, 3 in the picture); (b) expectation of an event (situation 4); (c) generalization or law about events (situation 5). Situation 1, where the speaker and listener are in contact with the same objective field, is divided by our language into the two conditions, 1*a* and 1*b*, which it calls present and past, respectively. This division is unnecessary for a language which assures one that the statement is a report.

Hopi grammar, by means of its forms called aspects and modes, also makes it easy to distinguish among momentary, continued, and repeated occurrences, and to indicate the actual sequence of reported events. Thus the universe can be described without recourse to a concept of dimensional time. How would a physics constructed along these lines work, with no *T* (time) in its equations? Perfectly, as far as I can see, though of course it would require different ideology and perhaps different mathematics. Of course *V* (velocity) would have to go too. The Hopi language has no word really equivalent to our 'speed' or 'rapid'. What translates these terms is usually a word meaning intense or very, accompanying any verb of motion. Here is a clue to the nature of our new physics. We may have to introduce a new term *I*, intensity. Every thing and event will have an *I*, whether we regard the thing or event as moving or as just enduring or being. Perhaps the *I* of an electric charge will turn out to be its voltage, or potential. We shall use clocks to measure some intensities, or, rather, some *relative* intensities, for the absolute intensity of anything will be meaningless. Our old friend acceleration will still be there but doubtless under a new name. We shall perhaps call it *V*, meaning not velocity but variation. Perhaps all growths and accumulations will be regarded as *V*'s. We should not have the concept of rate in the temporal sense, since, like velocity, rate introduces a mathematical and linguistic time. Of course we know that all measurements are ratios, but the measurements of intensities made by comparison with the standard intensity of a clock or a planet we do not treat as ratios, any more than we so treat a distance made by comparison with a yardstick.

A scientist from another culture that used time and velocity would have great difficulty in getting us to understand these concepts. We should talk about the intensity of a chemical reaction; he would speak of its velocity or its rate, which words we should at first think were simply words for intensity in his language. Likewise, he at first would think that intensity was simply our own word for velocity. At first we should agree, later we should begin to disagree, and it might dawn upon both sides that different systems of rationalization were being used. He would find it very hard to make us understand what he really meant by velocity of a chemical reaction. We should have no words that would fit. He would try to explain it by likening it to a running horse, to the difference between a good horse and a lazy horse. We should try to show him, with a superior laugh, that his analogy also was a matter of different intensities, aside from which there was little similarity between a horse and a chemical reaction in a beaker. We should point out that a running horse is moving relative to the ground, whereas the material in the beaker is at rest.

One significant contribution to science from the linguistic point of view may be the greater development of our sense of perspective. We shall no longer be able to see a few recent dialects of the Indo-European family, and the rationalizing techniques elaborated from their patterns, as the apex of the evolution of the human mind, nor their present wide spread as due to any survival from fitness or to anything but a few events of history— events that could be called fortunate only from the parochial point of view of the favored parties. They, and our own thought processes with them, can no longer be envisioned as spanning the gamut of reason and knowledge but only as one constellation in a galactic expanse. A fair realization of the incredible degree of diversity of linguistic system that ranges over the globe leaves one with an inescapable feeling that the human spirit is inconceivably old; that the few thousand years of history covered by our written records are no more than the thickness of a pencil mark on the scale that measures our past experience on this planet; that the events of these recent millenniums spell nothing in any evolutionary wise, that the race has taken no sudden spurt, achieved no commanding synthesis during recent millenniums, but has only played a little with a few of the linguistic formulations and views of nature bequeathed from an inexpressibly longer past. Yet neither this feeling nor the sense of precarious dependence of all we know upon linguistic tools which themselves are largely unknown need be discouraging to science but should, rather, foster that humility which accompanies the true scientific spirit, and thus forbid

that arrogance of the mind which hinders real scientific curiosity
and detachment.

CROSS-CULTURAL COMPARABILITY IN THE MEASUREMENT OF MEANING

CHARLES E. OSGOOD

The world is rapidly shrinking—politically, socially, and psychologically.
Recent developments in the technology of transportation and communication are annihilating both space and time. These same developments are
making it possible to conduct social and behavioral science research on an
international scale that is certainly rewarding scientifically and perhaps
essential practically, if we are to survive along with our technology. Indeed,
there are many hypotheses about human nature that demand cross-
national designs, if we are to successfully disentangle what is common to
the human species from what is specific to a particular language or culture.

But comparisons across cultures are extremely difficult for what
anthropologists call nonmaterial traits—things such as values, customs,
attitudes, feelings, and meanings. Many years ago Edward Sapir and
Benjamin Lee Whorf phrased what would now be called the hypothesis
of psycholinguistic relativity. According to this hypothesis, how we
perceive, how we think and even how we formulate our basic philosophies
depend upon the structure of the language we speak. If this were literally
and completely true, then comparisons across language barriers would be
impossible. The Sapir-Whorf hypothesis has been shown to apply to
certain aspects of language—for example, the way in which the lexicon
of any language arbitrarily carves up the world denotatively does influence
the perceptual and conceptual processes of its users. But, our research is
making it clear that there are other aspects of language—particularly the
way it represents affect and the way affect mediates metaphor and
symbolism—for which universality rather than relativity seems to be the
rule.

Let me begin by asking you to do the impossible—to imagine a
space of some unknown number of dimensions. This will be our hypothetical
semantic space. Just like all self-respecting spaces, this one has an origin,

From "Cross-Cultural Comparability in Attitude Measurement Via Multilingual
Semantic Differentials" by Charles E. Osgood, in *Current Studies in Social Psychology*
edited by Ivan D. Steiner and Martin Fishbein. Copyright © 1965 by Holt, Rinehart
and Winston, Inc. Adapted and reprinted by permission of Holt, Rinehart and Winston,
Inc.

which we define as complete "meaninglessness"—this is like the neutral grey center of the color space. If we think of the meaning of any word or concept as being some particular point in this space, then we could represent it by a vector out from the origin to that point (for example, x and y in Figure 4). The longer the vector, the further out in semantic space (concept x), the more "meaningful" the concept; the shorter the vector, the nearer the origin of the space (concept y), the less intensely meaningful the concept—this being analogous to saturation in the color space. Vectors may also vary in their direction within this n-dimensional space, and we equate direction with the "quality" of meaning—like the way colors may vary in hue, including the white to black axis. It should also be noted that if we are dealing with an Euclidean space—which is the simplest assumption about Nature to start with—then the less the distance between the endpoints of vectors in our semantic space, the more similar in meaning should be the concepts they represent.

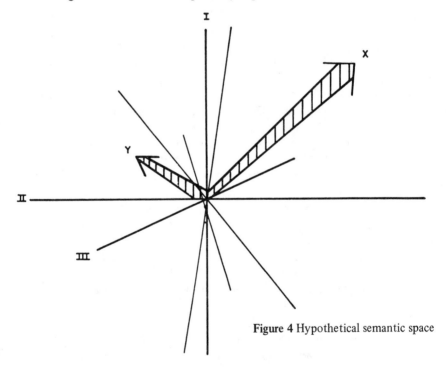

Figure 4 Hypothetical semantic space

One more analogy with the color space will prove useful to us: Just as complementary colors are defined as points equidistant and in opposite directions from the origin of the color space, which when mixed together in equal proportions cancel each other out to neutral grey, so we may think of verbal opposites as defining straight lines through the origin of the semantic space and cancelling each other out to meaninglessness when mixed. As a matter of fact, this is exactly the way dictionary-makers define pure or logical opposites in language—their meanings cancel each other out, component for component.

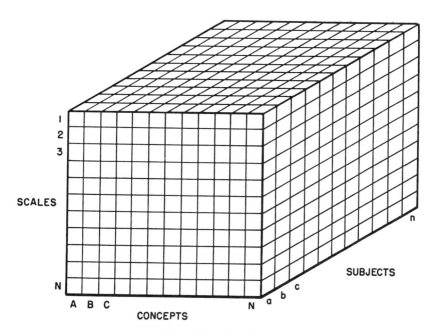

Figure 5 A cube of data

Now imagine a whole set of different straight-line "cuts" through this space, as suggested by the fine lines in Figure 4. Each would be defined by a different pair of opposites—*hard-soft, excitable-calm, good-bad, fair-unfair, hot-cold, noisy-quiet, large-small,* and so forth—creating a veritable pincushion of qualitative dimensions. In order to locate a particular person's meaning of a particular concept, say "white rose buds," we might now play a special game of "Twenty Questions" with him: (1) Is this concept *beautiful* or *ugly*? It is *beautiful*—so it must be in the upper half of the total space. (2) Is it *hard* or *soft*? It is *soft*—so it must be upward and to the right. (3) Is it *noisy* or *quiet*? It is *quiet*—so it must be in the octants away from us rather than near us in Figure 4. Thus, with only three binary questions, we could decide in which of eight octants of the space was "—white rose buds": or, if each straight-line "cut" were scaled into seven discriminable steps, for example, from *extremely beautiful* through neutral to *extremely ugly*, as we have actually done in our work, then each decision would reduce uncertainty by six-sevenths, and only three "cuts" would differentiate a space having 343 discrete regions.

But to talk about "directions" in any space one has to have some reference coordinates. Is the up-down, north-south, east-west of the semantic space to be completely arbitrary, or is there some "natural" built-in structuring, analogous to the gravitational and magnetic determinants of geophysical space? This question is an empirical one, and the logical tool is some variant of factor analysis. . . .

When a group of people judge a set of concepts against a set of semantic scales, a cube of data is generated, as shown in Figure 5. The rows are defined by scales, the columns by the concepts being judged, and the "slices" from front to back by the subjects doing the judging. Each cell represents with a single value how a particular subject rated a particular concept against a particular scale. . . .

During the past decade or more we have analysed many such data cubes collected from English-speaking Americans. Much of this work has been summarized by Osgood, Suci & Tannenbaum (1957). Despite deliberate and independent variations in the rules for sampling scales and concepts and in the kinds of subjects used, three dominant, orthogonal factors have kept reappearing: An "evaluative" factor (represented by scales like *good-bad, kind-cruel,* and *honest-dishonest*), a "potency" factor (represented by scales like *strong-weak, hard-soft* and *heavy-light*) and an "activity" factor (represented by scales like *active-passive, fast-slow* and *hot-cold*). What this means is that there are at least three "directions" in the semantic space that are regions of relatively high density, in the sense of containing many highly correlated scales representing similar modes of qualifying. Evaluation, potency and activity appear to be the most salient modes of qualifying experience. Of course, there are additional factors, other dimensions in the semantic space—indeed, a long train of them of decreasing importance and increasing uniqueness.

Is this basic evaluation-potency-activity framework common to all people? Within the English-speaking American community we have made many comparisons—between old people and young, between males and females, between Eisenhower Republicans and Stevenson Democrats, and even between schizophrenics and normals. The results of all these and many more comparisons can be stated quite succinctly: In no case has there been convincing evidence for differences in the underlying factors. But is it possible that this semantic system is restricted to Americans who speak the English language? Let me now tell you something about our attempt to determine if this affective meaning system varies with language and culture or is, indeed, panhuman. . . .

We start with a list of 100 familiar concepts that have been selected by linguists and anthropologists as being "culture fair" and that have survived a stringent translation test with bilinguals in all of the six language families represented in our sample. (We have been working with Japanese, Cantonese in Hong Kong, Kannada in Southern India, Hindi in Northern India, Farsi in Afghanistan and Iran, Arabic in Lebanon, Turkish, Finnish, Serbo-Croatian in Yugoslavia, Polish, and a number of Western Indo-European languages: Dutch, Flemish, French, Swedish and English.) This original list of 100 translation-equivalent concepts, like "house," "man," "sky," "hand," "future," "dog," and "anger," is the only point at which translation is involved and could influence the results. From this point on, everything is done in the native language, with native monolingual subjects and with indigenous research personnel.

The first step is to have 100 young high-school-level boys in each country give the first qualifiers (adjectives in English) that occur to them when each of the 100 concepts is given as a stimulus—for example, to the word for "tree" in his language one boy might say *tall*, another *green*, another *big*, and so forth. This basketful of 10,000 qualifiers (100 subjects times 100 concepts) is shipped to Illinois, where, using IBM and Illiac high-speed computers, we determine a rank order of these various ways of qualifying experience in terms of their total frequency of usage, diversity of usage across the 100 nouns, and independence of usage with respect to each other—in other words, we are looking for the most characteristic, productive and independent qualitative dimensions in each language. . . .

The 60 or 70 highest ranked qualifiers are shipped back to the field, where their opposites are elicited and they are made into bipolar scales— the highest ranked 50 surviving this process being kept. Then another group of young males rate the original 100 concepts against these 50 scales, 200 subjects being divided into subgroups of 20 judging subsets of 10 concepts because this task is so time-consuming. Thus we generate a cube of semantic data, 100 concepts times 50 scales times 20 subjects, in each language/ culture community. These data are returned to Illinois, where standard correlation, factor analysis and rotation procedures are applied by our computers. Such analyses of each cube of data yield a unique solution for each language/culture community; nevertheless, it is gratifying to be able to report that for the 12 communities carried through this stage so far, evaluation, potency and activity are identifiable as the first three factors in magnitude—and usually in that order. . . .

What is the purpose of all this busy work in many lands and many tongues? The first, purely scientific purpose has been to demonstrate that human beings the world over, no matter what their language or culture, do share a common meaning system, do organize experiences along similar symbolic dimensions. In contradiction to Benjamin Lee Whorf's notion of "psycholinguistic relativity," here is at least one aspect of language behavior that is universal. A second, more practical purpose of this research is to develop and apply instruments for measuring "subjective culture"—meanings, attitudes, values, customs and the like—instruments that can be shown to be comparable across languages and thereby break through the language barrier. The demonstration of common semantic factors makes it completely feasible to construct efficient "semantic differentials" for measuring the meanings of critical concepts cross-culturally, with reasonable confidence that the yard-stick being employed is something better than a rubber band. It is now possible to ask questions like: "How does the meaning of the self vary from culture to culture?" "How do attitudes toward leadership and authority vary around the world?" "Is a common subjective culture developing among the world's elites?"—and be reasonably sure that the answers are not artifacts of translation.

Now, given this long introduction, let me turn directly to the matter of measuring attitudes cross-culturally. Despite the plethora of definitions of "attitude," there seems to be general consensus that (a) they are learned and implicit, (b) that they may be evoked either by perceptual signs or linguistic signs (c) that they are predispositions to respond evaluatively to these signs, and (d) that the evaluative predispositions may fall anywhere along a scale from "extremely favorable" through "neutral" to "extremely unfavorable."

In all of the general factor analyses of affective meanings we have done to date, the first and dominant factor—usually accounting for about twice as much variance as any other—has always been clearly identifiable as Evaluation. Furthermore, being a bipolar factor, graded in intensity in both directions from a neutral point, it meets the criterion of reflecting predispositions from "extremely favorable" through "neutral" to "extremely unfavorable." It is also clear that, in the general mediation theory of meaning of which our semantic differential measuring operations are part, meanings of concepts are implicit reactions to either perceptual or linguistic signs, and they are learned. The evaluative factor of semantic differentials thus seems to meet all the criteria for a measure of attitude, and it is therefore tempting to simply define "attitude" toward any concept as its projection, onto the evaluative factor in the total meaning space. . . .

You will recall that the factors obtained from different language/ culture communities were found to be truly pancultural in the direct, mathematical sense that the scales from these different language/culture communities were found to be highly correlated when used in rating the standard 100 concepts. We will now take the four scales for each community which load highest and most purely on the pancultural evaluative factor and use their composite value for each concept, transposed to a + 3 to − 3 scale, as an *SD-attitude-score*—that is, a semantic-differential-determined attitude score for each concept. The scales used in this analysis, both in the native language and in approximate English translation, are given in Table 1. You will note that although they are not—in many cases translation equivalents, they do maintain a common evaluative feeling-tone.

Before presenting some illustrative results, I would like to offer a few words of caution about interpretation. First, these data were collected in the course of the "tool-making" phases of our work and hence the concepts were not selected for their relevance to attitude measurement. Second, due to the large number of judgments involved in the concept-on-scale task,

Table 1. Scales contributing to SD-attitude-scores for seven language/culture communities

	Native Language	*English Translation*
American English	nice-awful sweet-sour good-bad happy-sad	
Dutch	prettig-naar gezellig-ongezellig mooi-lelijk gelukkig-ongelukkig	pleasant-unpleasant cozy-cheerless pretty-ugly happy-sad
Belgian Flemish	aangenaam-onaangenaam plezierig-vervelend gezellig-ongezellig prachtig-afschuwelijk	agreeable-disagreeable pleasant-boring cozy-cheerless magnificent-horrible
French	sympathique-antipathique rassurant-effrayant gai-triste gentil-méchant	likeable-repugnant calm-frightened happy-sad nice-awful
Finnish	hauska-ikava valoisa-synkka makea-hapan onneton-onnellinen	nice-awful light-gloomy sweet-sour happy-sad
Japanese	気持よい — 気持悪い 快よい — 不快な 有難い — 迷惑な ようにはしい-悲しい	pleasant-unpleasant comfortable-uncomfortable thankful-troublesome happy-sad
Indian Kannada	ದಯಾಳು - ಕ್ರೂರ ಒಳ್ಳೆಯ - ಕೆಟ್ಟ ಸುಂದರ - ವಿರೂಪ ಸೂಕ್ಷ್ಮ - ಒರಟು	merciful-cruel good-bad beautiful-ugly delicate-rough

subgroups of 20 subjects judged subgroups of 10 concepts; therefore, the N in each case is only 20. In our work with American subjects we have found factor-score differences as small as half a scale unit to be significant at beyond the 0.05 level for N's of this magnitude, but to be on the safe side I would use a full scale unit as a significance criterion here. Third, there appear to be real differences in scale-checking style between language/ culture groups; in the present case, the Flemish-speaking Belgians have SD-attitude-scores beyond plus or minus 1.5 in polarization for 56 of the 100 concepts, whereas the Finns and the Kannada-speaking Indians have only 6 and 9 concepts respectively reaching this degree of polarization. It is also true that inconsistencies in attitudinal direction among the individual subjects in a group will tend to cancel the composite scores toward neutrality, but since we are here interested in *cultural meanings,* not individual, this will not concern us. Finally, you should keep in mind the fact that the subjects are unmarried males of junior high-school age.

With these caveats in mind, let us turn to some results. Table 2 reports SD-attitude-scores for some concepts among our sample of 100 that are usually considered objects of attitude. Attitude toward "work" is most favorable for the Kannada-speaking Indians of Mysore and the Japanese, but actually slightly negative for the Flemish-speaking Belgians. The concept of "wealth" is quite positive in evaluation for Americans and Flemings but negative for Finns, Flemish and Finnish subjects have neutral or slightly negative attitudes toward "doctor," in contrast to the very favorable American attitude. For some reason—unknown to me at least— the Japanese have an extremely positive feeling about "luck." "Peace" is favored highly by everyone, and about equally if we take into account the differences in average polarization; but only for Indians and Americans is "policeman" a positive concept.

Table 3 presents sets of concepts that are universally favorable, neutral, or unfavorable—insofar as our small sample of seven language/ culture communities can be considered an adequate sample of the universe!

Table 2. SD-attitude-scores for some "Attitude objects" among standard 100 concepts

Concepts	Language/culture communities						
	American	Dutch	Flemish	French	Finnish	Japanese	Kannada
Work	0.5	0.7	−0.2	0.9	0.3	1.0	1.0
Wealth	1.3	0.5	1.2	0.9	−0.1	0.9	0.4
Doctor	1.6	1.0	−0.7	0.8	0.3	1.0	1.0
Luck	1.6	1.6	1.6	1.5	1.2	2.5	1.0
Peace	2.0	1.4	2.3	2.1	1.1	2.3	0.8
Policeman	0.8	−0.4	−0.3	−0.4	−0.5	0.0	1.0

Table 3. Concepts having favorable, neutral, and unfavorable
SD-attitude-scores among standard 100 concepts

Concepts   Language/culture communities

Favorable	American	Dutch	Flemish	French	Finnish	Japanese	Kannada
Girl	2.1	2.0	2.3	1.9	1.4	1.1	1.1
Love	2.2	2.1	2.2	2.0	1.8	1.3	1.4
Marriage	2.3	1.9	2.0	2.0	1.7	1.4	1.1
Mother	2.1	2.1	2.1	2.3	1.1	1.9	1.7
Pleasure	1.8	1.9	2.3	2.2	1.3	2.0	1.1
Friend	1.8	1.4	2.0	1.5	1.1	1.5	1.8
Freedom	2.3	2.0	2.1	1.9	1.9	2.2	1.6
Sympathy	1.3	1.3	2.1	2.1	1.4	0.8	1.0
Music	1.6	1.7	1.9	1.3	1.2	1.4	1.9
Sleep	1.8	1.2	1.7	1.2	1.4	1.6	0.4
Sun	1.6	1.8	1.7	2.1	1.2	1.2	0.1
Success	1.5	2.1	2.1	1.7	0.5	2.2	1.0
Neutral							
Wind	0.6	−0.3	−1.0	0.6	0.1	0.4	0.3
Heat	0.4	0.5	0.3	0.8	0.0	0.3	0.4
Stone	0.0	−0.6	0.2	0.2	−0.4	0.4	−0.8
Cloud	1.3	0.5	0.1	−0.5	0.2	0.5	0.7
Root	0.6	0.0	−0.1	0.1	−0.4	0.5	0.9
Rope	0.2	0.3	0.5	−0.1	−0.7	0.6	0.7
Knot	0.2	0.0	0.0	0.8	0.0	0.0	0.5
Unfavorable							
Pain	−1.4	−1.8	−2.3	−1.0	−1.2	−1.9	−0.7
Anger	−1.9	−1.1	−2.2	−1.3	−1.3	−1.5	−1.3
Guilt	−1.2	−1.3	−2.2	−1.3	−0.9	−2.1	−0.5
Fear	−1.4	−1.4	−2.0	−1.4	−1.4	−1.5	−0.3
Danger	−1.6	−1.8	−2.1	−0.9	−1.1	−2.0	−0.8
Punishment	−0.9	−1.1	−2.3	−1.6	−1.7	−1.1	−1.1
Crime	−1.9	−1.8	−1.9	−1.9	−1.5	−2.5	−0.6
Thief	−1.9	−2.0	−2.2	−1.4	−1.4	−2.5	−1.3
Snake	−0.5	−1.1	−1.6	−1.4	−0.4	−2.0	−0.5
Poison	−1.7	−1.6	−2.3	−1.6	−1.4	−2.2	−0.9
Battle	−1.8	−1.4	−1.7	−1.7	−1.8	−2.1	−0.5
Defeat	−1.5	−1.5	−1.7	−1.5	−1.4	−1.3	−0.4
Death	−0.9	−1.6	−2.0	−0.3	−1.3	−1.2	−0.9

"Girl," "love," "marriage" and "mother" are highly favorable notions, as
are "pleasure," "freedom," "success," "sympathy," and "friend"−all of
which is not too surprising. The list of universally unfavorable concepts
reads like a catalogue of human misery: the emotional states of "pain,"
"anger," "guilt," and "fear"; the conditions of "danger," "punishment,"
and "crime"; the specific threats posed by "thief," "snake," and "poison";
and then, at last, "battle," "defeat," and "death." Yet, among these

generally unfavorable notions, there are some interesting deviations: note the rather mild disapproval registered by the Indians (even taking into account their generally reduced polarization), as compared with the intensely negative attitudes of the Japanese; note also the relative lack of concern of the French for things like "pain," "danger," and "death" as compared with the Flemish-speaking Belgians.

It is interesting, but perhaps not surprising, that the evaluatively neutral concepts are all natural objects and phenomena. "Stone," "root," "knot," and "cloud" surely are not objects about which people are likely to have strong attitudes, nor are the natural phenomena of "wind" and "heat" (unless they are in excess, in which case they usually have special names like "tornado"). But this is not necessarily the case. The first set of concepts in Table 4 might have been expected to be attitudinally neutral, too, but they are not for all people in our sample. The linguistically and culturally close Dutch and Flemings have a highly favorable attitude toward "Wednesday"; all Indo-European language communities (Americans, Dutch, Flemish, and French) place a high valuation on "chair," in contrast to the non-Indo-European groups (Finnish, Japanese and Kannada); the Kannada-speaking Indians have, for them, an extremely positive feeling toward the "moon," while the Japanese feel similarly about "tree." Just why such affective investments should exist, I do not know, but I suspect they are reflections of uniqueness in subjective culture and should be of interest to cultural anthropologists.

Other comparisons in this table—which I have titled "Attitudinal Bits to Conjure With"—may have similar interest. The second set of concepts, all referring to human and kin classifications, display close similarities among the Indo-European language groups, who, I believe, also share the same kinship system. We also note that attitudes toward "women" are higher than toward "men" everywhere except in Japan—however, keep in mind that our subjects were boys between 14 and 16 years of age. The set of future-oriented concepts, "hope," "future," and "purpose," display an interesting pattern—they are all positively evaluated by Americans, French and Japanese, but are essentially neutral attitudinally for the Dutch, Flemings, Finns, and Indians. Does this necessarily imply that Americans, French and Japanese are more hopeful about the future and more purposefully striving toward it?

The next set of concepts suggests a paradoxical kind of denial mechanism: The Indians in Mysore rate "hunger" and "need" relatively positively, and yet (with the exception of "fruit") have relatively neutral attitudes toward the food concepts; on the other hand, the well-off Americans, Flemings, and Dutch have the most negative attitudes toward "hunger" (and the Flemings particularly toward "need"), yet display consistently positive attitudes toward the food concepts. It is as if those that have are most gratified with having and most concerned about being deprived! But, in the end, there is "laughter"; Americans and Flemings hold this form of social commentary in the highest esteem—Indians in the least.

Table 4. Attitudinal bits to conjure with

Concept	Language/culture community						
	American	Dutch	Flemish	French	Finnish	Japanese	Kannada
Wednesday	0.6	1.4	1.5	0.6	0.3	0.8	0.4
Chair	1.2	1.4	1.6	1.4	0.3	0.9	0.8
Moon	1.2	1.1	1.0	1.1	0.6	1.3	2.0
Tree	0.8	0.9	1.1	1.4	0.1	2.0	0.8
Husband	1.2	1.7	2.0	1.4	0.2	1.5	1.3
Father	1.9	1.2	1.4	2.2	1.0	1.9	1.4
Man	1.1	1.1	1.4	1.8	0.5	1.3	0.8
Woman	1.9	1.9	1.8	2.4	1.1	1.2	1.1
Mother	2.1	2.1	2.1	2.3	1.1	1.9	1.7
Girl	2.1	2.0	2.3	1.9	1.4	1.1	1.1
Hope	1.9	0.7	0.6	1.3	0.7	1.3	0.3
Future	1.4	0.7	0.5	1.2	0.3	1.1	0.5
Purpose	1.1	0.6	0.6	1.1	0.3	1.0	0.5
Hunger	−1.5	−1.3	−1.9	−0.3	−1.0	−1.2	0.5
Need	0.5	0.4	−2.7	0.0	0.1	0.9	0.7
Meat	1.6	0.7	1.5	0.7	−0.1	0.8	0.2
Bread	1.6	1.0	1.5	1.4	0.4	1.4	0.7
Fruit	1.5	1.4	2.2	1.5	0.7	1.7	1.5
Food	1.8	1.6	1.4	1.5	0.6	1.6	0.9
Laughter	1.9	1.2	1.9	1.6	1.1	1.2	0.2

REFERENCE

Osgood, C.E., Suci, G.J., & Tannenbaum, P.H. *The Measurement of Meaning.* Urbana: University of Illinois, 1957.

THE ACTOR AND THE OBSERVER:
DIVERGENT PERCEPTIONS OF THE CAUSES OF BEHAVIOR

EDWARD E. JONES and RICHARD E. NISBETT

When a student who is doing poorly in school discusses his problem with a faculty advisor, there is often a fundamental difference of opinion between the two. The student, in attempting to understand and explain his inadequate performance, is usually able to point to environmental obstacles such as a particularly onerous course load, to temporary emotional stress such as worry about his draft status, or to a transitory confusion about life goals that is now resolved. The faculty adviser may nod and may wish to believe, but in his heart of hearts he usually disagrees. The adviser is convinced that the poor performance is due neither to the student's environment nor to transient emotional states. He believes instead that the failure is due to enduring qualities of the student—to lack of ability, to irremediable laziness, to neurotic ineptitude.

When Kitty Genovese was murdered in view of thirty-nine witnesses in Queens, social scientists, the press, and the public marveled at the apathy of the residents of New York and, by extension, of urban America. Yet it seems unlikely that the witnesses themselves felt that their failure to intercede on the woman's behalf was due to apathy. At any rate, interviewers were unable to elicit comments from the witnesses on the order of "I really didn't care if she lived or died." Instead, the eyewitnesses reported that they had been upset, but felt that there was nothing they could or needed to do about a situation that in any case was ambiguous to them.

In their autobiographies, former political leaders often report a different perspective on their past acts from that commonly held by the public. Acts perceived by the public to have been wise, planful, courageous and imaginative on the one hand, or unwise, haphazard, cowardly, or pedestrian on the other, are often seen in quite a different light by the autobiographer. He is likely to emphasize the situational constraints at the time of the action—the role limitations, the conflicting pressures brought to bear, the alternative paths of action that were never open or that were momentarily closed—and to perceive his actions as having been inevitable. "Wise moves" and "blunders" alike are often viewed by the leader as

From Edward E. Jones and Richard E. Nisbett, *The Actor and the Observer: Divergent Perceptions of the Causes of Behavior,* © 1971 General Learning Corporation. Reprinted by permission of the publisher, General Learning Press.

largely inescapable under the circumstances. The public is more inclined to personalize causation for success and failure. There are good leaders who can cope with what the situation brings and bad leaders who cannot.

In each of these instances, the actor's perceptions of the causes of his behavior are at variance with those held by outside observers. The actor's view of his behavior emphasizes the role of environmental conditions at the moment of action. The observer's view emphasizes the causal role of stable dispositional properties of the actor. We wish to argue that *there is a pervasive tendency for actors to attribute their actions to situational requirements, whereas observers tend to attribute the same actions to stable personal dispositions.* This tendency often stems in part from the actor's need to justify blameworthy action, but may also reflect a variety of other factors having nothing to do with the maintenance of self-esteem. We shall emphasize these other, more cognitive factors but include also a consideration of the role of self-justification.

The proposition that actors attribute their behavior to situational constraints while observers attribute the behavior to dispositions of the actor is best characterized, perhaps, as an actuarial proposition. We acknowledge at the outset that there are undoubtedly many exceptions. In our opinion, though, there are good theoretical reasons for believing that the proposition is generally correct. We wish to explore what we believe to be powerful cognitive forces impelling actors to attribute their behavior to the environment and observers to attribute that same behavior to characteristics of the actor. The proposition has not been fully tested, but there are a few experiments that provide data consistent with it. We will now describe these experiments in order to supplement our selected anecdotes. . . .

Experimental Evidence Consistent with the Proposition

One set of experiments, while lacking data on actors themselves, indicates that observers are remarkably inclined to see behavior in dispositional terms. Three experiments were conducted by Jones and Harris (1967). In the first of these they asked their college student subjects to read essays or listen to speeches presumably written by fellow students. Subjects were asked to give their estimates of the communicator's real opinions. They were told either that the communicator had been assigned one side of the issue or that he had been completely free to choose a side. It is the "no choice" conditions that are of the most interest to us here. In one case the impression of no choice was created by telling subjects they were reading essays written for a political science course in which the instructor had required the students to write, for example, a "short cogent defense of Castro's Cuba." In another experiment subjects believed they were reading the opening statement by a college debater whose adviser had directed him to argue a specified side of the Castro topic. In a third experiment subjects believed they were hearing a tape recording of a subject in a psychology experiment who had been instructed to give a speech favoring or opposing segregation. Questionnaire responses showed that subjects easily distinguished between choice and no choice conditions in the degree of choice available to the communicator.

Despite the fact that the subjects seem to have clearly perceived the heavy constraints on the communicator in the no choice conditions, their estimates of the true opinions of the communicator were markedly affected by the particular position espoused. When subjects read an essay or speech supporting Castro's Cuba, they inferred that the communicator was pro-Castro. If the communication opposed Castro's Cuba, they inferred that the communicator was anti-Castro. Across the three experiments, the effect of taking a pro versus anti stand was a highly significant determinant of attributed attitude in no choice conditions, though the effect of position taken was roughly twice as great when the communicator had complete choice.

These results are extremely interesting if they may be taken as evidence that observers attach insufficient weight to the situational determinants of behavior and attribute it, on slim evidence, to a disposition of the actor. It may be, however, that something about the content of the speeches caused the subjects to infer that the communicator actually held the opinion he was advocating. If the communications were quite eloquent and drew on esoteric sources of knowledge, it would not be surprising to learn that observers inferred that the communicator held the opinion he was delivering. This does not seem to be the proper explanation of the results, however, in view of the following facts: (a) the communications were designed to be "neither polished nor crude;" "of a C+ quality" in the case of the political science essay; (b) in each experiment it was made clear that subjects had access to study materials to help them formulate their arguments; (c) in a later series of experiments, Snyder (unpublished data) found that when the communications used were the actual products of students under no choice conditions, the same effects found by Jones and Harris were obtained. A crucial feature of Snyder's experiments was that each subject wrote a no choice essay himself, to be delivered to another subject. Thus the subjects should have been clearly aware of the constraints involved and of the ease or difficulty of generating arguments for a position opposite to that privately held.

The Jones and Harris experiment provides evidence, then, that observers are willing to take behavior more or less at "face value," as reflecting a stable disposition, even when it is made clear that the actor's behavior is under severe external constraints. These results have been replicated both by Snyder and more recently by Jones, Worchel, Goethals, and Grumet (1971) with "legalization of marijuana" as the issue.

A second study providing data for observers only has been performed by McArthur (1970). Her study is quite relevant to our proposition if one is willing to lean heavily on intuitions about the causal attributions that would be expected of actors. Subjects were given a simple, one-sentence description of an action, such as "George translates the sentence incorrectly," "While dancing, Ralph trips over Jane's feet," "Steve puts a bumper sticker advocating improved automobile safety on his car." They were then asked why this action probably occurred: Whether it was something about the *person* that caused him to act this way ("Something about *George* probably caused him to translate the sentence incorrectly"), or something about the *stimulus* ("Something about the *sentence* probably caused George to translate it incorrectly"), or something about the *situation* ("Something about the *particular circumstances* probably caused George to translate it incorrectly"). If subjects found none of these simple explanations to be the likely one, they were allowed to give whatever explanation they though necessary to account for the behavior. These were then coded into complex explanations involving both person and stimulus, both person and circumstances, both stimulus and circumstances, or all three. (As it happened, only the person-stimulus combination was resorted to with very great frequency.)

It seems likely that if one were to ask a random sample of people who had mistranslated sentences, tripped over feet, or placed bumper stickers on their cars why they had performed their various actions, a rather high fraction of explanations would be pure stimulus attributions or mixed stimulus-circumstance attributions. We would expect answers such as "That sentence was difficult to translate," "It was dark and Jane doesn't cha-cha the way I do," "The AAA sent me this catchy bumper sticker in the mail." For McArthur's vicarious observers, however, such reasons were extremely infrequent, amounting to only 4 per cent of the total attributions. By far the greatest proportion of reasons given—44 per cent for each of these particular actions—were pure *person* attributions: George translates the sentence incorrectly because he is rather poor at translating sentences and Steve is the sort who puts bumper stickers on his car.

McArthur also presented her subjects with statements about emotional experiences, such as "John laughs at the comedian," "Sue is afraid of the dog," "Tom is enthralled by the painting." One would expect that in a random sample of people found laughing at comedians, being frightened by dogs, or being enthralled by paintings, most of the actors would explain their experiences in pure stimulus terms: The comedian is funny; the dog is scary; the painting is beautiful. For McArthur's observers, however, only 19 per cent of the attributions were pure stimulus attributions and the most frequent attributions (45 per cent of the total) were *person-stimulus interactions:* "Sue tends to be afraid of dogs and this is a very large one." Interestingly, one of the emotion items did produce a very high proportion (52 per cent) of pure stimulus attributions: "Mary is angered by the psychology experiment." Since subjects were at that moment participating in a psychology experiment, it is tempting to conclude that they were responding as actors rather than as observers.

It is possible that some unintended feature of McArthur's highly artificial situation forced attributions away from the stimulus and toward the person. Perhaps a different sample of statements or a more extended account of the behavior would yield different results. Nevertheless, the willingness of her subjects to invoke explanations involving dispositions of the person seems striking. One's strong intuition is that the actors themselves in real-life situations of the type described to McArthur's subjects would rarely interpret their behavior in dispositional terms.

McArthur (1970) completed a second experiment that is less open to criticism on methodological grounds. Subjects were induced to perform a particular act and a written account of the actor and the surrounding circumstances was presented to observers. It was then possible to compare the attributions made by the actor subjects with the later attributions made by observer subjects. McArthur obtained the consent of subjects to participate in a survey concerning interpersonal relationships and then asked the subjects why they had agreed to participate. As we would expect, subjects were inclined to attribute their participation to the importance of the survey and were not likely to attribute their participation to a general disposition to take part in such surveys. Observers exactly reversed this pattern, attributing subjects' participation primarily to a personal inclination to take part in surveys and only secondarily to the value of the survey.

McArthur's study comes very close to being a direct test of the proposition that actors attribute cause to situations while observers attribute cause to dispositions. It suffers, however, from the interpretive difficulty that information about the actor's behavior was given to observers only in printed verbal form. A study by Nisbett and Caputo (1971) avoided this problem by examining situations where more nearly equivalent forms of information were available to actors and observers.

In this study, they asked college students to write a brief paragraph stating why they had chosen their major field of concentration and why they liked the girl they dated most frequently. Subjects were asked to write similar brief paragraphs explaining why their best friends had chosen their majors and girl friends. It proved possible to code all of the answers, à la McArthur, into either stimulus attributions ("Chemistry is a high-paying field," "She's a very warm person") or person attributes ("I want to make a lot of money," "I like warm girls"). When answering for himself, the average subject listed roughly the same number of stimulus and person reasons for choosing his major and twice as many stimulus as person reasons for choosing his girl friend. When answering for his best friend, subjects listed approximately three times as many person as stimulus reasons for choosing the major and roughly the same number of stimulus as person reasons for choosing the girl friend. Thus, when describing either choice of a major or choice of a girl friend, subjects were more likely to use dispositional language for their best friends than for themselves. . . .

The Information Available to Actor and Observer

It is a truism that the meaning of an action can be judged only in relation to its context. It is central to our argument that the context data are often quite different for actor and observer and that these differing data prompt differing attributions. . . .

Much of the discrepancy between the perspectives of observer and actor arises from the difference between the observer's inferred history of everyman and the concrete individualized history of the actor himself. The actor has been exposed to a sequence of experiences that are to a degree unique, but the observer is constrained to work with the blunt conceptual tools of modal or normative experience.

Kelley (1967) has proposed that naive causal inference resembles the scientist's analysis of variance. The attributor possesses three different kinds of information that correspond to different causal possibilities: consensus information (do other actors behave in the same way to a given stimulus?); distinctiveness information (does the actor, and do other actors, behave in the same way to other stimuli?); and consistency information (does the actor, and do other actors, behave in the same way to the given stimulus across time and situational contexts?). The attributor then makes use of whatever information he has available in the "analysis of variance cube" formed by these three dimensions and makes the best causal inference he can. In Kelley's terms, the observer always lacks some of the distinctiveness and consistency information the actor possesses by virtue of knowing his own history. The observer may approach the actor's knowledge of these dimensions if he knows the actor well, but he cannot reach it. If the actor is unfamiliar to him, he knows nothing at all of this data set.

Because the actor knows his past, he is often diverted from making a dispositional attribution. If the actor insults someone, an observer, who may assume that this is a typical sample of behavior, may infer that the actor is hostile. The actor, on the other hand, may believe that the sample is anything but typical. He may recall very few other instances when he insulted anyone and may believe that in most of these instances he was sharply provoked. The actor's knowledge about the variability of his previous conduct—associated, in his mind, with different situational requirements—often preempts the possibility of a dispositional attribution. We suspect that because of the differences in the availability of personal history data, actors and observers evaluate each act along a different scale of comparison. The observer is characteristically normative and nomothetic: He compares the actor with other actors and judges his attributes accordingly. The actor, on the other hand, is more inclined to use an ipsative or idiographic reference scale: This action is judged with reference to his other previous actions rather than the acts of other actors. . . .

The difference in information available to actor and observer probably plays an important role in producing differential attributions, but this is not the whole story. There are good reasons for believing that the same information is differentially processed by actors and observers.

While it hardly seems debatable that actors and observers operate much of the time with different background data, the contention that actors and observers differ fundamentally in the *processing* of available data is bound to be more controversial. We believe that important information-processing differences do exist for the basic reason that *different aspects of the available information are salient for actors and observers and this differential salience affects the course and outcome of the attribution process.*

The actor and the observer are both reaching for interpretations of behavior that are sufficient for their own decision-making purposes. With unlimited time, and using the kinds of probes that emphasize a full deterministic picture of an action sequence, observers can probably reach attributional conclusions very similar to those of the actor. In the heat of the interaction moment, however, the purposes of actor and observer are apt to be different enough to start the inference process along distinctive tracks. . . .

The action itself—its topography, rhythm, style, and content—is more salient to the observer than to the actor. In establishing the reasons for this we may begin with the observation that action involves perceptible movement and change (by definition) and it is always to some extent unpredictable. While the environment is stable and contextual from the observer's point of view, action is figural and dynamic. The actor, however, is less likely to focus his attention on his behavior than on the environmental cues that evoke and shape it. In part this is because the actor's receptors are poorly located for recording the nuances of his own behavior. Many response sequences are preprogrammed and prepackaged, as it were, and do not require careful monitoring. The actor need not concern himself with his response repertory until there is conflict among the demands of the environment. Even then he will resolve the conflict in terms of perceived stimulus requirements. In short, the actor need not and in some ways cannot observe his behavior very closely. Instead, his attention is directed outward, toward the environment with its constantly shifting demands and opportunities.

These attentional differences should result in differences in causal perception. The actor should perceive his behavior to be a response to environmental cues that trigger, guide, and terminate it. But for the observer the focal, commanding stimulus is the actor's behavior, and situational cues are to a degree ignored. This leaves the actor as the likely causal candidate, and the observer will account for the actor's responses in terms of attributed dispositions.

The effect of these differential attribution tendencies is amplified by bias from another source, the tendency to regard one's reactions to entities as based on accurate perceptions of them. Rather than humbly regarding our impressions of the world as interpretations of it, we see them as understandings or correct apprehensions of it. The nature of this bias is perhaps easiest to see with young children, where it is much more extensive and profound than for adults. Philosophers and other adults make a distinction between the properties of entities that a three-year-old child does not make. The distinction is between those properties that have an existence apart from the transaction of a human being with the object and those properties that are the result of such a transaction. Properties of the former type include the bulk, shape, mass, and motion of an object. Most philosophers and almost all scientists and laymen would agree that such properties have an existence apart from the perception of them. Philosophers since the seventeenth century have designated these as primary qualities and have distinguished them from what are called secondary qualities, including taste, odor, sound, and color, which have no existence apart from the interaction of a sense organ with the object. The layman, it is important to note, does not ordinarily distinguish between primary and secondary qualities unless corrected by a philosopher. He does, however, distinguish in principle between the primary and secondary qualities on the one hand and what may be called evaluations on the other. Evaluations include judgments such as those concerning the goodness, beauty, or propriety of an object or action. Adults realize, at least intellectually, that evaluations do not have the status of perceptions, but are only interpretations or reactions.

How is it that a three-year-old correctly learns the distinction between evaluations and primary qualities and incorrectly learns to group the secondary qualities with primary qualities instead of with evaluations? The answer seems to be that the child learns that certain of his reactions to objects meet invariably with consensual validation while others do not. Once he learns the designation "blue," his judgment that an object is blue is almost never contradicted. He eventually learns, however, that not everyone agrees with his evaluations of objects as pretty, funny, or good. In terms of Kelley's (1967) analysis of variance analogy, the child comes to learn that certain of his reactions to entities are shared by all others and that he himself has those same reactions at all times and under all circumstances. Simultaneously, he learns that there are certain other types of reactions that may or may not be shared by others and that he himself does not invariably have. Before the analysis of variance cubes begin to fill in, however, the child believes that clowns are funny in the same way that balls are round. Funniness is experienced as a property of the clown.

It seems clear that the distinction between evaluations and primary qualities is never fully made. We never quite get over our initial belief that funniness is a property of the clown and beauty is in the object. The probable reason for this is the fact that there remains a considerable degree of consensus even for our most subjective evaluations. Almost always at least some people agree with our evaluations, and sometimes almost everyone agrees with our evaluations. Phenomenologically, the distinction between evaluations and primary qualities is merely a quantitative one, just as the initial basis for learning the distinction—the degree of consensus—is quantitative. Just as we erroneously feel that secondary qualities are primary, we continue to feel that our subjective evaluations are in some sense perceptions.

This confusion between what is inherent in the object and what is a reaction elicited by it comes close to what Heider labels "egocentric attribution":

> Attribution to the object. . .means more than the dependence of p's pleasure on the object. It also means that there is something enjoyable about the object.

The attractiveness is a quality of the object, just as is the sweetness of a fruit or the roughness of a terrain. Consequently, p's expectations, and therefore beliefs, refer not only to his own reactions to x on future occasions, but also the reactions of other people. The basic scheme is as follows: "Since my pleasure was aroused by x, x is positive, and therefore everyone will like it." An expectation of similarity between the reactions of others and the self is thus egocentrically determined" (1958, p. 158).*

Our responses to immediately impinging stimuli are therefore biased in two ways: they are too salient and they are too "real." These biases should have a pronounced effect on the interpretations given by an actor and an observer to the actor's behavior. The actor will experience his behavior as proceeding naturally from the attractions, compulsions, and restraints in his environment. For the observer, it is not the stimuli impinging on the actor that are salient, but the behavior of the actor. The observer will therefore tend to see the actor's behavior as a manifestation of the actor, as an instance of a quality possessed by him. For the actor to interpret his behavior as the result of a disposition, he would have to weight the impact of the immediate environment less heavily, regard his knowledge about the environment as mere evaluations that may or may not be shared, and recognize that others might not respond as he does to this particular environment. For the observer to interpret the actor's behavior as a response to his environment, he would have to weight the vivid, sense-impression data of the behavior itself less heavily and strain his empathic abilities to allow himself to imagine the vividness for the actor of the environmental cues he confronts. To the extent that actor and observer fail to accomplish these tasks, the actor will overattribute his behavior to the environment and the observer will overattribute the behavior to qualities of the actor. . . .

For the observer who is at the same time an actor, the tendency toward heightened salience of action should become more pronounced for several reasons. The fact that the observer is also caught up in action suggests that he will not be in a position to make leisurely appraisals of the setting and its contributions to unfolding behavior. Rather than being in a set to understand and evaluate the relative contributions of person and environment, the actor-observer will be tuned to process those cues that are particularly pertinent for his own next responses. Short-run behavior prediction is of paramount importance to the observer who is preparing his next act, and we suggest that the actor's behavior is more likely to seem pertinent for such predictions than the situational context evoking it. The acting organism probably does not operate at the peak of potential

---

*From Fritz Heider, *The Psychology of Interpersonal Relations* (New York: John Wiley & Sons, 1958). Reprinted by permission.

cognitive complexity, but it is likely to be attracted to convenient simplifying assumptions about the environment. One such simplifying assumption is that action implies a disposition to continue acting in the same manner and to act in such a manner in other situations as well.

A second consideration arises from the fact that the observer's presence and behavior may affect the actor's responses in ways not discerned by the observer. It is difficult for the active observer to evaluate the significance of his own presence because he is not often afforded clear comparative tests—tests that pit the stimulus contributions he generally makes against the stimulus contributions of others. In the situation we are now considering, where the observer is also an actor, the observer is likely to exaggerate the uniqueness and emphasize the dispositional origin of the other's responses to his own actions, actions the observer assumes to be perfectly standard, unexceptional, and unprovocative. . . .

In summary, the observer and the actor are likely to take different perspectives toward the same information. For the observer, the actor's behavior is the figural stimulus against the ground of the situation. The actor's attention is focused outward toward situational cues rather than inward on his own behavior, and moreover, those situational cues are endowed with intrinsic properties that are seen to cause the actor's behavior toward them. Thus, for the observer the proximal cause of action is the actor; for the actor the proximal cause lies in the compelling qualities of the environment. Finally, the tendency for the observer to attribute action to the actor is probably increased to the extent that the observer is also an actor and to the extent that both the observing and the observed actor are tied together in a mutually contingent interaction.

The Naive Psychology of Observers and Actors

The preceding discussion is likely to raise in the reader's mind a question as to who is correct, the actor or the observer. In the typical case, is behavior really caused by the actor or elicited by the environment? Put in these simplified terms, the question is of course unanswerable. All behavior is in one sense caused or produced by the actor. Except perhaps in acts such as the patellar reflex, all action involves some form of explicit or implicit decision process suggesting volition or personal causation.

The more pertinent and answerable question concerns the extent to which a particular setting is likely to evoke the same response across many persons. According to either the logic of Kelley's (1967) analysis of variance cube or of Jones and Davis' (1965) correspondent inference theory, a situation that evokes a response common to many persons is likely to be seen as causing the behavior. Situations that evoke varied or unique responses are much less likely to be seen as causal. Obversely, when a person acts in a similar fashion on many different occasions, the act is seen to reflect a personal disposition.

It is obviously safer to talk about *phenomenal* causality than to raise any questions concerning accuracy or objective causality. Nevertheless, it is interesting to consider the many occasions on which the observer appears to violate the rules set up for him by Kelley and by Jones and Davis—to make a dispositional inference when the data do not allow it. Without insisting that the actor is usually right, we can point to many instances where the observer's interpretation of behavior is simply wrong. The observer is wrong when he infers that an attitude is consistent with an essay written in response to a legitimate request. He is wrong when he thinks the nonintervening bystander is apathetic, or infers that the subject who agrees to help out for a handsome fee is a chronic volunteer. In each of these cases the observer seems to underestimate the power of the situation and to overestimate the uniqueness of the (in fact modal) response. . . .

Summary and Conclusions

Actors tend to attribute the causes of their behavior to stimuli inherent in the situation, while observers tend to attribute behavior to stable dispositions of the actor. This is due in part to the actor's more detailed knowledge of his circumstances, history, motives, and experiences. Perhaps more importantly, the tendency is a result of the differential salience of the information available to both actor and observer. For the observer behavior is figural against the ground of the situation. For the actor it is the situational cues that are figural and that are seen to elicit behavior. Moreover, the actor is inclined to think of his judgments about the situational cues as being perceptions or accurate readings of them. These cues are therefore more "real" as well as more salient than they are for the observer. Behavior is thus seen by the observer to be a manifestation of the actor and seen by the actor to be a response to the situation.

The observer often errs by overattributing dispositions, including the broadest kind of dispositions—personality traits. The evidence for personality traits as commonly conceived is sparse. The widespread belief in their existence appears to be due to the observer's failure to realize that the samples of behavior that he sees are not random, as well as to the observer's tendency to see behavior as a manifestation of the actor rather than a response to situational cues. . . .

REFERENCES

Heider, Fritz. *The Psychology of Interpersonal Relations.* Wiley, 1958.

Jones, Edward E. and Davis, Keith E. "From Acts to Dispositions: The Attribution Process in Person Perception," in Leonard Berkowitz (Ed.) *Advances in Experimental Social Psychology,* 2, New York: Academic Press, 1965.

Jones, Edward E. and Harris, Victor A. "The Attribution of Attitudes," *Journal of Experimental Social Psychology,* 3 (1967), pp. 1-24.

Jones, Edward E., Worchel, Stephen, Goethals, George R., and Grumet, Judy. "Prior Expectancy and Behavioral Extremity as Determinants of Attitude Attribution," *Journal of Experimental Social Psychology,* 7 (1971), pp. 59-80.

Kelley, Harold H. "Attribution Theory in Social Psychology," *Nebraska Symposium on Motivation,* 14 (1967), pp. 192-241.

McArthur, Leslie Z. "The How and What of Why: Some Determinants and Consequences of Causal Attribution." Unpublished Ph. D. dissertation, Yale University, 1970.

Nisbett, Richard E. and Caputo, G. Craig. "Personality Traits: Why Other People Do The Things they Do." Unpublished manuscript, Yale University, 1971.

CHAPTER
THREE

HOW DO PEOPLE
BECOME MORAL ACTORS ?

THE ISSUE OF MORAL DEVELOPMENT

Eight-year-old Laura and her five-year-old sister Judy come downstairs to play one Sunday morning while their parents are still asleep. They wander into the living room laying plans to play house when the older child spots an opened box of fancy chocolates on a table, left over from their parents' entertaining of the previous evening.

"Look, Judy, some candy," she says in a controlled, matter-of-fact voice.

"Oh boy," enthuses her sister, "let's have some."

"No, Judy, Mommy wouldn't want us to. They're for her parties. They're too expensive. It wouldn't be nice to take them."

"It's O.K., Laura. Mommy is sleeping," Judy replies, all the while keeping her eyes fixed greedily on the box.

Laura becomes more perturbed: "No Judy, it doesn't matter. It would be naughty to take them. They're Mommy's"

Judy edges cautiously toward the box. "It's O.K. Mommy is sleeping. There are lots, see. Anyway, I just want one." She reaches into the box.

"Judy!" says Laura, raising her voice excitedly and putting her hands on her hips, "you may not have one and that's all! They don't belong to you. Now you be a good girl and leave them alone!"

"But Laura," whines Judy "it's O.K. Mommy won't be angry. She's sleeping and I'm only going to have one, and anyway Mommy said if we found a box left over we could have some."

"No she didn't, Judy. You're lying."

"She did too."

"No she didn't." Laura moves toward Judy, bends slightly forward, and wags her finger. "You shouldn't lie, Judy. That's not nice. Only bad people lie."

"I didn't lie. I'm going to eat one." She quickly takes a chocolate and pops it into her mouth.

"Judy!" says Laura almost crying, "You're terrible. You took Mommy's candy.

Now she will be very upset. You stop that!"

"Its O.K. Mommy won't be angry. She's sleeping. Anyway she said it was O.K."

Laura begins to waver as she watches her sister chewing contentedly on the chocolate. "Did she really say that? Is what you said true?"

"Yep."

"I don't think it's true."

"It is."

Laura hesitates, starts to say something, then reaches into the box and takes a candy. As she begins to eat, she is once more overcome by doubt. "It's not fair Judy..."

"They're delicious. I'm going to eat one more."

"No, Judy, it's not fair!" yells Laura. "They don't belong to us. You wouldn't want someone to steal your candy. Only bad people steal. Like robbers."

"It's O.K., Laura, Mommy said..."

"It's not true. I'm going to ask Mommy and I'm going to tell her what we did." She runs out of the room half crying and heads for the stairs: "Mommy," she cries, "Mommy, Judy said that it was O.K. if ..."

Laura and Judy are wrestling with a moral dilemma. It may not seem like an overly serious one, but to Laura, at least, it is quite vexing and she is heavily involved. There is a choice to be made and she very much wants to make the right choice—the moral choice. Judy, too—thanks largely to her older sister—is aware that the situation is a matter of right and wrong. She enters into a moral dialogue with Laura doing her level best to cite relevant facts and arguments. And in the end she even achieves a victory of sorts: her sister is persuaded to take a chocolate. Both girls are coming to grips with moral rules. Neither gives in pell-mell to her hedonistic desires because both realize that there are, after all, certain constraining principles that mitigate against the selfish pursuit of personal pleasure. Indeed, Laura is so upset by her moment of weakness—by her violation of these principles—that she begins to cry and runs to confess to her mother.

In this small example, then, we see all the basic elements of a moral quandary. The actor faces a choice that will affect not merely himself, but others as well; he is tempted to choose in a manner that is selfishly expedient; he is aware of certain constraints (norms, rules, principles) that mitigate against a purely selfish choice; he is likely to experience an internally generated emotional reaction—call it guilt, regret anxiety—if he does not make the "right" choice. Behaving morally is no simple matter. It involves transcending one's own personal viewpoint and examining the situation with which one is confronted from a wider perspective—a perspective that includes not merely certain immediate others, but also certain more abstract rules or principles that are widely shared in our social system. If we did not all learn to do this to some extent, social decisions would be made solely by whomever was strongest and co-operative social life would be impossible. We can be sure, then, that every society gives the greatest importance to moral behavior, and, in fact, we all spend a good part of our childhood being taught the rules of moral conduct.

But what is involved in this process? How do people become moral actors? In terms of our little story, what is the difference between Judy and Laura? In what sense, and why, is Laura apparently more moral than Judy? These are the questions with which we deal in this section. They are questions which have no agreed upon answers. We shall examine three quite different frameworks, each of which construes the process of moral development quite differently: Learning Theory views it as a process of learning certain behaviors; Psychoanalytic Theory, as a process of internalizing certain standards; and Cognitive Developmental Theory as a process of developing certain modes of thought.

THE MAJOR VIEWS

Social Learning

Social learning theorists (represented in this chapter by Albert Bandura and Richard Walters) would say, rather simply, that the scene between Laura and Judy illustrates how people's behavior can be shaped by rewards and punishments. The essential difference between Laura and Judy is that the former has been around three years longer and, hence, has learned that taking her parents' candy is bad because it leads to punishment (or at least the withdrawal of rewards). Judy believes that if no one sees them there will be no trouble (she keeps pointing out that "Mommy is asleep"), but Laura knows better. She has probably tried to get away with things in the past, was caught and found herself in even worse trouble. She certainly has learned that an empty chocolate box is telltale evidence, something which Judy, with her lesser experience, would probably overlook. Both girls, then, are worried about the negative sanctions contingent on taking the chocolates. Judy is more adventurous because she thinks that her mother will never find out. Laura will not take that risk and only gives in when sorely tempted and partially convinced by her sister that "Mommy won't be angry." At any rate, this information gives her a measure of security. She can always forestall punishment by pleading that she was misled by her lying sister. In the past, she has learned that her mother is unlikely to be as upset with her if she did wrong without knowing.

But there is clearly much more to it than this. It is apparent that Laura has learned to exercise more self-control than Judy. Judy is more at the mercy of her impulses—she can't keep her eyes off the chocolates and can't stop thinking of how delicious they will taste. Laura can see the situation in the wider context of being a good girl or a naughty girl. When she does things that her mother likes, she is told she is a "good girl" or a "big girl" and her mother is especially nice to her. Thus, she feels important and worthwhile and strives to continue behaving this way even on her own. Because she is the older sister, she is particularly aware of the importance of being a "big girl," and this means modeling her behavior after her mother. The fact that her mother seems a powerful agent with access to many goods and privileges that she too wishes to control by becoming a "big girl," gives extra impetus to her modeling. It is clear from the dialogue that, at times, Laura is patterning herself after her mother. Certain phrases (e.g., "You may not have one and that's all. Now you be a good girl and leave them alone") are more characteristic of an adult speaking to a child than of one child speaking to another. Evidently, then, Laura gets a certain satisfaction out of dealing with the situation as her mother would and this contributes to the greater self-control that she manifests.

Finally, it can be noted that, in the past, Laura has evidently been subjected to punishments after having misbehaved. When she finally eats the chocolate, she apparently experiences a pang of almost uncontrollable anxiety that sets her crying. She then runs to confess to her mother partly to "get it over with"—to receive any punishment that may be forthcoming—and partly to explain her actions and re-instate herself in her mother's good graces.

To the learning theorists, then, moral behavior is acquired in the same way as any other learned behavior. More important, the principles that govern learning are the same for humans as they are for any other animal. In all cases, it is a matter of the proper application of rewards and punishments. To be sure, humans are the most complex of animals and, hence, their behavior requires an appropriately sophisticated analysis, but learning theorists are skilled at this task and quite capable of making the necessary subtle distinctions. Listen to Bandura and Walters as they break down various techniques of parental discipline into different types of reward and punishment:

> Any disciplinary act may involve in varying degrees at least
> two operations, the *presentation of a negative reinforcer* and *the*
> *withdrawal of a positive reinforcement.* For example, threats
> of loss of love in which the parents depict disasterous consequences
> to their health resulting from the child's behavior consist
> in the presentation of fear-arousing noxious stimuli; whereas
> threats of loss of love in which the restoration of parental
> affection and approval is made contingent on the child's
> conformity to parental wishes involves the withholding of positive
> reinforcement but little aversiveness. Similarly, a parent
> who inflicts little pain while impersonally administering mild
> physical punishment to a child obtains his effects primarily
> through the withholding of positive reinforcers, whereas a parent
> who administers very severe physical punishment while assuring
> the child of his love is dispensing positive reinforcers at the
> same time as he administers noxious stimuli (1963, p.189).

When these sorts of techniques are applied to moral behavior, the child gradually learns to become a moral actor. Of course, if they are applied badly, or applied to the wrong behavior, the child can just as easily become an immoral actor.

While the direct administration of rewards and punishments is the surest and most controlled way of shaping behavior, children can also learn from observing behavior models. A good many experimental studies have shown that children will readily imitate behaviors that are in some way striking or noteworthy. They are parti-cularly prone to imitate behaviors with clear reinforcing consequences, or models who appear to be competent, successful, or admirable. Since parents are very likely to fit the latter category, it is important that they "do as they say" lest their direct discipline techniques be undermined by their modeling.

We noted at the outset that before a person can be considered a moral actor, he must be capable of exercising a good deal of self-control—he cannot be solely under the control of external reinforcers administered by others. Learning theorists would not disagree with this but, for them, the issue is more complex. On the one hand, they would point out that no behavior is entirely autonomous or self-controlled because all behavior must be maintained by the presence of at least sporadic external reinforcers— no one will persist indefinitely in a response that never brings rewards. On the other hand, they would agree that some behaviors require only very sporadic reinforcement, while others can become part of such a complex behavior-chain that the source of reinforcement is no longer apparent. Modeling would be an example of the latter: if a child derives satisfaction from imitating the actions of an admired and potent parent, he may continue to reproduce this model's moral behavior for a long time even in the absence of more direct reinforcement. Avoidance learning would be an example of the former: if a child is severely punished in the act of stealing, the next time a similar situation arises he will experience fear and will refrain from stealing in order to avoid a repetition of the punishment. Such restraint will be reinforced by a reduction in fear but, more important, it will prevent the child from actually checking whether punishment would again be forthcoming. Hence, behaviors initially acquired to avoid severe negative reinforcement can be extremely long-lasting even though they stemmed from only one or two direct punishments. Experiments with animals have shown that an organism trained to avoid electric shocks by, say, pressing a bar at the sound of a buzzer, will persist in this behavior for extraordinary periods of time—long after the electric shock has been disconnected.

A major side-effect of severe negative reinforcement is the induction of strong emotional reactions (anxiety reactions) which, themselves, become conditioned to the situation preceding punishment. And this brings us to the problem of guilt. To learning theorists, guilt is simply an anxiety reaction that has the special feature of coming after the completion of a transgression rather than before. This timing is seen to be a consequence of the timing of the original punishment. As we noted above, if a child is punished before he can complete the act of stealing, then on future occasions the anxiety will precede the act and will seem like fear. If, however, the child is punished only after the act is completed, then in the future the anxiety will follow the act and will seem more like guilt. To be sure, learning theorists prefer to avoid terms like "fear" and "guilt" because they feel that such labels have too much surplus meaning— for them, all such anxiety reactions are quite similar, apart from their timing.

Perhaps the most important point here is that learning theorists do not see guilt as being associated specifically with moral transgressions. Instead, they see it as an anxiety-response that can occur in connection with any act regularly punished after the fact. Since parents cannot always, nor even often, catch their offspring in the act of misbehaving, a great many behaviors are likely to fall in this category.

Finally, it should be noted that, for learning theorists, moral development is a piecemeal operation. Honesty, consideration of others, and control of aggression may all be aspects of morality, but each must be learned separately. There is no particular reason to expect that a non-aggressive child will also be more honest or, for that matter, that a child who doesn't lie will also be less prone to cheat. Consistency across these various realms must be imposed from without, either by the presence of consistently moral models, or by the steadfast application of discipline techniques across realms.

Psychoanalytic Theory

To a psychoanalytic theorist (represented in this chapter by Sigmund Freud) the story of Laura and Judy illustrates the dramatic transformation that occurs when a child internalizes the moral values of his parents. The difference between Laura and Judy is the difference between night and day. Judy is pure ego (in the service of a salivating id): she is concerned only with the amoral issue of how to get the chocolates without being apprehended. To attain this end, she is quite willing to steal and, if one can take the word of her older sister, to lie as well. She fixates on the fact that, "Mommy is sleeping," and, hence, that it is really quite safe to go ahead if only her sister could be persuaded to do likewise. But Laura is not easy to persuade for she has developed a super-ego: she has incorporated certain moral standards that constrain her ego and prevent her from looking at the situation in strictly utilitarian terms. For her, stealing and lying are repugnant *because they are immoral* and not because they might lead to punishment. She continuously berates her sister for contemplating actions that are "naughty" and unworthy of a "good girl." But, of course, these statements have little impact on Judy, who as yet lacks the internal standards needed for their appreciation.

If we look carefully at Laura's behavior, we can see the root causes of her internalization as well as some further consequences of it. According to psychoanalytic theory, Laura internalized her moral standards by identifying with her mother's attitudes and behaviors, especially those associated with moral uprightness. Indeed, Laura's behavior bears all the earmarks of this crucial identification. The longer Judy persists, and hence, the more the situation takes on moral overtones, the more Laura's behavior resembles that of her mother. Not only does she use language that is reminiscent of an adult scolding a child, but she puts her hands on her hips and engages in other mannerisms that are probably characteristic of her mother. She does not merely reproduce those aspects of her mother's behavior that are especially appropriate, or obviously rewarding. Rather, she reproduces those that are most characteristic: tone, bearing, facial expressions—subtle aspects of demeanor and behavior. It is in this sense that psychoanalytic theorists would argue that Laura is not merely imitating her mother (as social learning theorists would say) but actually identifying with her in a deeper way.

Laura's remorse, following her moment of weakness when she takes one chocolate, also accords with the presumption that she has internalized moral standards through identification. Since these standards are not abstract concepts but embodiments of her mother, they are capable of punishing her in the same way as a parent. Laura, in effect, feels as if she were being punished by an internal authority. She feels guilty. After repeating, "It's not fair," half to herself, she runs from the room in tears to confess to her mother, thus risking real punishment in order to mollify her stern super-ego. In sum, psychoanalytic theorists can account for four aspects of Laura's behavior via the single concept "internalization through identification": (1) her self-imposed restraint, (2) her rejection of both stealing and lying, (3) her tendency to mimic her mother, and (4) her guilt reaction and desire to confess.

For psychoanalytic theorists, all behavior is the outcome of an interplay among three psychic mechanisms: the Id, the Ego, and the Super-ego. The id is the seat of the passions and is concerned only with satisfying sensual and aggressive drives in the most impulsive manner without regard to the external dangers that this might incur. The ego is the seat of rationality or reality-testing. It seeks to regulate the id by facilitating the gratification of its impulses when, and only when, this can occur without danger to the organism. The super-ego is the seat of moral prohibitions and it further constrains the ego by permitting it to satisfy id impulses only when this can be done in a moral and not merely safe manner. Within this framework, then, true moral behavior is behavior under the control of super-ego standards. Purely expedient actions—those that happen to conform to the canons of propriety because the ego realizes that deviance would be dangerous—are only superficially moral and do not fit this category. Thus, psycho-analytic theorists exclude from the moral realm many behaviors that learning theorists prefer to include.

How and why does the super-ego come into existence? This is a complicated question whose answer would require an in-depth analysis of that most important of childhood experiences: the Oedipus Complex. Freud discusses this matter in his essay and the details need not concern us here. In broad outline, however, the following events are assumed to occur. At a certain age (between 3 and 6 years) the child forms an intense, quasi-sexual attachment to his cross-sex parent. This leads to a partially real and partially imaginary jealous rivalry with the same-sex parent which comes to a head when the child, fully cognizant of his own smallness and helplessness, comes to believe that he will be brutally punished for his incestuous attachment. (Male children, for example, are presumed to have a fear of castration at the hands of their father.) To protect himself, the child finally abandons his attachment and forms, instead, an identification with the same-sex parent. This permits a vicarious continuation of the earlier direct relationship, but otherwise removes him from direct competition and permits a reconciliation with the same-sex parent. Though ambivalent, the identification is nonetheless intense and, as the child takes on the attitudes and behaviors of the parent, a basis for the super-ego is laid. Finally the child represses—*i.e.,* banishes from conscious memory—this whole turbulent period and the super-ego becomes an auton-omous, unconscious force that prevents him from engaging in a wide range of immoral actions. It is because this period is so turbulent—so filled with threats and prohibitions —that the super-ego becomes a stern disciplinarian capable of inflicting harsh punish-ments in the form of guilt.

Certain features of this process remain rather obscure. For one thing, the Oedipal situation is considerably more complicated for girls than for boys and Freud, himself, was never wholly satisfied with his formulation of it. For another, it is not entirely clear why the super-ego comes to contain only the moral prohibitions of the parent and not the myriad other attitudes that he or she might hold. But to pursue these matters would require a much more detailed analysis than we can afford here.* Whether or not one agrees with psychoanalytic theorists concerning the genesis of the super-ego, it is nonetheless important to recognize that the presumed existence of such a psychic structure accords with much of our everyday experience. We are all aware of

* For a discussion of the Oedipal situation in women, see Freud's "The Psychology of Women" in his *New Introductory Lectures on Psycho-analysis*, New York: W. W. Norton & Co., 1965.

having certain moral prohibitions whose origins are vague but which, nevertheless, prevent us from taking actions that might otherwise seem rational. And most of us have at some time experienced the strong guilt feeling and remorse that follow a violation of these prohibitions.

Cognitive Development

In examining the story of Laura and Judy, a cognitive developmentalist (represented in this chapter by Lawrence Kohlberg) would see neither two organisms shaped by their past history of reinforcement, nor a moral being trying to save an immoral one, but rather a debate between two moral philosophers—a debate that proves fruitless because the protagonists are departing from such different premises that neither could ever quite manage to convince the other. It is not that both children are unable to make cogent points within their own framework; it is simply that they are talking past each other. Nor is it accurate to say that Laura is moral while Judy is not. The only sense in which Laura is more moral is in the sense that she has already been through Judy's philosophy and has come to reject it in favor of a more sophisticated position. In short, Laura and Judy are at different stages of cognitive development. Both are moral actors but each understands morality in different terms.

Judy's cognitive abilities are less advanced than those of her older sister and, consequently, her moral philosophy conforms to a very early, or ego-centric, stage of moral development. For her, right and wrong actions are a matter of the physical or hedonistic consequences of such actions *to herself,* irrespective of the meaning or broader value of these consequences to others. If the chocolates taste good and if they can be taken without incurring punishment, then it is right to take them and that is the end of it. In repeatedly pointing out that "Mommy is sleeping," it is not that she is being cagey or trying to get away with something that she knows is wrong. It is simply that she believes that this paramount fact makes her proposed course of action right— the chocolates can evidently be appropriated without danger of punitive consequences. Laura, on the other hand, is further along in her cognitive development, and her moral thought corresponds accordingly to the third stage of moral development. For her, right and wrong is a matter of living up to the expectations of her family or group, thereby manifesting the qualities of a stereotypical "good person" and winning the approval of significant others. If Mommy would not want them to take the chocolates, or if "she would be angry," then it is simply wrong to take them. Moreover, as Laura repeatedly points out, stealing (and lying as well) are indicative of a "bad" person— they are "naughty" deeds not to be performed by "good girls." Laura, however, is not interested solely in conforming to expectations in order to win approval, she is also concerned with maintaining and justifying these expectations to others. This, too, is typical of her stage of development for she sees moral rules not in the purely ego-centric manner of her sister, but as a system that is "out there" with definite consequences for others as well as herself. Thus, she feels that it is her duty, as one who understands this system, to explain the rules to her sister and see that she abides by them.

Judy has evidently been around her older sister long enough to understand that Laura operates on a different wave length in these matters. She even comprehends this wave length sufficiently well to come up with a somewhat implausible but nevertheless commendable rule: "Mommy said that if we found a box left over we could have some." Laura does not really believe this rule, but she realizes that if it were a statement of fact, it would justify taking some chocolates. When sorely tempted by her sister's enthusiastic munching, she finally uses this rule to justify taking a chocolate herself. However, the dubious credibility of the rule convinces her almost immediately that her action was wrong and she experiences a sharp pang of remorse. With her own moral rectitude in doubt, and with Judy threatening to make short shrift of the remaining chocolates, she is pushed to the brink of tears and runs to her mother partly for re-assurance, but mostly to enlist reinforcements lest the moral order be shattered beyond repair.

For cognitive developmentalists, then, moral behavior is a function of moral judgment, and moral judgment is a function of certain universal stages of cognitive development. As a child grows older, his cognitive processes change in accordance with an invariant sequence of development that is destined to be repeated by all chil-dren in all parts of the world. One consequence of this development is that the child's conception of his world changes, as does his conception of morality.

Of the many psychologists who have contributed to an understanding of these processes of cognitive growth, one man stands out above all the rest: the Swiss psychol-ogist Jean Piaget. For better than half a century, beginning in 1920, he has studied the thought and behavior patterns of children from infancy to adolescence and set down his seminal theories and rich observations in a proliferation of scholarly books and articles. Piaget divided the child's cognitive development into four basic periods: sensory-motor intelligence (0 to 2 years), pre-operational thought (2 to 7 years), concrete operations (7 to 11 years), and formal operations (11 to 15 years).* These periods differ in many ways, but most centrally in the child's relative ability to differentiate between himself and his environment and, thus, to think abstractly.

During the *sensory-motor* stage, the child is capable of forming simple associ-ations between his sensory inputs and his motor outputs, though he does not really experience them as "his" in a meaningful way. He can, for example, learn that moving a hand a certain way will cause a rattle to make a noise and, while he may be capable of generalizing this to other nearby objects, he is not able to conceive of this in a way that even remotely approaches an abstract rule of cause and effect.

During the period of *pre-operational thought* the child acquires the use of language and with this comes a rudimentary form of intuitive logic that moves from "the particular to the particular." For example, if he sees that a particular object floats, he is now capable of predicting correctly that a second, identical object will also float. But his ability to make such predictions breaks down rapidly if the second object differs from the first because he is incapable of using abstract properties that go beyond surface appearance. More generally, his logical powers are limited by "ego-centrism" and by "realism." Realism is the tendency to confuse subjective perceptions with objective reality: *e.g.,* persons that are far away from him are really

---

* It should be noted that Piaget prefers to treat the two intermediate levels as sub-periods of the same basic period. However, the two are sufficiently different so that it will simplify our discussion to consider them separately. For a detailed synthesis of Piaget's work see J. V. Flavell (1963). For an eminently readable account of how children at different stages differ see Roger Brown (1965), pp. 197-245.

smaller, the moon is really no bigger than a balloon and it follows him about as he moves, water poured from a shallow pan into a narrow glass really grows in quantity, and so on. There is no conception of constancy or conservation and, in general, things are assumed to be as they appear. Ego-centrism is the tendency to confuse one's own perspective on events with those of others; whatever the child experiences in the way of sights, sounds, feelings, or even thoughts, he assumes that others are experiencing as well. Thus, it is not unusual for a child of three to call out, "What's this?" and expect a person in a different room to know to what he is pointing. More generally, he is essentially incapable of getting into another's shoes and experiencing an event from that other's perspective. Thus, if he wants something done for him, he cannot begin to understand why another might be unwilling or unable to accede to his repeated requests.

As the child moves forward into the period of *concrete operations,* he becomes able to comprehend more fully the subtle distinction between his own personal attributes and those of the fluctuating yet orderly world around him. His realism and ego-centrism gradually abate so that he acquires both constancy and conservation, as well as an ability to take the role of another. His logical thought is now capable of moving from "the particular to the general," though he is still unlikely to go from "the general to the general" or even from "the general to the particular." For example, he is capable of understanding that certain buoyant objects form a general class of objects that float, and he is even capable of predicting with some accuracy which entities will float and which will sink despite differences in appearance, but he is incapable of systematically inducing Archimedes' Principle or even of using it to make his predictions. Finally, as the child moves into the period of *formal operations,* he loses all traces of realism and ego-centrism and eventually becomes capable of performing all of the logical operations routinely performed by adults.

Even though each new period, or stage, differs from the preceding in content, and even though each represents a quantum jump in the child's cognitive development, it is important to recognize that they all share certain overarching, defining characteristics. First, all form a part of the same basic maturational sequence. In increasingly sophisticated ways, the child is always wrestling with the same basic problem: that of making sense of his surrounding environment and improving his ability to act upon it. Second, each new stage represents an equilibrium point in this continuing sequence. Although the child's cognitive functioning is constantly changing, it slows at these points to consolidate itself, so that the child actually spends somewhat more time within stages than between them. Third, these stages form an invariant and irreversible sequence because each is built on, incorporates, and flows out of, the preceding one. A child can neither skip a stage nor go back to an earlier one.* (However, his normal progress can be accelerated by providing a stimulating environment in which the child can interact with older children or otherwise practice the operations of an upcoming stage.) Finally, communication across any two stages tends to be a one-way street. A child at a higher stage can, if he tries, reproduce the cognitive functioning of

---

* Skipping a stage would be equivalent to understanding multiplication before understanding addition—a logical impossibility. Regressing a stage would be equivalent to preferring to solve a complex multiplication problem through repeated addition—a practical impossibility.

a lower stage, but a child at a lower stage can hardly comprehend, let along reproduce, the thought processes of a higher stage. A corollary is that the child always prefers to function at the highest stage of which he is capable. In this sense, each new stage is always better than the preceding one, so that cognitive development becomes a matter of improved capabilities and not of changed preferences

Piaget's pioneering work forms the basis for Lawrence Kohlberg's more specialized theory of moral development. Like a true cognitive developmentalist, Kohlberg views moral development as a maturational sequence comprising six stages—each stage reflecting a differing and increasingly sophisticated understanding of moral matters. These stages conform to the special defining characteristic noted above and, thus, constitute true developmental stages in Piaget's sense of the term. Since Kohlberg describes his system quite fully in the essay included here, we shall confine ourselves to noting a few of the connections between his stages and Piaget's more general theory of development.

The first two stages correspond roughly to the periods of late pre-operational thought and early concrete operations. Here, the child is influenced by his realism and ego-centrism so that he judges the morality of actions in terms of their physical or hedonistic consequences, or in terms of the physical power of those who enunciate rules. For example, his realism leads him to believe that more severely punished actions, or actions that do more physical damage, are more immoral regardless of intent or mitigating circumstances. And his ego-centrism prevents him from understanding these consequences except as they relate to himself. For example, stealing is considered wrong, not because it harms another but because it will be punished. Similarly, doing someone a favor is right not because it helps the other but because it will bring favors in return. Actually, this latter form of "concrete reciprocity" requires a certain diminution in ego-centrism: the child must be capable of understanding that others, too, appreciate favors. Moreover, it requires a rudimentary form of deductive reasoning: "Since favors are appreciated and since appreciated favors are repaid, it follows that doing favors for others will bring rewards." In this sense, by stage two the child is already into concrete operational thought.

The third stage corresponds roughly to the period of late concrete operations. Here the child conceives of morality in terms of being a good boy or a nice girl and, thus, strives to live up to positive expectations of his family or group. The abatement of realism leads to a diminished attention to the noisier physical consequences of actions, and to the greater appreciation of subtler aspects such as intent or mitigating circumstances. The disappearance of ego-centrism leads to a deeper understanding of others' expectations and, thus, to an improved knowledge of how to behave in socially approved ways. As yet, the child has little comprehension of the basis for moral rules, but he does understand that violations reflect badly on the violator, and that certain actions are bad because they do harm to others.

The fourth stage corresponds roughly to the early period of formal operations. Here the child has a law and order orientation to moral matters whereby he believes that moral rules must be strictly obeyed for their own sake because they are an embodiment of what is right and good. He still does not comprehend the basis for these rules—in other words, *why* they are right and good— but he does understand that they constitute an objective system and, thus, must be applied with equanimity to himself as well as others. Hence, he is now fully capable of moving from a general rule to a specific situation even when he is not directly involved in that situation.

Stages 5 and 6 reflect increasingly sophisticated understandings of the ultimate foundations of moral rules. They probably correspond to the late period of formal operations, although it is difficult to say because Kohlberg's stages finally go beyond Piaget's. Indeed, these last two stages may never be attained even by adults and, in any event, are unlikely to be reached before the age of 16 (or 20, or more in the case of Stage 6). As Kohlberg notes, although the ordering of the stages is invariant across cultures, there are substantial differences in the pace at which they are traversed as well as in the highest stage ordinarily attained by members of a given society. In other words, as in the case for Piaget's stages, a child can never move ahead until his cognitive processes have matured sufficiently, but his pace of development can be accelerated, retarded, or even stopped by the nature of his environment. Progress is a joint function of physical maturation coupled with a supportive and stimulating environment.

The position of cognitive developmentalists, then, has a certain inexorable logic: moral behavior is a matter of moral judgment, and moral judgment is a matter of cognitive processing, and cognitive processing is a function of cognitive development, and cognitive development is a maturational sequence that unfolds through stages. Therefore, the process of becoming a moral actor must be viewed and studied as a maturational process. Unlike psychoanalytic theorists, cognitive developmentalists see internalization of moral standards not as the culmination of one relatively brief event (Oedipal situation) but as a long gradual process. And unlike learning theorists, who concentrate on moral behavior, they concentrate on moral judgment. For the most part they assume that behavior will follow from, and be consistent with, judgment. But this is not always a safe assumption, especially in situations where temptation runs high—here, a person may very well know right and do wrong. Cognitive developmentalists have only recently turned their attention to the problem of just when and why a person will be disposed to follow through behaviorally on his moral judgment.

CONTRASTING THE VIEWS OF MORAL DEVELOPMENT

These ways of looking at how people become moral actors can be contrasted by examining their treatment of five issues:

1. What aspect of morality receives the greatest attention?
2. Is the process of becoming moral similar to or different from other socialization processes? Can acquiring morality best be understood as a special case of more general processes or in terms of its own unique nature?
3. Is the process continuous or discrete? Is morality acquired more or less cumulatively in small pieces or in large, discontinuous chunks?
4. Is the process reversible or irreversible?
5. How difficult or painful is it to become a moral actor?

Behavior, Feeling, or Judgment

It is possible to focus on behavior that is generally considered in the moral realm without regard to any subjective states of the actor. Alternatively, behavior can be viewed as symptomatic of subjective states whose mystery we must unravel to understand the nature of moral action. For learning theory, focusing on emotional states and moral judgments adds unnecessary baggage to our efforts to understand moral behavior. One can, of course, talk about human beings and rats refraining from some course of action because they would feel "guilty" if they performed it, but nothing is added to our understanding in using these terms. In this view, so-called moral behavior can be understood in terms of the process of reinforcement without invoking feelings or cognitions.

Psychoanalytic theory and cognitive development theory give their primary attention to internal states. For the former, the key process is internalization of the parents' standards through a process of identification. A person's emotional reaction—his feeling about his actions in the moral realm—is the key to whether or not the process has proceeded in a healthy fashion in his case. If he feels too little quilt for real transgressions, we consider him a psychopath; if he is burdened by guilt for no apparent reason, a different pathology is indicated. Emotional states are the primary means for monitoring the underlying process. When they are appropriate to moral conduct, we can infer a well-functioning ego under the proper guidance of the super-ego.

The internal state that cognitive development theory focuses on is the realm of moral judgment. We can understand how people become moral actors by examining their ways of reasoning about moral behavior—a cognitive ability that matures with time.

Learning, Identification, or Maturation

It is possible to view the process of becoming a moral actor as identical to other socialization processes. One simply applies the understanding of the more general process to this more specific realm. This is essentially the view taken by both learning theorists and cognitive developmentalists in spite of their differences about the nature of the larger process that must be understood. For learning theorists, moral learning follows general principles of learning; for cognitive developmentalists, it follows equally general principles of cognitive maturation. In neither case are we advised to understand the process *sui generis*.

Psychoanalytic theory, in contrast, does make more of an attempt to understand moral behavior in its own, unique terms. The uniqueness comes from the very special nature of the Oedipal situation: that never to be duplicated dilemma of early childhood. Though the resolution of this dilemma entails a more general process of "internalization through identification"—a process that recurs both before and after the Oedipal resolution—its role in forming the super-ego is so singularly shaped by the Oedipal dilemma as to constitute a unique process. Thus, the development of the super-ego cannot really be understood as a special case of a more general process, but provides its own mysteries for the theorist to unravel.

Continuous or Discrete Process

Does one become a moral actor bit by bit, in barely perceptible pieces? Or does the process involve, large, discontinuous jumps? For learning theorists, the process is a continuous one. If a child learns not to lie, he may or may not have learned not to cheat or steal. These are separate pieces of learning which he must acquire more or less independently.

For psychoanalytic theory and cognitive developmental theory, the learning of morality is more of a single piece. For psychoanalytic theory, the resolution of the Oedipal situation is the crucial formative event. The child's mental being before and after this crucial event is sharply different—as different as a fetus and an infant. The Oedipal conflict is the birth trauma of the super-ego.

Cognitive developmentalists also see discrete steps, but several rather than one giant step. While stages of development blend into each other, and one can find children in transition from one to another, we pause and consolidate at each new stage. Each stage has its own equilibrium, and the divisions made are not simply arbitrary points on a continuum, but are distinct regions with definite boundaries between them.

Reversible or Irreversible Process

Can the process of acquiring morality go in the other direction? Can a person become less of a moral actor than he was previously? Or does it only go in one direction, with pauses perhaps, but no turning back? For learning theorists, the process is necessarily reversible because all learning is reversible and there is no reason to think the learning of moral behavior is any different. Honest people can be taught to lie, cheat, and steal by the appropriate schedule of reinforcements.

The process is irreversible for the other two views. One cannot go back to the pre-Oedipal state; for better or worse the post-Oedipal child has a super-ego. The process is not complete. The super-ego may be weak and dominated by the id, a tyrant which the ego cannot control, but these states are still fundamentally different from that innocent age before the child knew sin. No matter what the ultimate outcome in the struggle between id and super-ego, the child never returns to the earlier state.

For cognitive developmentalists, the process is as irreversible as any maturational process. A higher stage of moral development involves a more sophisticated consciousness. While one can understand a more naive view, one can never obliterate one's own consciousness and become that naive person.

Painful or Natural Process

Do we become moral actors only with a painful and continuing struggle, or does it come more or less naturally and painlessly? The struggle is greatest in the psychoanalytic view and is never fully resolved. There is a continual tension coming from the id's pressure to satisfy impulses immediately and unconditionally, and the super-ego's restrictions and inhibitions on how such impulses may be satisfied. The ego coordinates, coping at the same time with the demands and constraints of the external environment. When it is successful, it is so only with struggle and effort, and even the best of us slips often.

The struggle is much more moderate for the learning theorists. Basically, the person must learn that there is no necessary correspondence between what is gratifying in the short run and what is rewarding over a longer period. Thus, he must learn that a tempting reward foregone today will often bring a bigger one tomorrow—or, at least, will avoid a worse punishment.

No particular struggle is indicated by the cognitive developmentalists. Some people never reach a very high stage of moral development; those who do reach a high stage pay no special price in gaining their maturity. Morality flows naturally out of man's cognitive capacities. To be sure, if one operates at a stage of moral thought that is either much lower or much higher than the generally accepted stage in one's own society, bitterness and conflict may ensue. But this is due to society's need for shared standards and not to any special difficulties associated with the process of moral development itself.

These, then, are the central issues we see running through the contrasting views of how people become moral actors. They are summarized in Chart 3.

Chart 3 Underlying Issues of How People Become Moral Actors

	Social Learning e.g., Bandura and Walters	Psychoanalytic Theory, e.g., Freud	Cognitive Development, e.g., Kohlberg
What aspect of morality receives the greatest attention?	Moral behavior	Moral feeling	Moral judgment
Is the process involved part of a more general process?	Yes, the learning process	Yes and no, it is a highly special case of the identification process	Yes, the cognitive development process
Is the process continuous or discrete?	Continuous and piecemeal	Discontinuous with one critical jump	Discontinuous with several distinct stages
Is the process reversible or irreversible?	Reversible, like all learning	Irreversible, like birth	Irreversible, like all maturational processes
How difficult and painful is it to become a moral actor?	Moderately—one must learn to surrender immediate gratification	Extremely—the conflict between man's nature and society's demands is always there	Hardly at all—any development flows fairly naturally from normal capacities

REFERENCES

Bandura, Albert and Walters, Richard H. *Social Learning and Personality Development.* New York: Holt, Rinehart, & Winston, 1963.

Brown, Roger. "The Development of Intelligence," in Roger Brown, *Social Psychology.* New York: Free Press, Division of MacMillan Co., 1965, Chapter 5.

Flavell, J.V. *The Developmental Psychology of Jean Piaget.* Princeton, New Jersey: D. Van Nostrand and Co., 1963.

THE DEVELOPMENT OF SELF-CONTROL

ALBERT BANDURA AND RICHARD H. WALTERS

Self-Reactions as Determinants of Social Control

The process of acquiring self-control has usually been described as one in which parental standards are incorporated, introjected, or internalized, a "supergo" is formed, or some inner moral agent that is a facsimile of the parents is developed to hold in check impulses that are "ego-alien." These descriptions are replete with terms that have considerable surplus meaning and that frequently personify the controlling forces. The superfluous character of the constructs becomes evident when one examines laboratory studies in which animals are trained not to exhibit behavior that the experimenter has arbitrarily selected as deviant. For example, Whiting and Mowrer (1943), using a socialization paradigm, taught rats, as a result of punishment, to take a circuitous route to a food reward instead of a considerably shorter and more direct one; the rats maintained this behavior for some time after punishments were withdrawn. The substitution of less direct, more effortful, and more complicated ways of obtaining reward exhibited by the animals parallels changes in children's behavior that result from social training and are ordinarily regarded as indices of the development of self- or impulse-control. However, no one would say that the rats in the Whiting and Mowrer study had internalized the superego of the experimenters or had introjected their standards. . . .

It is evident that [terms] such as those considered above give rise to semantic difficulties and do little to further the understanding of the acquisition and maintenance of self-control responses, which are undoubtedly a function both of fear of anticipated aversive reactions from others and of self-generated aversive stimulation. On the other hand, it is profitable to attempt to identify social influences that generate or intensify fear of others' disapproval or self-punitive responses for transgressions and defects, and factors that affect the size and nature of the groups that persons permit to influence their behavior. . . .

Discriminative Training in Self-control

Children must be taught to discriminate circumstances under which certain classes of behavior may be exhibited from those under which they are not socially acceptable, and to utilize only those forms of response that are appropriate for the occasion. For example, children are expected to refrain from showing physical aggression toward adults or initiating physical attacks on peers; yet, at the same time, boys are expected to relax controls if first attacked by peers and to make efforts to defend themselves, though usually with the restrictions that they do not employ implements that could result in serious injury or use defensive physical aggression against younger or weaker opponents. Moreover, in certain well-defined social contexts, particularly in competitive physical-contact sports, boys are expected not only to defend themselves from attack but also to initiate and maintain physically aggressive behavior. Similar kinds of discrimination are also required in adulthood. For the majority of the population exercise of self-control involves refraining from injurious forms of attack, even in the face of persistent instigation, and the attenuation of the more noxious forms of aggression. However, disciplinary agents, such as parents, police, and armed servicemen, are permitted much freer and more direct expression of aggression in certain well-defined social contexts. . . .

Acquisition of Self-control Through Modeling

Social-learning principles can aid in the understanding of all aspects of self-control, including the development of self-rewarding and self-punitive responses.

The influence of modeling is most clearly apparent in those societies in which the majority of adults consistently display self-denying or self-indulgent behavior. In societies in which denial or indulgence is a cultural norm, the children have little opportunity to observe any other patterns of behavior and consequently are forced to model themselves after the prevalent self-control patterns. . . .

Leighton and his associates (Hughes, Tremblay, Rapoport, and Leighton, 1960) present an account of life in a Nova Scotian county, in which both self-indulgent and self-denial subcultural patterns have co-existed for a number of generations. In "Lavallée," an Acadian community, children are strictly trained in the control of sexual, aggressive, and dependency behavior and are strongly pressured to achieve educational and vocational success. *"Evidently some of these demands are contagious, for the mothers say that their children demand teaching even before entering school"* (p. 133; italics not in original). Both parents spend a considerable amount of time in interacting with their children and thus in transmitting to them the adult patterns which predominate in this cohesive community. While the people of Lavallée emphasize material success, the wealthier members of the community are not expected to be self-indulgent; "the greater economic success a person has, the more he is expected to share it with his family, his church, and his community" (p. 157).

> In terms of time orientation, the main things in life are long-range goals—such as the salvation of the soul, the economic battering of the area, the preservation and the expansion of the Acadian group—*even though some of these are unlikely to be achieved by any individual in his lifetime. . . . Work is a moral activity.* and a man is enjoined not only to do it but also to take pride and pleasure in it under almost any circumstance. . . . Life without work would be life without meaning, and people who try only to get as much money as possible while doing as little as they can are disparaged (pp. 159-160; italics not in original).

Within the same Nova Scotian county there exists a group of settlements in which a very different pattern of life prevails. Community cohesion is lacking, and laziness, drunkenness, fighting, sexual promiscuity, thievery, and other criminal and antisocial activities frequently occur. In contrast to the parents of Lavallée, the parents in these "depressed" settlements are permissive and nondirective and have very low educational and occupational aspirations for their children. Through their own life patterns, they transmit to their children beliefs that work should be avoided, if possible, and that laws are to be defied; and they continually present to them models of drunken, aggressive behavior. Indeed, one of the prevailing sentiments among these people is that "the best thing to do in life is to escape from your problems as quickly as possible."

> The preference for drinking as the modal recreational pattern sets the keynote for this sentiment. The drinking in turn often leads to fighting, another way of attempting to obliterate rather than solve problems. Also popular, though, are some of the "fantastic" types of comic books and violent action movies, through which emotional releases and temporary escapes can be found. Recreation then, when enjoyed at all, tends to be at either of two extremes: the drinking which soon results in oblivion, or the fighting and related types of violent action. There is relatively little middle-ground, such as moderately

tempered parties or group games. So dominant is the drive for liquor that people are willing to spend exorbitant sums of money to get it from bootleggers after the Government liquor store is closed. They will also drink alcoholic substitutes such as vanilla if the need is not met with regular liquor (p. 307).

A child who grows up in this kind of atmosphere is unlikely to acquire, either through modeling or through reinforcement patterns, habits of self-denial and self-restraint by which he and his children might secure a more stable and prosperous pattern of life. . . .

The influence of models in modifying resistance to deviation has been demonstrated in experimental studies having relevance to the problem of deviation. S. Ross (1962) employed a toy-store situation in which nursery-school children alternated in the roles of customer and storekeeper. For children in a deviant-model condition, a peer model, who served as the experimenter's confederate, informed the children that upon completing the game they could select a *single* toy only. The model then proceeded to help himself to three toys. In the conforming-model condition, the model took only one toy and thus exhibited behavior that was consistent with his verbal prohibition. Children in the control group simply received the verbal prohibition. In each condition the peer model left the room while the children made their selections. Relative to the subjects in the conforming-model and the control groups, children who observed the deviant model violated the prohibition more often and exhibited more conflictful behavior as reflected in moralistic comments, self-reassurances about the deviation, self-directed hostility, and concealment while performing the misdeed. Some evidence that a conforming model reinforces the observer's self-controlling tendencies, and thereby reduces conflict in temptation situations, is provided by the finding that control children displayed significantly more conflictful behavior than those who witnessed the conforming model, although both groups were equally conforming. . . .

Acquisition of Self-Control Through Direct Reinforcement

In a number of investigations, the severity of parents' socialization pressures has been related to the extent to which children demonstrate self-control in temptation or achievement situations. The findings, though far from consistent, in general suggest that children who experience relatively early or severe socialization pressures tend to exhibit greater self-control than children who are more leniently trained (W. Allinsmith, 1960; Burton, Maccoby, and Allinsmith, 1961; Cox, 1962; Heinicke, 1953; Whiting and Child, 1953). Assuming that severity-of-socialization measures largely reflect the extent to which parents dispense rewards for conformity with parental standards and punish noncompliance, these results provide indirect evidence that patterns of parental reinforcement are important determinants of the habit strength of the self-control responses of children.

Laboratory studies of reward of aggressive responses provide the only experimental demonstrations of the effects of direct positive reinforcement on the occurrence of socially disapproved responses. Similarly, the role of punishment in the development of response inhibition, although sometimes over-emphasized in theoretical expositions, has rarely been explored in experimental studies of human behavior in social situations. The available evidence . . . suggests that punishment may have very diverse effects, depending on its timing, intensity, and nature, and on the status of the punitive agent.

According to Mowrer (1960a, 1960b), the execution of a deviant act involves a sequence of response-produced cues, each providing sensory feedback. A painful stimulus (punishment) can be presented at various points in this sequence and so lead to the relatively direct association of a fear response with the response-produced cues occurring at the time of punishment. If the punishment occurs only on the completion of a deviant act, the fear will be most strongly associated with the stimuli accompanying the actual commission of the deviation and less strongly with the stimuli produced by the agent's preparatory responses. On the other hand, punishment occurring early in the sequence should result in a relatively strong association of the stimuli accompanying certain preparatory responses and the emotion of fear; in this latter case, even the initiation of a deviant act may be quickly forestalled. Since, once an act is initiated, numerous not easily identifiable secondary reinforcers may serve to maintain and facilitate the response sequence, and thus counteract the inhibitory effect of fear, punishment administered early in a response sequence should more effectively prevent the actual commission of a deviant act than punishment administered only when the act has occurred.

Walters and Demkow (1963) investigated the effects of timing on children's resistance to temptation. Two groups of children were given a training session, during which they were instructed to look through a book, which was printed in Russian and contained no pictures, while the experimenter "did some work" in another room. An array of toys was set out in front of the children, who were forbidden to touch these during the experimenter's absence. An observer, secreted behind a one-way vision booth, observed each child's responses and administered punishments, in the form of a loud aversive sound, whenever the child deviated. Subjects who were assigned to an early-punishment condition were presented with the aversive stimulus as soon as they began reaching for a toy; subjects assigned to the late-punishment condition received the stimulus only after they had touched the toys. On a subsequent day, the subjects were again brought to the experimental room and once more left with the book, but this time they were not explicitly instructed to refrain from touching the toys. The results for boys, though not for the generally more inhibited girls, supported the hypothesis that early punishment is more effective than late punishment in producing response inhibition. . . .

Whereas punishments occurring early in a response sequence produce anxiety arousal that inhibits deviant behavior, self-punitive responses associated with the termination of punishment can have an anxiety-reducing function (Aronfreed, 1963a). In the former case, anxiety is reduced by the cessation of the deviant response; in the latter case, it is reduced through the occurrence of the self-punitive response. In neither case is there need to assume that some inner moral agent or faculty has played a role in regulating behavior.

Some suggestive evidence in support of the above interpretation is provided in studies of puppies by Black, Solomon, and Whiting (Mowrer, 1960b). These investigators noted that puppies who were physically punished for approaching attractive but forbidden food showed high resistance to temptation but few emotional responses after transgression, whereas puppies who were punished during the course of consuming the forbidden food were less likely to resist temptation but more likely to exhibit emotional behavior following deviation.

Black *et al* assume that the emotional behavior of their puppies was indicative of "guilt." However, there is no reason to suppose that emotional behavior following the commission of deviant responses is necessarily equivalent to a self-punitive reaction. In fact, if the completion of a deviant act is frequently paired with the onset of punishment, its commission will elicit anticipatory fear reactions rather than self-punishment. One may suspect that in the majority of cases in which a parent disciplines a child, the child deviates and then is punished; it is rare for the parent to make the termination of punishment contingent on the child's making a self-punitive response. The disciplinary procedures of most parents may consequently be more conducive to the development of fear than to the development of guilt. Indeed, children typically react to their own deviations by attempts to avoid punishment, which may take the form of flight, hiding, concealment, denying responsibility, or attribution of blame to others.

Self-punishment has usually been considered the prototype of guilt reactions. However, self-initiated reactions to deviation are more likely to take the form of apology, restitution, or confession, all of which are usually regarded as indices of guilt. All of these responses, including self-punitive ones, may vary in their function according to the circumstances in which they occur, the person to whom the response is directed, and the social training of the agent. In some cases such responses are aimed primarily at the termination or attenuation of punishment, while in other cases they are designed primarily to secure the reinstatement of positive reinforcers. For example, a child may learn to make self-critical statements as an effective way of forestalling or reducing aversive stimulation in the form of parental punishments and thus acquire a habit of employing self-critical statements as a means of controlling the behavior of others. This parallels an infrahuman organism's learning to press a mildly charged lever in order to avoid or reduce the administration of a painful shock which he cannot directly control. In contrast, a child may learn to criticize himself for transgression because self-criticism has proved a successful means of securing the reinstatement of his parents' affection and approval. In this case, the child's behavior parallels that of an animal who learns to press a mildly charged lever in order to obtain food. . . .

Reinforcement Patterns and Disciplinary Techniques

While there is some evidence to suggest that the influence of a particular disciplinary technique on the development of self-control is partly contingent on the operation of other variables, studies of children who show aggressively antisocial response patterns suggest that parental preference for physical punishment as a disciplinary practice is an antecedent of aggressively deviant behavior, while the use of reasoning fosters non-aggressive prosocial behavior (Bandura and Walters, 1959; Glueck and Glueck, 1950; McCord, McCord, and Zola, 1959). The differential effects of aggressive-punitive and nonaggressive disciplinary orientations are also reflected in Bandura's (1960) finding that parents of aggressive boys had made more use of verbal and physical punishment, deprivation of privileges, and isolation in disciplining their children than had parents of very inhibited boys. In contrast, the latter group of parents, consistently with their general behavior patterns, had made more use of reasoning and had more frequently attempted to restore positive relationships with their children when some disciplinary action had been required.

The effects of physical punishment are probably complex and highly dependent upon the intensity of the punishment and the manner in which it is administered. A parent who attempts to modify his child's behavior by inflicting severe physical punishments is providing an aggressive model from whom the child may learn aggressive means of responding in interpersonal situations. Although, because of fear of retaliation, the child may not counteraggress in his parent's presence, he may nevertheless model his behavior after that of his parent when he himself wishes to cope with or control the behavior of others. Indeed, Hoffman (1960) found that mothers who forced compliance with their demands through the use of power-assertive disciplinary techniques, which included verbal and physical aggression, had children who exhibited aggressive power-assertiveness in controlling the behavior of peers and resisted the influence attempts of both teachers and peers. In contrast, one aspect of the use of reasoning as a disciplinary technique may be that the parent provides an example of how to respond nonaggressively in frustrating social interactions. . . .

Whereas physical punishment is frequently an emotionally toned parental reaction to children's completed misdemeanors, reasoning is more likely to be used when the parent anticipates a deviation or interrupts its occurrence in order to forestall undesirable consequences. Thus, reasoning is more likely than physcial punishment to occur early in a deviant response sequence, so fostering resistance to deviation. Moreover, the administration of physical punishment is often poorly timed; in fact, unless the transgression is immediately discovered and the parent is present at the time of commission, the punishment is inevitably delayed. Even when the child's misbehavior is immediately noted, physical punishment may be postponed until the parent who usually administers this punishment is present. Since the child anticipates the punishment, he may be "on his good behavior" and thus be performing prosocial acts when the time for administration arrives. Although on most occasions parents symbolically reinstate the offense before punishing the child, the prosocial behavior, as well as the symbolized transgression, gets paired with the aversive stimulation. Although there is little evidence to indicate what precise effect it will have on the child, this procedure is certainly not the best way of promoting alternative prosocial modes of response.

Disciplinary methods may be most effective when termination of punishment is made contingent on the child's compliance with parental demands. In such cases, compliance either terminates the negative reinforcer or reinstates the positive reinforcer; in both cases, the desired behavior may be strongly reinforced. Threats of loss of love in which positive reinforcers are continuously withheld until the child complies with the parents' demands may thus be especially effective in establishing self-control. The finding of Sears, Maccoby, and Levin (1957) that mothers who used withdrawal of love as a preferred disciplinary technique tended to have children whose self-control was well developed, *provided that the mothers were warm and affectionate,* seems to support this point of view. However, if physical punishment or deprivation of privileges were used in a similar way, that is, if their termination were made contingent on the child's complying with his parents' demands, these techniques might be equally effective in establishing self-control (Hill, 1960). . . .

The Generality of Moral Behavior

The evidence cited earlier in this chapter indicates that resistance to deviation and other forms of self-control can be transmitted through parental modeling, which is likely to attenuate the effects of direct training. Thus, while parents may almost unconditionally label cheating as an undesirable activity, they may at the same time themselves display violations of social prohibitions that the child has opportunity to observe. Most parents frequently violate traffic laws, particularly those relating to speed limits and parking, sometimes with the child enlisted as a participant observer. They enter into discussions of how they can "pad" expense accounts or misrepresent their financial position on income tax returns; they appropriate materials from their businesses or offices for personal use, and constantly infringe minor social prohibitions. Moreover, it is not unusual for parents to boast of their success in outwitting public officials, whom they are apt to depict as easily corruptible, or as getting the better of a bargain through deliberate overrepresentation of the value of their goods or services.

Indeed, Wallerstein and Wyle (1947), in a study of 1,700 predominantly middle-class adults in New York State, found that even seriously deviant behavior was not uncommon among those supposedly law-abiding citizens. Sixty-four percent of the men and 29 percent of the women who were interviewed admitted "off the record" offenses that amounted to felonies under the State law, while 99 percent of the adults acknowledged one or more offenses sufficiently serious to have drawn a sentence of at least one year. Less serious unlawful behavior and breaches of social prohibitions are undoubtedly much more frequent. There can be little doubt that most children are provided with ample opportunities for observing deviation in their parents; such experiences may more than counteract inhibitions that have been established through direct training and may, in fact, promote the learning of means of circumventing social and legal prohibitions.

Even less generality of self-control might be expected in cases in which parents provide precise discriminative training, as they do, for example, in teaching control of aggression. While parents may demand strict self-control of their children's aggression in the home, they may at the same time encourage, instigate, and reward aggression in other situations. In fact, most parents, directly or through modeling, train their children to respond in a highly discriminative manner to situations to which aggression is a possible response; discriminative stimuli, such as the age, sex, and status of the subject, are expected to govern the occurrence, form, and intensity of the response. Under such circumstances, general inhibition of aggression is maladaptive rather than a normal outcome of social training.

In this discussion, emphasis had been placed on factors that make for specificity of self-control. This emphasis, however, is not meant to imply that self-control responses do not generalize to situations similar to those in which they were learned or that parental training is inevitably lacking in consistency. . . .

[Nonetheless] the preponderance of contrary findings casts considerable doubt on the utility of theories of morality which assume that self-control is mediated by a unitary, internal moral agent, such as a conscience, superego, or sense of moral obligation. They also call in question theories of moral development, such as that advanced by Piaget (1948 [1932]), in which moral orientations are assumed to emerge in children of specific ages. According to Piaget, one can distinguish two clear-cut stages of moral judgment, demarcated from each other at approximately seven years of age. In the first stage, defined as objective morality, children judge the gravity of a deviant act in terms of the amount of material damages and disregard the intentionality of the action. By contrast, during the second or subjective morality stage, children judge conduct in terms of its intent rather than its material consequences. However, Bandura and McDonald (1963), using a wide variety of verbally described social situations eliciting moral judgments, . . . found . . . that the developmental sequence proposed by Piaget is by no means predetermined or invariant.

In this study, children who exhibited predominantly objective or subjective moral orientations were assigned to one of three experimental conditions. One group of children observed adult models who expressed moral judgments counter to the group's orientation, and the children were reinforced with verbal approval for adopting the model's evaluative responses. A second group observed the models but received no reinforcement for matching the models' behavior. A third group had no exposure to the models, but each child was reinforced whenever he expressed moral judgments that ran counter to his dominant evaluative tendencies. . . . Following the treatment procedure, the stability and generality of the children's judgmental responses were tested in a different social situation in the absence both of the models and of the social reinforcement.

[Results showed that] children who were exposed to models and those who were positively reinforced for matching their models' moral judgments not only modified their moral orientations but also maintained these changes in their postexperimental judgmental behavior. . . . The so-called development stages were, thus, readily altered by the provision of adult models who consistently adopted moral orientations that ran counter to those displayed by the child. Increased consistency in the children's moral orientations resulted from consistency on the part of the model and generalized to the new set of social situations. As this study suggests, consistency in moral behavior is probably attained when parent models exhibit widely generalized resistance to deviation or self-punitive responses and at the same time use reinforcement patterns that are consistent with the behavioral examples they provide.

The assumption of a generalized self-control system has led to the practice of conceptualizing deviant response patterns in terms of deficient or overdeveloped superego. For example, a psychopath is depicted as lacking internal controls, whereas a neurotic is presented as suffering on account of an overdeveloped superego. Once he has adopted a unitary theory of morality, the clinician finds himself faced with paradoxes. For example, the psychopath is depicted as being impulse-ridden, yet at the same time as exercising effective control over his behavior in order to gain his own ends. He is said to be free of guilt and shame and yet to exhibit behavior that elicits punishment. These apparent contradictions would undoubtedly disappear if one knew the typical social-learning history of the psychopath and the way in which his discriminations were acquired. Similarly, Redl and Wineman (1955) have depicted "children who hate" as lacking controls from within. In order to account for the occasional resistance to temptation and self-punitive responses displayed by these children, Redl and Wineman invoke the concept of "islands of superego." Not only is their account open to serious misinterpretation, but such concepts as "islands of superego" have no explanatory value. More would have been gained by focusing on the nature of the discriminations that the children had learned than in elaborating the paradox that results from the assumption of a unitary internal moral agent.

REFERENCES

Allinsmith, W. "The Learning of Moral Standards," in D. R. Miller and G. E. Swanson (Eds.) *Inner Conflict and Defense.* New York: Holt, 1960, pp. 141-176.

Aronfreed, J. "The Origins of Self-criticism," *Psychological Review,* 1963.

Bandura, A. "Relationship of Family Patterns to Child Behavior Disorders," Progress Report, U. S. P. H. Research Grant M-1734. Stanford University, 1960.

Bandura, A. and McDonald, F. J. "The Influence of Social Reinforcement and the Behavior of Models in Shaping Children's Moral Judgements," *Journal of Abnormal and Social Psychology,* **67** (1963), pp. 274-281.

Bandura, A. and Walters, R. H. *Adolescent Aggression,* New York: Ronald, 1959.

Burton, R. V., Maccoby, E. and Allinsmith, W. "Antecedents of Resistance to Temptation in Four-year-old Children," *Child Development,* 32 (1961), pp. 689-710.

Cox, F. N. "Some Effects on Frustration: I. A Methodological Programme," *Australia Journal of Psychology,* 4 (1952), pp. 94-106.

Glueck, S. and Glueck, Eleanor. *Unraveling Juvenile Delinquency.* Cambridge: Harvard University Press, 1950.

Heinicke, C. M. "Some Antecedents and Correlates of Guilt and Fear in Young Boys," Unpublished Ph.D. dissertation, Harvard University, 1953.

Hill, W. G. "Learning Theory and the Acquisition of Values," *Psychological Review,* **67** (1960), pp. 317-331.

Hoffman, M. L. "Power Assertion by the Parent and its Impact on the Child," *Child Development,* **31** (1960), pp. 129-143.

Hughes, C. C., Tremblay, M., Rappaport, R. and Leighton, A. H. *People of Cove and Woodlot: Communities from the Viewpoint of Social Psychiatry.* New York: Basic Books, 1960.

McCord, W., McCord, Joan and Zola, I. K. *Origins of Crime: A New Evaluation of the Cambridge-Somerville Youth Study.* New York: Columbia University Press, 1959.

Mowrer, O. H. *Learning Theory and Behavior.* New York: Wiley, 1960a.

Mowrer, O. H. *Learning Theory and Symbolic Processes.* New York: Wiley, 1960b.

Piaget, J. *The Moral Judgment of the Child.* New York: Free Press, 1948.

Redl, F. and Wineman, D. *The Aggressive Child.* New York: Free Press, 1955.

Ross, S. "The Effects of Deviant and Nondeviant Models on the Behavior of Pre-school Children in a Temptation Situation," Unpublished Ph.D. Dissertation, Stanford University, 1962.

Sears, R. R., Maccoby, Eleanor E. and Levin, H. *Patterns of Child Rearing.* New York: Harper, 1957.

Wallerstein, J. A. and Wyle, C. I. "Our Law-abiding Law-breakers," *Probation,* **25** (1947), pp. 107-112, 118.

Walters, R. H. and Demkow, Lillian. "Timing of Punishment as a Determinant of Resistance to Temptation," *Child Development,* **34** (1963), pp. 207-214.

Whiting, J. W. M. and Child, I. L. *Child Training and Personality.* New Haven: Yale University Press, 1953.

Whiting, J. W. M. and Mowrer, O. H. "Habit Progression and Regression—A Laboratory Study of Some Factors Relevant to Human Socialization," *Journal of Comparative Psychology,* **36** (1943), pp. 229-253.

THE SUPEREGO, THE EGO, AND THE ID

SIGMUND FREUD

There is scarcely anything else in us that we so regularly separate from our ego and so easily set over against it as . . . our conscience. I feel an inclination to do something that I think will give me pleasure, but I aban-

Reprinted from *New Introductory Lectures on Psychoanalysis* by Sigmund Freud. Translated from the German and edited by James Strachey. By permission of W.W. Norton & Company Inc. Copyright 1933 by Sigmund Freud. Copyright renewed 1961 by W. J. H. Sprott. Copyright © 1964, 1965 by James Strachey.

don it on the ground that my conscience does not allow it. Or I have let myself be persuaded by too great an expectation of pleasure into doing something to which the voice of conscience has objected and after the deed my conscience punishes me with distressing reproaches and causes me to feel remorse for the deed. I might simply say that the special agency which I am beginning to distinguish in the ego is conscience. But it is more prudent to keep the agency as something independent and to suppose that conscience is one of its functions and that self-observation, which is an essential preliminary to the judging activity of conscience, is another of them. And since when we recognize that something has a separate existence we give it a name of its own, from this time forward I will describe this agency in the ego as the *'super-ego.'*

I am now prepared to hear you ask me scornfully whether our ego-psychology comes down to nothing more than taking commonly used abstractions literally and in a crude sense, and transforming them from concepts into things—by which not much would be gained. To this I would reply that in ego-psychology it will be difficult to escape what is universally known; it will rather be a question of new ways of looking at things and new ways of arranging them than of new discoveries. So hold to your contemptuous criticism for the time being and await further explanations. The facts of pathology give our efforts a background that you would look for in vain in popular psychology. So I will proceed.

Hardly have we familiarized ourselves with the idea of a super-ego like this which enjoys a certain degree of autonomy, follows its own intentions and is independent of the ego for its supply of energy, than a clinical picture forces itself on our notice which throws a striking light on the severity of this agency and indeed its cruelty, and on its changing relations to the ego. I am thinking of the condition of melancholia,* or more precisely, of melancholic attacks, which you too will have heard plenty about, even if you are not psychiatrists. The most striking feature of this illness, of whose causation and mechanism we know much too little, is the way in which the super-ego—'conscience,' you may call it, quietly—treats the ego. While a melancholic can, like other people, show a greater or lesser degree of severity to himself in his healthy periods, during a melancholic attack his super-ego becomes over-severe, abuses the poor ego, humiliates it and ill-treats it, threatens it with the direst punishments, reproaches it for actions in the remotest past which had been taken lightly at the time—as though it had spent the whole interval in collecting accusations and had only been waiting for its present access of strength in order to bring them up and make a condemnatory judgement on their basis. The super-ego applies the strictest moral standard to the helpless ego which is at its mercy; in general it represents the claims of morality, and we realize all at once that our moral sense

---

* [Modern terminology would probably speak of 'depression.']

of guilt is the expression of the tension between the ego and the super-ego. It is a most remarkable experience to see morality, which is supposed to have been given us by God and thus deeply implanted in us, functioning [in these patients] as a periodic phenomenon. For after a certain number of months the whole moral fuss is over, the criticism of the super-ego is silent, the ego is rehabilitated and again enjoys all the rights of man till the next attack. In some forms of the disease, indeed, something of a contrary sort occurs in the intervals; the ego finds itself in a blissful state of intoxication, it celebrates a triumph, as though the super-ego had lost all its strength or had melted into the ego, and this liberated, manic ego permits itself a truly uninhibited satisfaction of all its appetites. Here are happenings rich in unsolved riddles!

No doubt you will expect me to give you more than a mere illustration when I inform you that we have found out all kinds of things about the formation of the super-ego—that is to say, about the origin of conscience. Following a well-known pronouncement of Kant's which couples the conscience within us with the starry Heavens, a pious man might well be tempted to honour these two things as the masterpieces of creation. The stars are indeed magnificent, but as regards conscience God has done an uneven and careless piece of work, for a large majority of men have brought along with them only a modest amount of it or scarcely enough to be worth mentioning. We are far from overlooking the portion of psychological truth that is contained in the assertion that conscience is of divine origin; but the thesis needs interpretation. Even if conscience is something 'within us', yet it is not so from the first. In this it is a real contrast to sexual life, which is in fact there from the beginning of life and not only a later addition. But, as is well known, young children are amoral and possess no internal inhibitions against their impulses striving for pleasure. The part which is later taken on by the super-ego is played to begin with by an external power, by parental authority. Parental influence governs the child by offering proofs of love and by threatening punishments which are signs to the child of loss of love and are bound to be feared on their own account. This realistic anxiety is the precursor of the later moral anxiety.* So long as it is dominant there is no need to talk of a super-ego and of a conscience. It is only subsequently that the secondary situation develops (which we are all too ready to regard as the normal one), where the external restraint is internalized and the super-ego takes the place of the parental agency and observes, directs and threatens the ego in exactly the same way as earlier the parents did with the child.

The super-ego, which thus takes over the power, function and even the methods of the parental agency, is however not merely its successor but actually the legitimate heir of its body. It proceeds directly out of it, we

---

* ['*Gewissensangst*', literally 'conscience anxiety'.]

shall learn presently by what process. First, however, we must dwell upon a discrepancy between the two. The super-ego seems to have made a one-sided choice and to have picked out only the parents' strictness and severity, their prohibiting and punitive function, whereas their loving care seems not to have been taken over and maintained. If the parents have really enforced their authority with severity we can easily understand the child's in turn developing a severe super-ego. But, contrary to our expectation, experience shows that the super-ego can acquire the same characteristic of relentless severity even if the upbringing had been mild and kindly and had so far as possible avoided threats and punishments. We shall come back later to this contradiction when we deal with the transformations of instinct during the formation of the super-ego.

I cannot tell you as much as I should like about the metamorphosis of the parental relationship into the super-ego, partly because that process is so complicated that an account of it will not fit into the framework of an introductory course of lectures such as I am trying to give you, but partly also because we ourselves do not feel sure that we understand it completely. So you must be content with the sketch that follows.

The basis of the process is what is called an 'identification'—that is to say, the assimilation of one ego to another one, * as a result of which the first ego behaves like the second in certain respects, imitates it and in a sense takes it up into itself. Identification has been not unsuitably com-pared with the oral, cannibalistic incorporation of the other person. It is a very important form of attachment to someone else, probably the very first, and not the same thing as the choice of an object. The difference be-tween the two can be expressed in some such way as this. If a boy identifies himself with his father, he wants to *be like* his father; if he makes him the object of his choice, he wants to *have* him, to possess him. In the first case his ego is altered on the model of his father; in the second case that is not necessary. Identification and object-choice are to a large extent independ-ent of each other; it is however possible to identify oneself with someone whom for instance one has taken as a sexual object, and to alter one's ego on his model. It is said that the influencing of the ego by the sexual object occurs particularly often with women and is characteristic of femininity. I must already have spoken to you in my earlier lectures of what is by far the most instructive relation between identification and object-choice. It can be observed equally easily in children and adults, in normal as in sick people. If one has lost an object or has been obliged to give it up, one often compensates oneself by identifying oneself with it and by setting it up once more in one's ego, so that here object-choice regresses, as it were, to identification.

---

* [I.e. one ego coming to resemble another one.]

I myself am far from satisfied with these remarks on identification; but it will be enough if you can grant me that the installation of the super-ego can be described as a successful instance of identification with the parental agency. The fact that speaks decisively for this view is that this new creation of a superior agency within the ego is most intimately linked with the destiny of the Oedipus complex, so that the super-ego appears as the heir of that emotional attachment which is of such importance for childhood. With his abandonment of the Oedipus complex a child must, as we can see, renounce the intense object-cathexes which he has deposited with his parents, and it is as a compensation for this loss of objects that there is such a strong intensification of the identifications with his parents which have probably long been present in his ego. Identifications of this kind as precipitates of object-cathexes that have been given up will be repeated often enough later in the child's life; but it is entirely in accordance with the emotional importance of this first instance of such a transformation that a special place in the ego should be found for its outcome. Close investigation has shown us, too, that the super-ego is stunted in its strength and growth if the surmounting of the Oedipus complex is only incompletely successful. In the course of development the super-ego also takes on the influences of those who have stepped into the place of parents—educators, teachers, people chosen as ideal models. Normally it departs more and more from the original parental figures; it becomes, so to say, more impersonal. Nor must it be forgotten that a child has a different estimate of its parents at different periods of its life. At the time at which the Oedipus complex gives place to the super-ego they are something quite magnificent; but later they lose much of this. Identifications then come about with these later parents as well, and indeed they regularly make important contributions to the formation of character; but in that case they only affect the ego, they no longer influence the super-ego, which has been determined by the earliest parental imagos.

I hope you have already formed an impression that the hypothesis of the super-ego really describes a structural relation and is not merely a personification of some such abstraction as that of conscience. One more important function remains to be mentioned which we attribute to this super-ego. It is also the vehicle of the ego ideal by which the ego measures itself, which it emulates, and whose demand for ever greater perfection it strives to fulfil. There is no doubt that this ego ideal is the precipitate of the old picture of the parents, the expression of admiration for the perfection which the child then attributed to them. . . .

We have allotted [to the super-ego] functions of self-observation, of conscience and of [maintaining] the ideal. It follows from what we have said about its origin that it presupposes an immensely important biological fact and a fateful psychological one: namely, the human child's long dependence on its parents and the Oedipus complex, both of which, again, are intimately interconnected. The super-ego is the representative for us of every moral restriction, the advocate of a striving towards perfection—it is, in short, as much as we have been able to grasp psychologically of what is described as the higher side of human life. Since it itself goes back to the influence of parents, educators and so on, we learn still more of its significance if we turn to those who are its sources. As a rule parents and authorities analogous to them follow the precepts of their own super-egos in educating children. Whatever understanding their ego may have come to with their super-ego, they are severe and exacting in educating children. They have forgotten the difficulties of their own childhood and they are glad to be able now to identify themselves fully with their own parents who in the past laid such severe restrictions upon them. Thus a child's super-ego is in fact constructed on the model not of its parents but of its parents' super-ego; the contents which fill it are the same and it becomes the vehicle of tradition and of all the time-resisting judgements of value which have propagated themselves in this manner from generation to generation. . . .

The whole theory of psycho-analysis is, as you know, in fact built up on the perception of the resistance offered to us by the patient when we attempt to make his unconscious conscious to him. The objective sign of this resistance is that his associations fail or depart widely from the topic that is being dealt with. He may also recognize the resistance *subjectively* by the fact that he has distressing feelings when he approaches the topic. But this last sign may also be absent. We then say to the patient that we infer from his behaviour that he is now in a state of resistance; and he replies that he knows nothing of that, and is only aware that his associations have become more difficult. It turns out that we were right; but in that case his resistance was unconscious too, just as unconscious as the repressed, at the lifting of which we were working. We should long ago have asked the question: from what part of his mind does an unconscious resistance like this arise? The beginner in psychoanalysis will be ready at once with the answer: it is, of course, the resistance of the unconscious. An ambiguous and unserviceable answer! If it means that the resistance arises from the repressed, we must rejoin: certainly not! We must rather attribute to the repressed a strong upward drive, an impulsion to break through into consciousness. The resistance can only be a manifestation of the ego, which originally put the repression into force and now wishes to maintain it . . . .

[Formerly,] under the new and powerful impression of there being an extensive and important field of mental life which is normally withdrawn from the ego's knowledge so that the processes occurring in it have to be regarded as unconscious in the truly dynamic sense, we had come to understand the term 'unconscious' in a topographical or systematic sense. . . .

We [now] perceive that we have no right to name the mental region that is foreign to the ego 'the system *Ucs.*', since the characteristic of being unconscious is not restricted to it. Very well; we will no longer use the term 'unconscious' in the systematic sense and we will give what we have hitherto so described a better name and one no longer open to misunderstanding. Following a verbal usage of Nietzsche's and taking up a suggestion by Georg Groddeck [1923],* we will in future call it the 'id'.† This impersonal pronoun seems particularly well suited for expressing the main characteristic of this province of the mind—the fact of its being alien to the ego. The super-ego, the ego and the id—these, then, are the three realms, regions, provinces, into which we divide an individual's mental apparatus, and with the mutual relations of which we shall be concerned in what follows. . . .

You will not expect me to have much to tell you that is new about the id apart from its new name. It is the dark, inaccessible part of our personality; what little we know of it we have learnt from our study of the dream-work and of the construction of neurotic symptoms, and most of that is of a negative character and can be described only as a contrast to the ego. We approach the id with analogies. We call it a chaos, a cauldron full of seething excitations. We picture it as being open at its end to somatic influences, and as there taking up into itself instinctual needs which find their psychical expression in it, †† but we cannot say in what substratum. It is filled with energy reaching it from the instincts, but it has no organization, produces no collective will, but only a striving to bring about the satisfaction of the instinctual needs subject to the observance of the pleasure principle. The logical laws of thought do not apply in the id, and this is true above all of the law of contradiction. Contrary impulses exist side by side, without cancelling each other out or diminishing each other: at the most they may converge to form compromises under the dominating economic pressure towards the discharge of energy. There is nothing in the id that could be compared with negation; and we perceive with surprise an exception to the philosophical theorem that space and time are necessary forms of our mental acts. There is nothing in the id that corresponds to the idea of time; there is no recognition of the passage of time, and—a thing that is most remarkable and awaits consideration in philosophical thought—no alteration in its mental process is produced by the passage of time. Wishful impulses which have never passed beyond the id, but impressions, too, which have been sunk into the id by repression,

---

*   [A german physician by whose unconventional ideas Freud was much attracted.]

†   [In German '*Es*', the ordinary word for 'it'.]

††   [Freud is here regarding instincts as something physical, of which mental processes are the representatives.]

are virtually immortal; after the passage of decades they behave as though they had just occurred. They can only be recognized as belonging to the past, can only lose their importance and be deprived of their cathexis of energy, when they have been made conscious by the work of analysis, and it is on this that the therapeutic effect of analytic treatment rests to no small extent. . . .

We can best arrive at the characteristics of the actual ego, in so far as it can be distinguished from the id and from the super-ego, by examining its relation to the outermost superficial portion of the mental apparatus, which we describe as the system *Pcpt.-Cs.* * This system is turned towards the external world, it is the medium for the perceptions arising thence, and during its functioning the phenomenon of consciousness arises in it. It is the sense-organ of the entire apparatus; moreover it is receptive not only to excitations from outside but also to those arising from the interior of the mind. We need scarcely look for a justification of the view that the ego is that portion of the id which was modified by the proximity and influence of the external world, which is adapted for the reception of stimuli and as a protective shield against stimuli, comparable to the cortical layer by which a small piece of living substance is surrounded. The relation to the external world has become the decisive factor for the ego; it has taken on the task of representing the external world to the id—fortunately for the id, which could not escape destruction if, in its blind efforts for the satisfaction of its instincts, it disregarded that supreme external power. In accomplishing this function, the ego must observe the external world, must lay down an accurate picture of it in the memory-traces of its perceptions, and by its exercise of the function of 'reality-testing' must put aside whatever in this picture of the external world is an addition derived from internal sources of excitation. The ego controls the approaches to motility under the id's orders; but between a need and an action it has interposed a postponement in the form of the activity of thought, during which it makes use of the innemic residues of experience. In that way it has dethroned the pleasure principle which dominates the course of events in the id without any restriction and has replaced it by the reality principle, which promises more certainty and greater success. . . .

We are warned by a proverb against serving two masters at the same time. The poor ego has things even worse: it serves three severe masters and does what it can to bring their claims and demands into harmony with one another. These claims are always divergent and often seem incompatible. No wonder that the ego so often fails in its task. Its three tyrannical masters are the external world, the super-ego and the id. When we follow the ego's efforts to satisfy them simultaneously—or rather, to obey them

---

* [Perceptual-conscious.]

simultaneously—we cannot feel any regret at having personified this ego and having set it up as a separate organism. It feels hemmed in on three sides, threatened by three kinds of danger, to which, if it is hard pressed, it reacts by generating anxiety. Owing to its origin from the experiences of the perceptual system, it is earmarked for representing the demands of the external world, but it strives too to be a loyal servant of the id, to remain on good terms with it, to recommend itself to it as an object and to attract its libido to itself. In its attempts to mediate between the id and reality, it is often obliged to cloak the *Ucs.* commands of the id with its own *Pcs.* rationalizations, to conceal the id's conflicts with reality, to profess, with diplomatic disingenousness, to be taking notice of reality even when the id has remained rigid and unyielding. On the other hand it is observed at every step it takes by the strict super-ego, which lays down definite standards for its conduct, without taking any account of its difficulties from the direction of the id and the external world, and which, if those standards are not obeyed, punishes it with tense feelings of inferiority and of guilt. Thus the ego, driven by the id, confined by the super-ego, repulsed by reality, struggles to master its economic task of bringing about harmony among the forces and influences working in and upon it; and we can understand how it is that so often we cannot suppress a cry: 'Life is not easy!' If the ego is obliged to admit its weakness, it breaks out in anxiety—realistic anxiety regarding the external world, moral anxiety regarding the super-ego and neurotic anxiety regarding the strength or the passions in the id.

I should like to portray the structural relations of the mental personality, as I have described them to you, in the unassuming sketch which I now present you with:

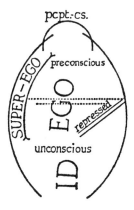

As you see here, the super-ego merges into the id; indeed, as heir to the Oedipus complex it has intimate relations with the id; it is more remote than the ego from the perceptual system. The id has intercourse with the external world only through the ego—at least, according to this diagram. It is certainly hard to say to-day how far the drawing is correct. In one respect it is undoubtedly not. The space occupied by the unconscious id ought to have been incomparably greater than that of the ego or the preconscious. I must ask you to correct it in your thoughts.

And here is another warning, to conclude these remarks, which have certainly been exacting and not, perhaps, very illuminating. In thinking of this division of the personality into an ego, a super-ego and an id, you will not, of course, have pictured sharp frontiers like the artificial ones drawn in political geography. We cannot do justice to the characteristics of the mind by linear outlines like those in a drawing or in primitive painting, but rather by areas of colour melting into one another as they are presented by modern artists. After making the separation we must allow what we have separated to merge together once more. You must not judge too harshly a first attempt at giving a pictorial representation of something so intangible as psychical processes. It is highly probable that the development of these divisions is subject to great variations in different individuals; it is possible that in the course of actual functioning they may change and go through a temporary phase of involution. Particularly in the case of what is phylogenetically the last and most delicate of these divisions—the differentiation between the ego and the super-ego—something of the sort seems to be true. There is no question but that the same thing results from psychical illness. It is easy to imagine, too, that certain mystical practices may succeed in upsetting the normal relations between the different regions of the mind, so that, for instance, perception may be able to grasp happenings in the depths of the ego and in the id which were otherwise inaccessible to it. It may safely be doubted, however, whether this road will lead us to the ultimate truths from which salvation is to be expected. Nevertheless it may be admitted that the therapeutic efforts of psycho-analysis have chosen a similar line of approach. Its intention is, indeed, to strengthen the ego, to make it more independent of the super-ego, to widen its field of perception and enlarge its organization, so that it can appropriate fresh portions of the id. Where id was, there ego shall be. It is a work of culture—not unlike the draining of the Zuider Zee.

REFERENCES

Groddeck, Georg. *Das Buch vom Es.* Vienna, 1923.

MORAL DEVELOPMENT

LAWRENCE KOHLBERG

It is usually supposed that psychology contributes to moral education by telling us appropriate *methods* of moral teaching and learning. A Skinnerian will speak of proper schedules of reinforcement in moral learning, a Freudian will speak of the importance of the balance of parental love and firmness which will promote superego-identification and so on. When Skinnerians and Freudians speak on the topic of moral education, then, they start by answering Yes to the question "Is virtue something that can be taught?" and go on to tell us how. In *Walden Two,* Skinner not only tells us that virtue comes by practice and reinforcement, but designs an ideal center which educates all its children to be virtuous in this way.

My own response to these questions was more modest. When confronted by a group of parents who asked me, "How can we make our children virtuous?" I had to answer like Socrates, "You must think I am very fortunate to know how virtue is acquired. The fact is that far from knowing whether it can be taught, I have no idea what virtue really is." Like most psychologists, I knew that science could teach me nothing as to what virtue is. Science could speak about causal relations, about the relations of means to ends but it could not speak about ends or values themselves. If I could not define virtue or the ends of moral education, could I really offer advice as to means by which virtue should be taught? Could it really be argued that the means for teaching obedience to authority are the same as the means for teaching freedom of moral opinion, that the means for teaching altruism are the same as the means for teaching competitive striving, that the making of a good storm trooper involves the same procedures as the making of a democratic leader? My response to all this was that either we must be totally silent about moral education or else speak to the nature of virtue.

The Bag of Virtues

American educational psychology is Aristotelian in that it divides the personality up into cognitive abilities, passions or motives, and traits of character. Moral character, then, consists of a bag of virtues and vices. One of the earliest major American studies of moral character, that of Hartshorne and May (1928-30), was conducted in the late twenties. Their bag of virtues included honesty, service and self-control. A more recent major study by Havighurst and Taba (1949) added responsibility, friend-

liness and moral courage to Hartshorne and May's bag. Aristotle's
original bag included temperance, liberality, pride, good temper, truth-
fulness and justice. The Boy Scout bag is well known, a Scout should be
honest, loyal, reverent, clean, brave.

Given a bag of virtues, it is evident how we build character. Children
should be exhorted to practice these virtues, should be told that happiness,
fortune and good repute will follow in their wake, adults around them
should be living examples of these virtues, and children should be given
daily opportunities to practice them. Daily chores will build responsibility,
the opportunity to give to the Red Cross will build service or altruism, etc.

You will hardly be surprised if I tell you that this approach to moral
education doesn't work. Hartshorne and May found that participation in
character education classes of this sort, in the Boy Scouts, in Sunday
school did not lead to any improvement in moral character as measured
by experimental tests of honesty, service and self-control, and more recent
research does not provide any more positive evidence as to the effects of
character-building programs.

The objection of the psychologist to the bag of virtues is that there
are no such things. Virtues and vices are labels by which people award
praise or blame to others, but the ways people use praise and blame toward others are not the ways in which they think when making moral decisions themselves. You or I may not find a Hell's Angel truly honest, but
he may. Hartshorne and May found this out to their dismay 40 years ago
by their monumental experimental studies of children's cheating and stealing. In brief, they and others since have found:

1.   You can't divide the world into honest and dishonest people. Almost
everyone cheats some of the time, cheating is distributed in bellcurve fashion around a level of moderate cheating.

2.   If a person cheats in one situation, it does not mean he will or will not
in another. There is very little correlation between situational cheating tests.
In other words it is not a character trait of dishonesty which makes a child
cheat in a given situation. If it were you could predict he would cheat in a
second situation if he did in the first.

3.   People's verbal moral values about honesty have nothing to do with
how they act. People who cheat express as much or more moral disapproval of cheating as those who don't cheat. More recently than Hartshorne
and May psychologists have studied moral character using psychoanalyti-
cally inspired words like "resistance to temptation," "conscience strength,"
"superego strength," and "moral internalization." However, they have
essentially used Hartshorne and May's tests and obtain similar results of
situational specificity.

A Study of Morality

But the question still beckons: how can one study morality? Current trends in the fields of ethics, linguistics, anthropology and cognitive psychology have suggested a new approach which seems to avoid the morass of semantical confusions, value-bias and cultural relativity in which the psychoanalytic and virtue approaches to morality have foundered. New scholarship in all these fields is now focusing upon structures, forms and relationships that seem to be common to all societies and all languages rather than upon the features that make particular languages or cultures different.

For twelve years, my colleagues and I studied the same group of 75 boys, following their development at three-year intervals from early adolescence through young manhood (Kohlberg, 1958, 1963, 1968; Kohlberg and Kramer, 1969; Turiel, 1966). At the start of the study, the boys were aged 10 to 16. We have now followed them through to ages 22 to 28. In addition, I have investigated moral development in other cultures—Great Britain, Canada, Taiwan, Mexico and Turkey.

Inspired by Jean Piaget's (1948) pioneering effort to apply a structural approach to moral development, I have gradually elaborated over the years of my study a typological scheme describing general stages of moral thought which can be defined independently of the specific content of particular moral decisions or actions. In our study of 75 American boys from early adolescence on, these youths were continually presented with hypothetical moral dilemmas, all deliberately philosophical, some of them found in medieval works of casuistry. It was on the basis of their reasoning about these dilemmas at a given age that we constructed the typology of definite and universal levels of development in moral thought.

The typology contains three distinct levels of moral thinking, and within each of these levels distinguishes two related stages. These levels and stages may be considered separate moral philosophies, distinct views of the social-moral world.

We can speak of the child as having his own morality or series of moralities. Adults seldom listen to children's moralizing. If a child throws back a few adult cliches and behaves himself, most parents—and many anthropologists and psychologists as well—think that the child has adopted or internalized the appropriate parental standards.

Actually, as soon as we talk with children about morality, we find that they have many ways of making judgments which are not "internalized" from the outside, and which do not come in any direct and obvious way from parents, teachers or even peers.

Moral Stages

The *preconventional* level is the first of three levels of moral thinking; the second level is *conventional,* and the third *postconventional* or autonomous. While the preconventional child is often "well-behaved" and is responsive to cultural labels of good and bad, he interprets these labels in terms of their physical consequences (punishment, reward, exchange of favors) or in terms of the physical power of those who enunciate the rules and labels of good and bad.

This level is usually occupied by children aged four to ten, a fact well known to sensitive observers of children. The capacity of "properly behaved" children of this age to engage in cruel behavior when there are holes in the power structure is sometimes noted as tragic (*Lord of the Flies, High Wind in Jamaica*), sometimes as comic (Lucy in *Peanuts*).

The second or *conventional* level also can be described as conformist, but that is perhaps too smug a term. Maintaining the expectations and rules of the individual's family, group or nation is perceived as valuable in its own right. There is a concern not only with *conforming* to the individual's social order but in *maintaining*, supporting and justifying this order.

The *postconventional* level is characterized by a major thrust toward autonomous moral principles which have validity and application apart from authority of the groups or persons who hold them and apart from the individual's identification with those persons or groups.

Within each of these three levels there are two discernible stages. Table 1 contains the dual moral stages of each level just described.

To understand what these stages mean concretely, let us look at them with regard to two of 25 basic moral concepts or aspects used to form the dilemmas. One such aspect, for instance, is "Motive Given for Rule Obedience or Moral Action." In this instance, the six stages look like this:

1. Obey rules to avoid punishment.
2. Conform to obtain rewards, have favors returned, and so on.
3. Conform to avoid disapproval, dislike by others.
4. Conform to avoid censure by legitimate authorities and resultant guilt.
5. Conform to maintain the respect of the impartial spectator judging in terms of community welfare.
6. Conform to avoid self-condemnation.

Table 1. Definition of Moral Stages

I. Preconventional Level

At this level the child is responsive to cultural rules and labels of good and bad, right or wrong, but interprets these labels in terms of either the physical or the hedonistic consequences of action (punishment, reward, exchange of favors) or in terms of the physical power of those who enunciate the rules and labels. The level is divided into the following two stages:

Stage 1: *The punishment and obedience orientation.* The physical consequences of action determine its goodness or badness regardless of the human meaning or value of these consequences. Avoidance of punishment and unquestioning deference to power are valued in their own right, not in terms of respect for an underlying moral order supported by punishment and authority (the latter being Stage 4).

Stage 2: *The instrumental relativist orientation.* Right action consists of that which instrumentally satisfies one's own needs and occasionally the needs of others. Human relations are viewed in terms like those of the market place. Elements of fairness, of reciprocity and equal sharing are present, but they are always interpreted in a physical pragmatic way. Reciprocity is a matter of "you scratch my back and I'll scratch yours," not of loyalty, gratitude or justice.

II. Conventional Level

At this level, maintaining the expectations of the individual's family, group, or nation is perceived as valuable in its own right, regardless of immediate and obvious consequences. The attitude is not only one of *conformity* to personal expectations and social order, but of loyalty to it, of actively *maintaining,* supporting, and justifying the order and of identifying with the persons or group involved in it. At this level, there are the following two stages:

Stage 3: *The interpersonal concordance or "good boy–nice girl" orientation.* Good behavior is that which pleases or helps others and is approved by them. There is much conformity to stereotypical images of what is majority or "natural" behavior. Behavior is frequently judged by intention—"he means well" becomes important for the first time. One earns approval by being "nice."

Stage 4: *The "law and order" orientation.* There is orientation toward authority, fixed rules, and the maintenance of the social order. Right behavior consists of doing one's duty, showing respect for authority and maintaining the given social order for its own sake.

III. Post-conventional, Autonomous, or Principled Level

At this level, there is a clear effort to define moral values and principles which have validity and application apart from the authority of the groups or persons holding these principles and apart from the individual's own identification with these groups. This level again has two stages:

Stage 5: *The social-contract legalistic orientation.* Generally has utilitarian overtones. Right action tends to be defined in terms of general individual rights and in terms of standards which have been critically examined and agreed upon by the whole society. There is a clear awareness of the relativism of personal values and opinions and a corresponding emphasis upon procedural rules for reaching consensus. Aside from what is constitutionally and democratically agreed upon, the right is a matter of personal "values" and "opinion." The result is an emphsis upon the "legal point of view," but with an emphasis upon the possibility of changing law in terms of rational considerations of social utility (rather than freezing it in terms of Stage-4 "law and order"). Outside the legal realm, free agreement, and contract is the binding element of obligation. This is the "official" morality of the American government and Constitution.

Stage 6: *The universal ethical principle orientation.* Right is defined by the decision of conscience in accord with self-chosen *ethical principles* appealing to logical comprehensiveness, universality, and consistency. These principles are abstract and ethical (the Golden Rule, the categorical imperative); they are not concrete moral rules like the Ten Commandments. At heart, these are universal principles of *justice,* of the *reciprocity* and *equality* of the human *rights* and of respect for the dignity of human beings as *individual persons.*

In another of these 25 moral aspects, the value of human life, the six stages can be defined thus:

1. The value of human life is confused with the value of physical objects and is based on the social status or physical attributes of the possessor.

2. The value of human life is seen as instrumental to the satisfaction of the needs of its possessor or of other persons.

3. The value of human life is based on the empathy and affection of family members and others toward its possessor.

4. Life is conceived as sacred in terms of its place in a categorical moral or religious order of rights and duties.

5. Life is valued both in terms of its relation to community welfare and in terms of life being a universal human right.

6. Belief in sacredness of human life as representing a universal human value of respect for the individual.

I have called this scheme a typology. This is because about 50 per cent of most people's thinking will be at a single stage, regardless of the moral dilemma involved. We call our types *stages* because they seem to represent an *invariant developmental sequence.* "True" stages come one at a time and always in the same order.

All movement is forward in sequence, and does not skip steps. Children may move through these stages at varying speeds, of course, and may be found half in and half out of a particular stage. An individual may stop at any given stage and at any age, but if he continues to move, he must move in accord with these steps. Moral reasoning of the conventional or Stage 3-4 kind never occurs before the preconventional Stage-1 and Stage-2 thought has taken place. No adult in Stage 4 has gone through Stage 6, but all Stage-6 adults have gone at least through 4.

While the evidence is not complete, my study strongly suggests that moral change fits the stage pattern just described.

As a single example of our findings of stage-sequence, take the progress of two boys on the aspect "The Value of Human Life." The first boy, Tommy, is asked, "Is it better to save the life of one important person or a lot of unimportant people?" At age 10, he answers, "All the people that aren't important because one man just has one house, maybe a lot of furniture, but a whole bunch of people have an awful lot of furniture and some of these poor people might have a lot of money and it doesn't look it."

Clearly Tommy is Stage 1: he *confuses* the value of a human being with the value of the property he possesses. Three years later (age 13) Tommy's conceptions of life's values are most clearly elicited by the question, "Should the doctor 'mercy kill' a fatally ill woman requesting death because of her pain?" He answers, "Maybe it would be good to put her out of her pain, she'd be better off that way. But the husband wouldn't want it, it's not like an animal. If a pet dies you can get along without it—it isn't something you really need. Well, you can get a new wife, but it's not really the same."

Here his answer is Stage 2: the value of the woman's life is partly contingent on its hedonistic value to the wife herself but even more contingent on its *instrumental* value to her husband, who can't replace her as easily as he can a pet.

Three years later still (age 16) Tommy's conception of life's value is elicited by the same question, to which he replies: "It might be best for her, but her husband—it's a human life—not like an animal; it just doesn't have the same relationship that a human being does to a family. You can become attached to a dog, but nothing like a human you know."

Now Tommy has moved from a Stage-2 instrumental view of the woman's value to a Stage-3 view based on the husband's distinctively human *empathy* and love for someone in his family. Equally clearly, it lacks any basis for a universal human value of the woman's life, which would hold if she had no husband or if her husband didn't love her. Tommy, then, has moved step by step through three stages during the age 10-16. Tommy, though bright (I.Q. 120), is a slow developer in moral judgment. Let us take another boy, Richard, to show us sequential movement through the remaining three steps.

At age 13, Richard said about the mercy-killing, "If she requests it, it's really up to her. She is in such terrible pain, just the same as people are always putting animals out of their pain," and in general showed a mixture of Stage-2 and Stage-3 responses concerning the value of life. At 16, he said, "I don't know. In one way, it's murder, it's not a right or privilege of man to decide who shall live and who should die. God put life into everybody on earth and you're taking away something from that person that came directly from God, and you're destroying something that is very sacred, it's in a way part of God and it's almost destroying a part of God when you kill a person. There's something of God in everyone."

Here Richard clearly displays a Stage-4 concept of life as sacred in terms of its place in a categorical moral or religious order. The value of human life is universal, it is true for all humans. It is still, however, dependent on something else, upon respect for God and God's authority; it is not an autonomous human value. Presumably if God told Richard to murder, as God commanded Abraham to murder Isaac, he would do so.

At age 20, Richard said to the same question: "There are more and more people in the medical profession who think it is a hardship on everyone, the person, the family, when you know they are going to die. When a person is kept alive by an artificial lung or kidney it's more like being a vegetable than being a human. If it's her own choice, I think there are certain rights and privileges that go along with being a human being. I am a human being and I have certain desires for life and I think everybody else does too. You have a world of which you are the center, and everybody else does too and in that sense we're all equal."

Richard's response is clearly Stage 5, in that the value of life is defined in terms of equal and universal human rights in a context of relativity ("You have a world of which you are the center and in that sense we're all equal"), and of concern for utility or welfare consequences.

At 24, Richard says: "A human life takes precedence over any other moral or legal value, whoever it is. A human life has inherent value whether or not it is valued by a particular individual. The worth of the individual human being is central where the principles of justice and love are normative for all human relationships."

This young man is at Stage 6 in seeing the value of human life as absolute in representing a universal and equal respect for the human as an individual. He has moved step by step through a sequence culminating in a definition of human life as centrally valuable rather than derived from or dependent on social or divine authority.

In a genuine and culturally universal sense, these steps lead toward an increased *morality* of value judgment, where morality is considered as a form of judging, as it has been in a philosophic tradition running from the analyses of Kant to those of the modern analytic or "ordinary language" philosophers. The person at Stage 6 has disentangled his judgments of—or language about—human life from status and property values (Stage 1); from its uses to others (Stage 2), from interpersonal affection (Stage 3), and so on; he has a means of moral judgment that is universal and impersonal. The Stage-6 person's answers use moral words like "duty" or "morally right," and he uses them in a way implying universality, ideals, impersonality: He thinks and speaks in phrases like "regardless of who it was," or ". . . I would do it in spite of punishment."

Cultural Universality

When I first decided to explore moral development in other cultures, I was told by anthropologist friends that I would have to throw away my culture-bound moral concepts and stories and start from scratch learning a whole new set of values for each new culture. My first try consisted of a brace of villages, one Atayal (Malaysian aboriginal) and the other Taiwanese.

My guide was a young Chinese ethnographer who had written an account of the moral and religious patterns of the Atayal and Taiwanese villages. Taiwanese boys in the 10-13 age group were asked about a story involving theft of food. A man's wife is starving to death but the store owner won't give the man any food unless he can pay, which he can't. Should he break in and steal some food? Why? Many of the boys said, "He should steal the food for his wife because if she dies he'll have to pay for her funeral and that costs a lot."

My guide was amused by these responses, but I was relieved: they were of course "classic" Stage-2 responses. In the Atayal village, funerals weren't such a big thing, so the Stage-2 boys would say, "He should steal the food because he needs his wife to cook for him."

This means that we have to consult our anthropologists to know what content a Stage-2 child will include in his instrumental exchange calculations, or what a Stage-4 adult will identify as the proper social order. But one certainly doesn't have to start from scratch. What made my guide laugh was the difference in form between the children's Stage-2 thought and his own, a difference definable independently of particular cultures.

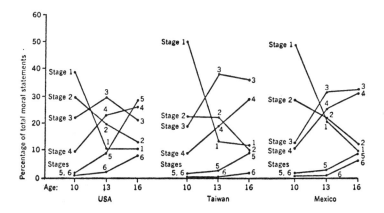

Figure 1 Middle class urban boys in the U.S., Taiwan, and Mexico. At age 10, the stages are used according to difficulty. At age 13, Stage 3 is most used by all three groups. At age 16, U.S. boys have reversed the order of age 10 stages (with the exception of 6). In Taiwan and Mexico, conventional (3-4) stages prevail at age 16, with Stage 5 also little used.

Figures 1 and 2 indicate the cultural universality of the sequence of stages which we have found. Figure 1 presents the age trends for middle-class urban boys in the U.S., Taiwan and Mexico. At age 10 in each country, the order of use of each stage is the same as the order of its difficulty or maturity.

In the United States, by age 16 the order is the reverse, from the highest to the lowest, except that Stage 6 is still little-used. At age 13, the good-boy, middle-stage (Stage 3) is most used.

The results in Mexico and Taiwan are the same, except that development is a little slower. The most conspicuous feature is that at the age of 16, Stage-5 thinking is much more salient in the United Stages than in Mexico or Taiwan. Nevertheless, it *is* present in the other countries, so we know that this is not purely an American democratic construct.

Figure 2 shows strikingly similar results from two isolated villages, one in Yucatan, one in Turkey. While conventional moral thought increases steadily from ages 10 to 16 it still has not achieved a clear ascendency over preconventional thought.

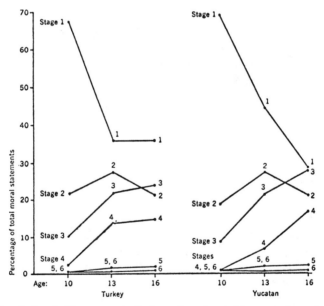

Figure 2 Two isolated villages, one in Turkey, the other in Yucatan, show similar patterns in moral thinking. There is no reversal of order, and preconventional (1–2) thought does not gain a clear ascendancy over conventional stages at age 16.

Trends for lower-class urban groups are intermediate in the rate of development between those for the middle-class and for the village boys. In the three divergent cultures that I studied, middle-class children were found to be more advanced in moral judgment than matched lower-class children. This was not due to the fact that the working-class children heavily ignored some one type of thought which could be seen as corresponding to the prevailing middle-class pattern. Instead, middle-class and working-class children move through the same sequences, but the middle-class children move faster and farther.

This sequence is not dependent upon a particular region, or any region at all in the usual sense. I found no important difference in the development of moral thinking among Catholics, Protestants, Jews, Buddhists, Moslems and atheists. Religious values seem to go through the same stages as all other values.

In summary, the nature of our sequence is not significantly affected by widely varying social, cultural or religious conditions. The only thing that is affected is the *rate* at which individuals progress through this sequence.

Implications of Universal Stages

Why should there be such a universal invariant sequence of development? In answering this question, we need first to analyze these developing social concepts in terms of their internal logical structure. At each stage, the same basic moral concept or aspect is defined, but at each higher stage this definition is more differentiated, more integrated and more general or universal. When one's concept of human life moves from Stage 1 to Stage 2 the value of life becomes more differentiated from the value of property, more integrated (the value of life enters an organizational hierarchy where it is "higher" than property so that one steals property in order to save life) and more universalized (the life of any sentient being is valuable regardless of status or property). The same advance is true at each stage in the hierarchy. Each step of development then is a better cognitive organization than the one before it, one which takes account of everything present in the previous stage, but making new distinctions and organizing them into a more comprehensive or more equilibrated structure. The fact that this is the case has been demonstrated by a series of studies indicating that children and adolescents comprehend all stages up to their own, but not more than one stage beyond their own (Rest, 1969). And importantly, *they prefer this next stage.*

We have conducted experimental moral discussion classes (Blatt and Kohlberg, 1969) which show that the child at an earlier stage of development tends to move forward when confronted by the views of a child one stage further along. In an argument between a Stage-3 and Stage-4 child, the child in the third stage tends to move toward or into Stage 4, while the Stage-4 child understands but does not accept the arguments of the Stage-3 child.

Moral thought, then, seems to behave like all other kinds of thought. Progress through the moral levels and stages is characterized by increasing differentiation and increasing integration, and hence is the same kind of progress that scientific theory represents. Like acceptable scientific theory— or like *any* theory or structure of knowledge—moral thought may be considered partially to generate its own data as it goes along, or at least to expand so as to contain in a balanced, self-consistent way a wider and wider experiential field. The raw data in the case of our ethical philosophies may be considered as conflicts between roles, or values, or as the social order in which men live.

The social worlds of all men seem to contain the same basic structures. All the societies we have studied have the same basic institutions—family, economy, law, government. In addition, however, all societies are alike because they *are* societies—systems of defined complementary roles. In order to *play* a social role in the family, school or society, the child must implicitly take the role of others toward himself and toward others in the group. These role-taking tendencies form the basis of all social institutions. They represent various patternings of shared or complementary expectations.

In the preconventional and conventional levels (Stages 1-4), moral content or value is largely accidental or culture-bound. Anything from "honesty" to "courage in battle" can be the central value. But in the higher postconventional levels, Socrates, Lincoln, Thoreau and Martin Luther King tend to speak without confusion of tongues, as it were. This is because the ideal principles of any social structure are basically alike, if only because there simply aren't that many principles which are articulate, comprehensive and integrated enough to be satisfying to the human intellect. And most of these principles have gone by the name of justice.

The Concept of Justice

Now let me point out that justice is not a character trait in the usual sense. You cannot make up behavior tests of justice, as Hartshorne and May did for honesty, service and self-control. One cannot conceive of a little set of behavior tests that would indicate that Martin Luther King or Socrates were high on the trait of justice. The reason for this is that justice is not a concrete rule of action, such as lies behind virtues like honesty. To be honest means don't cheat, don't steal, don't lie. Justice is not a rule or a set of rules, it is a moral principle. By a moral principle we mean a mode of choosing which is universal, a rule of choosing which we want all people to adopt always in all situations. We know it is all right to be dishonest and steal to save a life because it is just, because a man's right to life comes before another man's right to property. We know it is sometimes right to kill, because it is sometimes just. The Germans who tried to kill Hitler were doing right because respect for the equal values of lives demands that we kill someone who is murdering others in order to save their lives. There are exceptions to rules, then, but no exceptions to principles. A moral obligation is an obligation to respect the right or claim of another person. A moral principle is a principle for resolving competing claims, you versus me, you versus a third person. There is only one principled basis for resolving claims, justice or equality. Treat every man's claim impartially regardless of the man. A moral principle is not only a rule of action but a reason for action. As a reason for action, justice is called respect for persons.

As another example of our Stage 6, *orientation to universal moral principles,* let me cite Martin Luther King's letter from a Birmingham jail.

> There is a type of constructive non-violent tension which is necessary for growth. Just as Socrates felt it was necessary to create a tension in the mind so that individuals could rise from the bondage of half-truths, so must we see the need for non-violent gadflies to create the kind of tension in society that will help men rise from the dark depths of prejudice and racism.
>
> One may well ask, "How can you advocate breaking some laws and obeying others?" The answer lies in the fact that there are two types of laws, just and unjust. One has not only a legal but a moral responsibility to obey just laws. One has a moral responsibility to disobey unjust laws. An unjust law is a human law that is not rooted in eternal law and natural law. Any law that uplifts human personality is just, any law that degrades human personality is unjust. An unjust law is a code that a numerical or power majority group compels a minority group to obey but does not make binding on itself. This is difference made legal.
>
> I do not advocate evading or defying the law as would the rabid segregationist. That would lead to anarchy. One who breaks an unjust law must do so openly, lovingly, and with a willingness to accept the penalty. An individual who breaks a law that conscience tells him is unjust, and willingly accepts the penalty of imprisonment in order to arouse the conscience of the community over its injustice, is in reality expressing the highest respect for the law.

King makes it clear that moral disobedience of the law must spring from the same root as moral obedience to law, out of respect for justice. We respect the law because it is based on rights, both in the sense that the law is designed to protect the rights of all and because the law is made by the principle of equal political rights. If civil disobedience is to be Stage 6, it must recognize the contractual respect for law of Stage 5, even to accepting imprisonment. That is why Stage 5 is a way of thinking about the laws which are imposed upon all while a [stage 6] morality of justice which claims to judge the law can never be anything but a free personal ideal. It must accept being put in jail by its enemies not of putting its enemies in jail.

Both logic and empirical study suggest there is no shortcut to autonomous morality, no Stage 6 without a previous Stage 5.

Moral Judgment and Moral Action

Our claim is that knowledge of the moral good is one. We now will try to show that virtue in action is knowledge of the good. We have already said that knowledge of the good in terms of a bag of virtues that comes from opinion or conventional belief is not virtue. An individual may believe that cheating is very bad but that does not predict that he will resist cheating in real life. Espousal of unprejudiced attitudes toward Negroes does not predict to actual action to assure civil rights in an atmosphere where others have some prejudice. However, true knowledge, knowledge of principles of justice does predict to virtuous action. With regard to cheating, the essential elements of justice are understood by both our Stage-5 and Stage-6 subjects. In cheating, the critical issue is recognition of the element of contract and agreement implicit in the situation, and the recognition that while it doesn't seem so bad if one person cheats, what holds for all must hold for one. In a recent study, 100 sixth-grade children were given experimental cheating tests and our moral judgment interview. The majority of the children were below the principled level in moral judgment, they were at our first four moral stages. Seventy-five percent of these children cheated. In contrast, only 20% of the principled subjects, that is, Stages 5 or 6, cheated. In another study conducted at the college level only 11% of the principled subjects cheated in contrast to 42% of the students at lower levels of moral judgment.

In the case of cheating, justice and the expectations of conventional authority both dictate the same behavior. What happens when they are opposed?

An experimental study by Stanley Milgram (1963) involved such an opposition. Undergraduate subjects were ordered by an experimenter to administer increasingly more severe electric shock punishment to a stooge victim in the guise of a learning experiment. In this case, the principles of justice involved in the Stage-5 social contract orientation do not clearly prescribe a decision. The victim had voluntarily agreed to participate in the experiment and the subject himself had contractually committed himself to perform the experiment. Only Stage-6 thinking clearly defined the situation as one in which the experimenter did not have the moral right to ask them to inflict pain on another person. Accordingly, 75% of the Stage-6 subjects quit or refused to shock the victim as compared to only 13% of all the subjects at lower stages.

A study of Berkeley students carries the issue into political civil disobedience. Berkeley students were faced with the decision to sit in the

Administration building in the name of political freedom of communication. Haan, Smith, and Block (in press) administered moral judgment interviews to over 200 of these students. Again the situation was like the Milgram situation. A Stage-5 social contract interpretation of justice, which was held by the University administration, could take the position that a student who came to Berkeley came with foreknowledge of the rules and could go elsewhere if he didn't like them. About 50% of the Stage-5 subjects sat in. For Stage-6 students, the issue was clear-cut and 80% of them sat in. For students at the conventional levels, Stages 3 and 4, the issue was also clear-cut and only 10% of them sat in. These results will sound very heartwarming to those of us who have engaged in protest activities. Protesting is a sure sign of being at the most mature moral level. However, there was another group who was almost as disposed to sit in as the Stage-6 students. These were our Stage-2 instrumental relativists, of whom about 60% sat in. From our longitudinal studies, we know that most Stage-2 college students are in a state of confusion. In high school most were at the conventional level, and in college they kick conventional morality searching for their thing, for self-chosen values, but cannot tell an autonomous morality of justice from one of egoistic relativism, exchange and revenge. Our longitudinal studies indicate that all of our middle-class Stage-2 college students grow out of it to become principled adults.

I make the point to indicate that protest activities, like other acts, are neither virtuous nor vicious; it is only the knowledge of the good which lies behind them which gives them virtue. As an example, I would take it that a Stage-6 sense of justice would have been rather unlikely to find the Dow Chemical sit-in virtuous. The rules being disobeyed by the protesters were not unjust rules, and the sit-in was depriving individuals of rights, not trying to protect individual rights. Principled civil disobedience is not illegitimate propaganda for worthy political causes, it is the just questioning of injustice.

Having, I hope, persuaded you of one view of virtue, let us briefly consider how it may be taught. In a sense, this view implies that knowledge of the good is always within but needs to be drawn out. In a series of experimental studies (Rest, Turiel, and Kohlberg, 1969; Rest, 1969), we have found that children and adolescents prefer the highest level of thought they can comprehend. Children comprehend all lower stages than their own, and often comprehend the stage one higher than their own and occasionally two stages higher though they cannot actively express these higher stages of thought. If they comprehend the stage one higher than their own, they tend to prefer it to their own. This fact is basic to moral leadership in our society. While the majority of adults in American society are at a conventional level, Stages 3 and 4, leadership in our society has usually been expressed at the level of Stages 5 and 6, as our example of Martin Luther King suggests.

Returning to the teaching of virtue as a drawing out, the child's preference for the next level of thought shows that it is greeted as already familiar, that it is felt to be a more adequate expression of that already within, of that latent in the child's own thought. If the child were responding to fine words and external prestige he would not pick the next stage continuous with his own, but something else.

Let us now suggest a different example of the sense in which moral teaching must be a drawing out of that already within. At the age of four my son joined the pacifist and vegetarian movement and refused to eat meat, because as he said, "it's bad to kill animals." In spite of lengthy hawk argumentation by his parents about the difference between justified and unjustified killing, he remained a vegetarian for six months. Like most doves, however, his principles recognized occasions of just or legitimate killing. One night I read to him a book of Eskimo life involving a seal-killing expedition. He got angry during the story and said, "You know there is one kind of meat I would eat, Eskimo meat. It's bad to kill animals so it's all right to eat them."

For reasons I won't detail, this eye for an eye, tooth for a tooth concept of justice is Stage 1. You will recognize, however, that it is a very genuine though four-year-old sense of justice and that it contains within it the Stage-6 sense of justice in shadowy form. The problem is to draw the child's perceptions of justice from the shadows of the cave step by step toward the light of justice as an ideal form. This last example indicates a truth not indicated by our experimental example, the truth that the child initially turned from the dark images of the cave toward the light is still convinced that his dark images best represent the truth. The child is initially quite confident of his moral knowledge, of the rationality and efficacy of his moral principles. The notion that the child feels ignorant and is eager to absorb the wisdom of adult authority in the moral domain is one which any teacher or parent will know is nonsense. Let me give another example. Following a developmental timetable, my son moved to an expedient Stage-2 orientation when he was six. He told me at that time, "You know the reason people don't steal is because they're afraid of the police. If there were no police around everyone would steal." Of course I told him that I and most people didn't steal because we thought it wrong, because we wouldn't want other people to take things from us and so on. My son's reply was, "I just don't see it, it's sort of crazy not to steal if there are no police."

The story indicates that, like most ordinary fathers, I have no great skill in teaching true virtue. My son, of course, has always been virtuous in the conventional sense. Even when he saw no rational reason for being honest, he received A's on his report card on the bag of virtues of obedience, responsibility, and respect for property. Unlike what we usually think, it is quite easy to teach conventionally virtuous behavior but very difficult to teach true knowledge of the good.

The first step in teaching virtue, then, is the Socratic step of creating dissatisfaction in the student about his present knowledge of the good. This we do experimentally by exposing the student to moral conflict situations for which his principles have no ready solution. Second, we expose him to disagreement and argument about these situations with his peers. Our view holds that if we inspire cognitive conflict in the student and point the way to the next step up the divided line, he will tend to see things previously invisible to him.

In practice, then, our experimental efforts at moral education have involved getting students at one level, say Stage 2, to argue with those at the next level, say Stage 3. The teacher would support and clarify the Stage-3 arguments. Then he would pit the Stage-3 students against the Stage-4 students on a new dilemma. Initial results with this method with a junior high group indicated 50% of the students moved up one stage and 10% moved up two stages. In comparison, only 10% of a control group moved up one stage in the four-month period involved (Blatt and Kohlberg, 1969).

Obviously the small procedures I have described are only a way station to genuine moral education. As my earlier comments suggested, a more complete approach means full student participation in a school in which justice is a living matter.

REFERENCES

Blatt, M., and Kohlberg, L. The effects of a classroom discussion program upon the moral levels of preadolescents. *Merrill Palmer Quarterly,* 1969 (in press).

Haan, N., Smith, M. B., and Block, J. Political, family, and personality correlates of adolescent moral judgment. *Journal of Personality and Social Psychology,* 1968, *10* (3), 183-201.

Hartshorne, II., and May, M. A. *Studies in the nature of character:* Vol. 1. *Studies in deceit.* Vol. 2. *Studies in self-control.* Vol. 3. *Studies in the organization of character.* New York: Macmillan, 1928-1930.

Havighurst, R. J., and Taba, H. *Adolescent character and personality.* New York: Wiley, 1949.

Kohlberg, L. The development of modes of moral thinking and choice in the years ten to sixteen. Unpublished doctoral dissertation, University of Chicago, 1958.

Kohlberg, L. The development of children's orientations toward moral order: 1. Sequence in the development of moral thought. *Vita Humana,* 1963, *6,* 11-33.

Kohlberg, L. Stage and Sequence: the cognitive developmental approach to socialization. In D. Goslin (Ed.). *Handbook of socialization theory.* Chicago: Rand McNally, 1969.

Kohlberg, L., and Kramer, R. Continuity and discontinuity in moral development from childhood to adulthood. *Human Development,* 1969 (in press).

Milgram, S. Behavioral study of obedience. *Journal of Abnormal and Social Psychology,* 1963, *67* (4), 371-378.

Piaget, J. *The moral judgment of the child.* Glencoe, Ill.: Free Press, 1948 (originally published, 1932).

Rest, J. Hierarchies of comprehension and preference in a developmental stage model of moral thinking. Unpublished doctoral dissertation, University of Chicago, 1969.

Rest, J., Turiel, E., and Kohlberg, L. Level of moral development as a determinant of preference and comprehension of moral judgments made by others. *Journal of Personality and Social Psychology,* 1969 (in press).

Turiel, E. An experimental test of the sequentiality of developmental stages in the child's moral judgments. *Journal of Personality and Social Psychology,* 1966, *3* (6), 611-618.

CHAPTER FOUR
WHAT MAKES MEN AND WOMEN DIFFERENT ?

THE ISSUE OF SEX-ROLES AND TEMPERAMENT

What are little boys made of?
   Snakes and snails and puppy dog tails.
What are little girls made of?
   Sugar and spice and all that's nice.

Father: (to five-year old daughter) Julie, what's the difference between girls and boys?

Julie: Well. . . you know, Daddy.

Father: No, what?

Julie: Well, boys have penises and girls have (vulvas).

Father: Uh-huh, anything else?

Julie: Girls have longer hair than boys.

Father: Yes, but how about the way they act? Do girls and boys act differently?

Julie: (looking around at nearby people) Uhmmm, . . . boys wear pants. . . and some girls do too.

Father: Who do you like better, girls or boys?

Julie: Girls.

Father: Why?

Julie: 'Cause they're nicer.

Father: What do they do that's nicer?

Julie: I don't know. They're just nicer, Daddy. But some boys are nice too.

Father: (to seven-year old daughter) Leah, what's the difference between boys and girls?

Leah: That's hard. . . well, boys like to play rougher, you know. I mean they like games like hockey and football that I don't really like as much.

Father: I see. Anything else?

Leah: Well, boys are sometimes mean. They tease us. Like when the girls are just sitting around talking, the boys will tease us and play tricks. You know, they're sort of against us.

Father: Yes, I see. Can you think of any other differences?

Leah: Well, boys almost never play with dolls, and they don't like to play house much either. They like to play frisbee or hide-and-seek, or things like that.

Father: (to eleven-year old daughter) Jenny, in what ways are boys and girls different?

Jenny: Do you mean in personality, clothes, or what?

Father: Like in the way they act, or their personality.

Jenny: Boys tease more than girls. They're meaner. Girls are lots of times more open.

Father: What do you mean "more open"?

Jenny: A lot of times boys won't tell anybody about something, but girls will tell a lot of people.

Father: What about other differences?

Jenny: Not all boys and girls are like this, but girls like to go shopping more and talk. A lot of times girls have more patience. Boys like to fool around more.

Father: (to nine-year old son) Josh, in what ways are boys and girls different?

Josh: There's hardly any difference.

Father: Do boys and girls act in different ways in any situations?

Josh: It depends on the person. There are ways that they are supposed to act differently.

Father: How are they supposed to act differently?

Josh: Boys are supposed to act boyish—like not liking girls—at least at my age.

Father: What is acting boyish?

Josh: Not liking girls, being interested in sports, athletics. Boys are supposed to be more athletic.

Father: How are girls supposed to act?

Josh: They're not supposed to be as athletic—at least that's what people say.

In the United States, a *real* boy climbs trees, disdains girls, dirties his knees, plays with soldiers, and takes blue for his favorite color. A real girl dresses dolls, jumps rope, plays hopscotch, and takes pink for her favorite color. When they go to school, real girls like English and music and "auditorium"; real boys prefer manual training, gym, and arithmetic. In college boys smoke pipes, drink beer, and major in engineering or physics; the girls chew Juicy Fruit gum, drink cherry cokes, and major in Fine Arts. The real boy matures into a "man's man" who plays poker, goes hunting, drinks brandy, and dies in the war; the real girl becomes a "feminine" woman who loves children, embroiders handkerchiefs, drinks weak tea, and "succumbs" to consumption.

Roger Brown (1965, p. 161).

Man for the field and woman for the hearth;
Man for the sword and for the needle she;
Man with the head, and woman with the heart;
Man to command, and woman to obey;
All else confusion.

Alfred Lord Tennyson, from *The Princess*.

Now their separate characters are briefly these. The man's power is active, progressive, defensive. He is eminently the doer, the creator, the discoverer, the defender. His intellect is for speculation and invention; his energy for adventure, for war and conquest. . .But the woman's power is for rule, not for battle, and her intellect is not for invention or recreation, but sweet ordering, arrangement and decision. . .By her office and place she is protected from all danger and temptation. The man, in his rough work in the open world, must encounter all peril and trial—to him therefore must be the failure, the offence, the inevitable error; often he must be wounded or subdued, often misled, and always hardened.

John Ruskin, from *Of Queen's Gardens*.

What makes men and women different? The question may seem a little silly—the sort that provokes knowing glances. Even a five year old knows that the sexes have different genitalia. But we are not particularly concerned here with obvious physical differences in body shape, size, or functioning. We are concerned with differences in social role and, particularly, psychological temperament. Most women devote their lives to being housewives, mothers, and homemakers, or perhaps secretaries, teachers, clerks, social workers, and nurses. They are usually found in the home or in service and maintenance occupations. Most men spend their lives being bread-winners: crane operators, business executives, politicians, stock brokers, truck drivers, airline pilots, and doctors. They are usually found outside the home in higher status, instrumental occupations that entail mastery of the external environment. But men and women differ even more basically in character or temperament. Men are more masculine: more active, independent, aggressive, strong, dominant, steady, rational and unemotional. Women are more feminine: more passive, dependent, pacific, weak, submissive, gentle, sensitive, nurturant, flighty, intuitive, and emotional. Indeed, at least in our society, there is a stereotypical conception that "it is the function of the cool, stable, strong man to protect financially and to support the warm, gentle, dependent woman who, in return, bears and nurtures his children, cooks for him, and keeps his home" (Raines, 1972). This is an exaggeration, but not a very great one.

If these differences in role and temperament are no less obvious than the physical differences, they are a good deal less easy to understand. Why are men more masculine— more likely to be providers, leaders, and manipulators of the external environment?

Why are women more feminine—more likely to be nurturers, caretakers, followers, and sources of emotional support? Are these differences socially made or are they biologically born? Are they rooted in the biology of the human species or in the organization of its social environment? Are they inherited or learned? If inherited, how did this come to be? If learned, why are they taught?

These are the questions with which we deal in the ensuing section as we examine three divergent theories of sex-role-identity differentiation. Each of these theories provides quite a different framework for viewing and understanding the differentiation process. As is often the case with research problems that have an underlying nature-nurture controversy, it is relatively fruitless to try to settle the controversy directly. No carefully controlled experiment, even if it were ethically feasible, could hope to prove that sex differences in temperament are largely learned or largely innate. Even if it were possible, say, to raise a female in such a way that she developed a fully male temperament, this would not show the extent to which certain natural tendencies had to be overcome in the process. Similarly, if one turns to the anthropological literature in search of a natural (in the sense of typical) pattern for temperament differences, one, again, finds equivocal data. Cultural anthropologists—most notably Margaret Mead (1935)—have found considerable variety across human societies. While most societies do fit the Western pattern, there are a few in which male and female temperaments are very nearly the reverse. Thus, while the modal pattern can give support to the nature side of the controversy, the deviant cases can only be explained by the nurture side.

The point here is that, although the theories of sex-role differentiation we will examine take different sides on the nature-nurture controversy, they still cannot be proved by data bearing on this one issue. Rather, the controversy among them will have to be settled by data bearing on their other testable implications. In fact, the theories concentrate on explaining either how the temperament differences we observe today might have been selected by evolution or why they might have been created and perpetuated by society. Very briefly, before taking them up in more detail: the bio-evolutionist perspective sees temperament differences as stemming from a process of natural selection spanning 14 million years; the organizational-efficiency perspective sees them as flowing from the requirements of efficient family and societal organization; and the sexual politics perspective sees them as stemming from the perpetuation of a social system in which males politically dominate females.

THE MAJOR VIEWS*

Bio-Evolution

The bio-evolutionist perspective (represented in the readings by Lionel Tiger) believes that differences in temperament are rooted in biology which, in turn, was shaped by a process of natural selection. Males evolved toward masculinity and females toward femininity because this enhanced the survival capacities of the human species. To

---

* Throughout this section we have drawn on an excellent paper by Marcia Raines (1972) comparing theories of sex-role differentiation.

support such a proposition, it is necessary to show that at some point in the distant past men and women existed in an ecological setting which favored such a differentiation—a setting in which masculine men and feminine women were "fitter" and, thus, more likely to reproduce themselves. Though it is possible to reconstruct, to a limited extent, man's prehistory from remants found in archeological diggings and from observations of other primates, such efforts are necessarily tentative. They require weaving a plausible story around bits and pieces of solid evidence.

Tiger tells the following story. The differentiation of temperament, he maintains, began 14 million years ago when Man and his primate ancestors were hunter-gatherers living in loose bands. In their ecological setting, survival meant accomplishing three tasks: defense, food-gathering, and child rearing. Since women had to bear and feed the very young in any event, and since some division of labor is always efficient, women took to child care and other domestic concerns, while the more mobile males took up defense. This division of labor is still found among most terrestrial primates today. However, unlike other primates for which food-gathering is a joint activity, Ancient Man assigned this role exclusively to males. Why this should have been so is not entirely clear. Tiger suggests that is is because Man was at once carnivorous and capable of social communication so that, for him, food-gathering meant the cooperative hunting of big game. Because this task was complex and required constant interdependence, and because females were subject to periodic interruption for bearing and caring for offspring, it made sense for men to specialize in this as well. But whatever the initial reasons for such an arrangement, Tiger's essential argument is that, once established, it led to a biological differentiation between men and women consistent with the functions they performed. Men not only became faster, larger, and stronger but also more active, aggressive, dominant, and suited to dealing with the external environment in co-operation with other men. Women not only became smaller, slower, and weaker but also more passive, submissive, nurturant, and sensitive to the emotional needs of their mates and offspring.

Tiger, himself, is not really concerned with deriving all of these (as well as other) temperament differences that might be extracted from his line of argument. He concentrates primarily on two features of the male temperament: men's tendency to be socially dominant over women, and men's propensity to form close working relations with other men to the exclusion of women. Most of us might not see these rather complex traits as being rooted in temperament. But Tiger believes they are a very basic part of the male character, founded on inborn tendencies. He argues that the males' pre-historic role as co-operative hunters and warriors not only led to a natural selection of dominant males with leadership ability, but also to a selection of males who could bond with one another; who could form close working relationships with other males to the exclusion of females. As Tiger puts it, "just as selection for reproduction operated by establishing and consummating bonds between males and females, . . . so selection as a result of hunting depended on readiness of the organisms concerned [men] to form male-male bonds for these purposes and to reject male-female ones during the hunting period." He goes on to suggest that the current male domination of the political, economic, and military structures of society may be a remnant from the days of the hunter-warrior which has been bred into the human species. More specifically, he suggests that women's pre-historic experiences may have made them "biologically unprogrammed to dominate political systems," in part because they are less capable of inspiring "followership" (1969, p. 97).

Some of Tiger's speculations about male-bonding and male-dominance may seem a little implausible as well as unpalatable—especially to women. But one need not subscribe to the whole of his argument to experience the plausibility of the bio-evolutionist perspective. For them, temperament is like any other sex-linked trait; it is rooted in the genes and, thus, shaped by natural selection. Since ninety-nine per cent of man's history has been spent as a hunter-gatherer, it is this social arrangement that set the master pattern for masculine-feminine differentiation. Men evolved temperaments that enhanced their capacities for hunting and defending, while women evolved ones that enhanced their capacities for raising offspring and "keeping camp". Even though these temperaments may no longer be particularly useful today—especially in industrial societies—they linger on because biological evolution cannot begin to keep step with the accelerated pace of social change in the past few thousand years. Men continue to be the better organizers and providers, and women continue to be the better followers and nurturers.

Before leaving the biological perspective behind, it is worth considering briefly another variant of this approach which places less emphasis on evolution and more emphasis on post-birth psychological development. According to this view, masculine-feminine differentiation in temperament is but one aspect of personality or character development. This psychological process is not so much innate, in the sense of being genetically pre-programmed; rather, it is shaped by anatomical and physiological features and potentials that are present at birth. Put simply, temperament differentiation is a problem in the comparative personality development of men vs. women and, since such development is partly shaped by biology, it is necessary to approach the problem from the standpoint of basic male-female differences in anatomy and physiology.

This mode of analysis is associated with psychoanalytic theory and is well represented by the writings of Erik Erikson. He suggests that "a profound difference exists between the sexes in the experience of the groundplan of their body" (1968, p. 273) and that it is this biological difference that leads the sexes to develop their special temperaments. Women have a productive inner space—an internal structure of vagina and uterus, giving them the unique ability to bear and support life with their own bodies. Men have an intrusive penis, a stronger and heavier musculature, and, thus, a unique ability to deal actively and instrumentally with the external environment. As a consequence "women find their identities in the care suggested in their bodies and in the needs of their issue, and seem to take for granted that the outer world belongs to men" (1968, p. 274). In other words, women naturally tend to develop a more inward, receptive, peaceful, and nurturant temperament, while men tend to develop a more outward, intrusive, aggressive, and instrumental temperament.

In order not to misconstrue Erikson, it is important to emphasize that these natural tendencies are only tendencies—they are not biological imperatives incapable of being modified by counter-socialization. As he puts it: "Am I saying that 'anatomy is destiny'? Yes, it is destiny, insofar as it determines the range and configuration of physiological functioning and its limitation, but also, to an extent, personality configurations... [However] the physiological rock-bottom must neither be denied nor given exclusive emphasis. For a human being in addition to having a body, is *somebody,* which means an indivisible personality and a defined member of a group. . . . Each sex can transcend itself to feel and to represent the concerns of the other, . . . if permitted to do so by powerful mores" (1968, p. 285-286).

Like Tiger, then, Erikson accords to biology a prominent role in the development of temperament differences. Unlike him, he does not see male and female temperament as stemming directly from genes but, rather, indirectly through experiencing the "ground plan of their bodies" as they grow and develop. This ground plan does, of course, come to us by evolution, but that is only tangential for Erikson. Both men's views contrast with the remaining two perspectives to be examined which downplay biological considerations and look, instead, to principles of political and social organization.

Organizational Efficiency

According to this perspective (represented in the readings by Morris Zelditch) masculine-feminine differences can best be understood in terms of the organizational efficiency it offers the nuclear family. The nuclear family, as distinguished from the extended family, consists only of parents and their immediate offspring. This unit constitutes a discernible, separate, functioning group in virtually every human society and, since it must contribute to the solution of the most fundamental human problems—procreation and survival—its organization and efficiency are of vital importance. This is especially true in societies, such as our own, where the nuclear family actually lives and functions as an autonomous unit, sharply separated from other relatives. In many other societies, it is likely to merge into the extended family though always maintaining some degree of autonomy.

Apart from its ubiquity and centrality, the salient feature of the nuclear family, for this perspective, is that it is a small group. As such, it can be seen as subject to a series of problems and processes that have been well studied by small-group researchers in recent years (Bales, 1958; Slater, 1955). (Some of these are discussed in the introduction to Chapter Seven and in the associated reading by Sydney Verba.) Put very briefly, any small, problem-solving group must grapple with two sorts of problems. It must accomplish its manifest task: that thing out there must be mastered before it can feel successful; and it must maintain sufficient cohesion and positive mutual regard so that it does not literally disintegrate either in open conflict or in emotional exhaustion from the tension. Because these two needs are fundamental and universal, their solution, too, is relatively standard. As a small group evolves over time, two distinct roles begin to emerge: one filled by a "task specialist" who takes charge of the group's instrumental, problem-solving activity; the other filled by a "socio-emotional specialist" who plays a large role in relieving group tensions and restoring good feeling. The two roles are seldom filled by the same person for there appears to be an irreducible degree of strain in trying to carry out both (*e.g.*, a good task specialist should press and criticize, while a good socio-emotional specialist should listen and support). More generally, Parsons and Bales explain the emerging division of labor in this way: "The appearance of a differentiation between a person who symbolizes the demands of task accomplishment, and a person who symbolizes the demands of social and emotional needs, is implicit in the very existence of a system responsive to an environment. Any social system has both an "inside" and an "outside" aspect and a need to build a common culture that deals with both" (1955, p. 303).

Since the nuclear family is a small group "responsive to an environment," this analysis tells us we ought to expect a role-differentiation precisely of the sort that we do tend to find: one person who specializes in wresting from the external environment food, shelter, and safety for the family; and another who specializes in maintaining the internal order and emotional stability of the family.* There is no difficulty in understanding why it is the adult members of the nuclear family who fill these leadership roles, but why is it that men almost invariably draw the instrumental responsibilities while women draw the socio-emotional ones?

To answer this question adequately, it must be split into two questions—one about the historical past, and one about the present. Historically, the particular role allocation was in one sense arbitrary and in another sense quite practical. That is, although men could have become the socio-emotional specialists, it was simply more efficient to have the women do it. Parsons explains it this way: "In our opinion, the fundamental explanation for the allocation of roles between the biological sexes lies in the fact that the bearing and nursing of the very young necessarily fall to the woman, and thereby establish a presumptive primacy of the relationship between the mother and the small child; which, in turn, establishes a presumption that the man, who is exempted from these biological functions, should specialize in the alternative direction" (1955, p. 23). In other words, since the mother must care for the very young, it is efficient for her to specialize in the more nurturant socio-emotional area, leaving the male to cope with the more instrumental task of mastering the external environment.

So much for the historical past, but what about the present? In a modern society equipped with baby bottles and formula, it would not seem so hard for the male to assume responsibility for early child care and proceed to manage the other socio-emotional duties as well. The problem is that the male has not been socialized to assume these tasks, just as the female has not been socialized to assume the instrumental tasks. And this brings us to the explanation of differences in temperament from this perspective. Once the traditional role allocation had been established on grounds of historical efficiency, it became even more efficient to train the sexes early to assume their later role functions. Thus, males came to be socialized in such a way as to bring out instrumental traits—aggressiveness, rationality, and coolness under stress; while females came to be socialized so as to bring out socio-emotional traits—warmth, gentleness, receptivity, and emotional supportiveness. Just how natural these traits were for the two sexes is beside the point—*to an important degree temperament differences were socially engineered in order to aid each sex in the performance of its allocated role.*

But if in modern societies the original basis for role allocation is no longer so valid, why could the socialization pattern not be reversed? Theoretically it could, but in practice it is difficult. The pattern comes to take on a life of its own in the sense

---

* Several studies have documented the generality of this division of labor—see, for example, Barry, Bacon, and Child (1957).

that the men and women it produces come to be seen as natural and proper. Since masculine women and feminine men do not seem quite right to us, and since the traditional pattern does continue to permit an efficient division of duties within the nuclear family, it will continue to persist even after becoming largely arbitrary.

The organizational efficiency perspective, then, does not assume that masculine and feminine temperaments are natural in the sense of being rooted in genetics or anatomy, but it does not deny this possibility. Really, the issue is largely irrelevant to it, for its central tenet is simply that the differentiation of temperaments (whether created outright or merely reinforced) is highly functional for the nuclear family. Biology does play a role, but only the historical one of determining which sex could most efficiently be trained to perform which role within the nuclear family.

Sexual Politics

According to this perspective (represented in the readings by Kate Millett), temperament differences between the sexes can best be understood within a framework of political power. To put it baldly: men and women are the way they are because in virtually every human society men have held the lion's share of power and control, thus enabling them to appropriate for themselves the best roles and traits, and leaving women in subordinate positions and forcing on them complementary but less prestigeful traits.

Why would men wish to do this? More out of self-interest than maliciousness— due to their greater social power, they naturally played a major role in creating laws, institutions, and informal practices that served to perpetuate their privileged position by keeping women "in their places" performing convenient and essential functions of a subordinate sort. The central differences between the masculine and feminine character, then, are to be understood neither as a contrast between the nurturer and the hunter, nor as a contrast between the task and the socio-emotional specialist, but more nearly as a contrast between super-ordinate and subordinate. Men are strong, assertive, independent, active, aggressive, intelligent, rational, and controlled—in a word, superior. Women are weak, submissive, dependent, passive, docile, dumb, intuitive, and over-emotional—in a word, inferior.

Such contentions may seem a little implausible if not unpalatable—especially to men. But Millett sets out to explain and document them. She defines politics as "power-structured relationships and arrangements whereby one group of persons is controlled by another," and she notes that since men hold virtually all positions of authority in society, it is inevitable that women will be controlled by them. In her own words, ". . . our society, like all other historical civilizations, is a patriarchy. The fact is evident at once if one recalls that the military, industry, technology, universities, science, political office, and finance—in short, every avenue of power within the society, including the coercive force of the police, is entirely in male hands. As the essence of politics is power, such realization cannot fail to have impact."

Much of the remainder of her analysis is devoted to detailing this impact—to pointing out the convenient beliefs, laws, and informal arrangements that have been created in order to keep women in their subordinate positions. She refuses to accept biology as a valid foundation for the status, role, and temperament differences between the sexes, contending that there is no scientific basis for such a view, much less sufficient evidence to justify such a gross inequality in the distribution of social power. She attacks the evolutionary theory of Tiger, claiming that "since his evidence of inherent traits *is* patriarchal history and organization, his pretensions to physical evidence are both specious and circular." And she criticizes the "expedient myth" of a woman's inner space proposed by Erikson, contending that it is a theory based on "psychoanalysis' persistent error of mistaking learned behavior for biology" (1970, p. 243).

For Millett, the crucial factor in the differentiation of the sexes is socialization, learned behavior, or more precisely, the total process whereby both sexes learn and internalize a patriarchal ideology dictated by men. Albert Bandura (whose social learning approach to moral development we examined in Chapter Three) gives some sense of how the process begins:

> Sex-role socialization usually commences immediately after birth when the baby is named and both the infant and nursery are given the blue or pink treatment depending upon the sex of the child. Thereafter, indoctrination into masculinity and femininity is diligently promulgated by adorning children with distinctive clothes and hair styles, selecting sex-appropriate play materials and recreational activities, promoting associations with same-sex playmates, and generally through nonpermissive parental reactions to any deviant sex-role behavior (1969, p. 215).

If such socialization practices were changed, there is no reason why women could not come to manifest all the fine traits now ascribed to men. Or, for that matter, why men could not be manipulated into manifesting the same inferior traits now ascribed to women. But so long as any society remains a patriarchy—remains in the hands of men—no such change is likely to come about. Since, from the nuclear family upward, men are in control of the socializing institutions, it is more or less inevitable that pro-male practices and philosophy will be maintained. Why should men make changes against their own interests except perhaps in a paternalistic, mollifying fashion? More important, how would they ever come to consider such a change if both sexes are so imbued with the patriarchal ideology that there is virtually no one who can articulate, let alone justify, an alternative viewpoint?

Just as in the organizational efficiency perspective, here again socialization practices come to have a self-perpetuating quality. But for Millett, this quality extends to many other institutions in the society from the family to the legal system and beyond. All serve, however indirectly, to perpetuate male power and prejudices.

The end result, for a woman, of being processed by the totality of the patriarchal system is expressed by Germaine Greer as she sketches the feminine stereotype and then angrily rejects it:

> The stereotype is the eternal feminine. She is the sexual object sought by all men and all women. She is neither sex for she herself has no sex at all. Her value is solely attested by the demand she excites in others. All she must contribute is her existence. She need achieve nothing for she is the reward of achievement. She need never give positive evidence of her moral character because virtue is assumed from her loveliness, and her passivity. . . .
> Because she is the emblem of spending ability and the chief spender, she is also

the most effective seller of this world's goods. . . . .She may sit astride the mud guard of a new car, or step into it ablaze with jewels; she may lie at a man's feet stroking his new socks; she may hold the gas pump in a challenging pose, or dance through woodland glades in slow-motion in all the glory of a new shampoo; whatever she does her image sells. . . . Her [ubiquity and] dominion must not be thought to entail the rule of women, for she is not a woman. Her glossy lips and matte complexion, her unfocused eyes and flawless fingers, her extraordinary hair all floating and shining, curling and gleaming, reveal the triumph of cosmetics, lighting, focusing and printing, cropping, and composition. . . . She is a doll: weeping, pouting, or smiling, running, or reclining, she is a doll. . . .

Her essential quality is castratedness. She absolutely must be young, her body hairless, her flesh buoyant, and *she must not have a sexual organ.* . . . Her expression must betray no hint of humor, curiosity, or intelligence, although it may signify hauteur to an extent that is actually absurd, or smoldering lust, very feebly signified by drooping eyelids and a sullen mouth (for the stereotype's lust equals irrational submission), or, most commonly vivacity, and idiot happiness. . . . The occupational hazard of being a Playboy Bunny is the aching facial muscles brought on by the obligatory smiling.

So what is the beef? Maybe I couldn't make it. Maybe I don't have a pretty smile, good teeth, nice tits, a cheeky arse, a sexy voice. Maybe I don't know how to handle men and increase my market value, so that rewards due to the feminine [stereotype] will accrue to me. Then again, maybe I'm sick of the masquerade. I'm sick of pretending eternal youth. I'm sick of belying my own intelligence, my own will, my own sex. . . . I'm sick of the Powder Room. I'm sick of pretending that some fatuous male's self-important pronouncements are the objects of my undivided attention. . . . I'm sick of being a transvestite. I refuse to be a female impersonator. I am a woman, not a castrate (1971, pp. 50-53).

The desirable stereotype is easy to recognize; its oppressiveness is harder for some to see.

Unlike either the bio-evolution perspective or the organizational efficiency perspective, the sexual politics framework makes no real effort to explain the historical origins of sex-temperaments. How patriarchy started is of little concern, for it is its current existence that perpetuates the temperament differences. Perhaps, as Millett suggests, it was originally founded in the male's superior strength, or perhaps, as organizational efficiency suggests, it was founded on the male's specialization in the instrumental roles of society. But the point is that no historical origin yet proposed can explain or justify the present continuation of male dominance and of male-prejudiced temperament differences. In this sense, historical issues are of no particular use to this perspective. They explain nothing of interest.

CONTRASTING THE VIEWS OF SEX-ROLE AND TEMPERAMENT DIFFERENTIATION

These divergent views of how sex-role allocation and temperament differences came to be, can be contrasted by reviewing their answers to three questions:

1.   What is the central process that creates temperament differences?

2.   What principle determines the particular direction these processes take? Why are temperament differences the way they are?

3.   Are these differences largely imprinted in human nature, or largely learned from the social environment?

Central Process

Ultimately, temperament differences must be created by some orderly process. They are too consistent, too widespread, and too functional to suppose they could have arisen merely by chance. Each of the frameworks examined here, however, identifies a different, lawful process. For bio-evolution, that process is evolution itself—over a 14 million year period, the inexorable press for ecological fitness in a hunter-gatherer society led to the selection of masculine men and feminine women. For the organizational efficiency perspective, the central process is functional role-differentiation—the nuclear family, as a small group, could best manage its vital concerns if its instrumental and socio-emotional tasks were separated into two roles, each filled by a properly socialized masculine man and feminine woman. Finally, for the sexual politics perspective, the central process is power politics—since all societies are dominated by men, and since they thereby control the socializing institutions, the masculine and feminine stereotypes are perpetuated because it is in the interests of men to do so. In each case, then, we are operating within a quite different lawful system. For bio-evolution, the model is ecological survival; for organizational efficiency, it is social systems responsive to an environment; and for sexual politics, it is class interests and their embodiment in the institutions and ideology of the ruling class.

Guiding Principle

Any lawful process must be guided by some central principle that gives it its direction. These principles are the key to understanding the nature and shape of temperament differences. Evolution is guided by a natural selection of the fitter. The unfit, by definition, perish leaving the future to those who are biologically better equipped to survive. This principle, coupled with man's pre-historic natural setting, determined that males who could better hunt and fight, and females who could better nurture, would best survive to reproduce themselves. Fourteen million years later, men and women continue to manifest the traits locked in their genes by this selection.

In contrast, small groups responsive to an environment are guided by the requirements of organizational efficiency. Since any small social system has both instrumental and socio-emotional needs, and since it is difficult for the same person to manage both, it was most efficient for the tasks of the nuclear family to be divided between the sexes, with females becoming the socio-emotional specialists and males the instrumental ones. In the interests of further efficiency, socialization practices arose that served to instill temperament differences consistent with this division of labor.

Finally power politics are guided by class interests. Since men are the ruling class in every society, and since the traditional male temperament entails traits much more prestigeful and masterful than those of the female temperament, both the origin and nature of these prejudicial differences can be seen to be shaped by male self-interest. Directly or indirectly, intentionally or not, men have acted so as to perpetuate their power and social rewards while relegating women to an inferior position and identity.

Imprinted or Learned?

As noted at the outset of this chapter, the issue of the origin of sex-role-identity differences is laced with the nature-nurture controversy. Although it is always difficult to bring unequivocal data to bear on this controversy, one can still ask of each perspective: which side is it on? Does it see temperament differences as largely imprinted in the biological nature of the organism or as largly learned from the social environment?

For bio-evolution the answer is clear. Sex-differences are imprinted either directly in the genetic make-up of the human species, or else in the ground plan of its biological shape and functioning. According to Tiger, men and women have different traits from birth, and no amount of counter-training can greatly alter them. According to Erikson, men and women naturally develop after birth in accord with the ground plan of their bodies.

The organizational efficiency perspective takes a more ambiguous stand on the nature-nurture controversy. True, women were probably allocated the socio-emotional role because their biological make-up necessitated that they bear and nurse the very young, but it does not follow that they are naturally endowed with any other traits of the "expressive specialist." These other traits could well be instilled anew each generation by the process of socialization. Alternatively, it could be that the socializing process merely reinforces natural tendencies. The same two possibilities exist for men.

The sexual politics perspective, again, takes a clear stand on the controversy, opting strongly for social learning. According to this view, there is almost nothing natural about current differences in male and female temperament. They were born in the minds of men who wished to maintain their privileged positions vis-a-vis women, and they are perpetuated by an elaborate social system that instills them in its members from the very moment of birth when the newborn is tagged with a pink or blue bracelet. If the differences appear to be innate because they run so deep and so consistently, this only attests to the maleability of the human animal and to the thoroughness of the training schedules.

Chart 4 summarizes our discussion of the differences among the three perspectives.

REFERENCES

Bales, Robert F. "Task Roles and Social Roles in Problem-Solving Groups," in Maccoby E., Newcomb, T. and Hartley, E. (Eds.), *Readings in Social Psychology.* Third Edition, New York: Holt, Rinehart, and Winston, Inc. 1958.

Bandura, Albert. "Social-Learning Theory of Identificatory Processes," in Goslin, D.A. (Ed.), *Handbook of Socialization Theory and Research.* Chicago: Rand McNally, 1969.

Chart 4 Underlying Issues in Sex-Role and Temperament Differentiation

	Bio-evolution (*e.g.*, Tiger)	Organizational Efficiency (*e.g.*, Zelditch)	Sexual Politics (*e.g.*, Millett)
1. What central process creates temperament differences?	Evolution in a hunter-gatherer society	Functional role-differentiation in the nuclear family	Political organization in societies dominated by men
2. What guiding principle directs the process and shapes temperament?	Natural selection for hunter-warriors, and for domestic-nurturers	Organizational efficiency for handling instrumental and socio-emotional needs of the family	Men's self-interest in retaining dominance: masterly traits for themselves, subordinate ones for women
3. Are temperament differences imprinted in human biology, or learned from the social environment?	Imprinted either in the genes, or in the biological ground-plan of the human body	No clear position; possibly partly imprinted, but could also be entirely learned from socialization	Entirely learned from the socialization practices of a patriarchal society

Barry, H., Bacon, M. and Child, I.L., "A Cross-Cultural Survey of Some Sex-Differences in Socialization," in *Journal of Abnormal and Social Psychology*, (1957), **55**: 327-332.

Brown, Roger. "Roles and Stereotypes," Chapter 4 of his *Social Psychology*. New York: Free Press, Division of The Macmillan Co., 1965, pp. 152-191.

Erikson, Erik. "Womanhood and the Inner Space," in his *Youth, Identity and Crisis*. New York: W. W. Norton and Co., Inc., 1968, pp. 261-294.

Greer, Germaine. *The Female Eunuch.* New York: McGraw-Hill Book Co., 1971.

Mead, Margaret. *Sex and Temperament.* New York: Morrown, 1935.

Millett, Kate. *Sexual Politics.* Garden City, New York: Doubleday & Company, Inc., 1970.

Parsons, Talcott. "The American Family: Its Relations to Personality and to the Social Structure," in T. Parsons, and R. F. Bales, *Family, Socialization and Interaction Processes.* New York: Free Press Division of The Macmillan Co., 1955, pp. 10-26.

Parsons, Talcott and Robert F. Bales. *Family, Socialization and Interaction Processes.* New York: Free Press, Division of The Macmillan Co., 1955.

Raines, Marcia. "Four Theories of Sex-Role Differentiation," unpublished paper, Harvard College, (January, 1971).

Slater, Philip. "Role Differentiation in Small Groups," *American Sociological Review,* **20** (1955) 300-310.

Tiger, Lionel. *Men in Groups.* New York: Random House, 1969.

THE POSSIBLE BIOLOGICAL ORIGINS OF SEXUAL DISCRIMINATION

LIONEL TIGER

In this brief essay I want to comment about differences in male-female social organization. The suggestion is that, not unreasonably, these social differences bear relationship to biological realities of the human species which in turn are functions of human evolution and of a particular set of primate adaptations; these adaptations include both those uniquely our own and those we share with some other primates (with whom we find we share behavioural characteristics, just as earlier we were surprised to find that we share significant physical ones). The broad outlines of the argument are more fully presented in my book *Men in Groups* (1969), here, I want to discuss the significance this argument may have for our social theories and action.

From Lionel Tiger, "The Possible Biological Origins of Sexual Discrimination," *Impact of Science on Society,* Volume XX, No. 1 (1970). © UNESCO.

In essence, the position derives from the following set of ethnological observations and theories. The behaviour of animals evolves just as physical structure does, and both structure and function (which is a systematic way of saying behavior) reflect animals' evolutionary adaptation to their material and social environments. This adaptation is always mediated by processes of sexual selection which Darwin first explicitly described. The social behaviour of animals is, hence, not altogether sudden. It is not, in other words, only the expression of particular local and ephemeral circumstances. Even relatively complex social propensities can be programmed genetically. . . .

Hunting, the Master Pattern

It could be said that our most elaborate biological adaptation is to create culture. But if culture is our most complex concoction, it remains unchallenged by anthropologists and biologists that hunting is the master pattern of the human species. It is the organizing activity which integrated the morphological, physiological, genetic and intellectual aspects of the individual human organisms and of the population who compose our single species. Hunting is a way of life, not simply a 'subsistence technique', and it involves commitments, correlates and consequences spanning the entire biobehavioural continuum of the individual and of the entire species of which he is a member.

'That man achieved a worldwide distribution while still a hunter reflects the enormous universality of this kind of behavioral adaptation. . . . he practiced hunting for 99 per cent of his history. . . .' (Laughlin, 1968, p. 304). In other words, our practice of hunting was the infra-structural condition of our specialized evolution, and though it is tempting to see in this only a confirmation of theories of human bloodiness and evil, it remains the case that hunting was a co-operative activity and that in the acts of pursuit and slaughter there was selective advantage to those individuals able to work together, attuned to each others' needs, resources and states, and willing to mould their individual behaviour to the collective pattern of the group.

The critical subordinate section of this argument (for our purpose here) is that hunting was an all-male enterprise and that just as there was selection *for* co-operative hunting males, there was selection *against* both those females willing to hunt and those males agreeable to female participants in their hunts. The reasons for this proposition depend on a variety of individually disputable bits of evidence. But their over-all implications seem to point forcefully in the direction of an increased differentiation of male-female behaviour through evolution at the same time as there was probably a decreased physical differentiation.

Of course, differences in running methods, throwing skills, temperature adaptability, effects of physiological changes, etc., were clearly both the cause of and the effect of differentiated hunting experience. At the same time, the intriguing hypothesis remains that an important feature of this behavioural differentiation was the development of differing interests in and capacities for social bonding. Just as selection for reproduction operated by establishing and consummating bonds between males and females (and this was broadly programmed—for example, to follow puberty), so selection as a result of hunting depended on the readiness of the organisms concerned to form male-male bonds for these purposes while at the same time rejecting male-female ones during the hunting period. . . .

The fact that we have been a hunting species for probably one million years and possibly up to 26 million underlines the significance of this hypothesis of male-male linkages for the establishment of species-specific patterns of behaviour. These must remain influential today, if only as parameters in terms of which the force and effect of the patterns may be altered or vitiated by cultural factors and by the existential circumstances of particular individuals.

Biological Determination of Women's Role

But what has all this to do with women today?

At one level the role of biology in constraining the lives of women is obvious. Reproduction involves pregnancy and at least a short period of commitment to highly demanding offspring whose physical needs are not only inconsiderately recurrent but also who make psychological claims on mothers' time and energy. . . .

Though societies respond in various ways to the problem of aiding and mollifying the stresses of child-rearing, it remains the case that this process constitutes a real (if widely approved) impediment to following the same career pattern as men. A number of communities have provided for this by offering facilities for mothers which allow them time off from work—either on a short-term or long-term basis—opportunities for retraining after an absence, the maintenance of pension and other rights, etc., and the retention of 'equity' in a career line in an organization, industry, or in the community at large. Despite these provisions, however, females typically constitute a more floating segment of the labour market, work at lower rates of pay and in lower-level positions, and are more likely to be dismissed by organizations retrenching their personnel.

In general, it remains the case that females, in virtually every society, are to a large degree excluded from positions of power and substantial reward. They are clearly subdominant and even where they are educated as well as males and possess equal economic resources, they fail to achieve posts, properties or honorific awards in any degree comparable to those of males. Moreover, they find themselves largely outside the major political, economic and military decision-making processes of our time.

Of course, this is not to recommend this situation, but to identify once again the gap between the ideology of sexual equality and the reality of an only tentative and sporadic movement to this equality.

My point is that the reason for this hiatus between wish and reality is not simply the result of male churlishness, chauvinism or fear. Nor is it similar to the differences between the privileges and opportunities of different economic classes or races in stratified societies. Nor is it solely the result of a coercive process of socialization which condemns disadvantaged females to live equably and with misguided self-satisfaction. Simple-minded though it may seem, perhaps the difficulty females have faced arises in good measure because the rhetoric and the dream of equality have allowed communities to avoid coming to terms with real differences between the sexes—differences which go beyond the explicitly reproductive, and which have to do with the conduct of social affairs on even its most abstract and complex levels.

To help understand this suggestion in its proper context, it may be useful to look briefly at the social behaviour of other primate males and females, bearing in mind that we are primates ourselves—though different from all the others—and that it is possible that we share some ancient core patterns of 'genetically programmed behavioural propensity' just as we clearly have in common certain evident physical structures and processes.

Primate Sex Bonds and Group Structure

An obvious feature of primate behaviour to which primatologists pay attention early in their research is male-female differentiation. In some species there is relatively little, except for the bearing and immediate rearing of children. This is particularly so among arboreal creatures for whom the problems of defence are more easily solved by fleeing up a tree than by generating defensive social organization. On the other hand, among terrestrial groups such as the south African baboon, the demands of defence on the savannah have led to the evolutionary selection of males about twice as large as females, with large jaws and sharp canines, and in general physically equipped to defend the females and young of their communities.

A correlate of these defence patterns—which so far as we know involve males only—is that the males, both the dominant ones and the sub-adult ones, form 'bonds'—groups in which the individuals regard themselves as more significant to each other than to non-bond members. These are, in a real sense, 'personal' relationships, as distinct from aggregation-type encounters in which there is no real element of choice.

What is fascinating about these male bonds is that they seem to be associated with political dominance. This is, in turn, directly linked with the dominant males having the greatly preponderant sexual access to œstrus females. Thus, there is the clear implication that selection of males willing and able to form bonds with other males is a constant feature of these primates' reproductive function.

This introduces quite a new element into the whole matter of social bonds and their relationship to reproduction. Not only does a male animal have to want to and be capable of consummating an encounter with a fertile female, but to reproduce himself he must also be able to engage in relatively very long-term and elaborate social relationships with several other males. Though sub-adult males do form weak bonds (rather like human boys' gangs—and, as in the human, there are no female gangs), only dominant adult males seem to be able to form these with political effectiveness. The subdominant males appear to be incapable of forming strong bonds because even four or five of them are unable to combine to overthrow the leadership of the two or three dominants from whose bonds a great deal of super-individual power is generated.

Thus a picture emerges from generalizing about the terrestrial primates; it features the importance of bonds among males for the process of selection. An additional point of equal relevance is that the stability, order and defence of the community depend on the male-bonded individuals: politics and reproduction are closely linked. *Hence the Darwinian processes of natural selection involve a combination of sexual competence with females and social competence with males.* This in turn appears to stabilize communities, provide models for the young males, and seems, indeed, to conduce to the 'health' of females as well as dominant males.

(In one as yet unpublished study, it is noted that in a group of rhesus monkeys in which there was no male, the females were incapable of 'governing' the group and social tension and disorganization were constant. The introduction of but one adult male into the group corrected the situation immediately, and a more normal political and social pattern quickly returned).

What is relevant in all this to our concern here is that primate females seem biologically unprogrammed to dominate political systems, and the whole weight of the relevant primates' breeding history militates against female participation in what we can call 'primate public life'. . . .

The Genetic Foundation of Masculine Dominance

Let us return to the human case directly. In humans the bonding propensity of males—if it exists—would have been given an additional evolutionary emphasis by the function of hunting. It is important to remember that among non-human primates there is little if any differentiation between the sexes in the food-gathering activity. This is crucial, because if hunting in the human species was for males only, then a pre-existent male bonding pattern which we might have inherited along with the primates may have been strongly and unambiguously accentuated by our special human innovation of co-operative hunting. In other words, while in other primates the sexual division of labour had chiefly to do with defence and politics, in the human case this was expanded to include economics too, and herein may lie some of the resistance which human communities appear to show still to even the most sophisticated and ardent efforts to achieve sexual equality.

Every human community displays some sexual division of labour. The allocation of tasks may vary enormously. In one society a particular job will be for men and in another the same job for females. Some jobs will be done by both. But the significant regularity is that there is always some distinction between male and female work for some jobs and on some grounds. Sometimes these are linked to obvious physical factors: they involve speed, danger, muscular strength, etc. None the less, there is often no technological justification for the sexual distinction, and one is driven to the conclusion that the pattern of sexual division of labour may relate not only to real differences in skills, aptitudes, and interests, but to a core pattern of the human primate: that in some circumstances, particularly those defined as dangerous, important for the community, or involving matters of high moment, males will exclude females from their groups and engage in male bonding undisturbed.

That this may be both a deliberate and an infra-social, broadly unconscious pattern—in the same sense as the male-female bond, based on sexual attraction and reproduction, is both conscious and infra-social—underlines the difficulty of doing something about this; it aggravates the difficulty of knowing precisely how to go about obtaining female equality in the labour, political, and associated spheres.

In other words, I am suggesting that a species-specific pattern of *Homo Sapiens* is the creation of particular bonds between males, that these bonds are intrinsically related to political, economic, military, police and other similarly power- and dominance-centred social subsystems, that equal female colleagues—even one—could interfere with these bonding processes, that one reflection of this principle is the constant division of labour by sex, and that while conscious social management of these processes may of course alter or reverse them, the propensity to behave in this way will continue to manifest itself in each new generation until genetic change 'breeds it out'—a process which even under current circumstances is very improbable in any foreseeable future.

Of course, all this is impossible to prove in the sense that an exact and reproducible cause gives rise to an exact and reproducible effect. However, biologically speaking, a species is an experiment without a control group—except in so far as it bears systematic and acceptable comparison with other species—and in the human case we can use cross-cultural data to point toward items of behaviour which are common to all cultures, thus species-specific, and those which are clearly culture-specific. Hence, I have argued that the ubiquity of the male dominance and female exclusion patterns which can be identified is a serious indication of the possibility that these patterns may originate in our genetic codes, and in the interactions between genetic code and social group and particular circumstances in which individual codes work themselves out.

It should not surprise us that maleness and femaleness as biological categories have elaborate effects on even complex technologically based behaviour. Both are clearly biological features of the core of individual beings, and while there are many similarities between males and females, it is scientifically parsimonious to attend to the possibility that behavioural differences in other spheres are as significant as those in the reproductive. . . .

Male Bonds and Female Exclusion

The tendency for males to form bonds in work, fighting, politics, etc., and the more obvious but equally pervasive propensity for males and females to form at least ephemeral bonds centring round the process of sexual titillation and consummation, may be as formidable barriers to egalitarian female employment as the obvious ones directly related to reproduction. And an additional factor which has been often overlooked both by ethnographers and students of contemporary politics and economics is the apparent difficulty females have in forming the bonds necessary in order to manage structures involving power and wealth. Let us explore these factors in turn.

It should by now be clear that the proposition here is that if males bond because it is 'in the nature of the beast' to do so, then this places a considerable burden both on women seeking to join these bonds, and on those men willing to allow females into groups when this may signally affect the groups and the relations between group members.

One intriguing example of this phenomenon is the secret society; only exceptionally are these heterosexual. They are mostly all-male and when women do join them, this appears to mark the end of the society's particular drama and effect on its surroundings. This is, again, not to recommend a particular attitude or policy towards secret societies. But it is to suggest that they express certain effective propensities of the human male and that we can observe in these curious and unpredictable organizations a feature of male behaviour in the voluntary world which may find more formal expression in the more overt and legislated worlds of business, politics, etc.

Team sport is another example of this phenomenon; with the exception of tennis and skating, team sports are overwhelmingly unisexual. Except for the most violent of sports, there is no reason why rules governing female participation could not be introduced and appropriate numbers of women join teams. But I suggest that team sports depend on the bonding process and that female participation is anathema to this and would severely curtail the enjoyment of both players and spectators because of the distrubance of the male socio-dramaturgy of sport.

Perhaps both secret societies and sports will be seen by some as a wretched and retrogressive failure of males to embrace a modern and wholesome sexual egalitarianism. It may also be sensible to see them as rather complex projections of species-wide (and their incidence is species-wide) propensities for male bonding. In any event, they do exist (though secret societies are under considerable pressure, particularly in the United States) and represent a clue to what many men are concerned about and to the ways in which they willingly choose to spend their time.

If we apply the principles of these forms of association to other areas we can see that the rejection of female co-workers by males may stem from more than retrogressive pique, prejudice, lack of sympathy for females, or some other impetus regarded as malignant and uninformed. This means that coping with this rejection may involve dealing with subconscious processes which are possibly of ancient primate origin and which have for several million years and until just recently served very well for political and economic survival. What we may call 'the anti-female tradition', has its origins, then, not only in belligerent male chauvinist ideology and, in economic exploitation of females, but in a genetic process which evolved because pre-hominids found they could survive and reproduce better if they excluded females from the processes of political dominance, with survival further aided by the exclusion of females from the hunting party. . . .

The Female-Female Bond

Before concluding, I must make several remarks about another kind of bond, the female-female bond. The groups which females form appear to occupy themselves less with macro-structures of society than with micro-structures. In general, they seem to be less persistent over time and involve fewer people in associations having less organizational and technical complexity, both in humans and the other primates.

Recently there have been several sets of data published about primate groups in which female-managed 'kinship structures' are significant for the continuity of primate bonds across several generations, and even for the general guidance of the process of selection of male leaders (Reynolds, 1968). Perhaps further research may reveal the female bonds that exist in the other primates, and that these serve evolutionary functions, particularly in the critical sphere of rearing the young and, through socialization, establishing the continuity of the future with the present. Be that as it may, the fact is that in the human case there is a highly significant division of food-gathering labour—as distinct from non-human primates, among whom all able individuals find their own food—and this suggests that the factor of male bonding among humans may well have been more important than among the other (vegetarian) primates.

Should we find that primate females specialize in social organization and the maintenance of kinship patterns, this could accord with human data about the centrality of the domestic arena for female action. Necessarily, the facts of reproduction govern this at certain stages of the life cycle. Thus, there is the real possibility that selection has always favoured females who have surrounded themselves and their children with a group of kin and other females who provide information, security and the simple and necessary ease of social contact.

As much as solitary hunters face a difficult task, so do solitary mothers. In so far as biological processes can select for such gregarious characteristics, it is possible that a female bonding propensity does exist, with a focus on the relatively intimate matters of families and children rather than on the macro-structures involving war, hunting, defence, sport, religion and so on, which appear in virtually all cultures to obsess and stimulate human males. A host of present data about the reluctance of females to work for, vote for, or otherwise be associates of other females would then follow from this fact—if it should be proven to be a fact—that females in groups function best when occupied with tasks in the community consistent with those appropriate to their more limited familial ones.

Again, this is not to recommend this situation, nor to excuse the difficulty females have in penetrating male-dominated organizations or in contriving all-female dominated ones. My purpose is to note briefly that just as in pair-bonding or male-bonding, female-female bonding may involve biologically determined infra-social processes. The factor of sexual competition for the attention and (implicity) breeding potential of males is an additional restraint on the co-operation of females over extended periods of time and under various forms or degrees of social pressure.

I have tried to outline some of the parameters of biology within which efforts at social change may have to operate. Defining or describing a situation is not to excuse it, but presumably to provide some factual and theoretical basis for changing a system once it is understood. That the existing state of affairs is all involved with passionately felt prejudices. aspirations, fears and uncertainties makes it all the more necessary to ask why the position of women in society after society has remained unsatisfactory to idealistic and enterprising men and women.

The conspiracy theory of why this is so, and the class theory— curiously mixed as it is with an overtone of prejudice similar to that of racism—may be insufficient axes around which a discussion can revolve, for such discussion must also take into account what new biological and other data we have which may be pertinent.

Of course, there are limits to the utility of a biological model, too—it is too easy for some to say that what is true because of biology must always ren.ain social reality; but this is just not so. Our human biology is, however, the fundamental foundation on which social reconstitution must perforce be based. There can be no other foundation. And the task of ideologists and makers of public policy must be to incorporate biological reality into the idealism of their programmes and the scope of their extensions of human possibilities.

REFERENCES

Laughlin, William S. "Hunting: An Integrating Biobehavior System and Its Evolutionary Importance," in R. B. Lee and B. I. DeVore (Eds.), *Man the Hunter.* Chicago: Aldine, 1968.

Reynolds, Vernon. "Kinship and the Family in Monkeys, Apes, and Man," *Man,* 2 (June, 1968).

Tiger, Lionel. *Men in Groups.* New York: Random House, 1969.

ROLE DIFFERENTIATION IN THE NUCLEAR FAMILY

MORRIS ZELDITCH, JR.

The analysis of our own nuclear family structure reveals certain patterns of differentiation that we also see in other societies if we clearly distinguish the nuclear family from the extended kinship groupings in which, in a great many societies, they are incorporated. Parsons has pointed out that in this particular instance it is fruitful to begin analysis with the more *highly* differentiated social system of the United States, rather than the so-called "simple" nonliterate societies, because in our society the nuclear family is structurally isolated from extended kin solidarities and functionally differentiated from other systems. But the nuclear family is not something characteristic *only* of our society. Murdock, for instance, has stated flatly that it is a discernible functioning group in all societies entering his sample, and there have been only one or two exceptions reported in the entire anthropological literature.

In our system the marriage pair is given precedence as a solidary unit over any link with the *parents* of either member of the pair. The so-called simple nonliterate societies, on the other hand, often give precedence to solidarities with the family of orientation of one of the pair, or, in more complex forms, strong though differentiated obligations to both parental families. Even in the bilateral cases most closely approaching our own, the isolation of the nuclear family is not the distinguishing structural characteristic; rather a bilateral system generally functions to incorporate the nuclear family in a kin-oriented group, but one in which membership is fluidly structured from generation to generation.

Nevertheless, the nuclear family ordinarily *can* be distinguished, and does function as a significant group. This particular point, in fact, is responsible for a good many of the issues in the interpretation of matrilineal systems, which we will consider later, and a failure to distinguish the nuclear family from other kinship units in which it is incorporated is likely to confuse any sort of analysis of concrete kinship behavior.

The Generic Significance of Nuclear Family Structure

The nuclear family in our society has a particular pattern of roles which we now suggest has a *generic* significance. There is, in other words, an underlying structural uniformity which gives a baseline for the analysis of the range of variation usually noted.

A statement of this sort, of course, can be only hypothetical at this point. It is the purpose of this paper, however, to indicate that it is not *only* hypothetical. On what basis can we argue that this uniformity occurs? . . . .

We would argue that it is essentially fruitful to consider the nuclear family as a special case of a small group, and that the mode of differentiation observed in small groups has a generic significance which extends to any of its special cases. The fact that experimental groups are ephemeral compared to nuclear families (even those which are terminated after only a few months of existence) does not imply that the conclusions reached from these groups are ephemeral.

More generally, a nuclear family is a social system, and the peculiar attributes which distinguish it from other systems (its particular age-sex structure and primary function, for instance) should be examined *within* this more general context. All groups are subject to certain imposed *conditions* of existence; not that all groups exist, but that all groups that *do* exist meet these conditions. If we assume the existence of a nuclear family, therefore, we must inquire into the conditions of its existence. And certain of these conditions are common to all groups, appearing in such diverse forms as experimental groups and the family pattern of peasant Ireland.

Directions of Differentiation in the Nuclear Family

Among the conditions of a system's existence is at least a certain degree of differentiation along lines imposed by the orbits of the system's movement. Consider first the general pattern of differentiation which in broad outline appears from the experimental small group. There is a tendency for a *task leader* and a *sociometric star* to appear. Although there is some problem in clearly isolating the complex factors defining the task leader he seems to be associated with certain *behaviors* (in general terms, "task" behaviors; more specifically in giving suggestions, directions, opinions), and certain *attitudes* (involving, apparently, an inhibition of emotions and the ability to accept hostile reactions from others in the process of pressing a point, etc.). There are also, of course, reciprocal behaviors and attitudes on the part of other system-members towards the task leader. The sociometric star, although the term originally derives from attitudes taken toward ego by alters, also tends to show a certain pattern of behaviors and attitudes; namely, the *expression* of emotions, supportive behavior to others, the desire to please and be liked, and a more generalized liking for other members. The star may, of course, express negative reactions as well as positive supports; typically these are significant in releasing negative reactions (often through humor) of the group as a whole, reducing, in consequence, the general tension level. (The difference between a "leader," here, and one who fails to become a leader may very well lie, in part, in the capacity to express reactions felt by the group as a *whole*.)

From a general theoretical point of view this is *not* a fortuitous pattern of differentiation; it defines, in fact, the two basic conditions of the existence of a social system. In order to clarify and illustrate what we mean by this, we may take the nuclear family as a specific case; and it may be useful at the same time to begin with a differentiation logically prior to role differentiation itself.

Assume a time T_1 in which members of the nuclear family are dispersed somewhere in the external situation involved in devotion to the "task," or what we call "instrumental" activities. By either of these terms we mean here the manipulation of the object-world in order to provide facilities for the achievement of goals defined within the system. In our society, for instance, the husband typically goes to work in the morning, the mother shops or cleans up, the children go to school if they are old enough. In many other societies a similar dispersal, involving a departure of at least the husband-father (out hunting, or farming), often occurs. Now clearly, if there is no second occasion, T_2, during which the members of the system are *reunited*, the system will tend to disappear. It will no longer be identifiable as a system.

There is then, a most primitive level of differentiation here in the simple presence or absence of members on two different occasions. From this it is clear that one imperative of all social systems is integration, a coming together, which of course Durkheim emphasized a considerable time ago.

The other side of the coin, involving here a dispersal of members, introduces a more complex level of analysis. Although dispersal of system members is common during instrumental activities, it is not necessary to define what we are talking about. We merely suggest this as a first point of purchase on the type of analysis involved. Typically, in fact, the mother and children remain at some location symbolically associated with the system's existence—the home is the crucial symbol, of course—and there is always a *latent* existence to the system (*if* it is to reappear). This function of symbols, in giving latent existence to systems, is of obvious importance as a basis for their physical reintegration.

What is significant in the differentiation of these two occasions, however, is not the states of spatial dispersion and integration, physically, but the difference in behavior and attitudes involved. The system may in fact always act in concert from the present point of view, and still show the differentiation we are here concerned with.

Reverting to our time period T_1, then, assume that all members are physically adjacent but devoted to instrumental or task activities. The entire family, say, is out farming in the fields. These instrumental activities involve, in gross terms, the manipulation of objects (plows, or hoes, etc.), and an attitude composed of Parsons' pattern variables "specific, affectively neutral, universalistic, achievement-oriented," or in more gross terms a "rational" attitude towards the external situation, and an *inhibition* of emotions toward other members of the system. *In order for the system to continue as a system,* we now say, there must at some point be a *change* in attitude and behavior to integrative-expressive activities–to laughing, playing, release of inhibited emotions, the expression of affection for each other, a warmth and a symbolization of common membership through supportive, accepting behavior.

If we reverse our assumptions, we arrive at the same basic conclusion, something we were not able to do when we considered only physical presence or absence (we were not, that is, able to show why dispersion *had* to occur). Assume the time period T_2 in which all members are affectionate, responsive, emotionally warm and attached to each other, often symbolized in the meal-time break. The system *cannot* continue in this state forever. It must, at some point, change to the necessary activities–and the associated attitudes–involved in manipulating the facilities of the object world so that the family has the food, shelter, fire, etc., which the external situation can provide. The family then becomes reinvolved in the *task*, which, no matter how much integrative behavior there was before or will be after–and perhaps also at breaks during the task–must concentrate on *getting the job done.* It must, that is, at least for the time being, devote its attention to instrumental acts.

A considerable refinement is involved in the further differentiation of the structure of *roles* in the system. One clue, perhaps, is suggested by the earlier peripheral comment that while husband-father is away at work or in the fields, the mother very often stays at home symbolizing the integrative focus of the system (even though her activities may be primarily instrumental during this phase of family activity). The fact that it is the mother who stays home is not, for the present, significant although shortly it will become so. What *is* significant, is that *someone* stayed, and that someone is in fact *more* responsible for integrative-expressive behavior than the person who went off to work.

Why after all, are *two* parents necessary? For one thing, to be a stable focus of integration, the integrative-expressive "leader" can't be off on adaptive-instrumental errands all the time. For another, a stable, secure attitude of members depends, it can be assumed, on a *clear* structure being given to the situation so that an *uncertain* responsibility for emotional warmth, for instance, raises significant problems for the stability of the system. And an uncertain managerial responsibility, an unclear definition of authority for decisions and for getting things done, is also clearly a threat to the stability of the system.

We can say, then, that the system must differentiate behaviors and attitudes in order to continue to exist as a system; and that a further condition of stability is also that some specialization occur in responsibility for the attitudes and behaviors involved.

Age and Sex in the Nuclear Family

We actually want to examine two things in this paper. One is related to the generic significance of a certain pattern of differentiation. The relevant role-system, however, is indeterminate with respect to allocation when taken at this level. It is necessary to consider the nuclear family as a type of group peculiarly structured around age-sex differences in order to arrive at a hypothesis concerning who plays the instrumental and expressive roles.

Now any system, it should be noticed first, has a problem often considered peculiar to families, that is the processing of new recruits. While the "barbarian invasion" may be considered of special significance for the family, and thus to impose special conditions on its existence, the problem is in fact generic to all systems. Thus the family resembles other groups in this respect as well as in the more general terms discussed so far. What differs, and the difference is of crucial structural significance, is the age-sex matrix of the family, and with it the situational reference points for the allocation of *facilities* in the performance of roles. At the grossest level of analysis, for instance, the father is stronger than the son, so that he, rather than the son, is allocated to leadership roles in instrumental activities (with the possible, and amusing, exception of the polyandrous Marquesas).

At least one fundamental feature of the external situation of social systems—here a feature of the physiological organism—is a crucial reference point for differentiation in the family. This lies in the division of organisms into lactating and nonlactating classes. Only in our own society (so far as I know, that is) have we managed to invent successful bottle-feeding, and this is undoubtedly of importance for our social structure. In other societies necessarily—and in our own for structural reasons which have *not* disappeared with the advent of the bottle—the initial core relation of a family with children is the mother-child attachment. And it follows from the principles of learning that the gradient of generalization should establish "mother" as the focus of gratification in a diffuse sense, as the source of "security" and "comfort." She is the focus of warmth and stability. Thus, because of her special initial relation to the child, "mother" is the more likely expressive focus of the system as a whole.

The allocation of the instrumental leadership to the husband-father rests on two aspects of this role. The role involves, first, a manipulation of the external environment, and consequently a good deal of physical mobility. The concentration of the mother on the child precludes a *primacy* of her attention in this direction although she always performs *some* instrumental tasks. In addition to the managerial aspects of the role there are certain discipline and control functions of the father role. Consider, again, why *two* parents are necessary at all. The initial mother-child subsystem can do without the father (except that he provides food, shelter, etc., for this subsystem so that it need not split up to perform many of its own instrumental tasks). But *some* significant member of the nuclear family must "pry the child loose" from the mother-dependency so that it may "grow up" and accept its responsibilities as an "adult." There is necessarily a coalition of father and mother in this, or no stable socialization pattern develops. But the mother, by her special initial relation to the child is relatively more susceptible to *seduction* out of coalition. We may note, for instance, that one of the pathologies of family dynamics may arise because the father tends to be susceptible to seduction by daughters; and the very fact of his relative power in the coalition makes this *more* of a threat to the family as a system. The problem of the "weak, ineffectual" father is more significant than that of the "weak, ineffectual" mother. (Conversely, of course, and quite as significant, the problem of the "cold, unyielding" mother is more of a problem than the "cold, unyielding" father.) If, therefore, the female is allocated the integrative-supportive role, there must necessarily be an allocation of authority for discipline and relatively "neutral" judgment to the husband-father.

We may summarize the hypothesis we have stated then, in this way. Because the nuclear family is a special case of the more general class of social systems, and because it must meet certain conditions of existence common to all social systems, we suggest that:

1. If the nuclear family constitutes a social system stable over time, it will differentiate roles such that instrumental leadership and expressive leadership of the system are discriminated.

Because the nuclear family, on the other hand, has certain peculiar features not common to all systems, we are further able to state a certain hypothesis about the *allocation* of these roles to system-members. This peculiar feature is the age-sex matrix of the nuclear family and the differential distribution of facilities for the performance of the fundamental roles. We suggest that:

2. If the nuclear family consists in a defined "normal" complement of the male adult, female adult and their immediate children, the male adult will play the role of instrumental leader and the female adult will play the role of expressive leader. . . .

[Let us] consider the American middle-class case in reviewing the definitions we have given to instrumental and expressive leadership. From certain points of view the American middle-class family approaches most clearly to equal allocation (or "no allocation") of instrumental and expressive activities. The universalistic value schema (in which women are "just as good as" men) coupled with the general attitude toward the explicit expression of authority ("I'm agin it") apparently constitutes the limiting case of no differentiation at all. Underlying this broad value-schema, however, a rather clear differentiation occurs.

In the distribution of instrumental tasks, the American family maintains a more flexible pattern than most societies. Father helps mother with the dishes. He sets the table. He makes formula for the baby. Mother can supplement the income of the family by working outside. Nevertheless, the American male, by definition, *must* "provide" for his family. He is *responsible* for the support of his wife and children. His primary area of performance is the occupational role, in which his status fundamentally inheres; and his *primary* function in the family is to supply an "income," to be the "breadwinner." There is simply something wrong with the American adult male who doesn't have a "job." American women, on the other hand, tend to hold jobs *before* they are married and to quit when "the day" comes; or to continue in jobs of a lower status than their husbands. And not only is the mother the focus of emotional support for the American middle-class child, but much more exclusively so than in most societies (as Margaret Mead has pointed out in her treatment of adolescent problems). The cult of the warm, giving "Mom" stands in contrast to the "capable," "competent," "go-getting" male. The more expressive type of male, as a matter of fact, is regarded as "effeminate," and has too much fat on the inner side of his thigh.

The distribution of authority is legitimized on a different basis in the "democratic" family than in the so-called "traditional" one; but the father is "supposed" to remain the primary executive member. The image of the "henpecked" husband makes sense only on this premise. His "commands" are validated on the basis of "good judgment," rather than *general* obedience due to a person in authority. But when the mother's efforts at "disciplining" fail, she traditionally tells the errant child, "Wait till daddy gets home."

THEORY OF SEXUAL POLITICS

KATE MILLETT

In introducing the term "sexual politics," one must first answer the inevitable question "Can the relationship between the sexes be viewed in a political light at all?" The answer depends on how one defines politics. This essay does not define the political as that relatively narrow and exclusive world of meetings, chairmen, and parties. The term "politics" shall refer to power-structured relationships, arrangements whereby one group of persons is controlled by another. By way of parenthesis one might add that although an ideal politics might simply be conceived of as the arrangement of human life on agreeable and rational principles from whence the entire notion of power *over* others should be banished, one must confess that this is not what constitutes the political as we know it, and it is to this that we must address ourselves.

The following sketch, which might be described as "notes toward a theory of patriarchy" will attempt to prove that sex is a status category with political implications. Something of a pioneering effort, it must perforce be both tentative and imperfect. Because the intention is to provide an overall description, statements must be generalized, exceptions neglected, and subheadings overlapping and, to some degree, arbitrary as well.

The word "politics" is enlisted here when speaking of the sexes primarily because such a word is eminently useful in outlining the real nature of their relative status, historically and at the present. It is opportune, perhaps today even mandatory, that we develop a more relevant psychology and philosophy of power relationships beyond the simple conceptual framework provided by our traditional formal politics. Indeed, it may be imperative that we give some attention to defining a theory of politics which treats of power relationships on grounds less conventional than those to which we are accustomed. I have therefore found it pertinent to define them on grounds of personal contact and interaction between members of well-defined and coherent groups: races, castes, classes, and sexes. For it is precisely because certain groups have no representation in a number of recognized political structures that their position tends to be so stable, their oppression so continuous.

In America, recent events have forced us to acknowledge at last that the relationship between the races is indeed a political one which involves the general control of one collectivity, defined by birth, over another collectivity, also defined by birth. Groups who rule by birthright are fast disappearing, yet there remains one ancient and universal scheme for the domination of one birth group by another—the scheme that prevails in the area of sex. The study of racism has convinced us that a truly political state of affairs operates between the races to perpetuate a series of oppressive circumstances. The subordinated group has inadequate redress through existing political institutions, and is deterred thereby from organizing into conventional political struggle and opposition.

Quite in the same manner, a disinterested examination of our system of sexual relationship must point out that the situation between the sexes now, and throughout history, is a case of that phenomenon Max Weber defined as *herrschaft*, a relationship of dominance and subordinance. What goes largely unexamined, often even unacknowledged (yet is institutionalized nonetheless) in our social order, is the birthright priority whereby males rule females. Through this system a most ingenious form of "interior colonization" has been achieved. It is one which tends moreover to be sturdier than any form of segregation, and more rigorous than class stratification, more uniform, certainly more enduring. However muted its present appearance may be, sexual dominion obtains nevertheless as perhaps the most pervasive ideology of our culture and provides its most fundamental concept of power.

This is so because our society, like all other historical civilizations, is a patriarchy.* The fact is evident at once if one recalls that the military, industry, technology, universities, science, political office, and finance—in short, every avenue of power within the society, including the coercive force of the police, is entirely in male hands. As the essence of politics is power, such realization cannot fail to carry impact. What lingers of supernatural authority, the Deity, "His" ministry, together with the ethics and values, the philosophy and art of our culture—its very civilization—as T. S. Eliot once observed, is of male manufacture. . . .

I. Ideological

Hannah Arendt (1969) has observed that government is upheld by power supported either through consent or imposed through violence. Conditioning to an ideology amounts to the former. Sexual politics obtains consent through the "socialization" of both sexes to basic patriarchal polities with regard to temperament, role, and status. As to status, a pervasive assent to the prejudice of male superiority guarantees superior status in the male, inferior in the female. The first item, temperament, involves the formation of human personality along stereotyped lines of sex category ("masculine" and "feminine"), based on the needs and values of the dominant group

---

* No matriarchal societies are known to exist at present. Matrilineality, which may be, as some anthropologists have held, a residue or a transitional stage of matriarchy, does not constitute an exception to patriarchal rule, it simply channels the power held by males through female descent— e.g. the Avunculate.

and dictated by what its members cherish in themselves and find convenient in subordinates: aggression, intelligence, force, and efficacy in the
male; passivity, ignorance, docility, "virtue," and ineffectuality in the
female. This is complemented by a second factor, sex role, which decrees
a consonant and highly elaborate code of conduct, gesture and attitude
for each sex. In terms of activity, sex role assigns domestic service and
attendance upon infants to the female, the rest of human achievement,
interest, and ambition to the male. The limited role allotted the female
tends to arrest her at the level of biological experience. Therefore, nearly
all that can be described as distinctly human rather than animal activity
(in their own way animals also give birth and care for their young) is largely
reserved for the male. Of course, status again follows from such an assignment. Were one to analyze the three categories one might designate status
as the political component, role as the sociological, and temperament as
the psychological—yet their interdependence is unquestionable and they
form a chain. Those awarded higher status tend to adopt roles of mastery,
largely because they are first encouraged to develop temperaments of
dominance. That this is true of caste and class as well is self-evident.

II. Biological

Patriarchal religion, popular attitude, and to some degree, science as well
assumes these psycho-social distinctions to rest upon biological differences
between the sexes, so that where culture is acknowledged as shaping
behavior, it is said to do no more than cooperate with nature. Yet the
temperamental distinctions created in patriarchy ("masculine" and
"feminine" personality traits) do not appear to originate in human
nature, those of role and status still less.

The heavier musculature of the male, a secondary sexual characteristic and common among mammals, is biological in origin but is also
culturally encouraged through breeding, diet and exercise. Yet it is hardly
an adequate category on which to base political relations *within
civilization*.* Male supremacy, like other political creeds, does not finally

---

* "The historians of Roman laws, having very justly remarked that neither birth nor
affection was the foundation of the Roman family, have concluded that this foundation must be found in the power of the father or husband. They make a sort of
primordial institution of this power; but they do not explain how this power was
established, unless it was by the superiority of strength of the husband over the wife,
and of the father over the children. Now, we deceive ourselves sadly when we thus
place force as the origin of law. We shall see farther on that the authority of the
father or husband, far from having been the first cause, was itself an effect; it was
derived from religion, and was established by religion. Superior strength, therefore,
was not the principle that established the family." Numa Denis Fustel de Coulanges
(1873, pp. 41-42). Unfortunately Fustel de Coulanges neglects to mention how
religion came to uphold patriarchal authority, since patriarchal religion is also an
effect, rather than an original cause.

reside in physical strength but in the acceptance of a value system which is not biological. Superior physical strength is not a factor in political relations—vide those of race and class. Civilization has always been able to substitute other methods (technic, weaponry, knowledge) for those of physical strength, and contemporary civilization has no further need of it. At present, as in the past, physical exertion is very generally a class factor, those at the bottom performing the most strenuous tasks, whether they be strong or not. . . .

The question of the historical origins of patriarchy—whether patriarchy originated primordially in the male's superior strength, or upon a later mobilization of such strength under certain circumstances—appears at the moment to be unanswerable. It is also probably irrelevant to contemporary patriarchy, where we are left with the realities of sexual politics, still grounded we are often assured, on nature. Unfortunately, as the psycho-social distinctions made between the two sex groups which are said to justify their present political relationship are not the clear, specific, measurable and neutral ones of the physical sciences, but are instead of an entirely different character—vague, amorphous, often even quasi-religious in phrasing—it must be admitted that many of the generally understood distinctions between the sexes in the more significant areas of role and temperament, not to mention status, have in fact, essentially cultural, rather than biological, bases. Attempts to prove that temperamental dominance is inherent in the male (which for its advocates, would be tantamount to validating, logically as well as historically, the patriarchal situation regarding role and status) have been notably unsuccessful. . . .

Not only is there insufficient evidence for the thesis that the present social distinctions of patriarchy (status, role, temperament) are physical in origin, but we are hardly in a position to assess the existing differentiations, since distinctions which we know to be culturally induced at present so outweigh them. Whatever the "real" differences between the sexes may be, we are not likely to know them until the sexes are treated differently, that is alike. And this is very far from being the case at present. Important new research not only suggests that the possibilities of innate temperamental differences seem more remote than ever, but even raises questions as to the validity and permanence of psycho-sexual identity. In doing so it gives fairly concrete positive evidence of the overwhelmingly *cultural* character of gender, i.e. personality structure in terms of sexual category. . . .

Because of our social circumstances, male and female are really two cultures and their life experiences are utterly different—and this is crucial. Implicit in all the gender identity development which takes place through childhood is the sum total of the parents', the peers', and the culture's notions of what is appropriate to each gender by way of temperament, character, interests, status, worth, gesture, and expression. Every moment of the child's life is a clue to how he or she must think and behave to attain or satisfy the demands which gender places upon one. In adolescence the merciless task of conformity grows to crisis proportions, generally cooling and settling in maturity.

Since patriarchy's biological foundations appear to be so very insecure one has some cause to admire the strength of a "socialization" which can continue a universal condition "on faith alone," as it were, or through an acquired value system exclusively. What does seem decisive in assuring the maintenance of the temperamental differences between the sexes is the conditioning of early childhood. Conditioning runs in a circle of self-perpetuation and self-fulfilling prophecy. To take a simple example: expectations the culture cherishes about his gender identity encourage the young male to develop aggressive impulses and the female to thwart her own or turn them inward. The result is that the male tends to have aggression reinforced in his behavior, often with significant anti-social possibilities. Thereupon the culture consents to believe the possession of the male indicator, the testes, penis, and scrotum, in itself characterizes the aggressive impulse, and even vulgarly celebrates it in such encomiums as "that guy has balls." The same process of reinforcement is evident in producing the chief "feminine" virtue of passivity.

In contemporary terminology, the basic division of temperamental trait is marshaled along the line of "aggression is male" and "passivity is female." All other temperamental traits are somehow—often with the most dexterous ingenuity—aligned to correspond. If aggressiveness is the trait of the master class, docility must be the corresponding trait of a subject group. The usual hope of such line of reasoning is that "nature," by some impossible outside chance, might still be depended upon to rationalize the patriarchal system. An important consideration to be remembered here is that in patriarchy, the function of norm is unthinkingly delegated to the male—were it not, one might as plausibly speak of "feminine" behavior as active, and "masculine" behavior as hyperactive or hyperaggressive.

Here it might be added, by way of a coda, that data from physical sciences has recently been enlisted again to support sociological arguments, such as those of Lionel Tiger (1968) who seeks a genetic justification of patriarchy by proposing a "bonding instinct" in males which assures their political and social control of human society. One sees the implication of such a theory by applying its premise to any ruling group. Tiger's thesis appears to be a misrepresentation of the work of Lorenz and other students of animal behavior. Since his evidence of inherent traits is patriarchal history and organization, his pretensions to physical evidence are both specious and circular. One can only advance genetic evidence when one has genetic (rather than historical) evidence to advance. As many authorities dismiss the possibility of instincts (complex inherent behavioral patterns) in humans altogether, admitting only reflexes and drives (far simpler neural responses), the prospects of a "bonding instinct" appear particularly forlorn. . . .

III. Sociological

Patriarchy's chief institution is the family. It is both a mirror of and a connection with the larger society; a patriarchal unit within a patriarchal whole. Mediating between the individual and the social structure, the family effects control and conformity where political and other authorities are insufficient. As the fundamental instrument and the foundation unit of patriarchal society the family and its roles are proto-typical. Serving as an agent of the larger society, the family not only encourages its own members to adjust and conform, but acts as a unit in the government of the patriarchal state which rules its citizens through its family heads. Even in patriarchal societies where they are granted legal citizenship, women tend to be ruled through the family alone and have little or no formal relation to the state.

As co-operation between the family and the larger society is essential, else both would fall apart, the fate of three patriarchal institutions, the family, society, and the state are interrelated. In most forms of patriarchy this has generally led to the granting of religious support in statements such as the Catholic precept that "the father is head of the family," or Judaism's delegation of quasi-priestly authority to the male parent. Secular governments today also confirm this, as in census practices of designating the male as head of household, taxation, passports etc. Female heads of household tend to be regarded as undesirable; the phenomenon is a trait of poverty or misfortune. The Confucian prescription that the relationship between rule and subject is parallel to that of father and children points to the essentially feudal character of the patriarchal family (and conversely, the familial character of feudalism) even in modern democracies.

Traditionally, patriarchy granted the father nearly total ownership over wife or wives and children, including the powers of physical abuse and often even those of murder and sale. Classically, as head of the family the father is both begetter and owner in a system in which kinship is property. . . .

In contemporary patriarchies the male's *de jure* priority has recently been modified through the granting of divorce* protection, citizenship, and property to women. Their chattel status continues in their loss of

---

* Many patriarchies granted divorce to males only. It has been accessible to women on any scale only during this century. Goode states that divorce rates were as high in Japan during the 1880s as they are in the U.S. today (1964, p.3).

name, their obligation to adopt the husband's domicile, and the general
legal assumption that marriage involves an exchange of the female's
domestic service and (sexual) consortium in return for financial support.*

The chief contribution of the family in patriarchy is the socialization
of the young (largely through the example and admonition of their
parents) into patriarchal ideology's prescribed attitudes toward the
categories of role, temperament, and status. Although slight differences
of definition depend here upon the parents' grasp of cultural values, the
general effect of uniformity is achieved, to be further reinforced through
peers, schools, media, and other learning sources, formal and informal.
While we may niggle over the balance of authority between the personalities of various households, one must remember that the entire culture
supports masculine authority in all areas of life and—outside of the home—
permits the female none at all. . . .

IV. Economic and Educational

One of the most efficient branches of patriarchal government lies in the
agency of its economic hold over its female subjects. In traditional
patriarchy, women, as non-persons without legal standing, were permitted
no actual economic existence as they could neither own nor earn in their
own right. Since women have always worked in patriarchal societies, often
at the most routine or strenuous tasks, what is at issue here is not labor but
economic reward. In modern reformed patriarchal societies, women have
certain economic rights, yet the "woman's work" in which some two
thirds of the female population in most developed countries are engaged
is work that is not paid for. In a money economy where autonomy and
prestige depend upon currency, this is a fact of great importance. In
general, the position of women in patriarchy is a continuous function of
their economic dependence. Just as their social position is vicarious and
achieved (often on a temporary or marginal basis) though males, their
relation to the economy is also typically vicarious or tangential.

Of that third of women who are employed, their average wages
represent only half of the average income enjoyed by men. These are the
U.S. Department of Labor statistics for average year-round income: white
male, $6704, non-white male $4277, white female, $3991, and non-white

---

* Divorce is granted to a male for his wife's failure in domestic service and
consortium: it is not granted him for his wife's failure to render him financial
support. Divorce is granted to a woman if her husband fails to support her, but
not for his failure at domestic service or consortium. But see Karczewski versus
Baltimore and Ohio Railroad, 274 F. Supp. 169.175 N.D. Illinois, 1967, where
a precedent was set and the common law that decrees a wife might not sue for
loss of consortium overturned.

female $2816. The disparity is made somewhat more remarkable because the educational level of women is generally higher than that of men in comparable income brackets.* Further, the kinds of employment open to women in modern patriarchies are, with few exceptions, menial, ill paid and without status.† . . .

In terms of industry and production, the situation of women is in many ways comparable both to colonial and to pre-industrial peoples. Although they achieved their first economic autonomy in the industrial revolution and now constitute a large and underpaid factory population, women do not participate directly in technology or in production. What they customarily produce (domestic and personal service) has no market value and is, as it were, pre-capital. Nor, where they do participate in production of commodities through employment, do they own or control or even comprehend the process in which they participate. An example might make this clearer: the refrigerator is a machine all women use, some assemble it in factories, and a very few with scientific education understand its principles of operation. Yet the heavy industries which roll its steel and produce the dies for its parts are in male hands. The same is true of the typewriter, the auto, etc. Now, while knowledge is fragmented even among the male population, collectively they could reconstruct any technological device. But in the absence of males, women's distance from technology today is sufficiently great that it is doubtful that they could replace or repair such machines on any significant scale. Woman's distance from higher technology is even greater: large-scale building construction; the development of computers; the moon shot, occur as further examples. If knowledge is power, power is also knowledge, and a large factor in their subordinate position is the fairly systematic ignorance patriarchy imposes upon women.

Since education and economy are so closely related in the advanced nations, it is significant that the general level and style of higher education for women, particularly in their many remaining segregated institutions, is closer to that of Renaissance humanism than to the skills of mid-twentieth-century scientific and technological society. Traditionally patriarchy permitted occasional minimal literacy to women while higher

---

* See *The 1965 Handbook on Women Workers,* United States Department of Labor, Women's Bureau: "In every major occupational group the median wage or salary income of women was less than that of men. This is true at all levels of educational attainment." A comparison of the income received by women and men with equal amounts of schooling revealed that women who had completed four years of college received incomes which were only 47% of those paid to men with the same educational training; high school graduates earned only 38%, and grade school graduates only 33%.
† For the distribution of women in lower income and lower status positions see *Background Facts on Working Women* (pamphlet) U. S. Department of Labor, Women's Bureau.

education was closed to them. While modern patriarchies have, fairly recently, opened all educational levels to women,* the kind and quality of education is not the same for each sex. This difference is of course apparent in early socialization, but it persists and enters into higher education as well. Universities, once places of scholarship and the training of a few professionals, now also produce the personnel of a technocracy. This is not the case with regard to women. Their own college typically produce neither scholars nor professionals nor technocrats. Nor are they funded by government and corporations as are male colleges and those co-educational colleges and universities whose primary function is the education of males.

As patriarchy enforces a temperamental imbalance of personality traits between the sexes, its educational institutions, segregated or co-educational, accept a cultural programing toward the generally operative division between "masculine" and "feminine" subject matter, assigning the humanities and certain social sciences (at least in their lower or marginal branches) to the female—and science and technology, the professions, business and engineering to the male. Of course the balance of employment, prestige and reward at present lie with the latter. Control of these fields is very eminently a matter of political power. One might also point out how the exclusive dominance of males in the more prestigious fields directly serves the interests of patriarchal power in industry, government and the military. . . .

V. Force

We are not accustomed to associate patriarchy with force. So perfect is its system of socialization, so complete the general assent to its values, so long and so universally has it prevailed in human society, that it scarcely seems to require violent implementation. Customarily, we view its brutalities in the past as exotic or "primitive" custom. Those of the present are regarded as the product of individual deviance, confined to pathological or exceptional behavior, and without general import. And yet, just as under

---

* We often forget how recent an event is higher education for women. In the U.S. it is barely one hundred years old; in many Western countries barely fifty. Oxford did not grant degrees to women on the same terms as to men until 1920. In Japan and a number of other countries universities have been open to women only in the period after World War II. There are still areas where higher education for women scarcely exists. Women do not have the same access to education as do men. The Princeton Report states that "although at the high school level more girls than boys receive grades of "A," roughly 50% more boys than girls go to college." *The Princeton Report to the Alumni on Co-Education* (pamphlet), Princeton, N.J. 1968, p. 10. Most other authorities give the national ratio of college students as two males to one female. In a great many countries it is far lower.

other total ideologies (facism and colonialism are somewhat analogous in this respect) control in patriarchal society would be imperfect, even inoperable, unless it had the rule of force to rely upon, both in emergencies and as an ever-present instrument of intimidation.

Historically, most patriarchies have institutionalized force through their legal systems. For example, strict patriarchies such as that of Islam, have implemented the prohibition against illegitimacy or sexual autonomy with a death sentence. In Afghanistan and Saudi Arabia the adulteress is still stoned to death with a mullah presiding at the execution. Execution by stoning was once common practice through the Near East. It is still condoned in Sicily. Needless to say there was and is no penalty imposed upon the male corespondent. Save in recent times or exceptional cases, adultery was not generally recognized in males except as an offense one male might commit against another's property interest. In Tokugawa Japan, for example, an elaborate set of legal distinctions were made according to class. A samurai was entitled, and in the face of public knowledge, even obliged, to execute an adulterous wife, whereas a chōnin (common citizen) or peasant might respond as he pleased. In cases of cross-class adultery, the lower-class male convicted of sexual intimacy with his employer's wife would, because he had violated taboos of class and property, be beheaded together with her. Upper-strata males had, of course, the same license to seduce lower-class women as we are familiar with in Western societies.

Indirectly, one form of "death penalty" still obtains even in America today. Patriarchal legal systems in depriving women of control over their own bodies drive them to illegal abortions; it is estimated that between two and five thousand women die each year from this cause.

Excepting a social license to physical abuse among certain class and ethnic groups, force is diffuse and generalized in most contemporary patriarchies. Significantly, force itself is restricted to the male who alone is psychologically and technically equipped to perpetrate physical violence. Where differences in physical strength have become immaterial through the use of arms, the female is rendered innocuous by her socialization. Before assault she is almost universally defenseless both by her physical and emotional training. Needless to say, this has the most far-reaching effects on the social and psychological behavior of both sexes.

Patriarchal force also relies on a form of violence particularly sexual in character and realized most completely in the act of rape. The figures of rapes reported represent only a fraction of those which occur, as the "shame" of the event is sufficient to deter women from the notion of civil prosecution under the public circumstances of a trial. Traditionally rape has been viewed as an offense one male commits upon another—a matter of

abusing "his woman." Vendetta, such as occurs in the American South, is
carried out for masculine satisfaction, the exhilirations of race hatred, and
the interests of property and vanity (honor). In rape, the emotions of
aggression, hatred, contempt, and the desire to break or violate personality,
take a form consummately appropriate to sexual politics. . . .

VI. Psychological

The aspects of patriarchy already described have each an effect upon the
psychology of both sexes. Their principal result is the interiorization of
patriarchal ideology. Status, temperament, and role are all value systems
with endless psychological ramifications for each sex. Patriarchal marriage
and the family with its ranks and division of labor play a large part in
enforcing them. The male's superior economic position, the female's inferior one have also grave implications. The large quantity of guilt attached
to sexuality in patriarchy is overwhelmingly placed upon the female, who
is, culturally speaking, held to be the culpable or the more culpable party
in nearly any sexual liaison, whatever the extenuating circumstances. A
tendency toward the reification of the female makes her more often a
sexual object than a person. This is particularly so when she is denied human
rights through chattel status. Even where this has been partly amended
the cumulative effect of religion and custom is still very powerful and
has enormous psychological consequences. Woman is still denied sexual
freedom and the biological control over her body through the cult of
virginity, the double standard, the prescription against abortion, and in
many places because contraception is physically or psychically unavailable
to her.

The continual surveillance in which she is held tends to perpetuate the
infantilization of women even in situations such as those of higher education. The female is continually obliged to seek survival or advancement
through the approval of males as those who hold power. She may do this
either through appeasement or through the exchange of her sexuality for
support and status. As the history of patriarchal culture and the representations of herself within all levels of its cultural media, past and present,
have a devastating effect upon her self image, she is customarily deprived
of any but the most trivial sources of dignity or self-respect. In many
patriarchies, language, as well as cultural tradition, reserve the human
condition for the male. With the Indo-European languages this is a nearly
inescapable habit of mind, for despite all the customary pretense that
"man" and "humanity" are terms which apply equally to both sexes, the
fact is hardly obscured that in practice, general application favors the male

far more often than the female as referent, or even sole referent, for such designations.*

When in any group of persons, the ego is subjected to such invidious versions of itself through social beliefs, ideology, and tradition, the effect is bound to be pernicious. This coupled with the persistent though frequently subtle denigration women encounter daily through personal contacts, the impressions gathered from the images and media about them, and the discrimination in matters of behavior, employment, and education which they endure, should make it no very special cause for surprise that women develop group characteristics common to those who suffer minority status and a marginal existence. A witty experiment by Philip Goldberg (1968) proves what everyone knows, that having internalized the disesteem in which they are held, women despise both themselves and each other. This simple test consisted of asking women undergraduates to respond to the scholarship in an essay signed alternately by one John McKay and one Joan McKay. In making their assessments the students generally agreed that John was a remarkable thinker, Joan an unimpressive mind. Yet the articles were identical: the reaction was dependent on the sex of the supposed author.

As women in patriarchy are for the most part marginal citizens when they are citizens at all, their situation is like that of other minorities, here defined not as dependent upon numerical size of the group, but on its status. "A minority group is any group of people who because of their physical or cultural characteristics, are singled out from others in the society in which they live for differential and unequal treatment" (Wirth, 1945, p. 347). Only a handful of sociologists have ever addressed themselves in any meaningful way to the minority status of women. And psychology has yet to produce relevant studies on the subject of ego damage to the female which might bear comparison to the excellent work done on the effects of racism on the minds of blacks and colonials. The remarkably small amount of modern research devoted to the psychological and social effects of masculine supremacy on the female and on the culture in general attests to the widespread ignorance or unconcern of a conservative social science which takes patriarchy to be both the status quo and the state of nature.

What little literature the social sciences afford us in this context confirms the presence in women of the expected traits of minority status: group self-hatred and self-rejection, a contempt both for herself and for her fellows—the result of that continual, however subtle, reiteration of her

---

* Languages outside the Indo-European group are instructive. Japanese, for example, has one word for man (*otōko*), another for woman (*ōnna*) and a third for human being (*ningen*). It would be as unthinkable to use the first to cover the third as it would be to use the second.

inferiority which she eventually accepts as a fact (Hacker, 1951; Myrdal, 1944; Hughes, 1949; Watson, 1966; Dixon). . . .

The gnawing suspicion which plagues any minority member, that the myths propagated about his inferiority might after all be true often reaches remarkable proportions in the personal insecurities of women. Some find their subordinate position so hard to bear that they repress and deny its existence. But a large number will recognize and admit their circumstances when they are properly phrased. Of two studies which asked women if they would have preferred to be born male, one found that one fourth of the sample admitted as much, and in another sample, one half (Hacker, 1951; Bird, 1968). When one inquires of children, who have not yet developed as serviceable techniques of evasion, what their choice might be, if they had one, the answers of female children in a large majority of cases clearly favor birth into the elite group, whereas boys overwhelmingly reject the option of being girls.* The phenomenon of parents' prenatal preference for male issue is too common to require much elaboration. In the light of the imminent possibility of parents actually choosing the sex of their child, such a tendency is becoming the cause of some concern in scientific circles (Etzioni, 1968).

Comparisons such as Myrdal (1944), Hacker (1951), and Dixon draw between the ascribed attributes of blacks and women reveal that common opinion associates the same traits with both: inferior intelligence, an instinctual or sensual gratification, an emotional nature both primitive and childlike, an imagined prowess in or affinity for sexuality, a contentment with their own lot which is in accord with a proof of its appropriateness, a wily habit of deceit, and concealment of feeling. Both groups are forced to the same accommodational tactics: an ingratiating or supplicatory manner invented to please, a tendency to study those points at which the dominant group are subject to influence or corruption, and an assumed air of helplessness involving fraudulent appeals for direction through a show of ignorance. It is ironic how misogynist literature has for centuries concentrated on just these traits, directing its fiercest enmity at feminine guile and corruption, and particularly that element of it which is sexual, or, as such sources would have it, "wanton."

As with other marginal groups a certain handful of women are accorded higher status that they may perform a species of cultural policing over the rest. Hughes (1949) speaks of marginality as a case of status dilemma experienced by women, blacks or second-generation Americans who have "come up" in the world but are often refused the rewards of

---

* "One study of fourth graders showed ten times as many girls wishing they could have been boys, as boys who would have chosen to be girls," Watson (1966), p.477.

their efforts on the grounds of their origins. This is particularly the case with "new" or educated women. Such exceptions are generally obliged to make ritual, and often comic, statements of deference to justify their elevation. These characteristically take the form of pledges of "femininity," namely a delight in docility and a large appetite for masculine dominance. Politically, the most useful persons for such a role are entertainers and public sex objects. It is a common trait of minority status that a small percentage of the fortunate are permitted to entertain their rulers. (That they may entertain their fellow subjects in the process is less to the point.) Women entertain, please, gratify, satisfy and flatter men with their sexuality. In most minority groups athletes or intellectuals are allowed to emerge as "stars," identification with whom should content their less fortunate fellows. In the case of women both such eventualities are discouraged on the reasonable grounds that the most popular explanations of the female's inferior status ascribe it to her physcial weakness or intellectual inferiority. Logically, exhibitions of physical courage or agility are indecorous, just as any display of serious intelligence tends to be out of place.

Perhaps patriarchy's greatest psychological weapon is simply its universality and longevity. A referent scarcely exists with which it might be contrasted or by which it might be confuted. While the same might be said of class, patriarchy has a still more tenacious or powerful hold through its successful habit of passing itself off as nature. Religion is also universal in human society and slavery was once nearly so; advocates of each were fond of arguing in terms of fatality, or irrevocable human "instinct"— even "biological origins." When a system of power is thoroughly in command it has scarcely need to speak itself aloud; when its workings are exposed and questioned, it becomes not only subject to discussion, but even to change.

REFERENCES

Arendt, Hannah. "Speculations on Violence," *The New York Review of Books*, 12 (February 27, 1969).

Bird, Carolyn. *Born Female.* New York: McKay, 1968.

Dixon, Marlene. Unpublished manuscript, McGill University, no date.

Etzioni, Amitai. "Sex Control, Science, and Society," *Science* (September, 1968), pp. 1107-1112.

Fustel de Coulange, Denis Numa. *The Ancient City* translated by Willard Small, New York: Doubleday Anchor Reprint, 1873.

Goldberg, Philip. "Are Women Prejudiced Against Women?" *Transaction* (April, 1968).

Goode, William J. *The Family.* Englewood Cliffs, New Jersey: Prentice-Hall, 1964.

Hacker, Helen Mayer. "Women as a Minority Group," *Social Forces*, 30 (October, 1951).

Hughes, Everett C. "Social Change and Status Protest: An Essay on the Marginal Man," *Phylon,* **10** (1949).

Myrdal, Gunnar. *An American Dilemma.* New York: Harper, 1944.

Tiger, Lionel. *Men in Groups.* New York: Random House, 1968.

Watson, Godwin. "Psychological Aspects of Sex Roles," *Social Psychology, Issues and Insights.* Philadelphia: Lipincott, 1966.

Wirth, Louis. "Problems of Minority Groups," in Ralph Linton (Ed.), *The Science of Man in the World Crisis.* New York: Appleton, 1945.

PART
TWO
SOCIAL ENCOUNTERS

CHAPTER
FIVE
WHAT IS THE NATURE OF
FACE TO FACE INTERACTION?

THE ISSUE OF HUMAN INTERACTION

Most of our days are filled with a series of smoothly managed social interactions. We move from one situation to another, talking to complete strangers at one point and to friends and intimates at another. The substance of our interaction varies from complicated business transactions to delicate interpersonal ones. Typically, we are able to manage effortlessly this *tour de force* as we shift our demeanor and behavior quickly and automatically to make them appropriate for each different situation.

Of course, sometimes we stumble. We get embarrassed or embarrass others, we feel uncertain about the appropriateness of our responses, or we become irritated and the interaction reflects the strain. Nevertheless, we do pretty well most of the time—so well that we tend to take our success for granted. One need only witness the awkwardness of young children interacting with strangers to recognize that such a skill is acquired, frequently with difficulty, over many years.

Because we normally take this process so much for granted, this section is in the position of supplying answers where there are no apparent questions. But the questions are there, even if it takes some effort of the imagination to recognize that many aspects of face to face interaction require some explanation. What order or pattern is there in the myriad daily social interactions that fill our waking hours? How is this order maintained? What causes it to break down? How is it re-established? What insights can we glean about these interactions from various ways of describing and analyzing them?

THE MAJOR VIEWS

Impression Management

The art of impression management is apparently a fascinating one. Witness the popular success of Stephen Potter's books on *Gamesmanship, Lifemanship,* and *One-Upmanship* and, more recently, Eric Berne's *Games People Play.* The humor and appeal of these books comes from the shock of recognition. There we are, naked, our most subtle gambits exposed. We usually conceal them so well that we succeed even in fooling ourselves until what we do is finally pointed out. And, of course, the joke is even funnier when other people's favorite ploys are shown for what they are.

Take the Potter vignette below which seems only superficially dated, if at all, after more than 20 years. He describes a studied technique to which he gives the verb form "to Harvard." Its essence is to appear, even with examinations only two days off, totally indifferent to the impending crisis. One should be seen "walking calmly and naturally, out of doors, enjoying the scenery and taking deep breaths of air" (1955, pp. 24-25). Naturally, this presents greater difficulty during the winter examination period but Potter describes how one student named "FitzJames," managed the trick:

> J. FitzJames disappeared suddenly from College midway through January Reading Period just about the time his friends began studying in earnest. Then, on the day of his first exam, he would return, strolling into the examination-room five minutes late, dressed in a light Palm Beach suit and heavily tanned. Sitting down next to a friend, he would inspect his papers casually and begin to write slowly.
>
> Later, it becomes known that FitzJames has received an A in the course. What is the explanation? FitzJames has been holing himself up in a miserable rented room in Boston surrounded by the total reading assignment, including the optional books, and has been working like a dog for three weeks, stripped to the waist between two sun lamps (*Ibid*, p. 25).

Potter may have thought he was kidding in his excurses, but some social psychologists have quite seriously viewed impression management as the central organizing principle of social interaction. The crux of any interaction in this view is what the participants are saying about themselves through the things they do and say. Each person is faced with the problem of presenting himself to others. This presentation will emphasize some of his many attributes and will hide others. In a variety of ways— some of them unconscious—a person will attempt to control the impression of him that others develop. It follows that the analyst of social interaction should turn his attention to the techniques people employ in impression management and the conditions under which one or another technique is effective.

Goffman exemplifies this view in his discussion of *The Presentation of Self in Everyday Life* included in the readings for this chapter. He grants that an individual may have diverse goals in an interaction situation.

> He may wish [others] to think highly of him, or to think that he thinks highly of them, or to perceive how in fact he feels toward them, or to obtain no clear-cut impression; he may wish to ensure sufficient harmony so that the interaction can be sustained, or to defraud, get rid of, confuse, mislead, antagonize, or insult them. Regardless of the particular objective which the individual has in mind and of his motive for having this objective, it will be in his interest to control the conduct of the others, especially their responsive treatment of him. This control is achieved largely by influencing the definition of the situation which the others come to formulate, and he can influence this definition by expressing himself in such a way as to give them the kind of impression that will

lead them to act voluntarily in accordance with his own plan. Thus, when an individual appears in the presence of others, there will usually be some reason for him to mobilize his activity so that it will convey an impression to others which it is in his interests to convey.

Given this argument, it is not surprising that interactions in Goffman's world are surrounded by a heavy aura of calculation. This effect is increased by his use of theatrical analogy and imagery. Participants in social interaction are engaged in "performances" which can be evaluated (as an actor's can) in terms of technical excellence or sloppiness in producing intended effects.

Goffman seems to invite misinterpretation. His tone is flip and cynical and his examples frequently make us appear to be con men. Nevertheless, he is pointing out something much more profound than that we sometimes manipulate others by deliberately fostering a particular impression of ourselves. One-upmanship is a caricature, not a prototype, of impression management.

Goffman is sometimes misconstrued in the following manner. "He is talking about phonies," it is charged. "Some people are like that of course, but I see through them and detest them. I even admit that I'm sometimes a bit phony myself but I'm ashamed of it afterwards and I certainly don't concede that it is characteristic of my interaction with other people."

If Goffman is talking about phonies, then we are all phony. But this is not his message because he does not employ a distinction between a "real" self and a "presented" self. We know, for example, that a student acts differently when he interacts in class and when he interacts with his family. No doubt he feels more natural in the latter situation but this does not imply that he is presenting a false self in class.

Imagine a situation in which your mother insisted on accompanying you to class. This is, for reasons that are not immediately obvious, an extremely embarrassing situation for most students and the embarrassment really has nothing to do with phoniness. The self you present to your mother is different than the one you present to your fellow students and instructor. The situation is embarrassing because the two presented selves are somewhat contradictory and difficult to reconcile. This makes the impression management task an impossible one and the result is embarrassment at the mere anticipation of such an awkward interaction.

To argue that we present a different set of attributes to different people at different times is not to imply any falseness at all. Presumably, many of the attributes remain constant but their exhibition may require a different line. If one thinks of himself as unpretentious, his language may change when he talks to a janitor and to a professor. The same style of expression which is quite natural in one situation may seem stilted and pretentious in the other. He changes, not because he is phony, but because the demands of impression management in the two situations are different. Our understanding is retarded rather than enhanced by insisting that only one of these presented selves can be the real one.*

---

* The relationship of the self presented in social interaction to one's personal identity or self-concept is an interesting and important one. It is beyond our concern in this section on the nature of social interaction but is well-treated in Ralph Turner's "The Self-Conception in Social Interaction," (1968), in a discussion that is perfectly compatible with Goffman's view of social interaction.

We reject, then, the argument that Goffman is talking primarily about phoniness or the fostering of false impressions. Nor is there anything more than surface
justice to the charge that Goffman presents us as narrowly self-serving in all of our
interactions. Self-enhancement may be one operating motive, but it is not the only
impetus to impression management. Equally or, perhaps, even more important is the
desire to insure predictability and order, to signal other people what to expect from
you and what you expect from them. Impression management helps to avoid misunderstanding and embarrassment. All parties are presenting themselves in interaction situations as they develop a "working consensus" of what the situation is and who has
what claims that should be honored. It is not necessarily a real consensus based on the
honest expression of deep feelings (although it may be) but is simply a sufficient agreement for the purposes of the interaction.

Finally, there is a third impetus to impression management beyond maintaining
predictability and self-enhancement. Frequently we employ our efforts altruistically—to
help others to carry out their reciprocal task of self presentation and impression management. We overlook slips, ignore contradictions to claimed attributes, and employ
tact—not to defend ourselves but to protect others. And others are helping us to look
good at the same time, making our performance easier, giving us cues on how to improve it. This is hardly an image of combatants intent on putting each other down, and
it is just as much a part of Goffman's basic conception as is the more aggressive and
manipulative use of impression management. One shouldn't be distracted from the
more general conception by Goffman's examples of more competitive interaction.

Methods of Rule Recognition

A group of social psychologists who call themselves "ethnomethodologists" offer a
perspective on social interaction that is, like Goffman, indebted to the symbolic interaction tradition in many ways. But it also makes a sharp break with this tradition in
at least one fundamental respect. At the root, the difference is more ontological than
social psychological. For the symbolic interactionists (see Blumer, pp. 18-31), the
bridge between people rests on a bedrock of consensus; for the ethnomethodologists,
it rests on a thin crust.

Social interaction, in the world of the ethnomethodologists, has a vulnerable
foundation. We operate on an assumption of shared meanings and this works pretty
well if we don't raise too many questions about it. If, for the symbolic interactionists,
communication makes the world go 'round, one could almost say that lack of communication serves the same function for the ethnomethodologists. Garfinkel (1967,
p.30) argues, " 'Shared agreement' " refers to various methods for accomplishing the
member's recognition that something was said according to a rule . . . " and not to some
matching of meanings. We get along by tacitly accepting each other's explanations of
what we are doing and why. And woe be it to anyone who raises too many questions
about "what everyone knows."

The fundamental posture of the ethnomethodologists is to refuse to assume at
the outset that a social order exists "out there." To assume it before one starts examining social life is, in their view, to beg the question. The symbolic interactionists
make a matter of assumption something that properly should be the major object of

discovery. In adopting the ethnomethodologist posture, social interaction becomes fundamentally problematic. One cannot argue, as symbolic interactionists do, that we learn the shared meanings that exist in the community around us because the assumption of such shared meanings is not made.

The refusal to make this assumption leads them to a strategy involving the detailed study of how we actually manage our everyday life. Our remark at the beginning of this section that the management of our daily interactions is a *tour de force* is very much in the ethnomethodology spirit. It is fitting to pay "to the most commonplace activities of daily life, the attention usually accorded extraordinary events . . . to learn about them as phenomena in their own right" (Garfinkel, 1967, p.1).

For ethnomethodologists, we are all lay social psychologists, planning and explaining our behavior to ourselves and to others in the process of conducting our interaction. However, we are not very self-conscious about this process and we take our successful productions for granted. This fact makes life interesting for the ethnomethodologists, because it leaves them the task of discovering our management secrets even when we are unaware of them ourselves.

Normally, we prefer to illustrate a paradigm by reprinting something from one who uses it in his own work and thinking. There is an unfortunate problem in the case of ethnomethodologists—they write in a manner that tries the patience of the most tolerant reader. An impatient reader is not one who is likely to be receptive to a subtle and difficult point of view. We think we will serve the ethnomethodologists better in this case by reprinting a sympathetic account that one of us has written—but there is no guarantee, of course, that ethnomethodologists would accept this presentation of their views by someone who is not one of their own.

Social Exchange

We have encountered the social exchange paradigm earlier, (see Homans, pp. 14-17) focusing on its assumptions about the nature of man. Here we explore it as applied to our understanding of face-to-face interaction. We interact with others in this view because our net rewards from such interaction outweigh our costs and we terminate interactions when this condition no longer holds. Of course, this feeling of net profit must hold for the other party also—interactions will not continue unless they are reciprocally rewarding.

In his presentation of social exchange included in the readings in this chapter, Blau emphasizes that he is not offering a description of some special kind of interaction—of business relations, for example. That these arms-length relationships involve considerations of social exchange is, of course, quite obvious. The power of this paradigm is in its application to a very full range of social interaction, including many kinds that are not usually thought of in these terms. Some behavior is excluded—for example, behavior motivated by the "irrational push of emotional forces without being goal oriented," or by the threat of brute force—but every kind of goal oriented behavior is included. The paradigm applies to the pursuit of such non-economic values as duty, honor, justice, beauty, love, personal loyalty, or a political cause.

This orientation to social interaction is best illustrated by applying it to the type of situation that seems least likely to involve conventional notions of exchange. We have chosen Blau's *Excursus on Love* for this reason. It represents a limiting case for the paradigm. If it can be fruitfully applied to such intimate social interactions, then one should hardly need convincing of its usefulness in analysing relationships among acquaintances where the expectations of *quid pro quo* are so much more obvious and explicit.

CONTRASTING THE VIEWS OF HUMAN INTERACTION

These ways of looking at social interaction can be contrasted by examining their treatment of four issues:

1. What process is most central to social interaction?
2. How much consciousness do participants have of the process?
3. How important is their self-image in the process?
4. Is the participant's world the basic reality of social interaction?

Central Processes

McGrath (1964, p. 97) suggests that social interaction can be viewed as including three elementary processes: the flow of meanings, the flow of influence and control, and the flow of feeling or affect.

> Communication, the flow of meanings is the process by which the group assembles its task resources and performs its tasks. The flow of influence is the process by which the group reaches decisions, sets goals, directs its activities. The flow of affect, positive and negative, is the process by which . . . the group maintains (or fails to maintain) its solidarity.

The different views of social interaction give contrasting emphasis to different processes. The ethnomethodologists share the emphasis of the symbolic interaction tradition on the flow of meanings. Or to put it more precisely, they are concerned with the establishment and acceptance of meanings which may or may not be shared. The social exchange perspective emphasizes the flow of influence, although feelings may be among the most important commodities being traded. Still, influence is central and feelings are simply one resource for an individual to use in the pursuit of profitable outcomes.

Goffman is the most ambiguous on this dimension. His emphasis on the definition of the situation and establishing a working consensus would seem to suggest a central importance for the flow of meanings. In general, however, the flow of meanings is emphasized as a means of influence. Meaning is a strategic resource, not an objective of the interaction.

Consciousness of Participants

For the impression managers, the production of intended effects is at least semi-conscious and frequently fully conscious. Of course, it becomes second nature to us and we do not think about it anymore than we think about what we are doing when we are driving a car along a familar route in perfect weather. If things do not go smoothly, we think about it more. It is not an inaccessible process rooted in our unconscious, but rather is one subject to our conscious control when we choose to exercise it.

For the ethnomethodologists, the process is not at all a conscious one. This is true not because it is suppressed from consciousness, but because it is so basic that we have trouble understanding our own techniques of managing interaction. The process for the ethnomethodologists is more like walking than driving a car. We can do it perfectly well but we never think about how we do it. If we tried explaining how we manage to walk, we would find it extremely difficult to do so.

For the social exchangers, there is a quite high degree of consciousness. We know whether an interaction is rewarding or not and we learn how to get what we want or to withdraw from situations in which we can't get it. When we make mistakes, we realize it and draw some lessons from our errors for future associations. Again, the process is under our conscious control and is quite accessible.

Role of Self-Image in the Process

For Goffman, of course, the management of impressions is achieved largely by the kind of self one presents. The image we project is the primary instrument used to define the interaction situation. Self-image receives little or no special attention from the ethnomethodologists despite some kinship with Goffman's views in a number of other respects.

It is of importance for social exchange theorists. Blau argues,

> Social attraction is the . . . force that induces human beings to establish social associations on their own initiative and to expand the scope of their associations once they have formed . . . . A person who is attracted to others is interested in proving himself attractive to them for his ability to associate with them and reap the benefits expected from the association is contingent on their finding him an attractive associate and thus wanting to interact with him (1964, p. 20).

This implies the necessity of some self-consciousness about the self one is presenting, if only to appraise one's market value realistically in interaction with others. If one has highly valued attributes, then one expects a higher return in interacting with others. If they are not equally attractive, then the principles of fair exchange call for additional compensation in the form of gratitude, deference, power, or the like.

Basic Reality of the Participant's World

To what degree does a given view of social interaction accept the world perceived and experienced by those engaged in social interaction as the basic reality? To do so is to take the vantage point of the participant even granting that he may be only partly conscious of what he sees and feels. This is not an argument for solipsism—that is, the belief that nothing exists outside the perceiver. But the objective world ultimately must be described and interpreted by people. For some paradigms, the true or objective nature of the world is regarded as unavailable to scientist and layman alike. Or, it is felt to be an unnecessary and unfruitful starting point for analysis since reality is always mediated through the minds of men before they act upon it.

In contrast, one might emphasize the existence of an external reality that may or may not correspond to the participants' experience and perceptions. In this latter view, the participants are limited by factors which they do not control but which govern the interaction process in important respects. To be sure, their perceptions of the objective world may influence how they act, but the consequences of external reality impinge on them in important respects whether or not the participants know it.

Impression management emphasizes the participant's world as the central reality without ignoring system restraints. A bald, pot-bellied grandfather cannot decide to present himself as a debutante; nor can a carefree man be his jovial self at a funeral. But analysts such as Goffman are somewhat less concerned with the nature of the constraints than with the ingenuity used by a versatile actor in minimizing them.

The ethnomethodologists are even more radical in accepting the participant's reality as *the* reality. The social psychologist's or other observer's pretention to describe what is "really" going on is no more than merely another account to be studied. The participant's account and the scientist's "objective" account are precisely equal in their status as reality; the only difference is in their accounting rules and practices. The ethnomethodologist is always one step farther outside than the most outside observer, ready to study the latter's accounting process as an interesting datum.

External reality is given more importance by the social exchange theorists. Participants bring much from the external world into their social interaction. It sets the context. It endows participants with status, power, and, for that matter, with goals to pursue in face to face interaction. These givens from outside the interaction situation have important consequences for the nature of the transactions in which the participants engage.

These are the central issues we see running through the contrasting views of social interaction. They are summarized in Chart 5.

REFERENCES

Berne, Eric. *Games People Play.* New York: Grove Press, 1964.

Garfinkel, Harold. *Studies in Ethnomethodology.* Englewood Cliffs, New Jersey: Prentice-Hall, 1967.

McGrath, Joseph E. *Social Psychology: A Brief Introduction.* New York: Holt, Rinehart, & Winston, 1964.

Potter, Stephen. *Gamesmanship.* London: Rupert Hart-Davis, 1947.

Potter, Stephen. *Lifemanship.* London: Rupert Hart-Davis, 1950.

Potter, Stephen. *One-Upmanship.* New York: Holt, Rinehart, & Winston, 1955.

Turner, Ralph. "The Self-Conception in Social Interaction," in C. Gordon and K. J. Gergen (Eds.), *The Self in Social Interaction.* New York: John Wiley & Sons, Inc., 1968, pp. 93-106.

Chart 5 Underlying Issues on What Is the Nature of Social Interaction

	Impression Management (*e.g.*, Goffman)	Methods of Rule Recognition (*e.g.* Ethnomethodology)	Social Exchange (*e.g.*, Blau)
What process is most central to social interaction?	Flow of influence (Secondary: flow of meanings)	Flow of meanings	Flow of influence (Secondary: flow of feelings)
How much conscious-ness do participants have of the process?	Conscious or semi-conscious	Very little	Conscious or semi-conscious
How important is self-image in the process?	Very important	No special im-portance	Important
Is the partici-pant's world the basic reality of social interaction	To an import-ant extent	Yes	No

THE PRESENTATION OF SELF IN EVERYDAY LIFE

ERVING GOFFMAN

When an individual enters the presence of others, they commonly seek to acquire information about him or to bring into play information about him already possessed. They will be interested in his general socio-economic status, his conception of self, his attitude toward them, his competence, his trustworthiness, etc. Although some of this information seems to be sought almost as an end in itself, there are usually quite practical reasons for acquiring it. Information about the individual helps to define the situation, enabling others to know in advance what he will expect of them and what they may expect of him. Informed in these ways, the others will know how best to act in order to call forth a desired response from him.

For those present, many sources of information become accessible and many carriers (or "sign-vehicles") become available for conveying this information. If unacquainted with the individual, observers can glean clues from his conduct and appearance which allow them to apply their previous experience with individuals roughly similar to the one before them or, more important, to apply untested stereotypes to him. They can also assume from past experience that only individuals of a particular kind are likely to be found in a given social setting. They can rely on what the individual says about himself or on documentary evidence he provides as to who and what he is. If they know, or know of, the individual by virtue of experience prior to the interaction, they can rely on assumptions as to the persistence and generality of psychological traits as a means of predicting his present and future behavior.

However, during the period in which the individual is in the immediate presence of the others, few events may occur which directly provide the others with the conclusive information they will need if they are to direct wisely their own activity. Many crucial facts lie beyond the time and place of interaction or lie concealed within it. For example, the "true" or "real" attitudes, beliefs, and emotions of the individual can be ascertained only indirectly, through his avowals or through what appears to be invo!untary expressive behavior. Similarly, if the individual offers the others a product or service, they will often find that during the interaction there will be no time and place immediately available for eating the pudding that the proof can be found in. They will be forced to accept some events as conventional or natural signs of something not directly available to the senses. In Ichheiser's (1949) terms, the individual will have to act so that he intentionally or unintentionally *expresses* himself, and the others will in turn have to be *impressed* in some way by him.

The expressiveness of the individual (and therefore his capacity to give impressions) appears to involve two radically different kinds of sign activity: the expression that he *gives*, and the expression that he *gives off.* The first involves verbal symbols or their substitutes which he uses admittedly and solely to convey the information that he and the others are known to attach to these symbols. This is communication in the traditional and narrow sense. The second involves a wide range of action that others can treat as symptomatic of the actor, the expectation being that the action was performed for reasons other than the information conveyed in this way. As we shall have to see, this distinction has an only initial validity. The individual does of course intentionally convey misinformation by means of both of these types of communication, the first involving deceit, the second feigning.

Taking communication in both its narrow and broad sense, one finds that when the individual is in the immediate presence of others, his activity will have a promissory character. The others are likely to find that they must accept the individual on faith, offering him a just return while he is present before them, in exchange for something whose true value will not be established until after he has left their presence. (Of course, the others also live by inference in their dealings with the physical world, but it is only in the world of social interaction that the objects about which they make inferences will purposely facilitate and hinder this inferential process.) The security that they justifiably feel in making inferences about the individual will vary, of course, depending on such factors as the amount of information they already possess about him, but no amount of such past evidence can entirely obviate the necessity of acting on the basis of inferences. As William I. Thomas suggested:

> It is also highly important for us to realize that we do not as a matter of fact lead our lives, make our decisions, and reach our goals in everyday life either statistically or scientifically. We live by inference. I am, let us say, your guest. You do not know, you cannot determine scientifically, that I will not steal your money or your spoons. But inferentially I will not, and inferentially you have me as a guest (Volkart, 1951, p.5).

Let us now turn from the others to the point of view of the individual who presents himself before them. He may wish them to think highly of him, or to think that he thinks highly of them, or to perceive how in fact he feels toward them, or to obtain no clear-cut impression; he may wish to ensure sufficient harmony so that the interaction can be sustained, or to defraud, get rid of, confuse, mislead, antagonize, or insult them. Regardless of the particular objective which the individual has in mind and of his motive for having this objective, it will be in his interests to control the conduct of the others, especially their responsive treatment of him. This control is achieved largely by influencing the definition of the situation which the others come to formulate, and he can influence this definition by expressing himself in such a way as to give them the kind of impression that will lead them to act voluntarily in accordance with his own plan. Thus, when an individual appears in the presence of others, there will usually be some reason for him to mobilize his activity so that it will convey an impression to others which it is in his interests to convey. Since a girl's dormitory mates will glean evidence of her popularity from the calls she receives on the phone, we can suspect that some girls will arrange for calls to be made, and Willard Waller's finding can be anticipated:

> It has been reported by many observers that a girl who is called to the telephone in the dormitories will often allow herself to be called several times, in order to give all the other girls ample opportunity to hear her paged (1937, p. 730).

Of the two kinds of communication—expressions given and expressions given off—this report will be primarily concerned with the latter, with the more theatrical and contextual kind, the non-verbal, presumably unintentional kind, whether this communication be purposely engineered or not. As an example of what we must try to examine, I would like to cite at length a novelistic incident in which Preedy, a vacationing Englishman, makes his first appearance on the beach of his summer hotel in Spain:

> But in any case he took care to avoid catching anyone's eye. First of all, he had to make it clear to those potential companions of his holiday that they were of no concern to him whatsoever. He stared through them, round them, over them—eyes lost in space. The beach might have been empty. If by chance a ball was thrown his way, he looked surprised; then let a smile of amusement lighten his face (Kindly Preedy), looked round dazed to see that there *were* people on the beach, tossed it back with a smile to himself and not a smile *at* the people, and then resumed carelessly his nonchalant survey of space.
>
> But it was time to institute a little parade, the parade of the Ideal Preedy. By devious handlings he gave any who wanted to look a chance to see the title of his book—a Spanish translation of Homer, classic thus, but not daring, cosmopolitan too—and then gathered together his beach-wrap and bag into a neat sand-resistant pile (Methodical and Sensible Preedy), rose slowly to stretch at ease his huge frame (Big-Cat Preedy), and tossed aside his sandals (Carefree Preedy, after all).
>
> The marriage of Preedy and the sea! There were alternative rituals. The first involved the stroll that turns into a run and a dive straight into the water, thereafter smoothing into a strong splashless crawl towards the horizon. But of course not really to the horizon. Quite suddenly he would turn on to his back and thrash great white splashes with his legs, somehow thus showing that he could have swum further had he wanted to, and then would stand up a quarter out of water for all to see who it was.
>
> The alternative course was simpler, it avoided the cold-water shock and it avoided the risk of appearing too high-spirited. The point was to appear to be so used to the sea, the Mediterranean, and this particular beach, that one might as well be in the sea as out of it. It involved a slow stroll down and into the edge of the water—not even noticing his toes were wet, land and water all the same to *him!*—with his eyes up at the sky gravely surveying portents, invisible to others, of the weather (Local Fisherman Preedy) (Sansom, 1956, pp. 230-232).

The novelist means us to see that Preedy is improperly concerned with the extensive impressions he feels his sheer bodily action is giving off to those around him. We can malign Preedy further by assuming that he has acted merely in order to give a particular impression, that this is a false impression, and that the others present receive either no impression at all, or, worse still, the impression that Preedy is affectedly trying to cause them to receive this particular impression. But the important point for us here is that the kind of impression Preedy thinks he is making is in fact the kind of impression that others correctly and incorrectly glean from someone in their midst.

I have said that when an individual appears before others his actions will influence the definition of the situation which they come to have.

Sometimes the individual will act in a thoroughly calculating manner, expressing himself in a given way solely in order to give the kind of impression to others that is likely to evoke from them a specific response he is concerned to obtain. Sometimes the individual will be calculating in his activity but be relatively unaware that this is the case. Sometimes he will intentionally and consciously express himself in a particular way, but chiefly because the tradition of his group or social status require this kind of expression and not because of any particular response (other than vague acceptance or approval) that is likely to be evoked from those impressed by the expression. Sometimes the traditions of an individual's role will lead him to give a well-designed impression of a particular kind and yet he may be neither consciously nor unconsciously disposed to create such an impression. The others, in their turn, may be suitably impressed by the individual's efforts to convey something, or may misunderstand the situation and come to conclusions that are warranted neither by the individual's intent nor by the facts. In any case, in so far as the others act *as if* the individual had conveyed a particular impression, we may take a functional or pragmatic view and say that the individual has "effectively projected a given definition of the situation and "effectively" fostered the understanding that a given state of affairs obtains.

There is one aspect of the others' response that bears special comment here. Knowing that the individual is likely to present himself in a light that is favorable to him, the others may divide what they witness into two parts; a part that is relatively easy for the individual to manipulate at will, being chiefly his verbal assertions, and a part in regard to which he seems to have little concern or control, being chiefly derived from the expressions he gives off. The others may then use what are considered to be the ungovernable aspects of his expressive behavior as a check upon the validity of what is conveyed by the governable aspects. In this a fundamental asymmetry is demonstrated in the communication process, the individual presumably being aware of only one stream of his communication, the witnesses of this stream another. For example, in Shetland Isle one crofter's wife, in serving native dishes to a visitor from the mainland of Britain, would listen with a polite smile to his polite claims of liking what he was eating; at the same time she would take note of the rapidity with which the visitor lifted his fork or spoon to his mouth, the eagerness with which he passed food into his mouth, and the gusto expressed in chewing the food, using these signs as a check on the stated feelings of the eater. The same woman, in order to discover what one acquaintance (A) "actually" thought of another acquaintance (B), would wait until B was in the presence of A but engaged in conversation with still another person (C). She would then covertly examine the facial expressions of A as he regarded B in conversation with C. Not being in conversation with B, and not being directly observed by him, A would sometimes relax usual constraints and tactful deceptions, and freely express what he was "actually" feeling about B. This Shetlander, in short, would observe the unobserved observer.

Now given the fact that others are likely to check up on the more controllable aspects of behavior by means of the less controllable, one can expect that sometimes the individual will try to exploit this very possibility, guiding the impression he makes through behavior felt to be reliably informing. For example, in gaining admission to a tight social circle, the participant observer may not only wear an accepting look while listening to an informant, but may also be careful to wear the same look when observing the informant talking to others; observers of the observer will then not as easily discover where he actually stands. A specific illustration may be cited from Shetland Isle. When a neighbor dropped in to have a cup of tea, he would ordinarily wear at least a hint of an expectant warm smile as he passed through the door into the cottage. Since lack of physical obstructions outside the cottage and lack of light within it usually made it possible to observe the visitor unobserved as he approached the house, islanders sometimes took pleasure in watching the visitor drop whatever expression he was manifesting and replace it with a sociable one just before reaching the door. However, some visitors, in appreciating that this examination was occurring, would blindly adopt a social face a long distance from the house, thus ensuring the projection of a constant image.

This kind of control upon the part of the individual reinstates the symmetry of the communication process, and sets the stage for a kind of information game—a potentially infinite cycle of concealment, discovery, false revelation, and rediscovery. It should be added that since the others are likely to be relatively unsuspicious of the presumably unguided aspect of the individual's conduct, he can gain much by controlling it. The others of course may sense that the individual is manipulating the presumably spontaneous aspects of his behavior, and seek in this very act of manipulation some shading of conduct that the individual has not managed to control. This again provides a check upon the individual's behavior, this time his presumably uncalculated behavior, thus re-establishing the asymmetry of the communication process. Here I would like only to add the suggestion that the arts of piercing an individual's effort at calculated unintentionality seem better developed than our capacity to manipulate our own behavior, so that regardless of how many steps have occurred in the information game, the witness is likely to have the advantage over the actor, and the initial asymmetry of the communication process is likely to be retained.

When we allow that the individual projects a definition of the situation when he appears before others, we must also see that the others, however passive their role may seem to be, will themselves effectively project a definition of the situation by virtue of their response to the individual and by virtue of any lines of action they initiate to him. Ordinarily the definitions of the situation projected by the several different participants are sufficiently attuned to one another so that open contradiction will not occur. I do not mean that there will be the kind of consensus that arises when each individual present candidly expresses what he really feels and honestly agrees with the expressed feelings of the others present. This kind of harmony is an optimistic ideal and in any case not necessary for the smooth working of society. Rather, each participant is expected to suppress his immediate heartfelt feelings, conveying a view of the situation which he feels the others will be able to find at least temporarily acceptable. The maintenance of this surface of agreement, this veneer of consensus, is facilitated by each participant concealing his own wants behind statements which assert values to which everyone present feels obliged to give lip service. Further, there is usually a kind of division of definitional labor. Each participant is allowed to establish the tentative official ruling regarding matters which are vital to him but not immediately important to others, e.g., the rationalizations and justifications by which he accounts for his past activity. In exchange for this courtesy he remains silent or non-committal on matters important to others but not immediately important to him. We have then a kind of interactional *modus vivendi.* Together the participants contribute to a single over-all definition of the situation which involves not so much a real agreement as to what exists but rather a real agreement as to whose claims concerning what issues will be temporarily honored. Real agreement will also exist concerning the desirability of avoiding an open conflict of definitions of the situation. I will refer to this level of agreement as a "working consensus." It is to be understood that the working consensus established in one interaction setting will be quite different in content from the working consensus established in a different type of setting. Thus, between two friends at lunch, a reciprocal show of affection, respect, and concern for the other is maintained. In service occupations, on the other hand, the specialist often maintains an image of disinterested involvement in the problem of the client, while the client responds with a show of respect for the competence and integrity of the specialist. Regardless of such differences in content, however, the general form of these working arrangements is the same.

In noting the tendency for a participant to accept the definitional claims made by the others present, we can appreciate the crucial importance of the information that the individual *initially* possesses or acquires concerning his fellow participants, for it is on the basis of this initial information that the individual starts to define the situation and starts to build up lines of responsive action. The individual's initial projection commits him to what he is proposing to be and requires him to drop all pretenses of being other things. As the interaction among the participants progresses, additions and modifications in this initial informational state will of course occur, but it is essential that these later developments be related without contradiction to, and even built up from, the initial positions taken by the several participants. It would seem that an individual can more easily make a choice as to what line of treatment to demand from and extend to the others present at the beginning of an encounter than he can alter the line of treatment that is being pursued once the interaction is underway.

In everyday life, of course, there is a clear understanding that first impressions are important. Thus, the work adjustment of those in service occupations will often hinge upon a capacity to seize and hold the initiative in the service relation, a capacity that will require subtle aggressiveness on the part of the server when he is of lower socio-economic status than his client. W. F. Whyte suggests the waitress as an example:

> The first point that stands out is that the waitress who bears up under pressure does not simply respond to her customers. She acts with some skill to control their behavior. The first question to ask when we look at the customer relationship is, "Does the waitress get the jump on the customer, or does the customer get the jump on the waitress?" The skilled waitress realizes the crucial nature of this question. . . .
>
> The skilled waitress tackles the customer with confidence and without hesitation. For example, she may find that a new customer has seated himself before she could clear off the dirty dishes and change the cloth. He is now leaning on the table studying the menu. She greets him, says, "May I change the cover, please?" and, without waiting for an answer, takes his menu away from him so that he moves back from the table, and she goes about her work. The relationship is handled politely but firmly, and there is never any question as to who is in charge (1946, pp. 132-33).

When the interaction that is initiated by "first impressions" is itself merely the initial interaction in an extended series of interactions involving the same participants, we speak of "getting off on the right foot" and feel that it is crucial that we do so. Thus, one learns that some teachers take the following view:

> You can't ever let them get the upper hand on you or you're through. So I start out tough. The first day I get a new class in, I let them know who's boss . . . You've got to start off tough, then you can ease up as you go along. If you start out easy-going, when you try to get tough, they'll just look at you and laugh (Becker, 1952, p. 459).

Similarly, attendants in mental institutions may feel that if the new patient is sharply put in his place the first day on the ward and made to see who is boss, much future difficulty will be prevented.

Given the fact that the individual effectively projects a definition of the situation when he enters the presence of others, we can assume that events may occur within the interaction which contradict, discredit, or otherwise throw doubt upon this projection. When these disruptive events occur, the interaction itself may come to a confused and embarrassed half. Some of the assumptions upon which the responses of the participants had been predicted become untenable, and the participants find themselves lodged in an interaction for which the situation has been wrongly defined and is now no longer defined. At such moments the individual whose presentation has been discredited may feel ashamed while the others present may feel hostile, and all the participants may come to feel ill at ease, nonplussed, out of countenance, embarrassed, experiencing the kind of anomy that is generated when the minute social system of face-to-face interaction breaks down.

In stressing the fact that the initial definition of the situation projected by an individual tends to provide a plan for the co-operative activity that follows—in stressing this action point of view—we must not overlook the crucial fact that any projected definition of the situation also has a distinctive moral character. It is this moral character of projections that will chiefly concern us in this report. Society is organized on the principle that any individual who possesses certain social characteristics has a moral right to expect that others will value and treat him in a correspondingly appropriate way. Connected with this principle is a second, namely that an individual who implicitly or explicitly signifies that he has certain social characteristics ought to have this claim honoured by others and ought in fact to be what he claims he is. In consequence, when an individual projects a definition of the situation and thereby makes an implicit or explicit claim to be a person of a particular kind, he automatically exerts a moral demand upon the others, obliging them to value and treat him in the manner that persons of his kind have a right to expect. He also implicitly forgoes all claims to be things he does not appear to be and hence forgoes the treatment that would be appropriate for such individuals. The others find, then, that the individual has informed them as to what is and as to what they *ought* to see as the "is."

One cannot judge the importance of definitional disruptions by the frequency with which they occur, for apparently they would occur more frequently were not constant precautions taken. We find that preventive practices are constantly employed to avoid these embarrassments and that corrective practices are constantly employed to compensate for discrediting occurrences that have not been successfully avoided. When the individual employs these strategies and tactics to protect his own projections, we may refer to them as "defensive practices"; when a participant employs them to save the definition of the situation projected by another, we speak of "protective practices" or "tact." Together, defensive and protective practices comprise the techniques employed to safeguard the impression fostered by an individual during his presence before others. It should be added that while we may be ready to see that no fostered impression would survive if defensive practices were not employed, we are less ready perhaps to see that few impressions could survive if those who received the impression did not exert tact in their reception of it.

In addition to the fact that precautions are taken to prevent disruption of projected definitions, we may also note that an intense interest in these disruptions comes to play a significant role in the social life of the group. Practical jokes and social games are played in which embarrassments which are to be taken unseriously are purposely engineered. Fantasies are created in which devastating exposures occur. Anecdotes from the past—real, embroidered or fictitious—are told and retold, detailing disruptions which occurred, almost occurred, or occurred and were admirably resolved. There seems to be no grouping which does not have a ready supply of these games, reveries, and cautionary tales, to be used as a source of humor, a catharsis for anxieties, and a sanction for inducing individuals to be modest in their claims and reasonable in their projected expectations. The individual may tell himself through dreams of getting into impossible positions. Families tell of the time a guest got his dates mixed and arrived when neither the house nor anyone in it was ready for him. Journalists tell of times when an all-too-meaningful misprint occurred, and the paper's assumption of objectivity or decorum was humorously discredited. Public servants tell of times a client ridiculously misunderstood form instructions, giving answers which implied an unanticipated and bizarre definition of the situation. Seamen, whose home away from home is rigorously he-man, tell stories of coming back home and inadvertently asking mother to "pass the fucking butter." Diplomats tell of the time a near-sighted queen asked a republican ambassador about the health of his king.

To summarize, then, I assume that when an individual appears before others he will have many motives for trying to control the impression they receive of the situation. This report is concerned with some of the common techniques that persons employ to sustain such impressions and with some of the common contingencies associated with the employment of these techniques. The specific content of any activity presented by the individual participant, or the role it plays in the interdependent activities of an on-going social system, will not be at issue; I shall be concerned only with the participant's dramaturgical problems of presenting the activity before others. The issues dealt with by stage-craft and stage management are sometimes trivial but they are quite general; they seem to occur everywhere in social life, providing a clear-cut dimension for formal sociological analysis. . . .

Underlying all social interaction there seems to be a fundamental dialectic. When one individual enters the presence of others, he will want to discover the facts of the situation. Were he to possess this information, he could know, and make allowances for, what will come to happen and he could give the others present as much of their due as is consistent with his enlightened self-interest. To uncover fully the factual nature of the situation, it would be necessary for the individual to know all the relevant social data about the others. It would also be necessary for the individual to know the actual outcome or end product of the activity of the others during the interaction, as well as their innermost feelings concerning him. Full information of this order is rarely available; in its absence, the individual tends to employ substitutes—cues, tests, hints, expressive gestures, status symbols, etc.—as predictive devices. In short, since the reality that the individual is concerned with is unperceivable at the moment, appearances must be relied upon in its stead. And, paradoxically, the more the individual is concerned with the reality that is not available to perception, the more must he concentrate his attention on appearances.

The individual tends to treat the others present on the basis of the impression they give now about the past and the future. It is here that communicative acts are translated into moral ones. The impressions that the others give tend to be treated as claims and promises they have implicitly made, and claims and promises tend to have a moral character. In his mind the individual says: "I am using these impressions of you as a way of checking up on you and your activity, and you ought not to lead me astray." The peculiar thing about this is that the individual tends to take this stand even though he expects the others to be unconscious of many of their expressive behaviors and even though he may expect to exploit the others on the basis of the information he gleans about them. Since the sources of impression used by the observing individual involve a multitude of standards pertaining to politeness and decorum, pertaining both to social intercourse and task-performance, we can appreciate afresh how daily life is enmeshed in moral lines of discrimination.

Let us shift now to the point of view of the others. If they are to be gentlemanly, and play the individual's game, they will give little conscious heed to the fact that impressions are being formed about them but rather act without guile or contrivance, enabling the individual to receive valid impressions about them and their efforts. And if they happen to give thought to the fact that they are being observed, they will not allow this to influence them unduly, content in the belief that the individual will obtain a correct impression and give them their due because of it. Should they be concerned with influencing the treatment that the individual gives

them, and this is properly to be expected, then a gentlemanly means will
be available to them. They need only guide their action in the present so
that its future consequences will be the kind that would lead a just individual to treat them now in a way they want to be treated; once this is
done, they have only to rely on the perceptiveness and justness of the
individual who observes them.

Sometimes those who are observed do, of course, employ these proper means of influencing the way in which the observer treats them. But
there is another way, a shorter and more efficient way, in which the observed can influence the observer. Instead of allowing an impression of their
activity to arise as an incidental by-product of their activity, they can re-
orient their frame of reference and devote their efforts to the creation of
desired impressions. Instead of attempting to achieve certain ends by acceptable means, they can attempt to achieve the impression that they are
achieving certain ends by acceptable means. It is always possible to manipulate the impression the observer uses as a substitute for reality because
a sign for the presence of a thing, not being that thing, can be employed in
the absence of it. The observer's need to rely on representations of things
itself creates the possibility of misrepresentation.

There are many sets of persons who feel they could not stay in business, whatever their business, if they limited themselves to the gentlemanly means of influencing the individual who observes them. At some
point or other in the round of their activity they feel it is necessary to
band together and directly manipulate the impression that they give. The
observed become a performing team and the observers become the audience.
Actions which appear to be done on objects become gestures addressed to
the audience. The round of activity becomes dramatized.

We come now to the basic dialectic. In their capacity as performers,
individuals will be concerned with maintaining the impression that they are
living up the many standards by which they and their products are judged.
Because these standards are so numerous and so pervasive, the individuals who are performers dwell more than we might think in a moral
world. But, *qua* performers, individuals are concerned not with the moral
issue of realizing these standards, but with the amoral issue of engineering
a convincing impression that these standards are being realized. Our activity, then, is largely concerned with moral matters, but as performers we
do not have a moral concern with them. As performers, we are merchants
of morality. Our day is given over to intimate contact with the goods we
display and our minds are filled with intimate understandings of them; but
it may well be that the more attention we give to these goods, then the
more distant we feel from them and from those who are believing enough
to buy them. To use a different imagery, the very obligation and profit-
ability of appearing always in a steady moral light, of being a socialized

character, forces one to be the sort of person who is practiced in the ways of the stage . . . .

And now a final comment. In developing the conceptual framework employed in this report, some language of the stage was used. I spoke of performers and audiences; of routines and parts; of performances coming off or falling flat; of cues, stage settings and backstage; of dramaturgical needs, dramaturgical skills, and dramaturgical strategies. Now it should be admitted that this attempt to press a mere analogy so far was in part a rhetoric and a maneuver.

The claim that all the world's a stage is sufficiently commonplace for readers to be familiar with its limitations and tolerant of its presentation, knowing that at any time they will easily be able to demonstrate to themselves that it is not to be taken too seriously. An action staged in a theater is a relatively contrived illusion and an admitted one; unlike ordinary life, nothing real or actual can happen to the performed characters—although at another level of course something real and actual can happen to the reputation of performers *qua* professionals whose everyday job is to put on theatrical performances.

And so here the language and mask of the stage will be dropped. Scaffolds, after all, are to build other things with, and should be erected with an eye to taking them down. This report is not concerned with aspects of theater that creep into everyday life. It is concerned with the structure of social encounters—the structure of those entities in social life that come into being whenever persons enter one another's immediate physical presence. The key factor in this structure is the maintenance of a single definition of the situation, this definition having to be expressed, and this expression sustained in the face of a multitude of potential disruptions.

A character staged in a theater is not in some ways real, nor does it have the same kind of real consequences as does the thoroughly contrived character performed by a confidence man; but the *successful* staging of either of these types of false figures involves use of *real* techniques—the same techniques by which everyday persons sustain their real social situations. Those who conduct face to face interaction on a theater's stage must meet the key requirement of real situations; they must expressively sustain a definition of the situation: but this they do in circumstances that have facilitated their developing an apt terminology for the interactional tasks that all of us share.

REFERENCES

Becker, Howard S. "Social Class Variations in the Teacher-Pupil Relationship," *Journal of Educational Sociology,* 25 (April, 1952), pp. 451-465.

Ichheiser, Gustav. "Misunderstanding in Human Relations," Supplement to *The American Journal of Sociology,* 55 (September, 1949), pp. 6-7.

Sansom, William. *A Contest of Ladies.* London: Hogarth, 1956.

Volkart, E. H. (Ed.), *Social Behavior and Personality: Contributions of W. I. Thomas to Theory and Social Research.* New York: Social Science Research Council, 1951.

Waller, Willard. "The Rating and Dating Complex," *American Sociological Review,* 2 (1937), pp. 727-734.

Whyte, William F. "When Workers and Customers Meet," in William F. Whyte (Ed.), *Industry and Society.* New York: McGraw-Hill, 1946.

ETHNOMETHODOLOGY

WILLIAM A. GAMSON

Because so many of the rules and understandings that govern social interaction are taken for granted, special techniques are required to make them visible to the investigator and participants. The major technique is disruption. As Garfinkel (1967, p. 37) puts it, "Procedurally it is my preference to start with familiar scenes and ask what can be done to make trouble." Alan Funt, with his Candid Camera idea, stumbled onto the same principle. Lacking awareness of what they were doing, Funt and his colleagues frittered away their opportunities in titillation and amusement instead of exploiting the potential for insight into the subtleties of social interaction.

An ethnomethodologist is an Alan Funt with a serious interest in learning something from people's attempts to restore interaction to its normal state following a puzzling disruption. Witness, for example, what happens when an ethnomethodology student carries out an assignment in which she has been asked to seek clarification of the meanings of commonplace remarks (from Garfinkel, 1967, p. 43):

"On Friday night, my husband and I were watching television. My husband remarked that he was tired."

Wife:	How are you tired? Physically, mentally, or just bored?
Husband:	I don't know. I guess physically, mainly.
Wife:	You mean that your muscles ache or your bones?
Husband:	I guess so. Don't be so technical.
	(After more watching.)
Husband:	All these old movies have the same kind of old iron bedstead in them.

From previously unpublished article.

Wife:	What do you mean? Do you mean all old movies, or some of them, or just the ones you have seen?
Husband:	What's the matter with you? You know what I mean.
Wife:	I wish you would be more specific.
Husband:	You know what I mean! Drop dead!

The husband is irritated with his wife because she is suddenly and inexplicably refusing to participate in the assumed consensus on which their interaction depends. As with all our communication, the husband says a tiny fraction of what he intends to communicate and assumes that his spouse will understand the balance. This works quite well most of the time because the assumption goes unchallenged even though we know that a child, for example, may only be understanding a small fraction. It is very difficult, if not impossible, to continue interacting with someone like this wife who will not accept the assumed consensus. In this case, reaction is indignation because the husband correctly interprets the wife's refusal as deliberate. If he thought it was not deliberate, he might have called a psychiatrist instead of getting angry.

I am not above such mischief by proxy in my own social psychology classes. I asked the students to create an interaction situation in which their behavior was "unaccountable." In other words, they were to create a situation in which the other party is forced to recognize that the assumed consensus is lacking. The example I suggested to students was that they enter a store, choose an inexpensive object, and offer *more* than the normal asking price. It is important that they offer more rather than less because the latter behavior is definable without much difficulty as chiseling. But offering more is unaccountable and should be followed by alarm and strenuous efforts to render the behavior understandable.

Many students had difficulty with this assignment, but they also were quite inventive. One girl went into a local variety store where jelly beans, normally priced for 49¢ a pound, were on sale for 35¢. She engaged the sales girl in conversation about the various candies and finally asked for one-half pound of jelly beans. The sales girl wrapped them and asked for 18¢.

Student:	Oh, only 18¢ for all those jelly beans. There are so many of them. I think I will pay you 25 ¢ for them.
Salesgirl:	Yes, there are a lot and they are only 18¢ today on sale.
Student:	I know they are on sale but I want to pay 25¢ for them. They are worth at least that to me. I love jelly beans.
Salesgirl:	No, you see they are selling for 35¢ a pound today and you ordered one-half pound. Half of 35¢ is 18¢.

Student: (voice rising) I am perfectly capable of dividing 35¢ in half. That has nothing to do with it. It's just that I feel that they are worth more and I want to pay more for them.

Salesgirl: (suddenly becoming quite animated) What's the matter with you? Are you crazy or something? Everything in this store is overpriced. Those jelly beans cost the store about 3¢ . Now do you want them or should I put them back?

              (At this point, the student became quite embarrassed, paid the 18¢, and hurriedly left).

Another student took a two week book from the library and tried to check it out for exactly 10 days. The following dialogue ensued:

Librarian: It's a two week book, you can have it until the 22nd.

Student: But I am going out of town on the 18th and I only want it checked out until then.

Librarian: Well, you can return it early.

Student: No, I'm sorry I can't. I only return books when they are due. I feel I am entitled to them until then.

Librarian: (bewildered) It is a two week book.

Student: You said that before.

Librarian: Do you want to sign the book out?

Student: Yes, but only for 10 days.

              (At this point the librarian became upset and left to get a more senior staff member who proceeded to give the student a great deal of irrelevant information about the library. Several people began to gather around and the student grew embarrassed and signed the book out for two weeks.)

Several things are interesting about the above examples. It is not surprising that the puzzled victims take measures to normalize the interaction. They tend to assume that the student is confused or lacks information. Less obviously, they become acutely uncomfortable when this initial attempt to account for what is happening fails. The students *also* become extremely uncomfortable even though they know what is going on. In a great many cases, the students found themselves unconsciously rendering their behavior more accountable. Thus, one student above invented a passion for jelly beans and another an out-of-town trip. It is not just the target person but all participants in the interaction who experience the pressure to remove the threat to social interaction that this mischief has created.

The reaction to someone who refuses to accept "What Everyone Knows" with all its attendant vagueness is not simply the reaction of one who has been inconvenienced. It is mildly annoying to be asked to define one's terms in an argument when one is using language with some self consciousness and precision. It is downright threatening to be asked do so when one is using language with typical imprecision, because one's terms may hide a good deal of confusion and ignorance.

It is sometimes easier, for example, to teach graduate students than introductory students because graduate students allow one to get by with certain terms. They are too sophisticated to question such "simple" words as "role" or "institution." The failure to accept such socially warranted terms would place them outside of the guild. They learn the rules for using such language and don't ask embarrassing and threatening questions that might uncover the thinness of the underlying professional consensus. Introductory students may be subject to many similar pressures, but they are not expected to share the same corpus of concepts. Consequently, they have the same dangerous quality as the child who is too young to know that certain family affairs are not fit topics for discussion with outsiders. Part of socialization is learning to keep one's mouth shut about such embarrassing matters as the emperor's new clothes.

Some of the ethnomethodologist's interaction gambits are designed to demonstrate the extent to which we contruct our own unspoken, "shared" meanings even when none exist. We operate *as if* we share an underlying consensus regardless of whether we actually do and we interact *in ways that avoid discovering whether this assumed consensus is false.* Garfinkel recruited ten undergraduates "by telling them that research was being done in the Department of Psychiatry to explore alternative means to psychotherapy 'as a way of giving persons advice about their personal problems' " (1967, p. 79). Each subject was seen individually by a person represented as a student counselor in training. The subject was asked first to discuss the background of some problem that concerned him and then to address a series of questions to the counselor that could be answered by a "yes" or "no." The counselor heard the questions and gave the answers from an adjoining room by means of an intercom system. The subject was also asked to record his reactions between answers, but these reactions could not be heard by the counselor. Excerpts from an illustrative protocol follow (Garfinkel, 1967, pp. 80-85):

| Subject: | O.K., this is the situation. . . . I happen to be of the Jewish faith and I have been dating a Gentile girl now for about two months. My Dad is not directly opposed to this situation but I feel . . . that he is not exactly pleased with it. . . . He has never said don't date her, but |

at the same time he will come up with digs and sayings that make me feel very ill at ease about dating the girl. . . . Do you feel that I should continue dating this girl?

Experimenter: My answer is no.

Subject: No. Well, that is kind of interesting I. . . feel that there is really no great animosity between Dad and I but, well, perhaps . . . [the counselor] feels that greater dislike will grow out of this. . . . Maybe it is easier for an outsider to see certain things that I am blind to at this moment. . . . [turns on intercom] Do you feel that I should have a further discussion with Dad about this situation?

Experimenter: My answer is yes.

Subject: Well I feel that is reasonable. . . I guess if it is worthwhile to me, if I really want to continue to date her that I will go on and have this discussion with Dad. I really don't know what to say because I mean I am dating her. . . . [turns on intercom] If after having my conversation with Dad and he says to continue dating her, but at the same time he gives me an impression that he really does not want me to date her. . . should I still date the girl?

Experimenter: My answer is yes.

Subject: Well I am actually surprised at the answer. I expected a "no" answer on that. Perhaps this is because you are not quite aware of my Dad and his reactions. . . He seems to be the type of person that is sensitive and therefore he is very careful in the way that he will handle things. . . . Do you feel that I should tell the girl that I am dating the problems that I am having at home over her religion?

Experimenter: My answer is no.

Subject: Well once again I am surprised. . . . I personally feel that it is only right to tell her for if she is perhaps thinking more serious than I am, . . . it might be best for us to understand the full situation. . . . If I was to fall in love with this girl and want to make plans for marriage do you feel that it is fair that I should ask her to change her religion over to my belief?

Experimenter: My answer is no.

Subject: Well, no. Well, this has me stymied. No. Well, I honestly feel that I have been brought up in a certain way and I believe that she has too, and I feel pretty strong about the way that I believe. . . . I think that perhaps I would be tempted to ask her to change. . . . Do you feel that it would be a better situation if we were to get married. . .

that we bring our children up in a neutral religion other
than the two that we believe in?

Experimenter: My answer is yes.

Subject: Well, perhaps this would be a solution. If we culd find a
religion that would incorporate our two beliefs to a certain extent. . . . If we were to get married would it be
best for us to live in a new community where we will not
be in contact with our parents if we were getting a lot of
family pressure over religious differences?

Experimenter: My answer is no.

Subject: Well, I kinda tend to agree with this answer. I feel that
you wouldn't be accomplishing too much by running
away from the issue. . . . Do you feel that our children, if
there were any, would have any religious problems themselves because of us the parents and our difficulties?

Experimenter: My answer is no.

Subject: Well I really don't know if I agree with that or not. . . .
But I suppose that only time will tell if such problems
would come about.

After the interview was over, the subject was asked to give his reactions. He com-
mented in part as follows: "Well, the conversation seemed to be one-sided because
I was doing it all. . . I feel that it was extremely difficult for [the counselor] to
answer these questions fully without having a complete understanding of the personalities of the different people involved. . . . The answers I received I must say
that the majority of them were answered perhaps in the same way that I would
answer them to myself knowing the differences in types of people. One or two of
them did come as a surprise to me and I felt that. . . is for the reason that he is
not aware of the personalities involved and how they are reacting or would react
to a certain situation. . . . I felt that his answers as a whole were helpful and that
he was looking out for the benefit to the situation for the most part. . . I heard
what I wanted to hear in most of the situation presented. . . Perhaps I did not
hear what I really wanted to hear but perhaps from an objective standpoint they
were the best answer because someone involved in a situation is blinded to a certain degree and cannot take this objective viewpoint. . . . I honestly believe that
the answers that he gave me, that he was completely aware of the situation at
hand. . . . I guess that should be qualified. . . . When I said should I talk to Dad for
instance he was not positive what I was going to talk to Dad about. . . He knew the
general topic but he is now aware how close I am to Dad or how involved the conversation might get. . . . Well, this once again is bringing in personalities which he
is not aware of. The conversation and the answers given I believe, had a lot of meaning to me. I mean it was perhaps what I would have expected from someone who
fully understood the situation. And I feel that it had a lot of sense to me and made
a lot of sense."

It turns out, as the reader may have guessed, that the subject in the above demonstration was receiving a pre-programmed, random sequence of "yes" and "no" answers that was in no way contingent on his questions. The subject assumes, of course, that he is in a mutually contingent inter-action. The interesting point is the relative ease with which he is able to maintain this assumption *regardless* of the answers. This does not take place through some blind malleability or other-directedness on the part of the subject. He has his own opinions and is quite capable of disagreeing with the advice, but he finds it reasonable in its own terms. The counselor lacks information or perhaps is more objective, but nothing occurs to up-set the assumption of an underlying consensus. This consensus, however, is entirely of the subject's construction.

No real consensus need exist, in this perspective, for people to inter-act smoothly so long as all parties assume consensus and do not act in ways that challenge it. This is characteristic of social interaction, and it is only when ethnomethodologists poke their fingers through the thin crust and we see the strenuous efforts to restore the assumed consᴗ ꜱus, that we can recognize the considerable management task involved.

REFERENCES

Garfinkel, Harold. *Studies in Ethnomethodology.* Englewood Cliffs, New Jersey: Prentice-Hall, 1967.

EXCURSUS ON LOVE

PETER M. BLAU

Not all human behavior is guided by considerations of exchange, though much of it is, more than we usually think. Two conditions must be met for behavior to lead to social exchange. It must be oriented toward ends that can only be achieved through interaction with other per-sons, and it must seek to adapt means to further the achievement of these ends. The purview of this study is restricted to such behavior. Excluded from consideration, therefore, is behavior resulting from the irrational push of emotional forces without being goal oriented, for instance, a girl's irrational conduct on dates that is motivated by her unconscious con-flicts with her father. But a wide range of behavior is pertinent for a study of exchange, including goal-oriented conduct in love relations, and including particularly "wertrational" as well as "zweckrational" conduct, in Weber's terms. The former does not entail what is conventionally defined as rational action but, as Weber put it, "the action of persons who, regardless of possible cost to themselves, act to put into practice their convictions of what seems to be required by duty, honour, the pursuit of beauty, a religious call, personal loyalty, or the importance of some 'cause' no matter in what it consists" (1947, p. 116). In brief, social exchange may reflect any behavior oriented to socially mediated goals.

The fact that given actions of people have expressive significance and are not calculated to obtain specific advantages does not necessarily mean that their conduct is irrational but may mean that it is wertrational rather than zweckrational, that is, oriented to the pursuit of ultimate values rather than to the pursuit of immediate rewards. This is not simply a hair-splitting distinction. Expressive social conduct oriented to ideals and absolute values is of great importance in social life, but our understanding of it is not at all advanced by the assumption that it merely reflects idiosyncratic and irrational individual behavior. Radical political opposition, for example, cannot be explained without taking into account the expressive significance it has for supporters, and failure to do so is a serious shortcoming of formalistically rational models of politics. Such political opposition that expresses the resentment of the oppressed can, however, be derived from a conception of exchange without resort to the assumption that the push of irrational impulses or psychopathic personality traits drive individuals to become radicals. Similarly, in intimate relations of intrinsic significance, individuals often do favors for one another not in the expectation of receiving explicit repayments but to express their commitment to the interpersonal relation and sustain it by encouraging an increasing commitment on the part of the other. There is still an element of exchange in doing favors to strengthen another's commitment that one desires, though only in the broadest sense of the term.

The broad application of the notion of exchange raises the question of tautology. There is a great temptation to explore the fruitfulness of the concept by extending its scope and applying it to all social conduct. But the assumption of exchange theory that social interaction is governed by the concern of both (or all) partners with rewards dispensed by the other (or others) becomes tautological if any and all behavior in interpersonal relations is conceptualized as an exchange, even conduct toward others that is not at all oriented in terms of expected returns from them. To be sure, much conduct that appears at first sight not to be governed by considerations of exchange turns out upon closer inspection to be so governed, as we shall see, but this makes it still more important to specify a criterion that restricts the concept of exchange and precludes its use in tautological fashion. Social exchange as here conceived is limited to actions that are contingent on rewarding reactions from others and that cease when these expected reactions are not forthcoming. Ultimately, however, a negative answer to the question of whether the theoretical principles are tautological depends on the possibility of inferring empirically testable hypotheses from them, and some operational hypotheses will be inferred to illustrate that this possibility exists. . . .

Excursus on Love

Love is the polar case of intrinsic attraction. Whereas it finds undoubtedly its purest expression in the relation between mother and child, its development as the result of the increasing attraction of two independent individuals to one another can best be examined in a romantic relationship. Love appears to make human beings unselfish, since they themselves enjoy giving pleasure to those they love, but this selfless devotion generally rests on an interest in maintaining the other's love. Even a mother's devotion to her children is rarely entirely devoid of the desire to maintain their attachment to her. Exchange processes occur in love relations as well as in social associations of only extrinsic significance. Their dynamics, however, are different, because the specific rewards exchanged are merely means to produce the ultimate reward of intrinsic attraction in love relations, while the exchange of specific rewards is the very objective of the association in purely instrumental social relations. In intrinsic love attachments, as noted earlier, each individual furnishes rewards to the other not to receive proportionate extrinsic benefits in return but to express and confirm his own commitment and to promote the other's growing commitment to the association. An analysis of love reveals the element of exchange entailed even in intrinsically significant associations as well as their distinctive nature.

A man falls in love if the attractiveness of a woman has become unique in his eyes. "All that is necessary is that our taste for her should become exclusive." This happens, Proust continues, when we start to experience an "insensate, agonising desire to possess her" (1934, p. 177). The woman who impresses a man as a most desirable love possession that cannot be easily won and who simultaneously indicates sufficient interest to make ultimate conquest not completely beyond reach is likely to kindle his love. His attraction to her makes him dependent on her for important rewards and anxious to impress and please her to arouse a reciprocal affection that would assure him these rewards.

In the early stages of falling in love, the fears of rejection and dependence engendered by the growing attraction motivate each lover to conceal the full extent of his or her affection from the other and possibly also from himself or herself. Flirting involves largely the expression of attraction in a semi-serious or stereotyped fashion that is designed to elicit some commitment from the other in advance of making a serious commitment oneself. The joking and ambiguous commitments implied by flirting can be laughed off if they fail to evoke a responsive cord or made firm if they do. But as long as both continue to conceal the strength of their affection for the other while both become increasingly dependent on the other's affection, they frustrate one another. In the lovers' quarrels that typically ensue, as Thibaut and Kelley have pointed out, "each partner, by means of temporary withdrawal or separation, tests the other's dependence on the relationship" (1961, p. 66). As both are threatened by these quarrels with the possible end of their relationship, they are constrained to express sufficient commitment for it to continue. Of course, one may not be ready to do so, and the conflict may terminate their relationship.

Human beings evidently derive pleasure from doing things for those they love and sometimes make great sacrifices for them. This tendency results partly from the identification with the other produced by love, from the desire to give symbolic expression to one's devotion, from the function providing rewards has for strengthening a loved one's attachment to oneself, and perhaps partly from the process previously termed reverse secondary reinforcement. The repeated experience of being rewarded by the increased attachment of a loved one after having done a variety of things to please him may have the effect that giving pleasure to loved ones becomes intrinsically gratifying. Further feedback effects may occur. Since doing favors and giving presents are signs of love, a man's gifts and efforts for a woman may stimulate his own affection for her as well as hers for him, and a woman may encourage a man to give her things and do things for her not primarily out of interest in the material benefits but in order to foster his love for her. "Benefactors seem to love those whom they benefit more than those who have received benefits love those who have conferred them," said Aristotle (1926, p. 545).

The more an individual is in love with another, the more anxious he or she is likely to be to please the other.* The individual who is less deeply involved in a love relationship, therefore, is in an advantageous position, since the other's greater concern with continuing the relationship makes him or her dependent and gives the less involved individual power. Waller called this "the principle of least interest" (1951, p. 190-192). This power can be used to exploit the other; the woman who exploits a man's affec-

---

* Providing extrinsic benefits may be a substitute for proving oneself intrinsically attractive, as Proust (1934, p. 205) has noted: "For the moment, while he lavished presents upon her and performed all manner of services, he could rely on advantages not contained in his person, or in his intellect, could forego the endless, killing effort to make himself attractive."

tion for economic gain and the boy who sexually exploits a girl who is in love with him are obvious examples. Probably the most prevalent manifestation of the principle of least interest, however, is that the individual whose spontaneous affection for the other is stronger must accede to the other's wishes and make special efforts to please the other. Such an imbalance of power and extrinsic rewards is often the source and remains the basis of lasting reciprocal love attachments. Hence, the lover who does not express unconditional affection early gains advantages in the established interpersonal relationship. Indeed, the more restrained lover also seems to have a better chance of inspiring another's love for himself or herself.

Costly possessions are most precious, in love as elsewhere. A man's intrinsic attraction to a woman (and hers to him) rests on the rewards he expects to experience in a love relationship with her.* An analytical distinction can be made between his actual experiences—resulting from her supportiveness, her charming talk, her kisses, and so forth—and the value he places upon these experiences with her compared to similar experiences with other women. His gratifications are the product of the experiences themselves and the value he places on them. The ease with which he obtains the rewards of her love, however, tend to depreciate their value for him. This is the dilemma of love, which parallels the previously discussed dilemma of approval. Just as a person is expected to give approval to his associates, but his doing so too freely will depreciate the value of his approval, so is a woman under pressure to give evidence of her love to her admirer, but if she does so too readily the value of her affection to him will suffer.

How valuable a woman is as a love object to a man depends to a considerable extent on her apparent popularity with other men. It is difficult to evaluate anything in the absence of clear standards for doing so, and individuals who find themselves in such an ambiguous situation tend to be strongly influenced by any indication of a social norm for making judgments. Evaluating the intrinsic desirability of a woman is an ambiguous case of this kind, in which any particular man is strongly influenced by her general popularity among men that socially validates her value as a love object. Of course, a girl can only become generally popular by being attractive to many particular boys, but her attractiveness to any one depends in part on evidence that others find her attractive too. Good looks constitute such evidence, and so does her behavior on dates.

A woman whose love is in great demand among men is not likely to make firm commitments quickly, because she has so many attractive

---

* To make the following discussion less burdensome, it will refer largely to men's orientations to women, but it is assumed to apply, in principle, also to women's orientations to men, although there are, of course, sex role differences in specific practices, as will be noted.

alternatives to weigh before she does. The one who is not popular is more dependent on a man who takes her out and has more reason to become committed to him. A woman who readily gives proof of her affection to a man, therefore, provides presumptive evidence of her lack of popularity and thus tends to depreciate the value of her affection for him. Her resistance to his attempts to conquer her, in contrast, implies that she is in great demand and has many alternatives to choose from, which is likely to enhance her desirability in his eyes. Her reluctance to become committed helps to establish the value of her affection, partly because he takes it as an indication of her general desirability, notably in the absence of any direct knowledge of how desirable she appears to other men. To be sure, men sometimes discuss women among themselves, their desirability and even their behavior on dates, the social taboo on doing so notwithstanding, but these discussions only increase the importance a woman's restraint has for protecting the value of her affection. If a woman has the reputation of readily engaging in sexual affairs, the value of this expression of her affection greatly declines, largely because her sexual favors entail less commitment to, and ego support for, a man than those of a woman who very rarely bestows them.

To safeguard the value of her affection, a woman must be ungenerous in expressing it and make any evidence of her growing love a cherished prize that cannot be easily won. Ultimately, to be sure, a man's love for a woman depends on her willingness and ability to furnish him unique rewards in the form of sexual satisfaction and other manifestations of her affection. The point made here is *not* that a woman who fails to provide a man with sexual and emotional gratifications is more likely to win his love than one who does. The opposite undoubtedly is the case, since such gratifications are the major source of a lasting love attachment. The point made is rather that a man's profound love for a woman depends not only on these rewarding experiences themselves but also on the value he places upon them and that a woman who refrains from bestowing expressions of her affection freely increases the value of these expressions *when she does bestow them.* Of course, unless she finally *does* bestow these rewards, she does not profit from their increased value. This is precisely the reason for the dilemma. A woman promotes a man's love by granting him sexual and other favors, as demonstrations of her affection and as means for making associating with her outstandingly rewarding for him, yet if she dispenses such favours readily—to many men or to a given man too soon—she depreciates their value and thus their power to arouse an enduring attachment.

Social pressures reinforce the tendency to withhold early evidence of great affection. If most girls in a community were to kiss boys on their first dates and grant sexual favors soon afterwards, before the boys have become deeply committed, it would depreciate the price of these rewards in the community making it difficult for a girl to use the promise of sexual intercourse to elicit a firm commitment from a boy, since sexual gratifications are available at a lesser price. The interest of girls in protecting the value of sexual favors against depreciation gives rise to social pressures among girls not to grant these favors readily. Coleman's study (1961) of high schools shows that these pressures tend to take the form of making a girl's social standing contingent on her reputation in regard to her sexual behavior with boys. This social pressure, which helps to maintain the sexual favors of girls worthy of permanent commitments of boys, strengthens the position of girls in their exchange relations with boys in the courtship market (Waller and Hill, 1951, pp. 190-192). The situation among boys is complementary, which means that the social pressures here discourage early commitment. The aim of both sexes in courtship is to furnish sufficient rewards to seduce the other but not enough to deflate their value, yet the line defined by these two conditions is often imperceptible.

The challenge of conquest is an important element in the formative stages of a love relationship, and its significance as a catalyst for the development of a lasting attachment is dissipated by making conquest too easy. A basic function of the casual dating among young people is to provide opportunities for them to ascertain their own attractiveness as lovers and their chances in the competition for desirable mates. In dating—and to some extent in intimate sociable intercourse generally—an individual places the attractiveness of his own self on the market, so to speak, which makes success of extreme importance for his self-conception. The girls or boys who are successful in making many conquests of the other sex validate their attractiveness in their own eyes as well as those of others. In casual dating, therefore, girls and boys use each other to test their own attractiveness through conquests. A girl's resistance to being easily conquered constitutes a refusal to let herself be used as such a test object and a demand for a minimum commitment as a condition of her affection. By prolonging the challenge of the chase until a boy has become intrinsically attracted to her, a girl exploits the significance of conquest to promote a more fundamental attachment that makes this incentive for dating her superfluous. Since an interest in conquest may be a boy's primary initial reason for courting a girl, an easy conquest robs him prematurely of this inducement for continuing the relationship.

A girl's demonstrations of affection for a boy, moreover, imply a commitment by her and a demand for a countercommitment from him. If he was satisfied with the previous level of involvement and is not yet ready to commit himself further, such a demand for greater commitment may alienate his affection for her. Love is a spontaneous emotion that cannot be commanded, and the command to love her more implicit in the girl's expressions of increasing affection for him may act as an external restraint that withers the boy's existing affection for her. A boy's growing love for a girl he pursues is typically accompanied and spurred by an anxiety lest he lose his love object, but the fear of becoming too deeply involved that her great involvement arouses in him is incompatible with and corrodes the anxiety of losing her and the affection associated with it. Although he can take advantage of her greater commitment to obtain sexual favors from her, his exploitative orientation in doing so is not likely to stimulate an intrinsic attachment; and if his superego prevents him from exploiting her, he is likely to terminate the relationship under these circumstances. The jealousy characteristic of the more deeply involved lover constitutes an explicit demand for a more exclusive commitment on the part of the other, and it frequently provides the final stimulus for the less involved lover to withdraw from the relationship. The growth of love is often stifled by the pressure put on it by the other lover's too great affection.

Whereas the processes just considered discourage the free expression of affection in early courtship, lovers also experience pressures to express their feelings. If an individual is in love, he or she obtains gratification from declaring his love to the beloved and even "to shout it from the tree-tops." Identification with the person one loves makes rewarding him enjoyable, and rewarding him tends to involve some expressions of love for him. Besides, many actions of a girl that reward a boy and express her feelings for him are simultaneously rewarding for her, such as her willingness to kiss him. Flirting, moreover, gives rise to expectations that must later be fulfilled to maintain the love relationship. The conduct of the flirtatious girl implies that, although she may not yet be ready to let the boy hold her hand, continued association with her would ultimately bring these and much greater rewards. The implicit promises made in the course of flirting put subsequent pressure on lovers to live up to the expectations they have created and begin to provide at least some of the rewards promised. The result is a dynamic force of increasing rewards and commitments, since each new commitment creates further expectations, lest frustrated expectations lead to the termination of the relationship. The girl lets the boy kiss her, he takes her to the "prom," she permits some sex play, he ceases to date others, so does she, and he ultimately gives her the ring that formalizes their relation—unless, of course, these pressures toward stepped-up rewards and increasing commitments induce one of the lovers to discontinue the affair.

Finally, the gratifications a woman experiences as the result of being loved by a man are greatly enhanced if she loves him too, and this may unconsciously incline her to return his love. The love of a man animates a woman and makes her a more fascinating and attractive person. Going out with a man who is in love with her enhances her self-image as a captivating woman and thus probably affects her behavior to make her actually more charming and appealing. For a man's loving admiration to have pronounced effects on her self-image and conduct, however, his estimation of her must be of great significance for a woman, and the more she loves him the greater is its significance for her. A woman's love for a man who loves her, therefore, helps to make her a more charming and self-confident person, because it magnifies, as it were, the mirror that reflects and partly shapes her personality as a lover. Although a woman cannot will herself to love a man who loves her, the advantages she gains from reciprocating his love may unconsciously motivate her to do so.

Lovers, then, are under pressure to express affection for one another as well as under pressure to withhold expressions of affection. The basic dilemma is that a woman who freely provides evidence of her affection for a man in order to make associating with her more attractive to him thereby depreciates the value of her affection. The generic processes are the same for both sexes, although cultural sex role differences determine their specific forms. The willingness to enter into sex relations, for example, entails less of a commitment for a boy than for a girl in our culture, and he can more easily declare his love first, since this too tends to imply less of a commitment for a boy than for a girl. But those acts of a boy that signify his commitment to a girl, such as his introducing her to his parents or his giving her his fraternity pin, have essentially the same implications as her acts of commitment. If both lovers are interested in continuing the relationship, both are also interested in having the other commit himself or herself first and more deeply. Hence, there is an element of "brinkmanship" in courtship, with both partners seeking to withhold their own commitment up to the point where it would endanger the relationship, because courtship is a mixed game with some common and some conflicting interests*. . . .

One lover's apparent affection and increasing commitment sometimes stimulate the growth of the other's love for him, while they sometimes inhibit the other's love and cause the other to lose interest in the relation. What determines which is the case? The personality structure of the lovers is unquestionably the most important factor, but the social condition in the developing love relation also exerts an influence. Since lovers tend to suppress the strength of their growing affection for one another, a lover's own deepening involvement produces a state of tension. This state makes him anxious to receive evidence of the other's increasing affection for him, which would avert the danger of rejection and of one-

---

* Another dilemma posed by this mixed game is that the lover who expresses his eagerness to spend time with his beloved enables her to enjoy dates with him without revealing how eager she is to do so and without making the commitment implicit in such revelations.

sided dependence and permit him to ease suppressing his strong feelings of attraction. In this situation the eagerly anticipated expressions of affection of a woman tend to relieve a man's distress and intensify his love for her. If, on the other hand, there is no such reservoir of suppressed feeling and a lover is no more involved than is manifest, a woman's demonstrations of great affection for him are likely to alienate his affection for her, because they depreciate the value of her love, undermine the challenge of pursuing her, and make demands for stronger commitments than he is ready to undertake. In parallel fashion, a man's expressions of affection that meet a woman's suppressed desires tend to intensify her love for him, but if his affection far exceeds her feelings and desires it is likely to alienate her.

In brief, it seems that commitments must keep abreast for a love relationship to develop into a lasting mutual attachment. If one lover is considerably more involved than the other, his greater commitment invites exploitation or provokes feelings of entrapment, both of which obliterate love. Whereas rewards experienced in the relationship may lead to its continuation for a while, the weak interest of the less committed or the frustrations of the more committed probably will sooner or later prompt one or the other to terminate it. Only when two lovers' affection for and commitment to one another expand at roughly the same pace do they tend mutually to reinforce their love.

Conclusions

Social approval and personal attraction are basic sources of support for an individual's opinions and judgments, for his values and self-conception. The significance of another's approbation or admiration depends on its being accepted as genuine. In contrast to the services of an associate or his compliance, where his actions count rather than his underlying attitudes, the underlying orientation is what counts in expressions of approval and affection. Simulated approval and feigned affection have little value.

The significance of a person's expressions of approval or affection also depends on their being scarce. Individuals who hardly ever disapprove or who readily demonstrate affection for others thereby depreciate the value of their praise or their love. Whereas the simulation of approval and affection is highly condemned, their dissimulation is not seriously censured. False praise stamps a person as a sycophant; false agreement, as a liar; false show of affection, as dishonorable; but the person who fails to express approval when he could or who withholds evidence of affection that he feels is much less severely rebuked and is merely accused of being unappreciative or cold. Only simulation, not dissimulation, makes approval and affection unauthentic. Given this asymmetry, there is no conflict between the requirements that expressions of approval must be genuine and that they must be rare to be of importance for others.

A man's willingness to provide social support by giving approval makes his associates appreciate him, but if he freely offers praise he depreciates its value. Similarly, a woman's expressions of affection for the man who loves her make him appreciate her the more, but if she too readily gives evidence of her love she depreciates its value. This poses a dilemma, since individuals risk either antagonizing significant associates by withholding expressions of approval and affection or depreciating the value these expressions have for them. The dilemma is more pronounced in the case of love than in the case of approbation, because the significance of approbation rests to a greater extent on alternative foundations than that of love. A person's ability to contribute to the welfare of others, which commands their respect, and his power over them govern the value his approval has for them, and the effect of his lack of discrimination in bestowing approval on its value does not completely obliterate these other effects. A person's lack of restraint in demonstrating affection, on the other hand, is much more intimately bound up with the impression he makes as a lover and thus with the value of his love for another.

The significance of a person's approval or affection for others depends, furthermore, on their orientation to him. The respect of others for a man greatly increases the significance of his approval for them, and the adoration of others for a woman greatly enhances the significance of her affection for them. Men whose performance receives the commendation of highly respected persons care little about the approval of less respected persons, and women who are adored by the most desirable men care little about the admiration of less desirable ones. For his approval to be appreciated at all, the less respected person must be relatively undiscriminating in expressing it and praise performances of only mediocre quality, thereby further decreasing the value of his approval. Correspondingly, for her affection to be appreciated at all, the woman who is not greatly admired among men must be comparatively indiscriminate in expressing it and readily give evidence of her love for a man, thereby further decreasing the value of her affection.

The very endeavor to impress others in order to win their approval or admiration makes a person less impressive. The man whose eminence in his field is renowned can dispense with such endeavors. He can act naturally and be matter-of-fact, and he can even minimize his own accomplishments, since doing so does not detract from their evident importance but only increases the others' estimation of him. The man whose equally great achievements are not known in a particular group cannot impress them in the same fashion. Unless he tells them of his accomplishments, they have no basis for respecting him or for appreciating his modesty in speaking of his attainments in a deprecatory manner, yet his having to tell them that he is a man of distinction, however subtly, makes him less impressive. Similarly, the raving beauty's evident attractiveness frees her from the necessity to demonstrate that she is a captivating woman and permits her to be charming and unpretentious and thus to prove herself still more attractive. Once a baseline of social standing is established, it is relatively simple to make further gains, but establishing it is not so easy.

There are, then, numerous parallels between expressions of affection in love relations and expressions of approval in social associations generally. There are also some contrasts, however. The main source of the difference is that the conditions in a collective structure largely govern the significance of social approval while the conditions established by a pair of lovers themselves primarily govern the significance of their affection for one another, although pair relations modify the significance of approval and the broader social situation affects the significance of affection, too. The baseline of prestige that makes others appreciate an individual's approval and the baseline of attraction that makes others appreciate an individual's affection rest on different foundations, since prestige is typically more firmly rooted in the social structure than is attraction.

Although a woman's beauty and popularity make her initially attractive to a man, the significance of her love for him depends ultimately on his personal feeling of attraction for her, whereas the significance of the approval of a person of superior status is inherently greater than that of others, whatever an individual may think of him for idiosyncratic reasons. The judgment of his superior or of an expert in his field cannot rationally be dismissed by an individual, but there is nothing irrational about not being attracted to a woman who is beautiful and whom other men consider desirable. Finally, with the exception of the special case of physical beauty, what makes a woman a desirable love object is the impression she makes of being desirable, while the respect commanded by a man—or a woman, for that matter—is governed by his actual abilities and evaluated in terms of objective criteria. To be sure, the relevance of these abilities rather than others depends on the social standards of evaluation that prevail in the social structure, but this fact does not affect the fundamental distinction. The attractiveness of a person as a lover, or generally as a sociable companion, is primarily a function of the orientations of his particular associates to him, whereas the multiple supports on which status in a social structure rests—especially, though not only, in areas of instrumental achievement—make it comparatively independent of the orientations of particular associates.

REFERENCES

Aristotle. *The Nicomachean Ethics.* London: William Heinemann, 1926.

Coleman, James S. *The Adolescent Society.* New York: The Free Press, 1961.

Proust, Marcel. *Remembrance of Things Past,* Vol. I. New York: Random House, 1934.

Thibaut, John and Kelley, Harold H. *The Social Psychology of Groups.* New York: John Wiley & Sons, Inc., 1961.

Waller, Willard and Hill, Reuben. *The Family.* New York: Dryden, 1951.

Weber, Max. *The Theory of Social and Economic Organization.* New York: Oxford University Press, 1947.

CHAPTER
SIX

HOW DO PEOPLE CHANGE EACH OTHER'S ATTITUDES AND BEHAVIOR ?

THE ISSUE OF SOCIAL INFLUENCE AND ATTITUDE CHANGE

Jack Plummer and Ed Blalock are neighbors in a modest suburban sub-division on the outskirts of a major city. They work in different shops at a nearby plant. The two men have been raking leaves in their yards and are now resting and talking about the plant where they work.

Ed: It could be worse, I guess. I've been there eight years and I got a nice place to live in a decent neighborhood. But the way they treat you there, you know? They don't give a damn about you.

Jack: That's for sure. (and with rising feeling) I saw in the paper how much they made last year. And look what we got from them. Did you hear how they're screwing Chuck again?

Ed: No, what? Didn't he get that frame shop opening? I thought they'd promised it to him. He's been working there twenty years, right?

Jack: Right, but he's not getting the job. They're giving it to Edwards instead. He's the favorite over there you know, that ass-licker. "Edwards is more reliable" is what they said.

Ed: (smiles and shakes his head; then, after a pause) Yeah, yeah, you're right. Chuck had it coming after 20 years and he needed the extra bread too. But it doesn't surprise me, you know, with this 'incentive system' the company's been pushing. It sounds alright, you know, how each guy should be paid and promoted according to how much he turns out. That way, the people who are willing to work can move faster is what they say. . .I mean, hell, I don't want to wait until everyone dies before I can move up—but I know it's not fair to the older guys. Anyway, it's no good everyone trying to beat out everyone else. It's better to stick together.

Jack: Sure. The problem is the Local isn't working hard enough. They're lazy. If I ever get on the Union Council, I'd sure as hell tell'em that too.

Ed: Well, you've got my vote Jack.

A year has passed and both men have new responsibilities at the auto plant. Ed has been promoted to foreman in the wheel shop where he had been working and now supervises a crew of fifteen workers. As a managerial position, his new job calls for him to give up his Union membership and to be paid on an annual salary basis rather than hourly. He regularly attends meetings with other foremen to discuss management problems. Jack, on the other hand, is now Union steward for his section of the chassis shop. He is a member of the Union Local council and is expected to be a spokesman among the men for Union concerns. The relations between Ed and Jack have grown somewhat strained.

Ed: What do you mean, it's a rotten place? It's not paradise, but you can do a lot worse other places. You tell me one that's better. They take care of the men pretty damn well. Look at the benefits and how they replaced that equipment that the Union was saying was so dangerous. Just last month, I needed a new type of riveter and within two weeks. . .

Jack: Sure, they'll do anything that gets you to turn out more for them, but if it don't, they won't lift a finger for you. Look at what they did to Chuck– passed right over him and put a guy in there who's stoned half the day.

Ed: Christ, are you still harping on that. Look, Chuck is a nice guy but you know as well as I do that a guy that drinks like that—well, you can't promote him. Chuck's just serving his time in there. This other fellow has had some education and he knows what he's doing. The plain fact is that he's a better man on the job than Chuck is and he has it coming to him.

Jack: Shit! If a man's been around for 21 years, he can do the job or they would have canned him long ago. He's earned it, he sweated for it, and he should get it. Look, I don't have to tell you about car payments and house and all. Chuck has a kid getting out of high school this year, maybe wants to go to college, and he can't cut it on what he's getting. A man deserves something after putting in 21 years. He's no piece of goddam machinery you throw away when you've gotten your use out of it.

Ed: You know something, you're really beginning to sound like a crank—like a goddamned Union crank! Seniority, seniority. You don't give a shit who's willing to work and who isn't. The Union doesn't care about the workers really, just their dues. If they really cared about the men they'd be. . .

Jack: Wait a minute! The Union is doing a hell of a job. If it wasn't for the Union we'd be nowhere and the Local is in there fighting all the time. Chuck will get his promotion, you'll see. And wait until you see what we're asking on the new contract.

Ed: Well, more pay I can see.

Jack: Hey, I'm glad we still agree on something. (shakes his head slowly) You sure have changed, Buddy.

Ed: Me? You mean *you*. Where are you getting those radical ideas anyway?

Jack: Radical! I'm not saying anything different than what you used to. . .*

However much these men may wish to deny it, there is no question that their feelings and attitudes toward important matters *have* changed in the one year interim. These changes square with the nature of their new jobs. Ed sounds more like a foreman: protective of management, in favor of the profit-oriented incentive system, against the security-oriented seniority system, and anti-union. Jack has changed less: he has increased his former coolness toward management and his former preference for seniority over incentive, and he appears to have warmed considerably in his attitudes toward the Union. Apparently, the men's new social roles have altered their psychic make-up in some manner.

A social role is a pattern of expectations about how a person who occupies a social position ought to act. The social position may be a well-defined one like shop foreman, or an amorphous one like bus passenger. In either case, there are expectations about how the incumbent of the position should behave. A bus passenger is expected to step to the rear, to refrain from spitting or acting in a noisy and obstreperous manner, and not to stand too close to others if it is avoidable. A shop foreman ought to keep his men working efficiently, look after their on the job needs, carry out the policies of his superiors, and stand ready to defend these policies if necessary.

A new social role is also a new social context for the person involved. He finds himself interacting with a new set of people in related roles. A foreman attends meetings that he never attended before, makes new friendships, and sees new people both on and off the job. By changing their jobs, both Ed and Jack have entered at least partly new social worlds. Somewhere in the interactions in their new social world—or perhaps in the very decision to enter them—lies the explanation for their attitude changes.

To understand these changes, one needs a framework for explaining social influence. Social influence has occurred whenever a person's beliefs, attitudes, or behavior are notably altered as a consequence of some interpersonal event. To be interesting, the changes ought to overcome some resistance—ought to be in an area that the person really cares about. Such is the case for both Ed and Jack. But, as we shall see, the three frameworks to be examined put rather different interpretations on such instances of social influence. Briefly, in the "consistency" framework, they are viewed as efforts to reorganize one's beliefs and actions into more harmonious patterns; in the "functional" framework, they are viewed as attempts to better attain important personal goals; and in the "activation of commitments" framework, they are viewed as the inevitable follow-through on implicit commitments that have already been made.

---

* The preceding vignette is loosely based on a classic study of role change and attitude change by Seymour Lieberman (1956)

THE MAJOR VIEWS

Consistency

Not long ago, one of us took a four day camping trip through the Sinai desert with a group of people. It was not an easy trip. Along with the absence of such amenities as running water and toilets, we experienced two nights of severe sand storms. One of our friends, let's call him David, was full of complaints about the inconveniences. He had been dubious about going in the first place and every hard bump through the desert wadis seemed to confirm his doubts.

Shortly afterwards we encountered a friend who had not been on the trip. We, of course, told him how exciting it had been and dwelled on the beauties of the desert. But our mutual friend David, we suggested, had had a miserable time. Our friend was surprised; he had spoken to David only yesterday and had been told of nothing but the unparalleled beauties of the desert. He wouldn't have missed the trip for the world, David reportedly asserted.

There is no reason to think David was being hypocritical, for we felt the same way. In retrospect, each new hardship only seemed to enhance the beautiful moments. After all, only a fool would put up with such inconveniences for anything less than an incomparable and memorable experience—and by the end, showered and desanded, it certainly seemed to merit these adjectives.

David altered his attitude because he experienced it as inconsistent with the action he had taken. He had freely chosen to venture into the desert and to remain there several days despite the various hardships. What sense could it make to have done all this for a miserable recompense? David could not achieve cognitive harmony as long as he persisted in viewing the trip as worthless. Fortunately, even a difficult experience has its positive moments. And, with the distance of hindsight, David was able to resort his memories and emerge with a cheerful view of the trip—one that amply justified it.

The change in David's attitude is paralleled in such phenomena as hazing. Having gone through a difficult and unpleasant experience to achieve the goal of membership in some group or organization, the value of such membership is often enhanced—if one hasn't given up in disgust before reaching the goal. These examples are paradigms of a theory of social influence that emphasizes a strain toward cognitive consistency.

The core notion is exceedingly simple. It derives from the common-sense observation that a person's related attitudes, beliefs, and behavior tend to fit together in a consistent fashion. Consistency theory takes this generalization and, with a slight twist, transforms it into a motivational principle. If people are generally consistent, it argues, then why not assume that they are motivated to be this way?

Everything else follows from this one assumption. If it is true that people's cognitions always tend toward some sort of "harmony," "balance," or "consonance," then social influence can be accomplished in a straightforward fashion: disrupt a person's cognitive harmony at some strategic point and then let the aversion for inconsistency take its natural course. To be sure, accomplishing this in a reliable way can be tricky, for the person may restore cognitive harmony in an unexpected way. For example, try to convince a student to work harder by persuading him that drinking and debauchery are inconsistent with getting a good education and you might convince him to drop out of school. But, with foresight and a little luck, such inconsistency can usually be planted in such a way as to produce intended changes.

As is often the case with a theory based on simple, common-sense notions, as soon as one attempts to formalize it—to state it so that it can be rigorously applied and tested—one discovers that it is not so simple after all. And, indeed, the domain of consistency theory is filled with pitfalls for the unwary. For one thing, cognitive inconsistency is a *subjective* state having no necessary correspondence to an objective inconsistency. For example, a person may be quite comfortable with the realization that his views are inconsistent with those of others around him, particularly if he dislikes and distrusts these others. Indeed, discomfort might be greater if he found himself in agreement with disliked others. Thus, inconsistency in the sense of conflict between a person's attitudes and some contrary pressure from the environment does not necessarily imply subjective inconsistency. One must apply consistency theory from the perspective of the actor. It is only an inconsistency—regardless of what appears to an observer—if the person experiences it as inconsistent.

And this brings us to one of the thorniest problems in the formalization of consistency theory: defining subjective inconsistency. It is no simple matter: given two or more related cognitions held by a single person, how do we decide whether these cognitions will be experienced as inconsistent or not? There are half-a-dozen variants of consistency theory that differ precisely in the way that they answer this question. Moreover, these answers are complicated, involving different assumptions about what underlies harmonious cognitive functioning. These variants have been well described and compared by a number of writers—Zajonc (1960), Cohen (1964, pp. 81-99), Brown (1965, pp. 549-609)—and we will not review them here. Instead, we will focus on the variant of consistency theory that is discussed in the selection included here by Sherwood, Barron and Fitch: cognitive dissonance.

This variant was first developed by Leon Festinger and it defines cognitive inconsistency in a rather loose, common-sense fashion. Two cognitions are said to be dissonant (inconsistent) if, from the perspective of the actor, one *cognition implies the negation of the other.* This may sound rigorous—a matter of strict logic—but it isn't. Strictly speaking, there is nothing illogical, for example, about behaving in public contrary to one's private beliefs; or about deciding that a trying trip to the Sinai desert was absolutely worthless. Yet, we can easily sense that there is a psycho-logical contradiction here—that a person who engages in such behavior will experience dissonance, since such behavior fits poorly with related cognitive elements.

But what is the psycho-logical system that defines dissonance? Some cynics have suggested that none really exists; that if one wants to know whether two cognitions are dissonant, the only way to tell for sure is to "ask Leon Festinger." However, Roger Brown provides a useful general rule of thumb. He suggests that two cognitions are dissonant if, in the ordinary use of language, we would link them with the conjunction "but" rather than "and." In the above examples, it is clear that a person would ordinarily say, "I believe thus and so *but* I publicly acted in a contrary fashion" or "I suffered a lot of hardship and spent great effort to do this *but* it has very little value." The conjunction "and" does not seem as correct as "but" in these sentences.

"I dropped a stone but it didn't fall"; "I like him but he hates me"; "I worked hard for this but it is worthless to me"—all of these are dissonant pairs of cognitions even though they are logically consistent. Other variants of consistency theory define inconsistency in other ways, but all must wrestle with this same perplexing problem: the naive human actor does not operate by the rules of formal logic and, hence, inconsistency must be defined by referring to some special system of psycho-logic.

There is a second major issue which consistency theories must face. Why do people avoid inconsistency; why do they prefer consonance, balance, or harmony? Some theorists prefer to side-step this question and to concern themselves strictly with the consequences of the observed tendency—they take it as their starting point and devote their research solely to how different types of inconsistency will be resolved.

Ultimately, though, they assume that consistency is wired into our cognitive processes in some fashion—that it is an intrinsic part of the operation of the human mind. The original version of consistency theory suggested by Fritz Heider (whom we encountered in connection with attribution theory in Chapter 2) treated this issue quite explicitly in terms of principles of Gestalt psychology. Humans have innate preferences for "elegant," parsimonious, and meaningful cognitive structures. He suggested that certain "balanced" organizations had these properties to a greater extent than other patterns, and that the human mind sought these balanced patterns.*

Some consistency theorists have flirted with extrinsic explanations of the desire for cognitive harmony, suggesting that it is sought because it pays off in the world. For example, most of us like to think of ourselves as honest, rational, and competent. With such desires, it is unpleasant to acknowledge to ourselves or others that we misrepresented our views, acted against our best interests, or badly bungled an opportunity. Rather than admitting such unpleasant truths, it is sometimes easier and more pleasant to alter our attitudes to make the misrepresentation true, to change our interests to fit what we have, or to convince ourselves that the bungled chance was really for the best anyway.

Inconsistency, in this extrinsic argument, is not disliked for its own sake but for its unpleasant consequences. It is our opinion, however, that to accept this extrinsic argument is to abandon the consistency framework in favor of the functional one presented below. Consistency becomes, like many other things, instrumental to achieving desired goals such as self-esteem and social rewards. But it is no longer the primary motivator.

How would a consistency theorist understand the attitude changes in Ed and Jack toward their place of work? Ed knows that his own promotion is attributable to the incentive system and that the company wants him to support it. He is, therefore, especially receptive to arguments in its favor. "The company has been good to me and favors the incentive system *but* I am against it," is a dissonant cognition for him. Similarly, Jack is now a Union representative. "I represent the Union *but* I think it is doing a poor job," is dissonant for Jack and he soon becomes increasingly impressed with the effectiveness of the group he serves. Since one of the dissonant cognitions is

---

* We encountered the notion of innate psychological processes earlier (Chapter 3) in exploring the cognitive-developmental view of moral development (Kohlberg, pp. 131-148). This view is broader than a mere "press-for-consistency" but also posits an intrinsic structure in human cognition that produces a natural sequence of developmental stages.

fixed by the nature of their jobs, it is easier to resolve the inconsistency by changing their attitudes—especially if it is not really inconsistent with other beliefs they hold.

But attitudes exist in an interrelated system and one can't be changed without forcing others connected with it into line. When Ed moved from an ambivalent attitude to a positive one toward the incentive system, a new inconsistency was generated. His mildly positive feeling toward the Union came into conflict with his knowledge that the Union was strongly opposed to the incentive plan. Ed might have corrected this inconsistency in other ways—for example, by denying that the Union really opposed it or by deciding the Union was right in opposing it. But these methods of dissonance reduction would have only created new inconsistencies of an even more serious nature. Down-grading the Union was the easiest and cognitively most efficient method of correcting the imbalance.

While both men changed in symmetric ways, Ed changed more than Jack. Why is this? The consistency framework would suggest that Jack's new job situation was relatively more compatible with his former attitudes than was Ed's. His new post was only part time and he retained his place in the assembly line with his old associates. Furthermore, the stronger role he was now required to play in Union affairs was quite consistent with a stronger version of his old views. In contrast, Ed shifted off the assembly line, entered a new circle of associates with more pro-company views, and found himself having to argue policy positions that he formerly opposed. Thus, he needed to change more of his attitudes to restore harmony among them.

In sum, amount of attitude change in this framework is a function of the number and incompatibility of new cognitive inputs; or, conversely, the more harmoniously new elements can be incorporated into an existing cognitive system, the more stable attitudes will be.

Functionalism

Attitudes, in this view, are performing some function for the individual—they better enable one to achieve some social or psychological goal. If they are no longer doing their job for the person, they will be replaced by other attitudes that work better.

There are a group of professionals who earn their living by social influence— those who work for advertising agencies. Their strategy of influence essentially employs the functional framework. In devising marketing strategies, they seek to understand how a product they wish to sell can be linked to important personal goals. Thrift, beauty, charm, status, health, integrity, and sex-appeal are some of the many packages in which products are wrapped. Ultimately, the strategy is to convince people that there is a means-end relationship between the product and the desired goal and, in so doing, to increase positive attitudes toward the product. They can rely on conscious or unconscious motives, arguing explicitly that the product will lead to the good life or suggesting it more subtly.

The more subtle practitioners focus on what Katz, in the selection included here, calls the ego-defensive and value-expressive functions rather than the social adjustment or knowledge functions. The technique relies on understanding the unconscious meaning that various objects have for consumers. To illustrate, we quote Ernst Dichter on soup:

> Soup, while it is food, is at the same time more than food. It is a potent magic that satisfies not only the hunger of the body, but has something to do with the yearnings of the soul. People speak of soup as a product of some mysterious alchemy, a symbol of love which satisfies mysterious gnawings. . . . Eating soup is a fulfillment—it is the food for which people express their appreciation audibly and almost involuntarily. . . we can almost hear the "aah"—the release after the first warming, strength-giving spoonful.
>   . . . Soup has the power to satisfy. It is a product of kitchen magic, . . . of mother's mystic skill. When you have eaten this soup, it protects and heals, and gives you strength,—it gives you courage and the feeling of belonging (1960, p. 146).

Inner peace, warm memories, strength and belonging—these are attractive end-states, and once their connection with soup has been established, it becomes a technical matter to design a marketing strategy that will allow a particular brand to benefit from the connection in people's minds.

What ends or goal states need to be considered? Different functional theorists emphasize somewhat different answers but there is fairly general consensus on some three or four major ones:

1. Maintaining the positive regard of others (what Katz, in the selection here, calls "social adjustment");
2. Maintaining a satisfying self-conception (what Katz calls "ego-defense" and "value-expression"); and
3. Maintaining an accurate and meaningful view of the social environment (what Katz calls the "knowledge" function).*

We can illustrate the functional framework using the vignette about Ed and Jack. What important goals might the two men have achieved better by their attitude changes? All of the functions listed above seem relevant to some degree but the ego-expressive functions appear especially important for Ed. If his new attitudes were merely in the service of social adjustment—aimed only at obtaining the approval of management—then we might expect him to state the views he did while on the job, interacting with management types. But why maintain them before Jack who, he knows, disapproves of them? The answer must be that they are to some degree important to his concept of himself. Ed wanted to become a foreman—it is a welcome addition to his self-identity—and he wants to be a "good foreman." He has learned that those considered good fore-men speak well of management, oppose the seniority system, and favor the incentive system. He needs, for his own self-respect, to hold the attitudes that, in his view, a good foreman holds.

It is possible that the knowledge function may also be playing an important role here. Ed has probably been exposed to memos and conversations expounding the virtues of what management supports. Perhaps he now understands the implications of the incentive and seniority plans differently. This is not to say that management's views

---

* In addition to the theory by Katz in the selection included here, there are three other major statements of the functional framework—Smith, Bruner, and White (1956), Kelman (1961) and Raven (1965).

are more correct, but merely that his exposure to selective information in support of them makes them more convincing.

A similar case can be made for Jack's attitude changes. He also has an investment in being a "good" Union representative and is probably exposed one-sidedly to information in support of the views he now endorses. If his attitudes have changed less, it is because his new sub-identity is less different from his old one—he is still first and foremost a worker—and because his new role is less pervasive.

One of the virtues of the functional framework is that it permits a highly differentiated analysis. Many different processes of influence can be identified, each shaped by the different goal state to which it is tied. Katz, in the selection here, undertakes the central task of functional analysis: to unravel the conditions necessary to arouse and change attitudes that perform each of the separate functions discussed.

Activation of Prior Commitments

This framework is not concerned with why people enter into relationships entailing diffuse commitments (the reasons are legion), but with the consequences of having so entered. The basic consequence is a potentially entrapping mental set—specifically, a propensity to place a higher priority on fulfilling the duties of the relationship than on pursuing personal desires or preferences.

We illustrate with reference to a dramatic case of influence by activation of prior commitments: the Milgram experiments on obedience to authority. In setting up his experiments, Milgram utilized the simple fact that any person who agrees to serve as a subject in a psychological experiment implicitly commits himself to doing whatever the experimenter may request of him, so long as the request pertains to the experiment. Ordinarily, this is an innocuous state of affairs and many people are willing to do it, whether for money, or for course credits, or for science. However, Milgram's experimental procedure was not innocuous. He created a situation in which the subject gradually discovered that his duties entailed administering increasingly severe electric shocks to another subject.* These shocks were so severe that the victim screamed in pain, complained of a heart condition, pleaded and demanded to be released from the chair in which he was strapped, and finally appeared to lose consciousness entirely. But despite this incredible spectacle, the experimenter coolly persisted in ordering subjects to continue administering ever-higher intensity shocks. As Milgram reports in the reading included in this section, fully 62 per cent of the subjects placed in this situation were completely obedient: they continued to administer shocks until the experimenter finally told them they could stop.

It is hard to make much sense of such an outcome, especially if one begins asking questions such as, "Why would anyone want to risk killing a poor helpless fellow by electrocuting him?" The problem is that no subject "wanted" to do what he ended up doing. Each did it out of a sense of obligation. Put differently, the subject's behavior was *not* under the control of his *personal* desires, preferences, or judgment. In entering the role of subject, he implicitly committed himself to holding his own preferences and judgment in abeyance—to acting merely as an agent of the experimenter, thus allowing

---

* In reality, this other subject was a confederate of the experimenter not really being shocked. But, as far as the real subject knew, the shocks were absolutely authentic.

his own behavior to be controlled by the latter's preferences and judgment. In this way his own desires became completely subordinate to the experimenter's.

Perhaps this does not sound entirely convincing. After all, even granting that a person might unthinkingly make such a commitment, why would he be unable to renege on it once he sees clearly where it is leading him? A reasonable enough question, but one that seems to be more or less meaningless to someone who has in fact made such a commitment. Such a person will seek to prevent his personal preferences from interfering with the performance of his duties. Perhaps he simply does not allow himself to think of the possibility of refusing to continue, or perhaps he is unable to figure out how his personal preferences could be used to explain and justify a unilateral abrogation of his prior commitment. Either way, most subjects in the Milgram experiment apparently felt that they had no choice—that, like it or not, they had to follow through on what they had started.

It is interesting to examine some of the tactics that these subjects did use in trying to evade their fate, for these reveal most clearly how hopelessly trapped they were. One common tactic was to seek a point of reversibility in their commitment to the experimenter. Thus, many offered to return the pay they had received for acting as subjects. They hoped that the experimenter would take back the money and release them. But the experimenter, of course, refused to make the exchange, thus leaving them trapped.

Another tactic was to try and persuade the experimenter that he (the experimenter) really ought to decide to stop. This subjects did by forcefully pointing out to him the alarming facts of the situation: that the victim was yelling, that he wanted to stop, that he might be having a heart attack, that he might even be killed. Though quite agitated and most anxious to stop, these subjects apparently felt they could not do so without first persuading the experimenter of the wisdom of such a course. Evidently, only the experimenter could release them from their duties, and since he refused to be swayed, they remained trapped.

Though the overall level of obedience was staggering, it is well to remember that some 40 per cent of the subjects in the Milgram experiment did stop, many breaking off as soon as the victim's distress became apparent. How did these persons manage to undo their commitment? The answer requires some preliminary discussion. Though this will become clearer later, enough has been said to suggest that a person who is subject to generalized commitments is in a quasi-legalistic mental set. He must make judgments about the validity and applicability of a prior agreement to a current situation. Thus, the quality of his judgement—of his power of reason—is among the most important factors in such an influence situation. Being influenced or not comes down rather simply to one's interpretation of a past agreement. If the agreement can be denied, invalidated, or made inapplicable, its force evaporates; if it cannot, its force is irresistible.

The difference between obedient and disobedient subjects is that the latter took their commitment to be inapplicable to the sorts of requests being made by the experimenter. Rather than remaining trapped in the mental set of obedient subjects, they declared the agreement null and void. But, they did this not so much on grounds of personal preference, as on moral-legalistic grounds—invoking, as it were, higher level commitments. Some, for example, noted that the situation was unjust because the victim had not known what he was getting in for; others stated more simply that injuring another person for no good reason was just plain wrong, and they would not do it. Whatever the particular higher-level rationale, once it was used to invalidate the commitment, the subject felt free to break off. And, indeed, subjects who broke off early did so with remarkable ease, either refusing to take the experimenter's requests seriously, or else becoming quite perturbed with him.

Who were these disobedient subjects? Did they have unusual powers of reason or judgment? Lawrence Kohlberg (1968, pp. 389-397) thinks so. By administering a test of moral reasoning to subjects who had participated in the Milgram experiment, he was able to show that disobedient subjects tended overwhelmingly to be capable of higher levels of moral reasoning than obedient subjects. Recall (from Chapter 3 of this book) that Kohlberg's theory of moral development is a cognitive one that posits an invariant sequence of stages of moral thought, with each higher stage entailing a more general and abstract understanding of moral matters. Since higher stages are characterized by an ability to use general moral principles without being distracted by the idiosyncratic features of specific situations, it seems plausible that higher-stage subjects would have been better able to reason through the invalidity of their agreement with the experimenter. Certainly, Kohlberg's data supports such an argument. He discusses these data briefly in the reading included in this book (see p. 131).

In addition to the compelling Milgram experiment, there are numerous other instances of influence by the activation-of-generalized commitments. First of all, the experimenter-subject relationship is but a special case of *legitimate authority* relationships. A legitimate authority is one who, by virtue of the position he occupies, has the right to make certain binding requests on others in reciprocal positions. The President can order armies into war; the bus driver can order passengers to the rear; and the safety patrol boy can order motorists to stop. Note that in each case the power resides not in their person but in the position. A sixth grade child is hardly overpowering as a person, but when he dons his day-glo orange strap, he attains the authority to stop motorists simply because they acknowledge his right to do so. They, like soldiers in the army, or passengers in a bus, have made generalized commitments that permit others in specified positions to control their behavior in particular situations.

Legitimate authority always has the potential for being abused. If a person has the proper credentials and training, he can enter into a position of authority, and once there, can use it to make dubious demands on his subordinates. Ordinarily this will result in loss of his position, but until the necessary official steps are taken he remains capable of perpetrating the sort of havoc illustrated by the Milgram experiments since his subordinates may be unclear about the precise limits of their commitments.

Legitimate authority aside, there are many other social relationships, entrance into which entails taking on generalized commitments: for example, friendship, marriage, and parenthood. By their nature, each involves generalized commitments to partners—diffuse obligations that may be both defined and called upon in the indefinite future. A friend in need has the right to expect extraordinary loyalty; a spouse ought to be loved and cherished, for better or worse; and a child ought to be cared for and supported in appropriate ways for many years. In each case, the details of how the commitment will be fulfilled cannot be known at the start; and yet it is made just the same. And once made, it leaves us vulnerable to obligations fully as onerous as those laid on subjects in the Milgram experiments. Like these subjects, we may not "want" to do what we have to do, but will do it just the same—that is, unless we can undo our prior commitment by mutual consent, or else (in some cases) have it "undone" through proper legal channels.

Another way of incurring unspecified obligations that may later be activated is by the mechanism of *reciprocity*. In a sparkling analysis, Alvin Gouldner (1960) argues that every human society has a norm that obliges people to reciprocate or re-pay benefits they have received from others. Such a norm is an important form of social cement—it places recipients in the debt of their benefactors, thus encouraging co-operation and discouraging exploitation. Moreover, it serves as a starting mechanism for relationships. There is little cost in being the first to give benefits to another, as long as the other will feel obliged to reciprocate. Yet, anyone who has received unwanted gifts or favors is well aware of the more onerous side of the norm of reciprocity. It is no accident that door-to-door salesmen typically begin their pitch by dispensing a free gift—at the very least, this obliges us to do them the courtesy of listening.

Gouldner notes that the exact nature of the "to-be-repaid" benefits is often left unspecified. Unlike dinner invitations, occasional favors may be repaid in myriad ways, and among these ways is simply doing something for the other when he asks it. Typically, we weigh our debt to another before acceding to any noxious requests, but sometimes our debt may be so great that we will feel obligated to acquiese to quite onerous requests. The popular novel and film, *The Godfather,* illustrates well the use of reciprocity to build a monumental power structure founded largely on generalized commitments. Strong-arm methods aside, the Godfather operated by doing immense favors for desperate people: saving their careers, their homes, their lives. In return, these others implicitly committed themselves to repay him at some future time, in some suitable way to be defined by the Godfather. By calling on these commitments, he was not only in a position to obtain anything that these others could get for him, but also to do bigger favors for evermore influential people, thereby steadily increasing his power.

The average person may be lucky enough never to need help so badly that he has to incur an open-ended debt of this nature, but he can scarcely exist socially without becoming subject to some obligations of reciprocity. In general, the more unanswered benefits one receives from another, the more the other has diffuse power over you—that is, the more he can expect you to repay him by doing his bidding irrespective of your personal preferences.

Examining the vignette about Ed and Jack within this framework one looks for initial, diffuse commitments which contained the seeds of their later attitude changes. Put more strongly, it involves looking for prior implicit agreements to change their attitudes in just the ways that they later did. Both men undertook new role commitments and some of these were quite detailed and explicit—for example, the specific role requirements associated with each man's new job. But other commitments were more diffuse. Neither man knew at the outset exactly what was entailed. Each entered his new position partly on faith, knowing that some of the obligations were unspecified and trusting that he wouldn't be asked to do something unacceptable.

As time passed, these obligations became more concrete. Representing management meant understanding and defending certain specific policies. Serving the Union required resisting management and rallying workers around important issues such as seniority. Each man changed his attitudes, then, to fulfill better his obligation in the new role. The prior commitment activated was the diffuse one of doing their jobs well. Having made it, they proceeded to do their best and probably never experienced a sense of choice about whether to accept or reject new obligations that surfaced. They simply did what was necessary given the responsibilities they had undertaken, a process so natural that neither was even aware of his own attitude change.

Social influence by activation-of-commitments, then, is the result of being called upon to carry through a diffuse commitment made earlier. At the moment of influence, a prior mental set intersects with the present request to form an irresistible obligation. This mental set is legalistic in nature: it orients one away from his personal desires and toward his duties in a relationship. This set may be conscious or subconscious. If subconscious, one remains essentially unaware of having the choice to refuse the request—much as one remains unaware of having the choice to leave a house by way of a window. If conscious, then one experiences the onerousness of the request but still works to suppress such feelings as irrelevant. In extreme cases, one may seek to evade his duty either by trying to persuade the agent to rescind the request, or by finding a justifiable reason for declaring the commitment invalid. If such courses fail, however, one is left trapped and must force himself to acquiesce.

CONTRASTING THE VIEWS OF SOCIAL INFLUENCE AND ATTITUDE CHANGE

The three frameworks for analyzing social influence can be contrasted by considering their answers to three basic questions:

1. Is the energizer of social influence basically internal (inside the person) or external?
2. What is the nature of the relationship between the agent of influence and the target?
3. What is assumed about the organization of the social world in which the target of influence functions?

Energizer of Change

Since social influence entails changing another's beliefs or behavior, any theory about this process must postulate some force that energizes or motivates change. This force may be intrinsic, rooted in the nature of the human mind and personality, or it can come from the social environment in which the person functions.

The consistency framework sees the energizer as internal. Cognitive imbalance may be stimulated by external events but these are merely the precipitants. The energy for change is internally generated as the mind tries to restore equilibrium as efficiently as possible.

In the functional framework, the basic energizer varies by function. The force for change is a desire to attain better important social and psychological goals. For the social adjustment function, the external world determines whether given attitudes and behaviors work—that is, whether rewards or punishments will be forthcoming. For other functions, the answer is less clear. The maintenance of a satisfying self concept and an accurate view of the world are essentially internal states. They provide the energy for change, and the outside world functions mainly to provide signals that activate them.

In the activation of commitments, the basic motivator is a sense of interpersonal obligation. This energizer is outside the person, a product of his social relationships. Once people make a commitment in a relationship, they tend to honor it—often without thinking much about it and even at the expense of personal hardship. If the prior commitment is diffuse in nature, it later allows the agent considerable leeway in controlling a subject's beliefs and behavior.

Relationship Between Agent and Target

In order to activate or unleash the force for change, an agent of influence must be in an appropriate position *vis-a-vis* his target. What, for each framework, is the nature of the relationship? In the consistency framework, the agent must be able to cue or trigger a subjective inconsistency in the target. In the functional framework, the agent is in the role of a goal facilitator. The agent either provides the means or points the way to a subject's goal achievement. Finally, in the activation of commitments, the agent must be able to activate an implicit contract between himself and the target. Successful influence depends on the subject accepting the validity of the agent's interpretation of the prior commitment.

Organization of the Social World

All frameworks assume a target of influence who functions in an ongoing social world. In some cases, this social world is one which need not be operative at the moment of influence. In consistency theory, for example, the person already has a set of cognitions which were acquired, of course, from the social world in which he exists. But once these have been taken in, nothing further needs to be assumed about an organized social system to set the influence process in motion. Other people might trigger a subjective inconsistency, but so might the physical environment. Others need not be present or organized in any particular way.

In functional theory, some set of ongoing interpersonal relationships are necessary for at least some of the functions to be fulfilled. This is most clear for the social adjustment function, but most functional theorists assume that other people play an essential role in mediating all functions.

Activation-of-commitments makes the strongest assumptions about an ongoing social structure. It assumes the existence of a normative order in which both agent and target participate and to which both are subordinate. In many cases, this order is embodied in a formal authority system with laws, but it can be merely an informal set of obligations as well. Social influence is assumed to operate only where some set of norms exist outside and above the particular relationship.

These, then, are some of the major differences among the views. They are summarized in Chart 6.

Chart 6 Underlying Issues on How People's Attitudes and Behavior are Changed

Questions	Cognitive Consistency, *e.g.,* Sherwood *et al.*	Functional, *e.g.,* Katz	Activation of Commitments, *e.g.,* Milgram
1. Is the energizer of change internal or external?	Internal: the mind flees from cognitive inconsistency	Mixed: depends on function	External: sense of interpersonal obligation
2. What is the nature of the relationship between agent and target?	Cue-giver of inconsistency	Goal-facilitator	Contractor
3. What is assumed about the ongoing social world?	Nothing, but other people sometimes trigger cognitive inconsistency	Ongoing interpersonal relationships	Ongoing normative order

REFERENCES

Brown, Roger. *Social Psychology.* New York: Free Press, Division of Macmillan Co., 1965.

Cohen, Arthur R. *Attitude Change and Social Influence.* New York: Basic Books, Inc., 1964.

Dichter, Ernst. *The Strategy of Desire.* New York: Doubleday, 1960.

Gouldner, Alvin. "The Norm of Reciprocity: A Preliminary Statement," *American Sociological Review* 25, 1960, 161-179.

Kelman, Herbert C. "Processes of Opinion Change," *Public Opinion Quarterly,* 25, 1961, 57-78.

Kohlberg, Lawrence. "Stage and Sequence: The Cognitive-Developmental Approach to Socialization," in D.A. Goslin (Ed.), *Handbook of Socialization Theory and Research.* Chicago: Rand McNally, 1968.

Lieberman, Seymour. "The Effects of Changes in Roles on the Attitudes of Role Occupants," *Human Relations,* 9, 1956, 385-402.

Raven, B. "Social Influence and Power," in I.D. Steiner and M. Fishbein (Eds.), *Current Studies in Social Psychology.* New York: Holt, Rinehart, & Winston, 1965.

Smith, M.B., Bruner, J.S. and White, R.W. *Opinions and Personality.* New York: Wiley, 1956.

Zajonc, Robert. "The Concepts of Balance, Congruity, and Dissonance." *Public Opinion Quarterly,* 24, 1960, 280-296.

COGNITIVE DISSONANCE: THEORY AND RESEARCH

JOHN J. SHERWOOD, JAMES W. BARRON, AND H. GORDON FITCH

In 1957, Leon Festinger put forth a little, but fascinating, theory in his book *A Theory of Cognitive Dissonance.* The book created an immediate sensation and has produced a decade of feverish research activity. It is a little theory because it is based upon a single principle and because it uses only a few concepts. Furthermore, it does not pretend to be a big theory; that is, it does not pretend to be a theory of behavior or personality. Yet at the same time, it is an important theory in that it is apparently useful in a wide variety of behavioral contexts—from studies of social problems and morality to the swimming of rats, from studies of attitude change and social influence to defense mechanisms. Finally, it is a fascinating theory because researchers have used it to make some "surprising" predictions that do not easily follow from common sense or from other psychological theories.

The theory of cognitive dissonance is frequently referred to as a social psychological theory. That is probably because Festinger is best known as a social psychologist and because the theory has proved to be particularly useful in areas of social psychological concern, such as attitude change, social influence, and conformity. More accurately, however, the theory of cognitive dissonance is a cognitive theory of motivation. The term "cognitive" comes from the Latin word for "knowing" and refers to processes of thought and perception.

Introduction to the Theory

The basic assumption underlying dissonance theory is that an individual *strives for consistency among his opinions, attitudes, and values.* Festinger replaced the word "consistency" with the more neutral term *consonance.* Similarly, "inconsistency" was replaced with a term having a less logical connotation—*dissonance.* So a restatement of the basic proposition is that there is "pressure to produce consonant relations among cognitions and to avoid dissonance" (Festinger, 1957, p. 9).

The existence of dissonance is assumed to be psychologically uncomfortable. It is an aversive motivational state that impels a person to try to reduce the dissonance and to achieve consonance. In addition to being motivated to reduce dissonance, the person actively avoids situations that are likely to increase the dissonance in his cognitive world.

A state of dissonance exists when a person holds, at the same time, two cognitions that are inconsistent with each other according to his psychological expectations. The two cognitions are said to be dissonant with each other if—for the person—the obverse of one cognition would follow from the other. Thus, if cognition A implies cognition B, then holding A and the observe of B—that is, not-B is dissonant. For example, "viewing oneself as an honest person" (A) and "behaving honestly" (B) are consonant, because B follows from A. On the other hand, "viewing oneself as an honest person" and the *obverse* of "behaving honestly"—such as "stealing from the poor box"—are dissonant conditions.

A cognition is any knowledge, belief, attitude, or value that a person holds about himself, about his behavior, or about his environment. Expectations about what cognitive relationships are consonant—that is, what follows from what—are acquired through an individual's experience, the mores of his culture, and his notions about logical relations between events. If a person were to stand in the rain and yet not get wet, the cognitions representing these two facts would be dissonant with each other because people usually learn from experience that getting wet follows from standing in the rain.

The amount or level of dissonance aroused is (1) a function of the ratio of dissonant to consonant cognitions, and (2) a function of the importance of each cognition to the person. Although the precise nature of these functions is an empirical question that is not yet fully understood, the basic relations between amount of dissonance and the cognitions held by an individual are represented by the following:

$$\text{Dissonance} = \frac{\text{Importance x Number of Dissonant Cognitions}}{\text{Importance x Number of Consonant Cognitions}}$$

This heuristic expression is not meant to be precise in terms of specific numbers or measurements but to suggest a number of relationships— for example, that dissonance will be reduced if the number or importance of consonant cognitions in a given situation is increased.

The meaning of "importance" is not clearly explicated in the original theory. A definition that seems to fit the theory is that "importance" refers to the instrumentality of the cognitions for the satisfaction of the individual's needs and values, particularly those central to his wider value system. However, at times, situations may become so salient as to attach temporary importance to otherwise peripheral cognitions.

The initial observational basis for Festinger's notion that people actively seek to avoid and reduce dissonance among cognitions came from trying to understand some bizarre rumors that started after a major earthquake in India in 1934. The rumors were recorded in an area where people felt severe and prolonged tremors but did not suffer any injury or witness any damage. These are samples of the rumors: "There will be a severe cyclone in the next few days," "There will be a severe earthquake on the lunar eclipse day," "A flood is rushing toward the province," and "In five days the fatal day will arrive. . . unforeseeable calamities will arise." These observations seem to contradict the widely accepted hedonistic assumption that people avoid unpleasant things, such as anxiety and the prospect of pain.

Some comparable data from people who were actually in an area of death and destruction in another natural disaster show a complete absence of rumors predicting further disaster. The data from the two communities do not agree with so-called common sense. Why should the occurrence of an earthquake—in the absence of death and destruction—be correlated with such frightening and exaggerated rumors, while people who were actually in an area of disaster did not invent such rumors? For Festinger, the rumors fell into place when viewed in terms of relations between cognitions. In the community that experienced only the shock of the earthquake but no suffering and destruction, Festinger assumed that the residents had a strong and persistent fear reaction yet could see nothing to fear. The *feeling* of fear in the absence of an adequate *reason* for fear was dissonant. The rumors predicting future disaster, if believed, provided the residents with cognitions that were consonant with being afraid. The rumors were, according to the theory, "fear justifying" rumors and thus a shared mechanism for dissonance reduction.

Examples of Dissonance Reduction

It is assumed that if a person holds two cognitions that are inconsistent with each other, he will experience dissonance—an aversive motivational state—and he will then try to reduce the dissonance and achieve consonance. Dissonance can be reduced in several ways, including increasing the number and/or importance of consonant cognitions. The fear justifying rumors, an example of the first method, served to reduce dissonance by adding new elements that were consonant with being afraid. An example of changing the importance of consonant cognitions is in the person who—rather than stop smoking in the face of its danger to health—increases the feeling of enjoyment he receives from smoking. He might also add new consonant elements, such as "Smoking is not so deadly as this publicity suggests: I run a far greater risk whenever I drive a car."

The smoker, instead of seeking to enhance the consonant aspects of his behavior, could act to remove the dissonant elements; he could give up smoking and thereby remove one major dissonance-producing cognition.

Or he could attempt to minimize the other by distorting or ignoring the claims of medical research on the relation between smoking and health, perhaps by carefully avoiding exposure to articles or arguments discussing the ill effects of smoking.

According to the theory, the individual will choose one or more of all these possible ways to reduce dissonance. As might be expected, there is no unambiguous way of predicting which he will select. However, the general rule for determining the mode of dissonance reduction is that of least effort; that is, the cognition least resistant to change will be changed. Resistance is in part determined by (1) the number of presently irrelevant cognitions with which the changed cognition will become dissonant, thereby creating new dissonance, and by (2) the importance of these newly relevant cognitions in terms of the person's system of values.

Moreover, although dissonance can be reduced by decreasing the number of dissonant cognitions, the theory is not clear on how that can be done. The ease with which reality can be changed (or distorted) depends, among other things, on the concreteness or abstractness of the cognition, the extent to which it is private or public, and the relative ambiguity or clarity of the reality that it represents. . . .

Commitment and Volition

The most extensive modification of dissonance theory as originally stated by Festinger has been that of Brehm and Cohen in their book *Explorations in Cognitive Dissonance* (1962). In their summary of the research literature on dissonance theory at that time, they demonstrated the predictive value of the theory in these situations: (1) the period after a free choice among *attractive alternatives* (decision making in which dissonance is a function of the relative number of favorable cognitions of the unchosen alternatives); (2) instances of forced compliance, in which a person is induced to *behave* in a manner inconsistent with his attitudes; and (3) situations in which a person is exposed to *information* inconsistent with his attitudes.

Brehm and Cohen's primary contribution, however, was in their demonstration of the importance of commitment and volition to the predictions of dissonance theory. According to Brehm and Cohen, "commitment provides a specification of the conditions under which one cognition follows from the obverse of another. . . . A central kernel of dissonance theory. . .is the notion that *a person will try to justify a commitment to the extent that there is information discrepant with that commitment*" (p. 300). They define "commitment" very simply as a decision (to do or not to do something) or a choice (and thereby a rejection of unchosen alternatives) or active engagement in a given behavior.

Presumably, when a person engages in a course of action discrepant from an attitude that he holds about this action, he will experience dissonance. He may reduce the dissonance by bringing his attitude into consonance or agreement with his behavior; that is, he might change his attitude about the behavior. An example is a high school student who praises ivy league schools and denigrates state universities and afterward discovers he cannot get into an ivy league school. If he then chooses to enter a state university, dissonance theory would predict his attitude toward state universities would become more favorable and, possibly, his attitude toward the ivy league more negative. By his actions he is now committed to a state university, and his actions are dissonant with his formerly critical attitude toward state universities. Of course, one's attitudes toward a state university might change for many other reasons, but in this example the student's entry into the state university is crucial. His entry is contrary to his attitude toward state universities, and it is likely that his attitude will become favorable in order to be more consonant with the fact that he is now attending the state university.

The crucial variable in commitment is *volition*, which refers to the degree of free choice involved in the decision to behave in an attitude-discrepant way. Thus, to the extent that the student in the example saw himself as being *forced* to attend a state university, the theory predicts he would experience less dissonance and, therefore, less pressure to change his attitudes about state universities than if he saw himself as making a *free* and uncoerced choice. A frequent, and non-obvious, finding in research on dissonance theory is the *less* the reward for engaging in an attitude-discrepant behavior, the greater the resultant attitude change is likely to be. Similarly, it has usually been found that the *less* the coercion used to force compliance or commitment, the greater the likelihood of attitude change. Presumably, a person finding himself committed to doing something contrary to his attitudes for a large reward or from coercion can deny responsibility for his behavior. He can externalize the reason he is doing what he is doing; that is, he can say to himself: "I don't really believe in this, but I really had no choice because I cannot afford to refuse such a large reward; therefore, I am justified in doing this even though I believe it is not what I should be doing." On the other hand, a person who receives a minimal reward or very slight coercion cannot justify his attitude-discrepant actions so easily. He is more likely to conclude: "I got myself into this situation, and because I don't normally do things in which I don't believe, there must really be something to the position I am advocating."

An Example of Research: The Effects of Temptation

Consider a person who is tempted by anticipation of reward to do something he thinks is immoral. If he performs such an act, dissonance will ensue between his knowledge that the act is immoral and his knowledge that he has done it. One way to reduce this dissonance would be to change his attitude—to decide, "It's not really so very bad."

As with other attitude-discrepant behavior that is a consequence of forced compliance, the amount of dissonance created decreases as the strength of the inducing force (temptation) increases. Therefore, one would expect, the *greater* the reward for performing an immoral act, the *less* the dissonance. The cognitions about the large reward received are consonant with performing the act; that is, the immoral act can be in some sense "justified" by the large reward.

How about the person who is tempted but resists? For him giving up the reward induces dissonance. He can reduce this dissonance by increasing the number and/or the importance of cognitions that are consonant with his behavior. If he has refrained from doing something he thinks is wrong—in spite of a reward—he can then convince himself the act is extremely immoral, thus justifying the behavior to which he has committed himself.

Whereas the person who *succumbs* to temptation and commits an act he considers immoral has less dissonance the greater the reward he gains, the person who *resists* temptation has more dissonance the greater the reward he forsakes.

These hypotheses were tested by Mills (1958) in an experiment with sixth graders. They were first given a questionnaire to measure the severity of their attitudes toward cheating. Then they participated in a contest in which they worked individually at a task involving eye-hand coordination. Three experimental conditions were created: (1) high temptation to cheat (offer of a large prize for outstanding performance on the task) together with low restraints against cheating (the students were given the opportunity to cheat while scoring their own performance); (2) low temptation (small prize) together with low restraint; and (3) high temptation together with high restraint (little opportunity to cheat). Cheating could be secretly detected by the experimenter. Some students cheated, some did not. One day later, the students were again asked about their attitudes toward cheating.

The findings generally supported dissonance theory. Attitude change scores showed on the average that those children who cheated tended to become more lenient toward cheating and that those who did not cheat became more critical of cheating. Students who cheated for a small prize became more lenient toward cheating than did those who cheated for a big prize. For the students who did not cheat, those giving up a large prize became more severe in their condemnation of cheating than did those who gave up only a small prize.

Finally, Mills' study showed that the effects of dissonance arousal are limited to cognitions directly relevant to the decision involved. Attitudes were also measured about other aggressive actions unrelated to cheating. But these attitudes were unaffected by the experiment. . . .

Situational Factors in the Arousal of Cognitive Dissonance

The Brehm and Cohen review makes it abundantly clear that commitment plays a critical role in the arousal or induction of cognitive dissonance. According to their definition, commitment follows a *decision* among alternatives. The crucial variable in producing commitment is *choice* or *volition*, so that the person feels responsible for and, in general, bound to the decision or the act. When the act is at odds with his private beliefs, dissonance is created.

It seems evident that the experience of dissonance should be higher if the actor sees his decision as volunatry—as his own decision—than would be the case if he is forced or required to engage in behavior discrepant with his private beliefs. In the latter case, dissonance can be avoided or reduced very simply: "I am being forced to do this; I really didn't have any choice. Therefore, it doesn't change my own beliefs about the matter at all." The research provided and reviewed by Brehm and Cohen indicates that people do in fact experience more dissonance under the condition of commitment than they do when they can satisfactorily externalize the responsibility for their discrepant behavior. A reasonable modification of the "formula" given previously suggests the relationship of commitment to the amount of dissonance induced:

$$\text{Dissonance} = \frac{\text{Degree of}}{\text{Commitment}} \times \frac{\text{Importance x Number of Dissonant Cognitions}}{\text{Importance x Number of Consonant Cognitions}}$$

We have a theoretical definition of commitment, but we still need to know how the concept has been defined operationally. Two techniques have received frequent experimental use. The first method of inducing commitment is to vary the degree of influence or persuasion utilized by the experimenter in getting the subject to engage in the attitude-discrepant behavior. For example, in order to produce a feeling of free choice and consequently high commitment, the experimenter might say to the subject, "I realize you are against issue X, but we are short of subjects and we really need someone to argue *for* issue X. Would you mind doing that?"

Usually the experimenter takes care *not* to appear overfriendly or overly in need of the subject's help; in fact, the experimenter may behave in an especially brusque fashion in order to prevent the subject from reducing dissonance by justifying his attitude-discrepant behavior with a cognition such as "I really don't believe what I am about to say, but he needs help, and anything to help science."

The second technique commonly used to induce commitment is differential reward. Paying some subjects a large amount of money for behaving in a particular way presumably reduces their choice in engaging in the attitude-discrepant behavior, whereas paying other subjects a small amount for the same behavior presumably induces high commitment. In the latter case, it would seem that the subjects value their integrity more than their small payment and might say to themselves: "I am responsible for this reprehensible act, and this isn't enough payment to justify what I am doing."

An example of the use of this technique is the classic Festinger-Carlsmith study (1959) using forced compliance with differential reward. They first had college students perform a boring experimental task. A third of the subjects (the control group) was then asked how they felt about the task, and they frankly described it as an unpleasant one. The two other groups had one duty to perform before they rated the task: They were paid to assist the experimenter by introducing the next subject, who was waiting outside, to the task by describing it as interesting and enjoyable. The required behavior was obviously discrepant with the subjects' own cognitions about the pleasantness of the task. The members of one group were paid \$1 for this attitude-discrepant behavior, and the others were paid \$20.

Dissonance theory predicts that one way to reduce the dissonance aroused would be to change one's attitude about the task to coincide with what he had just said about it—or decide that the task really wasn't so unpleasant. In addition, high reward for the behavior should lower the likelihood of attitude change because commitment to the expressed point of view is less than when one is paid very little.

The results of the experiment were that the group of subjects receiving \$20 rated the original task neutrally; in fact, their ratings were not significantly different from those of the control group. The subjects who made the same discrepant statements but were paid only \$1 rated the task as more pleasant and enjoyable than the other two groups did. These findings confirm the dissonance predictions that (1) making a statement discrepant with one's true evaluation tends to produce change in evaluation toward the position in the statement and that (2) the amount of change *decreases* as the amount of reward for making the statement *increases.**

One consequence of adding the commitment variable as an important one in the production of a state of cognitive dissonance has been that
a new question has been raised: Is it necessary for the person actually to
perform the discrepant behavior once he has committed himself to it in
order to produce attitude change, or is commitment alone sufficient to
produce attitude change in the direction of the position to which the
person is publicly committed but privately opposed? Brehm and Cohen
report a number of experiments in which commitment alone was sufficient
to produce some attitude changes. The question has, therefore, become
the relative *amount* of attitude change produced by commitment alone,
commitment with subsequent dissonant behavior, and dissonant behavior
alone (for example, improvisation of arguments against private attitude)
without choice or commitment in performing this behavior. Specification
of the conditions under which one of these techniques for inducing dissonance and subsequent attitude change is more effective than others has not
yet been systematically undertaken but is another area for continued
research.

At least two conclusions on the commitment variable have emerged.
First, this addition to dissonance theory has made the theory more explicit
and has been instrumental in generating further research. Second, the
variable of commitment seems to separate clearly dissonance theory from
a host of other currently popular cognitive consistency theories. It is clear
that other consistency theories do not account for this variable and that
it is a crucial one in dissonance theory in both extending it and indicating
a limitation in terms of attitude change techniques. . . .

Dissonance Reduction

Once dissonance has been aroused, theoretically, the person will be motivated to reduce it by using one or more of the various modes of dissonance
reduction that may be available. In a discussion of dissonance reduction,
two main questions should be considered. First, how may the person
reduce his dissonance? Second, what determines the preferred or chosen
mode of resolution?

---

* For two alternative interpretations of the findings of the Festinger and Carlsmith
study (1959), see D. J. Bem, "Self-perception: An Alternative interpretation of
cognitive dissonance phenomena, " *Psychological Review,* 74 (1967) 183-200; and the
incentive theory interpretation by A. C. Elms and I. L. Janis, "Counter-norm attitudes
induced by consonant versus dissonant conditions of role-playing," *Journal of
Experimental Research in Personality,* 1 (1965), 50-60. J.W. Brehm, (1965) answers the
criticisms of Elms and Janis in "Comment on 'Counter-norm attitudes induced by
consonant versus dissonant conditions of role playing ' " *Journal of Experimental
Research in Personality,* 1 (1965), 61-64.

To answer the first question, we shall outline three ways an individual may reduce the dissonance in a given situation: (1) revision of a dissonance producing *attitude*, (2) *selective exposure* to dissonant information, and (3) changing *behaviors* that produce dissonant cognitions.

Attitude Change

One of the most common forms dissonance research has taken requires that the subject find himself in a situation that contains dissonance for him because of some attitude he holds; that is, the subject's attitude toward some issue must be inconsistent with his behavior. A change in the attitude, as measured before and after performance of the behavior, is then said to be evidence for the psychological discomfort resulting from the inconsistency. Thus, the attitude change is theoretically motivated by and reduces the experience of dissonance. The discrepancy between a subject's attitudes and his behavior is often made salient by using either of two procedures termed "inadequate justification" and "effort expenditure."

The Festinger-Carlsmith study described previously, in which subjects were paid $1 or $20 for misrepresenting an experimental task by telling other subjects that it was enjoyable, is an illustration of the "inadequate justification" technique. Here it is assumed that a low reward is insufficient reason for the subject to express an attitude discrepant with one he privately holds; that this behavior is dissonant with his attitude; and that, because the behavior cannot be changed, the attitude will be changed. Subjects paid $20, on the other hand, had adequate justification for their behavior, and dissonance was thus not so strongly aroused.

The special significance of this design is in its implication that both high reward and strong coercion provide justification for attitude-discrepant behavior. Consequently, if one is interested in changing another's *attitude*, it is most effective to use as little reward or coercion as possible above some minimum amount in producing the necessary *behavior*. Note, however, that this behavior (or a commitment to behave in this way) must nevertheless occur.

The second experimental procedure for introducing a discrepancy between attitudes and behavior is "effort expenditure." This procedure focuses on the amount of effort the subject puts into an attitude-discrepant task. The more effort he expends (unpleasantness?), the more dissonance is aroused between the behavior on the task and the attitude toward the task. And one way to reduce the resulting discomfort is to change the attitude to fit more closely the behavior on the task (for example, to like the task more).

Yaryan and Festinger (1961) designed an experiment to examine this hypothesis. In order to show the effect of "preparatory effort" on one's belief in a future event, they asked subjects to prepare for an IQ test by studying an information sheet on which there were definitions essential to the test. The subjects were told that they were participants in a "techniques of study" experiment that was supposed to investigate the techniques, hunches, and hypotheses that students use to study for exams. The experimenter said that only half of them would later actually take the IQ test.

In the "high effort" condition, the subjects were asked to study the sheet and memorize the definitions; in the "low effort" condition, they were asked simply to glance over the definitions briefly and were told that they would have access to the sheet later if they were actually to take the test. After studying the material, the subjects gave their estimates of the probability that they were part of the group that would be taking the IQ test. The results showed that the high effort group considered themselves more likely to take the test.

The authors' interpretation of these results is that the more effort expended in preparation for a future event, the more dissonant is the cognition that the event may not occur. Thus, subjects in the high effort condition should believe more strongly in the likelihood of the occurrence of the event. This should be the case regardless of whether one is apprehensive about the event (considers it unpleasant) or whether one looks forward to it.

Selective Exposure

If a person holds two cognitions that are inconsistent with each other, it is theorized that he will try to find ways to reduce the feeling of dissonance caused by them. Searching for new cognitions that support the favored side of the dissonant pair would be one possibility; avoiding new cognitions that would increase the dissonance would be another. In situations in which a person has some control over the kind of information to which he is exposed, according to the principle of selective exposure, he will (1) seek out dissonance reducing information and/or (2) actively avoid dissonance increasing information.

One of the earliest dissonance studies is related to this hypothesis. Ehrlich, Guttman, Schonbach, and Mills (1957) looked at the selective reading of automobile advertisements by people who had just purchased a new car and by others who owned older cars. The researchers guessed that someone who had recently made an important decision in favor of one make of automobile would be more likely to read material favoring that make than would people who had either bought another make or not made a recent decision in favor of any automobile. They also expected new car owners to avoid reading materials that favored a brand other than the one they chose.

The first prediction, that owners of new cars read advertisements of their own car more often than of cars they considered but did not buy and more often than other cars not involved in the choice, was supported by the evidence. However, this experiment as well as several others, such as Mills, Aronson, and Robinson (1959), Rosen (1961), and Adams (1961), did not yield evidence confirming the proposition that dissonant information will be avoided in proportion to the amount of dissonance produced. It seems, then, that people tend to seek out dissonance *reducing* information, but they do not necessarily *avoid* dissonance *increasing* information.

Perhaps this rather consistent finding, which conflicts with a direct prediction of the theory, can suggest a direction in which attempts to modify the theory might proceed. We know that people seek consonant information but can also tolerate dissonant information. In fact, there is some more recent evidence (Feather, 1963) that not only do smokers not avoid information linking lung cancer and smoking but, if anything, show a slight preference for it. This finding has been replicated in an unpublished work by Brock in 1965. Canon (1964) has shown that even though information increases dissonance, it may also be *useful* to the individual. The utility of information may often be more important than the dissonance it arouses, in which case it will be carefully studied. Canon's data also suggests that people may expose themselves to dissonant information largely because it is dissonant—they can in this way develop counterarguments to refute the dissonant position (Weick, 1965, p. 1268).

An expansion of the basic dissonance idea in order to incorporate these findings could use the concept of "information processing." When people develop arguments and attitudes, they seem to require a certain amount of information on both sides of the question in order to feel justified in holding them. This means an individual may purposefully introduce dissonant cognitions. Dissonant and consonant information may be *processed* differently by the individual, but to assume that the latter is sought for the comfortable feeling it provides and that the former is unpleasant and therefore to be avoided, denied, or distorted is far too simple for a theory of human behavior.

Behavioral Changes

If behaving in a certain way produces cognitions that are inconsistent with some attitude, dissonance theory predicts that either the attitudes or the behavior will change. In order to demonstrate this concept experimentally, Weick (1964) devised a situation in which the subject could reduce dissonance only by changing the level of a behavior; other ways of reducing dissonance were blocked. Weick was able to show significant attitude change *and* behavioral change in the form of enhancement of and working harder at an experimental task in which subjects were provided insufficient justification for engaging in that task.

In this experiment, the subjects were first assembled in a group. The experimenter then came into the room and in a rather discouraged manner informed the subjects that he had just been told by the head of the psychology department that he would not be allowed to offer class credit to participants in the experiment as originally promised because he was not a member of the psychology department staff. The experimenter then said rather brusquely that anyone who wanted to leave could at that time but that they might as well stay and participate in the experiment. (A few subjects did get up and leave at this point.) The subjects who stayed then worked at a concept attainment task. The startling finding was that these subjects worked harder at the task and liked it better than did subjects in control groups, who initially thought that they would get experimental credit. (Actually, at the end of the experiment, all subjects were informed of the ruse and were given equal credit for participating.)

The surprising aspect of this outcome is that Weick was able to demonstrate an increase in productivity with a reduction in the reward offered—an outcome exactly opposite to what traditional incentive theory would predict. This outcome may be seen by comparing the experimental and control conditions. In the experimental group, the subjects thought they were *not* going to receive class credit, and they were staying for an experimenter who was anything but warm-hearted. The latter aspect hopefully eliminated the dissonance reducing cognition that one is really staying to help out a warm, deserving person. The experimental subjects worked harder and performed better than those who received the expected reward of class credit. The manipulation, moreover, produced behavioral change in the form of increased productivity—not merely attitudinal change.

Choosing Between Various Modes of Dissonance Reduction

Three ways of reducing dissonance have just been discussed, and these are by no means exhaustive. Changing the importance of relevant cognitions, or the importance of the entire set of cognitions, selective recall of dissonant information, perceptual distortion, and denial of commitment or volition are all possibilities. What, then, determines which of these alternatives will be used by a given individual in preference to others?

We mentioned earlier that Festinger's original conception was that an individual would prefer to reduce dissonance by making the least effortful change he could make. The cognition least resistant to change would be selected, in other words. Research on this hypothesis has raised a number of questions indicating that the picture may be more complicated; indeed, the principle may eventually need to be replaced by a better one.

Dissonance theory itself is not equipped to predict which means of reducing dissonance will be chosen. Dissonance theorists, however, have made attempts in this direction. For example, Weick (1964) has conducted research leading him to believe that people sometimes choose the method of dissonance reduction that affords the most *stable* resolution. If one has two inconsistent attitudes about some issue, it might be easiest simply to change one's attitude on one side of that issue and thus reduce dissonance. But if one *behaves* in a way that is consistent with one attitude but not the other (thus producing a behavioral commitment to the first), then one's position is solidified, less resistant to change, and more stable. Weick's research on behavioral change reinforces this notion; he feels that behavior can be used to *validate* a cognitive realignment.

REFERENCES

Adams, J. S. "Reduction of Cognitive Dissonance by Seeking Consonant Information," *Journal of Abnormal and Social Psychology,* **62** (1961), pp. 74-78.

Bem, D. J. "Self-perception: An Alternative Interpretation of Dissonance Phenomena," *Psychological Review,* **74** (1967), pp. 183-200.

Brehm, J. W. "Comment on 'Counter-norm Attitudes Induced by Consonant versus Dissonant Conditions of Role Playing'," *Journal of Experimental Research in Personality,* **1** (1965), pp. 383-387.

Brehm, J. W. and Cohen, A. *Explorations in Cognitive Dissonance.* New York: Wiley, 1962.

Canon, L. K. "Self-confidence and Selective Exposure to Information," in L. Festinger (Ed.), *Conflict, Decision and Dissonance.* Stanford California: Stanford University Press, 1964, pp. 83-95.

Ehrlich, D. et al. "Postdecision Exposure to Relevant Information," *Journal of Abnormal and Social Psychology,* **54** (1957), pp. 93-112.

Elms, A. C. and Janis, I. L. "Counter-norm Attitudes Induced by Consonant versus Dissonant Conditions of Role Playing," *Journal of Experimental Research in Personality,* **1** (1965), pp. 50-61.

Feather, N. T. "Cognitive Dissonance, Sensitivity, and Evaluation," *Journal of Abnormal and Social Psychology,* **66** (1963), pp. 157-163.

Festinger, L. *A Theory of Cognitive Dissonance.* New York: Harper, 1957.

Festinger, L. and Carlsmith, J. M. "Cognitive Consequences of Forced Compliance," *Journal of Abnormal and Social Psychology,* **58** (1959), pp. 203-210.

Mills, J. "Changes in Moral Attitudes Following Temptation," *Journal of Personality,* **26** (1958), pp. 517-531.

Mills, J., Aronson, E. and Robinson, H. "Selectivity in Exposure to Information," *Journal of Abnormal and Social Psychology,* **59** (1959), pp. 250-253.

Rosen, S. "Postdecision Affinity for Incompatible Information," *Journal of Abnormal and Social Psychology,* **63** (1961), pp. 188-190.

Weick, K. E. "Reduction of Cognitive Dissonance Through Task Enhancement and Effort Expenditure," *Journal of Abnormal and Social Psychology,* **68** (1964), pp. 533-539.

Weick, K. E. "When Prophecy Pales: The Fate of Dissonance Theory," *Psychological Reports,* **16** (1965), pp. 1261-1275.

Yaryan, R. B. and Festinger, L. "Preparatory Action and Belief in the Probable Occurrence of Future Events," *Journal of Abnormal and Social Psychology,* **63** (1961), pp. 603-606.

THE FUNCTIONAL APPROACH TO THE STUDY OF ATTITUDES

DANIEL KATZ

Nature of Attitudes: Their Dimensions

Attitude is the predisposition of the individual to evaluate some symbol or object or aspect of his world in a favorable or unfavorable manner. Opinion is the verbal expression of an attitude, but attitudes can also be expressed in nonverbal behavior. Attitudes include both the affective, or feeling core of liking or disliking, and the cognitive, or belief, elements which describe the object of the attitude, its characteristics, and its relations to other objects. All attitudes thus include beliefs, but not all beliefs are attitudes. When specific attitudes are organized into a hierarchical structure, they comprise *value systems.* Thus a person may not only hold specific attitudes against deficit spending and unbalanced budgets but may also have a systematic organization of such beliefs and attitudes in the form of a value system of economic conservatism. . . .

Four Functions which Attitudes Perform for the Individual

The major functions which attitudes perform for the personality can be grouped according to their motivational basis as follows:

1. *The instrumental, adjustive, or utilitarian function* upon which Jeremy Bentham and the utilitarians constructed their model of man. A modern expression of his approach can be found in behavioristic learning theory.

From Daniel Katz, "Functional Approach to the Study of Attitudes," *The Public Opinion Quarterly,* **24** (1960), pp. 168-192. Reprinted by permission of the author and *The Public Opinion Quarterly.*

2. *The ego-defensive function* in which the person protects himself from acknowledging the basic truths about himself or the harsh realities in his external world. Freudian psychology and neo-Freudian thinking have been preoccupied with this type of motivation and its outcomes.

3. *The value-expressive function* in which the individual derives satisfactions from expressing attitudes appropriate to his personal values and to his concept of himself. This function is central to doctrines of ego psychology which stress the importance of self-expression, self-development, and self-realization.

4. *The knowledge function* based upon the individual's need to give adequate structure to his universe. The search for meaning, the need to understand, the trend toward better organization of perceptions and beliefs to provide clarity and consistency for the individual, are other descriptions of this function. The development of principles about perceptual and cognitive structure have been the contribution of Gestalt psychology.

Stated simply, the functional approach is the attempt to understand the reasons people hold the attitudes they do. The reasons, however, are at the level of psychological motivations and not of the accidents of external events and circumstances. Unless we know the psychological need which is met by the holding of an attitude we are in a poor position to predict when and how it will change. Moreover, the same attitude expressed toward a political candidate may not perform the same function for all the people who express it. And while many attitudes are predominantly in the service of a single type of motivational process, as described above, other attitudes may serve more than one purpose for the individual. A fuller discussion of how attitudes serve the above four functions is in order.

1. *The adjustment function.* Essentially this function is a recognition of the fact that people strive to maximize the rewards in their external environment and to minimize the penalties. The child develops favorable attitudes toward the objects in his world which are associated with the satisfactions of his needs and unfavorable attitudes toward objects which thwart him or punish him. Attitudes acquired in the service of the adjustment function are either the means for reaching the desired goal or avoiding the undesirable one, or are affective associations based upon experiences in attaining motive satisfactions (Katz and Stotland, 1959). The attitudes of the worker favoring a political party which will advance his economic lot are an example of the first type of utilitarian attitude. The pleasant image one has of one's favorite food is an example of the second type of utilitarian attitude.

In general, then, the dynamics of attitude formation with respect to the adjustment function are dependent upon present or past perceptions of the utility of the attitudinal object for the individual. The clarity, consistency, and nearness of rewards and punishments, as they relate to the individual's activities and goals, are important factors in the acquisition of such attitudes. Both attitudes and habits are formed toward specific objects, people, and symbols as they satisfy specific needs. The closer these objects are to actual need satisfaction and the more they are clearly perceived as relevant to need satisfaction, the greater are the probabilities of positive attitude formation. . . .

2. *The ego-defensive function.* People not only seek to make the most of their external world and what it offers, but they also expend a great deal of their energy on living with themselves. The mechanisms by which the individual protects his ego from his own unacceptable impulses and from the knowledge of threatening forces from without, and the methods by which he reduces his anxieties created by such problems, are known as mechanisms of ego defense. A more complete account of their origin and nature will be found in Sarnoff (1960). They include the devices by which the individual avoids facing either the inner reality of the kind of person he is, or the outer reality of the dangers the world holds for him. They stem basically from internal conflict with its resulting insecurities. In one sense the mechanisms of defense are adaptive in temporarily removing the sharp edges of conflict and in saving the individual from complete disaster. In another sense they are not adaptive in that they handicap the individual in his social adjustments and in obtaining the maximum satisfactions available to him from the world in which he lives. The worker who persistently quarrels with his boss and with his fellow workers, because he is acting out some of his own internal conflicts, may in this manner relieve himself of some of the emotional tensions which beset him. He is not, however, solving his problems of adjusting to his work situation and thus may deprive himself of advancement or even of steady employment.

Defense mechanisms, Miller and Swanson (1960) point out, may be classified into two families on the basis of the more or less primitive nature of the devices employed. The first family, more primitive in nature, are more socially handicapping and consist of denial and complete avoidance. The individual in such cases obliterates through withdrawal and denial the realities which confront him. The exaggerated case of such primitive mechanisms is the fantasy world of the paranoiac. The second type of defense is less handicapping and makes for distortion rather than denial. It includes rationalization, projection, and displacement.

Many of our attitudes have the function of defending our self-image. When we cannot admit to ourselves that we have deep feelings of inferiority we may project those feelings onto some convenient minority group and bolster our egos by attitudes of superiority toward this underprivileged group. The formation of such defensive attitudes differs in essential ways from the formation of attitudes which serve the adjustment function. They proceed from within the person, and the objects and situations to which they are attached are merely convenient outlets for their expression. Not all targets are equally satisfactory for a given defense mechanism, but the point is that the attitude is not created by the target but by the individual's emotional conflicts. And when no convenient target exists the individual will create one. Utilitarian attitudes, on the other hand, are formed with specific reference to the nature of the attitudinal object. They are thus appropriate to the nature of the social world to which they are geared. The high school student who values high grades because he wants to be admitted to a good college has a utilitarian attitude appropriate to the situation to which it is related.

All people employ defense mechanisms, but they differ with respect to the extent that they use them and some of their attitudes may be more defensive than others. It follows that the techniques and conditions for attitude change will not be the same for ego-defensive as for utilitarian attitudes.

Moreover, though people are ordinarily unaware of their defense mechanisms, especially at the time of employing them, they differ with respect to the amount of insight they may show at some later time about their use of defenses. In some cases they recognize that they have been protecting their egos without knowing the reason why. In other cases they may not even be aware of the devices they have been using to delude themselves.

3. *The value-expressive function.* While many attitudes have the function of preventing the individual from revealing to himself and others his true nature, other attitudes have the function of giving positive expression to his central values and to the type of person he conceives himself to be. A man may consider himself to be an enlightened conservative or an internationalist or a liberal, and will hold attitudes which are the appropriate indication of his central values. Thus we need to take account of the fact that not all behavior has the negative function of reducing the tensions of biological drives or of internal conflicts. Satisfactions also accrue to the person from the expression of attitudes which reflect his cherished beliefs and his self-image. The reward to the person in these instances is not so much a matter of gaining social recognition or monetary rewards as of establishing his self-identity and confirming his notion of the sort of person he sees himself to be. The gratifications obtained from value expression may go beyond the confirmation of self-identity.

Just as we find satisfaction in the exercise of our talents and abilities, so we find reward in the expression of any attributes associated with our egos.

Value-expressive attitudes not only give clarity to the self-image but also mold that self-image closer to the heart's desire. The teenager who by dress and speech establishes his identity as similar to his own peer group may appear to the outsider a weakling and a craven conformer. To himself he is asserting his independence of the adult world to which he has rendered childlike subservience and conformity all his life. Very early in the development of the personality the need for clarity of self-image is important—the need to know "who I am." Later it may be even more important to know that in some measure I am the type of person I want to be. Even as adults, however, the clarity and stability of the self-image is of primary significance. Just as the kind, considerate person will cover over his acts of selfishness, so too will the ruthless individualist become confused and embarrassed by his acts of sympathetic compassion. One reason it is difficult to change the character of the adult is that he is not comfortable with the new "me." Group support for such personality change is almost a necessity, as in Alcoholics Anonymous, so that the individual is aware of approval of his new self by people who are like him.

The socialization process during the formative years sets the basic outlines for the individual's self-concept. Parents constantly hold up before the child the model of the good character they want him to be. A good boy eats his spinach, does not hit girls, etc. The candy and the stick are less in evidence in training the child than the constant appeal to his notion of his own character. It is small wonder, then, that children reflect the acceptance of this model by inquiring about the characters of the actors in every drama, whether it be a television play, a political contest, or a war, wanting to know who are the "good guys" and who are the "bad guys." Even as adults we persist in labeling others in the terms of such character images. Joe McCarthy and his cause collapsed in fantastic fashion when the telecast of the Army hearings showed him in the role of the villain attacking the gentle, good man represented by Joseph Welch. . . .

4. *The knowledge function.* Individuals not only acquire beliefs in the interest of satisfying various specific needs, they also seek knowledge to give meaning to what would otherwise be an unorganized chaotic universe. People need standards or frames of reference for understanding their world, and attitudes help to supply such standards. The problem of understanding, as John Dewy (1910) made clear years ago, is one "of introducing (1) *definiteness* and *distinction* and (2) *consistency* and *stability* of meaning into what is otherwise vague and wavering." The definiteness and stability are provided in good measure by the norms of our culture, which give the otherwise perplexed individual ready-made attitudes for comprehending his universe. Walter Lippmann's (1922) classical contribution to

the study of opinions and attitudes was his description of stereotypes and the way they provided order and clarity for a bewildering set of complexities. The most interesting finding in Herzog's (1944) familiar study of the gratifications obtained by housewives in listening to daytime serials was the unsuspected role of information and advice. The stories were liked "because they explained things to the inarticulate listener."

The need to know does not of course imply that people are driven by a thirst for universal knowledge. The American public's appalling lack of political information has been documented many times. In 1956, for example, only 13 per cent of the people in Detroit could correctly name the two United States Senators from the state of Michigan and only 18 per cent knew the name of their own Congressman (Katz and Eldersveld, 1961). People are not avid seekers after knowledge as judged by what the educator or social reformer would desire. But they do want to understand the events which impinge directly on their own life. Moreover, many of the attitudes they have already acquired give them sufficient basis for interpreting much of what they perceive to be important for them. Our already existing stereotypes, in Lippmann's language, "are an ordered, more or less consistent picture of the world, to which our habits, our tastes, our capacities, our comforts and our hopes have adjusted themselves. They may not be a complete picture of the world, but they are a picture of a possible world to which we are adapted" (1922, p. 95). It follows that new information will not modify old attitudes unless there is some inadequacy or incompleteness or inconsistency in the existing attitudinal structure as it relates to the perceptions of new situations.

Determinants of Attitude Arousal and Attitude Change

The problems of attitude arousal and of attitude change are separate problems. The first has to do with the fact that the individual has many predispositions to act and many influences playing upon him. Hence we need a more precise description of the appropriate conditions which will evoke a given attitude. The second problem is that of specifying the factors which will help to predict the modification of different types of attitude.

The most general statement that can be made concerning attitude arousal is that it is dependent upon the excitation of some need in the individual, or some relevant cue in the environment. When a man grows hungry, he talks of food. Even when not hungry he may express favorable attitudes toward a preferred food if an external stimulus cues him. The ego-defensive person who hates foreigners will express such attitudes under conditions of increased anxiety or threat or when a foreigner is perceived to be getting out of place.

The most general statement that can be made about the conditions conducive to attitude change is that the expression of the old attitude or its anticipated expression no longer gives satisfaction to its related need state. In other words, it no longer serves its function and the individual feels blocked or frustrated. Modifying an old attitude or replacing it with a new one is a process of learning, and learning always starts with a problem, or being thwarted in coping with a situation. Being blocked is a necessary, but not a sufficient, condition for attitude change. Other factors must be operative and will vary in effectiveness depending upon the function involved.

Arousing and Changing Utilitarian Attitudes

Political parties have both the problem of converting people with antagonistic attitudes (attitude change) and the problem of mobilizing the support of their own followers (attitude arousal). To accomplish the latter they attempt to revive the needs basic to old attitudes. For example, the Democrats still utilize the appeals of the New Deal and the Republicans still talk of the balanced budget. The assumption is that many people still hold attitudes acquired in earlier circumstances and that appropriate communication can reinstate the old needs. For most people, however, utilitarian needs are reinforced by experience and not by verbal appeals. Hence invoking the symbols of the New Deal will be relatively ineffective with respect to adjustive attitudes unless there are corresponding experiences with unemployment, decreased income, etc. Though the need state may not be under the control of the propagandist, he can exaggerate or minimize its importance. In addition to playing upon states of need, the propagandist can make perceptible the old cues associated with the attitude he is trying to elicit. These cues may have associated with them favorable affect, or feeling, though the related needs are inactive. For example, the fighters for old causes can be paraded across the political platform in an attempt to arouse the attitudes of the past.

The two basic conditions, then, for the arousal of existing attitudes are the activation of their relevant need states and the perception of the appropriate cues associated with the content of the attitude.

To change attitudes which serve a utilitarian function, one of two conditions must prevail: (1) the attitude and the activities related to it no longer provide the satisfactions they once did, or (2) the individual's level of aspiration has been raised. The Chevrolet owner who had positive attitudes toward his old car may now want a more expensive car commensurate with his new status.

Attitudes toward political parties and voting behavior are often difficult to change if there is no widespread dissatisfaction with economic conditions and international relations. . . .

The use of negative sanctions and of punishment to change utilitarian attitudes is more complex than the use of rewards. To be successful in changing attitudes and behavior, punishment should be used only when there is clearly available a course of action that will save the individual from the undesirable consequences. To arouse fear among the enemy in time of war does not necessarily result in desertion, surrender, or a disruption of the enemy war effort. Such channels of action may not be available to the people whose fears are aroused. The experiment of Janis and Feshbach (1953) in using fear appeals to coerce children into good habits of dental hygiene had the interesting outcome of a negative relationship between the amount of fear and the degree of change. Lurid pictures of the gangrene jaws of old people who had not observed good dental habits were not effective. Moreover, the group exposed to the strongest fear appeal was the most susceptible to counterpropaganda. One factor which helps to account for the results of this investigation was the lack of a clear-cut relation in the minds of the children between failure to brush their teeth in the prescribed manner and the pictures of the gangrene jaws of the aged. . . .

Arousal and Change of Ego-Defensive Attitudes

Attitudes which help to protect the individual from internally induced anxieties or from facing up to external dangers are readily elicited by any form of threat to the ego. The threat may be external, as in the case of a highly competitive situation, or a failure experience, or a derogatory remark. It is the stock in trade of demagogues to exaggerate the dangers confronting the people, for instance, Joe McCarthy's tactics with respect to Communists in the State Department. Many people have existing attitudes of withdrawal or of aggression toward deviants or out-groups based upon their ego-defensive needs. When threatened, these attitudes come into play, and defensive people either avoid the unpleasant situation entirely, as is common in the desegregation controversy, or exhibit hostility.

Another condition for eliciting the ego-defensive attitude is the encouragement given to its expression by some form of social support. The agitator may appeal to repressed hatred by providing moral justification for its expression. A mob leader before an audience with emotionally held attitudes toward Negroes may call out these attitudes in the most violent form by invoking the good of the community or the honor of white womanhood.

A third condition for the arousal of ego-defensive attitudes is the appeal to authority. The insecurity of the defensive person makes him particularly susceptible to authoritarian suggestion. When this type of authoritarian command is in the direction already indicated by his attitudes of antipathy toward other people, he responds quickly and joyously. It is no accident that movements of hate and aggression such as the Ku Klux Klan or the Nazi Party are authoritarian in their organized structure. Wagman (1955), in an experimental investigation of the uses of authoritarian suggestion, found that students high in ego-defensiveness as measured by the F-scale were much more responsive to directives from military leaders than were less defensive students.* In fact, the subjects low in defensiveness were not affected at all by authoritarian suggestion when this influence ran counter to their own attitudes. The subjects high in F-scores could be moved in either direction, although they moved more readily in the direction of their own beliefs.

A fourth condition for defensive arousal is the building up over time of inhibited drives in the individual, for example, repressed sex impulses. As the drive strength of forbidden impulses increases, anxiety mounts and release from tension is found in the expression of defensive attitudes. The deprivations of prison life, for example, build up tensions which can find expression in riots against the hated prison officials.

In other words, the drive strength for defensive reactions can be increased by situation frustration. Though the basic source is the long-standing internal conflict of the person, he can encounter additional frustration in immediate circumstances. Berkowitz (1959) has shown that anti-Semitic girls were more likely than less prejudiced girls to display aggression toward an innocent bystander when angered by a third person. . . .

The usual procedures for changing attitudes and behavior have little positive effect upon attitudes geared into our ego defenses. In fact they may have a boomerang effect of making the individual cling more tenaciously to his emotionally held beliefs. In the category of usual procedures should be included increasing the flow of information, promising and bestowing rewards, and invoking penalties. As has already been indicated, punishment is threatening to the ego-defensive person and the increase of threat is the very condition which will feed ego-defensive behavior. The eneuretic youngster with emotional problems is rarely cured by punishment. Teachers and coaches know that there are some children who respond to censure and punishment by persevering in the forbidden behavior. But what is not as well recognized is that reward is also not effective in modifying the actions of the ego-defensive person. His attitudes are an expression of his inner conflicts and are not susceptible

---

* The F-scale is a measure of authoritarianism comprising items indicative of both defensiveness and ideology.

to external rewards. The shopkeeper who will not serve Negroes because they are a well-fixated target for his aggressions will risk the loss of income incurred by his discriminatory reactions.

Three basic factors, however, can help change ego-defensive attitudes. In the first place, the removal of threat is a necessary though not a sufficient condition. The permissive and even supportive atmosphere which the therapist attempts to create for his patients is a special instance of the removal of threat. Where the ego-defensive behavior of the delinquent is supported by his group, the social worker must gain a measure of group acceptance so as not to be perceived as a threat by the individual gang members. An objective, matter-of-fact approach can serve to remove threat, especially in situations where people are accustomed to emotional appeals. Humor can also be used to establish a nonthreatening atmosphere, but it should not be directed against the audience or even against the problem. Cooper and Jahoda (1947) attempted to change prejudiced attitudes by ridicule, in the form of cartoons which made Mr. Biggott seem silly, especially when he rejected a blood transfusion which did not come from 100 per cent Americans. Instead of changing their attitudes, the subjects in this experiment found ways of evading the meaning of the cartoons.

In the second place, catharsis or the ventilation of feelings can help to set the stage for attitude change. Mention has already been made of the building up of tension owing to the lack of discharge of inhibited impulses. When emotional tension is at a high level the individual will respond defensively and resist attempts to change him. Hence, providing him with opportunities to blow off steam may often be necessary before attempting a serious discussion of new possibilities of behavior. Again, humor can serve this purpose. . . .

Conditions for Arousing and Changing Value-Expressive Attitudes

Two conditions for the arousal of value-expressive attitudes can be specified. The first is the occurrence of the cue in the stimulus situation which has been associated with the attitude. The liberal Democrat, as a liberal Democrat, has always believed in principle that an income tax is more just than a sales tax. Now the issue has arisen in his state, and the group in which he happens to be at the moment are discussing an increase in sales tax. This will be sufficient to cue off his opposition to the proposal without consideration of the specific local aspects of the tax problem. The second condition for the arousal of this type of attitude is some degree of thwarting of the individual's expressive behavior in the immediate past. The housewife occupied with the routine care of the home and the children during the day may seek opportunities to express her views to other women at the first social gathering she attends.

We have referred to voters backing their party for bread and butter reasons. Perhaps the bulk of voting behavior, however, is the elicitation of value-expressive attitudes. Voting is a symbolic expression of being a Republican or a Democrat. Party identification accounts for more variance in voting behavior than any other single factor. Though there is a minority who consider themselves independent and though there are minor shifts in political allegiance, the great majority of the people identify themselves as the supporters of a political party. Their voting behavior is an expression of this self-concept, and it takes a major event such as a depression to affect their voting habits seriously (Campbell, Converse, Miller, and Stokes, 1960).

Again, two conditions are relevant in changing value-expressive attitudes:

1. Some degree of dissatisfaction with one's self-concept or its associated values is the opening wedge for fundamental change. The complacent person, smugly satisfied with all aspects of himself, is immune to attempts to change his values. Dissatisfaction with the self can result from failures or from the inadequacy of one's values in preserving a favorable image of oneself in a changing world. The man with pacifist values may have become dissatisfied with himself during a period of fascist expansion and terror. Once there is a crack in the individual's central belief systems, it can be exploited by appropriately directed influences. The techniques of brain washing employed by the Chinese Communists both on prisoners of war in Korea and in the thought reform of Chinese intellectuals were essentially procedures for changing value systems.

In the brain washing of Chinese intellectuals in the revolutionary college, the Communists took advantage of the confused identity of the student. He had been both a faithful son and a rebellious reformer and perhaps even an uninvolved cynic. To make him an enthusiastic Communist the officials attempted to destroy his allegiance to his parents and to transfer his loyalty to Communist doctrines which could meet his values as a rebel. Group influences were mobilized to help bring about the change by intensifying guilt feelings and providing for atonement and redemption through the emotional catharsis of personal confession (Lifton, 1957).

To convert American prisoners of war, the Communists made a careful study of the vulnerability of their victims. They found additional weaknesses through a system of informers and created new insecurities by giving the men no social support for their old values (Schein, 1957). They manipulated group influences to support Communist values and exploited their ability to control behavior and all punishments and rewards in the situation. The direction of all their efforts, however, was to undermine old values and to supply new ones. The degree of their success has probably been exaggerated in the public prints, but from their point of view they did achieve some genuine gains. One estimate is that some 15 per cent of the returning prisoners of war were active collaborators, another 5 per cent resisters, and some 80 per cent "neutrals." Segal, in a study of a sample of 579 of these men, found that 12 per cent had to some degree accepted Communist ideology (Segal, 1957).

2. Dissatisfaction with old attitudes as inappropriate to one's values can also lead to change. In fact, people are much less likely to find their values uncongenial than they are to find some of their attitudes inappropriate to their values. The discomfort with one's old attitudes may stem from new experiences or from the suggestions of other people. Senator Vandenburg, as an enlightened conservative, changed his attitudes on foreign relations from an isolationist to an internationalist position when critical events in our history suggested change. The influences exerted upon people are often in the direction of showing the inappropriateness of their present ways of expressing their values. Union leaders attempt to show that good union men should not vote on the old personal basis of rewarding friends and punishing enemies but should instead demand party responsibility for a program. . . .

We have already called attention to the role of values in the formation of attitudes in the early years of life. It is also true that attitude formation is a constant process and that influences are continually being brought to bear throughout life which suggest new attitudes as important in implementing existing values. An often-used method is to make salient some central value such as the thinking man, the man of distinction, or the virile man, and then depict a relatively new form of behavior consistent with this image. The role of motivational research in advertising is to discover the rudimentary image associated with a given product, to use this as a basis for building up the image in more glorified terms, and then to cement the association of this image with the product.

Arousing and Changing Attitudes which Serve the Knowledge Function

Attitudes acquired in the interests of the need to know are elicited by a stimulus associated with the attitude. The child who learns from his reading and from his parents that Orientals are treacherous will not have the attitude aroused unless some appropriate cue concerning the cognitive object is presented. He may even meet and interact with Orientals without identifying them as such and with no corresponding arousal of his

Determinants of Attitude Formation, Arousal, and Change in Relation to Type of Function

Function	Origin and Dynamics	Arousal Conditions	Change Conditions
Adjustment	Utility of attitudinal object in need satisfaction. Maximizing external rewards and minimizing punishments	1. Activation of needs 2. Salience of cues associated with need satisfaction	1. Need deprivation 2. Creation of new needs and new levels of aspiration 3. Shifting rewards and punishments 4. Emphasis on new and better paths for need satisfaction
Ego defense	Protecting against internal conflicts and external dangers	1. Posing of threats 2. Appeals to hatred and repressed impulses 3. Rise in frustrations 4. Use of authoritarian suggestion	1. Removal of threats 2. Catharsis 3. Development of self-insight
Value expression	Maintaining self identity; enhancing favorable self-image; self-expression and self-determination	1. Salience of cues associated with values 2. Appeals to individual to reassert self-image 3. Ambiguities which threaten self-concept	1. Some degree of dissatisfaction with self 2. Greater appropriateness of new attitude for the self 3. Control of all environmental supports to undermine old values
Knowledge	Need for understanding, for meaningful cognitive organization, for consistency and clarity	1. Reinstatement of cues associated with old problem or of old problem itself	1. Ambiguity created by new information or change in environment 2. More meaningful information about problems

attitude. Considerable prejudice in this sense is race-name prejudice and is only aroused when a premium is placed upon social identification. Since members of a minority group have many other memberships in common with a majority group, the latent prejudiced attitude may not necessarily be activated. Prejudice based upon ego-defensiveness, however, will result in ready identification of the disliked group.

The factors which are productive of change of attitudes of this character are inadequacies of the existing attitudes to deal with new and changing situations. The person who has been taught that Orientals are treacherous may read extended accounts of the honesty of the Chinese or may have favorable interactions with Japanese. He finds his old attitudes in conflict with new information and new experience, and proceeds to modify his beliefs. In this instance we are dealing with fictitious stereotypes which never corresponded to reality. In other cases the beliefs may have been adequate to the situation but the world has changed. Thus, some British military men formerly in favor of armaments have changed their attitude toward disarmament because of the character of nuclear weapons. The theory of cognitive consistency later elaborated in this issue can draw its best examples from attitudes related to the knowledge function.

Any situation, then, which is ambiguous for the individual is likely to produce attitude change. His need for cognitive structure is such that he will either modify his beliefs to impose structure or accept some new formula presented by others. He seeks a meaningful picture of his universe, and when there is ambiguity he will reach for a ready solution. Rumors abound when information is unavailable. . . .

In the foregoing analysis we have attempted to clarify the functions which attitudes perform and to give some psychological specifications of the conditions under which they are formed, elicited, and changed. This material is summarized in the table. . . .

REFERENCES

Berkowitz, L. "Anti-Semitism and the Displacement of Aggression," *Journal of Abnormal and Social Psychology,* **59** (1959), pp. 182-188.

Campbell, A., Converse, P., Miller, W. and Stokes, D. *The American Voter.* New York: Wiley, 1960.

Cooper, E. and Jahoda, M. "The Evasion of Propaganda: How Prejudiced People Respond to Anti-prejudice Propaganda," *Journal of Psychology,* **23** (1947), pp. 15-25.

Dewey, J. *How We Think.* New York: Macmillan, 1910.

Herzog, H. "What Do We Really Know About Daytime Serial Listeners," in P.F. Lazarsfeld and F. Stanton (Eds.), *Radio Research 1942-1943.* New York: Duell, Sloan, and Pierce, 1944, pp. 3-33.

Janis, I. L. and Feshbach. "Effects of Fear-arousing Communications," *Journal of Abnormal and Social Psychology,* **48** (1953), pp. 78-92.

Katz, D. and Eldersveld, S. "The Impact of Local Party Activity Upon the Electorate," *Public Opinion Quarterly,* **25** (1961), pp. 1-24.

Katz, D. and Stotland, E. "A Preliminary Statement to a Theory of Attitude Structure and Change," in S. Koch (Ed.), *Psychology: A Study of a Science,* **3**, New York: McGraw-Hill, 1959, pp. 423-475.

Lifton, R. J. "Thought Reform of Chinese Intellectuals: A Psychiatric Evaluation," *Journal of Social Issues,* **13**, No. 3 (1957), pp. 5-20.

Lippmann, W. *Public Opinion.* New York: Macmillan, 1922.

Miller, D. R. and Swanson, G. E. *Inner Conflict and Defense.* New York: Holt, 1960.

Sarnoff, I. "Psychoanalytic Theory and Social Attitudes," *Public Opinion Quarterly,* **24** (1960), pp. 251-279.

Schein, E. H. "Reactions to Severe, Chronic Stress in American Army Prisoners of War of the Chinese," *Journal of Social Issues,* **13**, No. 3 (1957), pp. 21-30.

Segal, J. "Correlates of Collaboration and Resistance Behavior among U. S. Army POW's in Korea," *Journal of Social Issues,* **13**, No. 3 (1957), pp. 31-40.

Wagman, M. "Attitude Change and the Authoritarian Personality," *Journal of Psychology,* **40** (1955), pp. 3-24.

OBEDIENCE AND DISOBEDIENCE TO AUTHORITY*

STANLEY MILGRAM

The situation in which one agent commands another to hurt a third turns up time and again as a significant theme in human relations. It is powerfully expressed in the story of Abraham, who is commanded by God to kill his son. It is no accident that Kierkegaard, seeking to orient his thought to the central themes of human experience chose Abraham's conflict as the springboard to his philosophy.

War, too, moves forward on the triad of an authority who commands a person to destroy the enemy, and perhaps all organized hostility may be viewed as a theme and variation on the three elements of authority, executant, and victim. We describe an experimental program, recently concluded at Yale University, in which a particular expression of this conflict is studied by experimental means.

In its most general form, the problem may be defined thus: If x tells y to hurt z, under what conditions will y carry out the command of x and under what conditions will he refuse? In the more limited form possible in laboratory research, the question becomes: If an experimenter tells a subject to hurt another person, under what conditions will the subject go along with this instruction, and under what conditions will he refuse to

* This research was supported by two grants from the National Science Foundation: NSF G17916 and NSF G24152. Exploratory studies carried out in 1960 were financed by a grant from the Higgins Funds of Yale University. For a more detailed account of some of the earlier work in this program see Milgram (1963).

From Stanley Milgram, "Some Conditions of Obedience and Disobedience to Authority," *The International Journal of Psychiatry,* Vol. 6, No. 4 (October 1968). Reprinted by permission of the author. A more thorough analysis may be found in *Obedience to Authority* by Stanley Milgram (New York: Harper & Row, 1973).

obey? The laboratory problem is not so much a dilution of the general statement, as it is one concrete expression of the many particular forms this question may assume.

One aim of the research was to study behavior in a strong situation of deep consequence to the participants, for the psychological forces operative in powerful and lifelike forms of the conflict may not be brought into play under diluted conditions.

This approach meant, first, that we had a special obligation to protect the welfare and dignity of the persons who took part in the study; subjects were, of necessity, placed in a difficult predicament, and steps had to be taken to assure their well being before they were discharged from the laboratory. Toward this end, a careful, postexperimental treatment was devised and has been carried through for subjects in all conditions.*

Terminology

If y follows the command of x, we shall say that he has obeyed x; if he fails to carry out the command of x, we shall say that he has disobeyed x. The terms to obey and disobey, as used in this study, refer to the subject's overt action only, and carry no implication for the motive or experiential states accompanying the action.

To be sure, the everyday use of the word *obedience* is not entirely free from complexities. It refers to action within widely varying situations and connotes diverse motives within those situations: there is a difference in meaning of a child's *obedience* and a soldier's *obedience* and the love, honor, and *obey* of the marriage vow. However, a consistent behavioral relationship is indicated in most uses of the terms: in the act of obeying, a person does what another person tells him to do. Y obeys x if he carries out the prescription for action that x has addressed to him; the term

---

* It consisted of an extended discussion with the experimenter and, of equal importance, a friendly reconciliation with the victim. It is made clear that the victim did not receive painful electric shocks. After the completion of the experimental series, subjects were sent a detailed report of the results and full purposes of the experimental program. A formal assessment of this procedure points to its over-all effectiveness: 83.7 percent of the subjects indicated that they were glad to have taken part in the study; 15.1 percent reported neutral feelings; and 1.3 percent stated that they were sorry to have participated. A large number of subjects spontaneously requested that they be used in further experimentation. Four-fifths of the subjects felt that more experiments of this sort should be carried out, and 74 percent indicated that they had learned something of personal importance as a result of being in the study. Furthermore, a University psychiatrist, experienced in outpatient treatment, interviewed a sample of experimental subjects with the aim of uncovering possible injurious effects resulting from participation. No such effects were in evidence. Indeed, subjects typically felt that their participation was instructive and enriching.

suggests, moreover, that some form of dominance-subordination, or hierarchical element is part of the situation in which the transaction between x and y occurs.

A subject who complies with the entire series of experimental commands will be termed an *obedient* subject; one who at any point in the command series defies the experimenter will be called a *disobedient* or *defiant* subject. As used in this report, the terms refer only to the subject's performance in the experiment and do not necessarily imply a general personality disposition to submit to or reject authority.

Subject Population

The subjects used in all experimental conditions were male adults, residing in the greater New Haven and Bridgeport areas, aged 20 to 50 years, and engaged in a wide variety of occupations. Each experimental condition described in this report employed 40 fresh subjects and was carefully balanced for age and occupational types. The occupational composition for each experiment was: workers, skilled and unskilled: 40 percent; white collar, sales, business: 40 percent; professionals: 20 percent. The occupations were intersected with three age categories (subjects in 20's, 30's and 40's, assigned to each condition in the proportion of 20 percent, 40 percent, and 40 percent respectively).

The General Laboratory Procedure

The focus of the study concerns the amount of electric shock a subject is willing to administer to another person when ordered by an experimenter to give the "victim" increasingly severe punishment. The act of administering shock is set in the context of a learning experiment, ostensibly designed to study the effect of punishment on memory. Aside from the experimenter, one naive subject and one accomplice perform in each session. On arrival each subject is paid $4.50. After a general talk by the experimenter telling how little scientists know about the effects of punishment on memory, subjects are informed that one member of the pair will serve as teacher and one as learner. A rigged drawing is held so that the naive subject is always the "teacher," and the accomplice becomes the "learner." The learner is taken to an adjacent room and strapped into an "electric chair."

The naive subject is told that it is his task to teach the learner a list of paired associates, to test him on the list, and to administer punishment whenever the learner errs in the test. Punishment takes the form of electric shock, delivered to the learner by means of a shock generator controlled by the naive subject. The teacher is instructed to increase the intensity of electric shock one step on the generator for each error. The learner, according to plan, provides many wrong answers, so that before long the naive subject must give him the strongest shock on the generator. Increases in shock level are met by increasingly insistent demands from the learner that the experiment be stopped because of the growing discomfort to him. However, in clear terms the experimenter orders the teacher to continue with the procedure in disregard of the learner's protests. *Thus, the naive subject must resolve a conflict between two mutually incompatible demands from the social field. He may continue to follow the orders of the experimenter and shock the learner with increasing severity, or he may refuse to follow the orders of the experimenter, and heed the learner's pleas. The experimenter's authority operates not in a free field, but against ever mounting countervailing pressure from the person being punished.*

A few technical points need to be considered before describing the findings of the study. For the purpose of delivering shock, a simulated shock generator is used, with 30 clearly marked voltage levels that range from 15 to 450 volts (and each activated by one of 30 individual lever switches set in a horizontal line). The naive subject is given a sample shock of 45 volts to convince him of the authenticity of the instrument. The generator bears verbal designations that range from "Slight Shock" to "Danger: Severe Shock."

The responses of the victim are standardized on tape, and each protest is coordinated to a particular voltage level on the shock generator. Starting with 75 volts the learner begins to grunt and moan. At 150 volts he demands to be let out of the experiment. At 180 volts he cries out that he can no longer stand the pain. At 300 volts he refuses to provide any more answers to the memory test, insisting that he is no longer a participant in the experiment and must be freed. In response to this last tactic, the experimenter instructs the naive subject to treat the absence of an answer as equivalent to a wrong answer, and to follow the usual shock procedure. The experimenter reinforces his demand with the statement: "You have no other choice, you must go on!" (This imperative is used whenever the naive subject tries to break off the experiment.) If the subject refuses to give the next higher level of shock the experiment is considered at an end. A quantitative value is assigned to the subject's performance based on the maximum intensity shock he administered before breaking off. Thus any subject's score may range from zero (for a subject unwilling to administer the first shock level) to 30 (for a subject who proceeds to the highest voltage level on the board). For any particular subject and for any particular experimental condition, the degree to which participants have followed the experimenter's orders may be specified with a numerical value corresponding to the metric on the shock generator.

This laboratory situation gives us a framework in which to study the subject's reactions to the principal conflict of the experiment. Again, this conflict is between the experimenter's demands that he continue to administer the electric shock, and the learner's demands, which become increasingly more insistent, that the experiment be stopped. The crux of the study is to vary systematically the factors believed to alter the degree of obedience to the experimental commands, to learn under what conditions submission to authority is most possible and under what conditions defiance is brought to the fore. . . .

Immediacy of the Victim

This series consisted of four experimental conditions. In each condition the victim was brought "psychologically" closer to the subject giving him shocks.

In the first condition (Remote Feedback) the victim was placed in another room and could not be heard or seen by the subject, except that at 300 volts, he pounded on the wall in protest. After 300 volts he no longer answered or was heard from.

The second condition (Voice Feedback) was identical to the first except that voice protests were introduced. As in the first condition, the victim was placed in an adjacent room but his complaints could be heard clearly through a door left slightly ajar and through the walls . . . .

The third experimental condition (Proximity) was similar to the second, except that the victim was now placed in the same room as the subject and $1\frac{1}{2}$ feet from him. Thus visible as well as audible cues were provided.

The fourth, and final condition of this series (Touch-Proximity) was identical to the third, with this exception: the victim only received a shock when his hand rested on a shockplate. At the 150 volt level the victim again demanded to be let free and, in this condition, refused to place his hand on the shockplate. The experimenter ordered the naive subject to force the victim's hand onto the plate. Thus obedience in this condition required that the subject have physical contact with the victim in order to give him punishment beyond the 150 volt level.

Forty adult subjects were studied in each condition. The data revealed that obedience was significantly reduced as the victim was rendered more immediate to the subject. The mean maximum shock for the condition is shown in Table 1. Expressed in terms of the proportion of obedient to defiant subjects, we find that 34 percent of the subjects defied the experimenter under the Remote Feedback condition, 37.5 percent in Voice Feedback, 60 percent in Proximity, and 70 percent in Touch-Proximity.

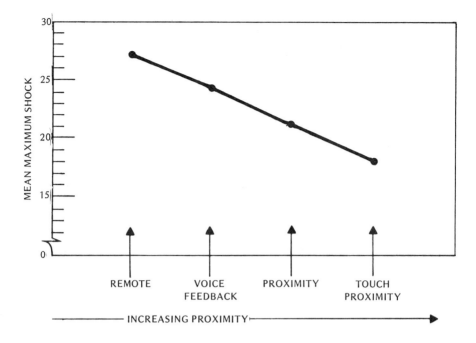

Figure 1. Experimental conditions

How are we to account for this effect? A first conjecture might be that as the victim was brought closer, the subject became more aware of the intensity of his suffering and regulated his behavior accordingly. This makes sense but our evidence does not support the interpretation. There are no consistent differences in the attributed level of pain across the four conditions (that is, the amount of pain experienced by the victim as estimated by the subject and expressed on a 14 point scale). But it is easy to speculate about alternative mechanisms.

Empathic Cues

In the Remote and to a lesser extent the Voice Feedback condition, the victim's suffering possesses an abstract, remote quality for the subject. He is aware, but only in a conceptual sense, that his actions cause pain to another person; the fact is apprehended, but not felt. The phenomenon is common enough. The bombardier can reasonably suppose that his weapon will inflict suffering and death, yet this knowledge is divested of affect and does not move him to a felt, emotional response to the suffering resulting from his actions. Other, similar observations have been made in wartime. It is possible that the visual cues associated with the victim's suffering trigger empathic responses in the subject and provide him with a more complete grasp of the victim's experience. Or it is possible that the empathic responses are themselves unpleasant, possessing drive properties that cause the subject to terminate the arousal situation. Diminishing obedience, then, would be explained by the enrichment of empathic cues in the successive experimental conditions.

Denial and Narrowing of the Cognitive Field

The remote condition allows a narrowing of the cognitive field so that the victim is put out of mind. The subject no longer considers the act of depressing a lever relevant to moral judgment, for it is no longer associated with the victim's suffering. When the victim is close, it is more difficult to exclude him phenomenologically. He necessarily intrudes on the subject's awareness because he (the victim) is continuously visible. In the remote conditions, his existence and reactions are made known only after the shock has been administered. The auditory feedback is sporadic and discontinuous. In the proximal condition the victim's inclusion in the immediate visual field renders him a continuously salient element for the subject. The mechanisms of denial can no longer be brought into play. One subject in the remote condition said: "It's funny how you really begin to forget that there's a guy out there, even though you can hear him. For a long time I just concentrated on pressing the switches and reading the words."

Reciprocal Fields

If in the Proximity condition, the subject is in an improved position to observe the victim, the reverse is also true. The actions of the subject now come under proximal scrutiny by the victim. Possibly, it is easier to harm a person when he is unable to observe our actions than when he can see what we are doing. His surveillance of the actions directed against him may give rise to shame, or guilt, which may then serve to curtail the action. Many expressions of language refer to the discomfort or inhibitions that arise in face-to-face confrontation. It is often said that it is easier to criticize a man "behind his back" than to "attack him to his face." If we are in the process of lying to a person, it is reputedly difficult to "stare him in the eye." We "turn away from others in shame" or in "embarrassment" and this action serves to reduce our discomfort. The manifest function of allowing the victim of a firing squad to be blindfolded is to make the occasion less stressful for him, but it may also serve a latent function of reducing the stress of the executioner. In short, in the proximal conditions, the subject may sense that he has become more salient in the victim's field of awareness. Possibly he becomes more self-conscious, embarrassed, and inhibited in his punishment of the victim. . . .

Proximity as a variable in psychological research has received far less attention than it deserves. If men were sessile it would be easy to understand this neglect. But we move about; our spatial relations shift from one situation to the next, and whether we are near or remote may have a powerful affect on the psychological processes that mediate our behavior toward others. In the present situation as the victim is brought closer to the man ordered to give him shocks, increasing numbers of subjects break off the experiment, refusing to obey. The concrete, visible, and proximal presence of the victim acts in an important way to counteract the experimenter's power and to generate disobedience.*

Closeness of Authority

If the spatial relationship of the subject and victim are relevant to the degree of obedience, would not the relationship of subject to experimenter also play a part?

There are reasons to feel that, on arrival, the subject is oriented primarily to the experimenter rather than to the victim. He has come to the laboratory to fit into the structure that the experimenter—not the victim—provides. He has come less to understand his behavior, than to *reveal* that behavior to a competent scientist, and he is willing to display himself as the scientist's purposes require. Most subjects seem quite concerned about the appearance they are making before the experimenter and one could argue that this preoccupation, in a relatively new and strange setting, makes the subject somewhat insensitive to the triadic nature of the social situation. In other words, the subject is so concerned about the show he

---

* It is difficult to convey on the printed page the full tenor of the victim's responses, for we have no adequate notation for vocal intensity, timing, and general qualities of delivery. Yet these features are crucial to producing the effect of an increasingly severe reaction to mounting voltage levels. In general terms, however, the victim indicates no discomfort until the 75 volt shock is administered, at which time there is a light grunt in response to the punishment. Similar reactions follow the 90 and 105 volt shocks, and at 120 volts the victim shouts to the experimenter that the shocks are becoming painful. Painful groans are heard on administration of the 135 volt shock and at 150 volts the victim cries out, "Experimenter, get me out of here! I won't be in the experiment any more! I refuse to go on!" Cries of this type continue with generally rising intensity, so that at 180 volts the victim cries out, "I can't stand the pain," and by 270 volts his response to the shock is definitely an agonized scream. Throughout, he insists that he be let out of the experiment. At 300 volts the victim shouts in desperation that he will no longer provide answers to the memory test; and at 315 volts, after a violent scream, he reaffirms with vehemence that he is no longer a participant. From this point on, he provides no answers but shrieks in agony whenever a shock is administered. This continues through 450 volts. Of course, many subjects will have broken off before this point.

is putting on for the experimenter, that influences from other parts of the social field do not receive as much weight as they ordinarily would. This strong orientation to the experimenter would account for the relative insensitivity of the subject to the victim, and would also lead us to believe that alterations in the relationship between subject and experimenter would have important consequences for obedience.

In a series of experiments, we varied the physical closeness and degree of surveillance of the experimenter. In one condition the experimenter sat just a few feet away from the subject. In a second condition, after giving initial instructions, the experimenter left the laboratory and gave his orders by telephone; in still a third condition, the experimenter was never seen, providing instructions by means of a tape recording activated when the subjects entered the laboratory.

Obedience dropped sharply as the experimenter was physically removed from the laboratory. The number of obedient subjects in the first condition (Experimenter Present) was almost three times as great as in the second, where the experimenter gave his orders by telephone. Twenty-six subjects were fully obedient in the first condition and only 9 in the second. (Chi Square, obedient vs. defiant in the two conditions, 1 d.f. $= 14.7; p < 0.001$). Subjects seemed able to take a far stronger stand against the experimenter when they did not have to encounter him face to face, and the experimenter's power over the subject was severely curtailed.

Moreover, when the experimenter was absent, subjects displayed an interesting form of behavior that had not occurred under his surveillance. Though continuing with the experiment, several subjects administered lower shocks than were required and never informed the experimenter of their deviation from the correct procedure. (Unknown to the subjects, shock levels were automatically recorded by an Esterline-Angus event recorder wired directly into the shock generator; this provided us with an objective record of the subjects' performance.) Indeed, in telephone conversations, some subjects specifically assured the experimenter that they were raising the shock level according to instruction while, in fact, they were repeatedly using the lowest shock on the board. This form of behavior is particularly interesting; although these subjects acted in a way that clearly undermined the avowed purposes of the experiment, they found it easier to handle the conflict in this manner than to precipitate an open break with authority.

Other conditions were completed in which the experimenter was absent during the first segment of the experiment, but reappeared at the point the subject definitely refused to give higher shocks when commanded by telephone. Although he had exhausted his power via telephone, the experimenter could frequently force further obedience when he reappeared in the laboratory.

Experiments in this series show that the physical *presence* of an authority is an important force contributing to the subject's obedience or defiance. Taken together with the first experimental series on the proximity of the victim, it would appear that something akin to fields of force, diminishing in effectiveness with increasing psychological distance from their source, has a controlling effect on the subject's performance. As the victim is brought closer, the subject finds it harder to administer shocks to him. When the victim's position is held constant relative to the subject and the authority is made more remote, the subject finds it easier to break off the experiment. This effect is substantial in both cases, but manipulation of the experimenter's position yielded the more powerful results. Obedience to destructive commands is highly dependent on the proximal relations between authority and subject.

Tension

The description of final scores does not fully convey the character of the subject's performance, and it would be useful to interrupt our reporting of quantitative relationships to remark on the subject's general reaction to the situation.

One might suppose that a subject would simply break off or continue as his conscience and temperament dictate. Yet this is very far from what actually happened. There were powerful reactions of tension and emotional strain in a substantial proportion of the participants. Persons were observed to sweat, tremble, stutter, bite their lips, and groan as they found themselves increasingly implicated in the experimental conflict. Some sense of the subject's mood can be gotten from a transcript of their remarks at break-off point. Here are the remarks of two defiant subjects:

> Is he banging?. . .Is he hurt out there? Well I don't want to be responsible for anything that happens to him. No I can't go on with it. I don't know whether he's all right or not. I mean he may have a heart condition or something; I wouldn't feel right doing it. He's banging for help. He's evidently in trouble or he wouldn't bang. . . .I don't see any sense to this—to knocking him out or something. I just can't see it. (Subject refuses to administer shocks) [Subject 0108]
>
> This man is banging. He wants to get out. . .I'm sorry. If the man wants to get out I'd just as soon stop. . . .I don't want to administer any more. [Extremely excited]. . .I will gladly refund the check, but I will not harm this man. . .I'm sorry, I will not give him any more if he obviously wants to get out. There is no money in the world that will make me hurt another individual. [Subject 010X]

And here is a transcript from an obedient subject. He began the experiment calmly, but became increasingly tense as the experiment proceeded. After administering the 150 volt shock, he began to address the experimenter in agitated tones:

150 Volts Delivered. You want me to keep going?

165 Volts Delivered. That guy is hollering in there. There's a lot of them here. He's liable to have heart condition. You want me to go?

180 Volts Delivered. He can't stand it! I'm not going to kill that man in there! You hear him hollering? He's hollering. He can't stand it. What if something happens to him?. . .I'm not going to get that man sick in there. He's hollering in there. You know what I mean? I mean I refuse to take responsibility. He's getting hurt in there. He's in there hollering. Too many left here. Geez, if he gets them wrong. There's too many of them left. I mean who is going to take responsibility if anything happens to that gentleman? [The experimenter accepts responsibility.] All right.

195 Volts Delivered. You see he's hollering. Hear that. Gee, I don't know. [The experimenter says: "The experiment requires that you go on,"] I know it does, sir, but I mean—huh—he don't know what he's in for. He's up to 195 volts.

210 Volts Delivered.

225 Volts Delivered.

240 Volts Delivered. Aw, no. You mean I've got to keep going up with the scale? No sir. I'm not going to kill that man! I'm not going to give him 450 volts! [The experimenter says: "The experiment requires that you go on."] I know it does but that man is hollering in there, sir.

Despite his numerous, agitated objections, which were constant accompaniments to his actions, the subject unfailingly obeyed the experimenter, proceeding to the highest shock level on the generator. He displayed a pronounced dissociation between word and action. Although at the verbal level he had resolved not to go on, his actions were fully in accord with the experimenter's commands. Although this subject did not want to shock the victim and found it an extremely disagreeable task, he was unable to invent a response that would free him from the experimenter's authority. Many subjects could not find the specific verbal formula that would enable them to reject the role assigned to them. Perhaps our culture does not provide adequate models for disobedience.

One puzzling sign of tension was the regular occurrence of nervous laughing fits. In the first four conditions, 71 of the 160 subjects showed definite signs of nervous laughter and smiling. The laughter seemed entirely out of place, even bizarre. Full blown, uncontrollable seizures were observed for 15 of these subjects. On one occasion, we observed a seizure so violently convulsive that it was necessary to call a halt to the experiment. In the postexperimental interviews, subjects took pains to point out that they were not sadistic types and that the laughter did not mean they enjoyed shocking the victim. . . .

When a person is uncomfortable, tense, or stressed, he tries to take some action that will allow him to terminate this unpleasant state. Thus, tension may serve as a drive that leads to escape behavior. But in the present situation, even where tension is extreme, many subjects are unable to perform the response that will bring about relief. Thus, there must be a competing drive, tendency, or inhibition that precludes activation of the disobedient response. The strength of this inhibiting factor must be of greater magnitude than the stress experienced, else the terminating act would occur. Every evidence of extreme tension is at the same time an indication of the strength of the forces that keep the subject in the situation.

Finally, tension may be taken as evidence of the reality of the situations for the subjects. Normal subjects do not tremble and sweat unless they are implicated in a deep and genuinely felt predicament.

Background Authority

In psychophysics, animal learning, and other branches of psychology, the fact that measures are obtained at one institution rather than another is irrelevant to the interpretation of the findings, as long as the technical facilities for measurement are adequate and the operations are carried out with competence.

But it cannot be assumed this holds true for the present study. The effectiveness of the experimenter's commands may depend in an important way on the larger institutional context in which they are issued. The experiments described thus far were conducted at Yale University, an organization that most subjects regarded with respect and sometimes awe. In postexperimental interviews, several participants remarked that the locale and sponsorship of the study gave them confidence in the integrity, competence, and benign purposes of the personnel; many indicated that they would not have shocked the learner if the experiments had been done elsewhere.

This issue of background authority seemed important to us for an interpretation of the results that had been obtained thus far; moreover, it is highly relevant to any comprehensive theory of human obedience. Consider, for example, how closely our compliance with the imperatives of others is tied to particular institutions and locales in our day-to-day activities. On request, we expose our throats to a man with a razor blade in the barber shop but would not do so in a shoe store; in the latter setting, we willingly follow the clerk's request to stand in our stockinged feet but resist the command in a bank. In the laboratory of a great University, subjects may comply with a set of commands that would be resisted if given elsewhere. *One must always question the relationship of obedience to a person's sense of the context in which he is operating.*

To explore the problem, we moved our apparatus to an office building in industrial Bridgeport and replicated experimental conditions without any visible tie to the University. . . .

As it turned out, the level of obedience in Bridgeport, although some what reduced, was not significantly lower than that obtained at Yale. A large proportion of the Bridgeport subjects were fully obedient to the experimenter's commands (48 percent of the Bridgeport subjects delivered the maximum shock vs. 65 percent in the corresponding condition at Yale.)

How are these findings to be interpreted? It is possible that if commands of a potentially harmful or destructive sort are to be per-ceived as legitimate, they must occur within some sort of institutional structure. But it is clear from the study that it need not be a particularly reputable or distinguished institution. The Bridgeport experiments were conducted by an unimpressive firm lacking any credentials: the laboratory was set up in a respectable office building with its title listed in the build-ing directory. Beyond that, there was no evidence of benevolence or competence. It is possible that the *category* of institution, judged accord-ing to its professed function rather than its qualitative position within that category, wins our compliance. Persons deposit money in elegant, but also seedy-looking, banks without giving much though to the differences in the security they offer. Similarly, our subjects may treat one laboratory as equally competent as another, so long as it *is* a scientific laboratory.

It would be valuable to study the subjects' performance in other contexts that go even further than the Bridgeport study in denying institutional support to the experimenter. It is possible that beyond a certain point, obedience disappears completely. But that point had not been reached in the Bridgeport office: almost half the subjects obeyed the experimenter fully.

Levels of Obedience and Defiance

One general finding that merits attention is the high level of obedience manifested in the experimental situation. Subjects often expressed deep disapproval of shocking a man in the face of his objections, and others denounced it as senseless and stupid. Yet many subjects complied even while they protested.

The proportion of obedient subjects greatly exceeded the expecta-tions of the experimenter and his colleagues. At the outset, we had conjectured that subjects would not, in general, go above the level of

"Strong Shock." In practice, many subjects were willing to administer the most extreme shocks available when commanded by the experimenter. For some subjects, the experiment provides an occasion for aggressive release. And for others, it demonstrates the extent to which obedient dispositions are deeply ingrained and are engaged irrespective of their consequences for others. Yet this is not the whole story. Somehow, the subject becomes implicated in a situation from which he cannot disengage himself. . . .

A situation exerts an important press on the individual. It exercises constraints and may provide push. Under certain circumstances, it is not so much the kind of person a man is as it is the kind of situation in which he is placed that determines his actions.

Many people, not knowing much about the experiment, claim that subjects who go to the end of the board are sadistic. Nothing could be more foolish as an over-all characterization of these persons. It is like saying that a person thrown into a swift flowing stream is necessarily a fast swimmer or that he has great stamina because he moves so rapidly relative to the bank. The context of action must always be considered. The individual, upon entering the laboratory, becomes integrated into a situation that carries its own momentum. The subject's problem, then, is how to become disengaged from a situation that is moving in an altogether unpleasant direction.

The fact that disengagement is so difficult testifies to the potency of the forces that keep the subject at the control board. Are these forces to be conceptualized as individual motives and expressed in the language of personality dynamics, or are they to be seen as the effects of social structure and pressures arising from the situational field?

A full understanding of the subject's actions will, I feel, require that both perspectives be adopted. The person brings to the laboratory enduring dispositions toward authority and aggression, and at the same time he becomes enmeshed in a social structure that is no less an objective fact of the case. From the standpoint of personality theory one may ask: What mechanisms of personality enable a person to transfer responsibility to authority? What are the motives underlying obedient and disobedient performance? Does orientation to authority lead to a short-circuiting of the shame-guilt system? What cognitive and emotional defenses are brought into play in the case of obedient and defiant subjects?. . .

Postscript

Almost a thousand adults were individually studied in the obedience research, and there were many specific conclusions regarding the variables that control obedience and disobedience to authority. Some of these have been discussed briefly in the preceding sections, and more detailed reports will be released subsequently.

There are now some other generalizations I should like to make that do not derive in any strictly logical fashion from the experiments as carried out, but which, I feel, ought to be made. They are formulations of an intuitive sort that have been forced on me by observation of many subjects responding to the pressures of authority. The assertions represent a painful alteration in my own thinking: and since they were acquired only under the repeated impact of direct observation, I have no illusion that they will be generally accepted by persons who have not had the same experience.

With numbing regularity, good people were seen to knuckle under the demands of authority and perform actions that were callous and severe. Men who are in everyday life responsible and decent were seduced by the trappings of authority, by the control of their perceptions, and by the uncritical acceptance of the experimenter's definitions of the situation into performing harsh acts.

What is the limit of such obedience? At many points we attempted to establish a boundary. Cries from the victim were inserted; they were not effective enough. The victim claimed heart trouble; subjects still shocked him on command. The victim pleaded that he be let free and his answers no longer registered on the signal box: subjects continued to shock him. At the outset, we had not conceived that such drastic proce- dures would be needed to generate disobedience, and each step was added only as the ineffectiveness of the earlier techniques became clear. The final effort to establish a limit was the Touch-Proximity condition. But the very first subject in this condition subdued the victim on command, and proceeded to the highest shock level. A quarter of the subjects in this condition perfomed similarly.

The results, as seen and felt in the laboratory, are to this author disturbing. They raise the possibility that human nature, or more specific- ally the kind of character produced in American democratic society, cannot be counted on to insulate its citizens from brutality and inhumane treatment at the direction of malevolent authority. A substantial propor- tion of people do what they are told to do, irrespective of the content of the act and without limitations of conscience, so long as they perceive that the command comes from a legitimate authority. If, in this study, an anonymous experimenter could successfully command adults to subdue a 50-year-old man and force on him painful electric shocks against his protests, one can only wonder what government, with its vastly greater authority and prestige, can command of its citizenry. (There is, of course, the extremely important and separate question of whether malevolent institutions could or would arise in American society. The present research contributes nothing to this issue.)

In an article titled "The Dangers of Obedience," Harold J. Laski (1929) wrote:

> . . .civilization means, above all, an unwillingness to inflict unnecessary pain. Within the ambit of that definition, those of us who heedlessly accept the commands of authority cannot yet claim to be civilized men.
>
> . . .Our business, if we desire to live a life not utterly devoid of meaning and significance, is to accept nothing which contradicts our basic experience merely because it comes to us from tradition or convention or authority. It may well be that we shall be wrong: but our self-expression is thwarted at the root unless the certainties we are asked to accept coincide with the certainties we experience. That is why the condition of freedom in any state is always a widespread and consistent skepticism of the canons upon which power insists.

REFERENCES

Laski, Harold J. The dangers of obedience. *Harper's Monthly Magazine,* 1929, 159: 1-10.

Milgram, S. Dynamics of obedience: Experiments in social psychology. Mimeographed report. *National Science Foundation,* January 25, 1961.

Milgram, S. Behavioral study of obedience. *J. abnorm. soc. Psychol.,* 1963, **67**: 371-378.

Miller, N. E. Experimental studies of conflict. In J. McV. Hunt (Ed.), *Personality and the Behavior Disorders,* New York: Ronald Press, 1944.

Scott, J. P. *Aggression.* Chicago: University of Chicago Press, 1958.

CHAPTER
SEVEN
WHAT MAKES
GROUPS DYNAMIC ?

THE ISSUE OF GROUP PROCESS

We've all been to meetings that leave us frustrated and depressed. Sometimes we've suspected in advance what might occur. Perhaps it was an evening meeting that we wanted to avoid but felt we couldn't. We knew the group involved well enough to anticipate that nothing would be accomplished and that we would probably be bored and frustrated as well. Here's a description of such a meeting.

It was scheduled for 8:00 PM but only two people were there before 8:15. Others wandered in and talked in twos and threes until about 8:40 when someone finally suggested that the meeting begin. Other people continued to come in while the meeting was in progress, some coming as late as 9:30.

The chairman announced one major item of business for the meeting—a proposal to carry out a fairly complicated action program, beginning almost immediately. The proposal was presented quite vaguely with few details specified. After a few questions of clarification, an argument ensued over whether the group should discuss the proposal at this time. Two people in the group argued that it is silly to discuss such a proposal without first settling a fundamental prior issue on which it is dependent. The prior issue was one that had frequently come up in the past and on which there was considerable disagreement in the group.

After a half hour of wrangling about the agenda, the group moved to a discussion of its general procedures. The chairman claimed he was not feeling well and one of the members who proposed an alternative agenda offered to chair the meeting if the group were willing to discuss the issue he proposed. No one challenged this suggestion and a fairly coherent discussion began about 9:15. However, during a lull in the discussion, a member who had been eating a large bag of pistachio nuts offered them to everybody. A spontaneous 'break' occurred while the nuts were passed around and several conversations started among small subgroups. When the group grew silent again, one of the members who came in about 9:30 said, "I came in late because I had to take a friend to the airport so would someone please explain to me why we're not discussing X [the original agenda item] . I thought that's what this meeting was about."

The new chairman grew very annoyed and berated the speaker for being so late and for then interfering with the discussion. His remarks were punctuated by repeated pauses to crack pistachio nuts with his teeth. The latecomer, feeling that he had an impeccable excuse for his tardiness, fought back and attacked the chairman for his past "egocentric" behavior. Several people attempted to mediate. This discussion led to a decision to return to the original agenda as there were several steps to be taken in the next 10 days if the group wished to proceed with the proposed action. As ten o'clock passed, some members left and others warned that they must leave very soon.

In response, several people who supported the proposed action suggested small interim steps to take place until the next meeting, but others opposed these as committing the group to the proposal before it had been adequately examined. The discussion of interim measures continued while several more people left and the meeting dwindled to less than half of its peak size. Finally, unable to come to any agreement, the supporters of the proposal insisted on another meeting to be held two days hence and the survivors of this meeting wearily agreed.

Why was this group so ineffectual? Its members were highly intelligent individuals as aware as any observer of how feckless their meeting was. Was something lacking or were there too many of the wrong ingredients? Some groups are able to carry out their tasks in a way that leaves the members quite satisfied with both the process and the product. Why not this one? What are the keys to understanding group process? What do we need to look at to understand what makes a group tick?

THE MAJOR VIEWS

Dynamic Leadership

The most popular explanation of group process is one which has been almost totally rejected by contemporary social psychologists. We represent it here by a sports story, "Storm over Second," rich in the cliches of this genre. Here is a collection of talented individuals, the Hawks, producing below their collective capacity and too proud to fight. They lack dynamic leadership—until the rookie from the wrong side of the tracks provides them with the spark they need. Note that the rookie provides them with very little direct assistance—his talent is adequate but no more, and he is performing below capacity because of injury. The assistance he provides is indirect—the sports cliche would call it "the intangibles"—but it makes the difference in this tale between a dynamic and a flat team.

The essence of this view of group process can be captured in a phrase : dynamic leaders make dynamic groups. The meeting group in the example described above was ineffective because it lacked the kind of leader whose skill could transform it from an aggregate of individuals into an effective instrument of the will of its members. Groups that function well are fortunate enough to have such leaders.

We do not help the case for this paradigm by representing it with the adventure magazine example "Storm over Second." Nevertheless, we take it seriously. It is stubbornly adhered to by students even when we tell them and present evidence to convince them that it is false. Of course, they dutifully acknowledge that it is false and are able to present to us, probably quite sincerely, the functional view of leadership described below. But it is quite obvious that when they begin to analyze the groups they are part of, they automatically slip back into the rejected paradigm. At a more fundamental level, they continue to believe that the dynamism of groups can be explained by the dynamism of their leaders.

Why did social psychologists reject this paradigm? Because it led them to an apparent dead end. If great leaders make great groups, then a significant research problem becomes the identification of the personality characteristics or traits of leaders. Frequently these traits were even assumed to be innate as in the expression "Leaders are born, not made."

Unfortunately, leadership studies turned up very few traits and those few had relatively low predictive value. Fiedler speaks for most social psychologists who have studied leadership when he writes, "The chances are that *anyone* who wants to become a leader can become one if he carefully chooses the situations that are favorable to his leadership style. The notion that a man is a 'born' leader, capable of leading in all circumstances, appears to be nothing more than a myth. If there are leaders who excel under all conditions, I have not found them in my 18 years of research" (1969, pp. 42-43).

If one can't find a good answer after a persistent search, he begins to wonder whether he is asking the right question. So it happened with the quest for personality characteristics of leaders. Not only the research question, but also the underlying view that great leaders make great groups suffered rejection. But the implication that we should be able to discover leadership traits perhaps is not an inevitable derivative of the paradigm. Let's examine it more closely.

Note the elements in "Storm over Second." An individual joins an ineffective team. He is no more talented in the performance of the group task than other members, but his presence enables the group to produce a great deal more than before. The value he has added to the team can be broken into two parts—his direct contribution to the task (for example, his hitting and fielding) and a residual, indirect contribution. This indirect contribution is widely recognized in the sports world and elsewhere and is typically given the name "leadership."

To distinguish this paradigm from subsequent ones, it is important that the leadership which the individual brings to the group is a quality that he possesses— granting that it will only come out in given situations. Individuals who have it are leaders; those who don't, are not leaders. One is creating a straw man to assume that this view postulates that an individual will exhibit leadership in all situations. A man who has it can produce it when needed, but this doesn't mean that he always will produce it anymore than a rich man will always spend money or a powerful man will always exercise influence. But it is definitely *not* true in this view that anyone can become a leader. The fact that sometimes an individual will surprise us by revealing leadership ability that we didn't know he possessed only reflects on our lack of perspicacity.

The sterility of the trait approach in this view results from the failure to recognize leadership as an *interactional competence.* It is, for example, like impression management, poise, or tact. There is no single set of behaviors or attributes that would measure poise since the interactional competence it reflects differs from situation to situation. Nonetheless, we are confident in saying that some people are unflappable and others are not. If one wanted to study poise, he probably would not learn a great deal by comparing the traits of poised and awkward people. But this does not disprove its existence, it only suggests that researchers must approach it differently.

The implication, then, is that if we want to understand what makes groups dynamic, we should study that very special and valuable kind of interactional competence known as dynamic leadership.

Functional Specialization

The point of departure here is to view the small group as a miniature social system.* All social systems must handle certain functional problems if they are to survive and prosper. This is true of a microsystem such as a committee just as much as it is true of a total society. Of course, the manner in which each solves its functional problems may be very different, but some solution must be found in both cases if the system is to work well.

The selection by Verba included in this chapter describes this approach, drawing on the seminal work of Robert F. Bales, Kurt Lewin and others (Bales, 1950). The functions that must be performed in the small group can be usefully thought of as falling into two general categories—those directly connected with the goal-oriented tasks of the group and those connected with keeping the group together and meeting the needs of individual members. The first of these functions is usually called external, task-oriented, or instrumental; the second is called internal, maintenance-oriented, social-emotional, or affective.

Basically, a bad meeting such as the one described above results from the failure of the group to solve these two central functional problems of all groups. It was unable to carry out the simplest tasks of settling on an agenda and moving toward a decision on a proposal, and it was equally unable to keep the group members together and functioning as a unit. Either failure can easily affect the other. Thus, participants grow frustrated and withdraw because the group is unable to perform its tasks; it is unable to perform its tasks because people come late, wander in and out, bicker with each other, and in other ways manifest low commitment.

The critical question for this paradigm becomes one of determining how these functions are effectively performed, and why they are not performed well in some groups. The analysis suggests that the two functions are closely related. On the one hand, they are complementary. Groups which perform effectively find it easier to keep their members happy. It is a common observation, for example, that teams that are winning have little trouble with internal dissension—all kinds of minor annoyances and slights are easily ignored in the glow of victory. On the other hand, groups which have highly committed members are able to call on their members to make personal sacrifices to help the group to achieve its instrumental goals. Success in handling internal problems can contribute substantially to external success.

* See the reading by Zelditch in Chapter 4, and the associated "organizational efficiency" perspective discussed in the Chapter introduction.

There is evidence, however, that in spite of this complementarity there is potential conflict in the performance of these functions. Acts designed to move a group toward its goal upset the equilibrium of the group and create inevitable tension. The tension is inherent in the group process rather than a result of incompetence or poor leadership. Efforts to influence people and reach a consensus generate resistance —at least in American groups with their egalitarian norms and strong emphasis on individual choice. Bales and Strodtbeck (1951) provide evidence of a rise in tension as the group moves through phases of orientation, evaluation, and control. Tension is highest when the press for decision becomes greatest near the end of the meeting. The common phenomenon of laughter and joking as a meeting ends is a sign of tension release.

Those who are most active in pushing the group toward a decision are likely to be the target of some hostility because of their efforts at control. Therefore, they are ill-suited to assume a role aimed at reducing the tension that their task efforts have generated. Consequently, other group members tend to become specialists in the handling of inter-personal relations in the group. There is a tendency for effective groups to develop a division of labor, with some individuals acting as instrumental leaders while others act as affective leaders. Mere division of labor is insufficient, though, if these different specialists fail to work together. A high degree of cooperation and mutual support between the two types of leaders is characteristic of the most effective groups.

Leadership, in this view, is a set of functions. Since every member of the group may perform these functions to some degree, it is misleading to talk about leadership as a special quality of a few individuals. Of course, individuals with certain traits will naturally gravitate to one or the other kind of leadership function. A warm, empathic person who is sensitive to interpersonal nuances often will make his contribution in the affective realm. A no-nonsense, impatient type will contribute in the instrumental realm.

One can study the personality characteristics of those who show great skill in handling the functional problems that all groups face. But this is not really the crucial question for understanding what makes a group tick. The primary issues are: to understand who is performing the basic functions, the nature of the skills involved in their performance, and how the coordination of these fundamental group tasks is handled.

Shared Unconscious Fantasies

We participate in groups at another more fundamental and unconscious level. Slater, in the selection included in this chapter, asserts, "I cannot see how an understanding of groups can proceed beyond its current level unless the unit of analysis in some way embodies that segment of an individual's instinctual life which he commits to a group." Groups are, in this view, a vehicle for our unconscious fantasies.

The dynamism of a group is a function of how much intensity or primitive energy its members invest in it. This is determined in turn by the extent to which the group serves as a vehicle for the expression of unconscious fantasies. If these fantasies are idiosyncratic to one member, they may serve more to distract the group rather than to provide it with its basic energy. But we are one species, and our Ids are not that different. Hence, groups frequently become a common vehicle rather than a private one. The selection by Slater illustrates the content of such collective fantasies.

The meeting described at the beginning of this chapter is difficult to analyze from this perspective because the description given is too superficial. In describing the manifest content of the interaction, what is *really* going on gets lost. The critical clues are contained in what people are doing with their bodies, the intensity of their verbal expressions, their slips, their metaphors, their imagery. Such apparently irrelevant behavior as eating pistachio nuts is in fact very important, although one needs the total context of such activity to interpret it reliably. A description designed to unravel the acting-out of unconscious fantasies in this meeting would look very different. But without this level of description, we are doomed to a superficial and inadequate understanding of what makes a group tick.

CONTRASTING THE VIEWS OF GROUP PROCESS

These ways of looking at group process can be contrasted by examining their treatment of three issues:

1.   What is the most fruitful way of thinking about the phenomenon of leadership?

2.   To what extent is a group regarded as a real entity rather than merely an abstraction to describe an interaction setting?

3.   To what extent does the manifest content of a group's interaction contain the basic information we need to understand group process?

Nature of Leadership

Each paradigm has a distinctive view of the phenomenon of leadership and its importance for group process. In the dynamic leadership perspective, it is regarded as an outstanding personal quality that certain individuals are able to contribute to a group. People possess this ability in varying degrees and they may or may not be motivated to use it on any given occasion. It is useful to think of this quality as an interactional competence that enables an individual to turn an aggregate of individuals into an effective unit.

For the functional specialists, leadership is best thought of as the performance of a set of vital group functions. One can call the people who perform these functions "leaders," but nothing is gained by using this label. On the contrary, it may obscure the fact that different people are performing different leadership functions and that many group members may be performing them to some degree. Rather than focusing on the qualities of leaders, this approach suggests that one should ask about the distribution of leadership functions among members of the group and the relationships between individuals specializing in different functions. Certain kinds of relationships—for example, cooperation between instrumental and affective specialists—lead to a more effective group process.

In the unconscious fantasy paradigm, leadership may be thought of as creativity in the expression of shared unconscious fantasies—the talent of a Lenny

Bruce or Norman Mailer, for example, Such genius is not necessarily a controlled skill. It stems from the ability to let oneself go, a willingness to hold nothing back so that normally repressed impulses and associations are publicly expressed. The product of such genius is an uneven one; much unconscious material is too raw or idiosyncratic to evoke a collective response. But when shared unconscious fantasies are tapped, a group will respond with intensity and fascination. A group that lacks this peculiar kind of leadership will be sterile in the production of unconscious material and will not engage its members in more than a superficial fashion.

Groups as Entities

It is possible to think of groups in two ways. For some, they are an entity with their own clear boundaries and special properties. Although one may talk of their elements, they have an integrity and wholeness just as an individual person does. They are real.

For others, groups are an abstraction that it is misleading to reify. The "real" entities are individuals and their relationships. The group is a setting rather than an entity. Group members share means and goals and "the group" is merely a convenient phrase to describe the setting in which an interdependent interaction occurs.

The dynamic leadership view treats groups as settings rather than entities. A leader sparks a team by inspiring its members to greater individual performance and selfless aid to teammates. The real elements are individuals and their relationships and the group is an abstraction.

For the functional specialization and unconscious fantasies views, groups are real entities. This is the essence of the former approach. A "function" is to a group as a "need" is to an individual. Just as an individual will starve if his need for food is not met, a group will collapse if its task and maintenance functions are not met. These functions can only be thought of as properties of a group and cannot be reduced to a description of the needs of individual members.

As for the other view, it is true that unconscious fantasies are properties of individuals. But the dynamic is provided by their becoming a property of the group. The hippopotamus in the Slater selection derives its potency from the fact that it has shared meaning for the group members. Although the meaning is a complex and unconscious one, it is a symbol of a collective rather than an individual fantasy.

Usefulness of Manifest Content

Can one learn from group process by taking at face-value what is said and done or must one read between the lines? For both the dynamic leadership and functional specialization views the manifest content contains most of the necessary material. While the source of dynamic leadership may remain somewhat obscure, its exercise is not disguised. The members of dynamic groups make a maximum effort for collective goals and one can discover this in their words and behavior. Baseball teams that "like to play ball" are "full of shout" as Holder puts it.

Similarly, one learns who is performing group functions by looking at the manifest content of the interaction. Individuals contributing in the affective area make remarks praising or supporting others; those contributing in the instrumental area make suggestions for carrying out group tasks. There is nothing especially hidden here.

The unconscious fantasy view requires more strenuous detective work. The manifest content provides the trappings for the real dynamics. Unconscious meanings cannot be discovered by taking expressions at face value. Such emotionally-charged material cannot be expressed directly but is necessarily revealed indirectly through symbols. The penetration of this meaning is a subtle and difficult process that begins where face value explanations end. It is typically those expressions where there is a discrepancy between the apparent content and the emotional intensity that alerts one to a second level of meaning. When there is a slip or an odd way of expressing something, when a face value explanation seems to leave something unaccounted for, one is at the gateway to the netherworld of unconscious symbolism.

These are the central issues we see running through the contrasting views of group process. They are summarized in Chart 7.

Chart 7 Underlying Issues on What Makes Groups Dynamic

	Dynamic Leadership (*e.g.*, "Storm over Second")	Functional Specialization (*e.g.*, Verba)	Unconscious Shared Fantasies (*e.g.*, Slater)
What is the most fruitful way of thinking about leadership?	A personal quality: an interactional competence	A set of group functions	A personal quality: a talent for expressing unconscious, shared fantasies
Is a group an entity or an abstraction?	An abstraction	An entity	An entity
Is manifest content adequate for understanding group process?	Yes	Yes	No—merely provides trappings

REFERENCES

Bales, Robert F. *Interaction Process Analysis: A Method for the Study of Small Groups.* Reading, Massachusetts: Addison-Wesley, 1950.

Bales, Robert F. and Strodtbeck, Fred L. "Phases in Group Problem Solving," *Journal of Abnormal and Social Psychology,* **46** (1951), pp. 485-495.

Fiedler, Fred. "Style or Circumstance: The Leadership Enigma," *Psychology Today,* **2** (1969), pp. 38-43.

STORM OVER SECOND

WILLIAM HOLDER

Carew went uptown on the subway, his left leg stretched out before him, easing the injured groin muscle. He hadn't bothered to buy a newspaper, for he knew what they'd be saying. He'd gone hitless again yesterday, and they'd be asking why the Hawks couldn't bring up a second baseman who could play ball. They'd be naming possibilities, quoting figures, explaining just why the Hawks were in their present slump.

He thought of Janey, slim and gentle and trusting, in the lovely small apartment he'd just left. The apartment they'd secured by a minor miracle when they'd come to town three weeks before. Janey had been smiling happily, working on some gayly colored curtains. The apartment was high up above the river, cooled by a gentle breeze that held a last trace of ocean freshness. Janey loved the place, loved the big city. She was making friends, eagerly making plans.

He wondered how he was going to tell her, tonight or tomorrow or the next day, that they'd have to get out. That she'd have to go back and live with her family, like before. It wouldn't be much fun, telling her that.

The leg, he knew, would be all right in a week or ten days. Which would be just a week or ten days too late. He'd pulled the muscle on his fifth day with the Hawks, sliding into second while stretching a single. The private doctor he'd consulted had told him a minimum of three weeks' complete rest was necessary.

And that was a laugh. You didn't come up to the Hawks on a break like this, then tell them to wait, that it would be three weeks before you'd be able to play ball. Somebody else might be able to do that, but not Eddie Carew.

Because he remembered the past too acutely, where you made your own breaks. The miserable coal towns of his childhood where poverty was an incurable disease; the semi-pro ball, and then the bush leagues, playing night game after night game for peanuts, doing four hundred miles overnight in a bus, and some of the time driving the bus.

And during all that time you had a dream. The big time. Good money and stability and playing with the best. Something to offer a girl like Janey, who had held so much love for him she had insisted it wasn't necessary to wait until the dream came true, but had married him while he was still playing in whistle-stops, in flag-down towns, in spite of what he said and what her family said.

You didn't think about playing with the Hawks—the best, the Gentlemen's Club. Just any spot in the big time. But you got sold up one rung of the long ladder, traded up another, and there you were, playing the tough, smart, all-out game you'd always played, with tough old Jig Taylor's Hawk farm team. Then, when Dalson broke his hand, early in June, you went all the way, a terrifying jump, and you wondered what the hell was going on.

And you were a little surprised to find that you had it. You made the plays and went up there and got the hits. The pitchers were good, but they threw with only one arm, and you could hit them. You knew, after the first few days, that you had it and you could stick. . .

He got off the subway at the ball park and walked to the players' entrance. He did not limp. He'd given no sign, even when he'd been hurt, that there was anything wrong with him. That was part of it. If he could hide the injury until the muscle was better, if he could get away with it, could stall.

Maybe he was playing it wrong. Maybe he should have told Burke about it right away, given himself an out. Then they would have sent him down the line, knowing they weren't seeing him at his best, and in a year, two or three years, he would have had another chance.

But the hell with that. When you got a break you took it and made the most of it. You shook off the tough years, the bitter years, and dug in.

Except that it wasn't working that way with him. He didn't think now they'd even let him stay until Dalson's hand was better. He'd heard they were bringing Johnson over from Newkirk.

He went into the dressing room, which was like no other he'd ever been in. It was quiet, possessing a certain dignity that was a very integral part of the Hawk club and that no other outfit owned, somehow. The Gentlemen's Club. You went out and you played fine baseball, but you did it without noise, without shouting. No roughnecks, no odd characters, ever played for the Hawks.

He dressed before his locker, in the small cubicle given to every player. The names were painted chastely on the lockers. J. SILERS, T. CORELLA, W. COFFEE. His own was plain and unadorned. He was a stranger, a visitor. Whoever was in charge of painting the lockers had been smart, had saved himself some trouble.

He went through the dugout into the warm sunlight of the field and looked around, still with a touch of the wonder he'd known on that first day, at the hugeness of the stadium. The stands were filling early. This series with the Blues was important, would be indicative of the

teams' relative behavior later in the season. The Blues had taken over
the league lead during the last week and were out in front by two games.

For five minutes he tossed a ball back and forth with Murphy, the
shortstop. Then the battling cage was wheeled into place and they went
out onto the field.

He heard the big voice he'd come to know so well in the last week.
There were others, a lot of others, but this one was special, a foghorn of
a voice.

"Hey, Carew! They still lettin' ya wear the suit? Whyn't ya go
home, ya bum?"

The big voice started the others. His personal chorus, his rooting
section. It would grow as the crowd increased and the noise would
reach a mighty peak each time he stepped up to the plate. They were
on him, and on him good, and it made him sore. He wasn't a rabbit-
eared guy, but this crowd had him down. They'd watched him for the
first few days, withholding their approval, and when he'd started to
go sour they'd jumped on him. The club was in a slump and they'd
tagged him with the blame.

Murphy said, "Don't let them bother you, kid. They just like to
shout."

"They don't bother me none," Carew said, and it was a lie.

He fielded a few with caution, trying to keep pressure off the leg.
And when his turn was coming up, he went in to bat, and this was
another lesson in restraint. He couldn't take his full cut. He had
altered his usual motion almost imperceptibly to favor the muscle, and
it was a hindrance. His hitting had fallen off after the first five days.

"Get outa there, ya bum!" the voice came down. "Give us
Dalson with one hand! Go back to that water-tank league, Carew!"

Carew laid down his bunt and went out to the field again, and
the big voice had assistance now. They didn't let up for a moment.
He was ruining their ball club, and they let him know it.

He took another turn at bat and another riding, then he went to
the dugout for a drink of water. Burke, sitting at the end of the bench,
looked at him without smiling. "They like you out there, Carew."

"The hell with them." Carew went out on the field again.

It was Burke's first year of managing the Hawks. Thomson had
been sick and had retired, but the talk went that the fact that the
Hawks had finished third, two years running, might have had a lot to
do with his retirement. Burke was a chunky, florid man who hugged
his corner of the bench, never spoke unnecessarily, and who knew more
baseball than anyone Carew had ever met. His eyes were alert, cynical.
He seemed to be waiting for something.

Maybe, Carew thought, he's waiting for Johnson to come over from Newkirk.

It was the Blues' turn on the field then, and instead of going to the clubhouse Carew sat on the bench and watched them. They were a noisy, raucous group; some young, some old; all tough and full of shout. They had half as much talent as the Hawks, twice as much hustle. They were leading the league now and had copped the pennant last year.

And he thought absently that here was the sort of club he belonged with, this was the kind of baseball he had been weaned on. These guys had no more dignity than a fish had feathers. They fought for every run, squawked at every decision, hustled every day until the last man was out. What they couldn't buy with their mediocre virtues, they stole.

He was surprised to hear Burke's voice. "You ever see them before, Carew?"

Carew shook his head. "They're new to me, except what I've heard. They sure like to play ball."

Burke might have sighed. Carew couldn't be sure. "They certainly like to play ball," the manager said.

And when the Blues were done with their batting practice and the Hawks took the infield for a workout, the Blues started to ride Carew. They'd heard the bunch in the stands, and they added some dainty embroidery of their own. But Carew could grin at that. It was something he was used to, something he could understand. He was new. They were working him over for what it was worth. It was part of the ball game.

It was time, and they took the field. Big Morton was working for the Hawks, and the crowd roared out when the first pitch to Tip Raney, the Blues' right-fielder, was a strike. It was the only way to begin a ball game.

But Raney waited Morton out, waited and got his walk.

And from first base he yelled down to Carew. His voice was sharp, held a note of viciousness. "Stay clear of that sack, busher, or I'll cut your leg off at the knee."

And from shortstop Murphy said, "Watch him. He's crazy."

And Raney came down, on the second pitch. Rivers, at the plate, was a right-handed hitter, and Carew took Coffee's throw. It was a touch high, and Carew straddled the bag, out of Raney's way. He brought the ball down for the tag, and Raney's left foot shot past his face while the right foot dug into his leg. Out of the corner of his eye he saw the umpire's arm jerk skyward, then he felt the sudden tug at the ball in his glove. He watched the ball roll halfway to the pitcher's box and saw the umpire's corrective gesture. Raney was safe. Morton recovered the ball.

Raney said, "Get smart, busher. Keep out of the way."

Carew looked at his leg. The spikes had hit at the roll of his pants, just below the knee, and had penetrated just enough to scratch him. He thought of the foot going past his face, and he started for Raney.

Murphy grabbed him from behind. "Whoa, kid! No rumpus. No mess."

Carew turned on him. "The slob almost took my eyes out! I'll . . ." And then he stopped. Raney was wearing a vicious grin, and he spat at Carew's feet. Murphy said, "Easy, Carew." And no one else on the field had moved. Silers was at his usual spot at third, facing the play, and even as Carew looked, Silers turned away.

The Hawks were a dignified club. They never brawled on the field. He remembered that now.

"Okay," he told Murphy, and walked over to his position.

The roared abuse came down from the stands. It was a little tough to take, on top of everything else, but it didn't really matter. For one stupid second he thought of Janey, fixing up the apartment she'd live in for another day or two. She'd be getting a rougher deal than he was taking.

Morton got the next man on a short fly to second, but the third batter singled cleanly to right and Raney went in with the first run. It was all they got for the inning.

Carew went in to the bench, and he felt Burke's eyes on him, but the manager did not speak. Carew sat down. Morton said, "You want to watch it, Carew. That was a fat run you gave them."

And Carew said nothing. He sat there and watched Morris set the Hawks down in order.

In the second inning Fontana, the Blues' shortstop, singled on the first pitch. Morton stuck out Ullis, trying to sacrifice. Shanks hit one down to Murphy at short, and Carew went over to cover the bag for the double play. Murphy's throw was nice. Carew made the force and got the ball away fast, and he knew he had the runner easily.

And Fontana, out by fifteen feet coming down from first, didn't bother to slide. He ran right into Carew, hit him like a runaway truck and knocked him sprawling and rolling to the other side of second base.

Carew got up slowly, waiting for the pulled muscle to collapse, aware only of that and of the roaring laughter that came down from the stands. The leg had not been further injured and that surprised him. He'd never been hit harder. Fontana looked at him and grinned, and Carew started for him. Murphy stepped between them and it was a tough moment. Carew tossed his glove back on the grass and went in to the bench. The great laughter of the stands crowded after him.

He went through the next few innings numbly, thinking that this was a hell of a way to go out. He was sorry now that he hadn't spoken to Burke about the injury when it had happened. It would have let him out of this mess.

The Blues got a run in the fourth and another in the fifth, but he was not involved. He was busy thinking of how he'd break this thing to Janey. He could see the change in her expression, the disbelief in her eyes, could see the tears suppressed in his presence but shed upon a silent pillow.

In the sixth, with two away and a man on third, the batter hit a ball though the box and over second base. Carew went for it, instinctively thinking of the leg. It was well hit and he made a backhand stab and the ball stuck in the glove. He jammed to a stop, turned and made his throw. It was a little low, a little to one side, but under the circumstances a good peg. Hammond reached for it, the ball hit his glove and skittered behind first. The run scored. The next hitter flied out.

Carew walked in to the bench, and his particular public gave him the business. There was no bounce in him now. All he wanted was for the ball game to finish. It didn't matter that Hammond had been given the error. Nothing mattered very much.

The bench was silent, and he was startled to hear Hammond's voice. The first baseman said, "Get 'em up, Carew. I haven't got a pick and shovel out there."

He stared for a moment, and then all the bitterness in him flooded out. He couldn't have stopped it for a million dollars.

He walked to a point in front of Hammond. He said, "Why you big Dutch slob, where do you want me to throw them, down your throat? You haven't got off the dime since I've been around this club. There's more stretch in a block of cement than there is in you." Hammond stared at him.

Morton was sitting next to the first baseman, and Carew lashed at him. "You've got a hell of a nerve, giving me a call because they got a lousy run off you. Hell, they've got *five* of them. And where I come from a ball club plays together. Raney tries to cut me comin' down from first, the next time he came up there you shoulda beaned him, but good."

His anger was inclusive. He swept a derisive hand along the bench "The lot of you! You play ball like you were doped. The Hawks. The Gentlemen's Club! A lousy bunch of halfdead dummies that can't get a run off a fathead like this Morris! Why—"

A voice cut in on him. It was Burke's. The manager said dryly, "You're up, Carew."

He went out and took the bat the kid handed him. He wasn't think-ing now. He didn't hear the noise that poured down on him. He walked to the plate, and Morris had an easy half-smile on his face and came in with the duster. Carew went back, landing on his haunches. He stepped in there again. Morris took his motion, threw one fast and outside. Carew maced it into right.

He made his turn, watched Raney take his time with the ball, and headed for second. Fontana was taking the throw as he came in. He hit the dirt and kicked the Blues' shortstop four feet to the other side of the sack.

There was silence in the park for a moment, and then the roar burst out. Fontana did not move. Brannick, the second baseman, came for Carew but the umpires were in on it now and the brawl died before it had a chance to get started. They walked Fontana around for a few minutes, then he looked at Carew and cursed and took his position.

And Murphy singled Carew in with the Hawks' first run.

In the first of the seventh Carew had his chance at Raney. Raney dumped a bunt in front of the plate and ran it out, and when he looked down at second, it wasn't necessary for him to say anything. Everybody in the park knew he was going down. Even Morton knew it.

It was a pitchout, and Coffee got the ball down on a line. Carew stood in front of the bag and a bit to the first-base side. He took the throw in his glove, got out of the way, and swept the ball down. He felt it hit hard.

Raney was out by three feet, sliding. He didn't quite reach the base. He rolled over twice, then got slowly to his hands and knees and noisily spat out two teeth. He got groggily to his feet and started for Carew. But even before he got up, the Blues were pouring out of the dugout. The umpires intervened, but it was a mess before they stopped it. Carew's lip was split, Raney, Brannick, Silers and Murphy were out of the game. Surprisingly, they had let him stay in. Morton struck out Rivers and Sullivan to end the inning.

Carew went in to the bench. The crowd was as noisy as before, but there was a difference in the thunder. *All* those whistles weren't derisive; *all* the voices weren't yammering for his blood.

In the dugout, Burke looked at him and with a motion of his head indicated the next seat. Carew sat down, mopping at his lip with a handkerchief. He said nothing. He was watching Gannon, the lead-off man, going up to the plate.

Burke said, "Bet you five he hits."

"He hasn't hit in four days."

Gannon lined the first pitch into left center for a clean double.

Burke said, "How's the leg?"

Carew looked at him.

"I knew it wasn't bad," Burke said, "You can't hide a really bad˙ one as well as you did. That's why I kept you in there."

Carew said, "Hell, I haven't been hitting. I can't get around out there."

"You got a bum leg and you're hittin' .270. Five points under what Dalson hit in his best year. In a year you'll be covering more ground." He pointed out to the field. Humphrey singled through the box, but Gannon was held at third. The crowd, Carew thought, was making a hell of a lot of noise and he wasn't even out there.

There was a conference out on the mound, but Morris stayed in.

Burke said, "Jig Taylor called me when Dalson was hurt, and told me he had a second baseman who liked to play ball."

Up at the plate, big Hammond swung at the first pitch. It rode on a line into the right-field stands, and the three runs scored. Morris went out of there.

The relief came in and warmed up. Burke said, "I didn't know whether you could play ball or not. Jig said you could wake this club up. I kept you in there, even with the bad leg, hoping for a day like today."

Carew said, "It's been quite a day." The coldness, the anger, had gone out of him. His neck muscles were relaxing and he felt a comfortable warmth creeping into him. He thought of Janey and started to grin, then killed it. He didn't know yet.

Corella was at the plate, and Carew started for the bat rack. He said, "I'm on deck."

Burke said, "Call it a day. Take a couple of weeks off and rest that leg. We'll get ten runs today. This club has the lead out."

Carew said, "Lemme hit," and Burke nodded.

Corella lined the first pitch to deep left field. He went into third standing up.

Carew went out on the field, and this time it was different. The crowd roared down, but it was pure excitement and expectancy now, and there was no hostility in it. Carew cocked an ear for a moment before he heard it. The foghorn. It bulled its way through the mass of sound. It said, "All right, all right! Be a hitter up there, Carew. Be a hitter, you tough busher!"

Carew stepped back. He walked to the dugout. He looked at Burke. He said, "There's something. My locker . . ."

Burke grinned at him. He said. "Okay. In pink paint."

Carew walked to the plate. He could hear only one voice. It said, "All right, kid. Be a hitter up there!"

LEADERSHIP: AFFECTIVE AND INSTRUMENTAL

SIDNEY VERBA

The purpose of this chapter is to explore one aspect of the leader-follower relationship as it is found in both small experimental groups and on-going social systems. This aspect is the dual function that the leadership structure of a group must perform if the group is successfully to reach the goal that brought it together. In attempting to achieve its goal, a group must . . . direct activities both towards the instrumental task it faces and toward the maintenance of the internal structure of the group. The group's internal maintenance function must be performed in such a way that the individual members find their participation in the group at least satisfactory enough to keep them from leaving the group. And, . . . it is the function of the group leadership to operate in both these areas—the instrumental and the internal group maintenance.

The importance of the affective tone and emotional aspects of the leader-follower relationship in political and other social situations has long been recognized. Individuals do not give their allegiance to a state or their support to a political leader solely because of the material benefits they receive in return. The decision on the part of a follower to accept the directive of a leader is based on more than a rational calculus of the advantages to be gained from that acceptance. Loyalty to a state, for instance, usually has an emotional component, reinforced by more or less elaborate systems of symbols and rituals. Though there has been much analysis of these non-rational aspects of politics insofar as they affect the individual political participant, there has been little systematic consideration of the dynamic interaction between emotional attachment and material outputs within the leader-follower relationship. . . .

The difficulties of the leadership position derive not merely from the fact that the leader must be active in both the instrumental and affective group tasks, but from the fact that these two tasks are closely related. The way in which the group functions in one area will influence functioning in the other. If group members have a satisfactory affective relationship with the leader, they will be more likely to accept his instrumental directives. On the other hand, if the level of member satisfaction with

Selections from Sidney Verba, *Small Groups and Political Behavior: A Study of Leadership* (copyright © 1961 by Princeton University Press), published for the Center of International Studies, Princeton University, pp. 142, 145-150, 158-164, 168. Omission of footnotes. Material referred to in list of references. Reprinted by permission of Princeton University Press.

group leadership is low, members may withdraw from the group, reject the group leader, or reject the group leader's instrumental directives. All these activities lower the instrumental effectiveness of the group. Conversely, the success or failure of the instrumental activity of the group will influence the affective rewards to the members. Group members may derive satisfaction directly from the successful completion of the instrumental task of the group or from certain other rewards that are the bi-product of that task completion. Insofar as the group cannot achieve its instrumental goal, satisfactions will be lowered. Maintaining a balance between the satisfactions of the group members and the task achievement of the group may well be the most important task of the group leader.

Equilibrium Problem

Maintaining the balance between affective satisfactions and instrumental performance is, however, a difficult and delicate task. Several studies of group process have suggested that attempts to direct the group toward the accomplishment of its instrumental task may be greeted by negative affective reactions on the part of group members. The theoretical and experimental work of Kurt Lewin and his associates first pinpointed the problem within small groups. In Lewin's theoretical formulation (1951), attempts to direct the group toward the group goal disturb the equilibrium of the group by restricting the freedom of the members. This in turn causes a negative reaction that can take two forms: it may take the form of a rejection of the instrumental directive, in which case equilibrium is restored by negating the directive's effect; or the reaction may be an acceptance of the directive accompanied by increased hostility toward the leader. In the latter case, equilibrium is restored but at a higher level of tension between leader and follower.

Examples of this process of negative reaction to directive leadership can be found in the classic experimental work of Lewin, Lippitt and White (1939) carried out under Lewin's direction. In these experiments with democratic and authoritarian group climates, it was noted that directives from an authoritarian leader, though followed, were accompanied by negative affective reactions on the part of the group members, expressed in hostility toward the leader, a scapegoat, or other groups. Furthermore, the acceptance of the leader's directives in the authoritarian situation was external rather than internal. When the leader left the room and the external pressure was removed, the group members ceased complying with the instrumental directive. Experimental work in field situations produced similar results; attempts to direct change in a group led to negative affective reactions on the part of the group members that in turn limited the effectiveness of the instrumental directive. Coch and French, for instance, found that an attempt by management to direct certain changes in the work process " . . . had the effect for the members of setting up management as a hostile power field. They rejected the forces induced by this hostile power field, and group standards to restrict production developed within the group in opposition to management" (1948, p.528). The problem of leadership is clearly presented by these examples. The achievement of the group's instrumental goal must proceed along with the continuing satisfaction of the individual needs of the group members, but frequently the attempts themselves to achieve the instrumental goal lower the level of affective satisfaction of the group members. This lowering will in turn feed back upon the instrumental achievement and hamper it. Thus the several tasks of the leader may not all be consistent with one another.

The treatment of the problem of control and instrumental achievement in the work of Lewin and his associates bears a significant resemblance to the treatment of the problem in the work of Robert F. Bales (1950) and his associates at the Harvard Laboratory of Social Relations. In the small experimental groups used by Bales in the formulation of his theoretical system, the formation of the group takes place around the instrumental task presented to the group by the experimenter. The initial differentiation among the group members evolves in response to the demands of this task. Certain members tend to become more active in directing the group toward the completion of its instrumental task. But attempts to control the group in relation to the instrumental task disturb the equilibrium of the group and cause tensions in the expressive-integrative area of the group's activities. These negative reactions to control attempts may, like the negative reactions found in the work of Lewin and his associates, be directed at the leader or at a group scapegoat.

Evidence for the negative reaction received by the group member who attempts to lead the group in the direction of instrumental task achievement is derived from six measures taken by Bales during the group experiments. Two measures are based on interaction counts using the Bales scheme; these are simply measures of the amount of interactions initiated and the amount received. After each group session the members are asked to rate all members on a sociometric test using three criteria: the member who contributed the best ideas to the group, the member who contributed the best guidance, and the member who was best liked. And after all four group sessions the members are asked to select the one who contributed the best leadership. The percentage of times the same group member occupies the highest position by more than one measure is calculated. Thus on one batch of experimental groups, Slater (1955) calculated the percentage of times that the individual selected as the best leader was highest by another criterion. The results follow:

The "best leader" was also ranked highest on guidance 80 percent of the time; on receiving, 65 per cent; on ideas, 59 per cent; on talking, 55 per cent; and on liking, 25 per cent. Clearly, the member who is best liked is rarely associated in the minds of the group members with the individual who is the best leader. Furthermore, Slater found that "liking" was not associated with any of the other measurements of leadership. The individual chosen highest by the socio-emotional criterion of best-liked was three times as likely to hold the highest position by that measure alone than were those who were most highly chosen by any other measure. Thus, those group members who are active in directing the group, or who are selected by the group members as having contributed to the instrumental task of the group, are not likely to receive choices on a sociometric test using an expressive criterion. The results clearly indicate that the individual who attempts to control the instrumental activities of the group lowers his chances to be highly thought of by the group according to an affective criterion.

External Relations of the Leader

The conflict between directing the group and maintaining one's acceptance by the group would seem to be the unique problem of the group leader. This conflict is heightened in the groups discussed above by the fact that the task toward which the instrumental leader directs the group is set for the group externally by the experimenter. Insofar as the task is set for the group externally rather than chosen by the group, attempts at instrumental control are more likely to engender negative reactions. This proposition is supported in an experimental study by Katz *et al* (1957) of a number of four-men groups. After the performance of one task, the groups were asked to select a leader for a second task. In some cases, the task was one that the group had chosen; in others, it was imposed by the experimenter. The results support the proposition that when the task is imposed upon the group externally, the negative reaction against the leader who attempts to direct the task activity will be greater. In those cases where the group performed a second task that it had selected for itself, all those who had been chosen as leaders after the first task were again so chosen at the end of the second. On the other hand, when the group was assigned a task that it had not selected, only one-third of those who had been chosen as leaders after the first task retained that position after the second . . . .

Group Accomplishment

The dilemma faced by the leader in reconciling the demands for satisfactory affective relations within the group and effective instrumental activity can, as has been shown, hinder the effective operation of the group. Insofar as the negative reactions of the followers reduce the extent to which they accept the instrumental directives of the leader or the extent to which the leader is motivated to undertake such instrumental directives, the leader will be forced to concentrate more and more on the socio-emotional aspect of group interaction and ignore the instrumental. This will be especially the case in those groups—such as the experimental groups with no previous experience together—in which the leader has not built up enough general prestige to allow him to survive some negative reactions without being rejected as leader. Though the long-run satisfactions of the group members may be greater if the instrumental task of the group is accomplished, the uncertain leader may not be able to ask the group members to delay their satisfactions until that later time. Until a stable leadership structure able to survive some negative affective reactions is developed, group task accomplishment will lag. This viewpoint is supported by several experimental studies comparing groups that have evolved stable leadership patterns with those that have not. Heinicke and Bales compared groups which had evolved a stable pattern of leadership and a high degree of group consensus as to who was the group leader, with groups in which there was greater fluctuation of leadership and less agreement as to who was the most influential in the group. They found that in the stable, high-consensus groups there was greater speed and accuracy in the solution of the problem presented to the group as well as greater member satisfaction. The unstable, low-consensus groups had to spend time on solving the problem of leadership that was used by the stable group for task accomplishment. Experimental work by March (1956) and Borg (1957) also found that groups with a stable pattern of leadership performed more effectively and spent less time in resolving internal group conflicts.

A stable leadership structure is important if the group is to accomplish its instrumental task. But such stability is difficult to achieve because of the conflicting demands for task accomplishment and affective satisfactions. Insofar as the group can achieve some satisfactory balance between the instrumental and the affective aspects of its interaction and a stable leadership structure is developed, the group will be effective and contribute to the satisfactions of its members. Insofar as such a balance cannot be reached and such a structure is not developed, groups will either fall apart or continue operating at high levels of tension. This problem, we can assume, is faced not only by small groups, but by larger organizations and political systems as well. Unless the unlikely prospect of a state totally run by coercion is to be considered, some minimum of acceptance of the system by the participants must be maintained at the same time that the organization or political system carries on instrumental activities that inhibit freedom and, presumably, lower the satisfactions of the members. The importance of affective relations in political systems and the acceptance by the followers of the leader's directives has long been recognized in political science. As Merriam has written: "No power could stand if it relied upon violence alone, for force is not strong enough to maintain itself against the accidents of rivalry and discontent. The might that makes right must be a different might from that of the right arm. It must be a right deep-rooted in emotion, embedded in feelings and aspirations . . ." (1934, p.102). The question must then be asked: how do social systems—whether small experimental groups, on-going groups, organizations or political systems—maintain a satisfactory level of affective integration at the same time that they carry on instrumental activities whose tendency may be to lower the degree of affective satisfaction of the participants?

CONFLICTING EXPECTATIONS: THEIR RESOLUTION IN SMALL GROUPS

The Two Leaders

To shed some light upon the way in which the conflict between instrumental and affective leadership is resolved, we turn first to the small group experimental literature. The resolution of the conflict in these small groups will then be compared with the resolution in larger, on-going social systems. In the small groups studied by Bales and his associates, the conflict between instrumental and affective leadership is resolved by a differentiation within the leadership role. In these groups different individuals tend to specialize in the instrumental leadership role and in the socio-emotional leadership role. The evidence for this role differentiation is found in the material cited above: those members highly selected by the group by an affective criterion were not likely to be selected by the group as having contributed to the instrumental task, nor were they likely to be active in giving the group direction toward the accomplishment of that task. On the other hand, the individual selected by the group as contributing the most to the external task (Best Ideas) was also highly selected as contributing most to the instrumental aspect of the internal group task (Best Guidance). High choice by one criterion was closely correlated with high choice by the other, and the individual rated lowest by one was likely to be lowest by the other. The findings by Bales and his associates that the leadership role tends to be split between a task-oriented instrumental leader and a "sociometric star" is supported by small group studies of other authors. Both Gibb (1950) and Olmstead (1959) found that affective choice did not correlate highly with choice by an instrumental criterion. And Cattell and Stice (1954) in a factor analysis of leader characteristics found that different characteristics are associated with leadership defined in "syntality" terms (i.e., in terms of contribution to changes in group productivity) and leadership defined by an affective sociometric criterion.

Activities of the Two Leaders

The fact that group leadership tends to be split between two individuals is reflected not only in the fact that group members choose different individuals by socio-emotional and instrumental criteria, but also in the fact that the behavior patterns of the individuals thus selected differ. When one looks at the interaction rates of the group members most highly selected on the basis of the socio-emotional and the instrumental (Best Ideas) criteria, one finds significant differences. The socio-emotional leader tends to initiate and receive more interactions in the socio-emotional categories of interaction than does the task specialist. He gives and receives more solidarity and tension-release interactions. The task specialist, on the other hand, is more active in giving opinions and suggestions; and he receives larger amounts of agreement, questions, and negative reactions. The difference between the behavior of the two leaders is best described by Slater: "The most salient general difference between the rates of interaction of the two types of leaders is the tendency for the Idea man to initiate interactions more heavily in Area B (Problem Solving Attempts) and the Best-liked man in Area A (Positive reactions). . . . On the Receiving end, the situation is largely reversed, with the Idea man receiving more agreement, questions and negative reactions, while the Best-liked man receives more problem solving attempts, and more solidarity and tension release. The general picture is thus one of specialization and complementarity, with the Idea man concentrating on the task and playing a more aggressive role, while the Best-liked man concentrates more on social emotional problems, giving rewards, and playing a more passive role" (1955, p.306). The qualitative ratings given the two leaders by the group members are thus reflected in their quantitative interaction rates.

The difference between the two specialists extends to the attitudes of these two group members. Not only do they specialize in certain areas of the group activity, but they receive their satisfactions from those areas. The instrumental leader, it has already been suggested, is relatively less motivated to receive positive affective responses from the group. His personal satisfactions derive not from the affective responses of the group members, but from the instrumental task directly. For the "sociometric star," on the other hand, " . . . *primary* satisfaction derives from his success in his role as promoter of solidarity and provider of opportunities for tension release . . . ." (1955, p.309). The socio-emotional leader also tends to be more accepting of the other group members, while the task specialist differentiates among the other members in the degree to which he accepts them. On the sociometric question in which the group members were asked to rate the other members on the degree to which they liked them, 42 per cent of the socio-emotional leaders did not differentiate among the members (they said, in effect, "I like everybody") while only 20 per cent of the task leaders did not so differentiate.

Relations Between the Two Leaders

The balance between affective tone and instrumental accomplishment is maintained in these groups, then, by the development of two leaders. The disturbance in the expressive area caused by the instrumental directives of the task leader is countered by positive affective reactions from the socio-emotional leader. In understanding this process, it is important to note the relations between the two leaders. Bales and Slater (1957) found that the two had close relations, one with the other. The task and socio-emotional leaders tended to interact more frequently with each other than did any other pair of members; and, what is equally significant, tended to agree more frequently with each other. In this way, it may be suggested, the task leader receives indirectly through the socio-emotional leader the expressive support that he could not directly obtain because of his instrumental role. That such a coalition between the two group leaders is important for the effective functioning of the group is suggested by a comparison made by Bales and Slater between High Status Consensus groups and Low Status Consensus groups. In the former type of group—in which, as was pointed out earlier, task accomplishment and member satisfaction are both higher—the relationships between the two leaders are statistically significant. In the Low Consensus groups, though there is a tendency for the two leaders to interact with each other, the pattern is neither as consistent nor as strong . . . .

Insofar as members are similar in age, insofar as they are similar in status in the external culture of the group, and insofar as the experimenter supplies no sanction for any particular leadership structure, any directive attempt by a group member will be looked upon as a challenge to the other members. With no status consensus among the group members at the beginning of interaction and no status guides, would-be leaders in the new experimental groups are placed in a clear power struggle. The increased vigor necessary to control the group increases the negative reaction to the leader and heightens the conflict between acceptance and instrumental control.

REFERENCES

Bales, Robert F. *Interaction Process Analysis: A Method for the Study of Small Groups.* Reading, Massachusetts: Addison-Wesley, 1950.

Bales, Robert F. and Slater, Philip E. "Notes on 'Role Differentiation in Small Decision Making Groups': Reply to Dr. Wheeler," *Sociometry,* **20** (1957), pp. 152-155.

Borg, Walter S. "The Behavior of Emergent and Designated Leaders in Situation Tests," *Sociometry,* **20** (1957), pp. 95-104.

Cattel, Raymond B. and Stice, G. F. "Four Formulae for Selecting Leaders on the Basis of Personality," *Human Relations,* **7** (1954), pp. 493-507.

Coch, Lester and French, John R. P. Jr. "Overcoming Resistance to Change," *Human Relations,* **1** (1948), pp. 512-532.

Gibb, Cecil A. "The Sociometry of Leadership in Temporary Groups," *Sociometry,* **13** (1950), pp. 226-243.

Katz, Elihu et al. "Leadership Stability and Social Change: An Experiment with Small Groups, " *Sociometry,* **20** (1957), pp. 36-50.

Lewin, Kurt. *Field Theory in the Social Sciences.* New York: Harper, 1951.

Lewin, Kurt, Lippitt, Ronald, and White, R. "Patterns of Aggressive Behavior in Experimentally Designed Social Climates," *Journal of Social Psychology,* **10** (1939) pp. 271-299.

March, James G. "Influence Measurement in Experimental and Semi-Experimental Groups," *Sociometry,* **19** (1956), pp. 260-271.

Merriam, Charles E. *Political Power.* New York: McGraw-Hill, 1934.

Olmstead, Michael S. "Orientation and Role in the Small Group," *American Sociological Review,* **19** (1959), pp. 741-751.

Slater, Philip E. "Role Differentiation in Small Groups," *American Sociological Review,* **20** (1955), pp. 300-310.

MICROCOSM

PHILIP E. SLATER

Our inquiry begins with a phenomenon which is familiar to many group leaders and which I have rather dramatically called the "revolt." The term is used variously to refer to a specific event—the "ganging up" of group members in some sort of hostile attack on the assigned group leader—and to a process—the group members' growing independence of, yet identification with, the leader. As will later become clear, one might argue that every interaction between leader and member represents this process microscopically, but for the moment let us concentrate our attention on the more explicit macroscopic event, which is easily described and exhibits more visible symbols. A modal description of such an event is provided for us by Bennis and Shepard:

> A group member may openly express the opinion that the trainer's presence and comments are holding the group back, suggest that "as an experiment" the trainer leave the group "to see how things go without him." When the trainer is thus directly challenged, the whole atmosphere of the meeting changes. There is a sudden increase in alertness and tension. Previously, there had been much acting out of the wish that the trainer were absent, but at the same time a conviction that he was the *raison d'etre* of the group's existence—that it would fall apart without him. Previously, absence of the trainer would have constituted desertion, or defeat, fulfilment of the members' worst fears as to their own inadequacy or the trainer's. But now leaving the group can have a different meaning. General agreement that the trainer should leave is rarely achieved. However, after a little further discussion it becomes clear that he is at liberty to leave, with the understanding that he wishes to be a member of the group, and will return if and when the group is willing to accept him . . . .
>
> An interesting parallel, which throws light on the order of events in group development, is given in Freud's discussion of the myth of the primal horde. In his version:
>
> "These many individuals eventually banded themselves together, killed [the father], and cut him in pieces . . . They then formed the totemistic community of brothers all with equal rights and united by the totem prohibitions which were to preserve and to expiate the memory of the murder . . ." (1950).
>
> The event is always marked in group history as a "turning point," "the time we became a group," "when I first got involved," etc. The mounting tension, followed by sometimes uproarious euphoria, cannot be entirely explained by the surface

events. It may be that the revolt represents a realization of important fantasies individuals hold in all organizations, that the emotions involved are undercurrents wherever rebellious and submissive tendencies toward existing authorities must be controlled . . . . (Bennis and Shepard, 1956, pp 424-425).*

THE ATTACK ON THE LEADER

The revolt against the leader represents the decay of the original religious fantasy. In real life the god never appears, so that the fantasy of his ultimate power and protection can be preserved indefinitely. In the training group the fantasied protector is present and visible, as well as increasingly human and fallible. The myth of the omniscient protector is thus constantly confronted with an annoying reality. This might be called the Problem of Chronic Epiphany. The living personage not only fails to protect, or solve, or give, but on the few occasions when he does speak often seems irrelevant, gauche, or schizoid.

Faced with these facts, the group member is forced back to one of two positions. He must believe either that the group leader is not omniscient but in fact incompetent or that he is indeed omniscient and is simply withholding his knowledge and guidance out of stubborn perversity. The latter view may seem self-contradictory, but it is a less shattering admission than the former and is of course reinforced when ever the group leader says anything clever or cryptic.

When this point is reached, the anger aroused by the leader's primordial deprivation of the group can be released. What is particularly compelling about the attack which follows, however, is the variety of fantasy themes associated with it: themes of group murder, of cannibalism, of orgy. Sometimes all of these appear together, sometimes one or two at a time, depending on the major area of tension existing in a specific group at a specific time. Let us therefore consider several of these themes separately, noting, however, the point of overlap.

A.   The Theme of Group Murder

This notion appears in two forms. First, it appears in vague and ominous prophecies concerning the fate of the leader which sometimes occur early in the life of the group. Second, it appears in the group's *post hoc* definition of the group revolt. What in prospect is presented as a polite

---

* From W.G. Bennis and H.A. Shepard, "A Theory of Group Development," *Human Relations*, 9, 1956. Reprinted by permission of Plenum Publishing Corporation.

and rational motion to conduct an experimental meeting without the leader is subsequently referred to as "the day we threw him out" or "the day we killed authority."

IIe. After the group had met for several weeks one member, Henry, suggested at the beginning of a session that he thought the group leader would "end up getting killed." He then proceeded to take a highly interpretive role for the remainder of the hour, using many of the leader's most characteristic speech mannerisms. The group members began to court Sandra, the most silent and inactive member, expressing their resentment and fear toward her but also their desire for her participation. At this point Henry said, "It almost sounds as if we were recruiting for something," and the discussion began to center around the desire for an external danger to focus their feelings of inadequacy and helplessness.

A week later Jim observed that he and other members often sat with hands clasped in a manner which resembled the leader's. It was then suggested that the function of this mannerism was to "hide a smirk." Amid much hilarity, resentment was expressed at the compulsiveness with which his title was always used in referring to him, and it was alternatively suggested that he be called solely by his last or solely by his first name. When one girl made reference to his dimpled smile, guilt set in over "knocking him off his pedestal." Paul, who was sitting twisting a scarf, was then asked jokingly if he was "getting ready to kill the king."

A week later the group was engaged in a discussion of the Twist. When asked what had stimulated the desire to dance, Laura replied, "we want to dance around in a circle with you in the middle—on a stake."

Two weeks later the group indulged in the pleasant fantasy (it was now mid-December) of having a picnic in May. First it was suggested that they eat ham—in part a sardonic reference to the killing of the "pig" in *Lord of the Flies* (an inexhaustible fountain of metaphorical references for this group). Then they gleefully decided to have a drunken party without the group leader, in the middle of which they would call him up defiantly to tell him he was being excluded. The group very quickly backed off from these fantasies, however, and expressed guilt over them.

IXb. In a short-term intensive training group the group leader was called away one day after a few meetings had been held. During his absence the group members, young business executives, set fire to his name card (each participant had such a card in front of him on the table) . . . .

Vb. Toward the end of the year one of the males in the group suggested asking the group leader to leave. In the discussion which followed there were some mild objections that it "wouldn't make any difference," since they "tend to forget he's here." One girl thought he should stay away at least a week if "anything really definite" were going to happen. Most members nevertheless seemed willing to "go along" with the suggestion. One boy then asked why this had been brought up, and another said, "Well I don't know. You think this is—that everybody is kind of mad at Dr. Bales or what?" Ray, who had suggested the move, said he was just curious. The problem then arose as to whether the group leader should be allowed to sit in the observation room, behind the one-way mirrors, where there were graduate student observers, and it was agreed that he should not. One member now added, "Why do you want to throw him out?" Again, curiosity was advanced as the reason. A girl now noted that, "This isn't the first time it's been brought up by any means."

Male .   No, but this is the first time instead of going around the table asking what everyone thinks of it and would he mind leaving and if everyone is in agreement then we'll do this; this is the first time we've had any decisive action, and I just wonder why—what happened in the last session?

Male :   There has been nothing special about our recent sessions. I think Ray's experiment is still valid.

There was comment at various points about Ray's "assumption of leadership" with regard to this question. One boy, who was reminded by one of the girls that he had always been opposed to having the leader leave, said, "No, not now. Just thinking about that when I questioned Ray—perhaps I should have told you that I've been thinking the same thing myself, lately, that I was wondering if anyone else had—that I could feel this idea mounting in the last number of sessions and I was wondering why—" and later, " . . . I want him to go but I keep thinking, so what if he does, what's going to happen to us?"

A girl remarked that she didn't "consciously feel mad" at the group leader now although she had at first, to which one of the males replied that "he's already dead." Although he dodged a question as to what he had meant by this the idea appeared again later, when two of the girls were discussing the notion that the group leader had inhibited the emergence of a peer leader and one suggested that Ray had made a "bid" for such leadership in recommending the expulsion. Ray denied any such motivation, whereupon one of the girls suggested he was trying to "make the group guilty and responsible for his death rather than take the responsibility on yourself." Ray said he didn't "consider this his death, actually, maybe it is his death, I don't know."

The objection was now made that the act was like a child running away from home through resentment of authority. They questioned that the leader's absence would make them "any more individuated," and argued that "if we're really going to be people who can separate themselves and become individuals we should be able to do so with Dr. Bales still here." This was dismissed as mere faintheartedness. One of the girls then asked the group leader if his feelings weren't "a little hurt by all this," and after some attempt to deflect this question as irrelevant, he responded to a solid feminine phalanx by admitting that it was "an odd feeling"—to the dismay of one boy who "never thought you'd take it that way."

The majority now concentrated its attention on the two members who seemed to object to the expulsion. One, Shirley, said it would serve no purpose and would make her feel guilty. They objected that she had been "very aggressive" toward the group leader, and had reacted to an earlier, unsolicited absence of the group leader as paternal abandonment, thus demonstrating that the expulsion *would* "make a difference." The male objector argued that it would simply be a diversion, but one girl opposed him on the grounds that "if Dr. Bales isn't the cause of it, who is?" And later, "he makes me so mad that I would like to throw something at him. You say something in a joking way and he—I have a feeling that he can see into all my motives."

They now confronted the problem of how to let the leader know when to return since there was some feeling that an absence of more than one session would be desirable. This resolved, someone realized that the group leader had not yet indicated whether in fact he would leave. Ray refused to be the one to ask, on the grounds that the responsibility should be shared. All announced together their willingness to do so, and one of the girls asked if the group leader would leave for the next session, to which he agreed.

During the first of the two sessions in which they met alone they decided to discuss—after a period of preliminary frolicking—some previously distributed excerpts from *The Golden Bough,* including the opening and closing passages concerning the Sacred Grove of Diana at Aricia, the quotation from the *Aeneid,* and the material on Dionysus from Book IV. Early in the conversation one boy asked, with regard to the struggle for the priesthood, "I don't see why anyone would want to kill him, frankly . . . who would want to be head-priest?" In reply one girl asked, "Who wants to be leader?" Later it was suggested that Aeneas' visiting of his dead father with the golden bough was a "symbolic killing" and a "triumphal visit," since "his father is out of the way and he is coming down with the branch in his hand." Another girl said, "I had the impression that his father would tell him something." A boy referred to the incident as "lording it over his father," a girl as "getting strength to go on, and getting authorization and permission and help . . . from the father-figure, the authority—" at which point the relevance to the immediate situation became manifest and amid laughter one of the girls asked where the golden bough was.

They now began gradually to shift to Dionysus, sibling rivalry, and the similarities between the Dionysian and Christian traditions with regard to the killing, eating, and annual resurrection of the god. One girl pointed out that in Christianity the eternal cycle of killing and retribution, exemplified by the priest at Nemi who kills the former priest to win the post and is killed when he himself can no longer defend it, is brought to an end, since the murder is forgiven. Another objected that "that's the worst retribution there could be as far as I'm concerned." They then discussed to what extent the sacrifice rituals were an expiation of guilt. One boy suggested that since gods and animals were at one time identified, the sacrifice fused appeasement and hostility towards the god. "The people feel inferior to the gods." They then began a long discussion or orgies and "guilt-ridden" religious sects, following which they returned to the priest at Nemi, asking, "What would compel a person to want to be King of the Wood?" Guilt and homicidal tendencies were suggested, then they wondered if there might be other rewards attendant upon the position. Diana, as the "virgin mother" was mentioned briefly, and

> someone asked if they were going to invite the group leader to return next time. They now expressed gratification at their performance, suggesting that they "did better without him," "worked a little harder," "made a lot of progress," and finally agreed to spend another session alone. (R. F. Bales, transcript)

This example illustrates most of the usual themes which occur in a group revolt. Particularly striking is the consistency with which the two contrary definitions of the event are juxtaposed: the rational, experimental curiosity and desire to test their level of independence on the one hand: on on the other, anger and revenge, fantasies of murder, guilt, and expiation. What is one moment discussed as if it were a respectful request is at another referred to as "throwing him out." This is typical and both definitions of the situation are accurate and genuinely felt.

Note also the references to past consideration of the question, and the sense of the idea "mounting" in the group over time. In no other situation can the difference between an individual and a collective impulse be so closely observed. The suggestion may be made countless times in countless forms, and the members may even take a poll, as was reported here, but until some point of readiness is reached it is not heard, or not felt, or not relevant, or purely academic, until suddenly it is mentioned and essentially agreed on without any discussion at all. Prior to this point a single verbalized dissent will scotch it, while after it is reached several vocal dissenters will be unable to offset the illusion of unanimity. The sense of mounting readiness is, of course, the growth of group solidarity and independence. This is the true revolt, the expulsion being merely a ritual expression, testing, and consolidation of it. The phrase "he's already dead" expresses this fact that independence and secularization of the leader have already been achieved. . . .

C.   The Theme of Cannibalism

> One day the brothers . . . came together, killed and devoured their father and so made an end of the patriarchal horde. United, they had the courage to do and succeeded in doing what would have been impossible for them individually. . . .Cannibal savages as they were, it goes without saying that they devoured their victim. . . .The violent primal father had doubtless been feared and envied model of each one of the company of brothers: and in the act of devouring him they accomplished their identification with him, and each one acquired a portion of his strength. The totem meal . . . would thus be a repetition and a commemoration of this memorable and criminal deed, which was the beginning of so many things. . . . (Freud, 1950, pp. 141-142)*

---

* Reprinted from *Totem and Taboo* by Sigmund Freud. Authorized translation by James Strachey. By permission of W.W. Norton and Company, Inc. and Routledge & Kegan Paul Ltd. Copyright 1950 by Routledge & Kegan Paul Ltd.

It will be recalled that the watershed of the revolt is the frustration of dependency needs by the group leader. He supplies not only the motive force for the revolt but also the means, since his nonresponsiveness forces them to talk about him rather than to him and thereby draws them together.

Since deprivation is thus the keynote of the attack on the leader, we should not be surprised to find such attacks often accompanied by oral manifestations of one kind or another, usually a group feast. The basis of this trend is best illustrated by a discussion in Group IIe, occurring in a meeting about three weeks before Christmas, when, amid much hilarity, the members decided that they should collectively apply to *The New York Times* as a candidate for the years' "100 Neediest Cases." Bion also notes the importance of the feeling of being starved (1949, p. 296).

IIf. It was the last meeting of the fall term and the discussion was extremely lethargic. The members became aware that they were waiting for the group leader to make an interpretation about their desultory conversation which would "get them going." They now considered the possibility that perhaps he would say nothing for the entire hour. They tried to interpret their own interaction but decided rather apathetically that all their interpretations were "meaningless." They then began to exchange examples of "meaningless" facts, particularly those used as "fillers" in newspaper columns. Danny reported one saying that the bean surplus in the United States would feed the entire population for an extended period. Helen quoted one which stated the average number of licks in an ice cream cone. Aaron raised the mathematical problem of how many facets there were to a pear.

IIb. It was shortly before Christmas vacation, and papers had been returned after the previous session. Despite many indications of anger over what were felt to be low grades there seemed to be great reluctance to discuss this in the group setting, and a long silence resulted when the group leader pointed out the contrast. Eve then remarked that she was "affected by a sense of—of inappropriateness of—of my reaction to—to my paper when I got it back." Roger described the reaction of several of them as "exaggerated. We sort of blew until the first black inky cloud passed and then we went our own separate ways, perhaps felt a little better for having exploded to someone who could understand what we meant." Gordon mentioned their preoccupation with who got what grade, and when others said this was typical of all courses, Eve disagreed: "We stood around like buzzards outside the door and as everyone came down the steps we pounced on them." There followed a long series of complaints about the leader's role ("He just sits there"), his treatment of the papers ("too many comments," "too few," etc.), their lack of preparation or "model" for the papers, their feeling of betrayal ("we hoped we had been moving toward what you wanted"), and some suspicion that the supposedly low grades had been given for some ulterior purpose. In the midst of this Brad, who was the most consistent of all the group members in protesting the lack of structure, said, "You have expressed the fact that we have not learned what you wanted us to learn and yet you will not *tell* us what we are trying to learn." A little later Madeline remarked, "You've got the golden key to the little box of A's and we can't have it." Vic wondered if after all their problems weren't their own, but John clouded this polarization by suggesting that the group leader must have a reason for "running the course in this way." Gordon and Roger then expressed openly their feeling of "intense competition" with other group members for the leader's approval. Eve said it was easy in group meetings to ignore the leader, but that writing a paper put her "at a complete loss." Joe said what if the leader were evaluating each comment, but others also protested their unselfconsciousness in the group setting. Roger then wondered if the grades would affect the structure of the group in the coming term.

This session is particularly interesting since it shows not only the sense of deprivation and the competition it generates, but also the approach to a solution. Through direct *expression* of the invidious impulses, the members achieve unity, and through similar expression of dependency needs, a step toward independence is taken. Once such feelings are shared they seem to lose their potency, perhaps because the act of sharing them in itself expresses a commitment to other group members and a relinquishing of the fantasy of a private and secret relationship with the leader.

IIg. About a month after the group began there was a period in which dependency needs seemed very acute. A session immediately following the one in which experiment myths were verbalized . . . began with comments about the Passover custom of leaving an empty chair at the table and a glass of wine for Elijah—wondering if the custom should be inaugurated in the group. Later on in the session Julie said that up to now she had been able to maintain a veneer of responsibility but today she felt childish and wanted someone else to do things. Neil had the fantasy of an entire society in which everyone simply lay down.

The next session was the day after Hallowe'en, and Penny passed out "Sugar Daddys" to everyone in the group, joking about the "totem" on the back of the wrapper. They then talked of how much personal revelation took place in meetings outside the class, and a few of their personal feelings toward one another were now exchanged. At the end of the hour, in response to an interpretation by the group leader concerning expressions of dependency, Margo told about a fantasy of having the entire group play "Trick or Treat" on the group leader. She and Julie then exchanged reports of feelings of jealousy and gratification about particularizing comments of the leader.

It is indeed an unusual group which does not at some point or another bring in food and pass it around, usually with great satisfaction and high spirits. At times this seems merely to express a dim beginning awareness that the group must "feed" itself. At other times it is clearly associated with aggression against the leader, and has the air of a kind of symbolic cannibalistic revenge on him for his failure to gratify their needs. Finally, one often finds signs that the act of eating expresses a desire to incorporate desired attributes of the leader, such as his knowledge and ability to interpret group behavior.

This notion that desirable attributes can be acquired by devouring their possessor is of course a familiar one:

> The Bushmen will not give their children a jackal's heart to eat, lest it should make them timid like the jackal; but they give them a leopard's heart to make them correspondingly brave. British Central Africa aspirants after courage consume the flesh and especially the hearts of lions, while lecherous persons eat the testicles of goats .... To restore the aged Aeson to youth the witch Medea infused into his veins a decoction of the liver of the long-lived deer and the head of a crow that had outlived nine human generations ... and when Sigurd killed the dragon Fafnir and tasted his heart's blood he thereby acquired a knowledge of the language of birds.... Again, the flesh and blood of *dead men* are commonly eaten and drunk to inspire bravery, wisdom, or other qualities for which those men were remarkable.... It is now easy to see why a savage should desire to partake of the flesh of an animal or man whom he regards as divine. By eating the body of the god he shares in the god's attributes and powers.... Thus the drinking of wine in the rites of a vine-god like Dionysus is not an act of revelry, it is a solemn sacrament. (Frazer, 1959, pp. 464, 466)*

As usual, it is impossible to find examples which express a single idea in isolation, but those which follow can be grouped roughly according to their relative emphasis on the three aforementioned themes of self-feeding, revenge, and identification.

Group members often express their feeling of deprivation by remarking that the group has a "father" but no "mother" (unless the group leader is a female). Sometimes there is banter about constructing or importing one, or assigning the role to any faintly nurturant or mature female in the group, but occasionally someone will appear with his or her mother in tow to "sit in" on the group. In one group (VIb), the oral quality of the latter maneuver was intensified by the fact that the boy who brought his mother to the group also distributed some jelly beans which she had given him.

> IIf. After they had been meeting for about seven weeks, the group leader entered one day with a pile of graded papers to return to the members. When asked if they would be handed out at the end of the hour he nodded. No move was made to obtain them any sooner, although it was their first grade

---

* Reprinted by permission of S. G. Phillips Inc., from *The New Golden Bough* by Sir James George Frazer, edited by Theodor H. Gaster, Copyright ©1959 by S. G. Phillips, Inc.

of any kind in the course and they were clearly anxious to see how well they had performed. Before long, the discussion drifted into the question of the meaningfulness of their sessions. They asked each other whether they thought they were "taking anything away" from the group, and while many claimed they were, and said that they missed the group when they were absent, they also felt that they were somehow "trivializing" everything they discussed, and wondered if perhaps all of their interaction wasn't a "distraction." This led to some talk of cognitive processes and someone mentioned the old saw about telling someone "don't think about 'hippopotamus.'" Many of them had never heard it and they were enormously intrigued with the notion, trying it out and weaving facetious comments around it. The group leader then suggested that perhaps the image pleased them because a hippopotamus was so large that if they all took some there would still be some left. This seemed to tickle them but they paid little attention to it and began talking about each other's love affairs, complaining finally that they still hid intimate details of their lives from each other. The group leader then suggested that it was hard for them to share with each other when they were so concerned with their papers, i.e., with competing for approval and rewards from him. He wondered if they were "too hungry" to share, a phrase which produced a wave of laughter followed by a series of efforts to get him to talk more. They then returned to the discussion. A few minutes before the end of the hour Helen announced she had to leave early to get to an exam across the campus, but said she did not want to leave without her paper. When the instructor made no response, Barbara reached over, seized the pile of papers, and passed them to Danny who distributed them.

At their next meeting they discussed this incident, which had delighted them, at some length. Danny brought an animal cracker shaped like a hippopotamus which they passed around the group but did not eat. The next session Aaron brought his mother. The following meeting occurred just prior to a vacation and only four members were present. Aaron was describing an affair with a fat woman who he compared in size first to the table around which they were seated and then, quite ingenuously, to a hippopotamus. This aroused laughter but no interpretation. A week later the theme recurred, this time in the form of the fantasy that they should form 12 groups (there were 12 members), each consisting of a member, a hippopotamus, and the group leader.

By now the hippopotamus had become a group symbol of considerable salience, although it was always treated facetiously and no one ever ventured to interpret it. Barbara and Miriam reported seeing china or wooden hippopotami in shops, having the impulse to buy one and present it to the group, and refraining on the ground that it would be thought presumptuous. A week later someone brought in a bag of potato chips which they passed around to eat. It was suggested jokingly that they were "eating the hippopotamus" and that this was equivalent to eating the group mother. Danny then remarked that they would "eat the group father later." A few

days after this incident they were anticipating a meeting when the group
leader was to be away. Although he had merely announced autocratically
that "there would be no class" on the day in question, they now decide
to meet without him. During the discussion, Dora, who had been fiddling
with a piece of paper, now suddenly announced that it was a hippopotamus,
since it had an "eye" and was "clearly a mother." They then tried to
remember how the symbol had first arisen, some even hypothesizing that
it came from assigned reading. They wondered if they would be
"eating the hippopotamus" on the day they were to meet alone, and began
to analyze the symbol a little in terms of their efforts to "make a mother
out of" the group leader. Someone then suggested that they would be killing
the hippopotamus when they were alone.

It should be clear from this example that the hippopotamus was a
complex symbol whose meaning centered around the dependency needs
of the group members. It arose first out of their effort "not to think
about" their papers, that is, their attempt to avoid lapsing into the
competitive authority-oriented structure of the traditional classroom.
But it also signified their wish for a less depriving more nurturant leader,
who would be something more than just an "eye." Finally, it stood for
their aggressive strivings for collective independence, such as the seizing
of the papers and the decision to meet alone. Thus it would seem to
be of precisely the same order as the totem animals of primitive clans,
which are also an attempt to gratify dependency needs through group
solidarity based on common experience. It furthermore bears some
resemblance to Freud's exposition in *Totem and Taboo:* the substitution of the totem animal for a paternal figure, the aggression against
this figure, the taboo on eating the totem, and the ritual violation of that
taboo. . . .

CONCLUSION

We have come some distance in our perambulations from the limited and
mundane context in which we began. It might be objected that the many
parallels drawn merely reflect a kind of grandiosity on our part, an
attempt to crowd all of life and history into the tiny shell of one particular
and even atypical variety of contemporary group experience. It might
further be argued that if one can attach so much significance to a few
groups of students and patients one could just as well attach it to a tree
or a flower or any other evolving entity. What, then, is the value of all
these connections? To the effort to facilitate the development of any
given kind of group ("therapeutic," "meaningful," "rewarding,"
"cohesive," "valid," or whatever) I am certain they will add very little.
To the attempt to understand the structure and process of such groups

they may help to agglutinate an apperceptive mass which could be either useful or distracting. The title of this book, however, betrays a broader interest, as well as a conviction that these resemblances are engaged by some underlying principle of human association.

A training or therapy group is a sophisticated product of a complex civilization. This fact has indeed made possible the establishment of these connections. It takes no great wit to perceive the relevance of religious symbolism when group members regularly utilize such symbolism. What we have observed in our examples is simply a tendency for group members to draw upon a rich cultural heritage in expressing their reactions to the difficulties of establishing and maintaining a complex set of interpersonal relationships.

Yet it seems reasonable to assume that their choices are not random, but reflect patterns of solution often essayed in the past, which are hence relevant even though not always successful. My argument is not that a training group recapitulates cultural evolution but that any group must recapitulate some of it, and that we are therefore under an obligation to make sense out of whatever recapitulations we find. A theory based solely on this experience is of necessity limited, but since this is true of all theories, we can only advance our approximation and make the best of it until something better comes along. . . .

[Does] the group recapitulate the family situation? This would be a reasonable theory but to derive everything from familial experiences is somewhat limiting. Would it not be more useful to say that a group member uses the leader to help differentiate himself from the group as a whole not simply because the leader "represents" the father in his unconscious, but because this *general device* for maximizing boundary-awareness tends to be first learned in the family, although it is applicable to a wide variety of situations? Thus, for example, the deification or at least magnification of leaders has always been important in achieving higher levels of cultural development, since it permits people to cooperate with one another with less anxiety at times when awareness of their separateness from an overpowering world has begun (perhaps aroused by large increases in the size of the group, change of locale, contact with other societies, etc.). Later, when the world becomes more manageable, limited, and understandable, democratization can occur.

But this is only the negative side of this complex process. We have also noticed that in order to *increase* consciousness, libido is invested in a leader or other individual (or subgroup) and then taken back. Such a person is not only permitted but encouraged to be narcissistic in ways that normally are negatively sanctioned. There seems to be a feeling, as I have suggested elsewhere (Slater, 1963), that this withdrawal and hoarding of libido on the part of the leader will ultimately confer a boon on the collectivity.

This seems to me to be one of the most essential meanings of the primal horde myth: that it is a colorful metaphor for the "inchworm" model of cultural locomotion discussed in the previous chapter. Libido is concentrated in a leader or other specialist, the remainder of the collectivity resting submissive and deprived (the sexually monopolistic father and the victimized sons). The leader or specialist, thereby freed from the obligation to reciprocate the love of his followers, now undertakes to solve a problem for the collectivity ("some cultural advance . . . some new weapon"). Upon achieving success, the members of the collectivity cash in their libidinal investment, with whatever dividends the leader or specialist has achieved for them (they kill, devour, identify with, mourn, venerate the father). But not all of their libido is freed: some is merely transferred to the collectivity and diffused among its members (the women of the family are renounced and exogamy is enforced).

In one sense this is simply the sociological analogue of the pseudopod or the mutation—the intrinsic propensity of living matter to experiment randomly from time to time (although the occasion and mechanism of this process remain largely unknown). But it also reflects the fact that libido, like money or any other form of energy, is most effective when concentrated. Our use of the investment metaphor was deliberate—by such spasmodic concentrations and diffusions of libidinal energy, wealth, and power, civilization has expanded itself. . . .

At the very least I would hope this book has suggested, even though it has not altogether escaped from, the imprisoning and blinding effects of the traditional psychological and sociological units of person and role. Sociologists have long been aware that it is impossible to make any headway with the common sense notion that a group is an association of persons, but largely on the grounds that a group is "more" than the sum of its component individuals. It might be more productive to stress the fact that it is also a good deal less. Unless we are to remain utterly fixated on physical bodies, it is apparent that a group is not a collection of individuals at all but only of pieces of them. If all of an individual were bound up in a group we could scarcely talk of an individual at all, nor of fears or of wishes for envelopment, since he would in fact be enveloped. This is indeed a serious bar to boundary-awareness in extremely primitive societies in which such a situation almost obtains. The elaboration of cross-cutting groups—age groups, sex groups, kinship groups, territorial groups—helps to minimize this condition, and this may in fact be one of the major functions of totemism. As a result of such cross-cutting groups an individual's libido is much diffused, and what we see of him in a given group is an arrangement of feelings, needs, and desires which in no respect constitute a representative sample of his personality.

This point has been made often. But I wonder if the favored sociological unit—the disembodied role, divested of the needs, the motives, the feelings which, however group-specific they may be, nonetheless derive from a breathing organism—has not also exhausted its limited fertility. While most progress in the sciences has come from systematically ignoring large portions of the data at any given time, I cannot see how an understanding of groups can proceed beyond its current level unless the unit of analysis in some way embodies that segment of an individual's instinctual life which he commits to a group.

REFERENCES

Bennis, Warren G. and Shepard, H. A. "A Theory of Group Development," *Human Relations,* 9 (1956), pp. 415-437.

Bion, W. R. "Experiences in Groups: IV," *Human Relations,* 2 (1949), pp. 295-303.

Frazer, J. G. *The New Golden Bough.* T. H. Gaster (Ed.), New York: Criterion Books, 1959.

Freud, S. *Totem and Taboo.* London: Kegan Paul, 1950.

Slater, Philip E. "On Social Regression," *American Sociological Review,* 28 (1963), pp. 339-364.

PART
THREE
PEOPLE AND INSTITUTIONS

CHAPTER EIGHT
HOW DO PEOPLE BECOME SOCIAL DEVIANTS ?

THE ISSUE OF DEVIANCE AND SOCIAL CONTROL

Brad Waverly is in prison.* At the age of 23, he has spent only 18 months of his last nine years at liberty in the community. His criminal record indicates he first appeared in court at the age of eight on charges of malicious mischief—breaking windows in a schoolhouse. Thereafter he was in constant trouble with the juvenile courts until finally, at the age of fourteen, he was sentenced to the State Reform School for theft. Within a few months of his release, he was arrested again in a nearby state, convicted of larceny, and sent to its state reformatory.

Shaken by his lengthy stay in this stricter institution, he returned to his home state determined to put to use the skills he had acquired as a carpenter in the reformatory wood-shop. But his efforts to find a job proved unsuccessful. His reputation as dishonest and unreliable—which grew steadily as more people learned of his criminal record—plagued him at every turn. Even when he was allowed to work, he was treated with such suspicion and contempt that he could not control his temper and invariably ended up being fired.

Maintaining friendships proved equally difficult. Though he tried to be pleasant and friendly, his past record continued to stigmatize his character. On two occasions when acquaintances were visiting him, police forced their way into his house to badger and question him about burglaries in the neighborhood. Understandably, his "friends" treated him curtly and somewhat skittishly. Even his girl friend was ambivalent. Though she loved him deeply, she could not decide if he was sufficiently "reliable" to marry. He, in turn, found himself unable to decide how he really felt about her—whether he really loved her.

Within a year of leaving the state reformatory, he was spending most of his time with drifters, ex-convicts, prostitutes, and other alienated people like himself. Together with some of them he planned a series of robberies, but was quickly arrested

---
* The following vignette is loosely based on the case history of a criminal psychopath reported by Robert White (1956, pp. 68-76).

and convicted, and sent to state prison. His arrest resulted from a bizarre episode. Mistakingly believing that the police were about to arrest him for a recent burglary, he stole a car and, in his haste to escape, turned a corner too quickly, overturning the car and forcing another off the road. Shaken and panicky, he confessed his crimes to the first man who came to his aid, and was quickly carted off to jail.

If we visit Brad Waverly in prison, we find a moody but sociable young man of strong build and anxious but intelligent expression. His intelligence, as measured by standard tests, is above average—about equal to the average college student. While in the state reformatory, he read widely and worked in the library as well as in the carpentry shop.

In the wake of his last arrest, his manner is subdued and dejected. At times he speaks slowly and haltingly, at other times quickly and bitterly. He describes his early life: home—a crowded three room apartment on the top floor of a tenement house; father—a part-time laborer who drifted away from the family when Brad was four; mother—a "cleaning woman" who toiled impossible hours to keep the family of four children alive, and who died at the age of 46 while Brad was serving his first term in the state reformatory. The atmosphere of neglect, tension, and hopelessness that pervaded his home life is guardedly communicated by Brad, as is the guilt over his failure to help his mother during her final illness and earlier.

He talks of the companionship he sought as a boy from neighborhood friends, of the gang he belonged to, of the good times they had, of the fights and trouble they got into. He speaks bitterly of his frustrating experiences in school. Try as he might, his teachers inevitably found fault with him—he always wound up feeling both stupid and bad. He seemed to have taken particular pleasure in vandalizing the school.

He tells of a gang member who, while in reform school, learned techniques of burglary and shop-lifting from other inmates, and returned to teach his new tricks to the gang. In describing his early experiences with stealing, Brad avidly recounts the excitement it entailed, and the pleasure it brought him to possess finally some of the things he had always wanted, including the sense of at last being "somebody."

As he describes his more recent and more lucrative burglaries, he shows no remorse, seemingly enjoying the chance to tell of them. Occasionally, however, there are flashes of bitter anger at police and employers who he felt never gave him the chance to go straight when he had wanted it. Toward his girl friend he remains strangely indifferent, shrugging off the probability that she will not wait for him until his release.

He tries to explain away the pattern of failures that has been his life, but his efforts are unconvincing. (Even working as a thief, a person of his intelligence ought not to have spent 85 per cent of his last nine years in prison.) He admits he has sometimes been careless in carrying out his burglaries, and that this has contributed to his arrests. But he claims that when planning a burglary, it never occurs to him that he may be caught; and that his propensity to leave tell-tale clues or to panic unnecessarily is due to a tremendous excitement that overtakes him as he works. Mostly, however, he claims he has just been very unlucky.

Brad Waverly is a social deviant. Repeatedly he has engaged in acts that his society deemed unacceptable and, as a consequence, he has been processed by the machinery of justice which has sought to control and reform him by sending him to a variety of penal institutions. If one asks how and why Brad became deviant, one finds no dearth of suggestive clues in his past history: economic deprivation, broken home, poor motivation, quick temper, bad companions, inadequate education, police harrassment, the stigma of his early criminal record, and so on. His life of repeated failures seems sadly overdetermined. But the task of a theory of deviance is to place these multiple factors into an overall framework that can explain the relative meaning and import-ance of each. In deviance, as in any sphere of life, one thing leads to another. Where shall we look to find the genesis and the important choice points in a deviant career?

Deviance is a peculiarly difficult phenomenon to pin down. Although its general nature is clear, it is no easy matter to find a single definition that would satisfy all three of the divergent frameworks to be examined in this section. *In a sense, deviance is any activity that violates the rules, norms, or laws of a social collectivity.* Rules are the mainstay of an orderly and predictable social life. People who break rules thus threaten the social fabric—the degree of threat depends on the importance of the rules violated. When Brad Waverly stole and destroyed other people's property, duly appoin-ted representatives of society apprehended him and sought to punish and reform him.

But to view deviance simply as rule-breaking behavior that threatens society can be quite misleading. Such a view underplays the possible arbitrariness of the rules themselves and, thereby, focuses too much attention on the deviant act and actor. Equally as important are the rules that make his acts deviant. Rules do not spring auto-matically from some sacred source. They are created by a social collectivity. Thus, there are necessarily two parties implicated in any instance of deviance: the rule-breaker and the rule-makers. True, a deviant is one who has broken a rule—or at least one who is thought to have broken a rule—but in a deeper sense he is simply a person who has engaged in certain acts. Were it not for the existence of rules that defined these acts as out of bounds, he would be no deviant at all. Moreover, if his actions went undetected, then rule or no rule, society would not consider him deviant. In this sense, *the making and enforcement of social rules plays at least as great a role in the creation of deviance as do the acts and actors that violate these rules.*

There are, thus, three sure-fire ways of reducing the incidence of deviance: stop the rule-breakers, change the rules that are being broken, or stop enforcing these rules. None can fail. Which method one favors in a given situation depends on whose side one happens to be on: the side of the social collectivity, or the side of the deviant.

The important point here is that, in defining deviance with a view to explaining it, it makes a difference whether one chooses to emphasize the commission of the act or its social definition and detection. Do we focus on the deviant actor and his motives, or on the social rules and their enforcement?

Clearly, each perspective will seem natural in certain circumstances. Al Capone and Martin Luther King both spent time in jail, but we tend to adopt different frame-works in explaining their respective imprisonments. When the social rules being violated appear just, it is easier to take them as given and to ask how and why a person might come to violate them. But when the social rules appear arbitrary, it is easier to take their violation for granted and to ask, instead, how and why a social collectivity might come to create and enforce such rules.

Even when only one of these perspectives seems natural, both have their value. Al Capone and Martin Luther King both had motives for their deviant acts, just as society had reasons for creating and enforcing the rules that they broke. Thus, deviance is inherently the product of an *interaction* between individuals' actions and society's rule-enforcement apparatus.

With this in mind, we turn to three divergent frameworks for understanding the origins of deviance. All three devote some attention to explaining the behavior of the deviant actor, though each emphasizes a different causal network. Some, however, do not treat society's rules and their enforcement as within their purview, preferring to take them as given—as outside the scope of their analysis.

To summarize each very briefly, before taking them up more carefully, the *psychopathology* framework sees deviance as originating in special persons who are inherently less capable of abiding by social rules; the *opportunity structure* framework sees deviance as stemming from social structures that impede persons from attaining desired ends without violating social rules; and the *labelling* framework sees deviance as flowing directly from the application of deviant labels to certain persons under certain circumstances.

THE MAJOR VIEWS

Psychopathology

Psychopathology literally means "sickness of the mind." And in this framework, represented in the readings by William and Joan McCord, deviance is seen essentially as the product of disturbed minds—as a result of a pathological inability to abide by social rules. We noted earlier that it is not always meaningful to take such a perspective. Sometimes social rules are oppressive, and sometimes special circumstances are compelling. In such cases, it makes little sense to invoke the pathological.

But adherents of this framework do not have such cases in mind. They concentrate more on crimes against people or property: crimes that are hard to dismiss as healthy rebellion; and they concentrate also on repeated offenders: crimes that are hard to explain by one-time compelling circumstances. In the case of Brad Waverly, for example, it is difficult to escape the feeling that his overall behavior pattern was a bit less than healthy, and that his deviance was only a part of this pattern. By concentrating primarily on cases such as this, psychopathologists are able to take the social rules as given, and to focus on the deviant actor and his antisocial motives.

What might lead a person repeatedly to violate apparently reasonable laws? Presumably some defect in his psychological make-up, a defect that might have its roots in biology and heredity or that might be the result of faulty socialization. Either way, it is located squarely within the individual and would be there whether or not social rules existed.

At one time, proponents of this school placed a good deal of emphasis on biological factors. Prior to the turn of the century, for example, Cesare Lombrosa maintained that many criminals had skulls of a distinctive size and shape, indicative of a more primitive psychic make-up. A few decades later, William Sheldon argued that juvenile delinquents were predominantly of a certain body-type, a type he called mesomorph—heavy-set and muscular with large hands and heavy bones. He maintained that this body-type tends to be associated with a distinctive temperament—an energetic, self-confident, callous, and even ruthless one—a temperament that is conducive to deviance. Extending this work in the early 50's, Sheldon and Eleanor Glueck confirmed that mesomorphs have a greater predisposition to delinquency, and argued that the combination of physical and emotional traits that they manifested suggested "some sort of internal disharmony" conducive to aggression and delinquency (Johnson, 1968, pp. 166-7). Most recently, the interest in biological factors received impetus from genetic research demonstrating that a certain chromosome mutation is found with unusual frequency among violent male criminals.

These biological theories all share the underlying premise that deviant tendencies are to some degree inherited, or at least are built into the structure of the body from birth. Such biological determinism has had relatively little currency in recent years. Instead, the trend has been to place the locus of causality outside the individual in his early environment.

According to this latter view, people acquire deviant tendencies from deficient socialization. Whether through sins of omission or commission, the future deviant is shaped by his early experiences in ways that later render him less capable of abiding by social rules—less able or willing to control his impulses and channel them into socially acceptable paths. Such a psychiatric perspective takes us deep into the realm of personality development, an area too vast to summarize comprehensively. But surely no one would question that early experiences can shape later personality, sometimes in very detrimental ways. Countless studies from a variety of standpoints have documented this connection (White, 1956).

The very term "psychopath" was originally coined by psychiatrists to label a particular type of abnormal personality. Clinical psychologist Robert White describes it:

> The people now diagnosed as psychopaths have this in common: They have developed in such a way that parental standards have never been introjected. They have failed to respond adequately to the process of socialization. . . .
>
> In interviews, [the psychopathic patient] makes an unusually pleasing impression: alert, well-informed, able to talk well. Intelligence is good and does not deteriorate. But one soon finds out that there is a marked absence of sense of responsibility in matters both great and small. . . .He does not accept blame for his conduct nor feel shame about it. He readily gives a plausible excuse for everything that has occurred. While he is able to reason satisfactorily, in some cases brilliantly, he shows the most execrable judgment about attaining his ends, whatever these may be. He gets into the same trouble over and over again, so much so that [one could] describe him as regularly failing to learn from experience. . . . On the side of affect there are grave difficulties. The psychopath seems incapable of real love and attachment. Strong, deep, and lasting feelings do not seem to exist (1956, p. 371).

This description appears to fit Brad Waverly exceedingly well: intelligent, shameless, repeatedly failing, incapable of love and attachment.

What might cause a person to become this way? White makes the following suggestion:

> We can make the hypothesis of a very early injury to affectionate relations, a serious deficit of gratifying love and care perhaps even in the first year of life. Lacking strong initial attachment to the mother, the child as he grows up may learn to adapt shrewdly enough to the realities around him and may become socialized to the extent of presenting a pleasing front; but the real meaning of his life is still the direct gratification of impulse, and this childlike value is not importantly tempered by close affectual ties, or by a feeling of involvement in the human community (1956, p. 372).

This hypothesis seems, again, quite pertinent to the case of Brad Waverly. Given the marginal and stressful conditions of his home life, it would hardly be surprising to learn that he suffered just such a damaging deficit of love in his earliest years.

Many other factors have been hypothesized to contribute to the psychopath's development—for example, an overwhelming sense of personal worthlessness and guilt that leads him, *unconsciously,* to seek punishment through repeated careless failures— but these need not concern us here. Some are discussed by the McCords in their essay included in this chapter. For our purposes, it is sufficient to make the point that the psychopath is believed to have been psychologically damaged by his early experiences, and that one manifestation of this damage is an inability to abide reliably by social rules.

It should also be noted, however, that the dichotomy we made earlier between biological theories and early experience theories is not so easy to maintain in the case of psychopaths. Some researchers, including the McCords, have proposed that innate biological factors probably contribute to the development of psychopathology. More generally, a number of researchers have found that certain personality traits are unusually common among deviants, and have sought to link these traits both to early experience *and* to biology.

Among the more intriguing of such theories is one developed by H. J. Eysenck. Working with innumerable personality tests and diverse populations of subjects, he has found through factor-analytic techniques* that most people's personalities can be described remarkably well using only two major dimensions: introversion-extroversion and emotional stability.†

Eysenck describes the introversion-extroversion dimension as follows:

> The typical introvert is. . .quiet and introspective,. . . reserved and distant except with intimate friends. He tends to plan ahead mistrusting the impulse of the moment. . . .He does not like excitement,. . .and keeps his feelings under close control. . . .He is reliable, somewhat pessimistic and places great value on ethical standards. [In contrast,] . . .the typical extrovert is sociable,. . .has many friends, needs to have people to talk to,. . .craves excitement, takes chances,. . . often acts on the spur of the moment, and is generally an impulsive individual. . . .

---

* For a brief discussion of factor-analysis and how it can be used to identify underlying dimensions, see the reading by Charles Osgood in Chapter Two of this volume.

† Eysenck refers to the emotional stability dimension as "neurotic-normal."

Altogether, his feelings are. . .[less] under control and he is. . .[less] reliable. (Eysenck and Rachman, 1965, p. 19).

The emotional stability dimension is more straightforward. At the unstable end are

people whose emotions are labile, strong, and easily aroused; they are moody, touchy, anxious, restless, and so forth. At the other extreme we have people whose emotions are stable, less easily aroused, people who are calm, even-tempered and carefree (1965, p. 20).

These two basic dimensions of personality appear to be largely independent of one another, thereby yielding four basic types of people: stable introverts (who are calm, steady, reliable, and reserved), stable extroverts (who are even-tempered, carefree, spontaneous and sociable), unstable introverts (who are moody, anxious, compulsive, and withdrawn), and unstable extroverts (who are touchy, restless, impulsive, and outgoing).

By this time the reader will have guessed Eysenck's findings with respect to deviance: numerous studies he reviews show that both adult criminals and juvenile delinquents are unusually prone to have personalities of the unstable extrovert type (Eysenck, 1965). Indeed, the traits of this type are not so different from those that both Sheldon and the Gluecks found to be associated with the mesomorph or, for that matter, from those commonly associated with the psychopath. In the extreme case, we have a person who may be quite sociable and outgoing in a devil-may-care sort of way, but who is also moody, unreliable, impulsive, quick-tempered, and prone to aggression. In short, a likely candidate for breaking social rules.

The question, of course, is what makes people introverted or extroverted, emotionally stable or unstable. The answer remains in doubt. Eysenck, while not denying that early experiences probably play a crucial role, suggests that the origins *may* be largely innate. We cannot, here, go into his evidence and his extrapolations. Suffice it to say that he believes introverts differ from extroverts primarily in being more susceptible to *cortical arousal* that threatens to bring cortical overload, which is counteracted by such inhibitory reactions as withdrawal and control. On the other hand, the emotionally unstable differ from the stable primarily in having a *more arousable autonomic system* which produces a greater emotional reactivity and lability. In this view, then, it is the particular combination of "uninhibited cortical activity" coupled with "a readily arousable autonomic system" which makes for a deviance-prone individual.

In sum, the psychopathology framework argues that deviants are special types of people—people who, by reason of their biological make-up or their early experiences, are simply less capable of living within the bounds of social rules. To understand deviance, then, one must study the deviant actor with a view to identifying the biological and psychological roots of his behavior.

Opportunity Structures

This framework, represented in the readings by Richard Cloward, differs sharply from the preceding in shifting the emphasis from psychological structure to social structure. Deviants are viewed not as abnormal people living in normal social settings, but rather as normal people living in abnormal social settings. They are people who have been deprived of the opportunity to build a satisfying life within the bounds of existing social rules and who, therefore, resort to illegitimate activities. They break rules neither because they are mentally ill nor because it suits their idiosyncratic personalities. They do so simply in a struggle to circumvent roadblocks that their social situation has placed between them and the aspirations that any of us legitimately have: success, status, income, and control over one's destiny. Deviance, then, is to be understood as an effort to obtain valued ends that cannot be attained by legitimate means.

This frame of analysis was first systematically developed by sociologist Robert Merton (1938) in a theoretical essay entitled "Social Structure and Anomie." Subsequently revised a number of times, this essay has continued to have a major impact on the sociological study of deviance. In it, Merton argued that pressure toward deviant behavior must be understood in terms of a "disjunction" between two major systems that exist in any society: culturally-valued goals and institutionalized means for attaining these goals.

Cultural goals are those ends that a society defines as "worth striving for." Every society, or smaller social system, will have a reasonably integrated hierarchy of success-goals which almost everyone within the system considers desirable. In the United States, for example, we place high value on such things as active mastery of the environment and material wealth. From scientists to businessmen, people receive power and prestige in proportion to their ability to attain such goals. In a smaller social system, such as an educational institution, there are more specific goals: students should strive for high grades; professors should publish scholarly writings. Again, status and prestige are accorded to those who best attain these goals.

Institutionalized means are those avenues that are considered to be:

> acceptable modes of reaching out for cultural goals. Every social system invariably couples its cultural objectives with regulations. . .governing the allowable procedures for moving toward these objectives. These regulatory norms are not necessarily identical with. . .[technical efficiency]. Many procedures which from the standpoint of particular individuals would be most efficient in securing desired values—the exercise of force, fraud, and power—are ruled out of the institutional area of approved conduct (Merton, 1957, p. 133).

In short, there are social rules that govern the means by which persons can legitimately pursue success-goals. Scientists must not advance knowledge by carrying out unethical experiments; businessmen must not make profits by fraudulent advertising; students must not obtain good grades by cheating on exams; and professors must not publish by fabricating their data.

When a social system is functioning well, cultural goals and institutionalized means are properly integrated. Not only are the legitimate means available and conducive to the success-goals, but norms proscribing the use of illegitimate means are strictly enforced. However, it sometimes happens that these two systems become disjointed. Perhaps access to legitimate means is closed off; or, perhaps the available means are not sufficiently conducive to the goals; or perhaps there is such an overwhelming emphasis on attaining the success-goals that the legitimacy of the means becomes secondary; or worse yet, all three could be true simultaneously. At any rate, when such a disjuncture exists, Merton refers to the social system as being in a state of "anomie" or normlessness: mechanisms regulating the pursuit of cultural goals have broken down.

It is but a small step from here to a theory of deviance. Persons who happen to find themselves in an anomic sub-system have problems: they cannot pursue the goals they have been taught to value through legitimate paths. What can they do? Merton suggests four types of deviant solutions that they can adopt.

1. *Innovation*—They can abandon legitimate means and pursue cultural goals by a variety of rule-breaking activities.

2. *Ritualism*—They can abandon cultural goals, continuing slavishly to adhere to legitimate paths despite having lost the hope of attaining any meaningful ends.

3. *Retreatism*—They can give up in frustration, forsaking both success-goals and legitimate means—in effect, dropping out of the social system, or existing at its margins without direction and without hope.

4. *Rebellion*—They can reject both cultural goals and institutionalized means, but in an angry, rebellious manner that leads to agitation for social change—for a better system with more equitable goals and means.

Of these four adaptations, the first, innovation, is deviance of the classic type: gainful law-breaking such as that pursued by Brad Waverly. Brad's history clearly fits the expected pattern. Born in a society that extolls material wealth, raised in the deprived environs of a slum, forced to attend schools concerned more with authoritarian discipline than with education, unable to afford college or training in any saleable skill, stigmatized by an early criminal record—it is small wonder that he turned repeatedly to stealing as a means of livelihood, status, and prestige. The wonder is that he ever tried to go straight at all. Perhaps he also had a somewhat aberrant personality, but the point is that *any* person placed in his position might have coped in similar fashion—possibly more successfully.

Because persons from the lower class tend to have the least access to legitimate avenues of success, Merton suggests that they are the most likely to use innovation as a way of coping with anomie. But this response is not limited to the lower class. In an educational institution, for example, we can find students who, having accepted the overreaching importance of grade-point-averages and feeling unable to do the requisite work, resort to techniques such as buying term papers from agencies willing to exploit their anomie. And similarly, we can find professors who, having accepted the paramount importance of publishing but unable to manage the work entailed, may resort to doctoring data or stealing ideas from colleagues.

Strictly speaking, the second type of adaptation, ritualism, is not a case of deviance as we have defined it, for no rule-breaking is entailed. Nonetheless, Merton views it as deviant because the actor has abandoned the pursuit of socially prescribed success-goals. Merton suggests that this mode of coping with anomie will be most common among persons who have only limited access to legitimate avenues for success, but who have strongly internalized norms against rule-breaking and, thus, find themselves unable to engage in innovation. Families with some hope of upward mobility, who have consequently trained their children to "play the game strictly by the rules," are most likely to produce offspring that slip into ritualism when the path upward turns out to be blocked. Merton hypothesizes that this might be most frequent among the lower-middle classes, for they are just likely enough to be able to rise by legitimate paths to make it worth their effort to try.

Once again, however, ritualism can be found in any social system suffering from anomie. Students who are incapable of producing work that brings high grades and unwilling to cheat may finally abandon academic honors as a goal, to become concerned only with the hollow exercise of meeting all minimun requirements by doing just *exactly* what is expected of them and no more. Similarly, professors may abandon hope of publishing worthwhile papers in leading journals, but still continue to go through the motions, churning out a worthless string of writings destined either to sit on their shelves or to appear in second-rate publications that no one reads.

According to Merton, the third form of adaptation, retreatism, is most likely to occur when a person has strongly internalized both legitimate means and cultural goals. Unable to bring himself to abandon the former and opt for innovation, and unable to bring himself to abandon the latter and opt for ritualism, he copes with his anomie by simply giving up—by withdrawing from the entire game in utter frustration. On the societal level, he may become a vagrant, bum, alcoholic, heroin addict, hippie drop-out, or psychotic. Though he remains marginally "in the society," he is not "of it": he does not partake in conventional life, refusing both to adhere to the mores of proper conduct and to seek after the ratified trappings of success. He may break only minor laws, but his life-style is widely at variance with the conventional.

At an educational institution, retreatism is not uncommon. Unable to justify the pursuit of grade point averages by fraudulent means, and unable to find meaning in blind conformity to academic rules, students may simply drop out—either seeking their future elsewhere, or else becoming "non-students" who continue to hang about the university without being part of its academic side. Similarly, professors may entirely abandon any scholarly pretentions.

The final mode of adaptation, rebellion, represents a rejection of both legitimate means and cultural goals while still remaining within the social system. The rebel may break laws but he does so neither with impunity nor out of purely selfish motives. He sees present structures as unjust and has a vision of a better society in which there can be greater opportunity to attain more meaningful goals.

Martin Luther King, for example, broke laws, not secretly in order to evade them, but openly in order to change them. In contrast to an Al Capone, who was concerned solely with the amoral issue of self-aggrandisement, King was concerned with the moral issue of opening a better life to victims of discrimination. Not all rebels are as gentle as he was. In their anger and frustration, and in the face of severe repression, many will naturally resort to more violent tactics and may, indeed, be forced to operate secretly. But they still differ from the amoral "innovator" in aspiring to create a society in which they could live happily as law-abiding citizens.

In recent years, educational institutions have had their share of rebels: students and faculty who have sought forcefully to change the structure in ways that made it more valuable and meaningful to those already within, more open to those disadvantaged groups traditionally excluded from it, and more responsible in its dealings with the wider society. The push for pass-fail grading, for self-tailored majors, for new areas of concentration, for new programs of financial aid, for different recruiting procedures, and for new regulations on ROTC and classified research have in the main been spear-headed by rebellious students and faculty, some of whom were willing to break rules and create havoc in order to dramatize their discontent.

Merton's work, then, provides a very general scheme for analyzing deviance. It suggests that deviance must be understood in terms of the legitimate opportunity structures available to people in different parts of a social system. Wherever such structures are unavailable, some form of deviance is likely. Which form depends on two things: how thoroughly people have internalized (or accepted) legitimate means, cultural goals, or both; and how capable they are of seeing the system as unjust and in need of change.

In one of the readings for this chapter, Richard Cloward proposes a very important addition to Merton's framework. He suggests that it is insufficient to consider only patterns of internalization and patterns of access to legitimate opportunity structures. He maintains it is necessary also to consider patterns of access to illegitimate means.

The frustration of blocked opportunities may be an important motivation for deviance, but by itself it is insufficient. To become deviant in any lucrative way requires more than motivation—it requires skills, materials, information, and organization. Society, after all, is geared to prevent deviance and, thus, to thwart any bumbling novice who might try his hand at burglary, forgery, armed robbery, or embezzlement. Even the rebel may find it hard to make progress without some organizational base.

In discussing ritualism and retreatism, Cloward suggests that these modes of adaptation may be due less to internal standards that inhibit a person from turning to illegitimate means, and due more to an inability to gain access to such means. Brad Waverly, for example, might well have ended up as a heroin addict or skid row bum were it not for the fact that he was able to learn the skills of burglary from other gang members and other reformatory inmates. Indeed, penal institutions are notoriously good locations for acquiring deviant skills.

Cloward's contribution, then, is to add a second set of opportunity structures to the set proposed by Merton. In the integrated framework, deviance comes to be understood not simply in terms of differential access to legitimate means, but also in terms of differential access to illegitimate means. The idiosyncracies of individuals need to be taken into account only to note the extent to which internalized standards might inhibit such individuals from engaging in illegitimate activities. In the light of Cloward's contribution, such individual factors become quite minor compared to the social structural ones.

Labelling

In this framework, represented in the readings by Howard Becker, deviance is viewed quite literally as the product of social definition. A person becomes deviant not so much when he breaks rules as when he is identified and treated as deviant by those who have the power to do so. To be sure, breaking rules is the surest way to acquire a deviant identity, but it is neither the only way, nor a guaranteed way.

Sometimes it is sufficient merely to be different. Anyone who has ever owned a motorcycle, worn his hair long, or dressed like a hippie knows from first hand experience that one can be accorded deviant status and treatment without having the slightest intention of breaking any rules. And conversely, as the Watergate scandal illustrated, some people can break important rules and still be accorded the status of respected government officials or business executives—at least for a while. There may be a high correlation between rule-breaking and the acquisition of deviant status, but a dispassionate look at social life indicates rather clearly that this correlation is far from perfect.

Labelling theorists, therefore, take very seriously the proposition that deviance is the product of an interaction between those who make and enforce rules on the one hand, and those who run afoul of these rules and their enforcers on the other. Deviance is not a static phenomenon that occurs at a moment in time, or that can be pinned to a particular, discrete rule-breaking act. It is a dynamic phenomenon—a drama with many actors that gradually unfolds over time.

Even a discrete episode begins simultaneously at many points: in the halls of the state legislature where a new drug law is passed, in a precinct police station where the word is passed to "get tough," in a student apartment where several people are partying and getting stoned, in a downstairs apartment where a woman is annoyed and calls the police. The drama reaches its climactic point when several students are arrested and taken off to jail, thus unwittingly becoming the central actors. But the story continues with new supporting actors in further scenes: more police at the station, a judge and jury in the courtroom, guards and wardens in prison, and those who, in the future, will learn of the students' criminal records.

A labelling theorist would be concerned with every phase of this drama, and with all of its principal actors. All of them together conspired to make the students deviant— to label them officially as undesirable outlaws.

Note, of course, that the students themselves are among the central actors, and, consequently, that one might wish to examine carefully the history leading up to their use of illegal drugs at the ill-fated party. [Indeed, Howard Becker has devoted several scholarly papers to analyzing the processes by which people become regular users of marijuana (1963, pp. 41-78)] . But labelling theorists would maintain that to focus exclusively on the rule-breakers and their motives is to obtain a biased and distorted picture. The rule-breaking was but one important element in a wider scenario.

How and why did the state legislature come to regulate who could partake of what kinds of substances? On what basis do people decide to call the police on their neighbors? When do policemen decide to "get tough" with offenders? Who are they trying to impress, and what are their general attitudes toward groups such as students? What does the judge see himself as doing when he passes sentence? Would the police, judge, and jury have acted any differently if those apprehended had had important political connections in the city? How does a prison parole board decide who will be paroled? Why do people stigmatize ex-offenders and continue to treat them as unsavory characters likely to repeat or engage in worse offenses?

These are the sorts of questions a labelling theorist would ask in order to get beyond the narrow issue of how and why the students came to break the drug laws. All of these questions, and more, need to be investigated before one can understand how the students acquired their status as deviants.

Why do theorists of this school place such a heavy emphasis on labelling? In part, because this is what officially creates deviance, and, in part, because it has onerous consequences for the ones who get labelled. Not only is it grounds for incarceration or other punishment, but it fixes a degrading blemish on the deviants' character: even after serving their time, they are likely to find that they are systematically discriminated against. In fact, some studies have shown that the mere fact of being arrested is enough to substantially diminish one's future chances of finding employment. And here we come back to opportunity structures. By closing off legitimate paths to status and income, the labelling process itself becomes implicated in a causal chain of further deviance.

Indeed, labelling theorists make a sharp distinction between primary deviance and secondary deviance. Primary deviance is the rule-breaking activity that first triggers the labelling process. Secondary deviance is the further rule-breaking and further labelling that results partly from the deleterious effects of the initial labelling. Primary deviance is often difficult to explain. People may first engage in illegal activities for a wide variety of personal and social reasons, just as they may end up being caught and convicted due to a wide variety of circumstances. But all primary deviants have the initial labelling experience in common, and this experience may be sufficiently far-reaching to force them permanently into a deviant career.

The point is starkly illustrated by Brad Waverly's story. We have already noted a variety of childhood experiences that may have impelled him to engage in his initial juvenile acts of vandalism and stealing. But it seems fairly clear that he did not seriously embark on burglary as a way of life until he found himself unable to find work, unable to find friends, and unable to avoid continual harrassment by the police. All this was a consequence of his earlier criminal record. It is almost as if society, once having labelled him as deviant, would not rest until it had forced him to prove again the accuracy of that label. If a single causal factor had to be extracted from his tangled life, a labelling theorist would surely point to the stigma acquired as a result of being sentenced to the state reformatory.

In sum, then, labelling theory views as overly narrow any analysis of deviance that focuses exclusively on the rule-breaker or his social environment. Rule-breaking is, at best, only half of the total picture. Rule-making and rule-enforcement must be subjected to the same degree of analysis. As Becker puts it,

> ". . .we must get these two possible foci of inquiry into balance. We must see deviance. . .as a consequence of a process of interaction between people, some of whom in the service of their own interests make and enforce rules which catch others who, in the service of *their* own interests, have committed acts which are labelled deviant."

CONTRASTING THE VIEWS OF DEVIANCE AND SOCIAL CONTROL

The three perspectives on social deviance can be summarized and compared in terms of their answers to the following three questions:

1. Where should one look to find the sources of deviance—where are they located?
2. Which societal sub-systems are most implicated in the production and control of deviance?
3. Are deviant persons in any essential way different from non-deviant ones?

Locus of Causal Sources

We have noted repeatedly that deviance is behavior that comes to be viewed as so-cially unacceptable and, hence, that elicits collective reactions aimed at punishing or correcting those individuals who engage in such behavior. Given the nature of the phe-nomenon, then, it is possible to concentrate on explaining either the causes of the behav-ior, or the causes of its being viewed as unacceptable and in need of correction. Either path can provide a more or less complete explanation. Without rule-breaking behavior there can be no deviance, and without rules and collective efforts to enforce these rules there can be no deviance either.

Of the frameworks considered here, the first two—psychopathology and oppor-tunity structures—concentrate primarily on explaining the rule-breaking behavior. The psychopathology perspective traces the sources of this behavior to characteristics of the individual actor—rule-breakers are people with special, often pathological, person-ality structures that render them less capable of abiding by social norms. In contrast, the opportunity structures perspective traces the sources of such behavior to structural pressures in the actor's immediate social environment—rule-breakers are people with limited access to legitimate opportunities, who are thus forced to resort to illegitimate means of attaining their ends.

In contrast to both of these frameworks, the labelling perspective attempts to explain not only the behavior of rule-breakers, but also that of rule-makers and rule-enforcers. It sees deviance primarily as a product of social definition, and seeks to en-compass all phases of the process by which given actors come to be officially labelled as deviants. Above all, it focuses on the formal and informal interactions that tran-spire between those who make and enforce rules, and those who are thought to have violated them.

Responsible Societal Sub-System

Once the causal locus of deviance has been spotted, we can proceed to locate those parts of society that are most responsible for its creation and prevention. If the sources of deviance lie within the rule-breaker's personality, it follows that those societal systems responsible for shaping personality are the most directly implicated. Person-ality, of course, may be shaped in part by biological factors beyond the control of society, but society is involved, through its socializing institutions. Thus, for the psychopathology perspective, it is these institutions that play the major role in dif-ferentiating deviants from non-deviants: the family, the mass media, the educational system, and the correctional system.

If the sources of deviance are located outside the individual in the opportunity structures of his immediate social environment, then it follows that patterns of access to legitimate and illegitimate means become the crucial features of a society. Thus, all societal systems that facilitate vertical mobility or that otherwise allow people to attain culturally valued ends become implicated in the creation and prevention of deviance, including the economic system, the educational system, the welfare system, systems of organized crime, and patterns of racial, ethnic, and sex discrimination.

Finally, if the sources of deviance are to be found in the social processes by which rule-breaking behavior is defined, detected, and treated, then the important societal sub-systems become the legislative, law-enforcement, and correctional institutions. And, in fact, labelling theorists concentrate primarily on studying these institutions, or their more informal counterparts.

Differences Between Deviants and Non-Deviants

In certain respects, deviants are by definition different from others: they break rules, get arrested, populate prisons, and are viewed askance by the social collectivity whose rules they have violated. But apart from their rule-breaking, and apart from the treatment they are accorded by society, are they in any essential way different from others?

According to both the labelling and opportunity structures frameworks, they are not. Labelling theorists might even question the presumption that deviants have necessarily broken rules, for, they would argue, all that really matters is that such people be seen as eminently capable of breaking rules. Once they are, they will be defined as deviants, and as far as labelling theorists are concerned, this is their *only* special characteristic.

Adherents to the opportunity structures perspective see deviants as rule-breakers, but they too reject the notion that deviants are special types of people. They are people like any others, coping rationally with problems imposed on them by the social environment they inhabit. Given the nature of their social setting, rule-breaking may well be an optimal response.

Chart 8 Underlying Issues on How People Become Social Deviants

	Psychopathology (*e.g.*, the Mc-Cords)	Opportunity Structures (*e.g.*, Cloward)	Labelling (*e.g.*, Becker)
1. Where are the sources of deviance located?	Within the deviant in the structure of his body and/or mind	Outside the deviant in the structure of his social environment	Between the deviant and society in the structure of their interaction
2. Which societal subsystems are most responsible for the production and prevention of deviance?	Socializing institutions	Institutions governing access to both legitimate and illegitimate opportunities	Legislative, law-enforcement, and correctional institutions
3. Are deviant persons basically different from non-deviant ones?	Yes, rule-breaking is but one manifestation of a defective personality	No, rule-breaking is a relatively rational response to a problematic environment	No, acquiring a deviant identity is a matter of social definition

Finally, and in contrast to both of the preceding frameworks, the psychopathology perspective sees deviants as special persons with distinctive personality defects. Rule-breaking is but one specific manifestation of this defect—a defect that has broader implications for their overall pattern of conduct. According to this view, then, it is possible to identify a psychopath or some other deviance-prone individual, quite apart from whether he has, as yet, broken any rules, and quite apart from whether society has begun to treat him as deviant. All that is required is a clinical interview or some appropriate battery of psychological tests.

Chart 8 summarizes our discussion of differences among the three frameworks.

REFERENCES

Becker, Howard. *Outsiders: Studies in the Sociology of Deviance.* New York: The Free Press, 1963.

Eysenck, H. J. and Rachman, S. *The Causes and Cures of Neurosis.* San Diego, California: Robert R. Knapp, 1965.

Johnson, Elmer H. *Crime, Correction, and Society.* Homewood, Illinois: The Dorsey Press, Revised Edition, 1968.

Merton, Robert K. "Social Structure and Anomie," *American Sociological Review,* 3, 1938, pp. 672-682.

Merton, Robert K. *Social Theory and Social Structure.* New York: The Free Press, Revised and Enlarged Edition, 1957.

White, Robert W. *The Abnormal Personality.* New York: The Ronald Press Co., Second Edition, 1956.

THE PSYCOPATH

WILLIAM McCORD AND JOAN McCORD

This 'landowner'. . . was a strange type, yet one pretty frequently to be met with, a type abject and vicious and at the same time senseless.

Dostoyevsky, describing *Fyodor Karamazov*

A sweaty crowd jammed the courtroom and gaped at a slender, passive young man sitting in the dock. He seemed detached from the melee, bored by the complicated legal process. If the papers had not splashed his picture across the front pages, few people would have known that this was the defendant, William Cook—"Billy the Kid"—brutal slayer of five human beings.

From *The Psychopath: An Essay on the Criminal Mind* by William McCord and Joan McCord © 1964 by Litton Educational Publishing, Inc. Reprinted by permission of Van Nostrand Reinhold Company.

In his few years of life, Cook had been a terrible scourge to society. His youth had been spent in fights, homosexual orgies, and robberies. His adult life, short as it was, had culminated in the killing of a fellow robber, in the murder of an innocent man and wife, and—most shockingly—in the shooting of their two children.

This was the day the crowd awaited. Today Billy Cook would "get what was coming to him." What could he possibly deserve but death? The crowd had little patience with the legal process that led to this moment. They despised the hairsplitting psychiatrists who had maintained that Cook was "mentally ill, although not insane." Few of the spectators understood the esoteric arguments among the expert witnesses. Three defense psychiatrists had asserted that Cook was "psychopathic." The prosecution agreed but added, to the joy of the crowd, "So what?"

As the judge read the sentence, a dissatisfied rustle swept through the crowd. Not death, but "300 years in Alcatraz" was Billy Cook's fate. Few heard or cared to hear what the judge so solemnly added: "Billy Cook is a symbol of society's failure."

To save itself from other Billy Cooks, society must come to understand the psychopathic personality. Psychopathy, possibly more than other mental disorders, threatens the safety, the serenity, and the security of American life. From the ranks of the psychopaths come political demagogues, the most violent criminals, the riot leaders, sexual misfits, and drug addicts. Psychologist Robert Lindner has observed: "Hydra-headed and slippery to the touch though it is, psychopathy represents the most expensive and most destructive of all known forms of abberrant behavior" (1948, p. 508). Not only does the psychopath cost society dearly, but he represents such a unique, fascinating example of the human species that the understanding of his disorder can contribute greatly to our general knowledge of human nature. For, . . . he rests at one extreme of the continuum of human variety: he is the unsocialized man, the "lone wolf,"' the stranger to social intercourse.

Just what is psychopathy? For 150 years, science has known of the psychopath's existence; for at least 140 years scientists have quarreled over the definition of his disorder. . . .Those who (to their sorrow) have dealt with psychopaths would recognize the fundamental profile given in the following paragraphs.

The Psychopath is Asocial

Society cannot ignore the psychopath, for his behavior is dangerously disruptive. He may be robbing a store or knifing another man; he may be peddling drugs or forging a check. No rule, however important, stops him. Since the bizarre, erratic behavior of the psychopath antagonizes society, he is often found in the social waste baskets: the prisons or the mental hospitals.

Because his behavior is so threatening, many people lose sight of the disorder which causes it. Much of psychology's confusion over the psychopath can be traced to a basic mistake: equating deviant behavior with the psychopathic personality.

The actions of the psychopath are only outward symptoms of a sick mind. Many other deviants—the professional criminal, the gang criminal, the sexual aberrant—exhibit dangerous behavior, but they do not share the character structure of the true psychopathic personality. Moreover, the definition of deviant behavior varies from culture to culture. . . .

Cook's murders might have been overlooked if his victims had been known German spies in the last war. Deviant behavior, then, is an inadequate criterion of psychopathy. At most, it may indicate the existence of a psychopathic character structure.

In almost every culture, the psychopath can be found. What he does will differ; what his society condemns will vary—but the purposeless rebel, the unsocialized misfit, the person who feels no guilt in breaking social mores can be found everywhere. Consequently, any adequate study of the psychopath must look beyond asociality.

The Psychopath is Driven by Uncontrolled Desires

There is no reason to believe that the psychopath has been born with desires different from those of other men. There, is, however, evidence that the psychopath expresses his desires in ways different from other men.

Hobbes said: "The wicked man is but the child grown strong." The psychopath is like an infant, absorbed in his own needs, vehemently demanding satiation. The average child, by the age of two, compromises with the restrictions of his environment. He learns to postpone his pleasure and to consider his mother's needs as well as his own. The psychopath never learns this lesson; he does not modify his desires, and he ignores the needs of others. In most respects, the psychopath is Narcissus, completely absorbed in himself, craving only his own pleasure.

Much of the psychopath's asociality can be traced to this quest for immediate pleasure. F. A. Freyhan (1951) observed: "The psychopath. . . is unsocial rather than anti-social." He does not purposefully attack society, but society too often blocks his way to fulfillment.

It seems probable, though not provable, that the psychopath has not learned to find pleasure in stability, for he seeks excitement in variety more than most human beings. The average man wants excitement, but he also wants security. The psychopath, however, often seems willing to sacrifice everything for excitement. His satisfactions have always been fleeting and highly changeable from childhood through maturity. Consequently, he seems to know no greater pleasure than constant change, and the search for excitement at any cost becomes an important motive. . . .

Unlike the normal person, or even the average criminal, the psychopath's adventures often seem purposeless. Even his crimes are rarely planned. He robs a store in a whim of the moment, not after careful consideration. He flits from woman to woman with volatile passion, never feeling prolonged attraction.

The psychopath has no stable goals. His life is dominated by fleeting desires which leave no space for farsighted planning. After many years of experience with criminal psychopaths, Robert Lindner observed: "Determined progress toward a goal—unless it is a selfish one capable of immediate realization by a sharply accented spurt of activity—the dynamic binding together of actual strands, is lacking" (1944, p. 13).

Lauretta Bender, a child psychiatrist who examined 800 psychopathic children, concluded that the most prominent trait of the psychopathic syndrome was "diffusely unpatterned impulsive behavior" (1942; 1947, p. 373).

The Psychopath is Aggressive

The psychopath's asociality often expresses itself in brutal aggression. He is not the passive neurotic who hurts no one but himself, nor the anxious psychotic who withdraws from human contact. The psychopath's uninhibited search for pleasure often clashes with the restrictions of his society; the conflict frequently results in aggressive action.

A notorious Baltimore murder illustrates the psychopath's quick-triggered aggression. Two men held up a milk wagon. Both carried loaded guns. The driver resisted. One criminal did not pull his gun. The other robber, a psychopath, used his gun to shoot and kill the driver. The panic which any animal experiences when faced with serious frustration more often causes the psychopath to react with aggression.

Why is the psychopath so inordinately aggressive? His childhood may account for the phenomenon. The psychopath is usually severely rejected, physically beaten, and emotionally deprived by his parents. . . .

As a child the psychopath has received pain from almost every part of his environment. Studies repeatedly indicate that painful treatment results in what has been called "aggressive action" (Allport, 1954, Chap. 22).

The normal man has learned to control aggression. He reacts to frustration with sublimation, with constructive action, with withdrawal—less often with aggression. The psychopath, on the other hand, characteristically reacts to frustration with fury. . . .He may temporarily seek control over his indiscriminate aggression, but this desire, like so many others, soon passes. Any control, however mild, again irritates him, and he rejects it.

The Psychopath Feels Little Guilt

When the normal man violates the moral strictures of his culture, a gnawing uneasiness grips him: his conscience hurts. But the psychopath—and this is a crucial trait—has few internalized feelings of guilt. In the usual sense, the psychopath has no conscience. He can commit any act with hardly a twinge of remorse.

William Cook illustrates the psychopath's guiltlessness through his dispassionate description of three murders: "The two little kids started crying, wanting water. I gave them some and she [their mother] drove a while—and I turned around and started shooting in the back seat and then turned back and shot her. She fell over against me and onto the floor" (Symkal and Thorne, 1951, p.311).

In the world of psychopathy, William Cook is no exception. After quenching the children's thirst, he shot them. It is this heartlessness of the psychopath which most strikingly sets him apart from the normal human being. The psychopath has the same desires as others; he dresses and talks in the same way. Yet a most important human element is missing: the sense of guilt.

Not only does this deficiency of guilt set the psychopath apart from the normal man, it also distinguishes him from other cultural deviants. Non-psychopathic criminals, for example, internalize an "underworld code of morality." For them, there can be "honor among thieves." If he breaches this code, the "normal" criminal feels remorse. The psychopath, however, has few values—either those of society or those of a gang. Dreikurs (1951) ascribes this to a lack of (Adlerian) common sense: ". . . our thinking in common, our participation in general ideas, in values and morals accepted by the whole group to which we belong." The Freudian labels the trait as an underdeveloped "superego." Both interpretations point to the psychopath's lack of inner controls. This guiltlessness is one of the central features of psychopathy. . . .

The Psychopath Has a Warped Capacity for Love

The psychopath has often been characterized as a "lone wolf." He seems cold and compassionless. He treats people as he does objects: as means for his own pleasure. Though he may form fleeting attachments, these lack emotional depth and tenderness, and frequently end abruptly in aggressive explosions. . . .

This warped capacity for love is so obvious that most social scientists regard it as the core of the psychopathic syndrome. A. H. Maslow connects lovelessness with the psychopath's aggression: "I have found it helpful in understanding psychopaths to assume that they have no love identifications with other human beings and can therefore hurt them or even kill them casually, without hate, and without pleasure, precisely as they kill animals who have come to be pests" (1954, p. 173). . . .

Either because he is incapable of forming them, or because his experience has not shown him how to form them, the psychopath wards off close attachments. Perhaps, as some psychoanalysts maintain, the psychopath fends off close relations because he fears being hurt. In any case, his lovelessness sets him apart as a uniquely isolated individual.

The Psychopathic Syndrome

Putting all the foregoing traits together, we see a picture of a dangerously maladjusted personality:

The psychopath is asocial. His conduct often brings him into conflict with society. The psychopath is driven by primitive desires and an exaggerated craving for excitement. In his self-centered search for pleasure, he ignores restrictions of his culture. The psychopath is highly impulsive. He is a man for whom the moment is a segment of time detached from all others. His actions are unplanned and guided by his whims. The psychopath is aggressive. He has learned few socialized ways of coping with frustration. The psychopath feels little, if any, guilt. He can commit the most appalling acts, yet view them without remorse. The psychopath has a warped capacity for love. His emotional relationships, when they exist, are meager, fleeting, and designed to satisfy his own desires. These last two traits, guiltlessness and lovelessness, conspicuously mark the psychopath as different from other men.

In this chapter we have discussed each of these traits separately. Although necessary for a clear analysis, such separation tends to create an artificial, unconnected picture of the psychopathic personality. A case study of a typical psychopath may serve to draw these disparate strands into a unified portrait of the psychopathic character structure.

In 1953 I spent many hours with "Howard Dever," discussing his life and future. Throughout our interviews he talked freely, controlling the situation with a glib stream of sophisticated conversation. His business suit, his conservative tie, and his clipped mustache proclaimed him as a successful young man "heading for the top." The setting of our talks—the Boston Psychopathic Hospital where Dever underwent observation before his trial for fraud, robbery and impersonation—belied this promise.

Dever, 35 years old, was born in a rural Vermont village. He hated the town and dismissed his childhood years with: "I got into trouble a lot, but they never put me in jail—not for a night." He disparagingly described his parents as "dull, stupid farmers." He pictured his father as a taciturn, forbidding person preoccupied with a country bank. His mother—"colorless, weak, lethargic"—didn't have the "gumption" to oppose his father's episodic rages. He added: "My parents really weren't so bad, though we were never close. They sent me money."

Although abnormally aggressive throughout childhood, Dever's official criminal record began during his high school years. His first job, when he was 14, ended abruptly as the town grocer caught Dever stealing $50 from the cash register. Despite his father's intervention, Dever's reputation as a "sneaky kid" grew until most townsmen ostracized him: "I became the scapegoat for everything that happened. Inspector Crooker would pick me up even if I wasn't doing a thing, just sitting on the curb."

At 16, Dever ran away to New York, where he led a life of larceny and dope peddling. His Manhattan career ended in 1941 when the Army drafted him. After three weeks in a Missouri boot camp, Dever went A.W.O.L. Military Police retrieved him in Vermont and sent him to a large Army prison at Vincennes. He hated the Indiana heat, his "crooked" companions, and the rough handling by Army police. "But I was lucky," he jovially admitted, "I was assigned a real Chicago lawyer for my courtmartial. Boy, was he a slicker. He sent to Missouri for my company records, proved my name was still on the roll during my A.W.O.L., and got me released."

Immediately after his acquittal, Dever walked from the courtroom and again deserted. Retrieved, he repeated the pattern. His record shows 14 absences without leave.

The Army shipped Dever overseas. In England, after more desertions, he was sent to the Oxford psychiatric hospital. From there, too, Dever escaped. Each episode involved alcoholic orgies in London, fist fights, and bizarre aggressive behavior. The baffled doctors tried insulin shock, electric shock, and Sodium Amytal analysis. These brought temporary improvement.

Dever was released and, through a military bureaucrat's mistake, given a plush assignment as a clerk in "Torch" headquarters. During the day, he intermittently fulfilled his duties as a filing clerk. At night, he retired to his own London flat (in direct violation of Army regulations). During his evening wanderings through Piccadilly, Dever met an English girl whom he later married.

In one of the last Nazi bombing raids, an explosion smashed one of Dever's legs. Given a medical discharge Dever headed back to America— leaving his wife on the day she delivered their first child. Several months later, his wife traced him to New York. She flew across the Atlantic and after an emotional reunion forgave him. Dever swore eternal faithfulness.

A week later he left for Florida without notifying his wife: "I met a guy in a bar, and he said he wanted to pull some jobs in Florida; would I go along? I said 'O.K.,' but I forgot to tell my wife. She didn't know where I was, but she took me back when I came home. It wasn't that I didn't like her—we got along O.K. I just had other things to do."

Dever's asocial behavior continued with almost monotonous regularity. He entered the automobile black market for a while, then moved to the selling of fraudulent bonds. He committed many burglaries and topped his career in Boston with the impersonation of an F.B.I. officer and the forging of a $5,000 check.

At the time of our talks, Dever faced trial in Boston on a 15-count indictment. New Jersey, Florida, and New York awaited his extradition. Summarizing his life, Dever said: "Hell, I didn't need the money. I just would get an idea and I'd go out and do it. Maybe I hurt somebody doing it, but I've had fun."

A comparison of Howard Dever with William Cook. . .shows the basic similarity in their character structures. Their malformed personalities expressed themselves in superficially different ways:. . .Cook, in brutal aggression; Dever, in sophisticated "confidence" crimes. Beneath these symptoms, however, they possess the same basic traits: an inability to control aggressive impulsiveness, persistent anti-sociality, a craving for primitive satisfaction, and a striking lack of guilt with a seriously defective capacity for loving others. . . .

Causes of Psychopathy

The evidence of neural defect in some psychopaths probably warrants the conclusion that brain damage plays a causative role. Injury to the forebrain sometimes deletes restraints, increasing impulsive and aggressive actions. But brain damage alone does not result in the distinctive characteristics of the psychopath: guiltlessness and lovelessness. Neural malfunction seems to be the catalyst which, in some cases, turns a rejected child into a psychopath. The proclivity for psychopathy found even in mildly rejected individuals, if aggravated by a neural system incompatible with inhibition, develops into the psychopathic syndrome.

Thus, there seem to be three causal patterns:

1. *Severe rejection, by itself, can cause psychopathy;*
2. *Mild rejection in combination with damage to the brain area (possibly the hypothalamus) which normally inhibits behavior, causes psychopathy;*
3. *Mild rejection, in the absence of neural disorder, can result in psychopathy if certain other influences in the environment fail to provide alternatives*

Specifically, in this third case, we would hypothesize that an environment characterized by mild rejection and, in addition, by a psychopathic parental model, by erratically punitive discpline, and by an absence of adult supervision results in a psychopathic pattern. This theory, we believe, reasonably synthesizes the superficially conflicting discoveries about the psychopath. Rejection, sometimes severe and sometimes complemented by neural or environmental defects, plays the paramount role. The psychopathic syndrome evolves from this rejection.

The psychopath's *inability to maintain close relations* seems due to his inexperience with affectional bonds. As a child, the psychopath was consistently rebuffed. He did not experience the satisfactions which accompany emotional attachment. Since he never developed ties of affection, he never acquired the ability to "empathize." Because he early learned that the world offered him no love, the psychopath reacts to other human beings with suspicious indifference. He doubts the sincerity of those who may seek to establish close relations. Though the psychopath might wish to develop an emotional attachment, he lacks the necessary techniques. His erratic, uninhibited, and aggressive behavior drives people from him.

Failure to develop a conscience flows logically from the psychopath's lovelessness. Almost all social scientists believe that the internalization of moral controls takes place primarily through the child's acceptance of his parents. The child and the parents strike an unconscious bargain: in return for the child's conformity to social restrictions, the parents give the child love. If the child fails to conform, disapproval follows. In time, the child looks ahead to the consequences of his acts. If he is about to misbehave, a gnawing fear warns that his parents might stop loving him. Thus, the inner anxiety eventually results in internalization of the parent's morality. The child has developed a rudimentary conscience (Heinicke, 1953).

There is, of course, a more positive aspect in this development of inner controls: not only does the child fear withdrawal of love, he also identifies with his parents. He loves them, and he wishes to emulate them. As Gordon Allport has pointed out, children who fear the loss of love develop the concept of "must," but the "ought" of behavior comes only through identification with parents and other moral symbols.

In a rejectant environment, love, the central element, is missing. Because the rejected child does not love his parents and they do not love him, no identification takes place. Nor does the rejected child fear the loss of love—a love which he never had—when he violates moral restrictions. Without love from the socializing agent, the psychopath remains *asocial.* And if love is too weak to countermand brain lesions which make socialization difficult, the child becomes a psychopath.

Since there is no real conscience in the psychopath, he allows uninhibited expression to whatever aggressive urges he has. *Aggression* seems intensified in the psychopath, although recent research with psychopathic children indicates that their aggressive drives may be no more pressing than the normal person's.

Since he does not have strong emotional ties, the psychopath does not understand the effects of his aggression on other people.

Impulsivity is also intimately connected with early rejection. As a child, parental love did not compensate the psychopath for moderating his behavior and, in at least some cases, neurological dysfunctioning weakened his inhibitory faculties. Thus, as an adult, his impulsivity is unchecked.

Although inconsistent and purposeless behavior is a product of impulsivity, it may also be due to a deficiency in the psychopath's ego. Harrison Gough (1948)(among many others) believes that the normal person's self-concept arises through emotional interaction with other people. The child records the evaluations of those around him and gradually absorbs these into his feeling toward himself. If these early evaluations are missing or are inconsistent, the child is unable to develop a coherent attitude about himself. Absence of long-range goals and erratic impulsivity may be due to the psychopath's underdeveloped attitude toward his "self."

The psychopath's *pleasure seeking*, like his other traits, seems primarily due to his early experiences. His emotional frustration, in all probability, increased the intensity of his desires. Because he so seldom experienced it, the psychopath craves pleasure with heightened intensity. Uninhibited by either conscience or attachment to others, the psychopath seeks immediate satisfaction for his whims.

Aggression, pleasure seeking, and impulsivity cause the psychopath to violate society's rules. These traits, in turn, come from deeper deficiencies: warped ability to form relations and consequent lack of conscience.

Thus, the psychopathic syndrome can be traced to early deficiency in affectional relations. Extreme emotional deprivation or moderate rejection coupled with other environmental conditions or with neural damage to inhibitive centers, best account for the development of psychopathy. Although this position obviously requires the confirmation of empirical research, the theory reconciles the two major discoveries: that all psychopaths are, in some degree, rejected, and that many psychopaths have a neural disorder.

REFERENCES

Allport, Gordon. *The Nature of Prejudice.* Cambridge: Addison-Wesley, 1954.

Bender, Lauretta. "Post-Encephalitic Behavior Disorder in Childhood," in Josephine B. Neal, *Encephalitis*, New York: Grune & Stratton, 1942.

Bender, Lauretta. "Psychopathic Behavior Disorders in Children," in R. Lindner and R. Seliger (Eds.), *Handbook of Correctional Psychology,* New York: Philosophical Library, 1947, pp. 360-377.

Dreikurs, A. (As quoted in) Gurvitz, M. "Developments in the Concepts of Psychopathic Personality," *British Journal of Delinquency,* 2 (1951), p. 96.

Freyhan, F. A. "Psychopathology of Personality Functions in Psychopathic Personalities," *Psychiatric Quarterly,* 25 (1951), pp. 458-471.

Gough, H. G. "A Sociological Theory of Psychopathy," *American Journal of Sociology,* 53 (1948), pp. 359-366.

Heinicke, C. "Some Antecedents and Correlations of Guilt and Fear in Young Boys." Harvard University Ph.D. Dissertation, June, 1953.

Lindner, Robert. "Psychopathy as a Psychological Problem," *Encyclopedia of Psychology.* New York: Philosophical Library, 1948.

Lindner, Robert. *Rebel Without a Cause—The Hypnoanalysis of a Criminal Psychopath.* New York: Grune & Stratton, 1944.

Maslow, A. H. *Motivation and Personality.* New York: Harper, 1954.

Symkal, Anthony and Thorne, Frederick C. "Etiological Studies of Psychopathic Personality," *Journal of Clinical Psychology,* 7 (1951), pp. 299-316.

ILLEGITIMATE MEANS, ANOMIE, AND DEVIANT BEHAVIOR

RICHARD A. CLOWARD

This paper represents an attempt to consolidate two major sociological traditions of thought about the problem of deviant behavior. The first, exemplified by the work of Emile Durkheim (1951) and Robert K. Merton (1957), may be called the anomie tradition. The second, illustrated principally by the studies of Clifford R. Shaw, Henry D. McKay, and Edwin H. Sutherland, may be called the "cultural transmission" and "differential association" tradition.* Despite some reciprocal borrowing of ideas, these intellectual traditions developed more or less independently. By seeking to consolidate them, a more adequate theory of deviant behavior may be constructed.

From Richard A. Cloward, "Illegitimate Means, Anomie, and Deviant Behavior," *American Sociological Review,* 24 (April 1959). Reprinted by permission.

* See especially the following: Clifford R. Shaw, (1931), Clifford R. Shaw et al., (1940); Clifford R. Shaw and Henry D. McKay (1942); Edwin H. Sutherland, (1937, 1947, 1949).

Differentials in Availability of Legitimate Means: The Theory of Anomie

The theory of anomie has undergone two major phases of development. Durkheim first used the concept to explain deviant behavior. He focussed on the way in which various social conditions lead to "overweening ambition," and how, in turn, unlimited aspirations ultimately produce a breakdown in regulatory norms. Robert K. Merton has systematized and extended the theory, directing attention to patterns of disjunction between culturally prescribed goals and socially organized access to them by *legitimate* means. In this paper, a third phase is outlined. An additional variable is incorporated in the developing scheme of anomie, namely, the concept of *differentials in access to success-goals by illegitimate means.*

Phase I: Unlimited Aspirations and the Breakdown of Regulatory Norms. In Durkheim's work, a basic distinction is made between "physical needs" and "moral needs." The importance of this distinction was heightened for Durkheim because he viewed physical needs as being regulated automatically by features of man's organic structure. Nothing in the organic structure, however, is capable of regulating social desires; as Durkheim put it, man's "capacity for feeling is in itself an insatiable and bottomless abyss." If man is to function without "friction," "the passions must first be limited. . . .But since the individual has no way of limiting them, this must be done by some force exterior to him." Durkheim viewed the collective order as the external regulating force which defined and ordered the goals to which men should orient their behavior. If the collective order is disrupted or disturbed, however, men's aspirations may then rise, exceeding all possibilities of fulfillment. Under these conditions, "de-regulation or anomy" ensues: "At the very moment when traditional rules have lost their authority, the richer prize offered these appetites stimulates them and makes them more exigent and impatient of control. The state of de-regulation or anomy is thus further heightened by passions being less disciplined precisely when they need more disciplining" (1951, pp. 247-257). Finally, pressures toward deviant behavior were said to develop when man's aspirations no longer matched the possibilities of fulfillment. . . .

In developing the theory, Durkheim characterized goals in the industrial society, and specified the way in which unlimited aspirations are induced. He spoke of "dispositions. . .so inbred that society has grown to accept them and is accustomed to think them normal," and he portrayed these "inbred dispositions": "It is everlastingly repeated that it is man's nature to be eternally dissatisfied, constantly to advance, without relief or rest, toward an indefinite goal. The longing for infinity is daily represented as a mark of moral distinction. . . ." And it was precisely these pressures to strive for "infinite" or "receding" goals, in Durkheim's view, that generate a breakdown in regulatory norms, for "when there is no other aim but to outstrip constantly the point arrived at, how painful to be thrown back!"

Phase II: Disjunction Between Cultural Goals and Socially Structured Opportunity. Durkheim's description of the emergence of "overweening ambition" and the subsequent breakdown of regulatory norms constitutes one of the links between his work and the later development of the theory by Robert K. Merton. In his classic essay, "Social Structure and Anomie," Merton suggests that goals and norms may vary independently of each other, and that this sometimes leads to malintegrated states. In his view, two polar types of disjunction may occur: "There may develop a very heavy, at times a virtually exclusive stress upon the value of particular goals, involving comparatively little concern with the institutionally pre-scribed means of striving towards these goals. . . . This constitutes one type of malintegrated culture," On the other hand, "A second polar type is found where activities originally conceived as instrumental are transmuted into self-contained practices, lacking further objectives. . . .Sheer conform-ity becomes a central value." Merton notes that "between these extreme types are societies which maintain a rough balance between emphases up-on cultural goals and institutionalized practices, and these constitute the integrated and relatively stable, though changing societies."

Having identified patterns of disjunction between goals and norms, Merton is enabled to define anomie more precisely: "Anomie [may be] conceived as a breakdown in the cultural structure, occurring particularly when there is an acute disjunction between cultural norms and goals and the socially structured capacities of members of the group to act in accord with them."

Of the two kinds of malintegrated societies, Merton is primarily in-terested in the one in which "there is an exceptionally strong emphasis upon specific goals without a corresponding emphasis upon institutional procedures." He states that attenuation between goals and norms, leading to anomie or "normlessness," comes about because men in such societies internalize an emphasis on common success-goals under conditions of vary-ing access to them. The essence of this hypothesis is captured in the follow-ing excerpt: "It is only when a system of cultural values extols, virtually above all else, certain *common* success-goals for the population at large while the social structure rigorously restricts or completely closes access to approved modes of reaching these goals *for a considerable part of the same population,* that deviant behavior ensues on a large scale" (1957, pp. 131-194). The focus, in short, is on the way in which the social struc-ture puts a strain upon the cultural structure. Here one may point to diverse structural differentials in access to culturally approved goals by legitimate means, for example, differentials of age, sex, ethnic status, and social class. Pressures for anomie or normlessness vary from one social position to another, depending on the nature of these differentials.

In summary, Merton extends the theory of anomie in two principal ways. He explicitly identifies types of anomic or malintegrated societies by focussing upon the relationship between cultural goals and norms. And, by directing attention to patterned differentials in the access to success-goals by legitimate means, he shows how the social structure exerts a strain upon the cultural structure, leading in turn to anomie or normlessness.

Phase III: The Concept of Illegitimate Means. Once processes generating differentials in pressures are identified, there is then the question of how these pressures are resolved, or how men respond to them. In this connection, Merton enumerates five basic categories of behavior or role adaptations which are likely to emerge: conformity, innovation, ritualism, retreatism, and rebellion. These adaptations differ depending on the individual's acceptance or rejection of cultural goals, and depending on his adherence to or violation of institutional norms. Furthermore, Merton sees the distribution of these adaptations principally as the consequence of two variables: the relative extent of pressure, and values, particularly "internalized prohibitions," governing the use of various illegitimate means. . . .

Apart from both socially patterned pressures, which give rise to deviance, and from values, which determine choices of adaptations, a further variable should be taken into account: namely, *differentials in availability of illegitimate means.* For example, the notion that innovating behavior may result from unfulfilled aspirations and imperfect socialization with respect to conventional norms implies that illegitimate means are freely available—as if the individual, having decided that "you can't make it legitimately," then simply turns to illegitimate means which are readily at hand whatever his position in the social structure. However, these means may not be available. As noted above, the anomie theory assumes that conventional means are differentially distributed, that some individuals, because of their social position, enjoy certain advantages which are denied to others. Note, for example, variations in the degree to which members of various classes are fully exposed to and thus acquire the values, education, and skills which facilitate upward mobility. It should not be startling, therefore, to find similar variations in the availability of illegitimate means.

Several sociologists have alluded to such variations without explicitly incorporating this variable in a theory of deviant behavior. Sutherland, for example, writes that "an inclination to steal is not a sufficient explanation of the genesis of the professional thief." Moreover, "the person must be appreciated by the professional thieves. He must be appraised as having an adequate equipment of wits, front, talking-ability, honesty, reliability, nerve and determination." In short, "a person can be a professional thief only if he is recognized and received as such by other professional thieves." But recognition is not freely accorded: "Selection and tutelage are the two necessary elements in the process of acquiring recognition as a professional thief. . . .A person cannot acquire recognition as a professional thief until he has had tutelage in professional theft, *and tutelage is given only to a few persons selected from the total population."* Furthermore, the aspirant is judged by high standards of performance, for only "a very small percentage of those who start on this process ever reach the stage of professional theft." The burden of these remarks—dealing with the processes of selection, induction, and assumption of full status in the criminal group—is that motivations or pressures toward deviance do not fully account for deviant behavior. The "self-made" thief—lacking knowledge of the ways of securing immunity from prosecution and similar techniques of defense—"would quickly land in prison" (1937, pp. 211-213). Sutherland is in effect pointing to differentials in access to the role of professional thief. Although the criteria of selection are not altogether clear from his analysis; definite evaluative standards do appear to exist; depending on their content, certain categories of individuals would be placed at a disadvantage and others would be favored.

The availability of illegitimate means, then, is controlled by various criteria in the same manner that has long been ascribed to conventional means. Both systems of opportunity are (1) limited, rather than infinitely available, and (2) differentially available depending on the location of persons in the social structure.

When we employ the term "means," whether legitimate or illegitimate, at least two things are implied: first, that there are appropriate learning environments for the acquisition of the values and skills associated with the performance of a particular role; and second, that the individual has opportunities to discharge the role once he has been prepared. The term subsumes, therefore, both *learning structures and opportunity structures.*

A case in point is recruitment and preparation for careers in the rackets. There are fertile criminal learning environments for the young in neighborhoods where the rackets flourish as stable, indigenous institutions. Because these environments afford integration of offenders of different ages, the young are exposed to "differential associations" which facilitate the acquisition of criminal values and skills. Yet preparation for the role may not insure that the individual will ever discharge it. For one thing, more youngsters may be recruited into these patterns of differential association than can possibly be absorbed, following their "training," by the adult criminal structure. There may be a surplus of contenders for these elite positions, leading in turn to the necessity for criteria and mechanisms of selection. Hence a certain proportion of those who aspire may not be permitted to engage in the behavior for which they have been prepared.

This illustration is similar in every respect, save for the route followed, to the case of those who seek careers in the sphere of legitimate business. Here, again, is the initial problem of securing access to appropriate learning environments, such as colleges and post-graduate school of business. Having acquired the values and skills needed for a business career, graduates then face the problem of whether or not they can successfully discharge the roles for which they have been prepared. Formal training itself is not sufficient for occupational success, for many forces intervene to determine who shall succeed and fail in the competitive world of business and industry—as throughout the entire conventional occupational structure.

This distinction between learning structures and opportunity structures was suggested some years ago by Sutherland. In 1944, he circulated an unpublished paper which briefly discusses the proposition that "criminal behavior is partially a function of opportunities to commit specific classes of crimes, such as embezzlement, bank burglary, or illicit heterosexual intercourse." He did not, however, take up the problem of differentials in opportunity as a concept to be systematically incorporated in a theory of deviant behavior. Instead, he held that "opportunity" is a necessary but not sufficient explanation of the commission of criminal acts, "since some persons who have opportunities to embezzle, become intoxicated, engage in illicit heterosexual intercourse or to commit other crimes do not do so." He also noted that the differential association theory did not constitute a full explanation of criminal activity, for, notwithstanding differential association, "it is axiomatic that persons who commit a specific crime must have the opportunity to commit that crime." He therefore concluded that "while opportunity may be partially a function of association with criminal patterns and of the specialized techniques thus acquired, *it is not determined entirely in that manner,* and consequently differential association is not the sufficient cause of criminal behavior" (emphasis not in original) (Cohen, Lindesmith, and Schuessler, 1956, pp. 31-35).

In Sutherland's statements, two meanings are attributed to the term "opportunity." As suggested above, it may be useful to separate these for analytical purposes. In the first sense, Sutherland appears to be saying that opportunity consists in part of learning structures. The principal components of his theory of differential association are that "criminal behavior is learned," and, furthermore, that "criminal behavior is learned in interaction with other persons in a process of communication." But he also uses the term to describe situations conducive to carrying out criminal roles. Thus, for Sutherland, the commission of a criminal act would seem to depend upon the existence of two conditions: differential associations favoring the acquisition of criminal values and skills, and conditions encouraging participation in criminal activity.

This distinction heightens the importance of identifying and questioning the common assumption that illegitimate means are freely available. We can now ask (1) whether there are socially structured differentials in access to illegitimate learning environments, and (2) whether there are differentials limiting the fulfillment of illegitimate roles. If differentials exist and can be identified, we may then inquire about their consequences for the behavior of persons in different parts of the social structure. Before pursuing this question, however, we turn to a fuller discussion of the theoretical tradition established by Shaw, McKay, and Sutherland.

Differentials in Availability of Illegitimate Means: The Subculture Tradition

The concept of differentials in availability of illegitimate means is implicit in one of the major streams of American criminological theory. In this tradition, attention is focussed on the processes by which persons are recruited into criminal learning environments and ultimately inducted into criminal roles. The problems here are to account for the acquisition of criminal roles and to describe the social organization of criminal activities. When the theoretical propositions contained in this tradition are reanalyzed, it becomes clear that one underlying conception is that of variations in access to success-goals by illegitimate means. Furthermore, this implicit concept may be shown to be one of the bases upon which the tradition was constructed.

In their studies of the ecology of deviant behavior in the urban environment, Shaw and McKay found that delinquency and crime tended to be confined to delimited areas and, furthermore, that such behavior persisted despite demographic changes in these areas. Hence they came to speak of "criminal tradition," of the "cultural transmission" of criminal values. As a result of their observations of slum life, they concluded that *particular importance must be assigned to the integration of different age-levels of offenders.* Thus:

> Stealing in the neighborhood was a common practice among the children and approved by the parents. Whenever the boys got together they talked about robbing and made more plans for stealing. I hardly knew any boys who did not go robbing. The little fellows went in for petty stealing, breaking into freight cars, and stealing junk. The older guys did big jobs like stick-up, burglary, and stealing autos. The little fellows admired the "big shots" and longed for the day when they could get into the big racket. Fellows who had "done time" were the big shots and looked up to and gave the little fellow tips on how to get by and pull off big jobs (Shaw, 1930, p. 54).

In other words, access to criminal roles depends upon stable associations with others from whom the necessary values and skills may be learned. Shaw and McKay were describing deviant learning structures—that is, alternative routes by which people seek access to the goals which society holds to be worthwhile. They might also have pointed out that, in areas where such learning structures are unavailable, it is probably difficult for many individuals to secure access to stable criminal careers, even though motivated to do so*. . . .

Other factors may be cited which affect access to criminal roles. For example, there is a good deal of anecdotal evidence which reveals that access to the upper echelons of organized racketeering is controlled, at least in part, by ethnicity. Some ethnic groups are found disproportionately in the upper ranks and others disproportionately in the lower. From an historical perspective, as Bell (1953) has shown, this realm has been successively dominated by Irish, East-European Jews, and more recently, by Italians. Various other ethnic groups have been virtually excluded or at least relegated to lower echelon positions. Despite the fact that many rackets (especially "policy") have flourished in predominantly Negro neighborhoods, there have been but one or two Negroes who have been known to rise to the top in syndicated crime. As in the conventional world, Negroes are relegated to the more menial tasks. Moreover, access to elite positions in the rackets may be governed in part by kinship criteria, for various accounts of the blood relations among top racketeers indicate that nepotism is the general rule (Frank, 1958). It has also been noted that kinship criteria sometimes govern access to stable criminal roles, as in the case of the pickpocket (Maurer, 1955). And there are, of course, deep-rooted sex differentials in access to illegal means. Although women are often employed in criminal vocations—for example, thievery, confidence games, and extortion—and must be employed in others—such as prostitution—nevertheless females are excluded from many criminal activities.

Of the various criteria governing access to illegitimate means, class differentials may be among the most important. The differentials noted in the preceding paragraph—age, sex, ethnicity, kinship, and the like—all pertain to criminal activity historically associated with the lower class. Most middle- or upper-class persons—even when interested in following "lower-class" criminal careers—would no doubt have difficulty in fulfilling

---

* We are referring here, and throughout the paper, to stable criminal roles to which persons may orient themselves on a career basis, as in the case of racketeers professional thieves, and the like. The point is that access to stable roles depends in the first instance upon the availability of learning structures. As Frank Tannenbaum says, "it must be insisted on that unless there were older criminals in the neighborhood who provided a moral judgement in favor of the delinquent and to whom the delinquents could look for commendation, the careers of the younger ones could not develop at all" (1938, p. 60).

this ambition because of inappropriate preparation. The prerequisite attitudes and skills are more easily acquired if the individual is a member of the lower class; most middle- and upper-class persons could not easily unlearn their own class culture in order to learn a new one. By the same token, access to many "white collar" criminal roles is closed to lower-class persons. Some occupations afford abundant opportunities to engage in illegitimate activity; others offer virtually none. The businessman, for example, not only has at his disposal the means to do so, but, as some studies have shown, he is under persistent pressure to employ illegitimate means, if only to maintain a competitive advantage in the market place. But for those in many other occupations, white collar modes of criminal activity are simply not an alternative.

Some Implications of a Consolidated Approach to Deviant Behavior

It is now possible to consolidate the two sociological traditions described above. Our analysis makes it clear that these traditions are oriented to different aspects of the same problem: differentials in access to opportunity. One tradition focusses on legitimate opportunity, the other on illegitimate. By incorporating the concept of differentials in access to *illegitimate* means, the theory of anomie may be extended to include seemingly unrelated studies and theories of deviant behavior which form a part of the literature of American criminology. In this final section, we try to show how a consolidated approach might advance the understanding of both rates and types of deviant conduct. The discussion centers on the conditions of access to *both* systems of means, legitimate and illegitimate.

The Distribution of Criminal Behavior. One problem which has plagued the criminologist is the absence of adequate data on social differentials in criminal activity. Many have held that the highest crime rates are to be found in the lower social strata. Others have suggested that rates in the middle and upper classes may be much higher than is ordinarily thought. The question of the social distribution of crime remains problematic.

In the absence of adequate data, the theorist has sometimes attacked this problem by assessing the extent of pressures toward normative departures in various parts of the social structure. For example, Merton (1957, p. 132) remarks that his "primary aim is to discover how some social structures exert a definite pressure upon certain persons in the society to engage in non-conforming rather than conforming conduct." Having identified structural features which might be expected to generate deviance, Merton suggests the presence of a correlation between "pressures toward deviation" and "rate of deviance."

> But whatever the differential rates of deviant behavior in the several social strata, and we know from many sources that the official crime statistics uniformly showing higher rates in the lower strata are far from complete or reliable, *it appears from our analysis that the greater pressures toward deviation are exerted upon the lower strata.* . . .Of those located in the lower reaches of the social structure, the culture makes incompatible demands. On the one hand they are asked to orient their behavior toward the prospect of large wealth. . . and on the other, they are largely denied effective opportunities to do so institutionally. *The consequence of this structural inconsistency is a high rate of deviant behavior* (1957, pp. 144-145).

Because of the paucity and unreliability of existing criminal statistics, there is as yet no way of knowing whether or not Merton's hypothesis is correct. Until comparative studies of crime rates are available the hypothesized correlation cannot be tested.

From a theoretical perspective, however, questions may be raised about this correlation. Would we expect, to raise the principal query, the correlation to be fixed or to vary depending on the distribution of access to illegitimate means? The three possibilities are (1) that access is distributed uniformly throughout the class structure, (2) that access varies inversely with class position, and (3) that access varies directly with class position. Specification of these possibilities permits a more precise statement of the conditions under which crime rates would be expected to vary.

If access to illegitimate means is *uniformly distributed* throughout the class structure, then the proposed correlation would probably hold— higher rates of innovating behavior would be expected in the lower class than elsewhere. Lower-class persons apparently experience greater pressures toward deviance and are less restrained by internalized prohibitions from employing illegitimate means. Assuming uniform access to such means, it would therefore be reasonable to predict higher rates of innovating behavior in the lower social strata.

If access to illegitimate means varies *inversely* with class position, then the correlation would not only hold, but might even be strengthened. For pressures toward deviance, including socialization that does not altogether discourage the use of illegitimate means, would coincide with the availability of such means.

Finally, if access varies *directly* with class position, comparative rates of illegitimate activity become difficult to forecast. The higher the class position, the less the pressure to employ illegitimate means; furthermore, internalized prohibitions are apparently more effective in higher positions. If, at the same time, opportunities to use illegitimate methods are more abundant, then these factors would be in opposition. Until the precise effects of these several variables can be more adequately measured, rates cannot be safely forecast.

The concept of differentials in availability of illegitimate means may also help to clarify questions about varying crime rates among ethnic, age, religious, and sex groups, and other social divisions. This concept, then, can be systematically employed in the effort to further our understanding of the distribution of illegitimate behavior in the social structure.

Modes of Adaptation: The Case of Retreatism. By taking into account the conditions of access to legitimate *and* illegitimate means, we can further specify the circumstances under which various modes of deviant behavior arise. This may be illustrated by the case of retreatism.

As defined by Merton, retreatist adaptations include such categories of behavior as alcoholism, drug addiction, and psychotic withdrawal. These adaptations entail "escape" from the frustrations of unfulfilled aspirations by withdrawal from conventional social relationships. The processes leading to retreatism are described by Merton as follows: "[Retreatism] arises from continued failure to near the goal by legitimate measures and from an inability to use the illegitimate route because of internalized prohibitions, *this process occuring while the supreme value of the success-goal has not yet been renounced.* The conflict is resolved by abandoning *both* precipitating elements, the goals and means. The escape is complete, the conflict is eliminated and the individual is asocialized" (1957, pp.153-154).

In this view, a crucial element encouraging retreatism is internalized constraint concerning the use of illegitimate means. But this element need not be present. Merton apparently assumed that such prohibitions are essential because, in their absence, the logic of his scheme would compel him to predict that innovating behavior would result. But the assumption that the individual uninhibited in the use of illegitimate means becomes an innovator presupposes that successful innovation is only a matter of motivation. Once the concept of differentials in access to illegitimate means is introduced, however, it becomes clear that retreatism is possible even in the absence of internalized prohibitions. For we may now ask how individuals respond when they fail in the use of *both* legitimate and illegitimate means. If illegitimate means are unavailable, if efforts at innovation fail, then retreatist adaptations may still be the consequence, and the "escape" mechanisms chosen by the defeated individual may perhaps be all the more deviant because of his "double failure."

This does not mean that retreatist adaptations cannot arise precisely as Merton suggests: namely, that the conversion from conformity to retreatism takes place in one step, without intervening adaptations. But this is only one route to retreatism. The conversion may at times entail intervening stages and intervening adaptations, particularly of an innovating type. This possibility helps to account for the fact that certain categories of individuals cited as retreatists—for example, hobos—often show extensive histories of arrests and convictions for various illegal acts. It also helps to explain retreatist adaptations among individuals who have not necessarily internalized strong restraints on the use of illegitimate means. In short, retreatist adaptations may arise with considerable frequency among those who are failures in both worlds, conventional and illegitimate alike.

Future research on retreatist behavior might well examine the interval between conformity and retreatism. To what extent does the individual entertain the possibility of resorting to illegitimate means, and to what extent does he actually seek to mobilize such means? If the individual turns to innovating devices, the question of whether or not he becomes a retreatist may then depend upon the relative accessibility of illegitimate means. For although the frustrated conformist seeks a solution to status discontent by adopting such methods, there is the further problem of whether or not he possesses appropriate skills and has opportunities for their use. We suggest therefore that data be gathered on preliminary responses to status discontent—and on the individual's perceptions of the efficacy of employing illegitimate means, the content of his skills, and the objective situation of illegitimate opportunity available to him.

Respecification of the processes leading to retreatism may also help to resolve difficulties entailed in ascertaining rates of retreatism in different parts of the social structure. Although Merton does not indicate explicitly where this adaptation might be expected to arise, he specifies some of the social conditions which encourage high rates of retreatism. Thus the latter is apt to mark the behavior of downwardly mobile persons, who experience a sudden breakdown in established social relations, and such individuals as the retired, who have lost major social roles (1957, pp. 188-189).

The long-standing difficulties in forecasting differential rates of retreatism may perhaps be attributed to the assumption that retreatists have fully internalized values prohibiting the use of illegitimate means. That this prohibition especially characterizes socialization in the middle and upper classes probably calls for the prediction that retreatism occurs primarily in those classes—and that the hobohemias, "drug cultures," and the ranks of the alcoholics are populated primarily by individuals from the upper reaches of society. It would appear from various accounts of hobohemia and skid row, however, that many of these persons are the products of slum life, and, furthermore, that their behavior is not necessarily controlled by values which preclude resort to illegitimate means. But once it is recognized that retreatism may arise in response to limitations on both systems of means, the difficulty of locating this adaptation is lessened, if not resolved. Thus retreatist behavior may vary with the particular process by which it is generated. The process described by

Merton may be somewhat more characteristic of higher positions in the social structure where rule-oriented socialization is typical, while in the lower strata retreatism may tend more often to be the consequence of unsuccessful attempts at innovation.

Summary

This paper attempts to identify and to define the concept of differential opportunity structures. It has been suggested that this concept helps to extend the developing theory of social structure and anomie. Furthermore, by linking propositions regarding the accessibility of *both* legitimate and illegitimate opportunity structures, a basis is provided for consolidating various major traditions of sociological thought on nonconformity. The concept of differential systems of opportunity and of variations in access to them, it is hoped, will suggest new possibilities for research on the relationship between social structure and deviant behavior.

REFERENCES

Bell, Daniel. "Crime as an American Way of Life," *The Antioch Review* (Summer, 1953), pp. 131-154.

Cohen, Albert, Lindesmith, Alfred, and Schuessler, Karl (Eds.), *The Sutherland Papers.* Bloomington, Indiana: Indiana University Press, 1956.

Durkheim, Emile. *Suicide.* translated by J. A. Spaulding and George Simpson, Glencoe, Illinois: Free Press, 1951.

Frank, Stanley. "The Rap Gangsters Fear Most," *The Saturday Evening Post,* (August 9, 1958), pp. 26ff.

Maurer, David W. *Whiz Mob: A Correlation of the Technical Argot of Pickpockets with Their Behavior Pattern,* Publication of the American Dialect Society, No. 24, 1955.

Merton, Robert K. *Social Theory and Social Structure.* Glencoe, Illinois: Free Press, 1957.

Shaw, Clifford R. *The Jack-Roller.* Chicago: University of Chicago Press, 1930.

Shaw, Clifford R. *The Natural History of a Delinquent Career.* Chicago: University of Chicago Press, 1931.

Shaw, Clifford R. *et. al., Delinquency Areas.* Chicago: University of Chicago Press, 1940.

Shaw, Clifford R. and McKay, Henry D. *Juvenile Delinquency and Urban Areas.* Chicago: University of Chicago Press, 1942.

Sutherland, Edwin. *Principles of Criminology.* 4th edition, Philadelphia: Lippincott, 1947.

Sutherland, Edwin (Ed.), *The Professional Thief.* Chicago: University of Chicago Press, 1937.

Sutherland, Edwin. *White Collar Crime.* New York: Dryden, 1949.

Tannenbaum, Frank. *Crime and the Community.* New York: Ginn, 1938.

RULES AND THEIR ENFORCEMENT:
A SEQUENTIAL MODEL OF DEVIANCE

HOWARD S. BECKER

Outsiders

All social groups make rules and attempt, at some times and under some circumstances, to enforce them. Social rules define situations and the kinds of behavior appropriate to them, specifying some actions as "right" and forbidding others as "wrong." When a rule is enforced, the person who is supposed to have broken it may be seen as a special kind of person, one who cannot be trusted to live by the rules agreed on by the group. He is regarded as an *outsider*. . . .

Definitions of Deviance

The outsider—the deviant from group rules—has been the subject of much speculation, theorizing, and scientific study. What laymen want to know about deviants is: why do they do it? How can we account for their rule-breaking? What is there about them that leads them to do forbidden things? Scientific research has tried to find answers to these questions. In doing so it has accepted the common-sense premise that there is something inherently deviant (qualitatively distinct) about acts that break (or seem to break) social rules. It has also accepted the common-sense assumption that the deviant act occurs because some characteristic of the person who commits it makes it necessary or inevitable that he should. Scientists do not ordinarily question the label "deviant" when it is applied to particular acts or people but rather take it as given. In so doing, they accept the values of the group making the judgment.

It is easily observable that different groups judge different things to be deviant. This should alert us to the possibility that the person making the judgment of deviance, the process by which that judgment is arrived at, and the situation in which it is made may all be intimately involved in the phenomenon of deviance. To the degree that the common-sense view of deviance and the scientific theories that begin with its premises assume

that acts that break rules are inherently deviant and thus take for granted
the situations and processes of judgment, they may leave out an important
variable. If scientists ignore the variable character of the process of judgment, they may by that omission limit the kinds of theories that can be
developed and the kind of understanding that can be achieved. . . .

Another sociological view is more relativistic. It identifies deviance
as the failure to obey group rules. Once we have described the rules a
group enforces on its members, we can say with some precision whether or
not a person has violated them and is thus, on this view, deviant.

This view is closest to my own, but it fails to give sufficient weight
to the ambiguities that arise in deciding which rules are to be taken as the
yardstick against which behavior is measured and judged deviant. A society
has many groups, each with its own set of rules, and people belong to
many groups simultaneously. A person may break the rules of one group
by the very act of abiding by the rules of another group. Is he, then,
deviant? Proponents of this definition may object that while ambiguity
may arise with respect to the rules peculiar to one or another group in
society, there are some rules that are very generally agreed to by everyone,
in which case the difficulty does not arise. This, of course, is a question of
fact, to be settled by empirical research. I doubt there are many such areas
of consensus and think it wiser to use a definition that allows us to deal
with both ambiguous and unambiguous situations.

Deviance and the Responses of Others

The sociological view I have just discussed defines deviance as the infraction of some agreed-upon rule. It then goes on to ask who breaks rules, and
to search for the factors in their personalities and life situations that might
account for the infractions. This assumes that those who have broken a rule
constitute a homogeneous category, because they have committed the
same deviant act.

Such an assumption seems to me to ignore the central fact about
deviance: it is created by society. I do not mean this in the way it is ordinarily understood, in which the causes of deviance are located in the
social situation of the deviant or in "social factors" which prompt his
action. I mean, rather, that *social groups create deviance by making the
rules whose infraction constitutes deviance,* and by applying those rules
to particular people and labelling them as outsiders. From this point of
view, deviance is *not* a quality of the act the person commits, but rather
a consequence of the application by others of rules and sanctions to an
"offender." The deviant is one to whom that label has successfully been
applied; deviant behavior is behavior that people so label.

Since deviance is, among other things, a consequence of the responses of others to a person's act, students of deviance cannot assume that they are dealing with a homogeneous category when they study people who have been labelled deviant. That is, they cannot assume that these people have actually committed a deviant act or broken some rule, because the process of labelling may not be infallible; some people may be labelled deviant who in fact have not broken a rule. Furthermore, they cannot assume that the category of those labelled deviant will contain all those who actually have broken a rule, for many offenders may escape apprehension and thus fail to be included in the population of "deviants" they study. Insofar as the category lacks homogeneity and fails to include all the cases that belong in it, one cannot reasonably expect to find common factors of personality or life situation that will account for the supposed deviance.

What, then, do people who have been labelled deviant have in common? At the least, they share the label and the experience of being labelled as outsiders. I will begin my analysis with this basic similarity and view deviance as the product of a transaction that takes place between some social group and one who is viewed by that group as a rule-breaker. I will be less concerned with the personal and social characteristics of deviants than with the process by which they come to be thought of as outsiders and their reactions to that judgment. . . .

The degree to which other people will respond to a given act as deviant varies greatly. Several kinds of variation seem worth noting. First of all, there is variation over time. A person believed to have committed a given "deviant" act may at one time be responded to much more leniently than he would be at some other time. The occurrence of "drives" against various kinds of deviance illustrates this clearly. At various times, enforcement officials may decide to make an all-out attack on some particular kind of deviance, such as gambling, drug addiction, or homosexuality. It is obviously much more dangerous to engage in one of these activities when a drive is on than at any other time. (In a very interesting study of crime news in Colorado newspapers, Davis (1952) found that the amount of crime reported in Colorado newspapers showed very little association with actual changes in the amount of crime taking place in Colorado. And, further, that peoples' estimate of how much increase there had been in crime in Colorado was associated with the increase in the amount of crime news but not with any increase in the amount of crime.)

The degree to which an act will be treated as deviant depends also on who commits the act and who feels he has been harmed by it. Rules tend to be applied more to some persons than others. Studies of juvenile delinquency make the point clearly (Cohen and Short, 1966). Boys from middle-class areas do not get as far in the legal process when they are apprehended as do boys from slum areas. The middle-class boy is less likely, when picked up by the police, to be taken to the station; less likely when taken to the station to be booked; and it is extremely unlikely that he will be convicted and sentenced. This variation occurs even though the original infraction of the rule is the same in the two cases. Similarly, the law is differentially applied to Negroes and whites. It is well known that a Negro believed to have attacked a white woman is much more likely to be punished than a white man who commits the same offense; it is only slightly less well known that a Negro who murders another Negro is much less likely to be punished than a white man who commits murder (Garfinkel, 1949).This, of course, is one of the main points of Sutherland's (1940) analysis of white-collar crime: crimes committed by corporations are almost always prosecuted as civil cases, but the same crime committed by an individual is ordinarily treated as a criminal offense.

Some rules are enforced only when they result in certain consequences. The unmarried mother furnishes a clear example. Vincent (1961, p. 3-5) points out that illicit sexual relations seldom result in severe punishment or social censure for the offenders. If, however, a girl becomes pregnant as a result of such activities, the reaction of others is likely to be severe. (The illicit pregnancy is also an interesting example of the differential enforcement of rules on different categories of people. Vincent notes that unmarried fathers escape the severe censure visited on the mother.)

Why repeat these commonplace observations? Because, taken together, they support the proposition that deviance is not a simple quality, present in some kinds of behavior and absent in others. Rather, it is the product of a process which involves responses of other people to the behavior. The same behavior may be an infraction of the rules at one time and not at another; may be an infraction when committed by one person, but not when committed by another; some rules are broken with impunity, others are not. In short, whether a given act is deviant or not depends in part on the nature of the act (that is, whether or not it violates some rule) and in part on what other people do about it. . . .

Whose Rules?

I have been using the term "outsiders" to refer to those people who are judged by others to be deviant and thus to stand outside the circle of "normal" members of the group. But the term contains a second meaning whose analysis leads to another important set of sociological problems: "outsiders," from the point of view of the person who is labelled deviant, may be the people who make the rules he has been found guilty of breaking.

Social rules are the creation of specific social groups. Modern societies are not simple organizations in which everyone agrees on what the rules are and how they are to be applied in specific situations. They are, instead, highly differentiated along social class lines, ethnic lines, occupational lines, and cultural lines. These groups need not and, in fact, often do not share the same rules. The problems they face in dealing with their environment, the history and traditions they carry with them, all lead to the evolution of different sets of rules. Insofar as the rules of various groups conflict and contradict one another, there will be disagreement about the kind of behavior that is proper in any given situation.

Italian immigrants who went on making wine for themselves and their friends during Prohibition were acting properly by Italian immigrant standards, but were breaking the law of their new country (as, of course, were many of their Old American neighbors). Medical patients who shop around for a doctor may, from the perspective of their own group, be doing what is necessary to protect their health by making sure they get what seems to them the best possible doctor; but, from the perspective of the physician, what they do is wrong because it breaks down the trust the patient ought to put in his physician. The lower-class delinquent who fights for his "turf" is only doing what he considers necessary and right, but teachers, social workers, and police see it differently. . . .

To the extent that a group tries to impose its rules on other groups in the society, we are presented with a second question: Who can, in fact, force others to accept their rules and what are the causes of their success? This is, of course, a question of political and economic power. Later we will consider the political and economic process through which rules are created and enforced. Here it is enough to note that people are in fact always *forcing* their rules on others, applying them more or less against the will and without the consent of those others. By and large, for example, rules are made for young people by their elders. Though the youth of this country exert a powerful influence culturally—the mass media of communication are tailored to their interests, for instance—many important kinds of rules are made for our youth by adults. Rules regarding school attendance and sex behavior are not drawn up with regard to the problems of adolescence. Rather, adolescents find themselves surrounded by rules about these matters which have been made by older and more settled people. It is considered legitimate to do this, for youngsters are considered neither wise enough nor responsible enough to make proper rules for themselves.

In the same way, it is true in many respects that men make the rules for women in our society (though in America this is changing rapidly). Negroes find themselves subject to rules made for them by whites. The foreign-born and those otherwise ethnically peculiar often have their rules made for them by the Protestant Anglo-Saxon minority. The middle class makes rules the lower class must obey—in the schools, the courts, and elsewhere. . . .

A Sequential Model of Deviance

It is not my purpose here to argue that only acts which are regarded as deviant by others are "really" deviant. But it must be recognized that this is an important dimension, one which needs to be taken into account in any analysis of deviant behavior. By combining this dimension with another—whether or not an act conforms to a particular rule—we can construct the following set of categories for the discrimination of different kinds of deviance.

Two of these types require very little explanation. *Conforming* behavior is simply that which obeys the rule and which others perceive as obeying the rule. At the other extreme, the *pure deviant* type of behavior is that which both disobeys the rule and is perceived as doing so.*

Types of Deviant Behavior

	Obedient Behavior	*Rule-breaking Behavior*
Perceived as deviant	Falsely accused	Pure deviant
Not perceived as deviant	Conforming	Secret deviant

The two other possibilities are of more interest. The *falsely accused* situation is what criminals often refer to as a "bum rap." The person is seen by others as having committed an improper action, although in fact he has not done so. False accusations undoubtedly occur even in courts of law, where the person is protected by rules of due process and evidence. They probably occur much more frequently in nonlegal settings where procedural safeguards are not available.

An even more interesting kind of case is found at the other extreme of *secret deviance.* Here an improper act is committed, yet no one notices it or reacts to it as a violation of the rules. As in the case of false accusation, no one really knows how much of this phenomenon exists, but I am convinced the amount is very sizable, much more so than we are apt to think. . . .

Simultaneous and Sequential Models of Deviance

The discrimination of types of deviance may help us understand how deviant behavior originates. It will do so by enabling us to develop a sequential model of deviance, a model that allows for change through time.

---

* It should be remembered that this classification must always be used from the perspective of a given set of rules; it does not take into account the complexities, already discussed, that appear when there is more than one set of rules available for use by the same people in defining the same act. Furthermore, the classification has reference to types of behavior rather than types of people, to acts rather than personalities. The same person's behavior can obviously be conforming in some activities, deviant in others.

But before discussing the model itself, let us consider the differences between a sequential model and a simultaneous model in the development of individual behavior.

First of all, let us note that almost all research in deviance deals with the kind of question that arises from viewing it as pathological. That is, research attempts to discover the "etiology" of the "disease." It attempts to discover the causes of unwanted behavior.

This search is typically undertaken with the tools of multivariate analysis. The techniques and tools used in social research invariably contain a theoretical as well as a methodological commitment, and such is the case here. Multivariate analysis assumes (even though its users may in fact know better) that all the factors which operate to produce the phenomenon under study operate simultaneously. It seeks to discover which variable or what combination of variables will best "predict" the behavior one is studying. Thus, a study of juvenile delinquency may attempt to discover whether it is the intelligence quotient, the area in which a child lives, whether or not he comes from a broken home, or a combination of these factors that accounts for his being delinquent.

But, in fact, all causes do not operate at the same time, and we need a model which takes into account the fact that patterns of behavior *develop* in orderly sequence. In accounting for an individual's use of marihuana, [for example] we must deal with a sequence of steps, of changes in the individual's behavior and perspectives, in order to understand the phenomenon. Each step requires explanation, and what may operate as a cause at one step in the sequence may be of negligible importance at another step. We need, for example, one kind of explanation of how a person comes to be in a situation where marihuana is easily available to him, and another kind of explanation of why, given the fact of its availability, he is willing to experiment with it in the first place. And we need still another explanation of why, having experimented with it, he continues to use it. In a sense, each explanation constitutes a necessary cause of the behavior. That is, no one could become a confirmed marihuana user without going through each step. He must have the drug available, experiment with it, and continue to use it. The explanation of each step is thus part of the explanation of the resulting behavior.

Yet the variables which account for each step may not, taken separately, distinguish between users and nonusers. The variable which disposes a person to take a particular step may not operate because he has not yet reached the stage in the process where it is possible to take that step. Let us suppose, for example, that one of the steps in the formation of an habitual pattern of drug use—willingness to experiment with use of the drug—is really the result of a variable of personality or personal orientation such as alienation from conventional norms. The variable of personal alienation, however, will only produce drug use in people who are in a position to experiment because they participate in groups in which drugs are available; alienated people who do not have drugs available to them cannot begin experimentation and thus cannot become users, no matter how alienated they are. Thus alienation might be a necessary cause of drug use, but distinguish between users and nonusers only at a particular stage in the process.

A useful conception in developing sequential models of various kinds of deviant behavior is that of *career*. Originally developed in studies of occupations, the concept refers to the sequence of movements from one position to another in an occupational system made by any individual who works in that system. Furthermore, it includes the notion of "career contingency," those factors on which mobility from one position to another depends. Career contingencies include both objective facts of social structure and changes in the perspectives, motivations, and desires of the individual. Ordinarily, in the study of occupations, we use the concept to distinguish between those who have a "successful" career (in whatever terms success is defined within the occupation) and those who do not. It can also be used to distinguish several varieties of career outcomes, ignoring the question of "success."

The model can easily be transformed for use in the study of deviant careers. In so transforming it, we should not confine our interest to those who follow a career that leads them into ever-increasing deviance, to those who ultimately take on an extremely deviant identity and way of life. We should also consider those who have a more fleeting contact with deviance, whose careers lead them away from it into conventional ways of life. Thus, for example, studies of delinquents who fail to become adult criminals might teach us even more than studies of delinquents who progress in crime. . . .

Deviant Careers

The first step in most deviant careers is the commission of a nonconforming act, an act that breaks some particular set of rules. How are we to account for the first step?. . . .

In analyzing cases of intended nonconformity, people usually ask about motivation: why does the person want to do the deviant thing he does? The question assumes that the basic difference between deviants and those who conform lies in the character of their motivation. Many theories have been propounded to explain why some people have deviant motivations and others do not. Psychological theories find the cause of deviant motivations and acts in the individual's early experiences, which produce unconscious needs that must be satisfied if the individual is to maintain his equilibrium. Sociological theories look for socially structured sources of "strain" in the society, social positions which have conflicting demands placed upon them such that the individual seeks an illegitimate way of solving the problems his position presents him with. (Merton's (1957) famous theory of anomie fits into this category.)

But the assumption on which these approaches are based may be entirely false. There is no reason to assume that only those who finally commit a deviant act actually have the impulse to do so. It is much more likely that most people experience deviant impulses frequently. At least in fantasy, people are much more deviant than they appear. Instead of asking why deviants want to do things that are disapproved of, we might better ask why conventional people do not follow through on the deviant impulses they have.

Something of an answer to this question may be found in the process of commitment through which the "normal" person becomes progressively involved in conventional institutions and behavior. In speaking of commitment, I refer to the process through which several kinds of interests become bound up with carrying out certain lines of behavior to which they seem formally extraneous. What happens is that the individual, as a consequence of actions he has taken in the past or the operation of various institutional routines, finds he must adhere to certain lines of behavior, because many other activities than the one he is immediately engaged in will be adversely affected if he does not. The middle-class youth must not quit school because his occupational future depends on receiving a certain amount of schooling. The conventional person must not indulge his interests in narcotics, for example, because much more than the pursuit of immediate pleasure is involved; his job, his family, and his reputation in his neighborhood may seem to him to depend on his continuing to avoid temptation.

In fact, the normal development of people in our society (and probably in any society) can be seen as a series of progressively increasing commitments to conventional norms and institutions. The "normal" person, when he discovers a deviant impulse in himself, is able to check that impulse by thinking of the manifold consequences acting on it would produce for him. He has staked too much on continuing to be normal to allow himself to be swayed by unconventional impulses.

This suggests that in looking at cases of intended nonconformity we must ask how the person manages to avoid the impact of conventional commitments. He may do so in one of two ways. First of all, in the course of growing up the person may somehow have avoided entangling alliances with conventional society. He may, thus, be free to follow his impulses. The person who does not have a reputation to maintain or a conventional job he must keep may follow his impulses. He has nothing staked on continuing to appear conventional.

However, most people remain sensitive to conventional codes of conduct and must deal with their sensitivities in order to engage in a deviant act for the first time. Sykes and Matza (1957) have suggested that delinquents actually feel strong impulses to be law-abiding, and deal with them by techniques of neutralization: "justifications for deviance that are seen as valid by the delinquent but not by the legal system or society at large.". . .

One of the most crucial steps in the process of building a stable pattern of deviant behavior is likely to be the experience of being caught and publicly labelled as a deviant. Whether a person takes this step or not depends not so much on what he does as on what other people do, on whether or not they enforce the rule he has violated. Although I will consider the circumstances under which enforcement takes place in some detail later, two notes are in order here. First of all, even though no one else discovers the nonconformity or enforces the rules against it, the individual who has committed the impropriety may himself act as enforcer. He may brand himself as deviant because of what he has done and punish himself in one way or another for his behavior. This is not always or necessarily the case, but may occur. Second, there may be cases like those described by psychoanalysts in which the individual really wants to get caught and perpetrates his deviant act in such a way that it is almost sure he will be.

In any case, being caught and branded as deviant has important consequences for one's further social participation and self-image. The most important consequence is a drastic change in the individual's public identity. Committing the improper act and being publicly caught at it place him in a new status. He has been revealed as a different kind of person from the kind he was supposed to be. He is labelled a "fairy," "dope fiend," "nut" or "lunatic," and treated accordingly. . . .

To be labelled a criminal one need only commit a single criminal offense, and this is all the term formally refers to. Yet the word carries a number of connotations specifying auxiliary traits characteristic of anyone bearing the label. A man who has been convicted of housebreaking and thereby labelled criminal is presumed to be a person likely to break into other houses; the police, in rounding up known offenders for investigation after a crime has been committed, operate on this premise. Further, he is considered likely to commit other kinds of crimes as well, because he has shown himself to be a person without "respect for the law." Thus, apprehension for one deviant act exposes a person to the likelihood that he will be regarded as deviant or undesirable in other respects.

In analyzing the consequences of assuming a deviant identity let us make use of Hughes (1945) distinction between master and subordinate statuses. Some statuses, in our society as in others, override all other statuses and have a certain priority. Race is one of these. Membership in the Negro race, as socially defined, will override most other status considerations in most other situations; the fact that one is a physician or middle-class or female will not protect one from being treated as a Negro first and any of these other things second. The status of deviant (depending on the kind of deviance) is this kind of master status. One receives the status as a result of breaking a rule, and the identification proves to be more important than most others. One will be identified as a deviant first, before other identifications are made. The question is raised: "What kind of person would break such an important rule?" And the answer is given: "One who is different from the rest of us, who cannot or will not act as a moral human being and therefore might break other important rules." The deviant identification becomes the controlling one.

Treating a person as though he were generally rather than specifically deviant produces a self-fulfilling prophecy. It sets in motion several mechanisms which conspire to shape the person in the image people have of him (Ray, 1961). In the first place, one tends to be cut off, after being identified as deviant, from participation in more conventional groups, even though the specific consequences of the particular deviant activity might never of themselves have caused the isolation had there not also been the public knowledge and reaction to it. For example, being a homosexual may not affect one's ability to do office work, but to be known as a homosexual in an office may make it impossible to continue working there. Similarly, though the effects of opiate drugs may not impair one's working ability, to be known as an addict will probably lead to losing one's job. In such cases, the individual finds it difficult to conform to other rules which he had no intention or desire to break, and perforce finds himself deviant in these areas as well. The homosexual who is deprived of a "respectable" job by the discovery of his deviance may drift into unconventional, marginal occupations where it does not make so much difference. The drug addict finds himself forced into other illegitimate kinds of activity, such as robbery and theft, by the refusal of respectable employers to have him around.

When the deviant is caught, he is treated in accordance with the popular diagnosis of why he is that way, and the treatment itself may likewise produce increasing deviance. The drug addict, popularly considered to be a weak-willed individual who cannot forego the indecent pleasures afforded him by opiates, is treated repressively. He is forbidden to use drugs. Since he cannot get drugs legally, he must get them illegally. This forces the market underground and pushes the price of drugs up far beyond the current legitimate market price into a bracket that few can afford on an ordinary salary. Hence the treatment of the addict's deviance places him in a position where it will probably be necessary to resort to deceit and crime in order to support his habit. The behavior is a consequence of the public reaction to the deviance rather than a consequence of the inherent qualities of the deviant act.

Put more generally, the point is that the treatment of deviants denies them the ordinary means of carrying on the routines of everyday life open to most people. Because of this denial, the deviant must of necessity develop illegitimate routines. The influence of public reaction may be direct, as in the instances considered above, or indirect, a consequence of the integrated character of the society in which the deviant lives. . . .

Ray (1961) has shown, in the case of drug addicts, how difficult it can be to reverse a deviant cycle. He points out that drug addicts frequently attempt to cure themselves and that the motivation underlying their attempts is an effort to show nonaddicts whose opinions they respect that they are really not as bad as they are thought to be. On breaking their habit successfully, they find, to their dismay, that people still treat them as though they were addicts (on the premise, apparently, of "once a junkie, always a junkie").

A final step in the career of a deviant is movement into an organized deviant group. When a person makes a definite move into an organized group—or when he realizes and accepts the fact that he has already done so—it has a powerful impact on his conception of himself. A drug addict once told me that the moment she felt she was really "hooked" was when she realized she no longer had any friends who were not drug addicts. . . .

Deviance and Enterprise: A Summary

Deviance—in the sense I have been using it, of publicly labelled wrongdoing—is always the result of enterprise. Before any act can be viewed as deviant, and before any class of people can be labelled and treated as outsiders for committing the act, someone must have made the rule which defines the act as deviant. Rules are not made automatically. Even though a practice may be harmful in an objective sense to the group in which it occurs, the harm needs to be discovered and pointed out. People must be made to feel that something ought to be done about it. Someone must call the public's attention to these matters, supply the push necessary to get things done, and direct such energies as are aroused in the proper direction to get a rule created. Deviance is the product of enterprise in the largest sense; without the enterprise required to get rules made, the deviance which consists of breaking the rule could not exist.

Deviance is the product of enterprise in the smaller and more particular sense as well. Once a rule has come into existence, it must be applied to particular people before the abstract class of outsiders created by the rule can be peopled. Offenders must be discovered, identified, apprehended and convicted (or noted as "different" and stigmatized for their nonconformity, as in the case of legal deviant groups such as dance musicians). This job ordinarily falls to the lot of professional enforcers who, by enforcing already existing rules, create the particular deviants society views as outsiders.

It is an interesting fact that most scientific research and speculation on deviance concerns itself with the people who break rules rather than with those who make and enforce them. If we are to achieve a full understanding of deviant behavior, we must get these two possible foci of inquiry into balance. We must see deviance, and the outsiders who personify the abstract conception, as a consequence of a process of interaction between people, some of whom in the service of their own interests make and enforce rules which catch others who, in the service of their own interests, have committed acts which are labelled deviant.

REFERENCES

Cohen, Albert K. and Short, James F. "Juvenile Delinquency," in R. K. Merton and R. A. Nisbet (Eds.), *Contemporary Social Problems.* New York: Harcourt, Brace & World, Inc., 1966.

Davis, James F. "Crime News in Colorado Newspapers," *American Journal of Sociology.* **56** (1952), pp. 325-330.

Garfinkel, Harold. "Research Notes on Inter- and Intra-Racial Homocide," *Social Forces,* **27** (1949), pp. 369-381.

Hughes, Everett C. "Dilemmas and Contradictions of Status," *American Journal of Sociology,* **50** (1945), pp. 335-359.

Merton, Robert K. *Social Theory and Social Structure.* New York: The Free Press of Glencoe, 1957.

Ray, Marsh. "The Cycle of Abstinence and Relapse Among Heroin Addicts," *Social Problems,* **9** (1961), pp. 132-140.

Sutherland, Edwin. "White Collar Criminality," *American Sociological Review,* **5** (1940), pp. 1-12.

Sykes, Gresham M. and Matza, David. "Techniques of Neutralization: A Theory of Delinquency," *American Sociological Review,* **22** (1957), pp. 667-669.

Vincent, Clark. *Unmarried Mothers.* New York: Free Press of Glencoe, 1961.

CHAPTER
NINE
WHAT CREATES
PERSONAL COMMITMENT
TO GROUPS AND ORGANIZATIONS?

THE ISSUE OF ALIENATION

"Central to alienation," Keniston writes, "is a deep and pervasive mistrust of any and all commitments, be they to other people, to groups, to American culture, or even to the self." Listen to the expression of this stance in these quotations from college students:

> "Emotional commitments to others are usually the prelude to disillusion and disappointment."

> " 'Teamwork' is the last refuge of mediocrity."

> "The whole idea of 'taking an active part in the life of the community' leaves me cold."

> "Of course there will be a war eventually. Very eventually. I'll let it bother me then.
> In my lifetime trees will get scarce.
> I would like to see more trees."

> "People by and large appear fairly stupid to me. I meet very few people whom I consider as having any insight into life. . . Under 'insight into life' I might list: the fact of life's ultimate futility, the stupidity of taking any small area of life and its activities as being more important than any other, the ability to see more than one side of everything."

> "For myself, society and others can go to Hell. If they have something worthwhile to say, I'll listen, but most often society has only a mold to force you into, destroying rather than creating."

> "I am also very intolerant, both of people and social, political, and business organizations. Without giving reasons, I shall name such things as student councils, the military, narrow-minded people, and 99% of life in America" (Keniston, 1965, p. 56-58, 66, 73).

And in these quotations from workers:

> "It's one of the most cutthroat places I ever worked in. I mean there's no sense of cooperation whatsoever. Everybody's looking out for Number One, and it's hard for me to work under these conditions. . . Standard will spend $20 with a time-study engineer on your back to save two cents. Well, it's that kind of place. So, when you work in that kind of place, you see, everybody has the same idea—get as much as he can, and the hell with the other guy."

> "We don't have time to visit, you might say. You can't leave your machine. That is, you could, to take care of yourself, but other than that, to go around visiting—no—they wouldn't allow that" (Lane, 1962, pp. 237-38).

Contrast this stance with the underlying attitude in these quotations, first from students:

> "It was only when I first began to do my first political activity which was—I can't remember, a boycott or peace work or something—but I really started to move personally. I started to put my mind to a project, an activity, a way of thinking. I really started to work hard in terms of learning how to do that stuff. . . I really put my personality into it. That's what I've been doing ever since."

> "The politics came after the people. There was always a personal relationship first."

> "My old man is very straight with the kids. That's been very important, because it has kept in the back of my mind all the time concepts like responsibility, seriousness: 'If you're going to work on this, you can't just do it on weekends.' I have this whole complex of ideas about carrying through with what you start, being serious about it, being confident about it. . . That kind of thing was in the back of my mind, nagging at me: 'You're not involved, you're not doing anything.' "

> "I still think I eventually want to go to graduate school. But I can see that I'm also becoming increasingly—I'm getting sucked into more full-time political involvement. I'm not sure I want to let that happen. . . For a while earlier this year, I had very little to do with political stuff. I really worked and read. I escaped and got lost in reading, and I enjoyed it for a while. And then I started listening to the radio, 'Another fifty thousand troops going to Vietnam,' and I would say, 'What the fuck am I reading this for. I've got to get back into some group.'. . . I don't want to neglect my studies and I don't want to neglect my social responsibilities, which means that you get very little sleep."

> "I've taken a lot of shit for the work I've done. When I was a kid, there were family problems, and then later, for being involved in Movement things. But I wouldn't trade it. It just seems to me that I have had what I consider great fortune—to grow up with the people I grew up with, and the situations I did, with the perceptions I have, and with the feelings that I have. I still feel very proud of the fact that I can cry, that things really dig me up inside, that I can cry when I'm happy" (Keniston, 1968, pp. 26-30, 38-43).

And from workers:

"It's an easy place to work in, y'know what I mean? The people who run it, they're easy going. We don't have any special time to smoke or have coffee—we do that anytime we want; we go down to the locker room. Of course, on my job, I'm responsible for it, so y'know, I have to be a little more on the ball than the other guys."

"I feel this fella's been doin' all right by me. . . this fella's got no pressure on top. I mean he leaves me alone. He'll set me on a job, and that's it."

"I feel lucky. I've found something that I'm suited for. Like the first box shop I ever went to, well, I learned how to run the machines in no time at all. . . I know quite a bit about the job; I know quite a bit about the machinery. Seems like I picked a lot of knowledge up; more—a lot more—than a lotta fellows been working there a lot longer than I have. Maybe it's because I take an interest in it, y'know? I mean a lotta fellows, their machine breaks down and y'know, you call a mechanic over. . . So a lotta guys will just take off and when it's fixed they'll come back. But I was never like that, y'know. I stick around and find out what's gotta be fixed. . . That's why I learned quite a bit more about a machine than a lotta fellows have" (Lane, 1962, pp. 233, 235, 243).

The first set of individuals express an emotional distance from other people, from groups, from collective effort, from organizations—in some cases, from life itself. They are uncommitted. The second group, although they may be highly critical of many aspects of organized social life, are involved in it. There are groups and organizations that they care about, feel part of, are motivated to participate in. There are some collective efforts for which they are ready to give of themselves if the need arises, groups for which they are willing to make personal sacrifices.

Commitment has both an attitudinal and a behavioral component. As an attitude, it is expressed in strong positive feelings about some groups, a feeling of being part of them and sharing their misfortunes and triumphs. As a behavior, it is expressed in actions which may involve personal sacrifices in the interest of group objectives, actions which share the burdens of membership as well as the benefits.

What produces this commitment to groups and organizations? Why do some individuals plunge into social life while others stand back and watch, detached? Why do individuals become committed to some groups and organizations and not others? What is it in a situation that operates to increase such commitments and what operates to diminish them?

THE MAJOR VIEWS

Interpersonal Trust

Commitment, in this first view, begins in the home. The key element is the ability to trust others, an ability that is impaired in some by a childhood that belies such a faith. Learning in some fundamental way that they cannot count on others to fulfill their basic emotional needs, they also learn to hold themselves back. He who invests nothing can lose nothing. And so, with an armor they have erected for the perils of family life, they march forth into the rest of organized social life.

Keniston, in the selection reprinted here, describes how the alienated characterize their fathers, emphasizing "qualities like detachment, reserve, inability to express affection, loneliness, and withdrawal from the center of the family." The fathers are men who, in spite of public success, are "failures in their own eyes, . . . disappointed, frustrated, and disillusioned. "

The mothers, in contrast, are vivid figures whose marriage has involved a renunciation and sacrifice. "To their sons," Keniston writes, "these women appear to have been talented, artistic, intense, and intelligent girls who gave up promise and fulfillment for marriage." Alienated students "often wonder aloud 'whether marriage was worth it' to their mothers."

The fundamental source of alienation, in this view, is in the incapacity of the individual. It is his armor that shuts out the opportunities that the world provides. Such a view invites the criticism that it is reductionist, that in emphasizing the personal history of the alienated, one is ignoring the alienating aspects of the society in which the individual operates.

No doubt there are versions of this view in which the person-society interaction is ignored, but Keniston, in particular, is very sensitive to this issue and has an especially ingenious way to meet it while keeping his basic paradigm intact. Since Keniston's personal stance toward society is a critical one, he is hardly likely to fall into the trap of seeing the uncommitted as maladjusted individuals who have failed to come to proper terms with an essentially benign social order.

Thus protected, he avoids the trap by discovering that there are other critical stances available. The critical and uncommitted can be contrasted with those who are both critical and committed. Since these other students are, like the alienated, critical of existing social institutions, it is not to the society as it exists that they give allegiance. Rather, they respond to the "alienating" aspects of society by committing themselves in various ways to movements for social change and to the groups and organizations that comprise such movements.

Thus, the alienated stance is only one of two possible and distinct varieties of dissent and cannot be understood by reference to the faults of social institutions, however real these may be. And in subsequent work on student "radicals," Keniston (1968) shows a childhood and personal history of the movement activist that is very different from that of the uncommitted described here.

Clearly the society is making a contribution to the production of the uncommitted, but the active dynamic element in this view is in the developmental history of the alienated. The society around them will determine the form such alienation will take— a return to nature, an experimentation with drugs, a flirtation with mystical religious movements, or whatever promises to answer the quest for community which the alienated seek. But the burden of loneliness that the individual carries remains his inheritance from a childhood that failed to provide the capacity for meaningful personal commitments.

Organizational Attraction

Give a person certain fundamental things in a social situation and he will become committed to his role in it. His personal history in this view, may affect the rapidity with which he makes or withdraws commitment, but the active, dynamic element is in the intrinsic characteristics of the organization. If it meets basic human needs, it will receive allegiance in return; if it fails to, it may gain people's compliance—their willingness to carry out tasks for external rewards or to avoid punishments—but it will not produce commitment in the sense we are using it here.

People may do their jobs without being committed. The behavioral test of commitment comes when they are asked to do more than usual—to be willing to give freely of their time and energy on occasions of special need. Lacking such a commitment, they expect time and a half for overtime.

What is it in a social situation that produces such commitment? We will focus, as Blauner does in the selection included here, on the organization of work. In doing so, we honor a century old concern with the alienating characteristics of modern industry, a tradition that has its roots in the early writings of Marx. But as a paradigm of commitment, the argument can be extended to any other situation involving collective effort —to participation in a political party, for example.

Blauner singles out four central attributes of the work situation which, if present, can be expected to generate commitment. The first centers on the powerlessness theme. If workers feel that they are unable to control the conditions under which they work, they will tend to develop a sense of alienation. Most central to this feeling, in Blauner's argument, is control over the immediate characteristics of the work situation—control over the rhythm and pace of the work. "You can't leave your machine," complains the worker quoted in the introduction. "We don't have any special time to smoke or have coffee. We do that anytime we want," says another worker with much more positive feelings about his job.

The second attribute focuses on meaninglessness. A sense of purpose in one's job contributes to commitment; a lack of it produces the opposite. Responsibility is intimately connected with this sense of purpose, as Blauner points out. "He'll set me on a job and that's it," says one worker with positive feelings toward his job. "Of course, on my job I'm responsible for it, y'know, I have to be a little more on the ball than the other guys," says another worker with similar feelings.

The third attribute focuses on social isolation. The person who feels a sense of camaraderie with fellow workers, who works cooperatively with others, who enjoys and finds opportunities for informal interaction and friendship with fellow workers will tend to be more committed than one who works in a setting which is structured to prevent the development of a network of social relations. " 'Teamwork' is the last refuge of mediocrity," says one of the uncommitted students quoted in the introduction. But its absence is a source of unhappiness to the worker who says, "I mean, there's no sense of cooperation whatsoever. Everybody's looking out for Number One, and it's hard for me to work under these conditions." "The politics came after the people," says a committed, politically active student.

The final attribute involves the self-estrangement theme. Work activity can be a means of personal self-expression rather than simply a means to an external reward— the paycheck. To the extent that it isn't, individuals will feel a distance from what they are doing, a heightened sense of time. Immersion in the present is characteristic of work which, by offering an intrinsic means of personal expression, leads to commitment. "I really put my personality into it," says a student about his political work. "I know quite a bit about the machinery, . . . I stick around and find out what's gotta be fixed," says one worker with pride.

These elements, then, determine whether a work situation is basically committing or alienating. Individuals, of course, bring different things to it and may respond in varying degrees, but this view directs our understanding to social organization rather than personal organization. The question becomes one of determining what specifically produces a sense of control, purpose, social integration, and personal self-expression; how do these factors interact with each other to produce commitment or its opposite.

A complaint about not being able to leave one's machine may seem trivial and unimportant if lifted out of context. It is a virtue of this perspective that it helps us to see such a complaint as a symptom of a much more fundamental situation—the inability to control the pace of one's work and to see this situation, in turn, as a central part of what produces personal commitment.

Side-Bets

In the views presented thus far, the sentiment is father to the act. The commitment process operates by the development of strong positive feelings and these increase one's willingness to make sacrifices for groups in which one believes. This final view reverses the order: one becomes committed through behavior, and then, psychological processes operate to bring attitudes into line.

The process runs like this. An individual undertakes something for a set of direct reasons. For example, he takes a job because he likes the work, the prestige, and the pay, and because it seems the best available to him at the time. Or, he marries a woman because he loves and admires her. Both of these acts involve a primary commitment—he undertakes direct obligations toward his job and his wife.

However, he now finds that he has made a series of what Becker, in the selection here, calls "side-bets." In particular, there are two types of side-bets, which Becker does not distinguish clearly, but which are implicit in his argument. The first type of side-bet involves a series of investments that an individual makes. In order to gain the rewards of membership in some group or organization, it is frequently necessary for the individual to put in energy, time, or other resources. Life is such that these investments must typically be made in advance of collecting the rewards. For example, a person might spend years preparing for a profession before he or she reaps the benefit of practicing it. The protection of the prior investment provides a secondary motivation for remaining in a situation that one would not choose if starting fresh. The investment represents his dues; having paid his dues, he continues rather than beginning again in some new situation where a fresh set of dues are required. Investments already made represent a kind of bet that one will continue because they are lost if one leaves.

There is a second, less obvious type of side-bet, although here the usage of the term seems more forced. When a person enters an enduring relationship, he undertakes in addition to direct obligations, a series of diffuse, unspecified, secondary obligations—the fine print in his unwritten contract. His job, for example, may call for him to conform to a lot of bureaucratic regulations that were never discussed or thought about when he decided to take the position. In his marriage, he may find that his wife has a profligate brother-in-law who needs to be bailed out of jail and he is under some obligation to do this. He has married no mere woman but a whole package of social relationships.

In fact, this view suggests, almost all commitments are of this open-ended sort; that is the basic nature of the process. We agree to something and we know—or, at least, we ought to know—that as part of the agreement, we may be asked to do some things the exact nature of which cannot be spelled out in detail in advance. The more specified such obligations are, the fewer side-bets of this type are involved. But virtually any agreement involving an enduring relationship carries with it some diffuse unspecified obligations.

The question remains why the individual feels he should honor such obligations. Note that the answer cannot be merely that he fears some punishment for failing to carry them out—for example, that he would lose his job if he didn't do what was expected. We would not describe him as committed unless he felt some sense of *duty* to carry out what may, at times, be unpleasant obligations involving some personal sacrifice or risk.

The answer is more implicit than explicit in Becker. To feel committed in such a situation, a person must feel that he has voluntarily agreed to a package of obligations of which the unpleasant ones are part. A responsible person keeps his promise—for self-respect and the respect of others. Thus, a person feels committed if he shares both a general cultural belief in the importance of keeping one's word *and* the belief that the specific thing being asked is a legitimate part of the general obligation he has undertaken. It is as if he thinks, "This is unpleasant but it's part of the job. I agreed to take the job and it wouldn't be right for me to shift the burdens to someone else." Or, in the case of the brother-in-law, he may think, "My wife is right in feeling that she has to help her brother. One should help one's family regardless of whether they deserve it or not. When I married her, I accepted a share of her obligations as part of the package."

There is no intention here to argue that people will always in fact feel committed and will always honor their obligations. They may rationalize their inaction by claiming that what is asked is not legitimate—that it is not in the unwritten contract to which they agreed. Or they may agree that they have an obligation, but find it so unpleasant that they present apologies and extenuating circumstances instead of fulfilling it. What is being offered here is an explanation of the pressures people feel to honor obligations, not an argument that the force of these pressures will always or typically overwhelm counter-forces to avoid unpleasant duties. What's noteworthy is that people experience such a commitment, not only with respect to the things they have specifically agreed to, but also with other, secondary obligations as well. And the pressure comes from a generalized side-bet that covers every voluntary agreement—the bet that one will keep one's promises, even implicit ones.

There are, then, these two kinds of side-bets: the bet implicit in making investments that one can't get back, and the generalized bet that one is a person who can be counted on to meet his or her obligations. Either of these can be entered into with varying degrees of awareness of just what one is committing oneself to. A man may be aware of such fine print as the profligate brother-in-law and still sign the marriage contract. One may know that once he has accepted a new job and moved with his family to another city, it will be no simple matter to change his mind. Or, more likely, such side-bets may be out of one's field of vision until, sometime later, something occurs to make them newly salient.

Since side-bets are typically of low salience compared to the primary reasons which lead one to enter a situation, this view of commitment carries with it an implication of commitment by drift. It is true that the individual by his own actions has gotten himself into the situation, but it is also true that typically he didn't quite know what he was getting into. He has acquired a good part of his commitment rather than sought it. The student quoted in the introduction who says, "I'm getting sucked into more full-time political involvement. I'm not sure I want to let that happen," is expressing this process at work.

We find, then, that individuals often remain in situations that are not especially rewarding compared to alternatives, and voluntarily carry out onerous and unpleasant obligations. They do so because they have become committed through a process of side-bets, typically made without forethought. These side-bets keep them operating because they don't want to sacrifice the heavy investments which they've already made or be untrustworthy promise breakers.

We must now face an issue that it has been convenient to avoid until now. Becker uses the term "commitment" in a more limited way than we are using it here. He is speaking of commitment as consistency in behavior—as sticking to something. But we have included in it an attitudinal and behavioral component—strong positive feelings as well as actions which share burdens.

There is little problem as far as the behavioral definition is concerned. Clearly, one does not need the concept to explain why people continue to stick to things that they find pleasurable and rewarding. Thus, Becker shares with us a concern for explaining what produces a willingness to shoulder burdens or make sacrifices. However, he is unconcerned with the other side of the commitment—the production of positive feelings. To make this comparable to our other views, we must add this component to Becker. We can do so by drawing on a social psychological tradition which emphasizes the psychological forces that bring attitudes and behavior into balance.

"It is a frequent observation," Aronson and Mills write (1959), "that persons who go through a great deal of trouble or pain to attain something tend to value it more highly than persons who attain the same thing with a minimum of effort." And so they reason, "individuals who go through a severe initiation to gain admission to a club or organization should tend to think more highly of that organization than those who do not go through the severe initiation to gain admission." They proceeded to test this idea with an experiment in which subjects who underwent a severe initiation did indeed perceive the group as being more attractive than did those who underwent a mild initiation or no initiation.

The mechanism invoked to explain this phenomenon is a need for cognitive consistency.* People don't want to feel that they have invested something for no good reason. So, once they have voluntarily made a sacrifice or investment, they have a psychological stake in discovering that it was worth it. If they are not getting a great deal, they could decide that they haven't really invested much, but this may

---

* See Chapter 6.

be difficult to do if their initiation into a group involves, for example, years of preparation and study. Frequently, a better method of achieving consistency is to raise their estimate of the value of what they are getting. They can do this easily enough by selective attention to positive features, ignoring or downgrading unpleasant aspects.

The bigger our investments in joining and the freer our decision to join, then the more likely we are to discover that the group or organization we belong to is "pretty damned good." It has to be, if we chose to join and invested so much. If we don't convince ourselves of this, we must live with the painful knowledge that we have wasted and sacrificed needlessly and unwisely. Thus, this psychological process works in tandem with the process of side-bets to produce commitment—including both strong positive feelings and sacrifices. Side-bets commit us behaviorally; the drive for consistency pulls our attitudes along.

CONTRASTING THE VIEWS OF ALIENATION

These ways of looking at the commitment process can be contrasted by examining their treatment of three issues:

1. Where is the primary locus of explanation in the commitment transaction?
2. What is the primary benefit that the individual realizes in becoming committed?
3. Do attitudes or behavior take priority in the commitment process?

Primary Locus of Explanation

Any view of commitment must recognize it as a transaction between the individual and the groups and organization he encounters. Commitment involves a push and a pull—an individual with characteristics that produce (or fail to produce) the push, and situations and social organizations that produce (or fail to produce) the pull. It is possible in the explanation to make either element in the transaction the dynamic one.

In the interpersonal trust paradigm, the differing capacities of individuals are given center stage. Some individuals have and others lack the ability to make meaningful commitments to a variety of groups and organizations. The push side of the equation is made problematic. In the organizational attraction view, the pull side becomes the issue; individuals with varying capacities are simply a given. Some organizations have and others lack the ability to induce meaningful commitments on the part of a variety of individuals.

Finally, the side-bets paradigm also puts emphasis on the pull side although the focus is more on the process than on the structural characteristics of organizations that invite commitment. The capacities of the individuals involved are not called into question. They encounter situations which, in varying degrees, pull them into commitments, usually with only partial awareness on their part.

Primary Benefit

If commitment is a transaction, then the individual must be both giving something and getting something. If he is willing to make sacrifices, presumably he receives something in return. This something need not be material or tangible, but it must provide a motivation for the sacrifices he makes. In the contrasting views, what are the benefits an individual derives in becoming committed?

In the interpersonal trust view, a committed individual gains community—a sense that he shares important goals and values with others and can count on them. The committed individual can rely on a community in times of crisis and know that he will receive needed support. In the organizational attraction paradigm, the individual gains the fulfillment of basic personal needs—needs which all individuals share to some degree. More specifically, he is able to fulfill personal needs for autonomy, responsibility, social affiliation, and self-expression. In the side-bets view, the individual receives the security of protecting the time, energy, and resources he has invested and the mental harmony of knowing that he has invested wisely.

Attitude-Behavior Priority

Commitment involves both attitudes and behavior but their order of appearance in the process varies in different views. For interpersonal trust and organizational attraction, the commitment process starts with the production of strong positive feelings of attachment. These then produce the motivation to action. Thus, the individual shares the burdens of membership in the groups or organizations that he really cares about.

The process is reversed in the side-bets paradigm. The individual finds himself committed in his actions. He has worked himself into a situation in which, if he continues, he must shoulder his share of the burdens of membership. But not to continue will involve the forfeiture of both the direct rewards that accrue to continuing members and the indirect rewards involved in the side-bets he has made along the way. Thus, for his peace of mind, the individual learns to care about the groups in which he has invested so much through his actions.

These then are the central issues we see running through the contrasting views of commitment and alienation. They are summarized in Chart 9.

Chart 9 Underlying Issues on What Creates Personal Commitment to
Groups and Organizations

	Interpersonal Trust (*e.g.,* Keniston)	Organizational Attraction (*e.g.,* Blauner)	Side-Bets (*e.g.,* Becker)
Where is the primary locus of explanation?	Push from individuals	Pull from social system	Pull from situation
What is the primary benefit that the individual realizes?	Community; secure support in time of need	Fulfillment of needs for autonomy, responsibility, social affiliation, and self expression	Protection of investments and mental harmony
Do attitudes or behavior take priority?	Attitudes	Attitudes	Behavior

REFERENCES

Aronson, Elliot and Mills. Judsons, "Effect of Severity of Initiation on Liking for a Group," *The Journal of Abnormal and Social Psychology,* **59** (1959), pp. 177-81.

Lane, Robert E. *Political Ideology: Why the American Common Man Believes What He Does,* New York: The Free Press, 1962.

Keniston, Kenneth. *The Uncommitted: Alienated Youth in American Society.* New York: Harcourt, Brace, and World, 1965.

Keniston, Kenneth. *Young Radicals: Notes on Committed Youth.* New York: Harcourt, Brace, and World, 1968.

THE ALIENATED:
REJECTION OF CONVENTIONAL ADULTHOOD

KENNETH KENISTON

This essay, written in 1964, grew out of the study of the psychological origins of alienation I conducted at Harvard in the late 1950's and early 1960's. As that study progressed I began to realize that whatever the psychological similarities between alienated students, their alienation was a reaction not only to their personal pasts but to the society around them. Psychological alienation resulted from an interaction between a complex, sometimes troubled childhood, and an equally complex, even more troubled society. The essay that follows is a summary of the first part of that equation.

Were I writing about these "alienated" students today, I would emphasize two issues that I did not sufficiently appreciate at the time. First, I would stress more than I did the developmental *function of alienation, and I would view the permanent choice of an alienated position as an example of development gone awry—as the response of a growing individual to the experienced failure of his search for people, ideals, groups, and institutions that genuinely merit his commitment. Second, I would emphasize more than I did the* historical context in *which alienation unfolds and expresses itself. For in the years since this research was completed, I have worked with many other students of comparable background and psychological makeup whose behavior and professed ideology differed, for cultural and historical reasons, from those of these students. For example, had psychedelic drugs been widely available during the years this study was conducted, I think these alienated students would have been strongly drawn to them. And, in the late 1960's, students of comparable psychological outlook were often immersed in a "hippie" subculture that adopted, at least on the surface, an ideology of love, openness, and genuine relatedness, instead of an ideology of distrust and cynicism. Indeed, one can view the hippie movement in part as a kind of informal (and often effective) therapy for alienated people, a subculture that expresses the discontents of the alienated while trying to provide new, communal, and loving ways of resolving their deep mistrust and frustration.*

Whatever the limitations of this account, I think that the psychological type I defined here is an enduring type, and that its occurrence in highly industrialized societies underlies many social movements now and in the future. The particular manifestations of this kind of psychological alienation will doubtless change in the years ahead. But its underlying roots lie deep in the structure of industrialized society, and until or unless that structure is changed, we will continue to have alienated youth. . . .

In order to study alienated individuals, we must first have some reliable way of identifying them. Over a period of several years my colleagues and I developed a series of highly intercorrelated questionnaire scales that enabled us to identify extremely alienated students. In the course of this study, we were able to define thirteen related alienated outlooks. If a student held one of these outlooks, he was extremely likely to hold the rest as well; if he disagreed with one, he was likely to disagree with the rest. These attitudes constitute a kind of empirical cluster or "alienation syndrome."

Amplifying the earlier work of Henry Murray and Anthony Davids, we eventually ended with the following thirteen alienation scales: (1) distrust ("Expect the worst of others and you will avoid disappointment"); (2) pessimism ("There is little chance of ever finding real happiness"); (3) resentment ("At times, some people make you feel like killing them"); (4) egocentricity ("You will certainly be left behind if you stop too often or too long to give a helping hand to other people"); (5) anxiety ("Whether he admits it or not, every modern man is a helpless victim of one of the worst ailments of our time—neurotic anxiety"); (6) interpersonal alienation ("Emotional commitments to others are usually the prelude to disillusion and disappointment"); (7) social alienation ("Trying to cooperate with other people brings mainly strains, rivalry, and inefficiency; consequently I much prefer to work by myself"); (8) cultural alienation ("The idea of trying to adjust to society as it is now constituted fills me with horror"); (9) self-contempt ("Any man who really has known himself has had good cause to be horrified"); (10) vacillation ("I make few commitments without some inner reservation or doubt about the wisdom of undertaking the responsibility or task"); (11) subspection ("First impressions cannot be relied upon; what lies beneath the surface is often utterly different"); (12) outsider ("I feel strongly how different I am from most people, even my close friends"); (13) unstructured universe ("The notion that man and nature are governed by regular laws is an illusion based on our insatiable desire for certainty"). Together these scales constitute the empirical definition of the "alienation syndrome."

These scales enabled us to select a small group of subjects for intensive clinical study. From a large group of volunteers, eighty-three male Harvard College sophomores with satisfactory academic standing were chosen for testing and were given these alienation scales and other questionnaires. On the basis of their scores three groups were selected for intensive clinical study: (1) a highly alienated group; (2) a highly nonalienated group; and (3) a third "comparison" group of students with medium scores on alienation. Including students drawn from this group and earlier groups, eleven alienated undergraduates, ten nonalienated undergraduates, and a comparison group of a dozen students were studied. The modal alienated student was in the most alienated 8 per cent of the college population; the typical nonalienated student was in the least alienated 8 per cent; and the members of the comparison group stood very near the middle.

All of these undergraduates took part in at least one year of the research study, and most of them were studied throughout the last three years of their college careers. During this time they gave approximately two hours a week to the research, for which they were paid. The research ranged over a wide variety of topics. All students wrote a lengthy autobiography and a detailed statement of their basic values and beliefs. All were repeatedly interviewed about matters autobiographical, ideological, vocational, ethical, and experimental. All took the 'Thematic Apperception Test' (T.A.T.), a test of fantasy in which students make up imaginative stories to twenty ambiguous pictures. In addition, all of the research subjects took part in a great variety of other specific psychological experiments. By the end of the three-year period, large amounts of information had been collected about almost every aspect of the individual's life.

The clinical study of alienation focused on the following questions:

1. What is the ideology of alienation as seen in these students? Written statements of basic values, interview material, and added questionnaire material helped answer this question.

2. What common characteristics of behavior and life style do these alienated students possess? Systematic studies of behavior in experimental groups, interview materials, and informal observations of the students in college helped answer this question.

3. What features of past life (infancy, family characteristics, childhood, adolescence) do these alienated students share? Written autobiographies and interviews provided most of the data here.

4. What are the central features of the fantasy life of alienated students? The T.A.T., reports of fantasies and dreams, and imaginative productions like poems, short stories, plays, and drawings were the basis for efforts to answer this question.

5. What hypotheses can be advanced that might explain the psychological basis of alienation? Here I sought for interpretations and hypotheses that might enable me to construct a coherent explanation of how alienation develops within the individual.

In an attempt to answer these questions the case records of each student were first studied independently. Then alienated students were systematically contrasted with the nonalienated and with the comparison group. In certain respects, of course, all three groups were similar; for example, all students in all three groups were intelligent and academically oriented, and most were from relatively privileged social backgrounds. But in the account to follow I will emphasize only those characteristics of the alienated students which were not found to the same degree among the nonalienated or the comparison group.

The Ideology of Alienation

Statistical studies had suggested that distrust was a primary variable in the alienation syndrome. Clinical investigations confirmed this finding. For alienated students distrust extends far beyond a low view of human nature; they also believe that intimacy ends in disillusion, that attachment to a group entails the loss of individuality, and that all appearances are untrustworthy. Nor can American culture be trusted: it is mechanical, boring, trashy, cheap, conformist, and dull. Any kind of positive commitment is viewed negatively: life is such that the alienated can never be sure of anything; every choice precludes equally desirable alternatives.

In addition, most alienated students are native existentialists. Few of them, when they began the research study, had read existentialist philosophers; yet they had often spontaneously arrived at a view of the world close to that of the most pessimistic existentialists like Sartre. And when later in their college careers they read such writers, it was usually with a sense of *déjà vu*. From middle adolescence on, alienated students had become increasingly aware of the darkness, isolation, and meaninglessness of life. The human condition as they had come to see it provides the basis for universal anxiety. The universe itself is dead, lacking in structure, inherently unpredictable and random. Individual life, too, is devoid of purpose and preordained form. Consequently, any meaning or truth that an individual finds is inevitably subjective and solipsistic. The "truth" that one man creates is not necessarily that of his fellows; and in writing about their "philosophies of life," the alienated stress that these are merely expressions of subjective and arbitrary belief. Morality, too, is seen as inevitably egocentric, arbitrary, and individualistic. Given the unpredictability of the future, long-range ethical idealism is impossible; the present becomes overwhelmingly important. Alienated students are usually moral "realists," who see immediate feeling, mood, and pleasure as the only possible guidelines for action.

Alienated undergraduates do not react stoically to this view of the world. On the contrary, their response is scorn, bitterness, and anger. Love and hate, they insist, are inseparable. Their own hostilities and resentment are close to awareness, and their scorn is especially intense when they confront those who are not alienated. They do not suffer fools gladly, and they consider most of their fellows fools. Indeed, their anger is so corrosive that it extends even to themselves. True to the logic of their position, they maintain that the consequences of self-knowledge are self-contempt and are quick to admit their own self-revulsion. Similarly, their resentment is expressed in their conviction that all men inevitably use each other for their own purposes, whatever their altruistic rationalizations.

Much of the explicit philosophy of these students is negative. They are, like Nietzsche (one of their favorite writers), philosophers with hammers, whose favorite intellectual sport is exposing the hypocrisy of others. They distrust all positive thinking and therefore find it almost impossible to agree with any questionnaire statement that clearly expresses an affirmative view. But despite the negative cast of their explicit views, the alienated share an implicit positive search in a common direction. Their philosophies emphasize the value of passion and feeling, the search for awareness, the cultivation of responsiveness, the importance of solitude, and the need somehow to express their experience of life. Their main values are therefore "expressive" or aesthetic, in that their main focus is the present, their main source is the self, and their main aim is the development of awareness, responsiveness, expressiveness, and sentience. Rejecting the traditional American values of success, self-control, and achievement, they maintain that passion, feeling, and awareness are the truest forces at man's disposal. For most of them the primary objective in life is to attain and maintain openness to experience, contact with the world, and spontaneity of feeling. Anything that might fetter or restrain their responsiveness and openness is opposed: the goal, as one student puts it, is "circumscribing my life as little as possible." And the same student goes on to say that he will some day be able to "express all or part of what I feel about life."

These alienated outlooks contrast sharply with "traditional" American views about the self, life, others, society, and the universe. Indeed each alienated view is a rejction of the conventional wisdom of our society. Thus, the unifying theme of the ideology of alienation is the rejection of what are seen as dominant American values, and unwillingness to accept the trusting, optimistic, sociocentric, affiliative, interpersonally oriented, and culturally accepting values which were, in less troubled times, the foundations of the American world view.

Alienation as a Style of Life

When we turn from alienated views of the world to the everyday life of alienated students, we find much less surface distinctiveness. Formal socioeconomic and demographic variables do not distinguish these students from their classmates, nor does a casual search through college records, high school records, or even police records. The alienated do not look different from their classmates, and the overt pattern of their daily activities shows relatively little that is distinctive. But if we examine not what they do but *how* they do it, we soon discover that the alienated have a characteristic life style that reflects and complements their alienation.

One crucial feature of this style of life is intellectual passion. In their approach to intellectual matters, these students are distinguished by their passionate concentration on a few topics of intense personal concern. They pursue their intellectual interests with such singleminded dedication that they almost completely disregard the conventional distinction between "work" and "goofing off" made by most of their classmates. Their capacity for intense intellectual concentration stands them in good stead during the last days before examinations, when they are capable of accomplishing extraordinary amounts of work. Moreover, when they are challenged in their work, and above all when their assignments strike some deep personal chord, they can become totally absorbed in intellectual work. Thus, despite erratic performances before examinations, the over-all averages of these students are about what was predicted for them on arrival in college.

Alienated students, when they become involved in extracurricular activities, are specifically drawn to those that allow them to express their artistic and "aesthetic" interests. But in whatever they do the style of their participation is alienated: it characteristically involves a preference for the role of the observer. Thus, as a group, they avoid positions of responsibility or, when accorded them, repudiate them immediately. One student, elected to an important national position, confounded everyone from his parents to his classmates by dropping out of college on the eve of assuming his new office. Since the alienated see all groups as destructive of individuality, they distrusted even the beatnik group which, during the years they were studied, flourished around the college: they found beatniks conformists and "not serious."

Their favored stance as detached observers led these students into semisystematic wanderings. Whenever they were confronted with a problem or conflict, they were likely to "take off," sometimes for a long walk at night, sometimes for a few years out of college. In all of these wanderings they seem to have been searching not so much for escape, as to immerse themselves in intense experience. Sometimes they found such experience. In their interviews and autobiographies there are occasional mentions of epiphanies, mystical experiences, and revelations of Everything in the garish pennants of a filling station, in the way the light of the setting sun falls through an archway, or in the smell of burning leaves.

Only on rare occasions did the alienated become active participants. In intellectual discussions in small groups, however, they are active, dominant, negative, and hostile, interrupting and correcting their fellows, impressing others with their scorn and contempt. But in stressful two-person situations, when confronted with an experienced and skilled antagonist, they find it difficult to express their anger at the time but later lapse into enduring resentment. Thus, direct expression of hostility to another person is not easy for these students; they find it most comfortable to channel their annoyance into intellectual discussions.

But despite their outward appearance of detachment from others, alienated undergraduates are highly though ambivalently involved with them. They are often simultaneously attracted to and somewhat fearful of an admired person—tempted to emulate him, but afraid that emulation might mean the sacrifice of their inner integrity. Given this ambivalence, it is understandable that these students tend to ruminate, often obsessively, about all close personal relationships. No friendship escapes detailed analysis from every point of view, every relationship becomes a matter of the preservation of identity. This ambivalent examination of relationships is especially pronounced with girls. Almost invariably, alienated students choose girls who are either profoundly dissatisfying to them or else strongly rejected by some crucial portion of their background. Thus, when they do become close to a girl, it is either to one who is described as passive, dependent, and subservient, or to one who is so totally unacceptable to their parents as to precipitate a complete break between the student and his family. In these relationships with girls, as in most of their relationships with other people, they combine an agonizing desire for closeness with a great fear of it.

In interviews as in questionnaires, alienated students are quick to admit their confusions, angers, anxieties, and problems. Given a list of neurotic symptoms, they check them all, describing themselves as confused, depressed, angry, neurotic, hostile, and impulsive. Yet the inference that these students are grossly disturbed can only be made with reservations. For one, they reject the value assumptions upon which most questionnaire measures of "maturity," "ego strength," and "good mental health" are based. Furthermore, they make a great effort to undermine any "defenses" that might protect them from unpleasant feelings. For most of these students, openness to their own problems and failings is a cardinal virtue; and they make a further point of loudly proclaiming their own inadequacies. Their drive to be totally honest with themselves and others makes them consistently put their worst foot forward.

But even when we make due allowance for the tendency of alienated students to exaggerate their own failings, many of these students are in fact confused, disoriented, and depressed. In interviews, their public face of contempt often gives way to private admissions of unhappiness and apprehension. Secretly, some harbor doubts that this unhappiness may be of their own making, rather than merely a consequence of the human condition. Thus, many alienated students can be aptly described in Erikson's terms as in a state of more or less intense identity diffusion. Their sense of themselves seems precarious and disunified; they often doubt their own continuing capacity to cope; they have little positive sense of relatedness to other people; the boundaries of their own egos are diffuse and porous. Strong in opposition these students are weak in affirmation; unable to articulate what they stand for, they have little sense of self to stand on. As a group, then, alienated students are not characterized by happiness, optimism, tranquillity, or calm; they are more notable for the intensity of their convictions, the vehemence of their scorn, the passion behind their search for meaning.

Alienation and the Personal Past

A careful examination of what alienated students tell us about their families and their earlier lives shows a remarkable consistency in their views. When discussing their mothers, for example, they frequently emphasize the renunciations and sacrifices their mothers have made. To their sons, these women appear to have been talented, artistic, intense, and intelligent girls who gave up promise and fulfillment for marriage. They also seem to their sons vivid, sensuous, and magnetic; and alienated students often wonder aloud "whether marriage was worth it" to their mothers. Throughout, these students express their special sympathy for and identification with their mothers and their sadness at their mothers' lack of fulfillment.

But the mothers of alienated sons have another set of common characteristics—dominance, possessiveness, excessive involvement with their sons, oversolicitude. The typical alienated student tells of his mother's intrusiveness, of her attempts to limit, supervise, and restrict his independence and initiative. And although few of the alienated admit that their mothers have been successful in controlling *them*, they do on the whole believe that their mothers have succeeded in controlling their fathers. Thus, it was Mother who paid Dad's way through college, it was Mother who made Dad's mind up to marry her, it is Mother who somehow decides how things are done in the family. Seen through her son's eyes, she emerges as a woman who has turned her considerable energies to the domination of her family.

About their fathers, alienated students volunteer less information than do most undergraduates. We already know that fathers are usually seen as dominated by mothers. Fathers are also described as men who, despite public success, are "failures in their own eyes," "apostates," disappointed, frustrated, and disillusioned men. But often, in addition, their college-age sons portray them as having once had youthful dreams which they were unable to fulfill, as idealists whose idealism has been destroyed by life. The precise agent of this destruction varies: sometimes it was Mother; sometimes it was the father's own weakness, particularly his inability to stand up against social pressures. So, despite their frequent scorn for their dominated fathers, alienated students retain much sympathy for the same fathers as they might have been—a covert identification with the fantasy of a youthful idealistic father.

In characterizing their fathers at present, however, the alienated again and again emphasize qualities like detachment, reserve, inability to express affection, loneliness, and withdrawal from the center of the family. Contrasted with the expressive, emotional, controlling, and dynamic mother, the father appears weak, inactive, detached, and uninterested. The greater portion of these students' current sympathies goes to their mothers, whose frustrations are seen as imposed from without, while their fathers are more often directly blamed for their failure to live up to their youthful dreams.

In their earliest memories alienated students make unusually frequent references to "oral" themes, that is, to issues of consuming, being nurtured and cared for, to food aversions, feeding problems, and in one student, to the assumption that his voracious nursing produced breast cancer in his mother. In these memories women are always present; men are striking by their absence. Although these subjects' fathers were usually present during their early childhood, it was the mother or other women who appeared to have mattered. Especially striking are idyllic recollections of happy times alone with Mother on vacations or family expeditions when Father was away from home. All of these memories suggest an unusually intense attachment between mother and son in early life.

In primary and secondary school alienated students, like most undergraduates at Harvard College, were capable intellectually and interested in their schoolwork. But they differ from many of their classmates in that they seem consistently to have prefered imagination, thought, and staying at home to outgoing activities with others; they speak less than most students of group activities and "running with the gang"; they usually describe themselves as quiet, homebound, unrebellious, and obedient children.

But during adolescence alienated students seem to have undergone even greater turmoil than most of their classmates. The symptoms of their turmoil are extremely varied: intense asceticism, tentative delinquency, vociferous rebellion, speeding, drinking, and, in one case, a halfhearted suicide attempt. From other evidence it seems that the arrival of adult sexuality was unusually disturbing to these young men. In discussing their sexual fantasies as college students, they emphasize to an unusual degree their desire for passivity, oblivion, and tranquillity, and often mention difficulties about being initiating and "aggressive" with women. Only a few alienated students have found sexual relationships fully satisfying, and many mention enduring feelings of anxiety, discomfort, or apprehension connected with sex. All of this suggests that one of the major problems in adolescence was especially great anxiety about assuming the traditional male sex role.

There is no mention of overt alienation in the life histories of these students until midadolescence—about the age of sixteen. At this age we hear accounts of growing feelings of cynicism, distance, estrangement, and scorn—initially for school classmates, later for parents and teachers, finally for all of society. In most cases these feelings appeared spontaneously, though sometimes they were precipitated by the views of a friend, a trip abroad, or some other specific event. This growing sense of alienation usually contrasted sharply with continuing academic and social success; and the contrast between inner alienation and outer success led to increasing feelings of estrangement from all those who accepted them merely at face value. Their alienation developed more or less in isolation and more or less spontaneously, it was usually only after they became alienated that these students sought out books and people who would confirm and support them in their alienation. Among the students studied, alienation could not be explained as the result of identification with an alienated parent; on the contrary, it always seemed to involve a sharp repudiation of perceived parental values.

Alienation in Fantasy

The fantasies of alienated students, as seen on the T.A.T., are different from the fantasies of other students both in style and in content. Stylistically, alienated fantasies are rich, vivid, imaginative, antisocial, unconventional, and sometimes bizarre. The typical alienated fantasy involves an inferior or unusually sensitive hero who becomes involved in a difficult relationship with another person. The relationship goes from bad to worse, leading to great resentment and hurt, especially on the hero's side. Efforts to repair the relationship invariably fail, and the hero is profoundly and adversely affected. This plot format contrasts sharply with the typical stories of nonalienated students, whose competent and superior heroes enter into positive and enduring relationships from which all concerned profit and grow.

Within this general plot format the alienated characteristically tells stories reflecting one or both of two major themes. The first of these is the loss of Eden. Alienated fantasies are distinctively concerned with the loss of supplies, with starvation, with forcible estrangement, and with a yearning to return to bliss. Sometimes these fantasies involve isolated heroes who die of starvation; more often they entail a hero who seeks to regain his union with a lost loved one, usually a woman. Alienated fantasies are a catalogue of yearnings for the past: undertakers enamored of their female subjects, ghoulish grave robbers, heroes obsessed with the recovery of the lost gods, grief-stricken husbands who crawl into their wives' graves, detectives searching for missing persons, lovers mourning the dead, husbands who kill themselves on their wives' coffins.

The same theme of reunion with a lost love is reflected in other stories where the hero loses himself in some warm, fluid, or embracing maternal medium. Some heroes are lured to their deaths by warm and friendly voices speaking from the sea or calling from the air. Other fantasies involve heroes who dive to the bottom of the ocean, never to return. Developmentally, these often archaic and weird stories seem to refer to an unconscious obsession with the lost early relationship with the mother. The fantasy of fusion with the lost maternal presence—a fantasy which exists somewhere in the hearts of all men—constitutes an obsessional theme for these college students.

A second important motif in alienated fantasy is the theme of a Phyrrhic Oedipal victory. Most college students, when given the Thematic Apperception Test, are at some pains to avoid stories which involve competitive rivalrous triangles: rivalry between men is usually minimized, and struggles between two men for the love of a woman are especially rare. The alienated, in contrast, take rivalrous triangles for granted, often importing them into stories where the picture in no way suggests this theme. Even more striking is the peculiar form and outcome of such fantasies. Again and again, it is the younger man who defeats the older man, but only to be overcome himself by some extraneous force. Attacks on fathers and father figures are almost inevitably successful: the father dies, the Minister of Interior Affairs is assassinated, the boss who has propositioned the hero's wife is killed. Or, in the many stories of political revolution told by these apolitical students, the established regime is seen as weak, corrupt, and easily overthrown. Traditional male authority topples at the first push.

Yet these stories of rebellion, rivalry, and revolution are, paradoxically, cautionary tales. The revolution succeeds, but it is followed by a disaster: the revolutionary murderer is assassinated by his own men; the revolutionary regime turns into a despotism worse than that which it overthrew; the avenged cuckold is killed in an automobile accident. These fantasies suggest that although traditional male authority is weak, its destruction leads to a new and worse tyranny.

These fantasies are consistent with the hypothesis that the rebellious son believes that he indeed succeeded in deposing his father, but that this deposition was followed by a new maternal tyranny. The victor was neither father nor son, but mother, who now dominates them both. Supporting this hypothesis is the fact that most alienated fantasies portray adult women as active, controlling, and possessive. In particular they restrain men's sexuality, aggressiveness, and nonconformity: they try to keep their sons from going out with girls; they keep men from fighting; they try to make their husbands settle down and conform—and almost invariably they succeed.

The dominant theme of relations between the sexes, then, is not love and intimacy but the control of men by women. When intimacy begins to seem possible, the story usually ends disastrously. Furthermore, women are not seen only as controlling and possessive but, on one occasion, as murderous and destructive: as lizard goddesses who eat their victims, apparently lovable ladies who murder their husbands, as emasculating and destructive figures. Fathers and older men, in contrast, are almost always portrayed as weak, corruptible, absent, or damaged. Men are controlled by women, and even men who initially appear strong eventually turn out to be fraudulent and weak.

Hypotheses about the Psychological Sources of Alienation

The themes of ideology, life style, past history, and fantasy summarized here are of course open to many different interpretations. In some respects the psychological origins of alienation are different for each alienated individual, and no composite account can hope to do justice to the uniqueness of each person. Nonetheless, the existence of many shared strands of belief, present feeling, past experience, and imagination suggests that in so far as we can take these students' accounts as an adequate basis for an explanation, general hypotheses about the psychological origins of alienation are possible.

One of the most striking findings of this study is the great similarity in the families of alienated students. Both parents seem to have been frustrated and dissatisfied. The mother's talents and emotionality found little expression within her marriage; the father's idealism and youthful dreams were crushed by the realities of his adult life. The mothers of alienated students seem to have turned their drive and perhaps their own frustrated needs for love onto their sons. Often, these mothers explicitly deprecated or disparaged their husbands. And confronted with this deprecation, the fathers of alienated students seem to have withdrawn from the family, becoming detached, embittered, and distant. Forced to choose between their families and their work, they almost to a man turned their energies outside of the family, leaving mother and son locked in a special alliance of mutual understanding and maternal control.

This basic family constellation is reflected and elaborated in fantasy. Unconsciously, alienated students seem to believe that they defeated their fathers, who are therefore seen as weak and inadequate models of male adulthood. Probably like most small boys, they attempted a "revolution" within the family in order to overthrow the tyrannical father and gain the exclusive love of the mother. But unlike most, these boys believe that their revolution succeeded in destroying male authority. Yet paradoxically, their apparent victory did not win them maternal love but maternal control, possessiveness, and oversolicitude. Furthermore, by displacing their fathers, they lost the right of every boy to a father he can admire. The son thus gained something very different from what he had wanted. At least in fantasy he found himself saddled with the possessive and intrusive mother, and he lost the youthful, idealistic father he could respect.

If these hypotheses are correct, they may help us to explain some of the other characteristics of these alienated students. For such a childhood experience would clearly leave a boy or even a college student with the unconscious assumption that apparently admirable men were really weak and impotent; and that apparently nurturing and loving women were really controlling, possessive, and even emasculating. Conventional adulthood as epitomized by the father—that is, the dominant value assumptions about adulthood in American society—would also seem unattractive and have to be rejected. Adult closeness with women would be frightening, as it would evoke fears of being dominated, controlled, and emasculated. Similarly, competition and rivalry would be avoided in everyday behavior, not out of the fear of failure, but from a fear of another Phyrric victory. Furthermore, the inability of our subjects' mothers to love them as sons, coupled with the apparently sudden change in the sons' image of the mother from that of a nurturer to an emasculator might help explain the persistence into early adulthood of recurrent fantasies about fusion with the maternal presence, the dominance of the theme of loss of Eden.

The psychological factors that predisposed these students toward alienation are thus complex and interrelated. The sense and the stance of alienation are partially reflections of the unconscious conviction of these subjects that they are outcasts from a lost Eden, alienated forever from their mothers' early love. then, too, the repudiation of conventional adulthood, of the dominant values of American society, is closely related to their unconscious determination not to let what happened to their fathers happen to them, and to covert identification with the fantasy of a youthful idealistic father before he was "broken" by life. Similarly, the centrality of distrust in the emotional lives and ideologies of alienated students is probably in part a reflection of an early family situation in which neither parent turned out to be what he or she had seemed to be. In a variety of ways, then, these students were prepared by their past experience and by the fantasies through which they interpreted this experience to be alienated from American culture.

Nonpsychological Factors in Alienation

An account of the psychological factors that predispose certain individuals to be alienated is by no means a complete or adequate account. For one, such an account will have, to many readers, an implicitly "reductive" quality: it may seem to suggest that alienation is "nothing but" a reflection of a particular kind of family constellation and childhood experience. It is far from my intention to "reduce" alienation to childhood history here; on the contrary, while the links between early experience and later alienation are clear, these links in no way entail that alienation is "nothing but" a reflection of unfortunate childhood. On the contrary, the childhood events and fantasies I have discussed here could be viewed as the fortunate and enabling factors that permitted these students to be aware of the very real deficiencies in their society to which their less alienated fellows remain obdurately blind.

Furthermore, this psychological account is, even in its own terms, far from complete. It is probable that the family factors I have outlined will dispose a young man to *some* kind of hesitancy about or repudiation of conventional adulthood. But these family factors alone do not suffice to explain why this hesitancy took the particular form of cultural alienation. For further explanations we would need to consider the early propensity of these students to solve problems with their imaginations rather than with their fists, their generally privileged social backgrounds, their very high talent, intelligence, and imaginativeness, and their very great sensitivity to the evils in themselves and in the world around them. We would have to consider the impact of talented and often artistic mothers on their eldest or only sons, and we would have to prepare a more adequate catalogue not only of the major psychological themes of alienation, but of the specific strengths and weaknesses of alienated students.

Another dimension omitted from this psychological account of alienation is even more important—it is the social and historical context and traditions within which these students live. Alienation of the sort here described is by no means an exclusively contemporary phenomenon; especially during the past two centuries in the Western world, many of the most creative men and women have been highly alienated from their own cultures. Furthermore, the precise forms, manifestations, and content of alienation are always given by the surrounding society; for example, during the years these students were studied, the late 1950's and early 1960's, there were few available student movements of social change and reform into which alienation might have been channeled. At least a few of these alienated students, had they been in college six years later, might have found a channel for the constructive expression of their alienation in the Civil Rights Movement or the peace movement.

Finally, this account of alienation is incomplete in the most fundamental way of all. Although alienated students are especially sensitized and predisposed toward alienation by their pasts, their alienation itself is a reaction *to* and *against* the society in which they live. In other words, alienation is a transaction between an individual and his society, and we can understand it adequately by examining not only the individual and his psychology, but the characteristics of the wider society as they impinge upon students like him. To attempt to characterize the major trends and pressures of American society is far beyond my topic here. But it should be said that the pressures and demands of modern American society seem to me profoundly alienating in many respects. Thus, we could with full justice ask of the *non*alienated why their individual psychology so blinds them to these "alienating" aspects of our society which the alienated perceive so sharply.

Alienation, then, as studied in this small group of talented college students, is the product of a complex interaction of psychological, sociological, cultural, and historical factors within the experience of each individual. It is not enough to attribute alienation solely to the characteristics of modern technological society—such an explanation makes it impossible for us to account for the majority of Americans who are not alienated. But it would be equally misleading to see alienation purely as an expression of individual psychology. Like most outlooks, alienation is the product of the inner world and the outer world as they come together in the developing individual's experience.

ALIENATION AND MODERN INDUSTRY

ROBERT BLAUNER

No simple definition of alienation can do justice to the many intellectual traditions which have engaged this concept as a central explanatory idea. One basis of confusion is the fact that the idea of alienation has incorporated philosophical, psychological, sociological, and political orientations. In the literature on the theory of alienation, one finds statements of the desired state of human experience, assertions about the actual quality of personal experience, propositions which link attitudes and experience to social situations and social structures, and programs for the amelioration of the human condition. My own perspective in this investigation is chiefly sociological, or perhaps social-psychological, in that alienation is viewed as a quality of personal experience which results from specific kinds of social arrangements.

This study also employs a multidimensional, rather than a unitary, conception of alienation. Alienation is a general syndrome made up of a number of different objective conditions and subjective feeling-states which emerge from certain relationships between workers and the sociotechnical settings of employment. Alienation exists when workers are unable to control their immediate work processes, to develop a sense of purpose and function which connects their jobs to the over-all organization of production, to belong to integrated industrial communities, and when they fail to become involved in the activity of work as a mode of personal self-expression. In modern industrial employment, control, purpose, social integration, and self-involvement are all problematic. In this chapter we discuss how various aspects of the technology, work organization, and social structure of modern industry further the four types of alienation which correspond to these non-alienated states: powerlessness, meaninglessness, isolation, and self-estrangement.

Powerlessness: Modes of Freedom and Control in Industry

A person is powerless when he is an object controlled and manipulated by other persons or by an impersonal system (such as technology), and when he cannot assert himself as a subject to change or modify this domination. Like an object, the powerless person reacts rather than acts. He is directed or dominated, rather than self-directing. The non-alienated pole of the powerlessness dimension is freedom and control. Freedom is the state which allows the person to remove himself from those dominating situations that make him simply a reacting object. Freedom may therefore involve the possibility of movement in a physical or social sense, the ability to walk away from a coercive machine process, or the opportunity of quitting a job because of the existence of alternative employment. Control is more positive than freedom, suggesting the assertion of the self-directing subject over such potentially dominating forces as employers or machine systems.

The degree of powerlessness a student imputes to manual workers in industry today depends not only on his sociological and political perspective but also on the aspects of freedom and control he selects as the most important. There are at least four modes of industrial powerlessness which have preoccupied writers on "the social question." These are (1) the separation from ownership of the means of production and the finished products, (2) the inability to influence general managerial policies, (3) the lack of control over the conditions of employment, and (4) the lack of control over the immediate work process. It is my contention that control over the conditions of employment and control over the immediate work process are most salient for manual workers, who are most likely to value control over those matters which affect their immediate jobs and work tasks and least likely to be concerned with the more general and abstract aspects of powerlessness.

The very nature of employment in a large-scale organization means that workers have forfeited their claims on the finished product and that they do not own the factory, machines, or often their own tools. Unlike the absence of control over the immediate work process, "ownership powerlessness" is a constant in modern industry, and employees, therefore, normally do not develop expectations for influence in this area. Today the average worker no more desires to own his machines than modern soldiers their howitzers or government clerks their file cabinets. Automobile and chemical workers, by and large, do not feel deprived because they cannot take home the Corvairs or sulfuric acid they produce.

Orthodox Marxism saw the separation from the means of production as the central fact of capitalism, the inevitable consequence of which would be the worker's general alienation from society. This has not happened: manual workers have required only steady jobs, reasonable wages, and employee benefits to put down at least moderate stakes in society and industry. Yet, despite the lack of any conscious desire for control in this area, we cannot know for certain whether or not the worker's alienation from ownership unconsciously colors the whole quality of his experience in the factory, as Erich Fromm (1955), for one, argues. The appeal of small-business ownership, stronger among manual than white-collar employees, suggests that there may be many workers like the automobile worker Ely Chinoy quotes, for whom employment itself is inherently alienating:

> The main thing is to be independent and give your own orders and not have to take them from anybody else. That's the reason the fellows in the shop all want to start their own business. Then the profits are all for yourself. When you're in the shop, there's nothing for yourself in it. So you just do what you have to do in order to get along. A fellow would rather do it for himself. If you expend the energy, it's for your benefit then (1955, pp. xvi-xvii).

Like the separation from ownership, another facet of industrial powerlessness, the lack of control over decision-making, is also common to the modern employment relationship. Large-scale organizations are hierarchical authority structures with power concentrated at the top, and manual workers have little opportunity to control the major decisions of the enterprise. And unlike the worker quoted above, most employees do not seem to resent this aspect of powerlessness, which they also tend to accept as a "given" of industry. The average worker does not want the responsibility for such decisions as what, for whom, and how much to produce; how to design the product; what machinery to buy; how to distribute jobs; or how to organize the flow of work. It is only when these decisions directly affect his immediate job and work load that he expects his labor organization to influence policy in his behalf—as the recent labor-management conflicts over work rules indicate.

A number of industrial reform movements have attempted to counteract this aspect of powerlessness. Early in the twentieth century, the classical advocates of workers' control—the socialist followers of Rosa Luxembourg in Germany, the American IWW, the French syndicalists, and the British shop-stewards' movements—raised the slogan of industrial democracy. But as labor reform movements became more sophisticated, they realized that large-scale production organizations cannot be governed directly and en masse. The sponsors of direct democracy gave way to the advocates of representative democracy and participation in management.

The most important recent examples of this trend are "joint consultation" in England, codetermination in Germany, and the workers' councils of eastern Europe. Yet the experience of these representative systems suggests that it is only the delegate or the participator, not the average worker, who actually feels he is influencing major decisions. Even those progressive firms which have encouraged mass participation in shop councils find that the average employee confines his interest to his own job and work group and leaves participation in the over-all plan to a select few.

A third aspect of industrial powerlessness, the lack of control over conditions of employment, is considerably more meaningful to American workers. Selig Perlman's (1949) characterization of the American working class as more "job conscious" than "class conscious" suggests that control of the opportunity for work itself within the oligarchic industrial system has been historically more relevant than the two more "revolutionary" aspects of control discussed above.

Under early capitalism, the worker could be hired and fired at will by impersonal forces of the market and personal whims of the employer. As a commodity subject to supply and demand factors, his employment depended on the extent of his skills and the phase of the business cycle. This is no longer the case. The most important innovations sponsored by American labor unions have been aimed at reducing the historic inequality of power in the contractual situation of employment. Collective bargaining, the contract, grievance procedures, arbitration, seniority provisions, hiring halls, and now "guaranteed annual wages" have all been partially successful attempts to increase the control of employees over their conditions of employment.

In addition, a number of economic changes have greatly reduced the worker's powerlessness in this area. The severity of periodic economic crises has diminished as industry and government have imposed major checks on the anarchy of a free competitive system. Technological requirements have increased the need for more skilled and responsible workers. Thus, the large corporation has recognized the advantage of a more permanent work force to its pursuit of economic stability and higher productivity.

As a result of these changes in economic life, technology, corporation policy, and union power, the worker's control over his employment is increasing in what Ralf Dahrendorf calls "post-capitalist society." The *worker*, who in classical capitalism was considered virtually a commodity or a cost of production and treated as a *thing*, is giving way to the *employee*, a permanent worker who is viewed much more as a *human being*. Many employees have job security based on seniority provisions or a *de facto* "common law" right to their jobs. The employment relationship no longer reflects merely the balance of power; it is more and more determined by a system of institutional justice.

Economic security is not distributed equally in the industrial structure, for the trends outlined above have not developed evenly. Some firms, industries, and specific occupations are extremely unstable in employment whereas others provide virtual tenure in jobs. Empirical studies constantly emphasize the important part which regularity of employment plays in workers' evaluations of particular jobs and companies. . . .

Both sociologists and socialists, in their emphasis on the assembly-line work situation, have provided much data on the powerlessness of the worker in the face of a dominating technological system. Despite the fact that the assembly line is not the representative work milieu, these scholars have rightly emphasized the central importance of the worker's relation to technology as a major condition of alienation. For when a worker is dominated and controlled by the machine system in the very process of his work, he, in effect, becomes reduced to a mechanical device. Reacting to the rhythms of technology rather than acting in some independent or autonomous manner, he approaches most completely the condition of *thingness,* the essence of alienation.

Studies of the assembly line show that workers greatly resent the dominance of technology and constantly try to devise ways to gain some measure of control over the machine system. The resentment against this kind of powerlessness may reflect an awareness of its special degrading and humiliating features, as well as the knowledge that there are many alternative kinds of work situations in factory employment.

The variations in control over the immediate activity of work are a principal focus of the present study. . . . Whether a worker controls his sociotechnical environment depends on his freedom of movement, freedom to make choices, and freedom from oppressive constraints. It is necessary to specify this final aspect of industrial powerlessness more precisely by distinguishing those individual freedoms which are the components or elements of control over the immediate activity of work. Of these, the most important is control over the *pace* of work.

A basic distinction can be made between those jobs which are machine paced, with the rhythms of work and the timing of the operator's actions depending on the speed of the machine or machine process, and those which are man-paced, in which the worker himself can vary the rhythms of his actions. This distinction can be seen in two occupations outside the factory. The man who takes money or issues tickets at the toll plaza of a bridge or highway has virtually no control over the pace of his work, since it is determined by the flow of traffic. He can only respond. An unskilled clerk in an office who adds columns of figures all day on an adding machine however, has considerable control over his work pace. Often he can slow down, speed up, or take a break at his own discretion, although supervisors and other clerks might have some influence over his work pace.

Control over the pace of work is critical because it sets a man apart from the machine system of modern technology. The pace of work is probably the most insistent, the most basic, aspect of a job and retaining control in this area is a kind of affirmation of human dignity. This freedom is also crucial because it influences other work freedoms.

For example, when a man can control his work rhythm, he can usually regulate the degree of *pressure* exerted on him. Some work environments, like automobile and textile factories, are characterized by considerable pressure, while others, like print shops and chemical plants, have a relaxed atmosphere. . . . In addition, *freedom of physical movement* is much more likely when a worker controls his own work rhythm and also when he is relatively free from pressure. In American industry today many jobs require the worker to stay close to his station for eight hours a day, while others permit a great deal of moving around the plant. The automobile assembly line is again an extreme example of restricted physical movement, whereas the work milieu of the print shop permits a high degree of this freedom. Many manual workers consider free movement quite important; the rather common preference of manual workers for truck-driving, railroad, and construction work rather than factory jobs often represents an aversion to physically confining "inside" work.

Control over work pace generally brings some *freedom to control the quantity of production.* Of course, workers cannot keep their jobs without a minimum production. But many are able to vary the hourly and daily output greatly, while others have no power at all to control this. Similar to this is the freedom to control the *quality* of one's work. When a man sets his own pace and is free from pressure, as are craft printers, he can take the pains to do a job up to his standards of workmanship; in machine paced systems with high-speed production, a worker's desire to put out quality work is often frustrated, as is the case with many automobile assemblers.

A final component of control over the immediate work process refers to *techniques.* In mass production there is generally little opportunity to make choices as to how to do one's job, since these decisions have been already made by engineers, time-study men, and supervisors. In other industrial settings, however, jobs permit some selection of work methods. There, workers can solve problems and use their own ideas.

These individual task-related freedoms—control over pace, freedom from pressure, freedom of physical movement, and the ability to control the quantity and quality of production and to choose the techniques of work—together make up control over the immediate work process. When rationalized technology and work organization do not permit the active intervention of the worker at any of these points, the alienating tendencies of modern industry, which make the worker simply a responding object, an instrument of the productive process, are carried to their furthest extremes.

Meaninglessness: Purpose and Function in Manual Work

A second dimension of alienation in industrial employment is meaningless-ness. Bureaucratic structures seem to encourage feelings of meaninglessness. As division of labor increases in complexity in large-scale organizations, individual roles may seem to lack organic connection with the whole structure of roles, and the result is that the employee may lack understanding of the co-ordinated activity and a sense of purpose in his work.

Karl Mannheim saw meaninglessness emerging in bureaucracies as a result of the tension between "functional rationalization" and "substantial rationality." Functional rationalization refers to the idea that in a modern organization everything is geared to the highest efficiency. The number of tasks and procedures required for a product or a service are analyzed, and the work is organized so that there is a smooth flow and a minimum of costs. The rationale of the technical and social organization is comprehended fully only by a few top managers (and engineers in the case of a factory), if indeed by anyone at all. But along with the greater efficiency and rationality of the whole, the substantial rationality of the individuals who make up the system declines. The man who has a highly subdivided job in a complex factory and the clerk working in a huge government bureau need only know very limited tasks. They need not know anyone else's job and may not even know what happens in the department of the organization next to them. They need not know how their own small task fits into the entire operation. What results is a decline in the "capacity to act intelligently in a given situation on the basis of one's own insight into the inter-relations of events" (1940, p. 59).

Meaning in work depends largely on three aspects of the worker's relationship to the product, process, and organization of work. The first factor is the character of the product itself. Working on a unique and individuated product is almost inherently meaningful. It is more difficult to develop and maintain a sense of purpose in contributing toward a standardized product, since this inevitably involves repetitive work cycles. The second point is the scope of the product worked on. It is more meaningful to work on the whole, or a large part, of even a standardized product, than to perform one's tasks only on a small part of the final product. Third, purpose and function increase when the employee's job makes him responsible for a large span of the production process, rather than a small restricted sphere.

Tendencies toward meaninglessness therefore stem from the nature of modern manufacturing, which is based on standardized production and a division of labor that reduces the size of the worker's contribution to the final product. Whereas many independent craftsmen of the preindustrial era made the entire product themselves, from the first step in the operations to the last, an automobile assembler may spend all his time putting on headlights and never have anything to do with any other operation. These alienating tendencies may be overcome when job design or technological developments result in a wide rather than a narrow scope of operations for the employee. Purpose may also be injected into relatively fractionized jobs when the worker develops an understanding of the organization's total function and of the relation of his own contribution to that larger whole. However, such understanding is less likely to lead toward a sense of purpose and function if the worker's responsibilities and scope of operations remain narrow.

Like powerlessness, meaninglessness is unequally distributed among manual workers in modern industry. The nature of an industry's technology and work organization affects the worker's ability to wrest a sense of purpose from his work task—substantial irrationality is not the fate of all modern factory employees. This mode of alienation is most intensified when production is carried out in large plants. In the small factory it is easier for the worker to see the relationship of his contribution to the enterprise as a whole. Team production also reduces meaninglessness. It is easier for factory workers to develop a sense of purpose when they are members of work crews which carry out the job jointly than for employees who do their work individually. Finally there is less alienation in process technology than in batch or assembly methods of production. In the former system, work is organized in terms of an integrated process rather than in terms of subdivided tasks, and the worker's span of responsibility and job assignment is enlarged. An increased sense of purpose and function in work for the blue-collar employee may be one of the most important by-products of automation, since this technical system brings about smaller factories, production by teams rather than individuals, and integrated process operations.

Social Alienation: Integration and Membership in Industrial Communities

In contrast to Marx, who emphasized the powerlessness of workers in modern industry and saw the solution to the modern social problem in "restoring" control to the workers over their conditions of work, the French sociologist Emile Durkheim saw *anomie* (normlessness) and the breakup of integrated communities as the distinguishing feature of modern society. The massive social processes of industrialization and urbanization had destroyed the normative structure of a more traditional society and uprooted people from the local groups and institutions which had provided stability and security.

The transition to industrialism brought about tendencies toward social alienation, not only in the larger society but also in the factories and mills. Although the use of physical force and the threat of starvation as "incentives" expressed the callousness of many indistrialists, it also reflected the fact that there was as yet no basis for an industrial community. With normative integration absent, machine-breaking, sabotage, strikes, and revolutionary activity not only represented protest against unbearable conditions but expressed the fact that workers had not yet developed a sense of loyalty to industrial enterprise or commitment to the new social role of factory employee.

In advanced industrial societies like the United States, the social alienation in factory employment characteristic of the early period has been greatly reduced. Even workers who lack control over their immediate work task and experience difficulty in achieving meaning and self-expression in the job may be spared the alienation of isolation, which implies the absence of a sense of membership in an industrial community. Membership in an industrial community involves commitment to the work role and loyalty to one or more centers of the work community. Isolation, on the other hand, means that the worker feels no sense of belonging in the work situation and is unable to identify or uninterested in identifying with the organization and its goals.

An individual community is made up of a network of social relationships which are derived from a work organization and which are valued by the members of the community. For many factory workers the plant as a whole is a community, a center of belongingness and identification, which mitigates feelings of isolation. It is quite common for workers to come to a factory thirty minutes early every day to relax in the company of their friends. It has been argued that the human contacts of the plant community are critical in making work which is in other ways alienating bearable for mass production workers. Beginning with the work of Elton Mayo and his associates, much research in industrial sociology has documented the role of informal work groups in providing a sense of belonging within the impersonal atmosphere of modern industry.

An industrial community also has a structure of norms, informal and formal rules, which guide the behavior of its members. Industrial organizations differ in the extent of normative integration, and this is important in determining the employee's sense of belonging to a cohesive work community. Industrial organizations are normatively integrated when there is consensus between the work force and management on standards of behavior, expectations of rewards, and definitions of fair play and justice, and when there are agreed upon "rules of the game" which govern the relations between employees and employers. The norms and practices through which workers are disciplined and laid off, assigned wage rates relative to the earnings of others, and awarded promotions, are especially critical. These matters affect the worker's sense of equity with respect to the allocation of rewards and the standards of distributive justice and therefore often determine his sense of alienation from, or integration in, the industrial enterprise.

Although the maturation of industrial society has generally reduced the worker's isolation, the implications of bureaucratic organization for social alienation are somewhat mixed. Bureaucracy's norm of impersonal administration emphasizes formal procedures, and in many cases this creates a feeling of distance between workers and management. And the bureaucratic principle of the rational utilization of all resources to maximize organizational goals furthers the tendency to view employees as *labor,* as means to the ends of profit and company growth. But bureaucratic administration also enhances normative consensus through its emphasis on universalistic standards of justice and "fair treatment" and thus makes it possible for employees to acquire the status of industrial citizenship. It is probably the policy and practices of individual firms, unique historical and economic conditions, and particularly the technological setting, that determines whether bureaucratization increases or decreases social integration in a specific situation.

Industries vary not only in the extent but also in the basis of normative integration and in the key institutions which are the center of the work community and the focus of worker loyalties. It is important to stress that the company need not be the major focus of the industrial community, as the advocates of what has been called "managerial sociology" tend to assume. In some cases, occupational groups and unions, in other situations, the local community as a whole, are more important presently and potentially. . . .

Self-Estrangement

Self-estrangement refers to the fact that the worker may become alienated from his inner self in the activity of work. Particularly when an individual lacks control over the work process and a sense of purposeful connection to the work enterprise, he may experience a kind of depersonalized detachment rather than an immediate involvement or engrossment in the job tasks. This lack of present-time involvement means that the work becomes primarily instrumental, a means toward future considerations rather than an end in itself. When work encourages self-estrangement, it does not express the unique abilities, potentialities, or personality of the worker. Further consequences of self-estranged work may be boredom and monotony, the absence of personal growth, and a threat to a self-approved occupational identity.

Self-estrangement is absent in two main situations: when the work activity, satisfying such felt needs as those for control, meaning, and social connection, is inherently fulfilling in itself; or when the work activity is highly integrated to the totality of an individual's social commitments. Throughout most of history the problem of work has been dealt with in the latter manner. Adriano Tilgher (1930), a historian of work ideologies, finds that the idea that work should be a creative fulfilment is peculiarly modern, with origins in the Renaissance. In many previous civilizations work was viewed as some kind of unpleasant burden or punishment. Our modern feeling that work should be a source of direct, immediate satisfaction and express the unique potential of the individual is probably a result of its compartmentalization in industrial society. In preindustrial societies "uninteresting" work was highly integrated with other aspects of the society—with ritual, religion, family, and community or tribal relationships, for example. Therefore it could not become simply a means to life, because it was an immediate part of life's main concerns.

A number of fateful social changes have contributed to the compartmentalization of work. Most basic was the market economy which, in severing the organic connection between production and consumption, between effort and gratification, set the stage for the instrumental attitude toward work. Second, the physical separation of household and workplace—an essential condition for the development of capitalism and bureaucratic organization, as Weber stressed—produced a hiatus between work life and family life. Third, with the secularization of modern society, the importance of the religious sanction in work motivation has declined; work and religion are now separated. Fourth, with the specialization brought about by industrial organization and the anonymity which urbanization has furthered, the average man's occupational role is not well known or understood: work is now separated from the community, as well as from the family and religion. Finally, the decline of the hours of work and the increase in living standards mean that less of life is devoted simply to problems of material existence. Time, energy, and resources are now available for other aspects of life, which compete with work for emotional loyalties and commitments.

Self-estrangement is experienced as a heightened awareness of time, as a split between present activity and future considerations. Non-alienated activity consists of immersion in the present; it is involvement. Alienated activity is not free, spontaneous activity but is compulsive and driven by necessity. In non-alienated activity the rewards are in the activity itself; in alienated states they are largely extrinsic to the activity, which has become primarily a means to an end. Marx expressed these notions in his early work on alienation, the *Economic and Philosophical Manuscripts:*

> In his work, therefore, [the worker] does not affirm himself but denies himself, does not feel content but unhappy, does not develop freely his physical and mental energy but mortifies his body and ruins his mind. The worker therefore only feels himself outside his work, and in his work feels outside himself. He is at home when he is not working, and when he is working he is not at home. His labor is therefore not voluntary, but coerced; it is *forced labor*. It is therefore not the satisfaction of a need; it is merely a *means* to satisfy needs external to it. Its alien character emerges clearly in the fact that as soon as no physical or other compulsion exists, labor is shunned like the plague. External labor, labor in which man alienates himself, is a labor of self-sacrifice, of mortification (No date, pp. 72-73).

Since self-estranged activity is a means to an end rather than an end in itself, the satisfaction is in the future rather than the present, and the tone of feeling approaches *detachment* rather than involvement. The man on the assembly line is thinking about that beer he will have when the whistle blows; the packing-house worker at Hormel goes home from work "so he can accomplish something for that day." The meaning of the job for the automobile worker is not the intrinsic activity itself but that "new car" or "little modern house," which the pay check, itself a future reward, brings closer.

Lack of involvement results in a heightened time-consciousness. If it were possible to measure "clock-watching," this would be one of the best objective indicators of this mode of alienation. The "over-concern" with time is central to Fred Blum's perceptive discussion of alienation in a meat-packing plant and suggests that self-alienation is not widespread in this kind of work. When Blum asked these workers whether they get bored on the job, a common response was that boredom was not a serious problem because "the time passes."

> How could the passage of time possibly neutralize the monotony of the job? Whatever the answer may be, there is no doubt but that the time does, as a rule, pass fast. A large majority of workers, when asked: "When you are at work does the time generally pass slow or fast?" indicated that it usually passes quickly.

Only a small minority feels that the time goes slowly. Many workers, however, intimated that sometimes the passage of time is slow and sometimes fast (1953, p. 82).

On the other hand, involvement in work may come from control, from association with others, and from a sense of its purpose. A man who is controlling his immediate work process—regulating the pace, the quantity of output, the quality of the product, choosing tools or work techniques—must be relatively immersed in the work activity. For most employees, when work is carried out by close-knit work groups, especially work teams, it will be more intrinsically involving and rewarding. And involvement and self-fulfilment is heightened when the purpose of the job can be clearly connected with the final end product or the over-all goals and organization of the enterprise.

REFERENCES

Blum, Fred. *Toward A Democratic Work Process.* New York: Harper & Bros., 1953.

Chinoy, Ely. *Automobile Workers and the American Dream.* New York: Doubleday & Company, 1955.

Fromm, Erich. *The Sane Society.* New York: Rinehart & Company, 1955.

Mannheim, Karl. *Man and Society in an Age of Reconstruction.* New York: Harcourt, Brace & Company, 1940.

Marx, Karl. *The Economic and Philosophical Manuscripts of 1844.* Moscow: Foreign Language Publishing House, no date.

Perlman, S. *A Theory of the Labor Movement.* New York: August M. Kelley, 1949.

Tilgher, Adriano. *Work: What It Has Meant to Men through the Ages.* New York: Harcourt, Brace & Company, 1930.

NOTES ON THE CONCEPT OF COMMITMENT

HOWARD S. BECKER

The term "commitment" enjoys an increasing vogue in sociological discussion. Sociologists use it in analyses of both individual and organizational behavior. They use it as a descriptive concept to mark out forms of action characteristic of particular kinds of people or groups. They use it as an independent variable to account for certain kinds of behavior of individuals and groups. They use it in analyses of a wide variety of phenomena: power, religion, occupational recruitment, bureaucratic behavior, political behavior, and so on.

In spite of its widespread use, the appearance of the concept of commitment in sociological literature has a curious feature the reader with an eye for trivia will have noticed. In articles studded with citations to previous literature on such familiar concepts as power or social class, commitment emerges unscathed by so much as a single reference. This suggests what is in fact the case: there has been little formal analysis of the concept of commitment and little attempt to integrate it explicitly with current sociological theory. Instead, it has been treated as a primitive concept, introduced where the need is felt without explanation or examination of its character or credentials. As is often the case with unanalyzed concepts used in an *ad hoc* fashion, the term has been made to cover a wide range of common-sense meanings, with predictable ambiguities.

In what follows, I consider the uses to which the concept of commitment has been put and the possible reasons for its increasing popularity, indicate the nature of one of the social mechanisms to which the term implicity refers, and develop a rudimentary theory of the social processes and conditions involved in the operation of this mechanism. Because the term has been used to express a varied assortment of ideas, it is fruitless to speculate on its "real" meaning. I have instead chosen one of the several images evoked by "commitment" and tried to make its meaning clearer. In doing so, I will unavoidably short-change those for whom the term evokes other of the associated images more strongly. The ultimate remedy for this injustice will be a classification and clarification of the whole family of images involved in the idea of commitment. . . .

Reprinted by permission of the publisher, The University of Chicago Press, from Howard S. Becker, "Notes on the Concept of Commitment," *American Journal of Sociology,* **66**: July, 1960. Copyright 1960, 1961 by The University of Chicago.

I.

What kind of explanation of consistent human behavior lies implicit in the concept of commitment? Clearly, the person is envisioned as having acted in such a way ("made a commitment") or being in such a state ("being committed") that he will now follow a consistent course. But, as the term is ordinarily used, the nature of this act or state of commitment is not specified; it appears to be regarded as either self-explanatory or intuitively understandable. If we use the concept in this way, the proposition that commitment produces consistent lines of activity is tautological, for commitment, whatever our intuitions about its independent existence, is in fact synonymous with the committed behavior it is supposed to explain. It is a hypothesized event or condition whose occurrence is inferred from the fact that people act as though they were committed. Used in this way, the concept has the same flaws as those psychological theories which explain behavior by referring to some unobserved state of the actor's psyche, this state deduced from the occurrence of the event it is supposed to explain.

To avoid this tautological sin, we must specify the characteristics of "being committed" independent of the behavior commitment will serve to explain. Schelling (1956), in his analysis of the process of bargaining, furnishes a hypothetical example whose analysis may help us arrive at a characterization of the elements of one of the mechanisms that might be called "commitment." Suppose that you are bargaining to buy a house; you offer sixteen thousand dollars, but the seller insists on twenty thousand. Now suppose that you offer your antagonist in the bargaining certified proof that you have bet a third party five thousand dollars that you will not pay more than sixteen thousand dollars for the house. Your opponent must admit defeat because you would lose money by raising your bid; you have committed yourself to pay no more than you originally offered.

This commitment has been achieved by making a *side bet*. The committed person has acted in such a way as to involve other interests of his, originally extraneous to the action he is engaged in, directly in that action. By his own actions prior to the final bargaining session he has staked something of value to him, something originally unrelated to his present line of action, on being consistent in his present behavior. The consequences of inconsistency will be so expensive that inconsistency in his bargaining stance is no longer a feasible alternative.

The major elements of commitment present themselves in this example. First, the individual is in a position in which his decision with regard to some particular line of action has consequences for other interests and activities not necessarily related to it. Second, he has placed himself in that position by his own prior actions. A third element is present, though so obvious as not to be apparent: the committed person must be aware that he has made the side bet and must recognize that his decision in this case will have ramifications beyond it. The element of recognition of the interest created by one's prior action is a necessary component of commitment because, even though one has such an interest, he will not act to implement it (will not act so as to win his side bet) unless he realizes it is necessary.

Note that in this example commitment can be specified independent of the consistent activity which is its consequence. The side bet not to pay more and the additional interest this creates in sticking to the original offered price occur independent of the fact of refusing to pay more. Were we to interview this clever bargainer before the final bargaining session, he presumably would tell us that he understood his interests could now be served only by paying no more.

Thus, whenever we propose commitment as an explanation of consistency in behavior, we must have independent observations of the major components in such a proposition: (1) prior actions of the person staking some originally extraneous interest on his following a consistent line of activity; (2) a recognition by him of the involvement of this originally extraneous interest in his present activity; and (3) the resulting consistent line of activity.

We cannot, of course, often expect social life to be of the classic simplicity of this economic example. Rather, interests, side bets and acts of commitment, and consequent behavior will seem confounded and irremediably mixed, and it will require considerable ingenuity to devise appropriate indexes with which to sort them out. But the economic example shows us the skeleton we can look for beneath the flesh of more complicated social processes.

II.

If we confined our use of commitment to those cases where individuals have deliberately made side bets, we would seldom bring it into our analyses of social phenomena. What interests us is the possibility of using it to explain situations where a person finds that his involvement in social organization has, in effect, made side bets for him and thus constrained his future activity. This occurs in several ways.

A person sometimes finds that he has made side bets constraining his present activity because the existence of *generalized cultural expectations* provides penalties for those who violate them. One such expectation operates in the area of work. People feel that a man ought not to change his job too often and that one who does is erratic and untrustworthy. Two months after taking a job a man is offered a job he regards as much superior but finds that he has, on the side, bet his reputation for trustworthiness on not moving again for a period of a year and regretfully turns the job down. His decision about the new job is constrained by his having moved two months prior and his knowledge that, however attractive the new job, the penalty in the form of a reputation for being erratic and unstable will be severe if he takes it. The existence of generalized cultural expectations about the behavior of responsible adult males has combined with his recent move, to stake his personal reputation, nominally extraneous to the decision about the new job, on that decision.

A person often finds that side bets have been made for him by the operation of *impersonal bureaucratic arrangements.* To take a simple instance, a man who wishes to leave his current job may find that, because of the rules governing the firm's pension fund, he is unable to leave without losing a considerable sum of money he has in that fund. Any decision about the new job involves a financial side bet the pension fund has placed for him by its rules.

The situation of the Chicago schoolteacher presents a somewhat more complicated system of side bets made by the operation of bureaucratic arrangements. Teachers prefer to teach middle-class children. To do so, they must be assigned to a school containing such children. Teachers can request assignment to as many as ten different schools; assignments are made, as openings occur, to the teacher whose request for a given school is of longest standing. New teachers are assigned to schools for which there are no requests, the lower-class schools teachers like least. The desirable schools have the longest list of requests outstanding, while less desirable schools have correspondingly shorter lists. The teacher in the lower-class school who desires to transfer must, in picking out the ten schools she will request, take into account the side bets the operation of the bureaucratic transfer system has made for her. The most important such bet has to do with time. If she selects one of the most desirable schools, she finds that she has lost a bet about the time it will take her to get out of her present position, for it takes a long time to reach the top of the list for one of these schools. She can instead choose a less desirable school (but better than her present situation) into which she can move more quickly, thus winning the side bet on time. This system of bets constraining her transfer requests has been made in advance by the bureaucratic rules governing requests for transfer.

One might ask in what sense the person's prior actions have made a side bet in these two instances. How has he, by his own act, placed himself in a position where his decision on a new job or request for transfer involves these other considerations? Is it not rather the case that he has had no part in it, being constrained by forces entirely outside himself? We can without sophistry, I think, locate the crucial action which has created the commitment in the person's acquiescence to the system, in his agreeing to work under the bureaucratic rules in force. By doing this, he has placed all the bets which are given in the structure of that system, even though he does not become aware of it until faced with an important decision.

Side bets constraining behavior also come into existence through the process of *individual adjustment to social positions.* A person may so alter his patterns of activity in the process of conforming to the requirements for one social position that he unfits himself for other positions he might have access to. In so doing, he has staked the ease of performance in the position on remaining where he is. To return to our earlier example, some Chicago schoolteachers chose to remain in a lower-class school for the lengthy period necessary to reach the top of the list for a very desirable middle-class school. When the opportunity to make the move came, they found that they no longer desired to move because they had so adjusted their style of teaching to the problems of dealing with lower-class children that they could not contemplate the radical changes necessary to teach middle-class children. They had, for instance, learned to discipline children in ways objectionable to middle-class parents and become accustomed to teaching standards too low for a middle-class school. They had, in short, bet the ease of performance of their job on remaining where they were and in this sense were committed to stay.

Goffman's (1955) analysis of *face-to-face interaction* suggests another way side bets are made through the operation of social processes. He notes that persons present to their fellows in any sequence of interaction an image of themselves they may or may not be able to live up to. Having once claimed to be a certain kind of person, they find it necessary to act, so far as possible, in an appropriate way. If one claims implicitly, in presenting himself to others, to be truthful, he cannot allow himself to be caught in a lie and is in this way committed to truth-telling. Goffman points out that the rules governing face-to-face interaction are such that others will ordinarily help one preserve the front he has put forward ("save face"). Nevertheless, a person will often find his activity constrained by the kind of front he has earlier presented in interaction: he finds he has bet his appearance as a responsible participant in interaction on continuing a line of activity congruent with that front.

This review of the social mechanisms through which persons make side bets extraneous to a particular line of activity that nevertheless later constrain that activity is not exhaustive. It serves only to point the direction for empirical study of side-bet mechanisms, in the course of which a more definitive classification might be made.

III.

As some of our examples indicate, commitments are not necessarily made consciously and deliberately. Some commitments do result from conscious decisions, but others arise crescively; the person becomes aware that he is committed only at some point of change and seems to have made the commitment without realizing it. By examining cases of both kinds, we may get some hints toward a theory of the genesis of commitments.

Such a theory might start with the observation that the commitment made without realization that it is being made—what might be termed the "commitment by default"—arises through a series of acts no one of which is crucial but which, taken together, constitute for the actor a series of side bets of such magnitude that he finds himself unwilling to lose them. Each of the trivial acts in such a series is, so to speak, a small brick in a wall which eventually grows to such a height the person can no longer climb it. The ordinary routines of living—the daily recurring events of everyday life—stake increasingly more valuable things on continuing a consistent line of behavior, although the person hardly realizes this is happening. It is only when some event changes the situation so as to endanger those side bets that the person understands what he will lose if he changes his line of activity. The person who contributes a small amount of each paycheck to a nontransferable pension fund which eventually becomes sizable provides an apposite illustration of this process; he might willingly lose any single contribution but not the total accumulated over a period of years.

If this is the case with commitment by default, we might conjecture that it is also true of commitments resulting from conscious decisions. Decisions do not of themselves result in consistent lines of action, for they are frequently changed. But some decisions do produce consistent behavior. We can perhaps account for this variety of outcomes of decisions by the proposition that only those decisions bolstered by the making of sizable side bets will produce consistent behavior. Decisions not supported by such side bets will lack staying power, crumpling in the face of opposition or fading away to be replaced by other essentially meaningless decisions until a commitment based on side bets stabilizes behavior.

We might also note that a consistent line of activity will often be based on more than one kind of side bet; several kinds of things valuable to the person may be staked on a particular line of activity. For instance, the man who hesitates to take a new job may be deterred by a complex of side bets: the financial loss connected with a pension fund he would lose if he moved; the loss of seniority and "connections" in his present firm which promise quick advance if he stays; the loss of ease in doing his work because of his success in adjusting to the particular conditions of his present job; the loss of ease in domestic living consequent on having to move his household; and so on.

IV.

For a complete understanding of a person's commitments we need one more element: an analysis of the system of values or, perhaps better, valuables with which bets can be made in the world he lives in. What kinds of things are conventionally wanted, what losses feared? What are the good things of life whose continued enjoyment can be staked on continuing to follow a consistent line of action?

Some systems of value permeate an entire society. To recur to Schelling's example of the canny house-buyer, economic commitments are possible only within the confines of a system of property, money, and exchange. A side bet of five thousand dollars has meaning only where money is conventionally valued.

However, it is important to recognize that many sets of valuable things have value only within a subcultural group in a society and that many side bets producing commitment are made within systems of value of limited provenience. Regional, ethnic, and social class subcultures all provide raw material for side bets peculiar to those sharing in the culture, as do the variants of these related to differing age and sex statuses. A middle-class girl can find herself committed to a consistently chaste line of behavior by the sizable side bet of her reputation that middle-class culture attaches to virginity for females. A girl who is a member of a social class where virginity is less valued could not be committed in this way; and, except for a few puritanical enclaves in our society, boys cannot acquire commitments of this kind at all, for male virginity has little value, and no side bet of any magnitude could be made with it.

More limited subcultures, such as those associated with occupational groups or political parties, also provide sets of valuables with which side bets can be made. These esoteric systems of value must be discovered if the commitments of group members are to be understood. For instance, the professional dance musician achieves job security by becoming known as a dependable man to a large group of employing band-leaders and to an even larger group of musicians who are not leaders but will recommend him for jobs they hear about. The dependable man is, among other things a man who will take any job offered him unless he is already engaged; by doing this, he shows that he will not let a leader who needs a vital man down. His reputation for not letting leaders down has economic value to him, for leaders who believe in that reputation will keep him working. When he is offered a job that he does not, for whatever reason, want, he finds himself committed to taking it anyway; by failing to do so, he would lose the reputation for dependability and the consequent steady supply of jobs the value system of the music business has bet for him on his consistency in always taking whatever job is offered.

In short, to understand commitments fully, we must discover the systems of value within which the mechanisms and processes described earlier operate. By so doing, we understand not only how side bets are made but the kind of counters with which they can be made; in fact, it is likely that we cannot fully penetrate the former without understanding the latter.

REFERENCES

Goffman, Erving. "On Face-Work," *Psychiatry,* **18** (August, 1955), pp. 213-31.

Schelling, Thomas C. "An Essay on Bargaining," *American Economic Review,* **46** (June, 1956), pp. 281-306.

CHAPTER TEN

HOW IS PUBLIC OPINION FORMED ON ISSUES OF PUBLIC POLICY?

THE ISSUE OF PUBLIC OPINION

The scene: The student union. Two students, Aaron and Bruce are sitting at a table drinking coffee. Aaron is reading the morning paper and Bruce is reading an assignment.

Aaron: I see the filibuster is still going on against the so-called safe streets bill. Have you been following this?

Bruce: Not too much. Something certainly needs to be done.

Aaron: Yes, but this bill gives the government a dangerous amount of power. You can't be sure that they won't use it against political dissenters and people like that.

Bruce: Yeh. I guess so. A lot of people don't feel safe though. Sometimes I even feel scared walking downtown alone in the daytime.

Aaron: O.K. but we don't want the cure to be worse than the disease.

(Three other people join the table: Aaron's girl friend, Carla; her roommate, Doris; and Doris' boyfriend, Ed. After an exchange of greetings, Aaron turns to Carla.)

Aaron: Did you see this business about Senator Marshall crying during the debate on the safe streets bill?

Carla: Really? He's doing a politically cour. . .

Ed: (interrupting) This man Marshall is a real demagogue. And a weakling. Any man who can't control his emotions better than that doesn't belong in public life.

Doris: (somewhat embarrassed) Oh, Ed. You don't really mean that, do you?

Carla: (angrily): That's a childish attitude. Here is a man who is risking his whole political career and getting all kinds of personal attacks and you call him a weakling.

Aaron: Don't you think, Ev, that he's fighting for an important issue?

Ed: The name is Ed. Sure the issue is important. Someone has to have the guts to treat the hoods and muggers the way they deserve—without getting tangled up in all this constitutional nonsense.

Doris: Oh, Wow! Is that how you really think, Ed?

Bruce: It's dangerous to give the government so much power.

Carla: So you think the Constitution is nonsense.

Ed: (raising his voice somewhat) I didn't say the Constitution was nonsense. Just that it shouldn't be used as an excuse for doing nothing. The men who wrote the Constitution would have known how to deal with criminals a lot better than people like Senator Marshall with his maudlin sentimentality.

Aaron: (still calm) You know, don't you, that the deans of the top ten law schools have issued a statement that in their opinion the bill is unconstitutional on at least seven different grounds.

Ed: (somewhat taken aback) That's their opinion.

Carla: You know better, of course, than the top ten constitutional lawyers in the country.

Doris: (to group) You know, Ed's views aren't really as extreme as they sound. He knows as well as we do that the issue of crime in the streets is very complicated.

Ed: Whoever said it was simple.

(A friend from the next table, Gary, has been listening and pulls his chair over.)

Gary: What's the great debate?

Aaron: On the merits of the safe streets bill.

Gary: Well, is it good for the Jews or bad for the Jews?

(they laugh)

Carla: (serious and still annoyed) I don't know how it is for the Jews but it sure ain't good for the blacks. I know whose apartments those cops are going to be barging into without warrants on the basis of "suspicion."

Aaron: I know this isn't true for you, Ed, but a lot of people are for this bill because it's a symbol of putting down black people.

Doris: Ed is no racist.

Ed: Who said anything about blacks? I'm talking about criminals, black or white. If you don't have the guts to punish what you think is wrong, then people won't do right. It's as simple as that.

Gary: I'll tell you though. The people I work with at the factory really see it as putting the blacks in their place. Almost all the black guys are against it if they care about it. Black or white though, that's what the issue is about for them, whether it is for you or not.

Ed: Look, I never said I was for this bill. As a matter of fact, I have serious crit-
         icisms. I just insist that something has to be done.

Aaron: Right, but the trick is to do it without violating a lot of important things
         like the right to privacy and due process.

Gary: Amen.

         (Ed and Doris excuse themselves and the conversation moves on to other
         things.)

There in the student union, a bit of public opinion is in the process of formation over
a hypothetical safe streets bill. How can one best understand the process operating
here and more generally? How do people come to believe what they do on issues of
public policy? How is public opinion formed?

THE MAJOR VIEWS

Personality

Twenty-five years ago, in the aftermath of World War II, social scientists were haunted
by the spectre of fascism. The fascist countries had just been defeated militarily, but
the memory of the triumphant mass movements of the 1930's was still fresh. And
there was no guarantee that the spectre might not appear again in some new guise,
perhaps even in America.

When something haunts social scientists, they exorcise it by doing research. In
this case, the result was a collection of studies that left its mark on an entire generation of social scientists, published under the title, *The Authoritarian Personality*
(1950). The research was guided, to quote the authors,

> by the conception of an individual whose thoughts about man and society
> form a pattern which is properly described as antidemocratic and which
> springs from his deepest emotional tendencies. Can it be shown that such
> a person really exists? If so, what precisely is he like?. . .What are the organ-
> izing forces within the person?

The distinction between opinion and personality is central to this view. As
McClosky states it in the selection included in this chapter,

> Personality is both a more general and more fundamental. . .term in the sense
> that it often underlies attitudes [and opinions] and furnishes the motive force
> that impels them. When one uses the term personality, one is talking about
> such things as needs, motives, affect, defense mechanisms, and the like; when
> one uses the term attitude [or opinion] , one is talking about implicit or ex-
> plicit beliefs regarding a specified class of objects.

The posture that an individual takes on public issues in this view stems from
basic personality needs. The authors of *The Authoritarian Personality* make explicit
the premise that underlies their work:

A primary hypothesis in this research is that an individual is most receptive to those ideologies which afford the fullest expression to his over-all personality structure. Thus, a person clinically described as strongly authoritarian, projective, and destructive is likely to be receptive to an anti-democratic ideology such as ethnocentrism—ultimately fascism as the total social objectification of these trends—because it expresses his needs so well.

The Authoritarian Personality offered a number of measures of personality and belief but undoubtedly the most widely used of them—and perhaps the most widely used questionnaire instrument of all time—is the F-scale. The F-scale was so called because it was intended to measure those personality traits that expressed "a predisposition or deep-lying receptivity to fascism."

The F-scale does not itself try to measure attitudes or opinions on public issues. The focus is not on politics or social institutions, but on personal values and beliefs about the nature of man and society. The scale contains a number of related sub-themes—for example, submissiveness to authority, a rejection of emotion and of attempts to look into one's own deeper motives and conflicts, contempt for weakness, intolerance of ambiguity, and general rigidity.

Some illustrative items from the F-scale will help to convey the characteristic world view of the authoritatian personality. To measure submission to authority, for example, people were asked to express agreement with the statement, "Every person should have complete faith in some supernatural power whose decisions he obeys without question." To measure the distrust of exploring feelings and motives, respondents expressed agreement or disagreement with the statement, "When a person has a problem or worry, it is best for him not to think about it but to keep busy with more cheerful things."

What might an advocate of this view see in the conversation about the safe streets bill in the beginning of this chapter? His attention would rather rapidly move to Ed because several of Ed's remarks suggest themes that are central to the authoritarian personality. Strength and weakness is a concern in several remarks—thus Senator Marshall is a "weakling" who can't control his emotions, and twice Ed mentions "having the guts" to do something. Submission to authority is suggested, although less clearly. He is quick to clarify a remark that might be interpreted as an attack on the founding fathers. Aaron's appeal to the authority of the ten law school deans might well have carried some weight with Ed and account for the apparent modification of his position in the course of the conversation. His distrust of emotional expression is indicated in his remarks about Senator Marshall's sentimentality and the inappropriateness of expressing emotions in public life.

A brief conversation is thin evidence for drawing conclusions about underlying personality dispositions compared to a battery of questionnaire scales and clinical tests. But an advocate of this view would have reasonable grounds for suspecting that he can understand a lot about Ed's attitude toward the safe streets bill *and* many other issues by gaining a better understanding of his personality. It's possible that others in the group are similarly influenced by personality factors in their own beliefs, but they give fewer grounds for such a presumption.

Many years and much research have passed since the publication of *The Authoritarian Personality*. The original studies were open to a variety of important methodological criticisms which need not concern us here. This work remains the prototype of the view that much can be gained in understanding how people come to believe what they do on public issues by looking at their underlying personality needs. With all its impact on the field though, *The Authoritarian Personality* still represents only a special case of the more general view. Authoritarianism is not the only personality syndrome that one might relate to public opinion. A wide variety of hypotheses in this mode are possible—for example, that men who are anxious about their sexual potency adopt very militant postures on issues of international conflict, or that permissive child rearing practices produce a "rebel" personality syndrome that leads to opposition to "the establishment" on any public issue. Similarly, one might try to understand the support or opposition to political candidates by the extent to which their image taps unconscious motives. To be concerned with whether a candidate can "stand up to the Russians" (or whoever the current devil may be) says more, in this view, about the personality needs of the observer than about his attitudes and ideology.

McClosky, in the selection included here, focuses on those underlying personality dispositions that lead to isolationism in the twentieth century. "Needs, motives, defenses, frailties, and fears color men's judgments about foreign affairs just as they do their evaluation of other matters," he writes. While he does not invoke the authoritarian personality as such, the personality syndrome that he identifies clearly owes a strong debt to *The Authoritarian Personality*. McClosky focuses on what he calls "aversive" personality dispositions—those that aim to "avoid, deny, deflect, shut out, or incapacitate other persons or related stimulus objects rather than to reach out to, embrace, accept, or involve them." The manifestation of this disposition sounds not very different from the authoritarian personality—a "generalized hostility, suspiciousness, misanthropy, inflexibility, a tendency toward 'we-they' distinctions, intolerance of differences, and so forth."

Without denying that isolationism is a complex political attitude shaped by many determinants, McClosky tries to impress upon us the extent to which it is "shaped by a complex set of personality variables, primarily of an aversive nature." In thus trying to understand public opinion on foreign policy by reference to underlying personality predispositions, McClosky is a good representative of this view in operation.

Group Influence

In the same years that *The Authoritarian Personality* was making its impact on the field, many social psychologists were, to use Katz and Lazarsfeld's phrase, "rediscovering the primary group." Of course, even social scientists were aware of the fact that most people are involved in social networks of frequently quite intense and intimate interpersonal relations. What needed rediscovering was not the fact itself, but its pervasive implications for a variety of areas, including the formation of public opinion.

The rise of the mass media had, in this view, over-impressed many observers who saw in it a technique of irresistible power in the molding of public opinion. The use of the new technology by the Nazi regime, and the central role played by propaganda minister Joseph Goebbels in this regime, led many to despair (and others, perhaps, to rejoice) at the helplessness of the masses in the face of this powerful tool. It was not for themselves that they feared, of course, feeling able enough to resist the irresistible. But hadn't millions of others, more easily led, already succumbed to such techniques as "the big lie"?

It must have been with considerable relief, then, that many social scientists embraced the idea that primary group relations placed an important constraint on the direct effect of the mass media. Be it poison or balm that is being dispensed, it does not pass directly through a hypodermic needle into the bloodstream of the unsuspecting individual, but is mediated by a complex set of person-to-person interactions.

This perspective, and the contrast it offers with *The Authoritarian Personality,* is well illustrated by a highly influential study of "Cohesion and Disintegration in the Wehrmacht during World War II" (Shils and Janowitz, 1948). The German Army in World War II proved quite resistant to allied propaganda attempts through most of the war. Only in the very late stages did its remarkable cohesion deteriorate and desertions occur in significant numbers. One hypothesis, in the spirit of the previous perspective, might have attributed this cohesion to the fanatic loyalty and blind obedience of these German soldiers,with their anti-democratic character structure, to their beloved Fuehrer.

On the basis of an array of data, including intensive interviews with captured German soldiers, the authors were led to reject the explanation that these men continued to fight because of ideology or blind devotion to an authority figure. They fought instead, the authors argued, because of loyalty to the friends with whom they shared the mud and trenches. As long as units remained intact and preserved the intense interpersonal relationships of men under fire, group cohesion was proof against the effectiveness of allied propaganda appeals. In the late stages of the war, when high casualties forced the German Army to combine units and fill them with large numbers of green replacements who were strangers to the group, these units began to disintegrate and allied propaganda began to have its effects for the first time.

The critical idea in this view of the public opinion process is to see it as a *normative* one. However controversial many public issues are in the society as a whole, there is frequently a consensus within small social groups. It shouldn't surprise anyone to discover, for example, that although all of his or her friends think that the smoking of marijuana should be legal, there are other groups in which the mere expression of such a permissive view would be regarded with outrage. We all live in circumscribed social worlds in which beliefs about many issues of public policy take on a normative character—that is, there is *a clear expectation about the views that a good member of the group ought to have* and those who fail to hold the "proper" views suffer accordingly. They lose status in the group and, in extreme cases, find themselves outcasts.

Not all issues are the subject of group norms. For many areas, there may be no clear expectation for group members. These issues are simply considered irrelevant for membership and a good group member is free to believe whatever he wants without fear of social ostracism. But, for any issue, we must ask under what conditions and in which groups it will become normative in the myriad social networks that make up public opinion.

The operation of this normative process on attitudes toward public issues was dramatically illustrated in the Bennington Study by Newcomb (1958). Newcomb studied the shift in political orientation by students as they moved through

Bennington College in the years 1935-39. Some individuals changed very little, but the general trend for the total group was a pronounced shift from "freshman conservatism to senior nonconservatism." Newcomb examined many factors to account for the shift but group influence emerged as the central theme. Nonconservatism was clearly normative in this community and both those who shifted and those who didn't felt it.

Many of Newcomb's quotations from his respondents reveal this normative process in operation. One girl, still conservative, explained, "I wanted to disagree with all the noisy liberals, but I was afraid and I couldn't. So I built up a wall inside me against what they said. I found I couldn't compete, so I decided to stick to my father's ideas. For at least two years I've been insulated against all college influences" (p. 269). A non-conservative describes her shift: "It didn't take me long to see that liberal attitudes had prestige value. But all the time I felt inwardly superior to persons who want public acclaim. . .I became liberal at first because of its prestige value. I remain so because the problems around which my liberalism centers are important. What I want now is to be effective in solving the problems" (p. 272). Another non-conservative states frankly, "I was so anxious to be accepted that I accepted the political complexion of the community here" (p. 273). Whether it is resisted or accepted, most of the Bennington students implicitly or explicitly acknowledged that group norms existed, promoting a nonconservative view on political issues. The content of such norms might differ at another school and might be less intense at a larger and more heterogeneous university, but many studies since the original Bennington research have documented a similar normative process among college students on issues of public policy.

People, of course, belong to many different groups simultaneously. A college student not only may have several circles of friends on campus but also a family and friends back home. The typical adult may belong to a church group, a civic group, a political group, an informal neighborhood social group, and an after-work group of friends from his or her job. Consequently, people sometimes find themselves under conflicting pressures: their various membership groups have a different consensus on public issues.

Such a state of conflicting pressures is not typical for two reasons. First, people tend to select their membership groups, mostly unconsciously, in a way that produces compatibility among them. Second, these different groups rarely care about the same issue with equal intensity. Friends on the job may be very involved on an issue that affects them directly—for example, fringe benefits—but have no consensus or collective concern about a proposed new housing law. Neighborhood friends may have exactly the reverse pattern of interests.

Nevertheless, on certain broad-ranging issues that affect many groups, some people are likely to find themselves in a quandary, torn between the conflicting pressures of their different friends and associates. Rather than emerging with some stable opinion, such people seem likely to end up either with no opinion or with an uncertain and unstable one. Indeed, studies of voting preferences in presidential campaigns have found that this is exactly what occurs. Lazarsfeld, Berelson, and Gaudet (1948), studying the 1944 campaign, identified a set of registered voters subject to "cross-pressures" as a consequence of belonging simultaneously to several groups with different candidate preferences. Compared to those who were not cross-pressured, these people had less interest in the campaign suggesting a tendency to withdraw from the issue as a way of handling the conflict. Furthermore, they were much more likely to vacillate in their candidate preference, taking the longest to make up their mind on how to vote if they decided to vote at all. Such a pattern is precisely what one would expect from a person subject to conflicting norms and expectations from others.

The emphasis on interpersonal influence does not ignore the role of the mass media. Katz and Lazarsfeld, in the selection included here, bring in the mass media through the idea of a "two-step flow of influence." Certain members of the group serve as "opinion leaders." These opinion leaders are not necessarily community notables or, in fact, different in any conspicuous way from other members of the group. Furthermore, the particular individuals who play the opinion leader role may differ from issue to issue. One may be an opinion leader in some cases simply because of greater interest and involvement in a particular issue area.

The opinion leaders, in this view, link the mass media and interpersonal influence. Opinion leaders frequently function as "gate-keepers," determining what information from the mass media will enter the group. As Katz and Lazarsfeld put it, "ideas often seem to flow *from* radio, [television], and print to opinion leaders and *from them* to the less active sections of the population."

An advocate of this view would see the whole process at work quite clearly in the conversation about the safe streets bill. Aaron is a good nominee for opinion leader. He feeds into the group information and arguments about the issue—for example, that the bill is seen as unconstitutional by ten law school deans, or that it might be used to suppress political dissent. These arguments are then available for other group members to buttress their beliefs. Thus, Bruce, who initially indicated little awareness of the bill, is able to produce an argument that "it is dangerous to give the government so much power,"and Carla, although she changes the law school deans to experts in constitutional law, is similarly making use of an input from Aaron.

The target of group influence is, of course, the deviant, Ed. He is subjected to considerable pressure in the short dialogue. His girl friend, although she later comes to his defense in an equivocal way ("Ed's views aren't really as extreme as they sound"), clearly lends her support to the general group norm about the safe streets bill ("Oh, wow! Is that how you really think, Ed?"). Carla's attack is most direct and harsh, but the others apply steady pressure also. Ed feels that he must defend himself against the suspicion that he is a racist, a heavy charge in such company.

Without admitting any change, Ed, in fact, moves into line with the group norm by denying support for the disliked bill. The group quickly moves to accept this concession and, the deviant thus chastened, the tension abates. Has Ed's attitude really changed? Would he now give a different response to a public opinion pollster who asked him about the bill? This depends on the further operation of the group process. One suspects that Ed's link to the group is mainly through his girl friend, Doris (Aaron, for example, doesn't even know his name accurately). If he is to become an accepted member of this friendship circle, he will clearly need to shift some attitudes on public issues. If, as seems more likely, he goes his separate way, Doris will then find herself in a situation of cross-pressures between the group and Ed. We can make some good guesses about her political opinions in the future, contingent on how she resolves this conflict. In sum, it is the process of interpersonal relations that provides the key to understanding the formation of opinion on public issues.

Organizing Frameworks

At the height of the American involvement in the Vietnam war, it was not uncommon for pollsters to uncover individuals whose opinions seemed to elude their conventional categories. Such individuals would warmly embrace the suggestion that the United States should increase its military efforts, perhaps even invading North Vietnam. But even as the interviewer was mentally coding them as "hawks," they would embrace with equal ardor the suggestion that the United States should withdraw its forces from Vietnam as soon as possible. Inconsistent? Only in the eyes of the beholder who has inappropriately imposed his own organizing framework on the unsuspecting respondent.

Belief systems such as "liberal," "conservative," "hawk," and "dove" undoubtedly are useful in understanding the public policy positions of *some* individuals. Once a person has been correctly identified as a political conservative, for example, we know something about him that enables us to predict with some success his view on any specific issue that is relevant for the liberal-conservative dimension. There is, thus, economy in being able to characterize him in terms of a general label since his various opinions are, in fact, systematically related to one another by means of a generalized belief system.

But what happens when we impose these labels on individuals whose ideas have no such interconnectedness? First, we lose the economy of the description—we are unable to predict successfully that he will hold one "conservative" position from knowing he held another. Thus, we gain no new information from the label. Worse yet, we mislead ourselves by imposing a false order upon his ideas. We are likely to assume he holds beliefs that he does not, and to misinterpret the beliefs that he does hold.

There is an unfortunate tendency to compound the error in a rather arrogant fashion when one discovers that an assumed organizing framework does not fit. Instead of blaming ourselves for having mistakenly imposed the wrong organizing framework, the hapless respondent is blamed for "logical" inconsistency. We would be better off to set about the task of discovering how people actually do organize their beliefs on public issues, rather than taking them to task for not fitting nearly into our liberal-conservative or hawk-dove dimensions.

This is essentially the task that Converse takes upon himself in the selection included in this chapter. He notes that such organizing frameworks as liberal-conservative fit a very small elite only and are not useful for understanding the opinions of at least 90 per cent of the American electorate. For the elite 10 per cent whom he labels ideologues or near-ideologues, it makes some sense to assume that there are, for example, hawks and doves on foreign policy and to ask them to choose among a set of alternatives ordered along this dimension.

But what of the others? If their ideas are not organized by some broad ranging belief system, what alternative framework exists by which they do organize their ideas? First, Converse suggests, one should expect to find many more or less independent clusters of ideas rather than a few grand unifying ones. Second, the organizing principles are more concrete, suggesting different levels of abstraction in their organizing frameworks.

At the highest level of abstraction are the already mentioned ideologues who do indeed use a relatively few broad-ranging, general dimensions to organize their beliefs. At the next level are those who organize their beliefs in terms of how issues affect the interests of various social groupings—workers, farmers, black people, women, etc. Converse writes,

> These people have a clear image of politics as an arena of group interests and, provided that they have been properly advised on where their own group interests lie, they are relatively likely to follow such advise. Unless an issue directly concerns their grouping in an obviously rewarding or punishing way, however, they lack the contextual grasp of the system to recognize how they should respond to it without being told by elites who hold their confidence.

Such people have what Converse calls "ideology by proxy."

A still less abstract organizing framework is one Converse calls "nature-of-the-times." Here the response is to mood rather than group interest. Are things going well or badly? If badly, then do something different—"throw the rascals out." If things are going pretty well,"leave well enough alone." If he felt things were going badly in Vietnam, for example, a respondent using this framework might well have endorsed apparently contradictory proposals as long as each proposed doing something new. He wasn't really telling the pollster that we should simultaneously invade and withdraw but that either alternative was preferable to the existing policy at that time.

Converse suggests, then, that there are three broad organizing frameworks—ideologues (and near-ideologues), group interest people, and nature-of-the-times people.* Can one discern these different frameworks in operation in the discussion of the safe streets bill? Aaron gives the clearest evidence of reacting to the bill in terms of ideology. In arguing against it, he invokes a series of civil liberties issues such as the right to privacy, due process, and the suppression of political dissent.

Gary is joking when he asks, "Is it good for the Jews or bad for the Jews?", but the question, with the appropriate group substituted, is at the heart of the group interest framework. Many issues become symbolic of group interest. Gary and Aaron both suggest that the safe streets bill is regarded by many people as anti-black. Neither says directly that he regards it as such but, if their perception is accurate, we have an important piece of information for understanding the opinions of group interest respondents. Within the group at the student union, it is a reasonable guess that Carla may be responding partly in these terms. She asserts as her own view, not simply how others see the bill, that it is bad for black people and it is reasonable to assume that her sympathies with this group are part of the reason for her opposition.

Finally, Bruce comes closest to a nature-of-the-times respondent in this group. He seems predisposed to be for the bill since he feels that something must be done about the crime problem. His focus is on the problem rather than on the proposed solution, and it is not hard imagining him assenting to many different proposed solutions

---

* He also notes another level—comprising about 1/5 of the American electorate—who have no discernible organizing framework at all by which we can understand their opinion on issues of public policy. In many cases, such individuals in fact have no opinion on public issues to be understood, and are entirely occupied with their private lives.

even if some of them are mutually contradictory.

In sum, it is useful to think of the students in the coffee shop, like the public at large, as composed of people with different organizing frameworks for dealing with public issues. We can't assume that an elite organizing framework such as "libertarian *versus* statist" or the like will be shared by all or even most of them. For even such an elite group as students, we must allow the possibility that group-interest or nature-of-the-times will be the operative framework in their opinion formation.

CONTRASTING THE VIEWS OF PUBLIC OPINION

These ways of looking at how public opinion is formed can be contrasted by examining their treatment of three issues:

1. With what elements does material from the mass media interact? What should one study to unlock the mystery of how public opinion is formed?
2. What is the locus of the key element? Is it internal to the individual or external?
3. To what extent are people consciously aware of the basis of their opinions on public issues?

Nature of Key Element

Each view of public opinion formation starts with some input from the mass media. Each sees the process as an interaction between this media content and a different element. For personality theorists, the media interact with unconscious needs and motives of individuals. What is it, they ask, that the different political objects—candidates, issues, political groups—symbolize for people at an unconscious level?

For group influence theorists, the issue is how media content interacts with the process of interpersonal influence in primary groups. What part of the media content will be transmitted to social groups and in what form? What filters will it pass through before it ultimately reaches the individual and how will it be transformed in the process?

For organizing framework theorists, the issue is whether and how media content will activate the appropriate organizing framework. A group-interest individual, for example, needs information on which groups are well or badly served by a proposal. A nature-of-the-times person needs to know if a vote for a candidate will "send them a message" that he wants sent. An ideologue may need more information on the exact implications of a proposal before he is confident in locating himself.

Locus of Key Element

For two of the views—personality and organizing framework—the key element is located inside the head of individuals. But while both look inside, one is motivational and the other cognitive. Rather than emphasizing more or less conscious thought processes, the personality view emphasizes underlying and frequently unconscious needs and motives. For the organizing framework view, although the thought processes may sometimes be simple-minded ones, they are still ways of coding and organizing the world of public policy.

For group influence theorists, the key element is external to the individual and is found in his interaction patterns with others. In spite of a broad range of cognitive and motivational differences, we are all assumed to be subject to the same interpersonal influence process. What is being transmitted, and how, is seen as more relevant than what is going on inside the head of the receiver.

Awareness

To what extent are individuals conscious of how their opinion is formed? Can we learn anything from asking them why they hold the opinions they do? And can we take their answers at face value or should we treat them as giving off unconscious cues rather than giving reasons?

For the personality view, people are largely unaware of why they are responding as they do. Their answers should not be regarded as reasons but should be examined for unintentional tips about what a political object symbolizes for the respondent. Political objects are ambiguous stimuli onto which respondents can project their unconscious needs. Asking them, "Why do you feel this way?" is akin to asking them to describe what they see in a Rorschach ink-blot.

For the group influence view, the level of respondent awareness is somewhat higher. If asked, the person may be able to say how his friends feel about the issue, but he won't necessarily volunteer or even admit that this is a reason for his opinion. But such interpersonal influence is not really inaccessible to him in the manner of unconscious motives. It just seems less socially commendable to most Americans to admit to being influenced by friends than to have arrived independently at an opinion through individual thought and study.

Finally, for the organizing framework view, the reasons given can essentially be taken at face value. This is not to say, of course, that respondents will identify their organizing framework by name ("I'm a nature-of-the-times man"), but that their answers can be viewed as reasons. A respondent who says, "I didn't really trust him. He seemed to want to change too many things all at once," is assumed to be expressing an image of a candidate that is, for him, a valid reason for opposing him. The candidate calls for change and the nature-of-the-times do not. Similarly, when a candidate is described as "no friend of the working man," this is again assumed to be a reason for the opposition of one who feels his group interest will not be well served by the candidate. It is assumed, then, that their reasons for holding the opinions they do are accessible to people, even if they can't always articulate them in the most elegant fashion.

These, then, are the central issues that we see running through the contrasting views of how public opinion is formed on issues of public policy. They are summarized in Chart 10.

Chart 10 Underlying Issues on How Public Opinion is Formed

	Personality, e.g., McClosky	Group Influence e.g., Katz & Lazarsfeld	Organizing Frameworks, e.g., Converse
With what elements does the content of the mass media interact?	Unconscious needs and motives	Interpersonal influence	Organizing frameworks
Where is the key element located?	Inside the individual	Outside the individual	Inside the individual
Is the individual aware of the basis of his opinion?	Unaware	Semi-aware	Aware

REFERENCES

Adorno, Theodore W.; Frenkel-Brunswik, Else; Levinson, Daniel J.; Sanford, R. Nevitt. *The Authoritarian Personality.* New York: Harper & Row, 1950.

Frenkel-Brunswik, Else; Levinson, Daniel J.; Sanford, R. Nevitt. "The Anti-Democratic Personality," in Newcomb, Theodore M. and Hartley, Eugene L. (Eds.), *Readings in Social Psychology.* New York: Holt, Rinehart, and Winston, 1947.

Lazarsfeld, Paul; Berelson, Bernard; and Gaudet, Hazel. *The People's Choice.* New York: Columbia University Press, 1948.

Newcomb, Theodore M. "Attitude Development as a Function of Reference Groups: The Bennington Study," in Maccoby, E. E., Newcomb, T. M. and Hartley, E. L. (Eds.), *Readings in Social Psychology,* Third Edition, New York: Henry Holt and Co., 1958.

Shils, Edward A. and Janowitz, Morris. "Cohesion and Disintegration in the Wehrmacht in World War II," *Public Opinion Quarterly,* 12 (1948), 280-315.

PERSONALITY CORRELATES OF FOREIGN POLICY ORIENTATION *

HERBERT McCLOSKY

In this paper I shall confine attention to the relation of personality factors to foreign policy orientations. I shall say little about the influence of these factors on the actual formulation of foreign policy. *A fortiori,* I shall ignore such questions as the influence of psychological variables on the roles played by various publics and policy elites in the decision-making process. These are, of course, important questions, but they are not the questions to which the present research is addressed. It is concerned, rather, to explore on various fronts the utility of psychological constructs for political belief, orientation, and activity. Foreign affairs is one of those fronts.

The major foreign policy orientation on which this chapter centers is that contained in the isolationist-nonisolationist distinction. . . .

Definitions

Despite variations, certain elements have been common to most public expressions of the isolationist point of view. One of these is a sense of disengagement from other nations, accompanied often by the conviction that American interests differ from and are incompatible with those of the rest of the world. To the traditional isolationist, there is no community of international interests, and Americans have little to gain by participating in international affairs. They have even less reason to be drawn into "entangling alliances," which are bound to be costly, dangerous, and incapacitating. The element of disengagement is the dominant feature of the isolationist persuasion. From it flows the desire to avoid joint action, the emphasis upon the unlimited and eternal sovereignty of nation-states, and the reluctance to commit the United States to any policy that would increase its obligations to foreign nations. In its more extreme form, the sense of disengagement passes from mere feelings of nonresponsibility for other nations into a ritualistic fear that sustained intercourse with them is

Reprinted with permission of The Macmillan Company from "Personality and Attitude Correlates of Foreign Policy Orientation" by Herbert McClosky, in *Domestic Sources of Foreign Policy* edited by James Rosenau. Copyright © 1967 by The Free Press, a Division of The Macmillan Company.

* This is publication A48 of the Survey Research Center. University of California, Berkeley. Support for the collection and analysis of data reported in this paper has been received from the Social Science Research Council and the Institute of Social Sciences, University of California, Berkeley. This investigation was supported in part by Public Health Research Grant MH-05837 from the National Institute of Health. I am greatly indebted to Paul Sniderman, Fellow at the University of California, for invaluable assistance in the preparation of this chapter.

bound to be contaminating. Not only will it diminish our freedom to act but it will debase and demoralize us. The nation's purity and vitality will be overcome by the decadence and corruption of the countries with which it is compelled to mingle. Thus the United States is portrayed, implicitly or explicitly, as innocent, naive, and trusting, a ready victim of unscrupulous foreign powers. . . .

A word might also be said about the terms *attitude* and *personality,* which figure so prominently in our analysis. By attitude I have in mind the generally accepted definition of the term, excellently stated by Selltiz and Cook "as a disposition to evaluate, or to respond to, an object or class of objects in a given way, this disposition being inferred from consistency of response to the object or members of the object class." By personality I mean a readiness or disposition to respond in a patterned way to stimulus objects of many different types across a range of subject areas. Whereas an attitude disposition is characteristically tied to a particular class of objects, a personality disposition may encompass more than one class of objects or behaviors and these objects need not be manifestly related. Personality is both a more general and more fundamental or genotypic term in the sense that it often underlies attitudes and furnishes the motive force that impels them. When one uses the term personality, one is talking about such things as needs, motives, affect, defense mechanisms, and the like; when one uses the term attitude, one is talking about implicit or explicit beliefs regarding a specified class of objects. One has an attitude toward foreigners, civil rights, political freedom, or international cooperation; but one exhibits a personality disposition when one's responses are marked by stimulus boundedness, a tendency to narrow the number and complexity of stimuli from the phenomenal field, premature closure and the rejection of incompatible material, cognitive restriction, a propensity for dichotomous distinctions, avoidance of trial-and-error behavior, and so forth. These will be recognized as the diagnostic responses of an inflexible personality. . . .

Isolationism: Background and Theory

In the mid-nineteenth century, a large number of Americans were undoubtedly isolationists. Many had little reason to be anything else. They were citizens of a vast continental power, safeguarded against military danger by two great oceans, secure against weak neighbors to the north and south, physically and culturally remote from the world's great centers. They lived, for the most part, in small, widely separated, rural communities, where they had little access to information about the rest of the world. Some were immigrants or the children of immigrants for whom Europe was a continent marked by unceasing quarrels, decaying aristocracies, political and religious oppression, rigid class stratification, and narrow opportunities. It was obviously a place to be avoided. The objective realities, as they appeared to many Americans of that day, made the isolationist point of view a "natural" one, easily learned and internalized, and (one assumes) sustained without help from any special psychological forces. . . .

No one can be certain whether the isolationists of the nineteenth century differed from the nonisolationists of that era in the same ways that isolationists and nonisolationists differ today. But one can scarcely ignore the contrast between America's insularity then and its "vulnerability" now. Apart from the fantastic changes in education, travel, communication, and exposure to other cultures, America's place in the international scene has been so drastically transformed as to defy comparison with that of earlier times. The United States has been engaged in wars on almost every continent, and has participated in numerous international organizations and alliances. Millions of Americans have lived or traveled abroad for extended periods of time. The oceans no longer safeguard American territory, and the lives of Americans have become interlaced with those of other nationals in countless ways.

One may wonder, then, whether isolationism is any longer a "natural," easily learned and accepted view, and whether the forces that once produced it are the same forces that are generating it now. Is isolationism today a "deviant" orientation, one that has different social and psychological meanings from those associated with it a hundred years ago? If, in light of contemporary realities, it is a less plausible and viable point of view than it once was, is it likely to win support from anyone who is not impelled towards it by strong inner needs? To what extent, in short, must we draw upon psychological explanations to account for the holding of isolationist beliefs in mid-twentieth century America?

That personality can be an important determinant of political attitudes has been too often confirmed by previous research to require extensive discussion here. Research on the relation of personality to foreign policy attitudes is less extensive, but the findings turned up on this question are consistent with those from other types of attitude research. There is, indeed, no reason to expect anything else. Needs, motives, defenses, frailities, and fears color men's judgments about foreign affairs just as they do their evaluation of other matters. In some ways, foreign policy offers an especially rich field for the play of personality variables. Many of the issues confronted have been heavily invested with symbolic meanings. They have, in some instances, occasioned struggle and sacrifice and have been dramatized as rallying points for mankind's hopes and fears. Often they present a highly ambiguous set of stimuli, thereby furnishing special opportunities for the engagement of psychological needs. Since they usually bespeak some type of conflict between nations, they furnish numerous occasions for the mobilization of appropriate affect (anger, anxiety, and the like). Sometimes they are incidents in the clash of rival ideologies, one or more of which may be intemperate in its claims. The prospect they raise is often one of danger to national pride, to independence, to territorial integrity, and even to survival.

There is reason to believe that the isolationist orientation is particularly susceptible to the influence of personality. As we shall see, isolationism offers numerous opportunities for marshalling aversive and appetitive dispositions, for the potentiation or projection of motives, for the activation of defense mechanisms, and for the ready translation of psychological needs (e.g. hostility) into appropriate attitude phenotypes. If it is also, as appears to be the case, a deviant view in contemporary American politics, it will be subject to those psychological factors that affect socialization, cognitive function, and the learning of norms.

It should not be necessary to state again that nothing I shall report here is meant to suggest that foreign policy attitudes are determined solely by personality. Obviously they also result from social learning, indoctrination, reference groups, ratiocination, and other nonpersonality influences. The stands men take on international questions are affected by time, geography, and social circumstance and by the configuration of forces in which personality variables are imbedded. In the present paper, however, the focus has been deliberately restricted and no attempt has been made to deal with the entire range of possible determinants.

Assumptions, Hypotheses, and Procedures

Owing to the profusion of variables employed in this study, the list of hypotheses that could possibly be investigated is unusually lengthy. It would burden the reader to face him at this point with the entire list, especially as some hypotheses will in any event need to be reiterated later in the chapter. Specific hypotheses, therefore, will be presented in subsequent sections, where they can be discussed simultaneously with the relevant findings. It might be helpful, however, to indicate at this time some of the major assumptions, general hypotheses, and theoretical considerations on which the analysis proceeded and on which the findings will, hopefully, throw some light. Principal among these are the following:

> Isolationism is in reality a complex political orientation that can originate in
> different ways and from diverse motives. It may spring from psychological
> needs and impulses as well as from social, intellectual, or political elements and
> it need not serve the same function or possess the same meaning for all persons who embrace it.

Personality variables are most likely to evoke isolationist responses when the elements of the former are psychologically close to, cognate with, or readily converted into, the components of the latter and when the stimulus objects ' (say, foreigners) afford adequate opportunity for the mobilization of appropriate effect (say, fear).

From a psychological standpoint, foreign policy attitudes are in principle no different from other political and social attitudes; they spring, together with other attitude phenotypes, from common personality genotypes (or from similar cognitive styles); many of these attitudes will often be more usefully (and more correctly) understood as part of a substantively diverse network of attitudes than as a unique stance arising wholly or largely out of elements intrinsic to the domain of international politics.

Isolationist beliefs will be strongly related to aversive rather than appetitive personality dispositions (i.e. response dispositions that aim to avoid, deny, deflect, shut out, or incapacitate other persons or related stimulus objects rather than to reach out to, embrace, accept, or involve them). This disposition will clearly manifest itself in generalized hostility, suspiciousness, misanthropy, inflexibility, a tendency toward "we-they" distinctions, intolerance of differences, and so forth.

Isolationism in its traditional form is, at the present stage of American life, a deviant political orientation, possessing many of the same characteristics and correlates that mark other extreme or deviant outlooks; support for isolationism, therefore, represents in part a failure of socialization.

Whatever interferes with the learning of political norms—ignorance, political apathy, cultural impoverishment, impaired cognitive functioning, restricted interaction, and even personality disorders—will increase the strength and frequency of isolationist sentiment. . . .

The exploration of these and other notions was carried out through the analysis of data collected from three extensive field surveys during the middle and late nineteen-fifties. I have described the sample and questionnaire procedures in previous publications and shall refrain, therefore, from an extended discussion of those matters here. (See McClosky, 1958; McClosky et al., 1960).

At least this much might be pointed out, however: the first of the three surveys was carried out on a cross-section sample of the population of Minnesota (n=1,082), with the cooperation of the Minnesota Poll. The second was a national cross section survey of 1,484 respondents, administered with the assistance of the American Institute of Public Opinion (Gallup Poll). The third, and most important for present purposes, was a mail survey of 3,020 Democratic and Republican leaders, ranging from office holders at the national levels of party and government to local officials and precinct workers. All had, two years earlier, served as delegates and alternates to the 1956 . . . Democratic and Republican conventions.

The questionnaires employed in the three studies had many similarities. All contained large batteries of attitude and personality scales of the self-administering type, together with numerous questions relating to political experience, personal background, political opinions, and social characteristics. . . .

Isolationism was one of the scales employed in all three studies. . . . The items were inititally drawn from materials published by, and about, active isolationist groups, and they express the sentiments that appeared most frequently in those writings. Built, like the other scales, from a much larger initial pool of items, it was reduced to a nine-item scale after testing and retesting. The items in the Isolationism scale are presented in Table 1, together with their item difficulties for the . . . samples.

Table 1 — The Isolationism Scale — Items and Item Frequencies

Items	Percentage Agree	
	National Leader Sample (n=3,020)	*General Population Sample (n=1,484)*
The best market for American goods is right here at home.	67%	51%
We almost have to restrict the amount of goods we let into this country because labor is so cheap in most other nations.	66	56
Most of the countries which have gotten economic help from America end up resenting what we have done for them.	61	54
These foreign wars America has been in are just part of the old quarrels Europeans have been having among themselves for centuries.	37	49
The federal government should be prevented from giving away any more of our wealth to foreign governments.	37	82
In spite of all the claims to the contrary, America can defend herself, as she has always done, without the aid of our so-called allies.	24	69
George Washington's advice to stay out of agreements with foreign powers is just as wise now as it was when he was alive.	23	75
By belonging to the UN we are running the danger of losing our constitutional right to control our own affairs.	17	55
Anytime American boys are found fighting on foreign shores, it is doubtful that the war is one that the United States should really be in.	17	30

In most of the analysis to follow, I have, for convenience of present-ation, classified respondents as high, middle, and low on each of the scales. The cutting points for these divisions were set by finding the arithmetic thirds in the distribution for the general population on each particular scale. Thus, those who score from 6 to 9 on the Isolationsim scale have been classified as high, or "isolationists"; those scoring from 3 to 5 have been called middle isolationists; and those scoring from 0 to 2 have been designated as low, or nonisolationists. . . .

Findings

For reasons that will become plain, isolationist beliefs are far more com-mon among the general population than they are among the political leaders. (See Table2.) Similarly, isolationism is more frequently expressed among the less educated than the more educated. Intellectuals, as the mean scores show, are least isolationist of all. By every criterion on which we have data, isolationism increases as political and social awareness decline: It is more common among the unthinking than among the informed seg-ments of the electorate, stronger among the poor, the culturally deprived, and any other groups who have been cut off from the mainstreams of the articulate culture. Some of the reasons for this will be considered at a later point. . . .

Table 2   Mean Scores on Isolationism for Three Levels of Articulateness* Among Party Leaders and Supporters

| | LEVEL OF ARTICULATENESS | | | | | | | | | | | |
| | Democratic Leaders | | | Republican Leaders | | | Democratic Followers | | | Republican Followers | | |
	H	M	L	H	M	L	H	M	L	H	M	L
Mean Isolationism Score	1.94	3.54	5.21	3.04	4.60	6.14	2.54	4.50	5.92	2.71	4.56	5.94
Number in Sample	638	1,047	103	384	782	66	76	527	222	83	415	125

*High articulates or intellectuals (H) are defined as college graduates who also score high on the Intellectuality scale. Low articulates (L) are persons of grade school education who score low on the Intellectuality scale.

ISOLATIONISM AND AVERSIVE PERSONALITY TRAITS

Need Aggression

Of all the personality states that one might expect, on theoretical grounds, to relate to isolationism, *n Aggression* and its concomitant aversive dispositions should be among the most powerful. The need to punish, reject, avoid, or contain others is very close to being a genotypic parallel of the values contained in the classical expressions of isolationism. Persons of more appetitive disposition are characterized by their openness to experience, their acceptance and trust of others, their tolerance of human foibles, their sympathy, and their desire to relieve human suffering. Clinical studies show that such persons carry less guilt and anxiety, impute less hostility to others, and are more willing to become involved with their fellow men. We expected, then, that persons of strong misanthropic inclinations would turn out substantially more isolationist than persons of more benign persuasion. We anticipated this correlation not because of any similarity in the substance of the values being correlated, for their content in no way overlaps. Take, for example, the Misanthropy index. A seventeen-item measure, it contains statements that bear entirely on one's feelings about mankind in general and various kinds of individuals in particular. (Typical items: "You have to be pretty choosy about picking friends." "I distrust people who try to be different from the rest of us." "People ought to be satisfied with what they have.") The other scales in Table 3, such as Hostility and Paranoia, are typical clinical scales designed to assess the genotypic personality states suggested by their names. Nothing in the face content of their items suggests a connection with isolationism either.

The connection is as powerful as we had predicted. As can be seen in Table 3, whereas 37 per cent of the isolationists in the political leader sample score high on the Misanthropy scale, only 2 per cent of the nonisolationists are misanthropic to the same degree. For the general population, the scores range from 65 per cent high to 4 per cent. Differences of comparable magnitude are apparent throughout the entire table for every sample (educated and uneducated) and every measure. Correlations computed on the intellectuals in both the elite and general population samples (not shown in this table) yield essentially the same results. Even for intellectual—and in some instances especially for intellectuals—the holding of isolationist beliefs is powerfully correlated with the disposition to punish, reject, and ridicule other men.

The scores on the Paranoia scale in Table 3 are equally consistent and impressive. Paranoia, of course, is a complex response disposition, but it may be understood in part as a projection of hostility. The paranoid tends

Table 3 — Isolationism and Misanthropy
(Percentages Down)

		ISOLATIONISM								
		National Leader Sample (n=3,020)			General Population Sample (n=1,484)					
					High Education*			Low Education*		
		H	M	L	H	M	L	H	M	L
		(643)	(1,150)	(1,227)	(199)	(359)	(229)	(358)	(260)	(79)
Scales										
Hostility	H	37	22	8	35	22	7	49	27	10
	M	48	48	38	47	42	35	41	50	41
	L	15	29	55	18	36	58	11	23	49
Paranoia	H	34	17	8	51	25	10	70	34	23
	M	36	35	24	32	35	26	21	37	29
	L	29	48	67	17	40	64	9	29	48
Misanthropy	H	37	15	2	45	25	5	67	42	13
	M	46	44	20	43	48	28	28	41	49
	L	17	41	78	12	27	67	4	16	38
F-Authoritarianism	H	38	15	3	43	20	3	67	34	6
	M	48	49	21	48	49	29	30	57	53
	L	15	37	76	9	31	68	3	9	41
Contempt for Weakness	H	36	20	8	31	19	8	47	25	8
	M	51	56	39	50	53	45	42	57	61
	L	13	24	54	19	28	47	11	17	32
Intolerance of Human Frailty	H	41	25	10	50	27	15	62	43	23
	M	47	50	45	44	53	45	31	42	46
	L	13	24	45	6	20	40	6	15	32

		Minnesota Sample Only (n=1,082)					
		High Education*			Low Education*		
		H	M	L	H	M	L
		(147)	(272)	(224)	(203)	(177)	(51)
Faith in People	H	9	32	48	11	32	27
	M	48	41	33	39	40	53
	L	43	27	19	50	28	20

*On these and subsequent tables High Education respondents are high school graduates and above; Low Education respondents are those who did not graduate from high school.

to impute to others the impulses and desires to which he is himself prey.
When he perceives others with suspicion, and regards them as deceptive,
conspiratorial, and diabolical, the paranoid is expressing his fear and aversion of others and his desire either to shut them out or to bring them
under control. The wish to dominate and to contain others is one of the
elements in the megalomania and grandiosity that so often mark the paranoid personality. No great leap is required to move from these response
dispositions to an orientation which holds foreigners and foreign nations
to be scheming and dangerous.

The Intolerance of Human Frailty and Contempt for Weakness
scales measure other aspects of the aggressive-aversive response. It may be
logically inconsistent for an isolationist simultaneously to fear the demonic power of others and to scorn them for their weaknesses. It is not, however, psychologically inconsistent. While he fears their power to harm him,
he loathes what he perceives to be their uncertain character, their shabby
morals, and their lack of pride in seeking his collaboration and sympathy.
Then, too, one who has a strong antagonism toward others is often led to
reject them on any ground or pretext that presents itself. The object of
the complaint is less telling in many cases than the impulse that gave rise
to it.

The data collected in the present study—only a small part of which is
being presented here—suggest that the relation between *n Aggression* and
isolationism is not unique. Persons of hostile disposition, it seems, fasten
upon various objects to vent their anger. Foreign nations are only one of
many classes of stimuli to which they respond in the same way. This is
not to suggest, of course, that persons of aggressive disposition will express their anger in all contexts. A person may be manifestly kindly in his
everyday life but fiercely antagonistic in his response to certain public questions. The manner of his response, after all, is a function not only of a general response disposition but of other factors as well, including the saliency
of the stimulus object. If he is indifferent to the state of the nation or its
place in the world, his hostility may be engaged scarcely at all. How strongly he aggresses also depends on whether it is safe to do so. A man who hesitates to disagree with his wife on any question whatever may not shy at
all from expressing his rage toward foreigners, foreign nations, or any other
groups outside his immediate household. . . .

Psychological Inflexibility

The parallels between psychological inflexibility and isolationism are not
so immediately apparent as were those shown in the case of *n Aggression.*
Nevertheless, there are reasons to expect inflexibility and isolationism to
be strongly and positively correlated. These reasons will become evident

from a description of the inflexible personality configuration.

In a study undertaken elsewhere to explore the nature of psychological inflexibility and its significance for political belief and behavior, we have conceptualized inflexibility as an attribute of the defense mechanisms (*e.g.,* reaction formation, rationalization, projection, denial, and the like). The inflexible person is one whose dependence upon these substitute expressions is extreme. Inflexibility, we believe, is a genotypic source trait, for the most part under aversive rather than appetitive control. Its manifest characteristics include an inclination toward black-white polarization and dichotomous distinctions, premature cognitive closure, stereotypic and automatized thought sequences, stimulus fixation, selective attention, and a narrowing of exposure to exclude unfamiliar persons and other stimulus objects. The inflexible person is also characterized by a strong need for order and autonomy, and is made acutely uncomfortable by ambiguity, uncertainty, contingency, complexity, and unfamiliarity. He tends, characteristically, to oversimplify by narrowing the phenomenal field and by assigning fixed, predictable roles to all the players. He is in a continual struggle against his own impulse life, and is rigidly constrained in the limits he imposes upon himself and others. Partly for these reasons, he is unusually susceptible both to hostility and anxiety. He is impatient with, and even angered by, differences and he accomodates poorly to novelty and change. He is severe in his judgments and intolerant of unconventionality. He is attracted to opinions that are categorical and dogmatic and he tends more than most to exclude incompatible information. Despite his elaborate defenses, he has low self-esteem, for which he often compensates by demeaning the motives and behavior of others. Individuals with this personality pattern often suffer a reduction in their capacity for interaction and an impairment in cognitive function.

Although this portrait is based on considerable evidence from our own research and the research of others, it is, of course, ideal-typical and inevitably overdrawn. Even so, we can easily see why individuals of inflexible personality might be expected to favor isolationist sentiments. The parallel, it seems, is far closer than we originally had reason to think. Isolationism offers its supporters a dichotomous choice, a polarization of forces so clearly etched as to contain little or no ambiguity. The world is made simple, with "them" on one side and "us" on the other. "They"—the nationals of other countries—are irrevocably estranged from "us" by culture, politics, language, manners, skin color, customs, and national character. These variations, which might intrigue some people, merely confound and repel the inflexible. He partitions the world in an effort to make order out of diversity, simplicity out of complexity, clarity out of confusion. He also manages in this way to reduce his anxiety about "strangers" who (as he characteristically sees it) freely gratify their impulses at the expense of character, duty, integrity, and independence. Why become involved with such people? Why rescue them from the misfortunes they have inflicted upon themselves?

Since it is important for the inflexible to achieve control and make the world manageable, he resists attachments that deprive him, or his country, of autonomy and initiative. Every treaty, every alliance gives hostages to disorder and uncertainty and strengthens potential enemies. A nation that looks to its own interests without regard for the demands of others is a nation that commands fate; a nation that allies itself with others becomes fate's pawn. Not only does it lose power over the behavior of other nations, but over its own affairs as well.

The strength of the relationship between isolationism on the one side and psychological inflexibility on the other is clearly evident in Table 4.

Table 4 – Isolationism and Inflexibility
(Percentages Down)

		ISOLATIONISM								
		National Leader Sample *(n=3,020)*			*General Population Sample* *(n=1,484)*					
					High Education			*Low Education*		
		H *(643)*	*M* *(1,150)*	*L* *(1,227)*	*H* *(199)*	*M* *(359)*	*L* *(229)*	*H* *(358)*	*M* *(260)*	*L* *(79)*
Scales										
Intolerance of	H	63	42	24	53	23	13	64	43	29
Ambiguity	M	24	29	26	34	37	30	26	35	25
	L	13	28	50	13	40	57	10	22	46
	H	62	51	35	54	32	25	57	38	18
Obsessive	M	21	22	25	20	29	24	23	27	33
	L	17	26	40	26	40	52	20	35	49
	H	46	32	16	53	30	21	65	48	28
Rigidity	M	28	28	24	26	28	23	22	24	37
	L	26	40	60	22	42	57	14	28	35
	H	30	17	8	27	8	3	43	18	4
Inflexibility	M-H	42	34	26	40	30	21	32	39	24
Index	M-L	21	30	33	22	35	29	19	27	37
	L	7	19	32	11	27	48	6	17	35

Among the political influentials, 63 per cent of the isolationists score high on intolerance of ambiguity, compared with 24 per cent of the nonisolationists. Differences of comparable magnitude hold for the general population, for Democratic and Republican leaders, and for both the educated and uneducated. The pattern is equally unmistakable when we examine the results on the Rigidity and Obsessiveness scales, and on the Inflexibility Index. Again it should be observed that the items on these scales are free of political content. All refer to comments about one's personal habits, one's feelings about carelessness, disorder, perfection, decisiveness, the manner of organizing one's work, and so forth. Nothing in the items suggests on their face a connection with isolationism.

Anxiety, Ego-Strength, and Feelings of Marginality

Both anxiety and low ego-strength are aspects of the aversive personality, for while they manifestly testify to dissatisfaction with oneself, they also carry heavy loadings of fear and rage and reflect an implicit wish to escape, avoid, or disarm others. The scales we have listed in Table 5 as measures of anxiety (Psychological Disorganization and Manifest Anxiety) refer primarily to constitutional states, such as restlessness, inability to concentrate, and excessive worry. . . .

Table 5 – Isolationism and Anxiety: Minnesota Sample Only
(Percentages Down)
(n=1,082)

		ISOLATIONISM					
		High Education			Low Education		
		H	M	L	H	M	L
		(147)	(272)	(224)	(203)	(177)	(51)
Scales							
Psychological	H	36	31	19	51	37	24
Disorgani-	M	37	39	40	33	34	29
zation	L	27	30	41	16	29	47
	H	26	22	13	37	22	10
Manifest	M	53	49	46	47	53	49
Anxiety	L	21	29	42	15	25	41

The scales in this table register in one fashion or another feelings of frustration, fear, disappointment, self-doubt, inadequacy, or failure. . . .

It is, of course, now well-established that such psychological states tend—through displacement, the frustration-aggression phenomenon, or the play of other defense mechanisms—to emerge in many of their victims as resentment and envy. As we have elsewhere observed (McClosky

& Schaar), 1965, those who strongly harbor these feelings "tend to project upon the external world the doubts and fears that dominate their own mental life." They are likely to be disgruntled and suspicious toward the world in general. This includes the international world, which mirrors for them the uncertainty, disorder, drift, and normlessness they are inclined to find everywhere.

On this reasoning, we would expect isolationism to be embraced by some people as a way of handling their own insecurities, doubts, and frustrations. Like ethnocentrism, to which it is closely related psychologically, an isolationist orientation would permit them not only to blame others (including other nations) for the bad fate that life has dealt them, but also to satisfy their impulse to punish, reject, and demean others, partly as retribution and partly as a way of bringing other men down to an even lower, more miserable level than their own. Foreign nations, it should be observed, represent a fairly safe target for such aggression. Not only can one usually assail them with impunity, but by doing so one can simultaneously demonstrate one's patriotism. . . .

In Table 6, we test more directly the hypothesis that isolationism is one expression, among others, of a general feeling of malaise or of alienation from the world as one finds it. The Alienation scale shown in that table refers primarily to feelings of personal isolation from primary groups and the absence of a nurturant environment. The Anomy scale assesses the degree to which individuals feel that the society is normless and lacking in direction and meaning. The Cruel World scale measures the tendency to regard the world as cold and indifferent, unconcerned with the respondent's fate. The Bewilderment scale, used only in the MB study, testifies to the respondent's feeling that the world is hopelessly complicated and unfathomable.

The response on each of these measures is uniformly in the predicted direction. Isolationists in both the political leader and general population samples register significantly stronger feelings of estrangement, bewilderment, and moral chaos. By an overwhelming margin, they are also disposed to regard the world as a hostile, dangerous, or indifferent place, populated by potential enemies and harboring innumerable threats. Similar findings turn up on a scale measuring pessimistic outlook on the world's future (not shown on this table), with isolationists scoring strongly pessimistic (in comparison with internationalists) by a ratio of approximately 5 to 1. The results on these scales are consistent for both parties and all education levels.

Whether the relationship between these personality measures and isolationism is causal or epiphenomenal is difficult to say. Like isolationism, they are all measures of dissatisfaction and fear. All refer to some

Table 6 — Isolationism and Feelings of Marginality
(Percentages Down)

		National Leader Sample (n=3,020)			General Population Sample (n=1,484)					
					High Education			Low Education		
		H	*M*	*L*	*H*	*M*	*L*	*H*	*M*	*L*
		(643)	*(1,150)*	*(1,227)*	*(199)*	*(359)*	*(229)*	*(358)*	*(260)*	*(79)*
Scales										
	H	25	17	12	35	26	17	54	33	24
Alienation	M	38	37	31	41	39	28	36	38	37
	L	37	47	57	24	35	55	11	29	39
	H	21	7	1	41	20	5	70	37	13
Anomy	M	48	38	18	46	46	30	25	45	49
	L	32	55	80	13	34	65	5	17	38
Cruel,	H	26	9	2	35	15	2	53	20	6
Indifferent	M	52	44	23	33	49	27	41	52	42
World	L	23	47	77	12	36	70	7	27	52

		Minnesota Sample Only (n=1,082)					
		High Education (n=643)			Low Education (n=431)		
		H	*M*	*L*	*H*	*M*	*L*
		(147)	*(272)*	*(224)*	*(203)*	*(177)*	*(51)*
	H	48	22	10	58	29	12
Bewilderment	M	33	42	32	33	42	29
	L	19	36	58	9	29	59

imagined hostile force that prevents happiness and the realization of one's desires. That they express concern about the world or the society rather than about oneself is really beside the point. Most people who score high on these measures are implicitly complaining about their own disappointments and frustrations, their feelings of being left out, and their sense of impotence and futility. They and the world have somehow diverged.

For many people, therefore, a preference for isolationism may be largely an expression of protest and resentment. I am not suggesting that no isolationist genuinely believes in the specific recommendations of the isolationist philosophy; among the political influentials, in fact, only a minority of the isolationists (approximately one-fourth) score high on the marginality measures. Nevertheless, one of the attributes of the isolationist persuasion is its association with a network of responses that bespeak frustration and disappointment. . . .

Summary

This paper has focused upon the personality . . . correlates of foreign policy orientation, with special attention to the isolationist-nonisolationist orientation. Isolationists and nonisolationists were compared on a large battery of personality and attitude scales, as well as on other measures. The samples employed in the surveys from which the data were taken included a national sample of 3,020 political leaders, a cross-section national sample of 1,484 adults, and a cross-section statewide sample of 1,082 Minnesota adults. A number of hypotheses were tested and the results evaluated.

It was found, among other things, that isolationism is a complex attitude that can be arrived at by different routes and understood in different ways. While it is obviously a political attitude influenced by political circumstances, reference groups, demographic factors, and other such determinants, it is also shaped to a considerable extent by a complex set of personality variables, primarily of an aversive nature. Such personality states as misanthropy, psychological inflexibility, manifest anxiety, and low self-esteem have a powerful influence on the attitudes one adopts toward other nations and toward foreign policy. Such personality factors, together with social opportunity and intellectual endowment, affect cognitive capacity and function, and these, in turn, further influence one's disposition to favor withdrawal from, or entrance into, international involvements. . . .

The isolationist orientation parallels closely other forms of belief that rely heavily upon dichotomous thought processes, that lack breadth of perspective, and that seek to exclude whatever is different, distant or unfamiliar. It also parallels other attitudes that are marginal or deviant in relation to the society. Like other deviant orientations, it signifies for some of its proponents a failure of socialization and an inadequate internalization of the norms. t is more common among those who are, by any criterion and for any reason, parochial and less common among those who are open to experience and are cosmopolitan in their perspective.

REFERENCES

McClosky, Herbert, "Conservatism and Personality," *American Political Science Review*, 52 (1958), pp. 27-45.

McClosky, Herbert, Hoffman, P., and O'Hara, R. "Issue Conflict and Consensus among Party Leaders and Followers," *American Political Science Review,* **54** (1960), pp. 406-427.

McClosky, Herbert and Schaar, J. "Psychological Dimensions of Anomy," *American Sociological Review,* **30** (1965), pp. 14-39.

Selltiz, C. and Cook, S. "Theory and Measurement of Attitudes," mineograph, no date.

THE PART PLAYED BY PEOPLE
IN THE FLOW OF MASS COMMUNICATION

ELIHU KATZ AND PAUL F. LAZARSFELD

The Part Played by People

During the course of studying the presidential election campaign of 1940, it became clear that certain people in every stratum of a community serve relay roles in the mass communication of election information and influence. (Lazarsfeld et al., 1948).

This "discovery" began with the finding that radio and the printed page seemed to have only negligible effects on actual vote decisions and particularly minute effects on *changes* in vote decisions. Here, then, was another of those findings which reduce belief in the magic of mass media influence. But the authors were not content to report only this unexpected negative finding. They were interested in how people make up their minds, and why they change them, and in effect, they asked, if the mass media are not major determinants of an individual's vote decision, then what is?

The Opinion Leader Idea and the Two-Step Flow of Communication

To investigate this problem, particular attention was paid to those people who changed their vote intention during the course of the campaign. When these people were asked what had contributed to their decision, their answer was: other people. The one source of influence that seemed to be far ahead of all others in determining the way people made up their minds was personal influence. Given this clue from the testimony of the voters themselves, other data and hypotheses fell into line. People tend to vote, it seems, the way their associates vote: wives like husbands, club members with their clubs, workers with fellow employees, etc. Furthermore, looked at in this way, the data implied (although they were not completely adequate for this new purpose) that there were people who exerted a disproportionately great influence on the vote intentions of their fellows. And it could be shown that these "opinion leaders"—as they were dubbed—were not at all identical with those who are thought of traditionally as the wielders of influence; opinion leaders seemed to be distributed in all occupational groups, and on every social and economic level.

The next question was obvious: Who or what influences the influentials? Here is where the mass media re-entered the picture. For the leaders reported much more than the non-opinion leaders that for them, the mass media were influential. Pieced together this way, a new idea emerged—the suggestion of a "two-step flow of communication." The suggestion basically was this: that ideas, often, seem to flow *from* radio and print *to* opinion leaders and *from them* to the less active sections of the population. . . .
We might say, perhaps, that as a result of investigating and thinking about the opinion leader, mass communications research has now joined those fields of social research which, in the last years, have been "rediscovering" the primary group.* And if we are correct, the "rediscovery" seems to have taken place in two steps. First of all, the phenomenon of opinion leadership was discovered. But then, study of the widespread distribution of opinion leaders throughout the population and analysis of the character of their relations with those for whom they were influential (family, friends, co-workers) soon led to a second idea. This was the idea that opinion leaders are not a group set apart, and that opinion leadership is not a trait which some people have and others do not, but rather that opinion leadership is an integral part of the give-and-take of everyday personal relationships. It is being suggested, in other words, that all interpersonal relations are potential networks of communication and that an opinion leader can best be thought of as a group member playing a key communications role. It is this elaboration—that is the tying of opinion leaders to the specific others with whom they are in contact—that completes the "rediscovery.". . . .

An Essay in Convergence

. . . The intellectual history of mass communications research is best characterized as a successive taking account of those factors which *intervene* between

---

* The "rediscovery," of the primary group is an accepted term by now, referring to the belated recognition that researchers in many fields have given to the importance of informal, interpersonal relations within situations formerly conceptualized as strictly formal and atomistic. It is "rediscovery" in the sense that the primary group was dealt with so explicitly (though descriptively and apart from any institutional context) in the work of pioneering American sociologists and social psychologists and then was systematically overlooked by empirical social research until its several dramatic "rediscoveries."

the mass media and their audience and, thus, which modify mass media effects. The central focus of the preceding section had to do with the introduction of the intervening variable of interpersonal relations. . . . Next, we want to scrutinize this notion of interpersonal relations, asking ourselves which elements of such social ties have most bearing on communications effectiveness. We shall try, in other words, to single out and examine those ingredients of informal primary groups which are, so to speak, the "active ingredients" as far as the mass communications process is concerned.

Our purpose, of course, is to try to point the way for the planning of research on the transmission of mass persuasion via the mass media—and, particularly, for the incorporation of a concern with interpersonal relations into the design of such research. By attempting to specify exactly which elements of person-to-person interaction might be relevant for mass media effectiveness, and by exploring what social science knows about the workings of these elements, we shall contribute, perhaps, to a more complex—yet, more realistic—formulation of a "model" for the study of mass persuasion campaigns.

Let us take as our starting point the several illustrations from mass media research set down above, and the thinking and research which constitutes the opinion leader tradition. If we reflect on these, and try to speculate about the specific ways in which interpersonal relationships might be said to affect the response of an individual to a communications campaign, we are led to two characteristics of interpersonal relations, each one of which seems to be a major key to our problem:

1. Interpersonal relationships seem to be *"anchorage" points for individual opinions, attitudes, habits and values.* That is interacting individuals seem collectively and continuously *to generate* and *to maintain* common ideas and behavior patterns which they are reluctant to surrender or to modify unilaterally. If this is the case, and if many, or most, of the ostensibly individual opinions and attitudes which mass media campaigns seek to modify are anchored in small groups, then the bearing of this aspect of group relations on the effectiveness of such campaigns will be well worth our attention.

2. Interpersonal relationships imply *networks of interpersonal communication,* and this characteristic seems to be relevant for campaign effectiveness in several interlocking ways: The "two-step flow" hypothesis suggests, in the first place, that these interpersonal networks are linked to the mass media networks in such a way that some people, who are relatively more exposed, pass on what they see, or hear, or read, to others with whom they are in contact who are less exposed. Primary groups, in other words, may serve as channels for mass media transmission; this might be called the

relay function of interpersonal relations. Secondly, it is implied, person-to-person influences may coincide with mass media messages and thus either counteract or reinforce their message. This might be called the *reinforcement function;* and, there is substantial reason to suspect, when the reinforcement is positive, the communication in question is likely to be particularly effective.

It is our guess that these two characteristics of small, intimate groups— (1) person-to-person *sharing of opinions and attitudes* (which we shall often refer to as "group norms") and (2) person-to-person *communications networks*—are the keys to an adequate understanding of the intervening role played by interpersonal relations in the mass communications process.

We propose now to turn to contemporary social science research to look for corroborating evidence for these hypotheses, and, in general, to see whether we might not in this way achieve a better understanding of just what such social relations have to do with the effectiveness of mass communications. . . .

Norms and Small Groups: The Shared Character of Opinions and Attitudes

Our focus is the primary group. We are thinking specifically of families, friends, informal work teams, etc., as well as those relatively more formal groupings of clubs and organizations of all kinds within which individuals are likely to form what we might call sociometric connections, that is, mutual attractions for each other as personalities. Such groups are usually characterized by their small size, relative durability, informality, face-to-face contact and manifold, or more or less unspecialized, purpose. We shall refer interchangeably to primary groups, small groups, intimate social ties, interpersonal relations or sometimes just to "others," with no attempt to be prematurely precise in our definitions. Our aim now is to see whether those who have studied such interpersonal relations can assist us in developing an idea of how to account for the role of *people* in the flow of mass media influence in modern society.

Our chief concern is with the hypothesis that such groups actively influence and support most of an individual's opinions, attitudes and actions. The evidence on this point is not yet very abundant, but what there is, is persuasive. We know, for example, from several studies that the members of a family are likely—except under certain conditions—to share similar attitudes on politics, religion, etc., and the same thing is true, we know, for most friendships. We know from a set of pioneering studies (which now constitute the core of what is called "reference group theory") that individuals seem often to have particular groups "in mind" when reporting their opinions. Here, then, is the suggestion that opinions are originated and maintained by an individual in common with specifiable others of his associates.

The fact that interacting individuals influence each other, or that an individual entering a new group is likely to adopt the thinking habits of that group is not an easy thing to prove because it almost always involves *disproving* the alternate hypothesis that individuals in a similar situation are each responding independently to the same external stimuli. Thus, even when it is demonstrated that Northern students attending Southern universities become increasingly prejudiced toward the Negro with each succeeding year at school (although never quite so prejudiced as the Southern students themselves), the authors cannot permit themselves to assert that the Northerners are adopting the attitude of their Southern classmates, because they must also show (and their data do not permit them to) that whatever it is that has caused prejudice in the Southerners is not also at work directly on the Northerners.

But although we do not yet have a mass of statistical evidence to demonstrate the *fact* that opinions, attitudes, decisions and actions are rooted in relatively small groups, we can feel much surer than we ordinarily might because we know from careful case studies some of the *reasons why* we are warranted in our expectation that this is the case. Several reasons have been put forward quite convincingly.

The Instrumental Function: The Benefits of Conformity

First of all, we might consider what can be called the *instrumental value*—the "benefits"—that can be derived from sharing the opinions and attitudes of those with whom an individual desires to be identified. We may cite here, as an illustration, Newcomb's (1952) well-known study of the political attitudes of a class of Bennington College girls. By beginning his study in the freshman year and recording changes in attitudes over the four-year period of college, Newcomb was able to show that those students who were positively oriented toward the college community and who aspired to be accepted or to achieve leadership tended to assimilate the liberal attitudes and sentiments which prevailed on campus, despite the strongly conservative family background from which they had come. On the other hand, Newcomb demonstrates, a major factor associated with non-acceptance of the prevailing political climate was a strong positive identification with the family group. Thus, the family group, on the one hand, and the small college community, on the other—each serving as "positive" or "negative" reference points of varying intensity—seemed to be associated with the steadfast conservatism of some of the girls and the increasing non-conservatism of the majority. In Newcomb's own words,

> In a membership group in which certain attitudes are approved (i.e., held by majorities, and conspicuously so by leaders) individuals acquire the approved attitudes to the extent that the membership group (particularly as symbolized by leaders and dominant subgroups) serves as a positive point of reference.

In other words, to the extent that a group is attractive for an individual, and to the extent that he desires acceptance as a member of that group, he will be motivated—whether he is aware of it or not—to accept that group's outlook.

Another set of findings supports the implications of Newcomb's study very neatly. In *The American Soldier,* Stouffer *et al.* (1949), compare the attitudes of those "green" soldiers (no combat experience) who had been sent as replacements to divisions composed of combat veterans, with the attitudes of equally "green" soldiers who were members of divisions composed only of others like themselves. Noting that 45% of the latter but only 28% of the former express attitudes reflecting a "readiness for combat," the authors indicate that this difference may derive from the two different social contexts in which these otherwise indistinguishable "green" troops were placed. It is suggested that those troops who found themselves in veterans' divisions were strongly influenced by the attitudes they encountered there since the combat veterans' own response to the same set of questions was overwhelmingly negative (only 15% indicated readiness for combat). The new men were seeking acceptance, it is argued, and they adjusted their opinions accordingly.

Conformity is not exacted from "new" members or potential members alone. Even long-time members who "deviate" too far from group opinion lose status, or may even lose membership in groups to which they already belong. Several recent experimental studies demonstrate this everyday fact quite well. In one study of a housing community by Festinger, Schachter and Back (1950)—(we shall refer repeatedly to this "Westgate" housing development study and to others by these authors, and their associates)—it was found that those who conformed least to the opinions of their immediate neighbors (as far as the particular item being studied was concerned) tended also to be the ones who were "underchosen" when people were asked in an interview to name their three best friends.* From another study by one of this same team of authors, (Schachter, 1951), we learn that when participants in clubs were asked, following their initial discussion periods, who among the participants they would like to see dropped from the club, those who had maintained extremely deviant opinions (these extremists were in the employ of the experimenter) were named most of all. . . .

---

* That is, they were not named as frequently as they named others.

In sum, all these studies seem to indicate that if an individual desires to attain, or maintain, an intimate relationship with others, or if he wants to "get somewhere" either within a group or via a group, he must identify himself with the opinions and values of these others. That does not necessarily mean that this identification is therefore rationally calculated. It may be quite unwitting. But conscious or not, the *consequences* of conformity or non-conformity which we have noted will remain the same.

Thus, from the "instrumental" point of view, we are led to expect that an individual's opinions will be substantially affected by the opinions of others whose company he keeps, or whose company he aspires to keep.

Providing a Social Reality

Let us now consider another of the reasons which may help explain our confidence in the assertion that individuals very largely share their opinions with other people who surround them. Here, we are thinking of the group not in instrumental terms (that is, not in terms of the "benefits" of conforming) but rather in terms of the function of the group as a provider of *meanings* for situations which do not explain themselves. Experimental social psychologists concerned with the impact of the group on perceptual processes, and particularly the late Kurt Lewin and those who continue in his tradition, have studied this phenomenon. The Lewinians have named it "social reality" and they explain it as follows:

> Experiments dealing with memory and group pressure on the individual show that what exists as "reality" for the individual is to a high degree determined by what is socially accepted as reality. This holds even in the field of physical fact: to the South Sea Islanders the world may be flat; to the European it is round. "Reality, " therefore, is not an absolute. It differs with the group to which the individual belongs (Lewin & Grabbe, 1945).

This concept provides an alternative or better, a supplementary, explanation for the soldiers' attitudes we reported above. Instead of attributing the attitude of the replacements (compared with their peers in all "green " divisions) simply to their motivation to be accepted in the veterans' outfits, we might have suggested there, as we shall here, that the "reality" of the combat experience toward which attitudes were being expressed might well have been different for those who were in daily touch with combat veterans as compared with those who were not. The Westgate study makes this point very well:

> The hypothesis may be advanced that the "social reality" upon which an opinion or an attitude rests for its justification is the degree to which the individual perceives that this opinion or attitude is shared by others. An opinion or attitude which is not reinforced by others of the same opinion will become unstable gen-

erally. There are not usually compelling facts which can unequivocally settle the question of which attitude is wrong and which is right in connection with social opinions and attitudes as there are in the case of what might be called "facts." If a person driving a car down a street is told by his companion that the street ends in a dead end, this piece of information may easily be checked against physical "reality." . . . The "reality" which settles the question in the case of social attitudes and opinions is the degree to which others with whom one is in communication are believed to share these opinions and attitudes (Festinger *et al.*, 1950, p. 168).

This is the way that stereotypes develop; and it is one of the reasons why ideas about what is real in religion or in politics vary from group to group. So many things in the world are inaccessible to direct empirical observation that individuals must continually rely on each other for making sense out of things. Several experimental studies illustrate this. For example, there is Sherif's (1952) now classic study which is perhaps the best single beginning point for a review of the twenty or so years of attention in experimental social psychology to the role of the small group as an influence on opinions, attitudes and actions. Sherif constructed experiments using the "autokinetic effect" which is the name given to the illusion of movement created by an actually stationary pinpoint of light when it is flashed on in a totally darkened room. He first tested each of his experimental subjects singly, asking them to make judgments about the number of inches the light "moved" each time it was lit. After each individual had developed a personal "norm" —that is, a modal number of inches—around which his judgments centered, Sherif brought his subjects together in groups of twos and threes, and asked them to repeat the experiment once more. Each of the subjects based his first few estimates on his previously established standard, but confronted, this time, with the dissenting judgments of the others each gave way somewhat until a new, group standard became established. Thus, knowing what each individual brought with him to the situation, Sherif was able to show how the effect of the judgments of others resulted in the convergence of substantially different private standards and the emergence of a shared norm. When the experiment was reversed—that is, when the group situation came first and the private situation second— individuals accepted the group standard as their own and carried it away with them into the private situation. The group norm thus became the norm of each group member. Interaction had given rise to a definition of "reality" which each participating individual retained.

Such laboratory experiments are sure to encounter a barrage of critical objections concerning the dangers of generalizing laboratory findings to "real life" situations. Often these warnings are very sound. Often, however, they are no more than pat pronouncements about the impossibility of studying human behavior in a laboratory. It may be interesting, then, to digress for a moment to consider some of the possible objections to the study we have just reported. Consider, for example, the arguments that (1) the situation was completely *unstructured* and therefore unreal, for, after all, nobody could know that the light did not move at all; (2) it was completely *without emotional affect* for the participating subjects—that is, they could not have cared much about the validity of their judgements; and (3) it was a situation where people were *forced* to make a decision in response to the artificial demands of the experimental situation. In short, these three objections taken together would imply that Sherif's experiment can be legitimately generalized only to situations where individuals are (1) forced to make decisions (2) about something they know nothing about and (3) about which they care not at all. The critic of laboratory experimentation too often retires at this point; but we shall continue. Let us suppose, now, that these objections are in fact valid and do limit the generalizability of Sherif's finding, as in fact they probably do. Still, that leaves us with a question: are there any real-life situations that resemble this laboratory one? And our answer happens to be—yes. Consider one: For very large numbers of people the presidential voting situation can be characterized as a situation where social pressures (1) force people to make a decision they would not otherwise make (2) between two candidates about whom they may know nothing and (3) about whom they may care not at all. In such a situation, for such people, we may expect informal groups to play a large part in defining the situation, and in influencing decisions. And let us add, that it would be wrong—in the case of almost any of the complex issues on which people in our society are expected to have opinions—to overestimate the objective verifiability of any social situation. . . .

The Group as a Target of Change

Now that we have seen that people, in close personal contact, are partners not only in creating and maintaining each other's ideas, but also in changing them, we must ask—for this was our motive in the first place—how this knowledge has been or might be applied to the study of influence attempts which originate *outside* the group. Translated into mass media language, this problem might read: Is there evidence that interpersonal relations act also to modify the effect of mass media campaigns on individuals?

Perhaps we can begin best with a negative statement: Everything we have seen so far would lead us to expect that an attempt to change an individual's opinion or attitude will *not* succeed if his opinion is one which he shares with others to whom he is attached, and if the others do not go along with the change. Kelley and Volkart (1952) in a study of Boy Scout troops, are able to demonstrate this proposition very clearly.

Two kinds of scouts were identified on the basis of an attitude questionnaire: those who valued their troop membership highly and those who did not. The authors set out to study whether those who valued their troop membership highly would show greater resistance to an attempt to change attitudes connected with Boy Scout life than those who did not feel strongly about their membership. This hypothesis was put to the test by introducing to the Boy Scout troop a guest speaker who, in his speech, implicitly attacked the worthwhileness of camping and of woodcraft, two of the chief concerns of Boy Scout lore. Following the speech, a questionnaire was administered to determine the degree to which the communication was effective in changing attitudes toward the two activities as they had previously been recorded in a "before" questionnaire. And the conclusions that were reached bear out the hypothesis, namely, that members of a group can be influenced to deviate from group-centered values to the extent that their group membership is less important for them. And the converse, is evident: Those who do value their group membership highly will resist outside attempts to change the opinions which they share with their group.

Unquestionably, when what is communicated assails prevailing opinions, attitudes or habits that are shared with highly valued others, then that influence attempt will surely be resisted. Here, then, is concrete evidence for one of the ways in which interpersonal relations intervene in the mass communications process to modify the effects of communications.

In the same way, it follows that an individual will more readily respond to an influence-attempt if he perceives that others support him in a proposed change. This hypothesis underlies the well-known "group decision" experiments pioneered by Kurt Lewin and his associates. Each of these studies is concerned with inducing change in individual behavior and, basically, each attempts to demonstrate the effectiveness of group discussion (followed by "group decision")for achieving change.

One of these studies compares the effectiveness of group discussion with private instruction (Lewin, 1952, p. 467): At a certain maternity hospital, it was customary to give instruction in child-care to new mothers before they were discharged, and this instruction was customarily given privately to one woman at a time. An experiment was devised to compare the relative effect of such individual instruction with group discussion. To do this, some mothers were given individual instruction as before, and others were formed into groups of six and guided in a discussion which culminated in a "decision"—that is, participants were asked to indicate, by a show of hands, whether they had decided to comply with the suggested program. The time devoted to the group discussion was not more than that devoted to a single mother in individual instruction, and the subject matter was the same in both situations. Follow-up interviews after two weeks

and after a month, indicated that participants in the group discussion adhered much more closely to the child-care program than did the mothers
who had received individual instruction. . . .

The bearing of these studies on our own problems should be clear.
We have come to small group research to learn something about the ways
in which interpersonal relations might "intervene" in the mass communications process, particularly in the communication of influence via mass
media "campaigns." Thus far we have focused on the fact that shared opinions and attitudes go along, hand in hand, with interpersonal relations; . . .
that interpersonal relations "intervene" by inducing *resistance* to those
influences which go counter to those ideas that individuals share with others they hold in esteem; and, on the other hand, that when individuals
share norms which are in harmony with an outside influence or when they
are willing to incorporate a proposed change into group norms, then interpersonal relations may act as *facilitators of change*. . . .

The Group and the World Outside: Implications for Mass Media Research

Earlier—and this is the opinion leader idea—it was hypothesized that person-to-person transmission may serve as a relay between people who are
exposed to mass media influence and others who are not. It was suggested,
too, that interpersonal influence may reinforce a mass media campaign. To
this point, however, we have been *assuming* that mass media influences
make their way, somehow, into interpersonal networks of communication
and, thus, we have been speculating about what happens when they get
there. . . .This, of course, has immediate and obvious implications for mass
media research and for a better understanding of the processes of effective
communication, *provided* that mass communications do, in fact, hook up
with these interpersonal networks.

Communicating to the Group

What evidence have we for the hypothesis that communications are relayed
according to a two-step formula? We can muster some impressive empirical evidence to indicate that this is so in several spheres of influence; but
the quantity of evidence is still quite modest and the areas explored quite
few. . . . What we shall attempt to do, however, is to try to specify some of
the ways in which influences originating outside a group may successfully
make their way inside to influence ideas or behavior. Thus, the following
pages will attempt to locate evidence which points to the kinds of links
that exist between systems of intragroup communication such as those
which we have just examined and the world "outside." If we can identify

some of these links then the relevance of interpersonal communications for mass media research will appear much more clear

Consider first the *situational* factor. Part of defining any situation involves the specification of a relevant environment. Minority groups in our society furnish good examples. For some situations, the relevant environment for these groups is the majority group, and thus, minority groups *nominate* ambassadors, so to speak, from among those who are able to relate the group to the majority. At other times and in other situations, the majority may be of little consequence compared, say, with the minority group's own culture, or the "old country"; the desire to relate to this other environment will give rise to quite a different set of relay roles. The characteristics of the kind of leadership which relates minority groups to the majority, in situations where the minority aspires to acceptance by the majority have been discussed by Myrdal in the case of the Negroes, and by Lewin in the case of the Jews. Merton (1949) makes a related point in his study of the interpersonal communication of news events in a small town. He finds that one kind of influential typically introduces "local" home-town news and quite another kind introduces "cosmopolitan" communications, implying, again, that there are different kinds of transmitters for different sorts of "outside" news.

If we ask which group members are more likely than others to serve as links between the group and some relevant environment, we shall find that our earlier discussion of structural and cultural factors is suggestive, too. Consider, for example, the kind of communications role which is assigned to an individual who is *located* at a strategic point in the group *structure* relative to some relevant environment. The boss's secretary, for example, may play this kind of role for the office workers; the member who has had social contact with the majority by virtue of his "position" in society may serve in the case of the minority group; the first family with a television set may have a structural head-start for influence transmission in the neighborhood.

Finally, there are those who have particular relay functions by virtue of their *cultural* roles. Adolescents, for example, are notorious for their determination to keep the family abreast of the latest in popular culture. Word of the newest song hit, or the latest movie release may reach the family only because the culture commends particular patterns of adolescent behavior. In a similar way, many of the interests of the members of the family are culturally determined and when news from one of these specialized areas passes to other family members it is thanks to the particular member in charge. The distribution of the sections of the Sunday paper among the family often reflects this division of interest; and when sports, for example, suddenly becomes the concern of all—during the

World Series, say—then the sports section reader, father perhaps, may become opinion leader.

These suggestions. . .have obvious implications for a discussion of communication *to* the group. Situational, structural, and cultural elements are as important in determining the selection of individuals who will link their peers to some relevant environment, as they are in determining the patterns and the key communicators within the group. Kurt Lewin (1952) had a name for these individuals who link interpersonal communications networks to something "outside": he called them "gatekeepers."

Gatekeeping means controlling a strategic portion of a channel— whether that channel is for the flow of goods, or news, or people—so as to have the power of decision over whether whatever is flowing through the channel will enter the group or not. . . .

A distinction needs to be made here between the role of *originator* of an idea and that of *transmitter* of the idea, and both of these must be distinguished from the role of *influential.* The gatekeeper, similarly, may be an originator only—in the sense that he introduces an idea to a group, but he may or may not serve also as a transmitter within the group and may or may not be influential at all. Whether or not gatekeeping leads to influentiality is an important problem, as a matter of fact, and one which is implicit in the following pages. . . .

The Traditional Community: Examples from International Communications Research

The new field of research which has developed from the vigorous programs in international communications allows us, among many other things, to return from our preoccupation with modern society to the kind of folk community so often described in the classical sociological writings and in the work of anthropologists. In the 1950's, however, we approached those communities with a new problem: What are the channels through which news of the world flows into the village and what, if any, are the attitudes of the villagers to foreign affairs and the world situation, and how are these attitudes formed?

In an article on the flow of world news into the tiny Greek village of Kalos, we find a discussion of several kinds of communications roles among this almost totally illiterate population (Stycos, 1952). The author describes the town's opinion leader—a teacher, one of the two men in the community who can read—and the process via which he receives a news-paper and conveys that part of its contents which he thinks worth conveying to those in the village who are concerned with the news. These recipients are called "opinion carriers," and it is suggested that they seek news either *per se* (Greek culture emphasizes knowledge) or as a means toward achieving prestige among others for whom they, in turn, serve as relayers.

The teacher is the community's only living link with the world out-side—both figuratively, in his role as the sole source of information in matters relating to extra-communal affairs, and literally because he makes an annual trip at the end of each school year to the big city. Thus, in our terms the teacher is gatekeeper for the community.

It is pertinent to contrast the role of the teacher as both gatekeeper and influential with the gatekeeping role of the tavern keeper who officially supervises the turning of the dial of the town's only radio. This role is called "information controller," and we are told that such people, usually illiterate and of low social status, are not in the least better informed or more influential. "They are merely people who, by nature of their occu-pation, are in a strategic position as regards the physical flow of radio communications. . . ."

A Summary of Implications

We have pointed to two ingredients of interpersonal relations which help to explain what there is about an individual's relatedness-to-others that might have bearing on the effectiveness of mass media influence-attempts.

The first ingredient singled out was group norms. It was shown that there is good reason to believe that very often, seemingly private opinions and attitudes are maintained by an individual in conjunction with small numbers of others with whom he is motivated to interact. It follows, therefore, that the success of an attempt to change an individual's opinion or attitude will depend, in some measure, on the resistance to or support for the proposed change which the individual encounters in his group.

The second ingredient singled out was person-to-person transmission. Here it was shown that there are patterned channels of communication between a group and "the world outside," and patterned channels of communication within the group. It follows, therefore, that those individ-uals who play key roles in these channels will have a major share in determining whether or not it will be circulated and whether or not it will be favorably received. We considered for a moment some of the ways in which these ingredients of interpersonal relations might block an influence-attempt stemming from the mass media and directed at an individual. For example, (1) the appropriate gatekeeper may not relay it; (2) an influential may not endorse it; (3) it may be perceived as going counter to norms shared with valued others.

To succeed, on the other hand, a proposed change may have to be identified with a valued group norm, or be endorsed as a new group norm; it may have to enlist the support of appropriate influentials and interpersonal transmitters; and it may have to make contact with an appropriate gatekeeper in order to reach the group at all.

This is what we mean when we say that interpersonal relations "intervene" in the mass communications process, and thus that communications research aiming at the study of short-run mass media effects must take systematically into account an individual's relatedness-to-others. The lesson is plain: No longer can mass media research be content with a random sample of disconnected individuals as respondents. Respondents must be studied within the context of the group or groups to which they belong or which they have "in mind"—thus, which may influence them— in their formulation of opinions, attitudes or decisions, and in their rejection or acceptance of mass media in influence-attempts.

REFERENCES

Festinger, Leon; Schachter, Stanley; and Back, Kurt. *Social Pressures in Informal Groups.* New York: Harper, 1950.

Kelley, Harold H., and Volkart, Edmund H. "The Resistance to Change of Group Anchored Attitudes," *American Sociological Review,* 17 (1952), pp. 453-465.

Lazarsfeld, Paul F., Berelson, Bernard, and Gaudet, Hazel. *The People's Choice.* New York: Columbia University Press, 1948.

Lewin, Kurt. "Group Decision and Social Change," in Swanson, G., Newcomb, T., and Hartley, E. (Eds.), *Readings in Social Psychology.* New York: Henry Holt, 1952.

Lewin, Kurt and Grabbe, Paul. "Conduct, Knowledge, and Acceptance of New Values," *Journal of Social Issues,* 1, No. 3 (1945), pp. 53-64.

Merton, Robert K. "Patterns of Influence: A Study of Interpersonal Influence and Communications Behavior in a Local Community," in Lazarsfeld, P. and Stanton, F. (Eds.), *Communications Research 1948-49.* New York: Harper, 1949.

Myrdal, Gunnar. *An American Dilemma.* New York: Harper, 1944.

Newcomb, Theodore M. "Attitude Development as a Function of Reference Groups," in Swanson, G., Newcomb, T. and Hartley, E. (Eds.), *Readings in Social Psychology.* New York: Henry Holt, 1952.

Schachter, Stanley. "Deviation, Rejection, and Communication," *Journal of Abnormal and Social Psychology,* 46 (1951), pp. 190-207.

Sherif, Muzafer. "Social Factors in Perception," in Swanson, G., Newcomb, T. and Hartley, E. (Eds.), *Readings in Social Psychology.* New York: Henry Holt, 1952.

Stouffer, Samuel *et al. The American Soldier: Studies in Social Psychology in World War II,* Vols. I and II, Princeton N.J.: Princeton University Press, 1949.

Stycos, J. Mayone. "Patterns of Communication in Rural Greek Village," *Public Opinion Quarterly,* 16 (1952), pp. 59-70.

THE NATURE OF BELIEF SYSTEMS IN MASS PUBLICS

PHILIP E. CONVERSE

Our focus in this article is upon differences in the nature of belief systems held on the one hand by elite political actors and, on the other, by the masses that appear to be "numbered" within the spheres of influence of these belief systems. It is our thesis that there are important and predictable differences in ideational worlds as we progress downward through such "belief strata" and that these differences, while obvious at one level, are easily overlooked and not infrequently miscalculated. The fact that these ideational worlds differ in character poses problems of adequate representation and measurement. . . .

I. Some Clarification of Terms

A term like "ideology" has been thoroughly muddied by diverse uses. We shall depend instead upon the term "belief system," although there is an obvious overlap between the two. We define a *belief system* as a configuration of ideas and attitudes in which the elements are bound together by some form of constraint or functional interdependence. In the static case "constraint" may be taken to mean the success we would have in predicting, given initial knowledge that an individual holds a specified attitude, that he holds certain further ideas and attitudes. We depend implicitly upon such notions of constraint in judging, for example, that, if a person is opposed to the expansion of social security, he is probably a conservative and is probably opposed as well to any nationalization of private industries, federal aid to education, sharply progressive income taxation, and so forth. Most discussions of ideologies make relatively elaborate assumptions about such constraints. Constraint must be treated, of course, as a matter of degree, and this degree can be measured quite readily, at least as an average among individuals. . . .

In the dynamic case, "constraint" or "interdependence" refers to the probability that a change in the perceived status (truth, desirability, and so forth) of one idea-element would *psychologically* require, from the point of view of the actor, some compensating change(s) in the status of idea-elements elsewhere in the configuration. The most obvious form of such constraint (although in some ways the most trivial) is exemplified by a structure of propositions in logic, in which a change in the truth-value of one proposition necessitates changes in truth-value elsewhere within the set of related propositions. Psychologically, of course, there may be equally strong constraint among idea-elements that would not be apparent to logical analysis at all, as we shall see.

We might characterize either the idea-elements themselves or entire belief systems in terms of many other dimensions. Only two will interest us here. First, the idea-elements within a belief system vary in a property we shall call *centrality*, according to the role that they play in the belief system as a whole. That is, when new information changes the status of one idea-element in a belief system, by postulate some other change must occur as well. There are usually, however, several possible changes in status elsewhere in the system, any one of which would compensate for the initial change. Let us imagine, for example, that a person strongly favors a particular policy; is very favorably inclined toward a given political party; and recognizes with gratification that the party's stand and his own are congruent. (If he were unaware of the party's stand on the issue, these elements could not in any direct sense be constrained within the same belief system.) Let us further imagine that the party then changes its position to the opposing side of the issue. Once the information about the change reaching the actor has become so unequivocal that he can no longer deny that the change has occurred, he has several further choices. Two of the more important ones involve either a change in attitude toward the party or a change in position on the issue. In such an instance, the element more likely to change is defined as less central to the belief system than the element that, so to speak, has its stability ensured by the change in the first element.

In informal discussions of belief systems, frequent assumptions are made about the relative centrality of various idea-elements. For example, idea-elements that are logically "ends" are supposed to be more central to the system than are "means." It is important to remain aware, however, that idea-elements can change their relative centrality in an individual's belief-system over time. Perhaps the most hackneyed illustration of this point is that of the miser, to whom money has become an end rather than a means.

Whole belief systems may also be compared in a rough way with respect to the *range* of objects that are referents for the ideas and attitudes in the system. Some belief systems, while they may be internally quite complex and may involve large numbers of cognitive elements, are rather narrow in range: Belief systems concerning "proper" baptism rituals or the effects of changes in weather on health may serve as cases in point. Such other belief systems as, for example, one that links control of the means of production with the social functions of religion and a doctrine of aesthetics, all in one more or less neat package, have extreme ranges.

By and large, our attention will be focussed upon belief systems that have relatively wide ranges, and that allow some centrality to political objects, for they can be presumed to have some relevance to political behavior. . . .

II. Sources of Constraint on Idea-Elements

It seems clear that, however logically coherent a belief system may seem to the holder, the sources of constraint are much less logical in the classical sense than they are psychological—and less psychological than social. This point is of sufficient importance to dwell upon.

Logical Sources of Constraint

Within very narrow portions of belief systems, certain constraints may be purely logical. For example, government revenues, government expenditures, and budget balance are three idea-elements that suggest some purely logical constraints. One cannot believe that government expenditures should be increased, that government revenues should be decreased, and that a more favorable balance of the budget should be achieved all at the same time. Of course, the presence of such objectively logical constraints does not ensure that subjective constraints will be felt by the actor. They will be felt only if these idea-elements are brought together in the same belief system, and there is no guarantee that they need be. Indeed, it is true that, among adult American citizens, those who favor the expansion of government welfare services tend to be those who are more insistent upon reducing taxes "even if it means putting off some important things that need to be done. . . ."

Psychological Sources of Constraint

Whatever may be learned through the use of strict logic as a type of constraint, it seems obvious that few belief systems of any range at all depend for their constraint upon logic in this classical sense. Perhaps, with a great deal of labor, parts of a relatively tight belief system like that fashioned by Karl Marx could be made to resemble a structure of logical propositions. It goes without saying, however, that many sophisticated people have been swept away by the "iron logic" of Marxism without any such recasting. There is a broad gulf between strict logic and the quasi-logic of cogent argument. . . .

[Such a gulf is] testimony to an absence of any strict logical constraints among such idea-elements, if any be needed. What is important is that the elites familiar with the total shapes of these belief systems have *experienced* them as logically constrained clusters of ideas, within which one part necessarily follows from another. Often such constraint is quasi-logically argued on the basis of an appeal to some superordinate value or posture toward man and society, involving premises about the nature of social justice, social change, "natural law," and the like. Thus a few crowning postures—like premises about survival of the fittest in the spirit of social Darwinism—serve as a sort of glue to bind together many more specific attitudes and beliefs, and these postures are of prime centrality in the belief system as a whole.

Social Sources of Constraint

The social sources of constraint are twofold and are familiar from an extensive literature in the past century. In the first place, were we to survey the combinations of idea-elements that have occurred historically (in the fashion suggested above), we should undoubtedly find that certain postures tend to co-occur and that this co-occurrence has obvious roots in the configuration of interests and information that characterize particular niches in the social structure. . . .

The idea-elements go together not simply because both are in the interest of the person holding a particular status but for more abstract and quasi-logical reasons developed from a coherent world view as well. It is this type of constraint that is closest to the classic meaning of the term "ideology."

The second source of social constraint lies in two simple facts about the creation and diffusion of belief systems. First, the shaping of belief systems of any range into apparently logical wholes that are credible to large numbers of people is an act of creative synthesis characteristic of only a miniscule proportion of any population. Second, to the extent that multiple idea-elements of a belief system are socially diffused from such creative sources, they tend to be diffused in "packages," which consumers come to see as "natural" wholes, for they are presented in such terms ("If you believe this, then you will also believe that, for it follows in such-and-such ways"). . . .

Such constraint through diffusion is important, for it implies a dependence upon the transmission of information. If information is not successfully transmitted, there will be little constraint save that arising from the first social source. Where transmission of information is at stake, it becomes important to distinguish between two classes of information. Simply put, these two levels are what goes with what and why. Such levels of information logically stand in a scalar relationship to one another, in the sense that one can hardly arrive at an understanding of why two ideas go together without being aware that they are supposed to go together.

On the other hand, it is easy to know that two ideas go together without knowing why. For example, we can expect that a very large majority of the American public would somehow have absorbed the notion that "Communists are atheists." What is important is that this perceived correlation would for most people represent nothing more than a fact of existence, with the same status as the fact that oranges are orange and most apples are red. If we were to go and explore with these people their grasp of the "why" of the relationship, we would be surprised if more than a quarter of the population even attempted responses (setting aside such inevitable replies as "those Communists are for everything wicked"), and, among the responses received, we could be sure that the majority would be incoherent or irrelevant. . . .

It is well established that differences in information held in a cross-section population are simply staggering, running from vast treasuries of well organized information among elites interested in the particular subject to fragments that could virtually be measured as a few "bits" in the technical sense. These differences are a static tribute to the extreme imperfections in the transmission of information "downward" through the system: Very little information "trickles down" very far. Of course, the ordering of individuals on this vertical information scale is largely due to differences in education, but it is strongly modified as well by different specialized interests and tastes that individuals have acquired over time (one for politics, another for religious activity, another for fishing, and so forth).

Consequences of Declining Information for Belief Systems

It is our primary thesis that, as one moves from the elite sources of belief systems downwards on such an information scale, several important things occur. First, the contextual grasp of "standard" political belief systems fades out very rapidly, almost before one has passed beyond the 10% of the American population that in the 1950s had completed standard college training. Increasingly, simpler forms of information about "what goes with what" (or even information about the simple identity of objects) turn up missing. The net result, as one moves downward, is that constraint declines across the universe of idea-elements, and that the range of relevant belief systems becomes narrower and narrower. Instead of a few wide-range belief systems that organize large amounts of specific information, one would expect to find a proliferation of clusters of ideas among which little constraint is felt, even, quite often, in instances of sheer logical constraint.

At the same time, moving from top to bottom of this information dimension, the character of the objects that are central in a belief system undergoes systematic change. These objects shift from the remote, generic,

and abstract to the increasingly simple, concrete, or "close to home."
Where potential political objects are concerned, this progression tends to
be from abstract, "ideological" principles to the more obviously recogniz-
able social groupings or charismatic leaders and finally to such objects of
immediate experience as family, job, and immediate associates.

Most of these changes have been hinted at in one form or another in
a variety of sources. For example "limited horizons," "foreshortened time
perspectives," and "concrete thinking" have been singled out as notable
characteristics of the ideational world of the poorly educated. Such
observations have impressed even those investigators who are dealing with
subject matter rather close to the individual's immediate world: his family
budgeting, what he thinks of people more wealthy than he, his attitudes
toward leisure time, work regulations, and the like. But most of the stuff
of politics—particularly that played on a national or international stage—
is, in the nature of things, remote and abstract. Where politics is concerned
therefore, such ideational changes begin to occur rapidly below the
extremely thin stratum of the electorate that ever has occasion to make
public pronouncements on political affairs. In other words, the changes
in belief systems of which we speak are not a pathology limited to a thin
and disoriented bottom layer of the *lumpenproletariat;* they are immediately
relevant in understanding the bulk of mass political behavior. . . .

III. Active Use of Ideological Dimensions of Judgment

Economy and constraint are companion concepts, for the more highly
constrained a system of multiple elements, the more economically it may
be described and understood. From the point of view of the actor, the
idea organization that leads to constraint permits him to locate and make
sense of a wider range of information from a particular domain than he
would find possible without such organization. One judgmental dimension
or "yardstick" that has been highly serviceable for simplifying and organizing events in most Western politics for the past century has been the
liberal-conservative continuum, on which parties, political leaders, legislation, court decisions, and a number of other primary objects of politics
could be more—or less— adequately located.

The efficiency of such a yardstick in the evaluation of events is quite
obvious. Under certain appropriate circumstances, the single word "conservative" used to describe a piece of proposed legislation can convey a
tremendous amount of more specific information about the bill—who
probably proposed it and toward what ends, who is likely to resist it, its
chances of passage, its long-term social consequences, and, most important,
how the actor himself should expect to evaluate it if he were to expend
further energy to look into its details. The circumstances under which such

tremendous amounts of information are conveyed by the single word are, however, two-fold. First, the actor must bring a good deal of meaning to the term, which is to say that he must understand the constraints surrounding it. The more impoverished his understanding of the term, the less information it conveys. In the limiting case—if he does not know at all what the term means—it conveys no information at all. Second, the system of beliefs and actors referred to must in fact be relatively constrained: To the degree that constraint is lacking, uncertainty is less reduced by the label, and less information is conveyed.

The psychological economies provided by such yardsticks for actors are paralleled by economies for analysts and theoreticians who wish to describe events in the system parsimoniously. Indeed, the search for adequate over-arching dimensions on which large arrays of events may be simply understood is a critical part of synthetic description. Such syntheses are more or less satisfactory, once again, according to the degree of constraint operative among terms in the system being described.

The economies inherent in the liberal-conservative continuum were exploited in traditional fashion in the early 1950s to describe political changes in the United States as a swing toward conservatism or a "revolt of the moderates." At one level, this description was unquestionably apt. That is, a man whose belief system was relatively conservative (Dwight D. Eisenhower) had supplanted in the White House a man whose belief system was relatively liberal (Harry Truman). Furthermore, for a brief period at least, the composition of Congress was more heavily Republican as well, and this shift meant on balance a greater proportion of relatively conservative legislators. Since the administration and Congress were the elites responsible for the development and execution of policies, the flavor of governmental action did indeed take a turn in a conservative direction. These observations are proper description.

The causes underlying these changes in leadership, however, obviously lay with the mass public, which had changed its voting patterns sufficiently to bring the Republican elites into power. And this change in mass voting was frequently interpreted as a shift in public mood from liberal to conservative, a mass desire for a period of respite and consolidation after the rapid liberal innovations of the 1930s and 1940s. Such an account presumes, once again, that constraints visible at an elite level are mirrored in the mass public and that a person choosing to vote Republican after a decade or two of Democratic voting saw himself *in some sense or other* as giving up a more liberal choice in favor of a more conservative one.

On the basis of some familiarity with attitudinal materials drawn from cross-section samples of the electorate, this assumption seems thoroughly implausible. It suggests in the first instance a neatness of organization in perceived political worlds, which, while accurate enough for elites, is a poor fit for the perceptions of the common public. Second, the yardstick that such an account takes for granted—the liberal-conservative continuum—is a rather elegant high-order abstraction, and such abstractions are not typical conceptual tools for the "man in the street." Fortunately, our interview protocols collected from this period permitted us to examine this hypothesis more closely, for they include not only "structured" attitude materials (which merely require the respondent to choose between prefabricated alternatives) but also lengthy "open-ended" materials, which provided us with the respondent's current evaluations of the political scene in his own words. They therefore provide some indication of the evaluative dimensions that tend to be spontaneously applied to politics by such a national sample. We knew that respondents who were highly educated or strongly involved in politics would fall naturally into the verbal shorthand of "too conservative," "more radical," and the like in these evaluations. Our initial analytic question had to do with the prevalence of such usage.

It soon became apparent, however, that such respondents were in a very small minority, as their unusual education or involvement would suggest. At this point, we broadened the inquiry to an assessment of the evaluative dimensions of policy significance (relating to political issues, rather than to the way a candidate dresses, smiles, or behaves in his private life) that seemed to be employed *in lieu of* such efficient yardsticks as the liberal-conservative continuum. The interviews themselves suggested several strata of classification, which were hierarchically ordered as "levels of conceptualization" on the basis of *a priori* judgments about the breadth of contextual grasp of the political system that each seemed to represent.

In the first or top level were placed those respondents who did indeed rely in some active way on a relatively abstract and far-reaching conceptual dimension as a yardstick against which political objects and their shifting policy significance over time were evaluated. We did not require that this dimension be the liberal-conservative continuum itself, but it was almost the only dimension of the sort that occurred empirically. In a second stratum were placed those respondents who mentioned such a dimension in a peripheral way but did not appear to place much evaluative dependence upon it or who used such concepts in a fashion that raised doubt about the breadth of their understanding of the meaning of the term. The first stratum was loosley labeled "ideologue" and the second "near-ideologue."

In the third level were placed respondents who failed to rely upon any such over-arching dimensions yet evaluated parties and candidates in terms of their expected favorable or unfavorable treatment of different social groupings in the population. The Democratic Party might be disliked because "it's trying to help the Negroes too much," or the Republican Party might be endorsed because farm prices would be better with the Republicans in office. The more sophisticated of these group-interest responses reflected an awareness of conflict in interest between "big business" or "rich people," on the one hand, and "labor" or the "working man," on the other, and parties and candidates were located accordingly.

It is often asked why these latter respondents are not considered full "ideologues," for their perceptions run to the more tangible core of what has traditionally been viewed as ideological conflict. It is quite true that such a syndrome is closer to the upper levels of conceptualization than are any of the other types to be described. As we originally foresaw, however, there turn out to be rather marked differences, not only in social origin and flavor of judgmental processes but in overt political reactions as well, between people of this type and those in the upper levels. These people have a clear image of politics as an arena of group interests and, provided that they have been properly advised on where their own group interests lie, they are relatively likely to follow such advice. Unless an issue directly concerns their grouping in an obviously rewarding or punishing way, however, they lack the contextual grasp of the system to recognize how they should respond to it without being told by elites who hold their confidence. Furthermore, their interest in politics is not sufficiently strong that they pay much attention to such communications. If a communication gets through and they absorb it, they are most willing to behave "ideologically" in ways that will further the interests of their group. If they fail to receive such communication, which is most usual, knowledge of their group memberships may be of little help in predicting their responses. This syndrome we came to call "ideology by proxy."

The difference between such narrow group interest and the broader perceptions of the ideologue may be clarified by an extreme case. One respondent whom we encountered classified himself as a strong Socialist. He was a Socialist because he knew that Socialists stood four-square for the working man against the rich, and he was a working man. When asked, however, whether or not the federal government in Washington "should leave things like electric power and housing for private businessmen to handle," he felt strongly that private enterprise should have its way, and responses to other structured issue questions were simply uncorrelated with standard socialist doctrine. It seems quite clear that, if our question had pointed out explicitly to this man that "good Socialists" would demand government intervention over private enterprise or that such a posture had traditionally been viewed as benefitting the working man, his answer would have been different. But since he had something less than a college education and was not generally interested enough in politics to struggle through such niceties, he simply lacked the contextual grasp of the political system or of his chosen "ideology" to know what the appropriate response might be. This case illustrates well what we mean by constraint between idea-elements and how such constraint depends upon a store of relevant information. For this man, "Socialists," "the working man," "non-Socialists" and "the rich" with their appropriate valences formed a tightly constrained belief system. But, for lack of information, the belief system more or less began and ended there. It strikes us as valid to distinguish such a belief system from that of the doctrinaire socialist. We, as sophisticated observers, could only class this man as a full "ideologue" by assuming that he shares with us the complex undergirding of information that his concrete group perceptions call up in our own minds. In this instance, a very little probing makes clear that this assumption of shared information is once again false.

The fourth level was, to some degree, a residual category, intended to include those respondents who invoked some policy considerations in their evaluations yet employed none of the references meriting location in any of the first three levels. Two main modes of policy evaluation were characteristic of this level. The first we came to think of as a "nature of the times" response, since parties or candidates were praised or blamed primarily because of their temporal association in the past with broad societal states of war or peace, prosperity or depression. There was no hint in these responses that any groupings in the society suffered differentially from disaster or profited excessively in more pleasant times: These fortunes or misfortunes were those that one party or the other had decided (in some cases, apparently, on whim) to visit upon the nation as a whole. The second type included those respondents whose only approach to an issue reference involved some single narrow policy for which they felt personal gratitude or indignation toward a party or candidate (like social security or a conservation program). In these responses, there was no indication that the speakers saw programs as representative of the broader policy postures of the parties.

The fifth level included those respondents whose evaluations of the political scene had no shred of policy significance whatever. Some of these responses were from people who felt loyal to one party or the other but confessed that they had no idea what the party stood for. Others devoted their attention to personal qualities of the candidates, indicating disinterest in parties more generally. Still others confessed that they paid too little attention to either the parties or the current candidates to be able to say anything about them.

The ranking of the levels performed on *a priori* grounds was corroborated by further analyses, which demonstrated that independent measures of political involvement all showed sharp and monotonic declines as one passed downward through the levels in the order suggested. Furthermore, these correlations were strong enough so that each maintained some residual life when the other two items were controlled, despite the strong underlying relationship between education, information, and involvement.

Table 1 Distribution of a Total Cross-Section Sample of the American Electorate and of 1956 Voters, by Levels of Conceptualization

		Proportion of total sample	*Proportion of voters*
I.	Ideologues	$2\frac{1}{2}\%$	$3\frac{1}{2}\%$
II.	Near-ideologues	9	12
III.	Group interest	42	45
IV.	Nature of the times	24	22
V.	No issue content	$22\frac{1}{2}$	$17\frac{1}{2}$
		100%	100%

The distribution of the American electorate within these levels of conceptualization is summarized in Table 1. The array is instructive as a portrait of a mass electorate, to be laid against the common elite assumption that all or a significant majority of the public conceptualizes the main lines of politics after the manner of the most highly educated. Where the specific hypothesis of the "revolt of the moderates" in the early 1950s is concerned, the distribution does not seem on the face of it to lend much support to the key assumption. This disconfirmation may be examined further, however.

Since the resurgence of the Republicans in the Eisenhower period depended primarily upon crossing of party lines by people who normally considered themselves Democrats, we were able to isolate these people to see from what levels of conceptualization they had been recruited. We found that such key defections had occurred among Democrats in the two bottom levels at a rate very significantly greater than the comparable rate in the group-interest or more ideological levels. In other words, the stirrings in the mass electorate that had led to a change in administration and in "ruling ideology" were primarily the handiwork of the very people for whom assumptions of any liberal-conservative dimensions of judgment were most far-fetched. . . .

V. Constraints among Idea-Elements

In our estimation, the use of such basic dimensions of judgment as the liberal-conservative continuum betokens a contextual grasp of politics that permits a wide range of more specific idea-elements to be organized into more tightly constrained wholes. We feel, furthermore, that there are many crucial consequences of such organization: With it, for example, new political events have more meaning, retention of political information from the past is far more adequate, and political behavior increasingly approximates that of sophisticated "rational" models, which assume relatively full information.

It is often argued, however, that abstract dimensions like the liberal-conservative continuum are superficial if not meaningless indicators: All that they show is that poorly educated people are inarticulate and have difficulty expressing verbally the more abstract lines along which their specific political beliefs are organized. To expect these people to be able to express what they know and feel, the critic goes on, is comparable to the fallacy of assuming that people can say in an accurate way why they behave as they do. When it comes down to specific attitudes and behaviors the organization is there nonetheless, and it is this organization that matters, not the capacity for discourse in sophisticated language.

If it were true that such organization does exist for most people, apart from their capacities to be articulate about it, we would agree out of hand that the question of articulation is quite trivial. As a cold empirical matter, however, this claim does not seem to be valid. Indeed, it is for this reason that we have cast the argument in terms of constraint, for constraint and organization are very nearly the same thing. Therefore when we hypothesize that constraint among political idea-elements begins to lose its range very rapidly once we move from the most sophisticated few toward the "grass roots," we are contending that the organization of more specific attitudes into wide-ranging belief systems is absent as well.

Table II gives us an opportunity to see the differences in levels of constraint among beliefs on a range of specific issues in an elite population and in a mass population. The elite population happens to be candidates for the United States Congress in the off-year elections of 1958, and the cross-section sample represents the national electorate in the same year. The assortment of issues represented is simply a purposive sampling of some of the more salient political controversies at the time of the study, covering both domestic and foreign policy. The questions posed to the two samples were quite comparable, apart from adjustments necessary in view of the backgrounds of the two populations involved.

Table II Constraint between Specific Issue Beliefs for an Elite Sample and a Cross-Section Sample, 1958[a]

	DOMESTIC				*FOREIGN*			
Congressional candidates	*Employment*	*Education*	*Housing*	*F.E.P.C.*	*Economic*	*Military*	*Isolationism*	*Party preference*
Employment	—	0.62	0.59	0.35	0.26	0.06	0.17	0.68
Aid to education		—	0.61	0.53	0.50	0.06	0.35	0.55
Federal housing			—	0.47	0.41	−0.03	0.30	0.68
F.E.P.C.				—	0.47	0.11	0.23	0.34
Economic aid					—	0.19	0.59	0.25
Military aid						—	0.32	−0.18
Isolationism							—	0.05
Party preference								—
Cross-Section Sample								
Employment	—	0.45	0.08	0.34	−0.04	0.10	−0.22	0.20
Aid to education		—	0.12	0.29	0.06	0.14	−0.17	0.16
Federal housing			—	0.08	−0.06	0.02	0.07	0.18
F.E.P.C.				—	0.24	0.13	0.02	−0.04
Economic aid					—	0.16	0.33	−0.07
Soldiers abroad[b]						—	0.21	0.12
Isolationism							—	−0.03
Party preference								—

a. Entries are tau-gamma coefficients, a statistic proposed by Leo A. Goodman and William H. Kruskal in "Measures of Association for Cross Classifications," *Journal of the American Statistical Association,* 49 (Dec., 1954), No. 268, 749. The coefficient was chosen because of its sensitivity to constraint of the scalar as well as the correlational type.

b. For this category, the cross-section sample was asked a question about keeping American soldiers abroad, rather than about military aid in general.

For our purposes, however, the specific elite sampled and the specific beliefs tested are rather beside the point. We would expect the same general contrast to appear if the elite had been a set of newspaper editors, political writers, or any other group that takes an interest in politics. Similarly, we would expect the same results from any other broad sampling of political issues or, for that matter, any sampling of beliefs from other domains: A set of questions on matters of religious controversy should show the same pattern between an elite population like the clergy and the church members who form their mass "public." What is generally important in comparing the two types of population is the difference in levels of constraint among belief-elements.

Where constraint is concerned, the absolute value of the coefficients in Table II (rather than their algebraic value) is the significant datum. The first thing the table conveys is the fact that, for both populations, there is some falling off of constraint *between* the domains of domestic and foreign policy, relative to the high level of constraint *within* each domain. This result is to be expected: Such lowered values signify boundaries between belief systems that are relatively independent. If we take averages of appropriate sets of coefficients entered in Table II however, we see that the stongest constraint *within* a domain for the mass public is less than that *between* domestic and foreign domains for the elite sample. Furthermore, for the public, in sharp contrast to the elite, party preference seems by and large to be set off in a belief system of its own, relatively unconnected to issue positions (Table III).

Table III Summary of Differences in Level of Constraint with and between Domains, Public and Elite (based on Table II)

| | *Average Coefficients* | | | |
	Within domestic issues	*Between domestic and foreign*	*Within foreign issues*	*Between issues and party*
Elite	0.53	0.25	0.37	0.39
Mass	0.23	0.11	0.23	0.11

While an assessment of relative constraint between the matrices rests only on comparisons of absolute values, the comparative algebraic values have some interest as well. This interest arises from the sophisticated observer's almost automatic assumption that whatever beliefs "go together" in the visible political world (as judged from the attitudes of elites and the more articulate spectators) must naturally go together in the same way among mass publics. Table II makes clear that this assumption is a very dangerous one, aside from the question of degree of constraint. For example, the politician who favors federal aid to education could be predicted to be more, rather than less, favorable to an internationalist posture in foreign affairs, for these two positions in the 1950s were generally associated with "liberalism" in American politics. As we see from Table II, we would be accurate in this judgment considerably more often than chance alone would permit. On the other hand, were we to apply the same assumption of constraint to the American public in the same era, not only would we have been wrong, but we would actually have come closer to reality by assuming no connection at all. . . .

To recapitulate, then, we have argued that the unfamiliarity of broader and more abstract ideological frames of reference among the less sophisticated is more than a problem in mere articulation. Parallel to ignorance and confusion over these ideological dimensions among the less informed is a general decline in constraint among specific belief elements that such dimensions help to organize. It cannot therefore be claimed that the mass public shares ideological patterns of belief with relevant elites at a specific level any more than it shares the abstract conceptual frames of reference. . . .

VII. THE STABILITY OF BELIEF ELEMENTS OVER TIME

All of our data up to this point have used correlations calculated on aggregates as evidence of greater or lesser constraint among elements in belief systems. While we believe these correlations to be informative indicators, they do depend for their form upon cumulations among individuals and therefore can never be seen as commenting incisively upon the belief structures of individuals.

It might then be argued that we are mistaken in saying that constraint among comparable "distant" belief elements declines generally as we move from the more to the less politically sophisticated. Instead, the configuration of political beliefs held by individuals simply becomes increasingly idiosyncratic as we move to less sophisticated people. While an equally broad range of belief elements might function as an interdependent whole for an unsophisticated person, we would find little aggregative patterning of belief combinations in populations of unsophisticated people, for they would be out of the stream of cultural information about "what goes with what" and would therefore put belief elements together in a great variety of ways.

For the types of belief that interest us here, this conclusion in itself would be significant. We believe, however, that we have evidence that permits us to reject it rather categorically, in favor of our original formulation. A fair test of this counterhypothesis would seem to lie in the measurement of the same belief elements for the same individuals over time. For if we are indeed involved here in idiosyncratic patterns of belief, each meaningful to the individual in his own way, then we could expect that individual responses to the same set of items at different points in time should show some fundamental stability. They do not.

A longitudinal study of the American electorate over a four-year period has permitted us to ask the same questions of the same people a number of times, usually separated by close to two-year intervals. Analysis of the stability of responses to the "basic" policy questions of the type presented in Table II yields remarkable results. Faced with the typical item of this kind, only about thirteen people out of twenty manage to locate themselves even on the same *side* of the controversy in successive interrogations, when ten out of twenty could have done so by chance alone.

While we have no comparable longitudinal data for an elite sample, the degree of fit between answers to our issue items and congressional roll-calls is strong enough to suggest that time correlations for individual congressmen in roll-call choice on comparable bills would provide a fair estimate of the stability of an elite population in beliefs of this sort. It is probably no exaggeration to deduce that, in sharp contrast to a mass sample, eighteen out of twenty congressmen would be likely to take the same positions on the same attitude items after a two-year interval. In short, then, we feel very confident that elite-mass differences in levels of constraint among beliefs are mirrored in elite-mass differences in the temporal stability of belief elements for individuals. . . .

In short, all these longitudinal data offer eloquent proof that signs of low constraint among belief elements in the mass public are not products of well knit but highly idiosyncratic belief systems, for these beliefs are extremely labile for individuals over time. Great instability in itself is *prima facie* evidence that the belief has extremely low centrality for the believer. Furthermore, it is apparent that any stability characterizing one belief sets an upper limit on the degree of orderly constraint that could be expected to emerge in static measurement between this unstable belief and another, even a perfectly stable one. While an aggregate might thus show high stability despite low constraint, the fact of low stability virtually ensures that constraint must also be low. This kind of relationship between stability and constraint means that an understanding of what underlies high instability is at the same time an understanding of what underlies low constraint.

The fact that we have asked these questions at more than two points in time provides a good deal of leverage in analyzing the processes of change that generate aggregate instability and helps us to illuminate the character of this instability. For example, in Figure 1 we discover, in comparing our indicators of the degree of instability associated with any particular belief as they register between t_2 and t_3 with the same figures for t_1 and t_2, that estimates are essentially the same. This result is an important one, for it assures us that within a medium time range (four years), differences among issues in degree of response stability are highly reliable.

Far more fascinating, however, is another property that emerges. Quite generally, we can predict t_3 issue positions of individuals fully as well from a knowledge of their t_1 positions alone as we can from a know-ledge of their t_2 positions alone. In other words, the turnover correlation between different time points for these issues tend to fit the scheme shown in Figure 1.

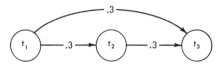

Figure 1 Pattern of Turnover Correlations between Different Time Points.

It can be shown that there is no single meaningful process of change shared by all respondents that would generate this configuration of data. In fact, even if we assume that there is a relatively limited number of change processes present in the population, we find that only two such models could generate these observations. The first of these models posits that some of the respondents managed in a deliberate way to locate them-selves from one measurement to another on the opposite side of an issue from the one they had selected at the preceding measurement. It would have to be assumed that a person who chose a leftish alternative on a certain issue in the first measure would be motivated to remember to seek out the rightish alternative two years later, the leftish again two years after that, and so on. Naturally, an assumption that this behavior characterizes one member of the population is sufficiently nonsensical for us to reject it out of hand.

Once this possibility is set aside, however, there is only one other model involving a mixture of two types of process of change that fits the observed data. This model is somewhat surprising but not totally implaus-ible. It posits a very sharp dichotomy within the population according to processes of change that are polar opposites. There is first a "hard core" of opinion on a given issue, which is well crystallized and perfectly stable over time. For the remainder of the population, response sequences over time are statistically random. The model does not specify what proportions of the population fall into these two categories: This matter is empirically independent, and it is clear that the size of the turnover correlations, between any two points in time is a simple function of these relative proportions. . . .

X. Conclusion

We have long been intrigued, in dealing with attitudinal and behavioral materials drawn from cross-section publics, at the frequency with which the following sequence of events occurs. An hypothesis is formed that seems reasonable to the analyst, having to do with one or another set of systematic differences in perceptions, attitudes, or behavior patterns. The hypothesis is tested on materials from the general population but shows at best some rather uninteresting trace findings. Then the sample is further subdivided by formal education, which isolates among other groups the 10% of the American population with college degrees or the 20% with some college education. It frequently turns out that the hypothesis is then very clearly confirmed for the most educated, with results rapidly shading off to zero within the less educated majority of the population.

We do not claim that such an analytic approach always produces findings of this sort. From time to time, of course, the hypothesis in question can be more broadly rejected for all groups, and, on rare occasions, a relationship turns out to be sharper among the less educated than among the well-educated. Nevertheless, there is a strikingly large class of cases in which confirmation occurs only, or most sharply, among the well educated. Usually it is easy to see, after the fact if not before, the degree to which the dynamics of the processes assumed by the hypothesis rest upon the kinds of broad or abstract contextual information about currents of ideas, people, or society that educated people come to take for granted as initial ingredients of thought but that the most cursory studies will demonstrate are not widely shared. As experiences of this sort accumulate, we become increasingly sensitive to these basic problems of information and begin to predict their results in advance. . . .

In this paper, we have attempted to make some systematic comments on this kind of phenomenon that seem crucial to any understanding of elite and mass belief systems. We have tried to show the character of this "continental shelf" between elites and masses and to locate the sources of differences in their belief systems in some simple characteristics of information and its social transmission.

The broad contours of elite decisions over time can depend in a vital way upon currents in what is loosely called "the history of ideas." These decisions in turn have effects upon the mass of more common citizens. But, of any direct participation in this history of ideas and the behavior it shapes, the mass is remarkably innocent. We do not disclaim the existence of entities that might best be called "folk ideologies," nor do we deny for a moment that stong differentiations in a variety of narrower values may be found within subcultures of less educated people. Yet for the familiar belief systems that, in view of their historical importance, tend most to attract the sophisticated observer, it is likely that an adequate mapping of a society (or, for that matter, the world) would provide a jumbled cluster of pyramids or a mountain range, with sharp delineation and differentiation in beliefs from elite apex to elite apex but with the mass bases of the pyramids overlapping in such profusion that it would be impossible to decide where one pyramid ended and another began.

CHAPTER
ELEVEN
WHY
DO PEOPLE REBEL
?

THE ISSUE OF THE ORIGINS OF SOCIAL MOVEMENTS

Berkeley, California: 1964. The Free Speech Movement (FSM): The beginning of the
student revolt. Part of an FSM song (quoted in Feuer, 1969):

> *I Walked Out in Berkeley* (Tune: "Streets of Laredo")
> As I was out walking one morning in Berkeley,
>   As I walked out in Berkeley one day,
> I spied an old man, all sad and dejected
>   His hands they were shaking, his hair it was gray.
> "I see by your books, boy, that you are a student"
>   These words he did say as I slowly walked by,
> "Come sit down beside me and hear my sad story."
>   He then shook his head and he gave a deep sigh.
> "It is here on the campus that I am the Chancellor
>   I push the buttons and run the whole show,
> These are my children but now they're ungrateful
>   They think they're adults and they think they are grown."

It started in the spring, when several persons complained to Alex C. Sherriffs,
vice-chancellor for student affairs, that noise from the bongo drums in the
Student Union Plaza was disruptive. Looking into the matter, Sherriffs found
not only bongo players in the plaza but also bicycle riders in pedestrian areas and
political hawkers at Bancroft and Telegraph. Increased political activity during the
spring, he noted, was producing a littered plaza, since students dropped leaflets
thrust upon them as they entered the campus. More seriously, persons with permits to set up tables on city of Berkeley property at the edge of the campus were
moving back onto the more spacious "no man's land"—a 26-foot-wide strip of
brick pavement that resembled the public sidewalk but actually belonged to the
University of California. Since the university forbade all political proselytizing,

such activity at this location technically was illegal. Sherriffs concluded that the office of the dean of students was not taking its policing functions seriously enough, and that something should be done before increased enrollment and the election campaign in the fall brought still greater activity in the area. (From Heirich, 1971).

Dean of students, Katherine Towle (quoted in Heirich, 1971):
"When I became dean of students in July of 1961, I inherited, more or less, the area out there, and the students did use it for their political action and social action activities, collecting funds and setting their tables up and handing out literature, and it didn't seem to pose any particular problem at that time. In fact, if I thought about it all, which I think was not very often, I–it seemed to me as sort of a safety valve, and there was no harm in what they were doing. . . ."

Freshman woman at Berkeley describing her motivation for participating in an FSM vigil (Heirich, 1971):
"This is my first year at Cal.; I was highly impressed by the concern, activity, and cross section of opinions displayed at the Bancroft-Telegraph area–and was highly shocked and infuriated when for, it seemed, absolutely no reason at all the school administration decided to eliminate this. [It was] . . . a wonderful area for bantering ideas around, informing people, and keeping them aware of the world around them. . . . If the administration's rules were followed it would seriously stifle the means of communication in this area, perhaps resulting in Cal becoming more apathetic like other colleges . . . . Perhaps if no one else had responded I would have grumbled, been sorry for the end of the Bancroft-Telly type area at Cal and done nothing except perhaps argue with friends on the matter; I am not a leader."

Anti-FSM student addressing FSM demonstrators (quoted in Heirich, 1971):
". . . some of them are down here because they say they've got an issue. I've been here for five years trying to get out of engineering school. I've seen 'em all the way from the time they were picketing ROTC. The thing that makes me personally sick–and this is our side of the issue–it seems like it's always the same people. I don't know whether you're students or not. But it looks like it's always the same people with a cause, every week!"

FSM leader Mario Savio, speaking at an FSM demonstration, addressing anti-FSM hecklers (quoted in Heirich, 1971):
"Look–the only reason that I took part in this is that I like Cal very much. I'd like to see it better. I'm not here to destroy something! We're all here to try to build something!"

Discussion by FSM leader Mario Savio (quoted in Feuer, 1969):
"The students are frustrated; they can find no place in society where alienation doesn't exist, where they can do meaningful work. Despair sets in, a volatile political agent. The students rebel against the apparatus of the university. This is the motive power of the student movement. I thought about it and my own involvement when I went to Mississippi where I could be killed. My reasons

were selfish. I wasn't really alive. My life, my middle-class life, had no place in society, nor it in me. It was not really a matter of fighting for constitutional rights. I needed some way to pinch myself, to assure myself that I was alive."

FSM leader Art Goldberg (reported in Heirich, 1971):
"Our first meetings were these huge meeting with almost always consensus. I would work, when I chaired the meeting, to get agreement from the right and agreement from a substantial segment of the left. . . ."

(Data reported in Heirich, 1971):
[Early in the controversy] . . . "students were asked to sign a 'petition of complicity,' saying that they had manned the political tables at Sather Gate and should be given the same treatment as the five students cited by the dean's office . . . . Using residence statistics from the university Housing office for fall, 1964, . . . one would expect that about half of the petition signers would be apartment dwellers, and about 10% residents of the Greek houses. (Housing statistics show 47.3% of the student body living in apartments, 10.4% in fraternities and sororities, that fall.) In fact, however, 83% of the petition signers lived in apartments and only 1% in Greek houses."

From the publication of a student political group, Slate, addressed to undergraduates (quoted in Heirich, 1971):
"This institution . . . does not deserve a response of loyalty and allegiance from you. There is only one proper response to Berkeley from undergraduates: that you organize and split this campus wide open!
From this point on, do not misunderstand me. My intention is to convince you that you do nothing less than begin an open, fierce, and thorough going rebellion on this campus. . . "

From the student newspaper, The Daily Californian:
"Another substantial concession was made by the University yesterday to the political groups protesting the Bancroft-Telegraph ban. . . . 'The Bancroft-Telegraph issue has alerted us to the free speech issue all over campus,' said one spokesman for the protesting groups. 'We won't stop now until we've made the entire campus a bastion of free speech.' "

Public Statement by Governor Edmund G. ("Pat") Brown:
"This is not a matter of freedom of speech on the campuses. . . This is purely and simply an attempt on the part of the students to use the campuses of the University unlawfully by soliciting funds and recruiting students for off-campus activities. This will not be tolerated. We must have—and will continue to have—law and order on our campuses."

Speech by FSM leader Mario Savio (quoted in Heirich, 1971):
"There is a time when the operation of the machine becomes so odious, makes you so sick at heart, that you can't take part; you can't even passively take part, and you've got to put your bodies upon the gears and upon the wheels, upon the levers, upon all the apparatus and you've got to make it stop. And you've got to indicate to the people who run it, that unless you're free, the machines will be prevented from working at all."

March, 1965:

> [Some months after the FSM protests had ended] , . . . "John Thomson, a non-student who had been active in radical political circles in New York City and who had moved to Berkeley after the Free Speech Movement, wandered onto campus holding a 5 by 8 inch piece of notebook paper in front of his chest. On the paper he had written the word 'Fuck.' He sat on the Student Union steps, near the street" (Described in Heirich, 1971).

Why all this unrest? What was this rebellion all about? Were students finding an outlet for a wide variety of individual problems? Were they rebelling against authority more generally, finding in the Free Speech issue a convenient vehicle? Were they especially vulnerable to mass action as unattached youth, away from home for the first time, living in scattered apartments on the fringes of the confusing and sometimes frightening Berkeley scene. Would they have rebelled anyway or was the content of the particular issue and the response of the administration important? Were they mainly joining with fellow students in order to exercise a greater degree of collective control over their lives at the University? Was the rebellion essentially a power struggle, carried out by unconventional means on the part of students because those were the means that seemed most available and effective to them? Are there common themes that run through rebellions, uniting Berkeley with urban riots and insurgencies around the world? Why, in fact, do people rebel?

THE MAJOR VIEWS

Personal Maladjustment

There is a long tradition, represented here in the selection by Eric Hoffer, that sees participation in mass movements as the politicization of a melange of individual problems. It is never more clearly expressed than in the soliloquy by the Marquis de Sade in Peter Weiss' brilliant play, "The Persecution and Assassination of Jean-Paul Marat as Performed by the Inmates of the Asylum of Charenton under the Direction of the Marquis de Sade" (better known as Marat/Sade):

> That's how it is Marat
> That's how she sees your Revolution
> They have toothache
> and their teeth should be pulled
> Their soup's burnt
> They shout for better soup
> A woman finds her husband is too short
> she wants a taller one
> A man finds his wife too skinny
> he wants a plumper one
> A man's shoes pinch
> but his neighbor's shoes fit comfortably
> A poet runs out of poetry
> and desperately gropes for new images

For hours an angler casts his line
Why aren't the fish biting
And so they join the Revolution
thinking the Revolution will give them everything
a fish
a poem
a new pair of shoes
a new wife
a new husband
and the best soup in the world
So they storm all the citadels
and there they are
and everything is just the same
no fish biting
verses botched
shoes pinching
a worn and stinking partner in bed
and the soup burnt
and all that heroism
which drove us down to the sewers
well we can talk about it to our grandchildren
if we have any grandchildren

Political grievances, in this view, are not the cause but merely the occasion or opportunity for rebellion. "A man is likely to mind his own business," Hoffer writes in the selection included here, "when it is worth minding. When it is not, he takes his mind off his own meaningless affairs by minding other people's business." Talents and other attributes are never equally distributed, the argument runs. Envy and jealousy are an inevitable part of social life. Some, through luck and talent, find they are life's winners; others are not so fortunate. And life's losers are sympathetic to any message that shifts responsibility from themselves to the system.

The personally maladjusted are ripe for rebellion. The messenger from the mass movement is a bearer of hope. One's burdens and frustrations are made to seem unjust and remedial; ones desires are made just and, through participation in the mass movement, achievable. But it is not merely the pull of hope that attracts people; it is the escape from the futility of their spoiled lives as well. "When our individual interests and prospects do not seem worth living for, we are in desperate need of something apart from us to live for," Hoffer writes.

How does such a paradigm apply to the Berkeley revolt? First of all, it suggests that one must look behind the surface issues such as free speech to more fundamental issues. After all, as Lewis Feuer observes, student rebellion is not a new or exclusively American phenomenon. History records many such rebellions in different historical periods, different countries, and different contexts. Some local issue becomes the focus of the rebellion but, to explain such a recurrent phenomena, one must look beyond the specific case.

Feuer (1969) writes:

A student movement. . . arises from a diffused feeling of opposition to things as they are. It is revolutionary in emotion to begin with, and because its driving energy stems largely from unconscious sources, it has trouble defining what it wants. It tries to go from the general to the particular, and to find a justifying bill of grievances; what moves it at the outset, however, is less an idea than an emotion, vague, restless, ill-defined, stemming from the unconscious.

The animus for student rebellion, in this view, is generational revolt. The rebellion precedes the cause. "It seems like it's always the same people" says the anti-FSM student quoted in the introduction. Savio himself, outside the heat of immediate combat, describes the motive power of the student movement as stemming more from a general existential alienation rather than immediate, concrete injustices. "My life. . . had no place in society, nor it in me."

Humiliation of the older generation is a dominant theme. The younger generation's mockery and glee at the discomfiture of their elders comes through clearly in the FSM parody on "The Streets of Laredo." The Chancellor is depicted as a pathetic figure—the defeated father with hands shaking and hair turned gray, bemoaning his loss of authority over the students.

Concessions only whet the appetite of such a movement. If there is a concession on the immediate issue of the Bancroft-Telegraph ban, the protestors respond that, "We won't stop now until we've made the entire campus a bastion of free speech." And this bastion, once secured, will surely become the sanctuary for new forays as inevitably as the plausible and high-sounding free speech movement was so quickly followed by the mischievous filthy speech movement over the right to use obscenity in public.

But if generational conflict is an ever present force, why don't student rebellions occur all the time? Because special conditions are necessary to politicize this motive and transform it into an active rebellion. Feuer (1969) writes:

Under fortunate circumstances [generational rebellion] may be resolved within a generational equilibrium. Under less happy circumstances, it becomes bitter, unyielding, angry, violent; this is what takes place when the elder generation, through some presumable historical failure, has become de-authorized in the eyes of the young.

Of course, other rebellions have other motive forces. Generation revolt is merely a special case of one particular kind of powerful, unconscious driving force. What student rebellions share with the more general category is the translation of individual discontent into collective behavior—the handling of personal frustration by directing the resultant aggressive impulses at political objects.

Mass Society

Personal anxiety and identity problems are part of the process in this view, but they are a misleading starting point. One starts with the observation that certain societies, during certain periods, experience large amounts of mass behavior and mass movements. Other societies experience very little. Personal crises, in this view, must be seen as a reaction to the particular state of the social system. Rebellion, in turn, is a symptom of social system breakdown, and we must seek understanding by examining the faulty social organization.

As Kornhauser states the argument in the selection here, we should look at mass movements as mass behavior that has become "organized around a program and [has acquired] a certain continuity in purpose and effort." But it retains the characteristics of mass behavior including "objectives [that] are remote and extreme; . . . activist modes of intervention in the social order; [the mobilization] of uprooted and atomized sections of the population; . . . [the absence of] an internal structure of independent groups."

Mass politics is the opposite of proximate politics. "The focus of attention is remote from personal experience and daily life," as Kornhauser puts it. "The mode of response to remote objects is direct. . . . Mass behavior also tends to be highly unstable, readily shifting its focus of attention and intensity of response." What produces such a volatile and, it would seem, undesirable kind of political behavior?

The basic problem lies in the weakness of "intermediate relations," the central defining characteristic of mass society. By intermediate relations is meant a set of group affiliations that lie between intimate, face-to-face primary groups and the State. Typical examples of such intermediate relations are those formed through work, church, and voluntary association. Each such tie embeds an individual in a different sub-community and together they produce a more proximate politics that filters and moderates an individual's political action. He remains focused on objectives that are real and concrete, that affect his daily life in direct ways. His interactions bring him close to reality, keeping him accountable, and hence, more responsible in his actions.

Group affiliations are not sufficient by themselves. To prevent mass politics, they must overlap with each other so that an individual shares one set of interests with some people and a different set with others. When these interests conflict, he can readily see the need for compromise. If some of his friends get their way completely, other friends will be hurt in the process. Furthermore, he can afford to accept less than total victory since he has only a few of his eggs in any one basket.

When these intermediate associations are lacking in the society as a whole or in some part of it, individuals experience a kind of social vertigo. They lack both anchor and compass and are adrift and available. Lacking close primary relations with others, the individual becomes a candidate for suicide or other forms of individual deviance; but lacking intermediate associations, he is a candidate for mass behavior that may take the form of messianic movements, fads and crazes, or political rebellion.

How does this argument apply to the Berkeley case.* We note, first of all, that students come from many different communities, many from highly protective environments. They are suddenly on their own, knowing few others at the University. They have no set of established groups to help guide them through the confusing set of stimuli and demands they encounter.

Second, most organized student groups at the University lack any meaningful affiliation with the adult world outside. Among political groups, Young Republicans

---

* Kornhauser himself is no longer as sympathetic to the line of argument that he helped to codify in *The Politics of Mass Society*, nor is there reason to think he would find it especially applicable to the particular case of the FSM. Another advocate might, however, and we present the case such a person might make.

and Young Democrats involve some ties, but only in the most tenuous fashion given the amorphous state of American political parties. Even then, such groups probably operate to discourage their members from more extreme forms of mass action. Fraternities and sororities are intermediate associations that provide, through their adult alumni, some modest ties with the world outside the University. It is very meaningful, in this view, that fraternity and sorority members were so grossly under-represented among FSM supporters while atomized apartment dwellers were so over-represented.

The Berkeley situation, then, is rich with the ingredients for rebellion. Take a large number of still unformed kids, rip them from the stabilizing environment of their home community, place them in a bewildering new environment with many others in the same state of insecurity, add the decline of the once powerful Fraternity and Sorority system as a means of integrating students—and finally, offer them a dramatic mass movement that provides the anchor and compass they lack. Mass movements grow, in this view, because they provide the individual with a substitute for the intermediate associations that he is unable to find in his regular social environment.

Relative Deprivation

This next view starts with an observation: people rarely rebel when things are at their worst; they rebel when things are improving. The observation itself is an old one. Alexis de Tocqueville, analysing the French revolution, wrote in 1856,

> So it would appear that the French found their condition the more unsupport-able in proportion to its improvement . . . Revolutions are not always brought about by a gradual decline from bad to worse. Nations that have endured patiently and almost unconsciously the most overwhelming oppression, often burst into rebellion against the yoke the moment it begins to grow lighter. The regime which is destroyed by a revolution is almost always an improvement on its immediate predecessor. . . . Evils which are patiently endured when they seem inevitable become intolerable when once the idea of escape from them is suggested.

How can this apparent paradox be resolved? The resolution is a very social psychological one. The benefits or deprivations that one is actually getting are only part of the story. We seem to forget this when we look at one group, docile under great deprivation, and wonder why it is so much less rebellious than another, more advantaged group.

The other half of the story is what people think they deserve. Stated simply, the greater the perceived discrepancy between what people are getting and what they think they deserve to get, the greater the tendency to rebellion. This "want-get" gap can be produced in a number of different ways but, unless it is present, there will be no animus to rebellion regardless of how great the absolute deprivation under which people are suffering.

How do people come to define what they deserve? There is a strong and universal tendency to determine this by comparing ourselves to what relevant others are getting. It is not always clear who the relevant others are, and this is a serious problem for the usefulness of this view. If people choose to compare themselves with those who are even more deprived, they will not be rebellious. There will be no gap or perhaps even a "guilt" gap in which individuals get more than they think they deserve. But frequently they compare themselves with those who receive much more than they do. If there were good reasons, in their eyes, why the group should receive more, it would not serve as a relevant comparison group to assess what they also deserve. So the other group is getting more for no good reason, and the people in question feel relatively deprived. Thus, it is not what a group is getting in absolute terms, but what it is getting relative to others that determines the degree of rebelliousness—hence the label, "relative deprivation."

With this view of rebellion, a central problem becomes the determination of the conditions under which relative deprivation will develop. Davies, in the selection here, presents an argument for one such set of conditions—a long period in which both benefits and expectations are rising followed by a sudden fall-off in benefits (and no corresponding decline in expectations). He calls this the "J-curve" theory of revolution, referring to the shape of the curve of benefits over time (labelled "actual need-satisfaction" in Figure 1, p. 531). The "J" may not be immediately apparent, having toppled over on its axis somewhat, but it is a convenient reminder of the general idea.

This is not the only path to the revolutionary state of mind as Davies points out.

> It may be that gratifications do not suddenly fall but continue to rise, but not so rapidly as expectations rise, with the result that the gap between the two widens without a downturn in gratifications. There may be cases in which violence breaks out after a steady but too slow rise in gratifications.

One way or another, then, relative deprivation develops. A group of people suddenly find that they are getting a great deal less than they think they deserve and expect. This produces a sense of frustration and injustice which in turn leads to anger. This anger is then expressed in aggression, directed either at the source of the deprivation or at some alternative, more convenient and vulnerable target.

Ideology plays an important role here as a creator of the revolutionary state of mind. By redefining for people what they deserve, a gap is created. What was thought to be inevitable or the will of God is redefined as the result of particular policies and of a particular social system and its agents. Ideology is a major vehicle for changing what people think they deserve. Of course, ideology can also be used by the potential target of rebellion as an instrument of social control, convincing people that they deserve what they are getting. In either case, it operates on rebellion by affecting expectations which, in turn, affect the amount of relative deprivation.

It is not hard to fit the events at Berkeley into this paradigm. Students had, for some time, been carrying on their political activity in a technically illegal area. Few of them realized this and they clearly regarded themselves as having a "right" to carry on this activity in this area. In any event, they had been using it for several years and, as even the Dean of Students Katherine Towle acknowledged, "it didn't seem to pose any particular problem. . . there was no harm in what they were doing." It was not only politically minded students but ordinary freshmen who felt "highly shocked and infuriated when for, it seemed, absolutely no reason at all, the school administration decided to eliminate this."

The ban on political activity on campus may have seemed reasonable enough in the less political 1950s but, by 1964, practices had eroded the original rules substantially. Along with changed practices came changed expectations. Many Berkeley students were highly involved in the civil rights movement and it seemed to them a matter of course that they should be able to hand out their leaflets and set up their tables in this natural area of student traffic. The ban on such activities created a sudden, sharp gap between their expectations of what they deserved and what other adult Americans had as a matter of right, and what they were now going to get. Thus, a rebellious state of mind was created which, fed by administration blunders of various sorts, led on to a dramatic all night sit-in in which almost 800 students were arrested. Berkeley, then, can be said to follow the general lines of the J-curve.

Interest Group Conflict

Rebellion, in this view, is best viewed as a conflict between an insurgent or challenging group and a set of authorities. Rebellion is simply the politics of the have-nots—the route of political action for those who feel unable to achieve their objectives through normal channels.

This paradigm suggests that the absence of rebellion is in need of explanation just as much as its presence. As Tilly puts it in the selection here,

> ... collective violence is one of the commonest forms of political participation. Why *begin* an inquiry into [the subject]... with the presumption that violent politics appear only as a disruption, a deviation or a last resort? Rather than treating collective violence as an unwholesome deviation from normality, we might do better to ask under what conditions (if any) violence disappears from ordinary political life.

Rebellion, here, is politics by other means. It is not some kind of irrational expression but is as instrumental in its nature as a lobbyist trying to get special favors for his group or a major political party conducting a presidential campaign. Tilly gives a list of reasons for

> hesitating to assume that collective violence is a sort of witless release of tension divorced from workaday politics: its frequent success as a tactic, its effectiveness in establishing or maintaining a group's political identity, its normative order, its frequent recruitment of ordinary people, and its tendency to evolve in cadence with peaceful political action.

In this argument, relative deprivation is endemic and explains little. Certainly, after the fact, one can go back and find some gap between what people were getting and what they thought they should get, but such gaps are ubiquitous in non-rebellion also. A similar argument is made about social strains. One can always find them, looking back, after a rebellion has occurred. That there will always be a variety of specific sources of discontent can be assumed; the question to answer is why, and under what conditions, groups will resort to relatively unlimited means in attempting to change things.

The proposed answer focuses on the distribution of power or resources in a society. Groups will use existing, legitimate channels of influence when they control significant resources and can bring them to bear on policy-makers. Such groups have no need for "rebellion" to achieve their political ends. Groups that are poor in resources and have little access to conventional channels will turn to protest and rebellion.

Powerless groups have special kinds of strategic problems. They can't call on existing resources, but must create their own on the basis of mass support. Or, if the supporting population is not a majority, they must find ways of bringing allies to their cause. As Lipsky (1968) writes, "The 'problem of the powerless' in protest activity is to activate 'third parties' to enter the implicit or explicit bargaining arena in ways favorable to the protesters. This is one of the few ways in which they can 'create' bargaining resources."

Take, for example, the students who participated in the FSM at Berkeley. Most of the leaders were experienced civil rights activists, veterans of direct action such as sit-ins, mass marches, the picketing of chain stores that discriminated, and a variety of local actions in the Bay Area. These were the politics that they knew how to use, not the politics of the board room or the labyrinth committee structure of the University bureaucracy. Furthermore, their experience in civil rights activity had left many with the conviction that such techniques were more effective than conventional channels, that at the very least they were necessary to grease the wheels of the ponderous bureaucracy. Later, when distrust became greater, many came to see the ordinary channels not as cumbersome and clumsy, but, instead, as clever and deceptive devices for preventing action.

The characteristic pattern of rebellion in this view is for a relatively powerless group to mobilize over some specific issue or grievance. In the course of the conflict, the group becomes more and more aware of its lack of power through conventional, institutional channels. At the same time, it comes to believe in the efficacy of unconventional methods, especially when these seem to produce a response—or at least a degree of attention to the problem—that was previously lacking. Add to this mix the fact that the protesting group is likely to share very little moral commitment to the usual "rules of the game." Lacking the cards to do well in the conventional game, they choose to play a different game.

Such groups are typically low in trust of conventional authorities. Low trust by itself does not move one to action, but when it is combined with the belief that rebellion has support and some chance of success, the mobilization to action can be bewilderingly rapid. Furthermore, groups low in trust will be more likely to use threats as a means of influence. They have little at stake to lose by alienating the powers that be and, no matter how poor in resources, they retain the capacity to make trouble—to make things unpleasant for those who seek a little peace and quiet in which to enjoy their share of society's spoils.

Ideology is important here for different reasons than in previous views. Ideology focuses and channels action and aims it at effective points. The role of ideology is to diagnose the sources of discontent and to prescribe the appropriate target and means of change. A poor ideology, of course, will lead a group into *cul-de-sacs* and dissipate its energies on futile and dangerous courses of action. A sound ideology will increase a group's awareness and effectiveness.

It is characteristic of this view to look at rebellion through the eyes of the rebel. Oglesby (1967) for example, makes this very explicit in his discussion of rebellion in the Third World:

> I make three assumptions. First, everyone who is now a rebel *became* a rebel; he was once upon a time a child who spoke no politics. The rebel is someone who has changed. Second, men do not imperil their own and others' lives for unimpressive reasons. They are sharp accountants on the subject of staying alive. When they do something dangerous, they have been convinced that not to do it was more dangerous. . . . Third, I assume that the rebel is much like myself, someone whom I can understand. He is politically extraordinary. That does not mean that he is psychologically so. My assumption is that what would not move me to the act of rebellion would not move another man.

Finally, there is a strong emphasis in this view on the interaction between two groups—the rebels on the one hand, the authorities on the other. Violence, when it occurs, is a product of this interaction and, as often as not, it is the agents of the authorities who fire the first shot. It is, in any event, a dynamic process in which one side's actions lead to responses by the other side which, in turn, become the stimulus for further actions back and forth in a chain. Escalation to violence is one possible outcome of such a process; compromise and peaceful resolution is another.

What happened, for example, to Mario Savio in the two months between the statements: (a) "We're all here to try to build something" and (b) "There is a time when the operation of the machine becomes so odious, makes you so sick at heart, that you can't take part . . . and you've got to put your bodies upon the gears and upon the wheels, upon all the apparatus and you've got to make it stop?" Savio was responding to the spiral of conflict in which he participated; his change in tone and mood reflected the response of many students. His words were not an expression of blind rage fueled by some personal problem. He was not hitting out blindly and irrationally at some inappropriate and irrelevant target. Anger there clearly was, but it was cold anger directed at the FSM antagonist in the spiral of conflict.

FSM leaders were, in this view, engaged in a power struggle with the University administration. Like any contestant, they worried about their strategy and tactics, their strengths and vulnerabilities. For such a "rebellion," mundane considerations such as holding their coalition together become important. "I would work . . . to get agreement from the right and agreement from a substantial segment of the left," said one FSM leader.

"We won't stop now until we've made the entire campus a bastion of free speech," an FSM spokesman told the Daily Californian. "We must have . . . law and order on our campuses," said Governor Pat Brown, using the ancient code words of all authorities under siege by insurgent groups. Only by examining the interaction between the contending parties can we hope to understand how almost 800 students could have seen this issue as being important enough to risk expulsion from school, arrest, and imprisonment. In the final analysis, it takes two to make a rebellion and the way in which authorities wage the conflict is as relevant as the actions and motives of the rebels.

CONTRASTING THE VIEWS OF THE ORIGINS OF SOCIAL MOVEMENTS

These ways of looking at rebellion can be contrasted by examining their treatment of five issues:

1.   Where is the active ingredient in rebellion located? What is the dynamic or volatile element in the total picture?

2.   Is rebellion more an instrumental act directed at achieving manifest goals, or an expressive act aimed at relieving unconscious tension?

3.   What does the individual get from participating in a rebellion?

4.   Is rebellion normal or abnormal for a healthy society?

5.   Is rebellion a corrective factor or a complicating factor for a society?

Active Ingredient

Any paradigm will recognize that a large array of factors are necessary to produce rebellion—some problems with the social system, some motivation and state of mind on the part of the rebels, some process of interaction with agents of social control. The operative differences among them center on the extent to which different ingredients are inert or active. Inert ingredients are those that are accepted as more or less constant and omnipresent. They do not carry the burden of explanation. Active ingredients are the ones toward which we are advised to direct our attention. Rebellions occur only among some people, some of the time, in some places. One must explain this variance, and this can be done only with an active, variable element.

The different paradigms call different active ingredients to our attention. For the personal maladjustment view, the active element is indicated by the label. Things will occur—wars and industrialization, for example—that will dislocate individuals. These are inert elements—they are part of the social environment in which we live. How individuals respond to their social environment is the variable element. Some have the knack of landing on their feet no matter what life throws at them; others gag on a silver spoon. The latter are the supporters of rebellions and we can understand the process best by learning to understand the nature of rebels.

In the mass society view, the active element shifts to the social system. More specifically, we are directed to the presence or absence of intermediate ties that guide an individual in his reactions to political issues. A society that fails to provide such a compass for its citizens invites mass movements by its default.

In the relative deprivation view, the active element links individuals to their social environment. The locus of relative deprivation is in the individual, but it focuses us on his perception of his social world. What he is actually getting is relevant. But how he feels about it—what he thinks he ought to be getting—is the critical, additional ingredient.

Finally, the group conflict paradigm emphasizes interaction between the rebels and the authorities they are challenging. Rebellion is one outgrowth of an interaction pattern that might have ended in other non-rebellious outcomes given the same inert elements of social strain, relative deprivation, and so forth.

Instrumental or Expressive

Rebellions always have some manifest concerns, whether vague or specific. The rebels want "freedom now," "free speech," "end the war," or "stop the expressway." One can take the rebels at face value and see them as trying to achieve their manifest goals through their rebellious acts. Or, one can regard the manifest goals as epiphenomena, while the real reasons for rebellion are more subtle and hidden from the consciousness of the rebels themselves. In this view, the rebels are expressing a sense of frustration and releasing tensions, using targets of convenience. Their malaise may come from broad social forces that they are hopelessly caught up in—for example, the impersonality of contemporary life, their inability to cope with the social environment, or the dislocations of modernization. They experience a diffuse discontent and find, in a mass movement, a way of giving vent to the frustrations they feel.

Both the personal maladjustment and mass society paradigms take an expressive view of rebellion. Basically, the rebel does not know why he is rebelling. Today, it may be for one cause, tomorrow for another one. But it is the process of rebelling that is important to him, not the achievement of the rebellion's goals.

The group conflict and relative deprivation paradigms take an instrumental view of rebellion. It is the essence of the group conflict view to see rebellion as an instrument of political change, used by a group faced with particular strategic problems and particular responses from the agents of social control. In the relative deprivation view, the manifest issues are also important. The group is getting less than it thinks it deserves and the rebellion aims at removing that gap. In both views, the rebel is concerned with the outcome, not with the process of rebelling.

The Individual's Stake

All views must explain what an individual receives from his participation in a rebellion. Their answers follow from the previous dimension. For the more expressive paradigms, personal maladjustment and mass society, the individual receives a sense of belongingness, of personal identity and worth. For Hoffer, he is escaping from a spoiled identity by submerging himself in group and cause; for mass society, there is less emphasis on escape and more on the way in which mass movements meet an individual need for social direction that is ordinarily supplied by intermediate ties.

For the more instrumental paradigms, the individual receives the hope of social change. For relative deprivation, the rebellion promises to give an individual what he thinks he deserves. Psychologically, it promises him harmony with his social environment as the want-get gap is eliminated. For the group conflict view, an individual hopes to get increased power or control over his life. If the rebellion is successful, the rebels will have a greater voice in determining policies that affect their interests and values.

Abnormality

Rebellion can be taken as a symptom of a sick society. In this view, it is pathological and abnormal and does not occur in societies that are functioning properly. Or, rebellion can be seen as no more "abnormal" than obedience. In this view, even the normal, healthy society will have rebellion, albeit for different reasons in different paradigms.

Mass society is the exemplar of the "rebellion is abnormal" view. The intermediate ties and overlapping groups of pluralist society are healthy; their breakdown is a pathology for which rebellion is one important symptom.

Rebellion is normal in the other views. In the personal maladjustment paradigm, it is normal because societies inevitably change, causing some disruption and strain, and individual talent and ability to cope is not evenly distributed among people. "When a great ship moves through the water," an advocate might say, "it will inevitably leave some turbulence in its wake. Those caught in the turbulence become rebels."

For different reasons, rebellion is normal in the relative deprivation view. The valued objects of a society—especially power, wealth, and prestige—are never equally distributed. Individuals inevitably will compare themselves with others and feel that they are getting less than they deserve. This gap will sometimes reach acute proportions through the normal operation of the system.

Finally, in the group conflict view, rebellion is as normal as conflict. Valued resources are scarce and the interests of different groups will inevitably clash. It is natural enough for the "haves" to keep as much power as they can to maintain what they have and equally natural for the "have-nots" to rebel when they lack institutional means for achieving their goals.

Corrective or Complicator

Rebellion may be normal without being healthy. In one view, it is essentially a force for change of the underlying conditions that gave rise to the rebellion. Rebellion is an anti-body that helps produce a corrective response that keeps pathologies from developing. In the other view, it is a symptom of either individual or societal problems. Moreover, it is a symptom with destructive secondary effects of its own that complicate and make more difficult potential solutions.

The mass society and personal maladjustment paradigms see rebellion as a complicator. It can promote the success of movements that are more lethal in their effects than the underlying disease. The danger is that demagogues will capture the rebellion and introduce changes that will worsen social conditions. Or, alternatively, that a totalitarian elite will capture the movement and use it as an instrument for the suppression of individual freedom.

The relative deprivation and group conflict paradigms see rebellion as a corrective. Rebellion can lead to a redistribution of power, wealth, or status, giving have-not groups a larger share of the pie. Of course, the response to rebellion may be less generous—the rebels may be crushed or ignored. Correction is not inevitable anymore than anti-bodies will always overcome the disease. Still, these paradigms see rebellion as a force for the adjustment of social inequality which, if responded to, can prevent more destructive forms of adjustment at later times.

These then are the central issues we see running through the contrasting views of rebellion and social movements. They are summarized in Chart 11.

Chart 11 Underlying Issues on Why People Rebel

	Personal Malad-justment, *e.g.,* Hoffer	Mass Society, *e.g.,* Kornhauser	Relative Dep-rivation, *e.g.,* Davies	Group Conflict, *e.g.,* Tilly
Where is the active ingred-ient in rebel-lion located?	The adjust-ment of indiv-iduals	Intermediate ties in the soc-ial system	Individual's perception of the social system	Interaction be-tween rebels and authorities.
Is rebellion in-strumental or expressive?	Expressive	Expressive	Instrumental	Instrumental
What does the individual get from the rebel-lion?	Sense of iden-tity and per-sonal worth	Sense of iden-tity and per-sonal worth	Hope of social change—more benefits	Hope of social change—more power
Is rebellion nor-mal or abnor-mal for a heal-thy society?	Normal	Abnormal	Normal	Normal
Is rebellion a corrective or complicating factor for a society?	Complicator	Complicator	Corrective	Corrective

REFERENCES

de Tocqueville, Alexis. *The Old Regime and the French Revolution.* New York: Harper, 1856.

Feuer, Lewis. *The Conflict of Generations.* New York: Basic Books, 1969.

Heirich, Max. *The Spiral of Conflict: Berkeley, 1964.* New York: Columbia University Press, 1971.

Lipsky, Michael. "Protest as a Political Resource," *American Political Science Review,* **62** (December 1968), pp. 1144–58.

Oglesby, Carl. "Vietnamese Crucible: An Essay on the Meanings of the Cold War," in Carl Oglesby and Richard Shaull, *Containment and Change.* New York: The Macmillan Company, 1967.

THE TRUE BELIEVER

ERIC HOFFER

There is in us a tendency to locate the shaping forces of our existence outside ourselves. Success and failure are unavoidably related in our minds with the state of things around us. Hence it is that people with a sense of fulfillment think it a good world and would like to conserve it as it is, while the frustrated favor radical change. The tendency to look for all causes outside ourselves persists even when it is clear that our state of being is the product of personal qualities such as ability, character, appearance, health and so on. "If anything ail a man," says Thoreau, "so that he does not perform his functions, if he have a pain in his bowels even . . . he forthwith sets about reforming– the world" (1937, p.96).

. . . Discontent by itself does not invariably create a desire for change. Other factors have to be present before discontent turns into disaffection. One of these is a sense of power.

Those who are awed by their surroundings do not think of change, no matter how miserable their condition. When our mode of life is so precarious as to make it patent that we cannot control the circumstances of our existence, we tend to stick to the proven and the familiar. We counteract a deep feeling of insecurity by making of our existence a fixed routine. We hereby acquire the illusion that we have tamed the unpredictable. Fisherfolk, nomads and farmers who have to contend with the willful elements, the creative worker who depends on inspiration, the savage awed by his surroundings–they all fear change. They face the world as they would an all-powerful jury. The abjectly poor, too, stand in awe of the world around them and are not hospitable to change. It is a dangerous life we live when hunger and cold are at our heels. There is thus a conservatism of the destitute as profound as the conservatism of the privileged, and the former is as much a factor in the perpetuation of a social order as the latter. . . .

For men to plunge headlong into an undertaking of vast change, they must be intensely discontented yet not destitute, and they must have the feeling that the possession of some potent doctrine, infallible leader, or some new technique they have access to a source of irresistible power. They must also have an extravagant conception of the prospects and potentialities of the future. Finally, they must be wholly ignorant of the difficulties involved in their vast undertaking. Experience is a handicap.

The men who started the French Revolution were wholly without political experience. The same is true of the Bolsheviks, Nazis and the revolutionaries in Asia. The experienced man of affairs is a latecomer. He enters the movement when it is already a going concern. It is perhaps the Englishman's political experience that keeps him shy of mass movements. . . .

Faith in a holy cause is to a considerable extent a substitute for the lost faith in ourselves.

The less justified a man is in claiming excellence for his own self, the more ready is he to claim all excellence for his nation, his religion, his race or his holy cause.

A man is likely to mind his own business when it is worth minding. When it is not, he takes his mind off his own meaningless affairs by minding other people's business.

This minding of other people's business expresses itself in gossip, snooping and meddling, and also in feverish interest in communal, national and racial affairs. In running away from ourselves we either fall on our neighbor's shoulder or fly at his throat.

The burning conviction that we have a holy duty toward others is often a way of attaching our drowning selves to a passing raft. What looks like giving a hand is often a holding on for dear life. Take away our holy duties and you leave our lives puny and meaningless. There is no doubt that in exchanging a self-centered for a selfless life we gain enormously in self-esteem. The vanity of the selfless, even those who practice utmost humility, is boundless.

One of the most potent attractions of a mass movement is its offering of a substitute for individual hope. This attraction is particularly effective in a society imbued with the idea of progress. For in the conception of progress, "tomorrow" looms large, and the frustration resulting from having nothing to look forward to is the more poignant. Hermann Rauschning (1941, p.189) says of pre-Hitlerian Germany that "The feeling of having come to the end of all things was one of the worst troubles we endured after that lost war." In a modern society people can live without hope only when kept dazed and out of breath by incessant hustling. The despair brought by unemployment comes not only from the threat of destitution, but from the sudden view of a vast nothingness ahead. The unemployed are more likely to follow the peddlers of hope than the handers-out of relief.

Mass movements are usually accused of doping their followers with hope of the future while cheating them of the enjoyment of the present. Yet to the frustrated the present is irremediably spoiled. Comforts and pleasures cannot make it whole. No real content or comfort can ever arise in their minds but from hope.

When our individual interests and prospects do not seem worth living for, we are in desperate need of something apart from us to live for. All forms of dedication, devotion, loyalty and self-surrender are in essence a desperate clinging to something which might give worth and meaning to our futile, spoiled lives. Hence the embracing of a substitute will necessarily be passionate and extreme. We can have qualified confidence in ourselves, but the faith we have in our nation, religion, race or holy cause has to be extravagant and uncompromising. A substitute embraced in moderation cannot supplant and efface the self we want to forget. We cannot be sure that we have something worth living for unless we are ready to die for it. This readiness to die is evidence to ourselves and others that what we had to take as a substitute for an irrevocable missed or spoiled first choice is indeed the best there ever was. . . .

Those who see their lives as spoiled and wasted crave equality and fraternity more than they do freedom. If they clamor for freedom, it is but freedom to establish equality and uniformity. The passion for equality is partly a passion for anonymity: to be one thread of the many which make up a tunic; one thread not distinguishable from the others. No one can then point us out, measure us against others and expose our inferiority.

They who clamor loudest for freedom are often the ones least likely to be happy in a free society. The frustrated, oppressed by their short-comings, blame their failure on existing restraints. Actually their innermost desire is for an end to the "free for all." They want to eliminate free competition and the ruthless testing to which the individual is continually subjected in a free society.

Where freedom is real, equality is the passion of the masses. Where equality is real, freedom is the passion of a small minority.

Equality without freedom creates a more stable social pattern than freedom without equality. . . .

Misfits

The frustration of misfits can vary in intensity. There are first the temporary misfits: people who have not found their place in life but still hope to find it. Adolescent youth, unemployed college graduates, veterans, new immigrants and the like are of this category. They are restless, dissatisfied and haunted by the fear that their best years will be wasted before they reach their goal. They are receptive to the preaching of a proselytizing movement and yet do not always make staunch converts. For they are not irrevocably estranged from the self; they do not see it as irremediably spoiled. It is easy for them to conceive an autonomous existence that is purposeful and hopeful. The slightest evidence of progress and success reconciles them with the world and their selves.

The role of veterans in the rise of mass movements has been touched upon earlier. A prolonged war by national armies is likely to be followed by a period of social unrest for victors and vanquished alike. The reason is neither the unleashing of passions and the taste of violence during wartime nor the loss of faith in a social order that could not prevent so enormous and meaningless a waste of life and wealth. It is rather due to the prolonged break in the civilian routine of the millions enrolled in the national armies. The returning soldiers find it difficult to recapture the rhythm of their prewar lives. The readjustment to peace and home is slow and painful, and the country is flooded with temporary misfits.

Thus it seems that the passage from war to peace is more critical for an established order than the passage from peace to war.

The permanent misfits are those who because of a lack of talent or some irreparable defect in body or mind cannot do the one thing for which their whole being craves. No achievement, however spectacular, in other fields can give them a sense of fulfillment. Whatever they undertake becomes a passionate pursuit; but they never arrive, never pause. They demonstrate the fact that we can never have enough of that which we really do not want, and that we run fastest and farthest when we run from ourselves.

The permanent misfits can find salvation only in a complete separation from the self; and they usually find it by losing themselves in the compact collectivity of a mass movement. By renouncing individual will, judgment and ambition, and dedicating all their powers to the service of an eternal cause, they are at last lifted off the endless treadmill which can never lead them to fulfillment.

The most incurably frustrated—and, therefore, the most vehement—among the permanent misfits are those with an unfulfilled craving for creative work. Both those who try to write, paint, compose, etcetera, and fail decisively, and those who after tasting the elation of creativeness feel a drying up of the creative flow within and know that never again will they produce aught worth while, are alike in the grip of a desperate passion. Neither fame nor power nor riches nor even monumental achievements in other fields can still their hunger. Even the wholehearted dedication to a holy cause does not always cure them. Their unappeased hunger persists, and they are likely to become the most violent extremists in the service of their holy cause.

The total surrender of a distinct self is a prerequisite for the attainment of both unity and self-sacrifice; and there is probably no more direct way of realizing this surrender than by inculcating and extolling the habit of blind obedience. When Stalin forces scientists, writers and artists to crawl on their bellies and deny their individual intelligence, sense of beauty and moral sense, he is not indulging a sadistic impulse but is solemnizing, in a most impressive way, the supreme virtue of blind obedience. All mass movements rank obedience with the highest virtues and put it on a level with faith: "union of minds requires not only a perfect accord in the one Faith, but complete submission and obedience of will to the Church and the Roman Pontiff as to God Himself." Obedience is not only the first law of God, but also the first tenet of a revolutionary party and of fervent nationalism. "Not to reason why" is considered by all mass movements the mark of a strong and generous spirit.

The disorder, bloodshed and destruction which mark the trail of a rising mass movement lead us to think of the followers of the movement as being by nature rowdy and lawless. Actually, mass ferocity is not always the sum of individual lawlessness. Personal truculence militates against united action. It moves the individual to strike out for himself. It produces the pioneer, adventurer and bandit. The true believer, no matter how rowdy and violent his acts, is basically an obedient and submissive person. The Christian converts who staged razzias against the University of Alexandria and lynched professors suspected of unorthodoxy were submissive members of a compact church. The Communist rioter is a servile member of a party. Both the Japanese and Nazi rowdies were the most disciplined people the world has seen. In this country, the American employer often finds in the racial fanatic of our South—so given to mass violence—a respectful and docile factory hand. The army, too, finds him particularly amenable to discipline.

People whose lives are barren and insecure seem to show a greater willingness to obey than people who are self-sufficient and self-confident. To the frustrated, freedom from responsibility is more attractive than freedom from restraint. They are eager to barter their independence for relief from the burdens of willing, deciding and being responsible for inevitable failure. They willingly abdicate the directing of their lives to those who want to plan, command and shoulder all responsibility. Moreover, submission by all to a supreme leader is an approach to their ideal of equality.

In time of crisis, during floods, earthquakes, epidemics, depressions and wars, separate individual effort is of no avail, and people of every condition are ready to obey and follow a leader. To obey is then the only firm point in a chaotic day-by-day existence.

The frustrated are also likely to be the most steadfast followers. It is remarkable that, in a co-operative effort, the least self-reliant are the least likely to be discouraged by defeat. For they join others in a common undertaking not so much to ensure the success of a cherished project as to avoid an individual shouldering of blame in case of failure. When the common undertaking fails, they are still spared the one thing they fear most, namely, the showing up of their individual shortcomings. Their faith remains unimpaired and they are eager to follow in a new attempt.

The frustrated follow a leader less because of their faith that he is leading them to a promised land than because of their immediate feeling that he is leading them away from their unwanted selves. Surrender to a leader is not a means to an end but a fulfillment. Whither they are led is of secondary importance.

REFERENCES

Rausching, Hermann. *The Conservation Revolution.* New York: G. P. Putnam's Sons, 1941.

Thoreau, Henry D. *Walden.* New York: Random House, 1937

THE POLITICS OF MASS SOCIETY
WILLIAM KORNHAUSER

Mass Behavior

Mass behavior is a form of collective behavior exhibiting the following characteristics. (a) *The focus of attention is remote from personal experience and daily life.* Remote objects are national and international issues or events, abstract symbols, and whatever else is known only through the mass media. Of course, not *any* concern for remote objects is a manifestation of mass behavior. Only when that concern leads to direct and activist modes of response can we speak of mass behavior. However, merely by virtue of the fact that mass behavior always involves remote objects certain consequences are likely to follow. Concern for remote objects tends to lack the definiteness, independence, sense of reality, and responsibility to be found in concern for proximate objects. The sphere of proximate objects consists of things that directly concern the individual: "his family, his buisness dealings, his hobbies, his friends and enemies, his township or ward, his class, church, trade union or any other social group of which he is an active member—the things under his personal observation, the things which are familiar to him independently of what his newspaper tells him, which he can directly influence or manage and for which he develops the kind of responsibility that is induced by a direct relation to the favorable and unfavorable effects of a course of action" (Schumpeter, 1947, pp. 258-9).

The sense of reality and responsibility declines as the object of concern becomes more remote:

> Now this comparative definiteness of volition and rationality of behavior does not suddenly vanish as we move away from those concerns of daily life in the home and in business which educate and discipline us. In the realm of public affairs there are sectors that are more within the reach of the citizen's mind than others. This is true, first, of local affairs. Even there we find a reduced power of discerning facts, a reduced preparedness to act upon them, a reduced sense of responsibility. . . . Second, there are many national issues that concern individuals and groups so directly and unmistakably as to evoke volitions that are genuine and definite enough. The most important instance is afforded by issues involving immediate and personal pecuniary profit to individual voters and groups of voters. . . . However, when we move still farther away from the private concerns of the family and the business office into those regions of national and international affairs that lack a direct and unmistakable link with those private concerns, individual volition, command of facts and methods of inference soon [decline] (Schumpeter, 1947, pp. 260-1).

(b) *The mode of response to remote objects is direct.* The lessening of the sense of reality and responsibility and effective volition with the greater remoteness of the focus of attention has particularly marked consequences when the mode of response is direct, rather than being mediated by several intervening layers of social relations. People act directly when they do not engage in discussion on the matter at hand, and when they do not act through groups in which they are capable of persuading and being persuaded by their fellows.

At times, people may act directly by grasping those means of action which lie immediately to hand. They may employ various more or less coercive measures against those individuals and groups who resist them (Heberle, 1951, p.378). For example, when large numbers of people feel that taxes are intolerably high, they may engage in quite different types of action. On the one hand, they may seek to change the tax laws by financing lobbyists, electing representatives, persuading others of their views by means of discussion, and so forth. These types of action are mediated by institutional relations, and are therefore subject to rules concerning legitimate modes of political action. On the other hand, people may seek to prevent others from paying their taxes and forcibly impede officials from collecting taxes, as in the instance of the Poujadists in France. This is direct action.

> Mass behavior is associated with activist interpretations of democracy and with increasing reliance on force to resolve social conflict. . . . The breakdown of normal restraints, including internalized standards of right conduct, and established channels of action . . . frees the mass to engage in direct, unmediated efforts to achieve its goals and to lay hands upon the most readily accessible

instruments of action. Ordinarily, even in countries having democratic constitutional systems, the population is so structured as to inhibit direct access to the agencies of decision. The electorate participates at specified times and in defined ways; it is not free to create *ad hoc* methods of pressure. The citizen, even when organized in a pressure group supporting, say, a farm lobby, can vote, write letters, visit his congressman, withhold funds, and engage in similar respectable actions. Other forms of activity are strange to him. But when this code has lost its power over him, he will become available for activist modes of intervention. . . . (Selznick, 1952, pp.293-4)

(c) Mass behavior also tends to be highly unstable, readily shifting its focus of attention and intensity of response. Activist responses are likely to alternate with apathetic responses. *Mass apathy* as well as mass activism is widespread in mass society. Mass apathy, like mass activism, is unstable and unpredictable, since it, too, is born of social alienation; and as an expression of resentment against the social order it can be transformed into extremist attacks on that order in times of crisis. In these respects, mass apathy differs from that indifference to public matters that is based on traditional conceptions of appropriate spheres of participation (for example, the indifference of women who believe that politics is a man's affair).

(d) When mass behavior becomes organized around a program and acquires a certain continuity in purpose and effort, it takes on the character of a *mass movement* (Blumer, 1946, p. 187). Mass movements generally have the following characteristics: their objectives are remote and extreme; they favor activist modes of intervention in the social order; they mobilize uprooted and atomized sections of the population; they lack an internal structure of independent groups (such as regional or functional units with some freedom of action). Totalitarian movements also possess these characteristics, but mass movements need not become totalitarian. The distinctive character of totalitarian movements lies in their effort to gain total control over their followers and over the whole society. Totalitarian movements are highly organized by an elite bent on total power, whereas mass movements tend to be amorphous collectivities, often without any stable leadership. The difference between the Communist movement and the I.W.W. is an example of the difference between a totalitarian movement and a mass movement.

Mass movements are miniature mass societies; totalitarian movements are miniature totalitarian societies. This parallelism implies the major similarity and the major difference between the two types of social movements: they both are based on atomized masses rather than on independent social groups, as are mass societies and totalitarian societies; on the other hand, the amorphous structure of the mass movement corresponds to the ease of access to elites in mass society, while the cadre organization of the totalitarian movement corresponds to the inaccessibility of the elite in totalitarian society. . . .

Weakness of Intermediate Relations

Weak intermediate relations leave elites and non-elites directly exposed to one another, and thereby invite widespread mass behavior; for in the absence of intermediate relations, participation in the larger society must be direct rather than filtered through intervening relationships.

The lack of strong independent groups undermines multiple proximate concerns, and thereby increases mass availability. Consider a man's relation to his work. While there often are important sources of intrinsic satisfaction derivable from the work itself, nevertheless the gratification derived from a sense of fellowship and control over the conditions of work are at least as important for firm occupational attachments. It is precisely these latter sources of interest and participation in work that require independent groups for their realization. Informal work groups supply some basis for fellowship and control at work, but with the growth in scale and complexity of the factory, office, and work institutions generally, they are insufficient. Therefore, all kinds of formal work associations, such as trade unions and professional associations, are needed. To the extent that they fail to develop, or, at the other extreme, themselves grow so far out of the reach of their members as to no longer be capable of providing the individual with a sense of participation and control, people are less likely to find the whole sphere of work an interesting and rewarding experience. Consequently, people may cease to care about their work, though of course they continue to work, despite their alienation from their jobs.

Similar factors shape a man's relation to his community. Unless a variety of forms of association are open to him, the individual is not likely to take an active interest in civic affairs—particularly in the metropolis, where the size of the population and the specialization of activities place a premium on voluntary associations as bases of political participation. Or, in the absence of associations such as the P.T.A. to provide channels of communication and influence between parents and school, the individual is less likely to develop or sustain interest and participation in the education of his children. Examples may be easily multiplied, but these are sufficient to suggest why independent groups are indispensable bases for the maintenance of meaningful proximate concerns.

The lack of a structure of independent groups also removes the basis for self-protection on the part of elites, because it permits direct modes of intervention to replace mediated participation in elites. In the first place, intermediate groups, even though they are independent of top elites, operate to protect these elites from arbitrary and excessive pressures by themselves being responsive to the needs and demands of people. They carry a large share of the burden of seeking to fulfill the interests of people who would otherwise have to rely exclusively on national agencies to minister to their needs. Secondly, the leaders of intermediate groups, irrespective of their particular aims (so long as these aims are not contrary to the integrity of the community), help to shore up the larger system of authority with which their own authority is inextricably bound. Third, intermediate groups help to protect elites by functioning as channels through which popular participation in the larger society (especially in the national elites) may be directed and restrained. In the absence of intermediate groups to act as representatives and guides for popular participation, people must act *directly* in the critical centers of society, and therefore in a manner unrestrained by the values and interests of a variety of social groups.

These reasons why the weakness of intermediate groups characterizes mass society are at the same time reasons why the strength of such groups characterizes the pluralist society. A strong intermediate structure consists of stable and independent groups which represent diverse and frequently conflicting interests. The opposition among such groups restrains one another's power, thereby limiting the aggregate intervention in elites; that is, a system of social checks and balances among a plurality of diverse groups operates to protect elites as well as non-elites in ways we have indicated. Furthermore, the separation of the various spheres of society—for example, separation of religion and politics—means that access to elites in one sphere does not directly affect elites in other spheres. The various authorities are more or less autonomous in their own spheres, in that they are not directly determined in their membership or policy by authorities in other spheres. These same factors protect non-elites from elites, since independent groups guard their members from one another, and since overlapping memberships among groups, *each of which concerns only limited aspects of its members' lives,* restrains each group from seeking total domination over its membership.

The state in pluralist society also plays a vital role in support of individual freedom, for it is above all the state which has the capacity to safeguard the individual against domination by particualr groups. Durkheim saw more profoundly than most that it is the *combination* of the state and what he called "secondary groups" that engenders individual liberty, rather than one or the other social structure alone. We shall quote him at length because he brings out with great clarity the special competence of each type of social structure for the advancement of individual freedom:

[The individual] must not be curbed and monopolised by the secondary groups, and these groups must not be able to get a mastery over their members and mould them at will. There must therefore exist above these local, domestic—in a word, secondary—authorities, some overall authority which makes the law for them all: it must remind each of them that it is but a part and not the whole and that it should not keep for itself what rightly belongs to the whole. The only means of averting this collective particularism and all it involves for the individual, is to have a special agency with the duty of representing the overall collectivity, its rights and its interests, vis-à-vis these individual collectivities . . . . It is solely because, in holding its constituent societies in check, it [the state] prevents them from exerting the repressive influences over the individual that they would otherwise exert. So there is nothing inherently tyrannical about State intervention in the different fields of collective life; on the contrary, it has the object and the effect of alleviating tyrannies that do exist. It will be argued, might not the State in turn become despotic? Undoubtedly, provided there was nothing to counter that trend. In that case, as the sole existing collective force, it produces the effects that any collective force not neutralized by any counter-force of the same kind would have on individuals. The State itself then becomes a leveller and repressive. And its repressiveness becomes even harder to endure than that of small groups, because it is more artificial. The State, in our large-scale societies, is so removed from individual interests that it cannot take into account the special or local and other conditions in which they exist. Therefore when it does attempt to regulate them, it succeeds only at the cost of doing violence to them and distorting them. It is, too, not sufficiently in touch with individuals in the mass to be able to mould them inwardly, so that they readily accept its pressure on them. The individual eludes the State to some extent—the State can only be effective in the context of a large-scale society—and individual diversity may not come to light. Hence, all kinds of resistance and distressing conflicts arise. The small groups do not have this drawback. They are close enough to the things that provide their *raison d'etre* to be able to adapt their actions exactly and they surround the individuals closely enough to shape them in their own image. The inference to be drawn from this comment, however, is simply that *if that collective force, the State, is to be the liberator of the individual, it has itself need of some counterbalance; it must be restrained by other collective forces, that is, by . . . secondary groups . . . it is out of this conflict of social forces that individual liberties are born* (Durkheim, 1958, pp. 62-3; italics added).

It has been said that medieval society was in fact essentially pluralist. But of course medieval society did not permit democratic control. The confusion here resides in the notion of pluralism: shall it be conceived as referring merely to a multiplicity of associations, or in addition, to a multiplicity of *affiliations?* Where individuals belong to several groups, no one group is *inclusive* of its members' lives. Associations have members with a variety of social characteristics (e.g., class and ethnic identities) and group memberships (e.g., trade unions may possess members who go to various churches, or even belong to church-affiliated trade union associations such as ACTU). Warner found that in Newburyport, Massachusetts, one-third of the 357 associations that were studied had members from three out of the six classes he identified, another third had members from four classes, and one-sixth from five or six classes. Almost two-thirds of the 12,876 members of associations belonged to associations in which four or more of the six classes were represented. Over three-fourths belonged to associations in which three or more of the ten ethnic groups were represented. Over one-half belonged to associations in which two or more of the four religious faiths were represented (Warner and Lunt, 1941, pp. 341, 346, 349). Such extensive *cross-cutting solidarities* favor a high level of freedom and consensus: these solidarities help prevent one line of social cleavage from becoming dominant, and they constrain associations to respect the various affiliations of their members lest they alienate them. Socially heterogeneous religious organizations are also important pluralistic agencies; they may be contrasted with situations in which religious and class lines tend to closely correspond, as in France where anti-clericalism is largely a working-class phenomenon. Political parties which draw their support from all major social segments constitute still another kind of cross-cutting solidarity. In this respect, the highly heterogeneous and decentralized American parties may be contrasted with the highly centralized, class-based Socialist parties and religious-based Catholic parties characteristic of European multiparty systems.

Our conception of pluralism includes that of multiple affiliations, which means that medieval society was not pluralist in our use of the term. So long as no association claims or receives hegemony over many aspects of its members' lives, its power over the individual will be limited. This is a vital point, because the authority of a private group can be as oppressive as that of the state.

A plurality of groups that are both independent and non-inclusive not only protects elites and non-elites from one another but does so in a manner that permits liberal democratic control. Liberal democratic control requires that people have *access* to elites, and that they exercise *restraint* in their participation. Independent groups help to maintain access to top-level decision-making by bringing organized pressure to bear on elites to remain responsive to outside influence. Each group has interests of its own in gaining access to elites, and has organized power not available to separate individuals for the implementation of these interests. These interests require not only that elites pay attention to the demands of the group, but also that other groups do not become so strong as to be able to shut off this group's access to the elite. Since independent groups seek to maintain their position by checking one another's power as well as the power of higher-level elites, the interaction of these groups helps to sustain access to decision-making processes in the larger society.

A plurality of independent groups also helps to regulate popular participation by integrating people into a wide range of proximate concerns. Where people possess multiple interests and commitments, attachments to remote objects, such as loyalty to the nation-state, are mediated by proximate relations. Therefore, people in pluralist society engage in relatively little *direct* participation in national decisions, not because elites prevent them from doing so, but because they can influence decisions more effectively through their own groups. Furthermore, people tend to be *selective* in their participation, limiting their direct involvement in the larger society to matters that appear to them of particular concern in light of their values and interests. Since pluralist society engenders a variety of values and interests, self-selective involvement in national politics tends to limit the number of people who are vitally concerned with any given issue. . . .

Social Classes and Mass Movements

Mass movements depend for their success on the weakness of existing institutions and on the intensive support of large numbers of people. The weakness of organizations in mass society allows them to be penetrated by mass movements. The population then becomes more easily absorbed by means of these captured organizations (as well as by direct mobilization into a movement), including satellite organizations designed to reach unorganized masses. In this section, we shall attempt to account for the kinds of people who flock to mass movements, especially during periods of acute crisis. We seek to show that totalitarian movements in particular mobilize people who are "available" by virtue of being socially alienated.

> [A totalitarian movement] depends on two distinct phenomena: on the one hand availability, itself created by a mental break with the milieu, and on the other hand the tendency toward millenarianism or secular religion. These two phenomena do not neccessarily go hand in hand: The "available" individuals or groups may be hostile to the Communist message, or on the other hand the appeal of the message may be so great that it creates a break, where none exists. . . . But in general the charm works on men who are already "available" as a result of a break with their milieu (Aron, 1953, p.9).

The theory of mass society seeks to account for certain fundamental characteristics of totalitarian movements by contrasting them with established political parties. Thus it views Communist and Fascist movements in terms of their *common* attributes: those which mark them off from genuine parties (including socialist, liberal, and conservative parties). These attributes, as Aron points out in the passage just cited, include a millenarian appeal and the mobilization of available people.

The totalitarian appeal has to be forthcoming, of course, before available people may be mobilized. There is nothing automatic about its presence. It requires the emergence of leaders capable of formulating an ideology and organizing a movement to carry it, as Lenin so well understood in his famous tract, "What Is To Be Done?" In the present study, we restrict ourselves to the task of stating conditions under which people are likely to be responsive to totalitarian leaders. However, even when there are totalitarian leaders capable of exploiting them, these conditions may not be sufficient. People who are responsive to a totalitarian movement at one time may turn to another kind of movement at another time. This proposition is illustrated by the results of a Swedish study which found that similar conditions favored the Communist movement in one area and a religious movement in another area:

> Conditions in both of the far-northern counties [of Sweden] were such as to breed radicalism. Both were subject to a rapid rate of colonization and industrial expansion during the past fifty to a hundred years. In both the climate was hard and life was dour. In the one, however, radicalism took a religious form; in the other a political form (Davison, 1954-55, p. 381).

Furthermore, Swedish public opinion data and census figures show that these two movements recruit similar kinds of people:

> Both religious radicals and the Communists are far more likely to attract men and young people than are more conservative groups—either religious or political. Here again the Communists and the religious radicals . . . seem to be competing for the allegiance of the same groups (Davison, 1954-55, p. 382).

The fact that some people turn to religious extremism rather than political extremism is fully compatible with mass theory. But of course the consequences for democracy will be very different depending on which of these alternatives gains a large following. It seems that people are more likely to seize the political alternative during periods of acute crisis. In the following pages, we seek to identify the kinds of people who are especially available for participation in totalitarian movements in such periods.

Up to this point, we have analyzed communism and fascism only insofar as they can be viewed as mass movements. But in order to formulate a fuller explanation of communism and fascism, it is also necessary to treat them as class movements. This means that part of the support for the Communist party is attributable to its being a working-class party, rather than a "mass" movement. Therefore, its social base is in certain respects and under certain conditions similar to that of democratic socialist parties. The analysis of the social base of working-class parties in general, as against those of the middle class, provides understanding that is missed by the analysis of the social base of mass movements in general, as against parties tied to the established order. Mass society theory does not account for the fact that Fascist movements draw their followers disproportionately from the middle classes, and that Communist movements draw their supporters disproportionately from the working classes. It is not contradicted by this class difference between fascism and communism, however, since common mass characteristics may subsist along with different class characteristics. On the contrary, just because fascism and communism are not similar in class composition, we cannot use class theory to account for their similarities, especially their totalitarianism. When organizations have as their central purpose the advancement of class interests, they tend to be restrained and limited by the exigencies of social situations and class traditions. Totalitarian movements, on the other hand, have few stable interests, traditions, or other affiliations of their members to restrain them either in their aims (which tend to be millennial), their methods (which tend to be violent), or control over their members (which tends to be total). Since in this study we are primarily concerned with *similarities* between the political extremes, we are emphasizing mass analysis. But because important *differences* also obtain among these groups, we must utilize class analysis in addition to mass analysis for a fuller description of their social composition.

Mass theory leads to the expectation that the unattached and alienated of all classes are more attracted to extremist symbols and leaders than are their class-rooted counterparts. Since workers tend to be less firmly attached to the social order than are middle-class people, they also tend to be less committed to democratic parties and civil liberties. Thus, in France and Italy, where the working class is poorly related to the social order, Communist movements are large and predominantly proletarian; whereas in Britain and the United States, where the working class is much less isolated from the society, Communist movements are small and ethnic. Middle-class people who lack strong attachments to the community also are more responsive to political extremism than are middle-class people who possess multiple social commitments. Thus, in France and Italy, where certain sections of the middle class are poorly related to the social order, a significant minority of the middle class supports mass movements (e.g. Poujadism in France and neo-Fascism in Italy); whereas in Britain and the United States, where the middle class is firmly attached to the social order, middle-class support for mass movements is practically non-existent (although the Mosley-led Fascists in Britain and the followers of G. L. K. Smith in the U. S., as well as certain sections of McCarthy's followers, constituted such support).

Intellectuals and peasants, small businessmen and industrial workers, when they lack social ties, alike find in the activism and millenarianism of mass movements more promising "solutions" to their plight than they do in the particularistic images of economic interest groups. Thus, mass theory looks to the breakdown of class identities as a critical process whereby people are freed to form new ties based on the commonly shared plight of mass men rather than the mutually exclusive plight of class men. In short, this approach finds in mass men rather than class men the shock troops in large-scale efforts to overturn democratic orders.

Consider the attributes of the early participants in the Nazi movement. They came from every stratum of German society:

> Princes without thrones, indebted and subsidized landlords, indebted farmers, virtually bankrupt industrialists, impoverished shopkeepers and artisans, doctors without patients, lawyers without clients, writers without readers, unemployed teachers, and unemployed manual and white-collar workers joined the movement. (Gerth, 1952, p. 105)

Consider the attributes of early participants in the Fascist movement in Italy:

> The composition of the Fascist movement also shows its mass-character. The Fascist flag was followed in the beginning by revolutionary syndicalists; by the *Arditi,* who could not forget the war; by discontented demobilized officers, who had no future but to become salesmen; by soldiers; by spirited youths; by loafers and professional criminals; by rich intellectuals who feared the workers, and by desperately poor intellectuals; by a mixture of "patriotic" agrarians, craftsmen and others. . . . *All the various layers of society* were represented, all social groups suspended in this crowd. (Lederer, 1940, pp. 86-7; italics added).

The Communist movement also recruits supporters from the uprooted members of all strata, albeit disproportionately from the working classes.

The analysis explores the hypothesis that all social classes contribute to the social base of totalitarian movements, and that in particular it is the socially uprooted and unattached members of all classes who support these movements first and in the greatest numbers. This implies that *unattached intellectuals, marginal members of the middle-class, isolated industrial and farm workers* have been among the major social types in totalitarian movements.

REFERENCES

Aron, Raymond. "Totalitarianism and Freedom," *Confluence,* 2 (June, 1953), pp. 3-20.

Blumer, Herbert. "Collective Behavior," in A. M. Lee (Ed.) *New Outlines of the Principles of Sociology.* New York: Barnes and Noble, 1946, pp. 165-222.

Davison, W. Phillips. "A Review of Sven Rydenfell's *Communism in Sweden,*" *Public Opinion Quarterly,* **18** (1954-55), pp. 375-388.

Durkheim, Emile. *Professional Ethics and Civic Morals.* New York: The Free Press, 1958.

Gerth, Hans H. "The Nazi Party: Its Leadership and Composition," in Robert K. Merton, *et al.,* (Eds.) *Reader in Bureaucracy.* New York: The Free Press, 1952, pp. 100-113.

Heberle, Rudolph. *Social Movements.* New York: Appleton-Century-Crofts, 1951.

Lederer, Emil, *State of the Masses.* New York: W. W. Norton, 1940.

Schumpeter, Joseph. *Capitalism, Socialism, and Democracy.* New York: Harper and Bros., 1947.

Selznick, Philip. *The Organizational Weapon.* New York: McGraw-Hill, 1952.

Warner, W. Lloyd and Lunt, P. *The Social Life of a Modern Community.* New Haven: Yale University Press, 1941.

THE REVOLUTIONARY STATE OF MIND

JAMES C. DAVIES

Civil violence, in our ignorance of its causes, often appears to be random, erratic, irrational. This appearance only betokens our ignorance of causes rather than any real randomness of revolutionary behavior. It is the product of natural laws more fundamental than any that men have adopted in writing or by custom—more fundamental than any written or unwritten constitution, any statute or city ordinance against unlawful assembly or disorderly conduct.

Explanations of fundamental, preconstitutional, preinstitutional causes of human behavior have been related to political consequences since Plato's *Republic* and Hobbes's *Leviathan.* In recent decades these fundamental principles have become far more clearly evident than they were even to Hobbes, that most magnificent integrator of speculative psychology and political theory.

As Aristotle observed in the 4th century before Christ and Hobbes twenty centuries later, we are now again becoming aware that civil disorders and revolutions begin in the minds of men. At least that is where revolutions acquire focus and direction. This assertion is so banal as to seem to need no saying, but the most current single assertion about revolution has been that it begins in group (economic, ethnic, or religious) conflict. There has been too little awareness of the human mind as a nodal, elemental factor.

Karl Marx was the most tenacious and prescient student of revolution in the 19th century and the most influential in the 20th. For him the unit of analysis was not the human being or his central nervous system but those vast nonindividual units called social classes. Marx did imply the mind, when he spoke of the class-consciousness of the proletariat. But "class-consciousness" and "the collective unconscious" are inexact shorthand terms, appropriate for easy and often monistic generalizations. Consciousness is more exactly a characteristic of individuals than of groups. Nevertheless, newspaper accounts and even academic studies of the civil disturbances among black people in the United States and university students throughout the world remain largely preoccupied with collectivities, rather than individuals, as the units of analysis. Sometimes such studies say that it all started with the demand in black slums for housing and jobs, or in universities for more and better professors and more student participation in making educational policy. They avoid saying that *any* individual, deprived of the steady means of physical survival or frustrated by careers that have been blocked without any visible purpose by tradition or by war, will become restless. They avoid looking into the minds of people.

Just why these demands are made by blacks or students is thus seldom considered on any general level. To many, it seems idle to consider that there may be common explanations applicable to the demands of black people and students and of those who made the Protestant Reformation and the great revolutions of the 20th century. To many, it is awesome and fascinating to read or witness disaster, whether it be the Black Death of early modern times in Europe or a lightning-caused fire in the green forest or a rioter-set fire in a black slum. The awe and the fascination produce little but fear and wonder. Seeing people die of the plague or witnessing a fire does not cure the plague or prevent the fire. . . .

The thesis is a fundamentally psychological one, referring to individuals rather than social aggregates: revolution is most likely to occur when a long period of rising expectations and gratifications is followed by a period during which gratifications (socioeconomic or otherwise) suddenly drop off while expectations (socioeconomic or otherwise) continue to rise. The rapidly widening gap between expectations and gratifications portends revolution. The most common case for this widening gap of individual dissatisfactions is economic or social dislocation that makes the affected individual generally tense, generally frustrated. That is, the greatest portion of people who join a revolution are preoccupied with tensions related to the failure to gratify the physical (economic) needs and the needs for stable interpersonal (social) relationships.

These are the ones, the following theory says, who are most likely to be the hewers of wood for scaffolds and the drawers of tumbrels—and to form the massive crowds that witness the execution of the old regime. The majority of revolutionaries thus are likely to be poor people at loose ends who have made some progress toward a new and better life and see themselves now failing to do so.

But socioeconomically deprived poor people are unlikely to make a successful rebellion, a revolution, by themselves. Their discontent needs the addition of the discontents developing among individuals in the middle class and the ruling class when they are rather suddenly deprived (socioeconomically or otherwise). Without the support of disaffected bourgeoisie, disaffected nobles, and disaffected intellectuals, the French Revolution might have been some kind of grand, episodic upheaval. But it would not likely have amounted to the successful assault on the political power structure that a revolution amounts to. The same may be said for the American Revolution. Those who signed the Declaration of Independence and/or became rulers of the new nation were gentlemen farmers like Washington and Jefferson rather than callous-handed yeomen, who became the rank and file of the Continental Army. The Russian Revolution, particularly in its 1905 phase, depended on the disaffection not solely of factory workers and peasants but also of urban bourgeoisie and—almost incredibly it seemed at first glance—of substantial numbers of the landed nobility.

The unit of analysis below is therefore not a vast or a small social aggregate, a peasantry or an elite, but consists of individual human beings. Whatever their state of advancement—from men who work with their hands and lose factory jobs or see prices fall for the product of their fields, to intellectuals who graduate from university with high honors and find themselves without jobs that fit their training—such individuals see a gap widening between their rising expectations and downturning gratifications. The interests of these visibly very different people may in the long run be directed counter to those of others with whom they, for a time, work together. But during the revolution they all share a high degree of frustration directed toward the government and the incumbent ruling "class." It is this frustrated state of mind, shared and focused on the government, that produces their cooperation.

In addition to the J curve hypothesis there are alternative and additional explanations for the development of the revolutionary state of mind. It may be that gratifications do not suddenly fall but continue to rise, but not so rapidly as expectations rise, with the result that the gap between the two widens without a downturn in gratifications. There may be cases in which violence breaks out after a steady but too-slow rise in gratifications. On the other hand, a close look at the events immediately preceding the outbreak of a period of violence always seems to reveal such acts as the violent suppression of a demonstration, the roughing-up of a worker or poor farmer or a black —or some other event in which there is a clearcut but scarcely visible downturn in the (mental) belief that rewards will continue to meet expectations. Tear gas or a billy club are not rising gratifications, nor do they produce rising expectations. They dash the expectation that tear gas will not be used and that the public park will at last be integrated. And so they hurt. . . .

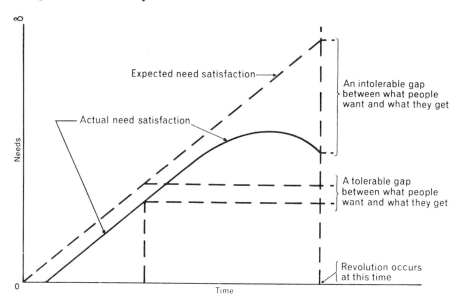

Figure 1. Need Satisfaction and Revolution.

Revolutions are most likely to occur when a prolonged period of objective economic and social development is followed by a short period of sharp reversal. The all important effect on the minds of people in a particular society is to produce, during the former period, an expectation of continued ability to satisfy needs—which continue to rise—and, during the latter, a mental state of anxiety and frustration when manifest reality breaks away from anticipated reality. The actual state of socioeconomic development is less significant than the expectation that past progress, now blocked, can and must continue in the future.

Political stability and instability are ultimately, dependent on a state of mind, a mood, in a society. Satisfied or apathetic people who are poor in goods, status, and power can remain politically quiet and their opposites can revolt, just as, correlatively and more probably, dissatisfied poor can revolt and satisfied rich oppose revolution. It is the dissatisfied state of mind rather than the tangible provision of "adequate" or "inadequate" supplies of food, equality, or liberty which produces the revolution. In actuality, there must be a joining of forces between dissatisfied, frustrated people who differ in their degree of objective, tangible welfare and status. Well fed, well educated high-status individuals who rebel in the face of apathy among the objectively deprived can accomplish at most a coup d'etat. The objectively deprived, when faced with solid opposition of people of wealth, status, and power, will be smashed in their rebellion as were peasants and Anabaptists by German noblemen in 1525 and East Germans by the Communist elite in 1953.

Before appraising this general notion in light of a series of revolutions, a word is in order as to why revolutions ordinarily do not occur when a society is generally impoverished when, as de Tocqueville put it, evils that seem inevitable are patiently endured. They are endured in the extreme case because the physical and mental energies of people are totally employed in the process of merely staying alive. The Minnesota starvation studies conducted during World War II indicate clearly the constant preoccupation of very hungry individuals with fantasies and thoughts of food. *In extremis,* as the Minnesota research poignantly demonstrates, the individual withdraws into a life of his own, withdraws from society, withdraws from any significant kind of activity unrelated to staying alive. Reports of behavior in Nazi concentration camps indicate the same preoccupation. In less extreme and barbarous circumstances, where minimal survival is possible but little more, the preoccupation of individuals with staying alive is only mitigated. Social action takes place for the most part on a local, face-to-face basis. In such circumstances the family is a—perhaps the major— solidary unit and even the local community exists primarily to the extent families need to act together to secure their separate survival. Such was life on the American frontier in the 16th through 19th centuries. In very much attenuated form, but with a substantial degree of social isolation persisting, such evidently is rural life even today. This is clearly related to a relatively low level of political participation in elections. As Zawadzki and Lazarsfeld (1935) have indicated, preoccupation with physical survival, even in industrial areas, is a force strongly militating against the establishment of the community-sense and consensus on joint political action which are necessary to induce a revolutionary state of mind. Far from making people into revolutionaries, enduring poverty makes for concern with one's solitary self or solitary family at best and resignation or mute despair at worst. When it is a choice between losing their chains or their lives, people will mostly choose to keep their chains, a fact which Marx seems to have overlooked.

It is when the chains have been loosened somewhat, so that they can be cast off without a high probability of losing life, that people are put in a condition of protorebelliousness. I use the term protorebelliousness because the mood of discontent may be dissipated before a violent outbreak occurs. The causes of such dissipation may be natural or social (including economic and political). A bad crop year that threatens a return to chronic hunger may be succeeded by a year of natural abundance. Recovery from sharp economic dislocation may take the steam from the boiler of rebellion. The slow, grudging grant of reforms, which has been the political history of England since at least the Industrial Revolution, may effectively and continuously prevent the degree of frustration that produces revolt.

A revolutionary state of mind requires the continued, even habitual but dynamic expectation of greater opportunity to satisfy basic needs, which may range from merely physical (food, clothing, shelter, health, and safety from bodily harm) to social (the affectional ties of family and friends) to the need for equal dignity and justice. But the necessary additional ingredient is a persistent, unrelenting threat to the satisfaction of these needs: not a threat which actually returns people to a state of sheer survival but which puts them in the mental state where they believe they will not be able to satisfy one or more basic needs. Although physical deprivation in some degree may be threatened on the eve of all revolutions, it need not be the prime factor, as it surely was not in the American Revolution of 1775. The crucial factor is the vague or specific fear that ground gained over a long period of time will be quickly lost. This fear does not generate if there is continued opportunity to satisfy continually emerging needs; it generates when the existing government suppresses or is blamed for suppressing such opportunity.

Some Conclusions

The notion that revolutions need both a period of rising expectations and a succeeding period in which they are frustrated qualifies substantially the main Marxian notion that revolutions occur after progressive degradation and the de Tocqueville notion that they occur when conditions are improving. By putting de Tocqueville before Marx but without abandoning either theory, we are better able to plot the entecedents of at least the disturbances here described.

Half of the general, if not common, sense of this revised notion lies in the utter improbability of a revolution occurring in a society where there is the continued, unimpeded opportunity to satisfy new needs, new hopes, new expectations. Would Dorr's rebellion have become such if the established electorate and government had readily acceded to the suffrage demands of the unpropertied? Would the Russian Revolution have taken place if the Tsarist autocracy had, quite out of character, truly granted the popular demands for constitutional democracy in 1905? Would the Cairo riots of January, 1952 and the subsequent coup actually have occurred if Britain had departed from Egypt and if the Egyptian monarchy had established an equitable tax system and in other ways alleviated the poverty of urban masses and the shame of the military?

The other half of the sense of the notion has to do with the improbability of revolution taking place where there has been no hope, no period in which expectations have risen. Such a stability of expectations presupposes a static state of human aspirations that some-times exists but is rare. Stability of expectations is not a stable social condition. Such was the case of American Indians (at least from our perspective) and perhaps Africans before white men with Bibles, guns, and other goods interrupted the stability of African society. Egypt was in such a condition, vis-a-vis modern aspirations, before Europe became interested in building a canal. Such stasis was the case in Nazi concen-tration camps, where conformism reached the point of inmates coopera-ting with guards even when the inmates were told to lie down so that they could be shot. But in the latter case there was a society with externally induced complete despair, and even in these camps there were occasional rebellions of sheer desperation. It is of course true that in a society less regimented than concentration camps, the rise of expectations can be frustrated successfully, thereby defeating rebellion just as the satisfaction of expectations does. This, however, requires the uninhibited exercise of brute force as it was used in sup-pressing the Hungarian rebellion of 1956. Failing the continued ability and persistent will of a ruling power to use such force, there appears to be no sure way to avoid revolution short of an effective affirmative, and continuous response on the part of established govern-ments to the almost continuously emerging needs of the governed.

R EFERENCES

Zawadzki, B. and Lazarsfeld, Paul F. "The Psychological Consequences of Unemployment," *Journal of Social Psychology,* **16** (1935), pp. 42-57.

THE CHAOS OF THE LIVING CITY

CHARLES TILLY

As life is disorderly, so is the city. But is the city itself the source of disorder? Since the rise of the industrial metropolis, generations of western men have proclaimed it so. The nineteenth-century sociologists who argued that the mobility, complexity, and scale of the modern city were bound to strip men of social ties, disorient them, and thus push them toward individual and collective derangement were simply articulating a well established tradition. The tradition has not yet died.

We find the precise tone in Baudelaire:

Swarming city, city of dreams
Where ghosts grab strollers in broad daylight . . .

How admirable it is, he tells us elsewhere, to join the few who are free of the spectral grasp:

And so you go your way, stoic, uncomplaining
Through the chaos of the living city . . .

"Through the chaos of the living city!" A great motto for the study of urban disorder.

"Under the aegis of the city," declares Lewis Mumford (1961, p.43) "violence . . . became normalized, and spread far beyond the centers where the great collective manhunts and sacrifical orgies were first instituted." Again we encounter the image of the city as destroyer, of urban life as the solvent of social bonds, of violence as the price paid for living on the large scale. While peasant revolts leave faded souvenirs here and there, the word "revolution" recalls city streets. As deprived millions limp hopefully into the cities of Africa or Latin America, political observers hold their breaths. When will the cities explode? Urbanization, it seems to go without saying, means social disorder.

It does, in a way. Huge wars and devastating revolutions only came into man's life with the flowering of cities. But whether urbanization and collective violence have a necessary or a contingent connection—or, indeed, any genuine casual connection at all—is far from clear.

Some small observations on the nature of that connection form the substance of this essay. I want to comment on the ways urbanization mi might incite or transform collective violence, raise some questions about the relationship between violent and nonviolent forms of political partici- pation, sketch some means for investigating the political consequences of urbanization, and review some relevant findings from a study of the evolution of political disturbances in France since 1830.

Why and how does urbanization affect collective violence? Sociolo- gists have some well-frozen ideas on the subject. After stressing the dis- ruptive personal effects of migration and the "frictions" produced by the rubbing together of urban and pre-urban value systems in expanding cities, Philip Hauser (1963, p.212) tells us that:

> Another group of serious problems created or augmented by rapid rates of
> urbanization are those of internal disorder, political unrest, and governmental
> instability fed by mass misery and frustration in the urban setting. The facts
> that the differences between the "have" and "have not" nations, and
> between the "have" and "have not" peoples within nations, have become
> "felt differences," and that we are expecting a "revolution in expectations,"
> have given huge urban population agglomerations an especially incendiary and
> explosive character.

In Hauser's view, the breaking of traditional bonds and the conflict of values feed disorder, while the swelling city's combination of misery and heightened hopes nearly guarantees it. Change produces tension, tension breaks out in collective explosions, and a form of action more frenzied than that of stable, developed countries erupts into life.

Hauser's analysis, I believe, sums up the predominant sociological position. Seen from the outside, the set of ideas looks solid and chinkless. From inside, it seems much less likely to withstand pressure. For one thing, it contains a notion of the equivalence of different types of dis- order. Personal malaise, moral deviation, crime and political upheaval are supposed to flow into each other.

Almost mystically, Louis Chevalier announces that essential unity: outside the major outbursts, he says,

> The political and social violence which has been studied so often and so
> minutely is replaced by other forms of violence—more continuous, more

complex, harsher, involving greater numbers, taking from the rise and the bulk of the masses their progress, their unity and their force. Here is another form of connection among crises: Private dramas, daily ones, add their weight to the public ones, developing outside them, but accumulating and culminating in them (Chevalier 1958, pp. 552-553).

Chevalier does not hesitate to call nineteenth-century Paris a sick city, or to consider misery, crime, suicide, street violence and popular rebellion so many expressions of the same pervasive pathology. That is one side of the standard sociological formulation.

Turn this set of ideas over. On the other side is stamped a complementary set: that there is a sharp disjunction between healthy and pathological social states, between the normal and abnormal, between order and disorder, which justifies treating different specimens of disapproved collective behavior as manifestations of the same general phenomenon—"deviance," The responses which other people give to the disapproved behavior win another general label—"social control."

Collective violence almost automatically receives both the complementary treatments. It is easy to treat as the final expression of a fundamental pathology which also shows up as a crime, delinquency, family instability or mental illness. It is even easier to treat as radically discontinuous from orderly political life. Long before Taine and Le Bon had dismissed the mass actions of the French Revolution as the work of demonic guttersnipes, Plato had shuddered over the outbreaks of man's "lawless wild-beast nature, which peers out in sleep," and James Madison had warned of

an unhappy species of the population . . . who, during the calm of regular government, are sunk below the level of men; but who, in the tempestuous scenes of civil violence, may emerge into the human character, and give a superiority of strength to any party with which they may associate themselves.

More recently, Hannah Arendt (1963: pp. 9-10) has argued that "violence is a marginal phenomenon in the political realm. . . ," that "political theory has little to say about the phenomenon of violence and must leave its discussion to the technicians," that "insofar as violence plays a predominant role in wars and revolutions, both occur outside the political realm." And the political realm, to Miss Arendt's mind, contains normal social life.

Here two ideas intertwine. One is that violence appeals to the beast in man and to the beasts among men. The other is that men in becoming violent step over an abyss which then separates them from coherent rationality.

Despite their devotion to death-dealing automobiles, aggressive detectives and murderous wars, it is true that men ring round most forms of interpersonal violence with extraordinary tabus and anxieties. Yet collective violence is one of the commonest forms of political participation. Why *begin* an inquiry into the effects of urbanization with the presumption that violent politics appear only as a disruption, a deviation or a last resort? Rather than treating collective violence as an unwholesome deviation from normality, we might do better to ask under what conditions (if any) violence disappears from ordinary political life.

That is, however, a mischievous question. The treatment of collective behavior in terms of change: tension, tension-release and the assumption of drastic discontinuity between routine politics and collective violence cling to each other. Most students of large-scale social change cling to both. Challenging either the fit between the two notions or their independent validity therefore smacks of rabble-rousing. Yet there are some alternatives we simply cannot ignore.

First, collective violence often succeeds. Revolutionaries do come to power, machine-breakers do slow the introduction of labor-saving devices, rioters do get public officials removed. The local grain riot, so widespread in western Europe from the seventeenth through the nineteenth centuries, often produced a temporary reduction of prices, forced stored grain into the market, and stimulated local officials to new efforts at assuring the grain supply (L. Tilly, 1971). I do not mean that, by some universal calculus, violence is more efficient than nonviolence. I simply mean that it works often enough in the short run, by the standards of the participants, not to be automatically dismissed as a flight from rational calculation.

Second, whether or not it succeeds in the short run and by the standards of the participants, collective protest is often a very effective means of entering or remaining in political life, of gaining or retaining an identity as a force to be reckoned with. Eugene Debs boasted that "no strike has ever been lost" and American advocates of Black Power consider their appeal the only means of mobilizing Negroes as an effective political force. Although there are always Revisionists to argue that the dispossessed will gain power more cheaply by circumventing revolution—even though the Revisionists are often right—collective violence does frequently establish the claim to be heard, and feared. In that sense, too, it can be a rational extension of peaceful political action.

Third, acts of collective violence often follow a well-defined internal order. The order goes beyond the Freudian logic of dreams or that symbolic correspondence Neil Smelser (1963) finds between the beliefs embodied in collective movements and the strains which produce them.

In many cases it is sufficiently conscious, explicit and repetitive to deserve the name "normative." Many western countries on the eve of intensive industrialization, for example, have seen a recurrent sort of redressing action against what the people of a locality consider to be violations of justice: mythical avenging figures like Rebecca or Ned Ludd, threats posted in their names, outlandish costumes (women and Indians being favorite masquerades), routine, focussed, roughly appropriate punishments inflicted on the presumed violators of popular rights (see Hobsbawm and Rude, 1968; Hobsbawm, 1969; C. Tilly, 1969). Disorder displays a normative order.

Fourth, the participants in collective violence are frequently rather ordinary people. Recent studies of popular disturbances in France, England and elsewhere have shifted the burden of proof to those who wish to claim that mass actions recruit from the lunatic fringe . . . . Not that these studies portray the recruitment as a kind of random sampling: real grievances, local economic conditions, established paths of communication, the character of local politics all help determine who take part. But the rioters and local machine-breakers commonly turn out to be fairly ordinary people acting on important but commonplace grievances. The "dangerous classes" stay out of sight.

Finally, the large-scale structural changes of societies which transform everyday politics through their effects on the organization, communication and common consciousness of different segments of the population also transform the character and loci of collective violence. As the scale at which men organize their peaceful political actions expands, so does the scale at which they organize their violence. As workers in mechanized industries become a coherent political force, they also become a source of disorder. The correlations are obviously complex and imperfect; that is precisely why they are interesting. But they are correlations rather than antitheses.

So there are five reasons for hesitating to assume that collective violence is a sort of witless release of tension divorced from workaday politics: its frequent success as a tactic, its effectiveness in establishing or maintaining a group's political identity, its normative order, its frequent recruitment of ordinary people, and its tendency to evolve in cadence with peaceful political action. The five points are debatable and worthy of debate . . . not to mention empirical investigation. To the extent that they are valid, they lead to somewhat different expectations from the usual ones concerning the development of political disturbances in the course of urbanization.

Urbanization *could* affect collective violence in three main ways: by disrupting existing social ties and controls, by exposing more

individuals and groups to urban institutions and living conditions, and
by changing relations between city and country. In fact, an abundant
(if largely theoretical and anecdotal) literature asserts the disturbing
effects of each of these changes. The disruption of ties and controls
is commonly supposed to incite disorder either by removing restraints
to impulses which would under normal circumstances be muffled or by
inducing anxiety in individuals detached from stable, orderly surroundings.
(Mass migration to cities is the standard example.) Exposure to urban
institutions and living conditions is usually considered to promote
collective violence in two respects: (1) by imposing intolerable privations
in the form of material misery and unfamiliar disciplines or (2) by
communicating new goals via heightened communication within large
groups sharing common fates and interests, and via the diffusion of
higher standards of comfort and welfare from the existing urban
population to the newcomers. Thus rapid urban growth is said to
exacerbate the "revolution of rising expectations." The changing
relations between city and country are often thought to engender
disturbance in the country itself as cities expand their claims for
goods, men, taxes, and subordination, while rural communities resist
those claims. Thus regions of distinct tribal character presumably
become ripe for rebellion.

If the disruption of existing ties and controls, the exposure of
individuals and groups to urban institutions and living conditions, and
the changing relations between city and country all uniformly
encourage collective violence, then matters are delightfully simple:
the pace and location of upheaval should be closely correlated with
the pace and location of urban growth. That hypothesis easily
lends itself to testing. The surprising thing is that it has not yet
been truly tested.

Even in the absence of good data on either side of the
relationship, however, we may legally doubt whether it is so
splendidly straightforward. In no western European country have
the peak years of urban growth since 1800 also been the peak years
of political upheaval. Such quantitative international studies as we
have of the twentieth century give relatively little weight to the
sheer pace of change in the explanation of the frequency of protest
and violence; instead, they tend to substantiate the importance of
political structure and of short-term deprivation. So a global
connection of upheaval to urban growth seems unlikely.

Happily, the various components of urbanization also lend themselves to separate analysis. We can, to some extent, isolate the political
correlates of rapid migration from rural areas to large cities, of miserable

urban living conditions, or of the expansion of central control into the rural backland. Rather than the amassing of case studies of violence or the statistical manipulation of general indices drawn from samples of whole countries, two strategies getting at differentials within countries seem particularly suitable. The first is to compare segments of the country—communities, regions, classes, as well as periods—in terms of the frequency and intensity of collective violence, of the forms violence takes, of the participants in it. Whereas international comparisons ordinarily make it tough to disentangle the correlates of urban poverty from those of rapid migration to cities, and case studies usually hide the significance of negative instances, systematic comparisons within countries promise the opportunity to examine the differences between turbulent and placid periods or settings in meaningful detail, with reasonable controls.

The second strategy is to separate—and, where possible, to index— the appearance of different *forms* of collective violence. This means eschewing summary indices of "turbulence" or "instability." It also means paying as much attention to variations in the form of collective outbursts as to shifts from calm to fury and back again. Here the illuminating work of George Rude or Eric Hobsbawm, who have depicted the characteristic preindustrial disturbances and stressed their replacement by other kinds of disturbances with the advent of industrialization, offers questions and hypotheses galore.

The power to close in on such hypotheses gives these two strategies their attraction. The ideas about urbanization and collective violence I earlier characterized as the standard sociological treatment immediately suggest predictions: those periods and regions in which the intensest urban growth goes on should be the richest in disturbances; misery, mobility and cultural diversity will have separate and roughly additive effects; while collective violence and other forms of "deviance" will be positively correlated in gross and will recruit in the same parts of the population, at a given level of urban concentration or a given pace of urbanization they will be negatively correlated, since they are alternative expressions of the same tensions; collective violence will recede as new groups become formally organized, integrated into the nation's political life.

There is surely something to all these hypotheses. They deserve checking. But the second thoughts on the nature of collective violence we encountered earlier suggest some different predictions: a weak connection of political disturbances with crime, misery or personal disorder; a corresponding rarity of the criminal, miserable or deranged in their ranks; a strong connection with more peaceful forms of political contention; a significant continuity and internal order to collective violence where it does occur; a long lag between urban growth and collective outbursts due to the time required for socialization, organization and formation of a common consciousness on the part of the newcomers; a tendency for disturbances to cluster where there is a conflict between the principal holders of power in a locality and more or less organized groups moving into or out of a *modus vivendi* with those holders of power; a marked variation of the form of the disturbance with the social organization of its setting. On the whole these hunches are harder to verify than those deducible from the standard sociological treatment. Still they can be tested, and should be . . . .

> [Tilly reviews an array of evidence from France during the period 1830 to 1960. He looks, for example, at the number of disturbances per year in France and finds that the high points did not correspond to the periods of rapid urban growth. He examines the specific places where violence was most likely to occur and finds no tendency for the fastest growing cities, or the most rapidly urbanizing administrative areas, to manifest more violence than the rest. The presence of cities is important but their rate of expansion is not. "The segments of the population with sufficient organization to carry on collective violence at a scale large enough to bother the authorities—and therefore to lead to violent encounters with troops, police, and others—were concentrated in the larger cities and their vicinities." Patterns of collective violence, he finds, tend to correspond to patterns of working class disturbances and strikes more generally.] *

The findings therefore cast doubt on theories which trace a main link between cities and protest through a process of disorganization. On the contrary, the whole array of evidence we have been examining suggests a positive connection between *organization* and conflict. The moderate relationship discovered earlier between collective violence in 1830-1832 and urban growth from 1821 to 1831, for instance, probably represents the appearance of new contenders for power in the largest industrial centers over the whole decade rather than individual disorientation or malaise at exposure to the modern city.

We are not, in any case, dealing with a constant pattern. Over the long run of the nineteenth and twentieth centuries, collective violence in France drifted away from the countryside and toward the cities faster than the population itself did, as the power and resources which mattered most politically concentrated in the great cities. Politics nationalized and urbanized simultaneously. In the short run, the extent of urban concentration of collective violence depended on the nature of the unresolved

---

* Editors' Note: This paragraph is our own summary of the material covered by Tilly in the approximately twenty pages we have omitted at this point from the original article.

political issues at hand. Food riots formed a more dispersed pattern than violent strikes; strikes were more scattered than major struggles for control of the national political apparatus. Since food riots, strikes, and major struggles for control followed different rhythms, the geographic pattern fluctuated. Perhaps the largest alternation went from battles for power at the center (which produced a high urban concentration of collective violence) and resistance to pressures from the center (which produced more disturbances at the periphery). In the period we are examining here, the revolutionary years 1830 and 1848 concentrated their violence in cities, while years of consolidation of central power like 1832 and 1851—both very turbulent times—spread their violence farther and more evenly.

Some of this alternation comes out in table 1, which chops up the entire period from 1830 to 1860 into five-year blocks. The table shows the striking contrast in overall participation between a revolutionary period like 1830-34 and a nonrevolutionary one like 1835-39. It also shows how much steeper the gradient of collective violence from rural to urban departments was in years of fundamental struggle for control of the state than in years of consolidation of state power; a comparison of 1845-49 (which includes, of course, the revolution of 1848) with 1850-54 (whose biggest violent conflict was the resistance to Louis Napoleon's 1851 coup, which eventually permitted him to move from elected president to emperor) makes that point dramatically.

Table 1 Participants in Collective Violence per 100,000 Population by Urbanity of Department, 1830-1859, Corrected to Annual Rates

Percent of population in cities of 10,000 or more	1830-34	1835-39	1840-44	1845-49	1850-54	1855-59
0.0	17	4	40	25	152	0
0.1-5.0	23	22	16	70	70	0
5.1-10.0	53	22	48	68	43	9
10.1-15.0	104	19	10	81	15	2
15.1+	731	57	64	689	86	0
Total	147	22	37	210	56	3
Total participants (Thousands)	240	41	64	371	101	5

The long trend and the short-term fluctuations both followed the same principle: nationalization of political conflict produces urbanization of collective violence. The principle has nothing to do with the disorganizing effects of urban life. It has a great deal to do with the location of groups of people mobilized to join different kinds of struggles for power. Explaining the actions of the participants in collective violence as responses to the chaos of the city discounts the reality of their struggle.

That is the general conclusion toward which all our explorations point. The absence of the uprooted, the continuity of different forms of conflict, their gradual change in response to shifts in the collective conditions of work and community life, the sheer lack of correlation between rapid urban growth or extensive in-migration and mass violence all challenge the cataclysmic theories of urbanization. And yet our evidence confirms that the distinctive social organization of cities—their hospitality to formal associations, the complexity of their communications systems, their widespread external relations, their gross patterns of segregation—strongly affects the character of the collective conflicts which occur within them. In that sense, urbanization, over the long run, transforms collective violence.

Through the chaos of living cities, what do we see? Certainly not the lawless disorder a romantic notion of urbanization has advertised. Not bucolic bliss, either. We see men held to their routines by commitments and controls, often dismayed by their routines, sometimes articulating and acting on their dismay, mostly singly, mostly in nonviolent ways, but occasionally being trained in another way of understanding and combatting the evils of their present situation, and joining with other men to strike out against the situation itself. There is a kind of order to the city's collective disorders, if not the one the forces of order would like to see prevailing.

It takes another poet, Christopher Fry, to state the theme properly: "There's no loosening, since men with men are like the knotted sea. Lift him down from the stone to the grass again, and, even so free, yet he will find the angry cities hold him." Angry cities, but not mad. Violent cities, but not pathological. Living cities, and in the last analysis not nearly so chaotic as widespread sociological ideas imply.

REFERENCES

Arendt, Hannah. *On Revolution.* London: Faber and Faber, 1963.

Chevalier, Louis. *Classes laborieuses et classes dangereuses.* Paris: Plon, 1958.

Hauser, Philip. "The Social, Economic and Technological Problems of Rapid Urbanization," in Bert Hoselitz and Wilbert Moore (Eds.), *Industrialization and Society*. The Hague: Mouton for UNESCO, 1963.

Hobsbawm, E. J. *Bandits*. New York: Delacorte, 1969.

Hobsbawm, E. J. and Rude, George. *Captain Swing: A Social History of the Great Agrarian Uprising of 1830*. New York: Pantheon, 1968.

Mumford, Lewis. *The City in History*. New York: Harcourt, Brace & World, 1961

Smelser, Neil J. *Theory of Collective Behavior*. New York: The Free Press, 1963.

Tilly, Charles. "Collective Violence in European Perspective," in Graham & Gurr, *Violence in America: Historical and Comparative Perspectives*. Washington, U.S. Government Printing Office, 1969.

Tilly, Louise. "The Food Riot as a Form of Political Protest in France." *Journal of Interdisciplinary History*, 1971.

CHAPTER
TWELVE
WHY DO PEOPLE
FIGHT WARS
?

THE ISSUE OF WAR AND PEACE

The New York Times, July 7, 1965:

> Saigon: Harsh and brutal measures have increased on both sides as the intensity
> of the war in South Vietnam has risen. . . . With a greater United States
> participation in the war, brutality has begun to occur among American troops
> as well. One American helicopter crewman returned to his base in the central
> highlands last week without a fierce young prisoner entrusted to him. He told
> friends that he had become infuriated by the youth and had pushed him out
> of the helicopter at about 1000 feet.

The New York Times, August 1, 1957:

> New York: The trouble started when forty members of the Egyptian Kings
> attacked five Jesters near the George Washington Bridge. Last Saturday, a
> Jester was stabbed by a member of the Dragons, a gang friendly to the Egyptian
> Kings. . . . The two gangs have been feuding for the last five weeks. . . .
> Detectives and patrolmen deployed throughout the area last night to prevent
> a resumption of hostilities between the Jesters and the Egyptian Kings.

St. Louis Post Dispatch, Mar. 6, 1966:

> Saigon: Bright flames spread quickly through the thatched roof. The American
> soldier threw his torch onto a part of the building not yet in flames and backed
> off from the intense heat. Sections of the roof began falling to the dirt floor
> of the deserted farmhouse and a shower of sparks splashed across the family
> altar. Buddhist religious scrolls smoldered and then burst into flames. The glass
> covering photographs of honored ancestors cracked and broke in the heat. Then
> the pictures themselves disappeared.
>
> It was a Viet Cong house, they said. As part of the war it was destroyed

together with neighboring homes. Whatever the sentiments of the villagers, the Viet Cong had used their hamlet to stage ambushes and attacks on government troops.

Spring 1972:

"When they hit you, you've got to hit them back with all you've got," President Nixon reportedly told a friend in Congress in explanation of his decision to order massive bombing of North Vietnamese ports and cities shortly after the North Vietnamese launched a new offensive.

The New York Times, May 3, 1965:

Defense officials do not like the terminology, but they readily concede that Vietnam has given the United States armed forces a "laboratory for war." Tactical theories are being tried, men trained and weapons tested. Each military service—Air Force, Army, Navy and Marines—is involved. . . . Among the gimmicks is the so-called Lazy Dog. This is a drum of steel pellets dropped from a plane that explodes at 6,000 feet. . . . A similar but more powerful weapon is the CBU for Cluster Bomblet Unit. Small fragmentation bombs are released from a drum against guerrilla units in the jungle.

General Maxwell Taylor, testimony, Department of Defense Appropriations for 1964: Hearings, 88th Congress, first session, Part I, pp. 483-4.

. . . Here we have a going laboratory where we see subversive insurgency, the Ho Chi Minh doctrine, being applied in all its forms. This has been a challenge not just for the armed services, but for several of the agencies of government, as many of them are involved in one way or another in South Vietnam, On the military side, however, we have recognized the importance of the area as a laboratory. We have had teams out there looking at the equipment requirements of this kind of guerrilla warfare. We have rotated senior officers through there, spending several weeks just to talk to people and get the feel of the operation, so even though not regularly assigned to Vietnam, they are carrying their experience back to their own organizations.

The Reader's Digest, August, 1968:

The hot line is a by-product of the Cuban missile confrontation. After that brush with nuclear disaster, President John F. Kennedy and Russian Premier Nikita Khrushchev had agreed that ordinary channels of communication were too cumbersome to deal with crises in an age of nuclear ICBMs. A direct wire was set up, with teleprinters in Moscow and in the National Military Command Center at the Pentagon. The Russians transmit in Russian, the Americans in English. At the Pentagon, a translator stands ready to relay any Kremlin message to the White House Situation Room. . . .

For three years and nine months, the line had remained blessedly quiet, carrying only test messages and New Year's Day greetings. Then, Monday morning, June 5, [1967] came the electrifying news that Moscow had activated it seriously for the first time. But the message was a reassuring one: The Soviet

Union would keep hands off the Middle East War, provided the United States
did the same. In a cautiously worded reply, Johnson agreed.

U.S. News and World Report, Sept. 23, 1968:

On Tuesday night, August 20, at 11:00 p.m. Central European time, the forces
of the Soviet Union and its allies went into Czechoslovakia. That was 6:00 p.m.,
Washington time. . . .
　　Promptly at 8:00 p.m. [Washington time], Ambassador Dobrynin's new
cadillac arrived at the White House . . . Mr. Johnson . . . chatted affably with
Mr. Dobrynin as a servant brought the Russian a scotch and soda, the President
a soft drink. At about 8:30 p.m., the Ambassador read the message from
Moscow to Mr. Johnson. This message said Soviet and satellite forces had
entered Czechoslovakia on "invitation" of Czechoslovak leaders, that this was
an internal matter between Communist governments and no business of the
U.S. . . . .
　　Secretary of State Dean Rusk, at New Haven, Conn. on Sept. 12. . . noted
that President Johnson and Eisenhower both saw the U.S. able to do little to
help Eastern Europe "without automatically engaging in general war with the
Soviet Union."

President Eisenhower's Farewell Address:

In the councils of government, we must guard against the acquisition of
unwarranted influence, whether sought or unsought, by the military-industrial
complex. The potential for the disastrous rise of misplaced power exists and
will persist. . . . Only an alert and knowledgeable citizenry can compel the
proper meshing of the huge industrial and military machinery of defense with
our peaceful methods and goals, so that security and liberty may prosper
together.

Newsweek, August 2, 1965:

New orders have been crackling out of the Pentagon, with requests sometimes
going out by telephone and telegram—rather than mail—to speed up the process.
American Machine and Foundry, for example, just got a $17 million order for
Mark 82 bomb assemblies. Some of the work is still classified, such as
Honeywell's $3.3 million order for BLU-3 cluster bombs. These are the high-
explosive anti-personnel bomblets being dropped on North Vietnam.

Honeywell advertisement in *Ordnance,* September-October, 1969:

Honeywell salutes the American Ordnance Association on a half century of
dedication to the nation's security. And supports the AOA in its efforts to
maintain industrial preparedness for defense. . . .
　　Our common goal with AOA—to maintain a constant state of readiness
through the best equipment possible.
　　We stand ready to build weapons that work, to build them fast, and to
build them in quantity. And always with one goal uppermost in mind: a more
effective military man now—and in the future.

Some Figures for Fiscal 1968:

> Total military expenditures for the United States and the Soviet Union combined $136,000,000,000
>
> Per capita *military expenditures,* U.S.A. and U.S.S.R. combined: $310 per person
>
> Per capita *gross national product,* Brazil: $310 per person

The chances are overwhelming that when these words are read there will be a war in progress somewhere in the world. Perhaps the United States will be a participant, perhaps not. In any event, it will be an interested party and potential participant in a wider war.

Why all these wars? Are they part of man's fighting nature? Are they part of the same phenomenon that produces assassinations and gang wars? Are they a result of the organization of the world into nation-states? Are they the product of calculation, accident, or impulse? Must they be understood in terms of arms races and war profiteers? What is it that brings people to engage in such costly conflicts again and again even though they know that they or those dear to them may kill or be killed?

THE MAJOR VIEWS

Personal Aggression

War must be understood, in this view, as one species of a larger genus—*fighting.* It is a special kind of fighting, of course. It takes place between groups rather than merely individuals; it is more organized, less spontaneous, and more deadly to bystanders than a fight between two small boys or large apes. Nevertheless, it is a member of the same genus and we can understand the species best if we start with the general characteristics that it shares.

This paradigm sometimes appears in rather simple-minded and unfruitful versions. For example, it is implicit in the assertion that there will always be war because man is innately aggressive. The evidence offered for such explanations is typically circular. One points to the frequency of wars and other fighting as evidence of the innate aggression which it is then asserted explains such behaviors. The selection included here, by Durbin and Bowlby, employs a much more sophisticated and defensible version. They do not argue either that fighting is a simple, direct expression of aggressive instincts in man or that war is inevitable.

They start by asking about the conditions that lead to fighting among both men and animals—for example, scarce possessions, intrusion of strangers, and frustration. They move from such general causes to those that are more specific to man, those that involve unconscious motives and defense mechanisms. What happens, they argue, is that personal aggressiveness becomes effectively disguised and rationalized. "Group life," write Durbin and Bowlby, "gives sanction to personal aggressiveness."

War, then, is rationalized personal aggression. Underneath the rhetoric about protecting "freedom" or even "national interest" lie more primitive motives. "When they hit you, you've got to hit them back." "We can't just cut and run."

"All's fair in war." "He wouldn't cooperate, so I pushed him out of the helicopter." "If we let them get away with this, we'll look like a pitiful, helpless giant."

Durbin and Bowlby do not argue that fighting is more "natural" than peaceful cooperation. Both are natural responses under the appropriate conditions. However, if war is simply a special form of fighting, we must recognize that just as the causes of fighting are ubiquitous, so are the causes of war. One can't eliminate provocations or prevent the operation of primitive, largely unconscious motives in propelling nations toward war. "There is no use in trying to get rid of men's aggressive inclinations," Freud wrote to Einstein in his famous open letter "Why War?" (1932).

But one can promote counter-forces—forces for peaceful cooperation. This task is made extremely difficult by the fact that both leaders and ordinary citizens share the primitive emotions that lead to war. And the leaders, those who ultimately make the fateful decisions, are especially skilled in using rhetoric that justifies fighting even as it disguises from themselves and others the underlying impulses of personal aggression.

Politics

Rationalization in the first view becomes reason in this one. "War is only a continuation of State policy by other means," wrote General Carl von Clausewitz, the intellectual father of this paradigm (p. xxiii). "The War of a community... always starts from a political condition, and is called forth by a political motive. It is, therefore, a political act.... [But] war is not merely a political act, but also a real political instrument, a continuation of political commerce, a carrying out of the same by other means" (p. 22-23).

Why do states resort to this instrument since it is always costly for at least one of the participants, and frequently for all of them? The answer lies in two parts: (1) the nature of the nation-state, and (2) the nature of the international system. The selection by Werner Levi, included here, reflects both parts.

The underlying conception of the state is provided by what its advocates rather arrogantly call the "realist theory of international politics." Morgenthau (1967) writes, "The main signpost that helps political realism to find its way through the landscape of international politics is the concept of interest defined in terms of power. ... We assume that statesmen think and act in terms of interest defined as power, and the evidence of history bears that assumption out" (p. 5). National power, then, is the objective of the nation-state. There is no assertion that this should be so but acceptance of the immutable "fact" that it is.

Personal motives and ideology are, in this view, distractions which blur our vision of the underlying reality. Individuals may act from a wide variety of personal motives but, in their role as foreign policy decision-makers, they are bound by organizational goals. And the goal of their particular organization, the State, is to protect or expand its power. Ideology is a means to this end; it can help one to win friends and influence people.

War is another means to national power. As Quincy Wright (1964) puts it in describing this paradigm, war is "the utilization by a group of violent means to remove political obstructions in the path of group policy. War is simply policy when speed is deemed necessary and political obstructions will not yield to persuasion" (p. 115). Note the cool, instrumental tone here—war is not hitting back or lashing out in some primitive fashion. It has little or nothing to do with such phenomena as the Egyptian Kings and the Jesters, with mass killers or assassins, or even with pushing prisoners out of helicopters. Personal aggression is a by-product and, when it is uncontrolled, an undesirable by-product. The prototype of the modern warrior is not the infantryman thrusting his bayonet and yelling "kill," but the bored B-52 pilot, living in a suburban home in Thailand, going on his daily bombing run to Vietnam to drop his "ordnance" on pre-selected targets that he can't see, using an automated "weapons delivery system."

But why do statesmen talk about the "aggression" of the enemy and person- alize the conflict? The answer is that the citizenry doesn't respond to such phrases as "protect the national interest" in the same way that it does to "Remember the Alamo." But one shouldn't confuse public relations with cause. Reasons for going to war are one thing; selling a war to the population is quite another.

There is no passion, hate, or aggression implicit in calling Vietnam a "laboratory for war," or in General Maxwell Taylor's testimony quoted in the introduction. Vietnam presented a challenge to the nation, the challenge of counter-insurgency. It was a new sort of challenge for the United States and presented unsolved problems. But we responded and learned, Taylor implies. Vietnam was a laboratory for problem solving.

The heads of major powers, in this paradigm, speak a common language in spite of ideological or other differences. They can sit down to a friendly drink before discussing a potential "issue" between them such as the Soviet invasion of Czechoslovakia. The United States can understand even though it doesn't approve of Soviet action. And it can understand that it is foolish to challenge an adversary on an issue that is peripheral to oneself but vital to the other side. Such a challenge means "automatically engaging in general war with the Soviet Union" and one does not engage in such wars to defend peripheral interests.

Realistic adversaries want to avoid miscalculations that can lead to an accidental war that nobody wants. Devices such as the "hot-line" between Washington and Moscow are welcomed by both. But this desire for communication should not be misinterpreted. It is not *misunderstanding* that is of concern, but *miscalculation*. The stakes between adversaries are real, not imaginary. Morgenthau writes (p. 504):

> The conception that international conflicts can be eliminated through inter- national understanding rests on the implicit assumption that the issues of international conflicts, born as they are of misunderstandings, are but imaginary and that actually no issue worth fighting about stands between nation and nation. Nothing could be farther from the truth. All the great wars that decided the course of history and changed the political face of the earth were fought for real stakes, not for imaginary ones. The issue in those great convulsions was invariably: Who shall rule and who shall be ruled?

The actual occurrence of war presents an apparent problem for this view. If the leaders of conflicting states are assessing their national interests accurately, there should never be a war. The potential loser would recognize that its national interest would not be furthered in such an arena and would avoid a military confrontation. However, such calculations are extremely difficult to make. "Wars arise unpredictably because governments know something but not everything," Quincy Wright (1954) writes. "Their image of other governments, of the world situation, and even of themselves, upon which their policies, decisions, and actions are based, is always in some measure distorted" (p. 115). Is the adversary's provocative troop movement a real threat, a mere bluff, or something in between? Is the militant speech mere bluster for domestic consumption or an indication that one has touched a sensitive nerve?

Miscalculation is only part of the answer. The international system is a peculiarly unstable conflict system. When the Egyptian Dragon-Jester conflict threatens to get out of hand, New York city policemen can deploy through their territory to keep the peace. If Jones and Smith cannot resolve their border dispute on the property line between their adjacent home sites, there is a legal system to adjudicate such matters.

Unlike most other conflict systems, the international system provides no superordinate authority to limit the means of conflict used. Mechanisms for negotiation are sparse and are frequently avoided when the State sees its vital interests at stake. The United States chose to use the United Nations during the Cuban Missile confrontation only *after* it had announced a partial-blockade of Soviet ships. The Soviet Union chose *not* to use the hot-line to communicate with Washington during its invasion of Czechoslovakia because to do so would have undermined its claim that the matter was an internal one, not an international dispute of interest to the United States.

A better communication link or better forum for negotiating conflicts is useful but limited, in this view. Its basic value is in preventing an unintended clash over relatively peripheral interests of the parties because of miscalculations about the intent of the other side. When vital interests are involved, a hot line may be no more than a more efficient vehicle for waging conflict rather than resolving it.

The nature of the State is, in this view, a given. States seek power; accept this fact, we are advised, instead of futilely inveighing against it. The path to peace is through increasing the stability of the international system. It is useful to think of this stability as a product of two factors—disagreements or conflicts between states and integrative ties. The first of these cannot be effectively solved. Some conflicts, of course, can be compromised. But basically one should work not on resolving conflicts but on increasing the capacity of the system to tolerate a given degree of conflict— that is, on integrative ties.

These integrative ties have two components—mechanisms for handling conflicts and mechanisms for achieving common goals. The hot line is an example of the former. Such devices help in limited ways; they are necessary but not sufficient. Once there are enough, it will help little to proliferate more. Mechanisms for achieving common goals are another matter. The key element here is to create interdependencies both at the governmental and non-governmental levels. By increasing interdependency, one increases the costs of war; if such ties can be made overwhelming, then actions which risk war will seem less and less attractive as means of pursuing national interest. Thus, France and Germany, who fought three wars with each other in the last century, are now linked economically through the European Economic Community in a manner that makes a fourth war between them highly improbable. But in the inter-

national system as a whole, such integration remains weak and the danger of war is
ever present.

Militarism

Suppose we grant that nations pursue what they conceive to be their "national interest."
How does it come about that this national interest gets defined in terms of military
power? How is it that foreign policy decision-makers can believe that this interest is
served by sending half-a-million sullen and resentful soldiers to participate in a civil
war thousands of miles away while the nation's cities explode in riots, its students
rebel in rage and frustration, and its intellectuals come to regard their own government as the most destructive and dangerous power in the world. Surely a reasonable
man might conclude that such a definition of "national interest" is, at the very least,
capricious.

National interest, in this view, is a highly ambiguous standard. It is subject to
variable interpretations and the process by which one or another definition comes to
be accepted is critical. One can't take this process for granted and assume that the
"national interest" is a stable feature of the world which "realistic" statesmen will
perceive in the same way. If there is consensus, it is an achieved consensus—the outgrowth of a complicated process within a country. To understand why people fight
wars, we must understand the internal forces in countries that lead statesmen to define
"national interest" in the particular way they do.

It is more than 30 years since Harold Lasswell (1941) asked whether we were
moving toward "a world of 'garrison states'—a world in which the specialists on
violence are the most powerful group in society. From this point of view, the trend of
our time is away from the dominance of the specialist on bargaining, who is the
businessman, and toward the supremacy of the soldier" (p. 455). Pilisuk and Hayden,
in the selection included here, write in this tradition, but rather than competition
between military and business elites for supremacy, they see a convenient and mutually
beneficial coalition.

Their argument is stated in terms of the United States, but the underlying logic
can be extended to other industrial states as well, including the Soviet Union. One
starts with the observation that certain groups in a modern, industrial state have a
vested interest in a high level of tension between their State and others. Military elites
find their position enhanced and their budgets increased when the nation regards itself
as under military threat from outside. The managers of defense industries find that
their organizations thrive and their personal position is enhanced under such conditions.
Political elites find that by forming alliances with such powerful and important groups,
their own political careers can be forwarded. And a host of subsidiary elites find that
there are spoils for them as well in cooperation with this powerful coalition. "I'm
doing basic research," claims the university scientist. "The only reason I go to the
Defense Department for funds is that that's where the money is."

The interest described above is not in war, but in *cold war*. War is disruptive and
costly, but a high state of international tension is not. "We arm to parley," says the
cold warrior without hypocrisy. "Peace is our profession," says the air force. There is

no reason to presume insincerity or conspiracy, no reason to think they are consciously self-serving. The argument is that their interests make them receptive to evidence of external threat and lead them to interpret reality in selective ways. Ideology provides, in this view, a justification and rationalization for self-interest rather than for unconscious personal aggression.

Military and industrial elites undoubtedly believe they live in a world where their nation's interest is threatened by powerful adversaries. It is a convenient belief, coinciding as it does, with self-interest, and one can search history for examples that support it. One must prepare in terms of an adversary's capabilities, the generals tell us, rather than its intentions. Intentions are ephemeral and changeable but capabilities are real and solid. "The prudent man hopes for the best but prepares for the worst," we are cautioned and, sure enough, the worst seems to come often enough in this self-fulfilling prophecy.

Challenge such ideology and it will be vigorously defended for it is a bulwark that, if breached, leaves vulnerable the underlying interest that it protects. If the Cold War has a large component of mythology, if "world communism" doesn't threaten the United States, then why spend so many billions for defense? And if less money is spent, what of those companies, like Honeywell, that "stand ready to build weapons that work, to build them fast, and to build them in quantity?" Ordnance—military weapons—means security, Honeywell agrees. And why should it question an equation that keeps new orders "crackling out of the Pentagon" and the Honeywell telephone ringing at the other end.

Although we know less about the process, presumably there are counterparts—generals, managers of arms industries, politicians—in the Soviet Union who find similar comfort in an atmosphere of external threat. They are as sincere as their American or Chinese counterparts in their concern for their country's national interest: Patriots all in a dance of death. The net result of this combination of ideology and interest is an arms race that leads the world's two largest military powers to spend an amount per citizen on military expenditures equal to the share of the *total national income* per citizen of Brazil.

A further result is a chronic state of high tension and great instability in which a spark may set off a war that is in nobody's interest. An atmosphere of chronic crisis is conducive to war and yet it is this very atmosphere that is encouraged by military interests. These are the processes one must understand, in this view, to answer the question "why war?"

CONTRASTING THE VIEWS OF WAR AND PEACE

These ways of looking at why people fight wars can be contrasted by examining their treatment of three issues:

1. What part of a country is the major instigator or driving force toward war?
2. What aspect of the process is most important to this major instigator.
3. Are the manifest issues about which nations fight reasons or rationalizations?

Major Instigator

Different elements in society can be seen as the major driving force that propels a nation toward war. For the personal aggression view, this force comes from the population itself. However much ideologies may disguise the fact, it is the people of a nation, with their reservoir of personal aggression, that provides the animus for the blood-letting.

For the politics paradigm, the driving force is the leadership of a country—the head of state and his advisors and fellow decision-makers in the foreign policy arena. Wars are created by politicians for reasons of State. They may miscalculate or blunder, of course, and the nature of the international conflict system makes it easy for quarrels to get out of hand. But, basically, statesmen are not pushed to war by forces from below or by military-industrial elites. We fight wars because statesmen have chosen to fight them or, at least, to go to the brink where they occasionally fall in, taking us along with them.

In the militarism view, the driving force comes not from accountable political elites but from military elites and their allies in the armaments industry and elsewhere. They are a major instigator of a high level of international tension, an unstable situation that sooner or later tilts into a war. They foster an atmosphere that stimulates personal aggression and xenophobia on the part of the population and brinkmanship on the part of foreign policy decision-makers.

Important Aspect

Viewed over time, war is a process with three aspects. First, one must prepare to fight, which means training soldiers, manufacturing weapons, building military alliances, and the like. Second, if such preparation fails to prevent war, one must fight, which means waging battles, capturing territory, bombarding the enemy, and the like. Finally, there is the outcome of the war, which means the terms of the peace treaty or settlement, the territory kept or lost, the reparations, changes in the regime of the belligerents, and the like.

Each view of the process emphasizes a different one of these aspects. For the personal aggression view, the fighting is the heart of the process. "Nailing the coonskin to the wall" is what it is about, not the preparation or the spoils. For the politics view, the outcome is the heart of the process. Nations go to war because they envision a peace settlement that is better than what they can get without war. This doesn't necessarily mean "spoils" in the crude sense of more territory or material wealth but can simply mean greater security or the removal of some grievance or threat to national power. Finally, preparation is the heart of the process in the militarism paradigm. Preparation, of course, is intended to prevent wars but, somehow, nations that are prepared to fight find reasons to do so. The arms race is the heart of the process, not the fighting that comes when the tinder-box is incidentally ignited or the peace treaty that temporarily extinguishes the fire. "Always with one goal uppermost in mind," as Honeywell puts it, "A more effective military man now—and in the future."

Reasons or Rationalizations

Official reasons are not taken at face value by any view. However, in one view they are regarded as simplifications and translations of the underlying reasons of State. In others, they are regarded as so many red herrings misleading leaders and led alike.

In the politics paradigm, the men who make war know what their objectives are and, aside from considerations of public relations, can tell them to you quite clearly. The reasons are conscious ones, centering around the maintenance or enhancement of the power of the State. For the other two views, statesmen don't really understand why why they are fighting. In the personal aggression paradigm, they are unable to see through the rationalizations of unconscious motive. They think they are protecting national interest when, in fact, they are irritated with the defiance of an adversary who will not bend to their will. In the militarism view, they are unable to see through the rationalizations that blend the interest of the state with the private interests of some of its most powerful citizens.

These are the central issues we see running through the contrasting views of war and peace. They are summarized in Chart 12.

Chart 12 Underlying Issues on Why Do People Fight Wars

	Personal Aggression, *e.g.* Durbin & Bowlby	Politics, *e.g.* Levi	Militarism, *e.g.* Pilisuk & Hayden
What is the major instigator towards war?	The people	Foreign policy decision-makers	The military and managers of defense industries
What is the heart of the process?	The fighting	The outcome, *i.e.,* the spoils	The preparation, *i.e.,* the arms race
Are the manifest issues reasons or rationalizations?	Rationalizations (for personal aggression)	Reasons	Rationalizations (for self interest)

REFERENCES

von Clausewitz, Carl. *On War.* New York: Barnes and Noble, 1968 (Written in 1832).

Freud, Sigmund. "Why War?" from Sigmund Freud, *Collected Papers,* 5, New York: Basic Books, 1959 (Written in 1932).

Lasswell, Harold. "The Garrison State," *The American Journal of Sociology,* 46 (1941), pp. 455-468.

Morgenthau, Hans. J. *Politics Among Nations.* New York: Alfred A. Knopf, 4th edition, 1967.

Wright, Quincy. *A Study of War.* Chicago: University of Chicago Press, 1964 (Originally published: 1942).

PERSONAL AGGRESSIVENESS AND WAR

E.F.M. DURBIN AND JOHN BOWLBY

The purpose of this article is to examine the bearing of some recent biological and psychological work upon the theories of the cause of war.

The authors hold that war—or organized fighting between large groups of adult human beings—must be regarded as one species of a larger genus, the genus of *fighting*. Fighting is plainly a common, indeed a universal, form of human behavior. It extends beyond the borders of humanity into the types of mammals most closely related in the evolutionary classification to the common ancestors of man and other apes. Wars between groups within the nation and between nations are obvious and important examples of this type of behavior. Since this is so, it must of necessity follow that the simplest and most general causes of war are only to be found in the causes of fighting, just as the simplest and most general causes of falling downstairs are to be found in the causes of falling down.

Such a simple thesis could hardly be expected to contain any important conclusion. Yet if the causes of war are to be found in their simplest form only in phenomena more widely dispersed in space and time than comparatively recent forms of political and economic organization, like the nation-state and the capitalist system, it must surely follow that theories tracing the cause of war either to capitalism or nationalism can only at the best contain part of the truth. Nevertheless, it is theories of this kind that are fashionable in the current discussions of the cause of war.

We shall revert at length to the bearing of our own views upon these theories. In the meantime, it is our primary task to examine some of the evidence recently collected on the extent and causes of fighting. The procedure that we propose to follow is to summarize and analyze the descriptive work that has been done upon fighting among apes, children, and civilized adults. . . and to use the conclusions to be derived from that work in the argument of this article. The empirical evidence that is available is far from complete, but we think that it is more than sufficient to sustain a number of most important conclusions about the effective causes of war.

Fighting, as we have already pointed out, is a form of behavior widely distributed through history and nature. It occurs in the form of group conflict throughout recorded time. It takes place spasmodically between individuals in civilized countries. It occurs among primitives, among

---

From "Personal Aggressiveness and War" by E. F. M. Durbin and John Bowlby in *War and Democracy* edited by Evan Durbin *et al.* (London: Routledge & Kegan Paul, 1938). Reprinted by permission.

children, and among apes. Whether one looks back through time or down-wards to simpler forms of social organization, it is a common practice for individuals to seek to change their environment by force and for other individuals to meet force with force.

But fighting, or the appeal to force, while universal in distribution, is not continuous in time. The most warlike groups and the most aggres-sive individuals spend considerable periods in peaceful toleration of, and positive cooperation with, other animals or persons. Most organized communities have enjoyed longer periods of peace than of war. The greater part of human activity—of man-hours—is spent, not in war, but in peaceful cooperation. The scientific problem is, therefore, twofold—why is there peaceful cooperation, and why does peaceful cooperation sometimes break down into war? The practical problem—at least, for lovers of peace—is how peaceful cooperation is to be preserved against the universal tendency exhibited in history for it to degenerate into war. . . .

The Simpler Causes of Fighting

Evidence taken from the observation of the behavior of apes and children suggests that there are three clearly separable groups of simple causes for the outbreak of fighting and the exhibition of aggressiveness by individuals (Isaacs, 1933).

One of the most common causes of fighting among both children and apes was over the *possession* of external objects. The disputed ownership of any desired object—food, clothes, toys, females, and the affection of others—was sufficient ground for an appeal to force. On Monkey Hill disputes over females were responsible for the death of thirty out of thirty-three females. Two points are of particular interest to notice about these fights for possession.

In the first place they are often carried to such an extreme that they end in the complete destruction of the objects of common desire. Toys are torn to pieces. Females are literally torn limb from limb. So overriding is the aggression once it has begun that it not only overflows all reasonable boundaries of selfishness but utterly destroys the object for which the struggle began and even the self for whose advantage the struggle was undertaken.

In the second place it is observable, at least in children, that the object for whose possession aggression is started may sometimes be desired by one person only or merely because it is desired by someone else. There were many cases observed by Dr. Isaacs where toys and other objects which had been discarded as useless were violently defended by their owners when they became the object of some other child's desire. The grounds of possessiveness may, therefore, be irrational in the sense that they are derived from inconsistent judgments of value. Whether sensible or irrational, contests over possession are commonly the occasion for the most ruthless use of force among children and apes.

One of the commonest kinds of object arousing possessive desire is the notice, good will, affection, and service of other members of the group. Among children one of the commonest causes of quarreling was "jealousy" —the desire for the exclusive possession of the interest and affection of someone else, particularly the adults in charge of the children. This form of behavior is sometimes classified as a separate cause of conflict under the name of "rivalry" or "jealousy." But, in point of fact, it seems to us that it is only one variety of possessiveness. The object of desire is not a material object—that is the only difference. The object is the interest and affection of other persons. What is wanted, however, is the exclusive right to that interest and affection—a property in emotions, instead of things. As subjective emotions and as causes of conflict, jealousy and rivalry are fundamentally similar to the desire for the uninterrupted possession of toys or food. Indeed, very often the persons, property of which is desired, are the sources of toys and food.

Possessiveness is, then, in all its forms a common cause of fighting. If we are to look behind the mere facts of behavior for an explanation of this phenomenon, a teleological cause is not far to seek. The exclusive right to objects of desire is a clear and simple advantage to the possessor of it. It carries with it the certainty and continuity of satisfaction. Where there is only one claimant to a good, frustration and the possibility of loss is reduced to a minimum. It is, therefore, obvious that, if the ends of the self are the only recognized ends, the whole powers of the agent, including the fullest use of his available force, will be used to establish and defend exclusive rights to possession.

Another cause of aggression closely allied to possessiveness is the tendency for children and apes greatly to resent the *intrusion of a stranger* into their group. A new child in the class may be laughed at, isolated, and disliked and even set upon and pinched and bullied. A new monkey may be poked and bitten to death. It is interesting to note that it is only strangeness within a similarity of species that is resented. Monkeys do not mind being joined by a goat or a rat. Children do not object when animals are introduced to the group. Indeed, such novelties are often welcomed. But when monkeys meet a new monkey or children a strange child, aggression often occurs. This suggests strongly that the reason for the aggression is fundamentally possessiveness. The competition of the new-comers is feared. The present members of the group feel that there will be more rivals for the food or the attention of the adults.

Finally, another common source of fighting among children is a failure or *frustration* in their own activity. A child will be prevented either by natural causes such as bad weather or illness or by the opposition of some adult from doing something he wishes to do at a given moment—sail his boat or ride the bicycle. The child may also frustrate itself by failing, through lack of skill or strength, to complete successfully some desired activity. Such a child will then in the ordinary sense become "naughty." He will be in a bad or surly temper. And, what is of interest from our point of view, the child will indulge in aggression—attacking and fighting other children or adults. Sometimes the object of aggression will simply be the cause of frustration, a straightforward reaction. The child will kick or hit the nurse who forbids the sailing of his boat. But sometimes—indeed, frequently—the person or thing that suffers the aggression is quite irrelevant and innocent of offense. The angry child will stamp the ground or box the ears of another child when neither the ground nor the child attacked is even remotely connected with the irritation or frustration.

Of course, this kind of behavior is so common that everyone feels it to be obvious and to constitute no serious scientific problem. That a small boy should pull his sister's hair because it is raining does not appear to the ordinary unreflecting person to be an occasion for solemn scientific inquiry. He is, as we should all say, "in a bad temper." Yet it is not, in fact, really obvious either why revenge should be taken on entirely innocent objects, since no good to the aggressor can come of it, or why children being miserable should seek to make others miserable also. It is just a fact of human behavior that cannot really be deduced from any general principle of reason. But it is, as we shall see, of very great import-ance for our purpose. It shows how it is possible, at the simplest and most primitive level, for aggression and fighting to spring from an entirely irrelevant and partially hidden cause. Fighting to possess a desired object is straightforward and rational, however disastrous its consequences, compared with fighting that occurs because, in a different and unrelated activity, some frustration has barred the road to pleasure. The importance of this possibility for an understanding of group conflict must already be obvious.

These are the three simplest separate categories of cause we are able to observe in the evidence. One further point, however, remains to be made about the character of the fighting that occurs among apes. It is a marked characteristic of this fighting that, once it has broken out anywhere, it spreads with great rapidity throughout the group and draws into conflict individuals who had no part in the first quarrel and appear to have no immediate interest whatever in the outcome of the original dispute. Fighting is infectious in the highest degree. Why? It is not easy to find an answer. Whether it is that the apes who are not immediately involved feel that some advantage for themselves can be snatched from the confusion following upon the rupture of social equilibrium or whether real advantages are involved that escape the observation of the onlooker is not at present determined. Or it may be that the infectiousness of fighting is irrational in the same way that the irrelevant expression of aggression due to frustration is irrational. Whatever the explanation, the fact remains that fighting spreads without apparent cause or justification—that "every dog joins a fight," in other and older words. This excitability and the attraction which fighting may possess for its own sake are likely to be a source of great instability in any society. It is one of the most dangerous parts of our animal inheritance.

So much for the simpler forms of aggression. It is now time to consider the light thrown by anthropological and psychoanalytic evidence upon the behavior of adult human beings.

The Further Causes of Aggressive Behavior

So far the material from which we have sought illumination has been derived from the simple behavior of children and apes. We must now consider more complicated behavior. There are, as we have already pointed out, at least two relevant attitudes—anthropology and the case histories recorded by psychoanalysts. The present authors have most unfortunately not been able through lack of time and assitance, to survey the vast mass of anthropological material in detail, but even such a slight study as they have been able to make suffices to show the very great importance of other causes of fighting among primitive peoples.

Before we begin this task it is necessary to make one preliminary and simple observation about the nature of adult aggression in general. It is of first importance to realize that, as far as aggressiveness and fighting are concerned, there is no noticeable improvement in the *behavior* of adults compared with that of the most savage animals and children. If anything, it is more ruthless. The recent history of Europe establishes this conclusion with horrible insistence. There is no form of behavior too ruthless, too brutal, too cruel for adult men and women to use against each other. Torture is becoming normal again; the knuckle-duster and the whip, other more refined instruments of flagellation, and the armory of mental pain are the commonplace instruments of prisons and concentration camps from Japan to Spain. Men and women have been shot down without trial, soaked in petrol and burned to death, beaten to unrecognizable masses of flesh and bone, hanged by the hair and hands until they die, starved and tortured with fear and hope during the "reigns of terror" that have accompanied and succeeded the civil wars in Russia, Italy, Poland, Austria, Germany, and Spain. Cruelty knows no boundary of party or creed. It wears every kind of shirt. And over all of us there hangs, perpetual and menacing, the fear of war. No group of animals could be more aggressive or more ruthless in their aggression than the adult members of the human race.

Are there then no differences between the aggression of more primitive beings and that of adult men? We suggest that there are only two differences. In the first place the aggression of adults is normally a group activity. Murder and assault are restricted to a small criminal minority. Adults kill and torture each other only when organized into political parties or economic classes or religious denominations or nation-states. A moral distinction is always made between the individual killing for himself and the same individual killing for some real or supposed group interest. In the second place, the adult powers of imagination and reason are brought to the service of the aggressive intention. Apes and children, when they fight, simply fight. Men and women first construct towering systems of theology and religion, complex analyses of racial character and class structure, or moralities of group life and virility before they kill one another. Thus they fight for Protestantism or Mohammedanism, for the emancipation of the world proletariat or for the salvation of the Nordic culture, for nation or for king. Men will die like flies for theories and exterminate each other with every instrument of destruction for abstractions.

The differences of *behavior* are therefore not substantial. The form is the same, the results are the same. Group fighting is even more destructive than individual fighting. A machine gun or a bomb is no less lethal because its use can be shown to be a necessity of the class war or noble because it brings the light of Italian civilization to the Abyssinian peoples. Now it might be argued that there is no continuity of character between the wars of civilized people and fighting of the simpler orders. We cannot, however, see any reason for supposing so. Indeed, the only question of interest appears to us to lie in the matter of causation. Are the causes exactly the same, or are they changed in any important way by the greater powers and complexity of the adult human mind?

We are therefore brought back to the question: What are the causes of aggressiveness in adult human beings? We would maintain that anthropology and psychoanalysis suggest a number of ways in which the powers of the human mind change and add to the causes of aggression. There appear to be at least three different mechanisms discernible in the material of these two sciences.

Animism

The first and most obvious of these is the cause of war revealed so very plainly by the study of primitive intergroup conflict. It consists in the universal tendency to attribute all events in the world to the deliberate activity of human or parahuman *will*. All happenings, whether natural and inevitable, or human and voluntary, are attributed to the will of some being either human or anthropomorphically divine. If a thunderstorm occurs or a hurricane visits a village or a man is killed by a tiger, the evil is attributed either to the magic of a neighboring tribe or the ill will of demons and gods. In the same way, good fortune, however natural, is attributed to the deliberate intention of some other being. This universal tendency in the human mind is termed "animism."

It is certain that this imaginative tendency on the part of human beings leads to war. It is obvious why it should. If evil is attributed to the direct malice of neighboring and opposing groups, the only possible protection against further evil lies in the destruction of the source of ill will. It is, however, of great importance whether the supposed enemy is human or supernatural. If it is spiritual, the natural reply will be placatory sacrifices or the harmless ritual of beating or burning or making war upon the evil spirit. . . . But if the supposed author of evil is not supernatural but human, the results are neither harmless nor amusing. If the typhoon is attributed to the magic of neighboring peoples or of dissident minorities within the tribe, then the destruction of the enemy, root and branch, is the only safe course. Hence after a thunderstorm or an accident the restless fears and hatred of the tribe will find expression in a primitive war against neighboring tribes or the stamping out of some hapless group of victims within it. Enemies without and traitors within must be exterminated.

We think it difficult to exaggerate the frequency and importance of this cause of fighting in human societies of all degrees of civilization. It is a universal tendency among the simpler people of all nations to attribute evil to some person or group of persons. It is present everywhere in party politics. Every evil is loaded upon political opponents. Socialists attribute all disasters, whether economic or political, to capitalists or the capitalist class. Conservatives think it obvious that the last uncontrollable and world-wide depression in trade was due to the bad government of the Socialists in this country. Other movements find different and more peculiar scapegoats in the bankers or the Jews or the Russians. In each case what is noticeable and dangerous is that a vast power and a deep malignity is attributed to the inimical group. The supposed malignity is often purely illusory. The attributed power transcends all reality. When the open conflict of party politics is suppressed by an authoritarian regime, the tendency is exaggerated rather than reduced. Some unfortunate minority within the group—the Jews or the kulaks—become the source of all evil, the scapegoat of all disaster. Or an overwhelming hatred is conceived for another nation. Out of these real terrors and derivative hatreds merciless persecutions and international wars are likely to spring. . . .

We have now completed our survey of the causes of aggression in human beings. We have suggested that there is no substantial difference in behavior, that adults are just as cruel—or more so—just as agressive, just as destructive, as any group of animals or monkeys. The only difference in our view is one of psychological and intellectual mechanism. The causes of simple aggression—possessiveness, strangeness, frustration—are common to adults and simpler creatures. But a repressive discipline drives the simple aggression underground—to speak in metaphors—and it appears in disguised forms. These transformations are chiefly those of displacement and projection. These mechanisms have as their immediate motive the reduction of anxiety and the resolution of the conflicts of ambivalence and guilt. They result in the typical form of adult aggressiveness—aggressive personal relations of all kinds—but above all in group aggression: party conflict, civil war, wars of religion, and international war. The group life gives sanction to personal aggressiveness. The mobilization of transformed aggression gives destructive power to groups. Aggression takes on its social form. And to justify it—to explain the group aggression to the outside world and to the group itself in terms that make it morally acceptable to the members of the group—great structures of intellectual reasoning—theories of history and religion and race—are built up. The impulses are rationalized. The hatred is justified. And it is typical of the complexity of human affairs that something in these theories is always true. But most is false, most of it a mere justification of hatred, a sickening and hypocritical defense of cruelty. This is particularly true of the political persecutions of dictatorships. We must now try to apply the conclusions of this evidence to the theory of the causes of war.

We hold that the evidence summarized above suggest a certain theory of the causes of war. In the absence of government—the organization of force to preserve the peace—we hold that a group of monkeys or children or men can only achieve, at the best, an unstable social equilibrium. It may well be that an appreciation of the advantages of cooperation and an agreement to continue it will preserve the peace for some time. But underneath there is a powerful and "natural" tendency to resort to force in order to secure the possession of desired objects or to overcome a sense of frustration or to resist the encroachment of strangers or to attack a scapegoat. Fighting and peaceful cooperation are equally "natural" forms of behavior equally fundamental tendencies in human relations. Peaceful cooperation predominates—there is much more peace than war—but the willingness to fight is so widely distributed in space and time that it must be regarded as a basic pattern of human behavior. The cause of the transition from one to the other is simply when some change in the circumstances of the group alters the balance between the desire for cooperation and the conflicting desire to obtain self-regarding ends in force. New females are introduced into the community of monkeys, food runs short, rain falls, or a new toy is given to a group of children. The pre-existing balance of desires is disturbed. The advantages to be gained by aggression grow greater. Fighting begins and spreads throughout the group. Social equilibrium is destroyed. Of course, we are not arguing that any real advantage is secured by the appeal to force. In the vast majority of cases the parties to a struggle would all be better off had they been able to continue cooperating with each other. All that we wish to insist upon is the universality of the tendency not to think so and the consequent willingness of minorities to fight.

What differences are made to the operation of these primitive forces by the development of more complex societies and cultures? For the moment we are not concerned with the prevention of aggression. To this vital matter we shall return. We are only concerned with the form of its expression. What activities of a developed society influence the form aggression takes? We suggest that there are two such activities—that of education and that of government.

The character of parental and familial control we have already discussed. Insofar as the emotional education of the child throughout human society involves appetitive frustration and insofar as intellectual education develops powers of reasoning and imagination, the forms of aggression change. It is rationalized, explained, and justified. It is displaced and projected. Above all, it is expressed in the life and activities of groups. Religious, economic, and political groups—churches, classes, and parties—release for the individual the aggression he dares not express for himself. And the greatest of all these groups—at least in the modern world—is the state. It is by an identification of the self with the state and by the expression of aggression through it that the individual has in recent times chiefly exhibited his aggressive impulses. Not exclusively so, for religious war and civil war have played an important part, but the great wars and the great loss of life have been in wars between nation-states.

It is natural that it should be so because the nation-state normally succeeds in preventing or controlling all other forms of aggression. The existence of government—with its apparatus of force—enormously increases the penalties of private aggression. Not only does the rationalizing mind and the conscience of mankind condemn private fighting and killing, but the social will to cooperation creates an instrument of force to control and punish any criminal minority that disturbs the peace. Hence private aggression is not only condemned by the conscience, it is also punished by the law. And so long as the state maintains supreme power, the same thing is true of all kinds of group aggression other than its own. Political and racial parties are prevented from taking the law into their own hands. Tendencies to civil war are successfully repressed. In such circumstances it is natural, in our view, that transformed aggression should be chiefly canalized by, and flow unimpeded through, the state organization of common endeavor and military adventure. In the service of the state the rationalized and transferred impulses of men find their last remaining and freest outlet.

What, then, causes the state to embark on war? We offer two conclusions in answer to this question. In the first place, as we have already mentioned, the expression of aggression on a group scale appears to restore to it simplicity and directness. In the civilized adult the original and simple causes for fighting are forgotten and overlaid with every kind of excuse and transformation. But when aggression is made respectable by manifestation through the corporate will of the group, it resumes much of its amoral simplicity of purpose. Indeed, positive moral obligation becomes attached to it. Nations will fight for simple possession, or through hatred due to animism, or because of national frustration, in a direct and shameless way that would be quite impossible for their individual members. The mutual approval of the members of the group makes conscienceless aggression possible. Hence states will fight for the same reasons as children fight. But not only for those things. In the second place states may fight, in our submission, because of the pressure of transformed aggression within their members. The members of the state may be so educated, so frustrated, and so unhappy that the burden of internal aggression may become intolerable. Such peoples—or the dominant groups within them—may constitue in a real sense aggressive nations. They have reached a point at which war has become a psychological necessity. Ambivalence is so severe, internal conflict so painful, fear and hatred of the scapegoat so intense, that a resolution of the crisis can only be found in war. In such cases war will be fought without adequate objective cause. It will have an objective occasion, some trifling incident or dispute, but the real effective causes will be elsewhere, within the tormented souls of the members of the aggressor nation. Such national neuroses can exhibit any or all of the general psychological mechanisms that we have already examined—animism, displacement, the projection of impulse, or the projection of conscience. Thus nations will exhibit the aggressiveness typical of apes and also the much more complex and obscure aggressiveness typical of humanity. They will fight because they are disciplined, because they are divided against themselves, because they have constructed mythical enemies and conjured terrors out of the darkness, because they are paranoid or sadistic. The balance of impulse between cooperation and force has been shifted against the advantages of peace.

This, then, is our theory of international war. War occurs because fighting is a fundamental tendency in human beings—a form of behavior called forth by certain simple situations in animals, children, human groups, and whole nations. It is a fundamentally pluralistic theory of international war. If the theory is true, then it follows that nations *can* fight only because they are able to release the explosive stores of transformed aggression, but they *do* fight for any of a large number of reasons. They may fight because of simple acquisitiveness or simple frustration or a simple fear of strangers. They may fight because of displaced hatred or projected hates or fears. There is no single all-embracing cause—no single villian of the piece, no institution nor idea that is wholly to blame. . . .

Let us at once make clear that there is nothing in the least alarmist or defeatist in the theory here advanced. We do not hold, nor think it possible to hold, that, because war is a chronic social disease, it is neccessarily an incurable disease. Not only have we emphasized throughout this article that the forces making for peaceful cooperation have been more powerful in history than the forces making for war, but we have not yet considered the implications of our evidence for the theory of the *cure* of war—the therapeutic as distinct from the causal problem. . . . All that it is necessary to do at this stage is to repeat and emphasize these three points:

Far more of the time and vitality of any nation has been absorbed in past history by the activities of peaceful cooperation than by war. The impulses to peace are therefore more powerful than the impulses to war. Hence the problem—how can they be further strengthened?

The governments of states have been successful in preserving comparative peace within their countries for centuries at a time. Is it not possible, then, that the expression of aggression can be permanently prevented or controlled by government?

We have only argued that the social and educational environments of the past have in fact produced certain "quantities" of aggression. Is it possible that different societies and different educations might produce less?

REFERENCES

Isaacs, Susan. *Social Development in Young Children.* London: Routledge, 1933.

ON THE CAUSES OF WAR AND THE CONDITIONS OF PEACE

WERNER LEVI

One of man's fundamental problems is to live in peace with his fellow men. He cannot live alone. Yet, in coexistence with others, conflicts inevitably arise. It is therefore characteristic of individuals, alone or organized in groups, to seek power for the satisfaction of their interests. Lest this lead to an eternal state of war, men organize themselves to reap the greatest benefit from cooperation and to reduce as much as possible conflict and strife. In particular, it is the minimum goal of social organization that the satisfaction of vital interests—usually bodily integrity and survival—should not lead to violent conflict but should, rather, be assured by peaceful methods or, failing these, by the application of supreme coercive power which is socialy organized and usually vested in a central authority.

The social organization of the state is intended to provide adequate means for peaceful adjustment of conflicts and to obviate the need for individual violence. Even when the means prove inadequate, the state simply does not permit violence—except as a matter of self-defense. The individual's personal accumulation of power is limited to most kinds of power short of physical force. As a compensation the state guarantees, as a minimum, the physical integrity and survival of the contestants in a conflict. This arrangement rests upon a habitual way of life and mental attitudes of the citizens indicating the existence of a community. The more complete the integration of the members into the community, the more successful.

In the international society, that loose association of states, the situation is basically different. Relations between states are ordered by routine practices and a vast network of international organizations promoting and regularizing the satisfaction of national interests. Much expedient cooperation exists between states, with well-established rules, regulations, and institutions. Innumerable conflicts of interest are resolved by accommodation and adjustment, either mutual or one-sided, depending upon the power relationship of the states involved. But this possibility is severely restricted because the society of states lacks an organized authority endowed with the legitimate supreme coercive power to guarantee the integrity and survival of each state, which is in turn merely an indication of the absence of any sense of solidarity among the peoples of the world.

From Werner Levi, "On the Causes of War and the Conditions of Peace," *Journal of Conflict Resolution.* 4 (December, 1960). Reprinted by permission.

Every state is the guardian and guarantor of all its own interests. It must be ready to defend them at all times and for this purpose must possess power. In contrast to intrastate conditions, the possession of power cannot be limited to the non-physical kind because national interests may be threatened which a state wishes to defend by force. The time when such a vital threat may arrive is unpredictable, and the nature of the threat is unknown. Therefore, the quest for power becomes inevitably permanent, though not for this reason all-consuming. It is conditioned by its relation to the goals the state pursues, by its relation to the power of other states, by the capabilities of the state, by the intensity of the state's will to survive integer, and by the results of the interrelations of these factors.

The quest for power becomes a major occupation of the state and a standard by which most aspects of its life and activities are measured, no matter how relative the magnitude of the desired power may be. It can be granted that, as states usually assert for the diplomatic record, they do not seek power for its own sake; they do so merely as a means to the end of satisfying their needs. For the nature of power, they can argue with cogency up to a point, like that of money, allows it to be accumulated and stored, to be expended for a great variety of unforeseeable ends at a time of need (25, p. 7). But whatever the end of the search for power and whatever its qualifications and limitations, the possibility remains that it can itself lead to violent conflict. States may become rivals in vying for elements of power or in one attempting to become more powerful than the other. The paradox here is that the search for power, even if only to have it available for a future conflict of interests, may itself become a source of violent conflict. This is an unending process because power as such has become a vital interest to some states. The search for it becomes necessary to guard against the consequences of this search. Thus, until another way is found to guarantee satisfaction of a state's interest, especially those it considers vital (or until states disappear), the possibility of violent conflict is a built-in feature of the nation-state system in the modern world (16, 22).

This fact can easily enough explain the mutual suspicion among states and their potential hostility. Here is genuine conflict. No amount of good will among nations, understanding among peoples, elimination of stereotypes, or clarification of semantic difficulties can obliterate it. Better knowledge of each other among peoples may gradually lead to greater integration on the way to a community and thereby reduce the chances of violence as a solution of conflict; but it cannot abolish conflict (4). It is therefore quite erroneous to assume, as has often been done, that states have violent conflicts because their citizens are aggressive, militaristic, and nationalistic. It is often the other way around: citizens assume these characteristics or are being prepared for warfare because there are real conflicts between states which may have to be solved with violence. The vicious circle is that a potential threat to their state makes citizens bellicose, and their bellicosity makes them appear as a threat to other states. Under the prevailing system the citizen must live in an anticipation of violence and take the necessary precautions, including readiness for war. Polls in many European and some American states showed that anywhere from one-third to three-quarters of the people consulted did not think it was possible to live in peace (8, pp. 125-216, question 3a).

This expectation of war does not, however, have to lead to war in accord with the assertion that "expectations determine behavior" (9, p. 15). For the expectation may produce behavior which either leads to its fulfilment or to its frustration. History is full of proof that governments have genuinely tried to avoid wars, knowing their potential existence. One of the reasons why they have sometimes failed is that they did not or could not choose the right means to avoid it. In a nation-state system, with the close identification of the citizen with his state, the anticipation of violence regularly leads the citizen to turn to his own community for increased security rather than to attempt integration with the threatening state for the sake of reducing the chance of violence (15, p. 19).

There are relations between states to which this general description does not apply. Not all states are hostile to each other, or, at any rate, not all consider every other state a potential threat to vital interests. Albania and Honduras are not anticipating violent conflict, nor are Norway and Great Britain, nor Canada and the United States. Such states either are not rivals for interests or power; or there is enough sentiment of community between them to obviate violence; or they repress violence for the sake of unity against a common enemy. They may still have conflicts of interest, but for a variety of reasons, including possibly the technical inability to be violent with each other or much simultaneous cooperation, they do not consider the use of violence. Such reasons may change, of course, or new causes may produce violence. Colombia was engaged in violent conflict with North Korea under United Nations action in the name of collective security. There was no reason for this in the direct relations between the two states, but for reasons sufficient to the Colombian government the violent conflict between the two states existed nevertheless, and very likely North Korea as such had very little to do with these reasons. As peace becomes increasingly indivisible and as technical developments enable—in the future—even small states to possess weapons which can reach any point on the globe and wipe out any state in the world, the chances for violent conflict between two

states hitherto geographically, politically, and in every other way remote
from each other, increase; just as—a compensating virtue—the chances for
their integration and growth into a community also become greater.
With such a community come the patterns of behavior facilitating peaceful solution of conflict and making the application of coercive power by
the supreme authority only one of the means of conflict solution and
an increasingly rare one.

In the meantime, while states continue to fight each other, almost
all conceivable and some inconceivable reasons have been given why they
use violence in the solution of some of their conflicts. Supernatural
powers, the state-system, social institutions, the character of groups, and
the nature of man have been named as the causes of war (34, 5, 17, 33,
12, 7, 18). If supernatural causes are disregarded, the common denominator of the rest is, sooner or later in the argument, man. But whether, as
the constitution of UNESCO asserts, it is the mind of man or some other
part, is a matter of debate—so is whether it is man as an individual or a
member of a group.

The number of natural traits held responsible as the cause of war is
almost unlimited. As so often with psychological explanations of personal
or social phenomena, any trait can somehow be made to serve as explanation. A man with an inferiority complex may either become a dictator or
a mouse! There are many reasons for these kinds of alternatives: the same
natural trait can find many different outlets, depending upon the opportunities which the environment offers; man is a complex of psychological
factors from whose interaction behavior results, so that no one factor can
be singled out; many psychological factors which appear mutually
exclusive in the abstract can nevertheless in practice produce the same
action. If the explanations of all psychologists are accepted as valid, the
whole spectrum of natural traits of man is covered as cause of war—which
is no explanation at all, for it is obvious that the nature of human beings
is responsible for human actions. In most cases, therefore, only certain
natural traits or psychological factors are singled out by various authors
to account primarily for the existence of war.

One group of these factors can be classified as destructive: aggressiveness, hostility, rivalry, bias and prejudice, hatred, sadism, projection of
one's own shortcomings upon the enemy. Another group contains factors
calling for balancing or compensation, such as boredom, thirst for
adventure, social frustration, insecurity, to which war offers the alternative of excitement and personal license. A third group refers to ego
fulfilment: need for prestige, status, and recognition; desire to be wanted,
wish for possessions. There is, finally, the not very frequently cited group
of constructive factors allegedly causing people to go to war: sense of

sacrifice, neighborly love, contribution to the community, sense of mission.

The protagonists of the theory that these psychological factors are the causes of war maintain that they can find particularly good expression in war and, without further ado, they jump to the conclusion that they are the cause. As one author put it, "eventually the growing hostility and the military preparation do lead to war, each side believing that the war was made necessary by the actions of the other" (13, p. 132). Unfortunately, things are not so simple. Even as a description of events this statement is not borne out by the facts, for there are innumerable instances in history of states being both hostile and militarily prepared without war breaking out between them. Things become even more complicated when the causes of war are sought in group conflict, regardless of one's concept of the group.

Depending upon that concept, various explanations have been given to make the peculiar characteristics of the group responsible as the cause of war: in a group the individual loses the customary social restraints, so that he can act aggressively against the enemy as he would not against a fellow member of his community; or, in joining a group, the individual's destructive drives become magnified and war offers itself as an outlet. Tensions between states, which can exist in the absence of concrete conflicts, have been blamed for the outbreak of violence (24, pp. 427-30). Or, it has been claimed, tensions and conflicts within a state are externalized for the sake of maintaining the national community and war results. Psychoanalysts blame unconscious remnants of man's earliest past which survive in the group and perpetuate war as an institution.

Some value cannot be denied to these attempts at explaining wars through psychological factors since it is men who are making wars. But they are not the whole explanation. Indeed, they leave many crucial questions unanswered. When, for instance, will certain natural traits or psychological drives find outlets in war, and when in something more peaceful? Why did German fight German before the political unification of Germany, and why has such a contingency been practically unthinkable since? How are these traits and drives of millions of individual citizens suddenly crystallized into a state of war against a specific enemy at a given moment? What these explanations fail to do is to indicate how these human factors are translated into violent conflict involving all citizens, regardless of their individual nature, and performed through a highly complex machinery constructed over a period of years for just such purpose.

There is always the missing link in these fascinating speculations about the psychological causes of war between the fundamental nature of man and the outbreak of war. It is fairly easy to understand how a conflict of interest can lead to personal violence in a face-to-face situation between two or a very few people. But this situation is vastly different from conflict between two states, each possibly composed of hundreds of millions of individuals. It then becomes evident that the natural traits of the citizenry cannot, by themselves, directly be related to international violence and adequately explain the origin of wars. Even on the assumption that the cause of war lies somehow in the total population of a state, these explanations need qualifications and refinements and amplifications whose character becomes clearer when psychological factors are more closely related to the nature of modern wars and the citizen's role in them.

In this connection the distinction between the causes and the conditions of war is of relevance (22, p. 224; 32, epilogue). In practice such a distinction may not be easily feasible, and there is danger that its definition may deteriorate into semantics. Nevertheless, there is good purpose in separating, as has often been done, the circumstances which are necessary prerequisites for war (sometimes called the "deeper" or "underlying" causes) and those which are directly resulting in war. The possession of weapons, for instance, is an indispensable condition of modern war, but not necessarily its cause. The occupation of an enemy's territory, if the enemy resists, is a cause of war, and so is the enemy's resistance. Usually, the psychological factors and human traits can be classified as conditions of war more correctly than as causes.

The example of the invading enemy brings to mind another distinction which might be equally difficult to make in practice, but which nevertheless raises questions unanswered by the theories on psychological causes of war. There are aggressive wars and defensive wars. Regardless of what the parties themselves claim, it is objectively possible for a government to start a war in the conviction that its country is about to be attacked and that its action is truly defensive. It would seem that the differing motivation behind these two types of wars requires different psychological explanation, even though the wars will all look alike (27, pp. 43-47).

In fact the failure of most psychological explanations of war to distinguish between different kinds of wars is another one of their weaknesses. Contrary to the usual assumption, wars are not always the same thing. In addition to being different regarding the aggressor and defender, wars can differ in regard to the kind of violence used, the weapons employed, the number and types of people involved, and several other things. Although the actual soldiers doing the fighting may have certain characteristics in common, from the standpoint of explaining on psychological grounds the origin of wars, it makes a basic difference whether Indian tribes fight, or armies hired by princes meet in battle, or the German people fight the French people in a total war.

The juxtaposition of these types of war shows clearly that each provides quite a different "environment," meaning: supplies quite different outlets for human traits and psychological drives. In modern wars there are never enough "aggressive" men flocking to the recruiting stations, while on the home front attractive salaries for war work seem to have greater attraction than the psychic rewards of a contribution to the war effort. Everywhere men are drafted into armies. Their and the general public's fighting spirit is aroused by government effort at great expense and not always successfully. How, for instance, can these explanations fit into their scheme Britain's war on Egypt in 1956 which had to be stopped because (among other reasons) a large section of the British public did not want to fight it? In some armies more than half the men who were supposed to shoot did not pull the trigger. At home from ten to twenty people are required in order to maintain one man at the front lines, most often continuing to do their routine work. In future push-button wars, any psychic satisfaction in war at the home front will be even further reduced. Usually, the mass at home has to be stirred up by an enormous propaganda campaign to become bellicose—after the war has started or is about to start—and the stimulus of revenge or defense of the fatherland soon has to be replaced by "war aims" conjuring up visions of a beautiful, peaceful future world. In brief: in the long run, the more effective appeals to keep people in a fighting spirit are not to aggressiveness and hatreds but to the desire for lasting peace and greater welfare. This is no conclusive argument against the possibility that people may yearn for war for other reasons. But, first, it is not likely that people switch their attitudes so radically from pro to con regarding war so quickly; second, it is, historically, extremely rare to find before modern wars appeals arousing sentiments designed directly to cause a war (19, p. 199; 27, p. 34); and, third, when preparation for war is compared, chronologically, to warlike appeals to the public, it will be found that the appeals begin at a considerably later moment, if not after the outbreak of the war; just as stereotypes of one people about another are often adjusted to suit the demands of the war.

The long and complex preparations needed for modern wars make it quite inconceivable that they result from some sudden, collective impulse of the state's citizenry. Whatever destructiveness and aggressiveness may be part of man's nature, "it is not a part of his native behavior to combine these into strategy and tactics, into armies and sea power and air forces, all controlled for the purposes of the State" (31, p. 254). This is all the more true as the majority of citizens, even in the best-educated countries, are notoriously uninterested in foreign affairs and uninformed about the course of international events. When polled, these citizens may express a phobia against foreigners in general or against a particular people, but there is no evidence that this has ever been strong enough to lead them to demand war or prepare for it. Indeed the relative insignificance of such phobias and stereotypes about other peoples as causes of war can best be discovered in the fact that a people has found itself allied with another people in war about which it had worse ideas than about the common enemy. A *Fortune* poll in 1939, for instance, showed that 6.9 per cent of American pollees considered themselves most friendly to the Germans, while only 0.9 per cent considered themselves friendly to the Russians (8, p. 117). Similarly, Great Britain was at war with Germany twice in modern times, although the British people consistently show a sentimental preference for Germans over Frenchmen.

The weaknesses in attempts to give individual psychological or natural traits as causes of war can be found, *mutatis mutandi,* in group psychology. Whatever the accepted theory about group behavior and group tensions, the need remains to explain how these characteristics of the group are organized and translated into war (27, p. 44; 28, p. 83). For it should be clear that, while man is endowed with certain psychological qualities, the environment of every individual man determines how these qualities become effective and what results they will produce. What may be said about psychological contributions to the outbreak of war, if "man in general" is considered, is that the institutionalization of war does indeed provide numerous and convenient outlets for psychological drives which might otherwise be channeled into different directions or be sublimated to produce different results. To some citizens the outbreak of war might thus become a pleasant prospect and lead to emotional readiness for it. But this is, essentially, a passive readiness, which is, besides, produced in almost every citizen in modern times by his civic training and his habitual way of life. This is an indispensable condition for war as long as it remains a mass war. Such readiness is, however, not the same thing as being a cause of war. It will be even less relevant when the perfection of missile warfare might conceivably lead to the ending of a war before anybody has had a chance to develop any feelings about it.

The relevance of psychological or natural traits upon war becomes greater with a better differentiation among groups and individuals in a state and the role they play in the shaping of the state's destiny (18, p. 47-50; 11, p. 32). Since obviously some citizens are more important than others in relation to the decision to make war, the failure to distinguish between them has led of necessity to such a generalization of explanations in psychological terms that they are not very fruitful. The nature of those making decisions within a state and of those prominently influencing these decisions is not only of importance in uncovering the origin of wars but may also be easier of investigation than the people as a whole. Even then, however, personal natural factors are likely to be only among the conditions of war. Even the most powerful dictator in a modern state cannot determine policy, least of all policy directed toward war, entirely according to his whims. Like all policy-makers, he is dependent upon many conditions over which he has no or little control. He too is part of the environment in which he lives and which contributes to the shaping of his personal character, though he may not be very conscious of this, while consciously many elements of the situation in which he must make his decision will enter into his calculations.

This brings into focus a possible cause of war which has been too often neglected in the preoccupation with finding psychological reasons: the use of war deliberately as an instrument of foreign policy. It is true that anyone considering war today as a political means must be, in a manner of speaking, "insane." Yet historical evidence is convincing in demonstrating that modern wars did not result from emotional outbursts or accumulated frustrations by either decision-makers or the general public. Instead, they were preceded by long and cool-headed preparations and finally started after carefully calculated decisions. Mr. Anthony Eden's memoirs—to take only a very recent example—show quite clearly that military action against Egypt in the Suez crisis in 1956 was much discussed by the British cabinet and in contacts with the United States Department of State and was eventually undertaken on the basis of a fairly unemotional conclusion that British interests in the Suez Canal made it worthwhile.

It is quite possible that the motivations of those who wish to use war as a means to reach certain goals are irrational, also that non- or irrationality affects the judgment of the instrumental usefulness of war in the particular situation. The decision-maker can hardly help seeing the world through his own eyes. This is natural and therefore unavoidable. But this is merely saying that there are limits to man's rationality and that these limits are among the conditions for peace and war which must be studied. Nevertheless, the decision to go to war has usually been made, as history shows, upon careful deliberation of the usefulness of war as an instrument and can largely be understood as such. Indeed, since usually many individuals contribute to the making of the war decision, the chances are very good that the variations and peculiarities of their natural traits have canceled out each other and that the decision has been arrived at upon the merits of war as a desirable instrument (1, 10). That decision-makers take war into their calculations at all will remain true as long as war remains an institution. Only as the use of violence between contesting parties becomes suppressed as it has been, generally, within many states, will this possibility change.

The fundamental difficulty in discovering the cause of war is that any fact, to be the cause, requires a particular conjunction of conditions not any one of which may itself be directed toward war. War is a social situation, a complex of relationships developing out of the interplay of a great many factors (27, p. 33; 34, II, p. 1284; 20, p. 45). This interplay is unique and many different variations can be responsible for some fact or facts becoming causes of war. Hence the impossibility of specifying what particular facts may cause wars. Hence, also, the experience that roughly similar historical situations may in one case end in war and in another not. One and the same factor in a number of situations will not always have the same result. The possession of weapons, for instance, is a condition always present in situations leading to war and may therefore appear as co-responsible. Yet, in other situations (Switzerland during World War II) it not only fails to lead to war but may contribute to the preservation of peace. Obviously the context in which the possession of weapons occurs is of decisive importance. The conclusion appears inevitable that no generally valid specifiable factor causes war but that, instead, only a particular constellation of factors can produce the conditions of war in which a factor or factors can become effective as causes. To overlook this nature of war has been a shortcoming in most of the attempts to look to the nature of man as the cause of wars. What most of these attempts have done is to search for all possible elements present in the situation to explain the origin of war. What they have usually not done is to try to discover whether there are missing elements whose presence would lead to the avoidance of the use of violence.

Yet this discovery is not difficult when states are considered, in which the use of intergroup violence has become a rarity and the exception for the solution of conflicts. It will then be found that the relative peacefulness within states was not achieved by changing human nature, altering human psychology, or eliminating conflict. It was not even achieved by eliminating hatreds between groups, discrimination, false stereotypes, prejudices, bias, rivalry, or competition—all of which continue in some of the most peaceful (internally) states with an intensity matching that of nationalism. Only the use of violence as a normal and accepted pattern of social relations has disappeared. To the extent that it has so disappeared, it did so by the addition of new behavior patterns, that is to say institutions, leading to the integration of hitherto separated groups into a community.

Once a group has grown into a comminity (20, pp. 1-27; 2, pp. 205-06; 29, pp. 12-14; 23, p. 28), its members habitually act in conformity with a sense of solidarity, unity, and cohesion which normally excludes violence as a means for the solution of conflicts between them. An organization has evolved which reinforces from without the habit of peaceful relations originating in the attitudes within the members, with a continual interaction between the two. Thus a community possesses the ideological and material restraints necessary to make warfare among its members practically unthinkable. It provides outlets for personality factors in the great variety of its institutions, such as legislatures, public opinion media, plurality of interest groups with overlapping memberships, which in their totality guarantee peaceful change and perform fundamental peace-preserving functions. The monopoly of coercion by a central authority—i.e., force and violence—is largely a result of these institutions and exists primarily for emergency situations. But also, its existence provides the citizen with that sense of security which makes him trust in the success of these peace-preserving institutions. In a community, conflicts of interest are adjusted without violence for the sake of higher interests in the preservation of the community which the contestants share. The use of violence is simply not considered either because of a common higher loyalty to the community, or because of learned habitual behavior and inner compulsion of social responsibility, because of fear of effective sanction against antisocial behavior made possible by the creation of the community or because of all these and possibly other reasons.

Unfortunately for the peace of the world, the growth of groups into such a community is a slow process. Many of the organizations calling themselves states in Asia and Africa today can hardly be described as communities in this sense, for they lack, above all, the peace-preserving plurality of interest groups which allows them to develop a common loyalty toward the state as such and therewith that sense of security which is one of the foundations of peaceful behavior (21, pp. 25-29). The development of a community requires high frequency and great intensity of contact between its members, directly or indirectly through shared experiences of almost any kind. The more they have things spiritual and material in common, the greater is the chance that a community will develop (30, pp. 18-74). It is for this reason (and not for reason of eliminating conflict) that all those enterprises undertaken for the sake of bringing about "better understanding" among nations may, in the long run, have the effect of diminishing the use of violence in international relations (3, p. 40). There may be a faster and less complicated way to stop violence. The means of war may become such that their use will guarantee the destruction of the user as well as the enemy. Then the uselessness of war as an instrument might lead to the elimination of war.

REFERENCES

Abel, T. "The Element of Decision in the Pattern of War," *American Sociological Review,* **VI** (1941), 853-59.

Angell, Robert C. "Discovering Paths to Peace." In International Sociological Association, *The Nature of Conflict.* Paris: UNESCO (1957), 204-23.

————. "Government and Peoples as Foci for Peace-Oriented Research," *Journal of Social Issues,* XI (1955), 36-41.

Bernard, Jessie. "The Sociological Study of Conflict." In International Sociological Association, *The Nature of Conflict,* Paris: UNESCO (1957), 33-117.

Bernard, L. L. *War and Its Causes.* New York: Henry Holt & Co., 1944.

Blum, Fred. *Toward a Democratic Work Order.* New York: Harper & Bros., 1953.

Bouthoul, G. *Les guerres, éléments de polémologie.* Paris: Payot, 1951.

Buchanan, William, and Cantril, Hadley. *How Nations See Each Other: A Study in Public Opinion.* Urbana: University of Illinois Press, 1953.

Cantril, Hadley (Ed.). *Tensions that Cause Wars.* Urbana: University of Illinois Press, 1950.

Deutsch, Karl W. "Mass Communications and the Loss of Freedom in National Decision-making," *Conflict Resolution,* I (1957), 200-211.

Farber, Maurice L. "Psychoanalytic Hypothesis in the Study of War," *Journal of Social Issues,* XI (1955), 29-35.

Findings of the Conference on the Cause and Cure of War, Washington, D.C., 1925.

Gladstone, Arthur. "The Conception of the Enemy," *Conflict Resolution,* III (1959), 132-37.

Glover, Edward. *War, Sadism and Pacifism,* London: George Allen & Unwin, 1946.

Haas, Ernst B., and Whiting, Allen S., Jr. *Dynamics of International Relations.* New York: McGraw-Hill Book Co., 1956.

International Sociological Association, *The Nature of Conflict.* Paris: UNESCO, 1957.

Johnsen, Juli E. *Selected Articles on War—Cause and Cure.* New York: H.W. Wilson Co., 1926.

Kelman, Herbert C. "Societal, Attitudinal and Structural Factors in International Relations," *Journal of Social Issues,* XI (1955), 42-56.

Klineberg, Otto. *Tensions Affecting International Understanding.* New York: Social Science Research Council, 1950.

Levi, Werner. *Fundamentals of World Organization.* Minneapolis: University of Minnesota Press, 1950.

————. "The Fate of Democracy in South and Southeast Asia," *Far Eastern Survey,* XXVIII (1959), 25-29.

Mack, Raymond W., and Snyder, Richard C. "The Analysis of Social Conflict—Toward an Overview and Synthesis," *Conflict Resolution,* I (1957), 212-48.

May, Mark A. *A Psychology of War and Peace.* New Haven, Conn.: Yale University Press, 1943.

Morgenthau, Hans J. *Politics among Nations.* New York: Alfred A. Knopf, 1960.

Nitze, Paul M. "Necessary and Sufficient Elements of a General Theory of International

Relations." In William T. R. Fox, *Theoretical Aspects of International Relations.* Notre Dame: University of Notre Dame, 1959.

Oppenheim, Felix E. "Rational Choice," *Journal of Philosophy,* **L** (1953), 341-50.

Röpke, Wilhelm. *Internationale Ordnung.* Erlenbach-Zürich: Eugen Rentsch, 1945.

Rüstow, Alexander. "Zur soziologischen Ortsbestimmung des Krieges," *Friedenswarte,* **XXXIX** (1939), 81-94.

Schwarzenbe.ger, Georg. *Power Politics.* London: Stevens & Sons, 1951.

Smend, Rudolf. *Verfassung und Verfassungsrecht.* München: Duncker & Humblot, 1928.

Stratton, George M. *Social Psychology of International Conduct.* New York: D. Appleton & Co., 1929.

Tolstoy, Leo. *War and Peace.*

Waltz, Kenneth N. *Man, the State, and War.* New York: Columbia University Press, 1959.

Wright, Quincy. *A Study of War.* Chicago: University of Chicago Press, 1942.

IS THERE A MILITARY-INDUSTRIAL COMPLEX WHICH PREVENTS PEACE?: CONSENSUS AND COUNTERVAILING POWER IN PLURALISTIC SYSTEMS*

MARC PILISUK AND THOMAS HAYDEN

Introduction

The term "military-industrial complex" is very much in the literature. If its most sinister depictions are correct, then the peace researcher who works with the hope that his research may actually improve chances for world peace is wasting his time. A research finding, like a bit of knowledge, is always double-edged in what it portends for application. The project which tells us the surest steps to peace, tells us with equal certainty the steps

From Marc Pilisuk and Thomas Hayden, "Is There a Military Industrial Complex Which Prevents Peace? : Consensus and Countervailing Power in Pluralistic Systems," *The Journal of Social Issues,* 21 (1965), pp. 67-117. Reprinted by permission.

* Research relevant to this paper was made possible by a series of small grants from the Christopher Reynolds Foundation, The Society for Psychological Study of Social Issues, The Institute for Policy Studies, and the University of Michigan Phoenix Memorial Project. Appreciation is also due to Michael Locker and Anatol Rapoport for review and assistance with the manuscript and to the University of Michigan's Mental Health Research Institute and Center for Research on Conflict Resolution for the use of facilities. A slightly revised and updated version of this paper appears in Perrucci, Robert and Pilisuk, Marc (eds.) *Triple Revolution Emerging: Social Problems in Depth,* Boston: Little, Brown, 1971.

which must be bypassed if peace is shunned. If there exists an omnipotent elite, committed to militarism, then there is simply no basis for hope that voices for peace have gotten, or can get, an influential channel into inner policy circles. If, on the other hand, the pluralist thesis can be said to apply in full even to basic policy directions of preparedness for war or for peace, then some influential decision makers must be eagerly awaiting the research findings on paths to peace with intentions to press for their immediate application.

Because we agree with neither of the above positions, because we believe that most research workers in this area tend either to ignore or to over-rate the potential consequences of their work to peace, and because we feel that consideration of the conditions which dictate major directions of policy is essential for an evaluation of any contribution to peace research, we are bringing the concept of the "military-industrial complex" to both the microscope and the scalpel. The implications of this inquiry point to a research approach which does have relevance to the decision process and to the most central agencies of social change, and resistance to change, within American society. . . .

In the United States there is no ruling group. Nor is there any easily discernible ruling institutional order, so meshed have the separate sources of elite power become. But there is a social structure which is organized to create and protect power centers with only partial accountability. In this definition of power we are avoiding the Weber-Mills meaning of *omnipotence* and the contrary pluralist definition of power as consistently *diffuse*. We are describing the current system as one of overall "minimal accountability" and "minimal consent." We mean that the role of democratic review, based on genuine popular consent, is made marginal and reactive. Elite groups are minimally accountable to publics and have a substantial, though by no means maximum, freedom to shape popular attitudes. The reverse of our system would be one in which democratic participation would be the orienting demand around which the social structure is organized.

Some will counter this case by saying that we are measuring "reality" against an "ideal," a technique which permits the conclusion that the social structure is undemocratic according to its distance from our utopian values. This is a convenient apology for the present system, of course. We think it possible, at least in theory, to develop measures of the undemocratic in democratic conditions, and place given social structures along a continuum. These measures, in rough form, might include such variables as economic security, education, legal guarantees, access to information, and participatory control over systems of economy, government, and jurisprudence.

The reasons for our concern with democratic process in an article questioning the power of a purported military-industrial complex are twofold. First, just as scientific method both legitimizes and promotes change in the world of knowledge, democratic method legitimizes and promotes change in the world of social institutions. Every society, regardless of how democratic, protects its core institutions in a web of widely shared values. But if the core institutions should be dictated by the requisites of military preparedness, then restrictions on the democratic process, i.e., restrictions in either mass opinion exchange (as by voluntary or imposed news management) or in decision-making bodies (as by selection of participants in a manner guaranteeing exclusion of certain positions), then such restrictions would be critical obstacles to peace.

Second, certain elements of democratic process are inimical to features of militarily oriented society, and the absence of these elements offers one type of evidence for a military-industrial complex even in the absence of a ruling elite. Secretary of Defense Robert McNamara made the point amply clear in his testimony in 1961 before the Senate Armed Services Committee:

> Why should we tell Russia that the Zeus development may not be satisfactory? What we ought to be saying is that we have the most perfect anti-ICBM system that the human mind will ever devise. Instead the public domain is already full of statements that the Zeus may not be satisfactory, that it has deficiencies. I think it is absurd to release that level of information. (Military Procurement Authorization Fiscal Year 1962)

Under subsequent questioning McNamara attempted to clarify his statement that he only wished to delude Russian, not American, citizens about U.S. might. Just how this might be done was not explained.

A long established tradition exists for "executive privilege" which permits the President to refuse to release information when, in his opinion, it would be damaging to the national interest. Under modern conditions responsibility for handling information of a strategic nature is shared among military, industrial, and executive agencies. The discretion regarding when to withhold what information must also be shared. Moreover, the existence of a perpetual danger makes the justification, "in this time of national crisis" suitable to every occasion in which secrecy must be justified. McNamara's statement cited above referred not to a crisis in Cuba or Viet Nam but rather to the perpetual state of cold war crisis. And since the decision about what is to be released and when, is subject to just such management, the media became dependent upon the agencies for timely leaks and major stories. This not only adds an aura of omniscience to the agencies, but gives these same agencies the power to reward "good" journalists and punish the critical ones.

The issues involved in the question of news management involve more than the elements of control available to the President, the State Department, the Department of Defense, the Central Intelligence Agency, the Atomic Energy Commission or any of the major prime contractors of defense contracts. Outright control of news flow is probably less pervasive than voluntary acquiescence to the objectives of these prominent institutions of our society. Nobody has to tell the wire services when to release a story on the bearded dictator of our hemisphere or the purported brutality of Ho Chi Minh. A frequent model, the personified devil image of an enemy, has become a press tradition. In addition to a sizeable quantity of radio and television programming and spot time purchased directly by the Pentagon, an amount of service, valued at $6 million by *Variety,* is donated annually by the networks and by public relations agencies for various military shows (Swomley, 1959). Again, the pluralistic shell of an independent press or broadcasting media is left hollow by the absence of a countervailing social force of any significant power.

The absence of a countervailing force for peace cannot, we have claimed, be demonstrated by an absence of conflicting interests among powerful sectors of American society. Indeed, such conflicts are ever-present examples of American pluralism. Demonstrating the absence of a discussion of the shared premises, among the most potent sectors of society, would go far in highlighting the area of forced or acquiescent consensus. But even the absence of debate could not complete the case unless we can show how the accepted premises are inconsistent with requisites of a viable peace-time social system. It is to this question: of the compatibility of the unquestioned assumptions of American society with conditions of peace, that we now turn. The "core beliefs" which we listed as unchallenged by any potent locus of institutionalized power are:

a) Efficacy is preferable to principle in foreign affairs (thus military means are chosen over non-violent means);

b) Private property is preferable to public property; and

c) Limited parliamentary democracy is preferable to any other system of government.

What characteristics of a continuing world system devoid of military conflict fly in the face of these assumptions?

We identify three conditions for enduring peace which clash with one or more of the core beliefs. These are: 1) the requirements for programming an orderly transition and the subsequent maintenance of a non-defense economy within a highly automated and relatively affluent society; 2) the conditions for peaceful settlement of internal disputes within underdeveloped countries and between alien nations and commercial interests; and 3) the conditions under which disparities in living standards between have and have-not nations can be handled with minimum violence.

If one pools available projections regarding the offset programs, especially regional and local offset programs, necessary to maintain economic well-being in the face of disarmament in this country, the programs will highlight two important features. One is the lag time in industrial conversion. The second is the need for coordination in the timing and spacing of programs. One cannot reinvest in new home building in an area which has just been deserted by its major industry and left a ghost town. The short-term and long-term offset values of new hospitals and educational facilities will differ in the building and the utilization stages and regional offset programs have demonstrable interregional effects (Reiner, 1964). Plans requiring worker mobility on a large scale will require a central bank for storing job information and a smooth system for its dissemination. Such coordination will require a degree of centralization of controls beyond the realm which our assumption regarding primacy of private property would permit.

Gross intransigence can be expected on this issue. Shortly after Sperry Rand on Long Island was forced to make major cutbacks of its professional and engineering staff to adapt to the termination of certain defense contracts, the union approached Sperry's management with the prospect of collaborating in efforts to commence contingency plans for diversification. The response, by Carl A. Frische, President of Sperry Gyroscope, a division of Sperry Rand, remains a classic. There must be no "government-controlled mechanisms under the hood of the economy." He suggested, with regard to such planning, that "we let Russia continue with that." (*Long Island Sunday Press,* February 23, 1964). Sperry is an old-timer in defense production. Its board of directors average several years older than the more avant garde board of directors of, say, General Dynamics. But the prospect of contingency planning will be no more warmly welcomed in the newer aeroframe industry (which is only 60% convertible to needs of a peace-time society), (McDonagh and Zimmerman, 1964). Private planning, by an individual firm for its own future does occur, but, without coordinated plans, the time forecast for market conditions remains smaller than the lag time for major retooling. A lag time of from six to ten years would not be atypical before plans by a somewhat over-specialized defense contractor could result in retooling for production in a peace-time market. In the meantime, technological innovations, governmental fiscal or regulatory policies, shifts in consumer preferences, or the decisions by other firms to enter that same market could well make the market vanish. Moreover, the example of defense forms which have attempted even the smaller step toward diversification presents a picture which has not been entirely promising (Fearon and Hook, 1964). Indeed, one of several reasons for the failures in this endeavor has been that marketing skills necessary to compete in a private enterprise economy have been lost by those industrial giants who have been managing with a sales force of one or two retired generals to deal with the firm's only customer. Even if the path of successful conversion by some firms were to serve as the model for all individual attempts, the collective result would be poor. To avoid a financially disastrous glutting of limited markets some coordinated planning will be needed.

The intransigence regarding public or collaborative planning occurs against a backdrop of a soon-to-be increasing army of unemployed youth and aged, as well as regional armies of unemployed victims of automation. Whether one thinks of work in traditional job market terms or as anything worthwhile that a person can do with his life, work (and some means of livelihood) will have to be found for these people. There is much work to be done in community services, education, public health, and recreation, but this is people work, not product work. The lack of a countervailing force prevents the major reallocation of human and economic resources from the sector defined as preferable by the most potent institutions of society. One point must be stressed. We are not saying that limited planning to cushion the impact of arms reduction is impossible. Indeed, it is going on and with the apparent blessing of the Department of Defense (Barber, 1963). We are saying that the type of accommodation needed by a cutback of $9 billion in R & D and $16 billion in military procurement requires a type of preparation not consistent with the unchallenged assumptions.

Even the existence of facilities for coordinated planning does not, to be sure, guarantee the success of such planning. Bureaucratic institutions, designed as they may be for coordination and control, do set up internal resistance to the very coordination they seek to achieve. The mechanisms for handling these bureaucratic intransigencies usually rely upon such techniques as bringing participants into the process of formulating the decisions which will affect their own behavior. We can conceive of no system of coordinated conversion planning which could function without full and motivated cooperation from the major corporations, the larger unions, and representatives of smaller business and industry. Unfortunately it is just as difficult to conceive of a system which would assure this necessary level of participation and cooperation. This same argument cuts deeper still when we speak of the millions of separate individuals in the "other America" whose lives would be increasingly "administered" with the type of centralized planning needed to offset a defense economy. The job assignment which requires moving, the vocational retraining program, the

development of housing projects to meet minimal standards, educational
enrichment programs, all of the programs which are conceived by middle-
class white America for racially mixed low income groups, face the same
difficulty in execution of plans. Without direct participation in the formulation of the programs, the target populations are less likely to participate
in the programs and more likely to continue feelings of alienation from the
social system which looks upon them as an unfortunate problem rather
than as contributing members. Considering the need for active participation
in real decisions, every step of coordinated planning carries with it the
responsibility for an equal step in the direction of participatory democracy. This means that the voice of the unemployed urban worker may
have to be heard, not only on city council meetings which discuss policy
on the control of rats in his dwelling, but also on decisions about where a
particular major corporation will be relocated and where the major resource
allocations of the country will be invested. That such decision participation
would run counter to the consensus on the items of limited parliamentary
democracy and private property is exactly the point we wish to make.

Just as the theoretical offset plans can be traced to the sources of
power with which they conflict, so too can the theoretical plans for
international governing and peace-keeping operations be shown to conflict
with the unquestioned beliefs. U.S. consent to international jurisdiction in
the settlement of claims deriving from the nationalization of American
overseas holdings or the removal of U.S. military installations is almost
inconceivable. Moreover, the mode of American relations to less-developed
countries is so much a part of the operations of those American institutions which base their existence upon interminable conflict with Communism that the contingency in which the U.S. might have to face the question
of international jurisdiction in these areas seems unreal. Offers to mediate
with Cuba by Mexico, with North Viet Nam by France, are bluntly rejected.
Acceptance of such offers would have called into question not one but all
three of the assumptions in the core system. International jurisdictional
authority could institutionalize a means to call the beliefs into question. It
is for this reason (but perhaps most directly because of our preference for
forceful means) that American preoccupation in those negotiations
regarding the extension of international control which have taken place,
deal almost exclusively with controls in the area of weaponry and police
operations and not at all in the areas of political or social justice.

The acceptance of complete international authority even in the area
of weaponry poses certain inconsistencies with the preferred "core beliefs."
Non-violent settlement of Asian-African area conflicts would be slow and
ineffective in protecting American interests. The elimination, however, of
military preparedness, both for projected crises and for their potential

escalation, requires a faith in alternate means of resolution. The phasing of the American plan for general and complete disarmament is one which says in effect: prove that the alternatives are as efficient as our arms in protection of our interests and then we disarm. In the short term, however, the effectiveness of force always looks greater.

The state of world peace contains certain conditions imposed by the fact that people now compare themselves with persons who have more of the benefits of industrialization than they themselves. Such comparative reference groups serve to increase the demand for rapid change. While modern communications heighten the pressures imposed by such comparisons, the actual disparities revealed in comparison speak for violence. Population growth rates, often as high as three percent, promise population doubling within a single generation in countries least able to provide for their members. The absolute number of illiterates as well as the absolute number of persons starving is greater now than ever before in history. Foreign aid barely offsets the disparity between declining prices paid for the prime commodities exported by underdeveloped countries and rising prices paid for the finished products imported into these countries (Horowitz, 1962). All schemes for tight centralized planning employed by these countries to accrue and disperse scarce capital by rational means are blocked by the unchallenged assumptions on private property and limited parliamentary democracy. A recent restatement of the principle came in the report of General Lucius Clay's committee on foreign aid. The report stated that the U.S. should not assist foreign governments "in projects establishing government owned industrial and commercial enterprises which compete with existing private endeavors." When Congressman Broomfield's amendment on foreign aid resulted in cancellation of a U.S. promise to India to build a steel mill in Bokaro, Broomfield stated the case succinctly: "The main issue is private enterprise vs. state socialism." (*The Atlantic,* September, 1964, p. 6.) Moreover, preference for forceful solutions assures that the capital now invested in preparedness will not be allocated in a gross way to the needs of underdeveloped countries. Instead, the manifest crises periodically erupting in violence justify further the need for reliance upon military preparedness.

We agree fully with an analysis by Lowi (1964) distinguishing types of decisions for which elite-like forces seem to appear and hold control (redistributive) and other types in which pluralist powers battle for their respective interests (distributive). In the latter type the pie is large and the fights are over who gets how much. Factional strife within and among military industrial and political forces in our country are largely of this nature. In redistributive decisions, the factions coalesce, for the pie itself is threatened. We have been arguing that the transition to peace is a process of redistributive decision.

Is there, then, a military-industrial complex which prevents peace? The answer is inextricably imbedded into the mainstream of American institutions and mores. Our concept is not that American society contains a ruling military-industrial complex. Our concept is more nearly that American society *is* a military-industrial complex. It can accomodate a wide range of factional interests from those concerned with the production or utilization of a particular weapon to those enraptured with the mystique of optimal global strategies. It can accommodate those with rabid desires to advance toward the brink and into limitless intensification of the arms race. It can even accommodate those who wish either to prevent war or to limit the destructiveness of war through the gradual achievement of arms control and disarmament agreements. What it cannot accommodate is the type of radical departures needed to produce enduring peace.

The requirements of a social system geared to peace, as well as the requirements for making a transition to such a social system, share a pattern of resource distribution which is different from the one the world now has. Moreover, these requirements for peace are, in significant measure, inconsistent with constraints set by the more enduring convergencies among power structures in the United States. The same is true whether one speaks of allocation of material or of intellectual resources. Both are geared to the protection of the premises rather than to avenues of change. We are not saying that war is inevitable or that the changes cannot be made. We are saying that the American political, military, and industrial system operates with certain built-in stabilizers which resist a change in the system. If there is to be peace, as opposed to detente or temporary absence of war, marked changes will be needed. Whether this society can or will accommodate to such changes is a question which is fundamentally different from the questions posed by most studies conventionally grouped under the rubric of peace research. One difference which marks the question of capacity to accommodate is in the theoretical conception or model of the cold war which is assumed. And a second distinction lies in the manner in which the end product of the research may be suited to meet the social forces (as apart from the intellectual arguments) which promote long-term changes in policy.

Role of the Peace Scholars

In recent years, intellectual attention to the problem of peace has usually been directed to the problem of averting war. The context of this problem is that of the non-zero-sum game in which the players have both a joint common advantage (in averting nuclear war) and a bargaining problem in deciding upon the competitive distribution of other non-sharable advantages. Much of the intellectual attention from social scientists has been directed to problems of trust, controls, and assurances of good faith— problems relevant to protecting the common advantage. Meanwhile the strategists have tended to give relatively greater emphasis to the problem of competitive advantage. There have been clashes between these two groups of intellectuals but both share, and both assume that foreign adversaries also share, the assumption that nuclear war ought to be avoided. The question is one of means to that end and of risks to be taken.

In the question of permanent peace with its contingent institutions, there is no such fundamental agreement about the desirability of the end. In fact, we have argued that there exists a large area of consensus which precludes the very set of contingent institutions which may be needed for lasting peace. Without certain shared end values, research on the part of peace protagonists cannot be used as a rational wedge in policy debate. The clash is with a social system some of whose very bases of organization run counter to the requirements of stable peace. Under such circumstances, there are zero-sum components to the conflict. Some institutions and some status positions within the society must change and some may actually have to perish if certain newer ones are to thrive. Research in this area becomes what most researchers who are justly sensitive about their scientific objectivity dread—a part of a political struggle. Dorwin Cartwright has called power "the neglected variable" in studies of interpersonal behavior (Cartwright, 1959). The scarcity of good empirical studies of the power to effect or constrain national policies shows an even greater area of neglect. Whatever the reasons for this neglect, there seems a need to follow the course once set by Freud if we are ever to learn about, and eventually make changes in, this taboo area.

Another departure intended by the type of research we shall suggest may be seen by a brief comparison with a sample of questions now being tackled by inquiry into problems of peace. Look, for example, at each of the following questions:

How will detection and punishment be regulated in the event of violations in an arms control agreement? What system of jurisdiction and policing could replace national armed forces? What institutionalized channels could be created to replace war as an expression of individual or social aggression? What sequences of events have led to escalation of conflicts in the past and how can these sequences be altered? How will the electronics industry, or Southern California, get along without defense contracts? What sequence of arms reduction and what type of inspections and controls would prevent a successful surprise attack during the disarmament process? When are unilateral gestures likely to be reciprocated?

Taken together, these questions and variations of them comprise a remarkably wide slice of the entire peace research movement (as intellectually popular as it has become on financially sparse resources). The questions are doubtlessly important ones, but they hold in common a certain format of answers. Each project seeks, and some find, as an answer to its research, a scheme which—*if* it were enacted—would promote enduring peace. Why the plan is not enacted is usually not asked, or, if asked at all, then answered within the framework of basic assumptions which protect the status quo. The propensity of scholars seems often to be an equation of their own ability to understand ways to treat a problem with the actual resolution of the problem. This may have been true for small pox but it is, so far, not true for over-population, and this understanding by itself falls many steps short of implementing the treatment for problems of war and peace. In the case of war and peace the discovery of answers could be irrelevant to their application—could be, that is, unless directed to foci of emergent power and change within the system. By and large, the efforts of the peace intellectuals have not been so directed.

We do not mean this as an indictment against the peace research movement. As an activity which institutionalizes means to support scholars who wish to devote their professional talents to the quest for peace, the movement is admirable. Moreover, it is a young movement still groping for its major task and hence capable of learning. But the nature of the current outputs by these scholars, the policy suggestions which they make as reflections of their intellectual inquiry, suggest a common denominator of difficulties.

The better known among the proposals are associated with the names of Charles Osgood (GRIT), Stephan James (peace hostage exchange), Ralph Lapp and others (finite deterrence), J. David Singer (gradual accretion of U.N. custody for major weapons), John Strachey (militarily enforced peace through Soviet-American alliance), Morton Deutsch (suspicion-reducing and trust-building steps), Herbert Kelman (neutral international armies), Amitai Etzioni (gradual reduction of military programs to finite levels and reinvestment in economic offensives), Quincy Wright and others (building of interpersonal and organizational ties which transcend the cold war), S. I. Hayakawa (listening), Anatol Rapoport (ideological debate), Louis Sohn and others (word federal government), Jermoe Frank and Louis Sohn and others (world federal government), Jerome Frank and others (education in non-violence), Erich Fromm (major unilateral arms reduction), and so forth. Several of the authors of these and related proposals have provided us with the arguments necessary to demonstrate that each of the plans offered is "not feasible." Usually the basis for the judgment of not feasible lies in the intransigence of the very conditions which that particular plan was designed to overcome. Psycho-logic and self-fulfilling prophecy prevents as well as necessitates a reversal in the arms race. Nationalism prevents as well as necessitates the growth of international friendships, armies, and governmental agencies. Without a theoretical model of what is or is not tractible in the social system, a marked tendency exists toward seeing the system and its basic assumptions as relatively immobile but for the cracks provided by one's own insight.

That the various proposals do not all agree on whether tensions or weapons must be first to go, or whether international institutions must precede or follow international allegiances, is not a critical problem. Each of the hypotheses presented in the plans may well be true but none may ever be tested. The specification of alternatives in the cold war is necessary. But just offering the alternatives does not serve to generate new goals for a society. Were the goals of our society appropriate to world peace all of these proposals, and many far more exotic than these, would already have been tried. Conversely, the military strategy proposals which have been either tried or subjected to serious policy consideration are not always more reasonable than the works of the peace scholars.

That the fault is not in the plans but in the absence of a market for them may be seen in a plan offered, in jest, by Anatol Rapoport which has much logical merit. Briefly, it suggests that teams of high ranking officers of the major powers, rather than civilian diplomats, be given the task of negotiating an agreement on general and complete disarmament. If the teams should fail, they are painlessly put to death and replaced by the next team, and so on. The plan assures a) that knowledge of the military requisites for national security will not be missing from consideration, b) that a demilitarization of society will come one way or another, and c) that those who advocate that we should be willing to die for our country would be given the opportunity to do so. What is missing here, as in each of the other plans, is the social force necessary to try the plan. . . .

Obviously, we have not answered our own question of whether there exists a military-industrial complex which can prevent peace. We have argued that the conditions of a stable peace will differ markedly from the conditions of temporary avoidance of war and that constellations of powerful and divergent interests coalesce on certain policies which work against social change.

REFERENCES

Barber, Arthur. "Some Industrial Aspects of Arms Control," *Journal of Conflict Resolution,* 7 (September, 1963), pp. 491-495.

Cartwright, Dorwin. "Power: A Neglected Variable in Social Psychology," in Dorwin Cartwright (Ed.), *Studies in Social Power.* Ann Arbor, Michigan: Research Center for Group Dynamics, 1959.

Fearon, H. E. and Hook, R. C., Jr. "The Shift from Military to Industrial Markets," *Business Topics,* 12 (Winter, 1964), pp. 43-52.

Horowitz, David. *World Economic Disparities: The Haves and the Have-Nots.* Santa Barbara, California: Center for the Study of Democratic Institutions, 1962.

Lowi, Theodore J. "American Business, Public Policy, Case-Studies, and Political Theory," *World Politics,* 16 (July, 1964), pp. 676-715.

McDonagh, James J. and Zimmerman, Steven M. "A Program for Civilian Diversifications of the Airplane Industry," in the U.S. Senate Subcommittee on Employment and Manpower, *Convertibility of Space and Defense Resources to Civilian Needs.* Washington: U. S. Government Printing Office, 1964.

Reiner, Thomas. "Spatial Criteria to Offset Military Cutbacks." Paper presented at the University of Chicago, Peace Research Conference, November, 1964.

Swomley, J. M. Jr. "The Growing Power of the Military," *The Progressive,* 23 (January, 1959), pp. 10-17.